THE

AMERICAN BOARD

OF

COMMISSIONERS FOR FOREIGN MISSIONS.

BY

ANDREW P. PEABODY.

[From the North American Review, for April, 1862.]

BOSTON:
PRINTED FOR THE BOARD.
1862.

THE

AMERICAN BOARD OF FOREIGN MISSIONS.

Memorial Volume of the First Fifty Years of the American Board of Commissioners for Foreign Missions. Fifth Edition. Boston. 1862. 8vo. pp. 464.

THE institution whose Jubilee this volume commemorates was one of those providential institutions which are not made, but grow, — are not formed in accordance with any antecedent plan or theory, but shaped by the work that they find to do. This mode of development is an essential condition of success. Had a body of enterprising Christian philanthropists, fired with the hope of the world's regeneration, assembled in 1810, and established an extensive, ambitious organization, sending emissaries through the churches to arouse zeal and collect funds, and proclaiming a grand crusade against heathenism, the flourish of trumpets that heralded their undertaking would hardly have died away before it was dishonored and abandoned. But in this case the organization was modestly framed to meet an exigency which justly assumed the form of a divine mandate. Of an incredulous world it hardly obtained "leave to be." It enlarged its proportions only as its work and the means of performing it accumulated upon its hands. It grew from within outward, claiming increased confidence and subsidies by meeting the trust already reposed in it, and by using to the best advantage the funds already in its treasury. It has become the most noble charity in our land, simply because it has given so full proof of its efficiency as to refute skepticism, disarm opposition, and conciliate lukewarmness.

The virtual author of this association was Samuel J. Mills, who was graduated at Williams College in 1809. He had "overheard his mother say, that she had devoted him to the service of God as a missionary." Impressed with this remembrance, he formed with four fellow-students an association, in which they pledged themselves personally to this work. He retained the holy purpose when he became a member of the Andover Theological Seminary, and in the first year of his novitiate he entered, with Newell, Judson, Nott, and Hall, into an association similar to that of Williams College. They offered themselves as missionaries to the General Association of Massachusetts, and the American Board was instituted to enable them to enter upon their work. Rev. Drs. Spring and Worcester were the fathers of the infant organization. What it was at the outset, and what it has effected, may be best seen from the following summary in Dr. Hopkins's Semi-Centennial Discourse : —

"At its first meeting but five persons were present, and at its second but seven. Its receipts, the first year, were but a thousand dollars. Now its meetings are like the going up of the tribes to Jerusalem; and its annual receipts are three hundred and fifty thousand dollars. Then it had no missions, and it was not known that any heathen country would be open to them. Now its mission stations belt the globe, so that the sun does not set upon them, and the whole world is open. It has collected and disbursed, with no loss from defalcation, and no suspicion of dishonesty, more than eight millions of dollars. It has sent out four hundred and fifteen ordained missionaries, and eight hundred and forty-three not ordained; in all, twelve hundred and fifty-eight. These have established thirty-nine distinct missions, of which twenty-two now remain in connection with the Board; with two hundred and sixty-nine stations and out-stations, employing four hundred and fifty-eight native helpers, preachers, and pastors, not including teachers. They have formed one hundred and forty-nine churches, have gathered at least fifty-five thousand church-members, of whom more than twenty thousand are now in connection with its churches. It has under its care three hundred and sixty-nine seminaries and schools, and in them more than ten thousand children. It has printed more than a thousand millions of pages, in forty different languages. It has reduced eighteen languages to writing, thus forming the germs of a new literature. It has raised a nation from the lowest forms of heathenism to a Christian civilization, so that a larger proportion of its people can read than in New England. It has done more to extend and to diffuse in this land a knowledge of different countries and people than any or all other agencies, and the reaction upon the churches of this foreign work has been invaluable." — pp. 16, 17.

Greatly to the embarrassment and sorrow of its projectors, but to their subsequent joy and gratitude, a double seed, with the elements of a divergent growth, was planted at the very outset. Two of the first missionaries of the Board became Baptists on their way to India. An appeal was thus made to another numerous and powerful body of Christians to sustain their new-born brethren in the work to which they had consecrated themselves. Thence originated the Baptist Missionary Union, whose history runs along with that of its elder sister in letters of light, illustrated by the Christian heroism of Judson and the noble women who successively bore the cross at his side, by the gentleness and courage, the incredible endurance and triumphant death, of Boardman, and by numerous other honored names, which formed the subject of one of our papers in an earlier volume of this journal.

We do not propose to enter into the history of the American Board. The volume before us could be abridged within our proposed limits only by reducing it to a dry digest of names, dates, and statistics. We hope that it will be read in its entireness by all who are interested in its subject. It has been compiled with the utmost care and skill by Dr. Anderson, who has been identified with the Board from 1824 till the present day, and has been for thirty years its Corresponding Secretary. We trust that the time may yet be far distant when our successors will record in full his manifold services, primarily to the cause of his Divine Master among the unevangelized, but *pari passu* to good letters, sound learning, and liberal Christian fellowship. His narrative style is perspicuous and fluent, swelling in genial fervor with the greatness of its theme, digressing gracefully for the discussion of such points as crave argumentative treatment, and presenting the entire subject of missions in the most attractive form to all who love the Gospel or their race.

The quiescence from which the churches of our land were roused by the formation of this Board was an utterly unchristian state. The legitimate Gospel can have no statics, but only dynamics, so long as there remains a nation or a soul not under its influence. It is in its Founder's purpose an unrestingly aggressive force. The church that makes of itself a close corporation, and furnishes the means of religious nurture only to its pew-holders,—its members bringing their own shallow cups to the fountain of salvation, and never proffering a draught to a thirsty outside brother, — has no title to be regarded as a church of Christ. The prime law of our religion is diffusive love; love imparts what it most prizes; and he can know little of the blessedness of Christian faith and hope who yearns not to make his fellow-men partakers of that blessedness. Yet, in the discussion upon the charter of the Board in the Senate of Massachusetts, it was gravely opposed on the ground "that it was designed to afford the means of exporting religion, whereas there was none to spare from among ourselves." It was well rejoined by the late venerable Judge White, that "religion was a commodity of which the more we exported the more we had remaining." Thus did it prove on experiment. The missionary enterprise returned its priceless revenue of vitalizing and fertilizing energy to its supporters long before its direct effects were conspicuous. Philanthropy thenceforth became, not the prerogative of a few, but the law of the whole Church. The spirit which first went forth for the victims of Hindoo and Burman superstition was not slow in detecting heathenism at home. The various classes of the unprivileged were sought out, and brought under appropriate means of instruction or reformation. Seamen, prisoners, slaves, the poor of our great cities, the dwellers in frontier settlements, neglected children, profligate women, — all were gradually taken into the scope of Christian charity, and there now remains hardly a body of worshipers which has not some one or more of these great causes among its foremost objects of interest, and either of organized action or of informal co-operation. These statements apply not to one denomination, but to all. True, the cause of foreign missions depends chiefly on two or three of our largest religious bodies. Of the others, some lack the requisite means; some have not a sufficiently close cohesion to make combined effort on an extended field practicable; while others are doubtful of the permanent results of such labors, so long as they are liable to be thwarted and neutralized by the vices of civilization that follow on every track on which intercourse is opened. But where the action has not been aided or emulated, the reaction has been profoundly felt, and the sects and the serious Christian believers that are doing little or nothing for the extension of the area of Christendom confess only the stronger obligation to aid in making the existing Christendom more worthy of its name.

Meanwhile, we can not overestimate the power of character which has grown out of the missionary work. It has brought back the heroic age of the Church, and has placed before the world such illustrious examples and verifications of the effective power of the Gospel as had hardly been witnessed since the apostles passed on to their reward. The contributions thus made to the store of religious biography are invaluable, and, next to the life of the all-perfect Author and Finisher of our faith, there is no instrumentality for the creation and growth of personal piety to be compared with this. Our older readers will remember the intense enthusiasm aroused, and the earnest impulses given, by the Memoir of Harriet Newell, the wife of one of the first band of missionaries, who died at the Isle of France at the age of nineteen. Eminently endowed by nature and by grace, fitted as few women have been for the most arduous of all services to her kind,, she undoubtedly effected more for the cause of missions and of Christ by her death, than she could have effected by the longest life. The consecration of her girlhood in its budding promise commended the work to universal Christian sympathy; while the beautiful traits of her character — the strong and brave heart, with the tenderness, modesty, and refinement of the true woman, all intensified and glorified by the martyr-spirit, and tested by exposures and sufferings which, though since exceeded, then had no precedent or parallel — were a felt demonstration of the faith that energized and the hope that gladdened her. This was but the first of a long and precious series of life-records, — Dr. Anderson enumerates more than forty, — of which there is not one that has not had its Divine mission in rebuking skepticism, awakening conviction, urging Christians to a more devoted life, and inspiring new and more vigorous endeavors for the growth of religion in the world. In our own pages, we have had within the last few years no more fruitful or profitable themes than the Lives of Judson and Stoddard, — the former in every dimension one of the greatest men of his age, arrested in early infidelity by an agency hardly less signal than the miracle which converted Paul from a persecutor to an apostle, and thenceforth devoting the fire of genius, the powers of a giant intellect, and the wealth of profound erudition, with a singleness of purpose seldom equaled, never surpassed, to the diffusion of the Gospel, — the latter peculiarly fitted to adorn the highest places of literary culture, rejecting the most flattering and honorable overtures, that he might wear his life out in untold privation and sacrifice among the mountains of Persia. Such men do not live or die to themselves. They reproduce something of their own likeness, not alone on the arduous paths they trod, but in unnumbered homes and quiet walks of duty, in humble scenes, in the susceptible hearts of children, in our colleges, in our rural parsonages, and wherever is a chord that can vibrate at the touch of what is most noble, generous, and holy.

In connection with this department of our subject, we ought not to forget the biographies of the deceased Corresponding Secretaries of the Board, of whom four have been commemorated in volumes, and a fifth in the pages of the Missionary Herald. These were all marked men, closely identified with their work, bringing to it strong minds and fervent hearts, and taking into their characters the heroic elements with which it is fraught. The first of these was Rev. Dr. Samuel Worcester, a pioneer in the cause, whose prescient mind saw in its very inception its destined triumph, and whose plastic and organizing ability was second to no agency in its early success and rapid growth. Though a keen controversialist, he was preeminently "a man of the beatitudes," uniting with the hardiest features of character — a strenuous purpose and an indomitable will — all the amenities of the Christian gentleman. In his declining health, he sought renewed strength where most men in his condition would have expected only a grave, among the Cherokee Indian tribe, where a flourishing mission had been established. He attained his goal, witnessed the achievements of Christian civilization among the rude aborigines, mingled his last prayers with those of the missionaries and their converts, and sank to his rest in the forest, where, through his instrumentality, already "instead of the thorn was the fir tree, instead of the brier the myrtle."

Jeremiah Evarts, a lawyer by profession, succeeded him, and after ten years of earnest and exhausting toil died, like his predecessor, on a journey undertaken too late to repair the waste of an overtasked body and mind. Dr. Anderson justly, if not with too guarded panegyric, says of him, —

"He had a mind and a heart that made him a prince in the domain of intellect and of goodness. He was far-seeing, cautious, earnest, firm, conciliatory, — every thing, in short, to render him an eminently suitable person to conduct one of the grandest of human enterprises. His memorial is in the record of his wise plans successfully carried out, of his untiring labors cheerfully performed, of his manifold sacrifices patiently submitted to, and of the joy unspeakable and full of glory that filled his soul while the gate of heaven was opening to receive him." — p. 125.

Rev. Elias Cornelius, D. D., was appointed Mr. Evarts's successor, but died — also at a distance from his home — before he had assumed the active duties of his office. He had, however, at an earlier period served as an agent of the Board among the Indians in the south-west, and had been largely instrumental in arrangements designed to promote those arts of civilization without which there may be sporadic cases of conversion from heathenism, but no permanent and transmissible Christian institutions. He was a man of rare powers and graces, beloved as a pastor, eloquent as a preacher, of rich and varied culture, of singular executive ability, and of ardent and consistent piety.

The work of the Board had so increased as to demand a division of labor, and Rev. Benjamin B. Wisner, D. D., was chosen one of three Corresponding Secretaries in 1832. His character is well sketched by Dr. Anderson.

"Dr. Wisner had the rarest qualifications for a secretaryship in a great missionary institution. His spirit, naturally somewhat overbearing, had been softened by a partial failure of health and pastoral trials. Cheerful, social, rejoicing in the usefulness of his associates and of all about him, his fine conversational powers made him a most agreeable companion. His public spirit made him ready for every good work; and such was his love for work, that he seemed never to grow weary in well-doing. He did every thing promptly and thoroughly, and little things and great things equally well; not with eye-service, or to have glory of men, but because he loved to be doing good, and because nature and grace made him happy in doing with his might what his hand found to do. So it was always and every where; and this made him the man for committees and sub-committees, on which he was generally to be found, when work was to be done trenching largely upon the hours usually appropriated to rest and sleep. He was a model of a business man — wakeful, cheerful, collected, judicious, laborious, devoted, disinterested. It was no mere official interest he had in his duties. The public welfare was his own. He felt a responsibility for the course of events. His heart was in the great cause of missions — in every part of it.

"His forte was executive. But he had great power also in debate in deliberative bodies. As a writer, he did not readily adapt himself to the popular mind. There was a lack of fancy and imagination, of the discursive and illustrative power, and of flow in thought and style — defects that may have been owing to some infelicity in the manner of his education. But, as an extemporaneous debater, he would have commanded attention on the floor of either House of Congress. At the very outset of the discussion, he seemed to have an intuitive perception of the leading points, in their natural relations and order, and to be at once prepared for a logical, instructive, convincing argument. This always gave him influence in deliberative bodies, where his tact and ability seemed never to be at fault.

"His mental powers came early to maturity; and comparing his labors and influence with those of other men, he needed not threescore years and ten to stand with the more favored men in the impression made upon his age. Yet his early death has ever seemed among the greater mysteries of God's holy providence." — pp. 217, 218.

Dr. Wisner was succeeded by Rev. William Jessup Armstrong, D. D., who lost his life in the wreck of the steamer Atlantic, in 1846. In the fearful scene from which he was translated he moved among his companions, calmly and trustingly, with words of consolation and hope; as the crisis approached, his fellow-passengers crowded around him, "because," said one, "it seemed safer to be near so good a man;" and, as he was swept into the sea, he gave utterance to his "perfect confidence in the wisdom and goodness of Him who doeth all things well."

These men were, indeed, selected for their offices because they were men of eminent powers, large influence, and surpassing excellence. But it is not too much to say that it was the missionary cause that made them fit to conduct it, that they were educated for their office by the momentous interests which that office gave into their charge, and that thus alone were they raised from the rank and file of well-to-do Christians to the foremost places in the sacramental host. With Dr. Worcester, indeed, there is reason to believe that the world-embracing plan had an independent origin, though not prior to the Williams College union; — it would appear that he had meditated and talked of it before he had listened to the appeal of Mills and his companions. We can not doubt that his soul was enlarged and exalted by the great thought, and that his whole life flowed ever after in a fuller current of religious emotion, energy, and efficiency. His successors were not chosen for their work, but made by it. They were put into their office because they had previously devoted themselves with ardor, wisdom, and distinguished success to other departments of the service, or had manifested a profound and fruitful interest in it. We are led to similar reflections on looking over the lists of the various office-bearers and the corporate members of the Board. We find among them a large number of the very men whose characters would denote, not mere Christian culture, but the operation of the strongest forces which our religion can bring to bear upon the human soul — men whose lives must needs have been formed under the overmastering influence of some great religious idea, toward which they have reached on and up, till the extensor muscles of the spiritual man have gained preternatural vigor, and the apprehensive faculties have acquired a superlative aptness, keenness, and precision as to all things human and divine. Nor let it be thought that we are pursuing a mere fancy. In all departments of life men are thus trained and developed. They elect their spheres of thought and action, and then are enlarged, dwarfed, or rounded to the measure they have chosen. The natively great thus become small, and the natively small, great. The American Revolution shaped the men who controlled its movement. Paltry party politics shape after a widely different type the men who seem their masters and mystagogues. Why should not the noblest conception which can enter the human soul, the most godlike service which can be rendered by human wisdom and charity, equally give tone to life and character?

We have devoted as much of our space as we can now afford to the biographical literature of missions, yet have conveyed to those who are not familiar with it but a faint idea of its affluence. To pass to another department, the American pulpit has given utterance to no eloquence surpassing that which has been called forth on the various occasions presented by the exigencies of this enterprise, in anniversary, ordination, and funeral sermons. Dr. Wayland's Sermon on the Moral Dignity of the Missionary Enterprise remains unequaled for grandeur of thought and style. Its periods roll on as if fraught full with the glory of a regenerated world. It sent a glow of zeal and joy through the Christian hearts of the land, and, if we remember aright, was reproduced in other tongues, and well nigh made the circuit of the globe. Similar in strain, and striking every vein of feeling that could have its pulses quickened by the theme, have been the numerous discourses of which we have a list in the volume before us. Dr. Hopkins's Semi-Centennial Discourse is stamped with the massive features of his intellect, — not artistically wrought, but displaying a wonderful compression of narrative, argument, and emotion, most forcefully combined and interfused, and falling upon the reader as in his energetic utterance it must have fallen upon the hearer, with an absolutely irresistible weight of conviction. We quote the closing paragraphs.

"What the precise blending is to be of those two great elements of change, tendencies and personal interposition, or how long the unchecked current of tendencies is to run, it is not for us to say. God makes haste slowly. The bud is formed, and then winter intervenes. The baffled spring lingers. According to geology, the days were long while tendencies did their tardy work of upheavings and deposits. For four thousand years the ages were in preparation for the coming of Christ. But at length God said, 'Let us make man;' at length 'the Desire of all nations' came. Personality asserted a visible supremacy, tendencies were seen to be flexible to will, and special interposition reached its high-water mark, up to the present time.

"But we now wait for another and broader movement. We think that prophecy and converging tendencies both indicate that we are nearing, and rapidly too, a point from which a new epoch is to open. As at the coming of Christ there were musings and forebodings, and the quickened sense caught presage of coming change, so it is now. The very air is full of its voices. The fig tree puts forth leaves. For the first time since the dispersion of men, is the world waking up to the consciousness of itself as one whole. Hardly yet do we comprehend fully the great thought of the Master, that 'the field is the world.' In their early dispersions, men diverged as upon a plain. That plain they now find to be a globe, upon which divergence becomes approximation and ultimate unity. The circuit of that globe, with every continent, and island, and ocean that it rolls up to the sunlight, or buries in its shadow, is now known; and this it is that we are to conquer for Christ. How wide the field, compared with that of primitive missions! How wide the work now, compared with it then! Never before was there such a theater for the action of moral forces; never before were there such forces to act; or such subordination of nature to them, giving them new facilities, and instruments of mightiest power; and never before were these forces taking their positions, and mustering themselves in such relations, as now. The old issues and specters of fear are passing. The papacy is reeling; the crescent is waning; idolatry is tottering; infidelity is shifting its ground and hesitating; the masses are upheaving. The power of those great principles of liberty and equality, which *are* Christ's Gospel on its human side, is beneath them, like that of the earthquake, and oppression and slavery are seeing the hand writing upon the wall, and the joints of their loins are being loosed. And Christians are praying and giving, and when the cry comes for special help they hear it; and there are joy and thanksgiving in ten thousand hearts this night that they do; and the battalions in the great army are nearing each other, and the shout of each becomes more distinct in the camp of the other; and to-night we lift *our* shout, and hold forth the hand of fellowship in this work to all who love the Lord Jesus. And more than all, the Spirit of God is poured out, and revivals are extending, and these showers of divine grace so descend as to show what 'the great rain of his strength' may be. Now the field rounds itself out into some proportion to the love of God in sending his Son; now that achievement comes up into its place for which the mighty energies that have been perverted in war and worldliness were intended; now we see the full contrast between the solitary Sufferer upon Calvary and his work; and looking upon him and upon it, we say, Yes, thou Man of sorrows, thorn-crowned and buffeted, it shall all be thine. He 'shall give thee the heathen for thine inheritance, and the uttermost parts of the earth for thy possession.' Looking upon him and upon it, we join our voice to that of the heavenly host, saying, 'Worthy is the Lamb that was slain, to receive power, and riches, and wisdom, and strength, and honor, and glory, and blessing.'

"Brethren, we rejoice that we live in this day, and may have a part in this work. It is not for us 'to know the times or the seasons, which the Father hath put in his own power.' It is not for the husbandman to bring on the summer. It is for him to sow and plant, and wait the movement of the heavens. So let us, so let every Christian, go forth — weeping if need be — bearing precious seed; let us sow beside all waters; let *us* see that there shall be the handful of corn upon the top of every mountain, and *God* will see that 'the fruit thereof shall shake like Lebanon.'" — pp. 34–36.

Its services to learning and science merit especial commemoration in treating of the missionary enterprise. In philology and in descriptive and physical geography more has been effected within the last half-century by this agency than by all others, and in our own country the contributions of the missionaries of the American Board to these branches of knowledge have borne to other researches and discoveries a proportion which it would be impossible to estimate, and which, could it be stated in figures, would seem almost mythical. The mere scholar may gratify his taste and win his desired meed of fame by manipulating preëxisting materials, by editing a new text of a well-known author, or propounding a new theory for familiar facts, or making a generalization which simplifies a science without adding to its contents; while the missionary must lay the foundation of his work, for the most part, by learning what civilized man had not learned before. The scene of his labors is, we will suppose, some previously unexplored region of Asia or Africa. He must first select a base line for his spiritual triangulation. He must measure the whole field over which his operations are to extend. He must ascertain the position of its mountain chains, the course of its rivers, the trend of its coast, the directions in which it is permeable. He must warily stretch his cordons of communication through its whole length and breadth. In the absence of great thoroughfares and established modes of intercourse, he must obtain all his bearings with scientific accuracy. A thoroughly constructed map is an almost inevitable result of his exploration. Then he must acquire the language of the natives. He has no grammar or vocabulary, probably no conventional written signs for his guidance. Slowly and tentatively he must ascertain the names of familiar objects, then the inflections of words, the particles, the syntax. In his careful and measured synthesis, he must embrace all that constitutes the conventional grammar of the tongue, before he can utter his message or commence the labor of translation. Meanwhile, he has the yearning of a solitary man for communion with his kind, the profounder yearning of a Christian soul to utter the Word of light and life to the benighted and the dying. Under this mighty impulse, the seemingly hopeless work grows and glows. The barbarous jargon is mastered. Its sounds, which he learned to articulate only by painful torture of the vocal organs, are reduced to alphabetic expression. The Saviour's words are committed in their strange garb to the mission press. A vocabulary follows. A new language is given to the learned world, to be analyzed, classified, traced to its analogues in other tongues, and fused into the still fluent and Protean science of linguistics.

At the same time, our missionary must enter on a still more intricate department of research — the human, moral, spiritual geography of the province which he is to annex to Christendom. He must ascertain the past and present of the race, if he would shape its future. Custom, tradition, faith, ritual, government, domestic life, — in all these are instrumentalities which he must use, or obstacles which he must surmount, or vices which he must cure. He can afford to remain ignorant of nothing that can be known. His are not the cursory observations, the sweeping inductions, the gratuitous inferences, of the mere traveler, nor yet the partial, one-idea investigations of the scientific explorer. He associates himself with the home-life of those who will give him entrance. He is with the suffering and the dying. His superior knowledge and skill are resorted to in emergencies of peril. As soon as he can win a convert to his religion, he has gained an avenue through which he can penetrate into mysteries else sealed; and as his band of believers grows, he is brought into familiar conversance with a new phase of humanity. His materials are embodied in his periodical reports, or they accumulate in his hands till he can furnish his volume or volumes of descriptions and experiences; and in either form they become a rich repertory of authentic facts in ethnology, available equally for the purposes of science, enterprise, and philanthropy.

Yet more, the missionary can hardly fail to render services of the last importance in that science of so vast moment and so vague dimensions, for which our own age has coined the appropriate term *humanics*. In modern civilized society, it is almost impossible so to eliminate the accidental and variable in man's condition from the innate and indestructible elements of his nature, as to determine the ultimate facts with regard to his constitution, capacities, and intuitions. An overestimate of these is fatal in practice; for it leads to the ignoring and disallowing of those reputedly divine means of culture which promise to supplement the deficiencies of nature. On the other hand, an unduly low estimate of man as he is in himself creates the expectation of, and cherishes the belief in, the perpetual intrusion of supernatural agents upon the sphere of human action, and nurses enfeebling and baneful superstitions. The former is the tendency of our time; and even a candid consideration of the positive arguments in favor of revelation is superseded, in many minds, by a flattering philosophy of human nature. On the Christian hypothesis, the facts that seem to legitimate this philosophy are easily accounted for. Christian ideas have so pervaded the common thought and feeling of civilized nations, that none can wholly escape their influence; and many notions, impulses, and sentiments which can be traced to no express teaching, and are therefore deemed the spontaneous outgrowth of the soul, are in fact breathed in from a circumambient atmosphere, which, if analyzed, would betray the modifying influence of Christianity. In fine, this element can not be eliminated in our study of civilized man. Man *plus* Christianity, even though the last exist in too small proportion for the spiritual benefit of the individual, is the compound presented to the philosopher of the nineteenth century. The missionary, on the other hand, has the rare opportunity of contemplating humanity as it is in itself — of ascertaining what man, left to his own light and strength, can know, and do, and attain. And if the result of his observations be the confirmation of his traditional faith, — the profound conviction that man's nature lacks and needs what a revelation from God alone can supply, — who can reject conclusions based on such premises? If the naturalism which in so many quarters seeks to supersede the simple faith of our fathers finds no support from the psychological phenomena of heathenism, the irresistible inference is, that its inductions have been drawn from too narrow a range of facts, and are therefore unworthy of reliance.

Still further, there are various departments of expressly theological science to which the missionaries of our age have brought large accessions. Their labors are wrought, in great part, among those nations of the East whose manners, habits, and customs have been stereotyped from time immemorial, and among those features of Oriental scenery which are the same now as in the days of Abraham, Isaiah, and Christ. Much of the imagery of the Scriptures needs for its illustration precisely such knowledge as lies on their daily walks. Many transactions recorded in Holy Writ are explained and verified only by such observations as are forced upon their regard. Many modes of thought and turns of expression are made clearly intelligible only by the surviving ideas and idioms of the Eastern nations which fall within the scope of their researches. An intelligent and Christian Asiatic once said to us, "A great deal of the material of your commentaries on the Bible is wholly worthless to me. Things often seem perfectly natural to me which a commentator will waste pages in endeavoring to reconcile with probability." Such being the case, who can estimate the services rendered in the department of biblical criticism alone by a band of educated men who love the Bible, and whose duties lie among scenes, objects, and people identical with, or closely resembling, those commemorated in the sacred record?

There are also some portions of ecclesiastical history that lie open to the missionary as to no one else. Of the Eastern churches, much more than has ever been written remains unwritten and unknown. But the materials for reproducing what has not yet found record exist in part in tradition, in part in ecclesiastical rites and institutions, and in theological symbols and ideas which have manifestly been transmitted from a remote antiquity. The missionary who seeks to make real the ostensible Christianity of these representatives of the early separatists, must needs enter into their ecclesiastical life, in order to recast it; must become conversant with their ancestral opinions, in order to replace them by better; must learn their traditions, in order to separate from them their admixture of falsity and error. We are to look, then, primarily to this source — and we have already the first-fruits of such an expectation — for effective researches in this large, interesting, and instructive department of the history of the Church, — for lines of testimony that shall carry us back to the time when primitive Christianity had its pure white light broken into varying hues by refracting media.

Such would be our reasonable anticipations at the hands of

missionaries in the various realms of literature and science. How far such expectations have been realized may be ascertained in part from the volume before us, — yet only in small part, as missionary associations other than the American Board have rendered similar incidental aid to good letters and substantial knowledge. As regards geography, in every region that has been opened to the curiosity of the present generation, if we except the region of the Amoor, missionaries have been the pioneer explorers. They have penetrated Africa in every direction, and their carefully written and ably illustrated volumes, filled with what they have seen and experienced, and vivified by the humane sentiment which pervades them throughout, stand in strong contrast with the jejune, spiritless sketches of some secular tourists, and the exciting myths and exaggerations of others. Dr. Anderson, in company with Rev. Eli Smith, one of the missionaries of the Board, made the earliest exploration of the Morea and the Greek islands after the establishment of Grecian independence, and the resultant volume was warmly welcomed by the Royal Geographical Society of London, as having made extensive and valuable additions even to what the English had learned of a region so much frequented by their ships of war, and under safer auspices by their men of letters. The researches of the same Rev. Eli Smith and Rev. H. G. O. Dwight (whose recent death by a railroad accident in Vermont, after his escape from unnumbered perils by land, by water, and "among false brethren," has sent a thrill of grief through the country) in Asia Minor, Georgia, and Persia, and among the Nestorian and Chaldean Christians in Oroomiah and Salmas, were published in 1833, and shortly after republished in London, with the highest commendation from the most distinguished authorities. On our own continent, an exploring tour beyond the Rocky Mountains, undertaken by direction of the Board by Rev. Samuel Parker, "first made known a practicable route for a railroad from the Mississippi to the Pacific."

We would here refer briefly to two works of signal merit, which have been reviewed at length in the pages of this journal. Williams's "Middle Kingdom" remains unrivaled as the most full and accurate account of China — its inhabitants, its art, its science, its religion, its philosophy — that has ever been given to the public. Its minuteness and thoroughness are beyond all praise. Rev. D. O. Allen's "India, Ancient and Modern," with an admirable abridgment of the history of India, contains a detailed and exhaustive statement of the present condition of that country, and of the various nationalities, religions, and governments that occupy and divide its soil.

On the geography of Palestine the prime authority, acknowledged as such throughout the learned world, is Robinson's "Biblical Researches," with its invaluable apparatus of maps. Of missionary agency in the production of this work Dr. Anderson makes the following statement: —

> "Here it is not improper to claim, as belonging, in an important degree, to this department of the literature of the Board, the great modern authority on the geography of Palestine, Robinson's 'Biblical Researches.' Without the preparations made by the mission at Beirût, and especially by the Rev. Eli Smith, who accompanied Dr. Robinson in his explorations, such a work would have been impossible. To a great extent, the present Arabic names of places mentioned in the Bible are the old Hebrew names, modified according to certain rules which Mr. Smith perfectly understood. With the assistance of well-informed natives, he had prepared a complete list of all the small districts into which Palestine is divided, with their several locations, and lists, nearly perfect, of all the names of places in each of these districts. By means of these lists, every day's work could be planned to the best advantage, as the travelers knew what they could search for with any hope of success, and very nearly where to search for it. Nor was it a slight advantage, that Mr. Smith was perfectly familiar with the language, character, and habits of the people among whom these explorations were to be made, whose aid they often needed, and whose acquiescence in their proceedings was always necessary; and that he was personally known and esteemed by many of them, and especially by those whose friendly influence was most important. Dr. Robinson, in his published 'Researches,' has fully acknowledged the value of this assistance; but it requires a better understanding of the circumstances than many readers possess, fully to appreciate the amount of his acknowledgment." — pp. 380, 381.

Of literature illustrative of the Bible, we know of no work so well arranged, so affluent, so equally adapted to the purposes of reference by the scholar and of familiar use by the ordinary reader, as "The Land and the Book," by Rev. W. M. Thomson, who had been for twenty-five years a missionary in Syria and Palestine.

But time fails us for our enumeration. We have given but a few titles among scores that equally deserve our grateful commemoration. We ought not, however, to omit emphatic mention of the "Missionary Herald," a periodical containing reports from all the missionary stations, with accurate statistics embracing every department of knowledge on which the researches of its contributors can throw light. If we were to leave out of thought its prime purpose of enkindling and sustaining zeal in the great work of evangelizing the world, and to regard it solely as a journal for the dissemination of knowledge and the advancement of learning, it would easily hold the first place among the periodicals of the age.

But we have not yet entered upon the most arduous and recondite literary labors performed by these soldiers of the cross. In philology they have accomplished more than all the learned world beside. The publications of the American Board in and concerning foreign languages number already nearly two thousand titles, in nearly forty different tongues. Many of these are translations of the entire Bible. Many are vocabularies and grammars of languages previously unknown to civilized man, and in not a few instances of languages previously unwritten. Who can estimate the amount of patient, intricate, baffling toil involved in these issues of the missionary press! How completely does it distance and throw into the shade the labors of retired scholars, in the shelter of well-stocked libraries, surrounded by reference-books, cheered by the sympathy of men of kindred tastes, and urged on by the anticipated plaudits of the erudite public in all lands! The missionary has no thought of fame; his only impulse — the noblest, indeed, and the mightiest of all — is the desire to save his fellow-men from spiritual death, and to enlarge the empire of Him whose are all souls, and to whom is destined "the kingdom and the dominion under the whole heaven."

We have purposely confined ourselves to the reflex influence of missions on Christendom. We have not time to present the immeasurably larger and more beneficent results that have ensued from their direct action. Nor, indeed, would it be possible by any statement to do them justice. The early history of every mission must almost necessarily be barren of the outward evidences of success. A great work must be wrought out of sight, before any thing can appear. Patient and obscure toil must build the coral reef under the waters of superstition and idolatry, before there can be lodgment for soil or seed where Christian philanthropy has resolved that there shall be "a garden of the Lord." It may require a heavier outlay of time and money, zeal and strength, to make the first convert, than to gather in thousands at a later period. While we are writing, our eyes have rested on the statistics of the Ahmednuggur mission, which received but nine church-members from 1831 to 1835 inclusive, and three hundred and sixty-three from 1856 to 1860 inclusive. This great increase is attributed by Dr. Anderson to the distribution of missionaries in various districts; but such distribution can take place only after the ground is thoroughly surveyed, the language learned, the press in activity, and the interest of native helpers and sympathizers secured. But the sunken foundation, once laid, is laid for all time. The researches put on record, the language reduced to form and brought to knowledge, the translations executed, will remain available for future laborers, even should the field be for a season deserted, or should adverse causes thwart for a while the best directed endeavors.

At all the stations of the American Board, we have what is far better than a flattering array of figures — satisfactory evidence that the preliminary work has been faithfully wrought, or is now in hopeful progress. At several of them, there are large native churches, or clusters of churches embracing an extended territory. From some of them there are going forth enlightening and reforming influences, which are already forcefully felt in the political, social, and religious condition of the respective countries. Among the Oriental Christians, in some instances, the missionaries, judiciously availing themselves of such Christian forms, usages, and institutions as they found surviving, are, without violent revolution, gradually infusing the almost obsolete elements of a working religion and a practical devotion. In other cases, it has been impossible to "put the new wine into the old bottles," and it has been found necessary to establish churches side by side with the ancient ecclesiastical order.

But the American Board has not merely made aggressions on Paganism, or modified heathen rudeness and barbarity, or restored something of the spirit of Christ where it found his name. Foreign missions are, in its theory, but a temporary institution. Its design is not to keep the less enlightened nations always in leading-strings, and dependent for religious influence, guidance, and restraint on foreign teachers and distant charity. The work of the missionary is complete only when his services are superseded. The true test of his success is in the degree to which this result is attained or approached. The conversion of an entire nation or tribe has had, we believe, till the present century, no precedent since the final establishment of Christianity in the countries of Northern Europe. Under the auspices of the American Board, nations have been Christianized. The Cherokees are a Christian people. Their constitution requires a belief in the Christian religion of all who hold office under it. Their laws provide for the daily reading of the Scriptures in their schools. They number about twenty-one thousand souls, and are making constant progress in the arts of civilized life. The Choctaws, whose remnant is about one third as numerous as that of the Cherokees, are also a converted people; and not far from one fourth of the whole population — a large proportion — are members of Christian churches. The Tuscaroras enjoy the same distinction, and many of their youth are making such proficiency in the elements of an English education as to promise large usefulness to those of their own and succeeding generations. The territories of these nations are no longer occupied as missionary stations, though the people still enjoy in part the oversight and religious services of other than their own native teachers. There remains the case of the Sandwich Islands, — in its providential preparatives, in its thoroughness, and in its good promise of permanence, perhaps the most remarkable instance of national conversion on the records of the Christian church. The story is best told in the following statement made to the Board at its annual meeting in 1853: —

"The mission to the Sandwich Islands left the United States, October 23, 1819, and first saw the Islands early in the following April. God prepared their way; one of the strangest of revolutions having occurred just before their arrival. The national idols had been destroyed, the temples burned, the priesthood, tabus, and human sacrifices abolished. All this, however, was only a removal of obstacles. It really did nothing to improve the character of the people, nor could it alone have ameliorated their condition.

"The horrid rites of idolatry had ceased; but the moral, intellectual, social desolation was none the less profound and universal. Society was in ruins, and could not exist at a much lower point; and it was there the mission commenced its work. What desolation was there in the native mind, as regards all useful knowledge! The language was unwritten, and of course there were neither books, schools, nor education. The nation was composed of thieves, drunkards, and debauchees. The land was owned by the king and his chiefs, and the people were slaves. Constitutions, laws, courts of justice, there were none, and no conception of such things in the native mind. Property, life, every thing, were in the hands of arbitrary, irresponsible chiefs, who filled the land with discord and oppression.

"But that people has become a Christian nation; not civilized, in the modern acceptation of the term; not able, perhaps, to sustain itself unaided in any one great department of national existence. Laws, institutions, civilization, the great compact of social and political life, are of slower growth than Christianity. A nation may be Christian, while its intellect is but partially developed, and its municipal and civil institutions are in their infancy. In this sense, the Hawaiian nation is a Christian nation, and will abide the severest scrutiny by every appropriate test. All the religion they now have claims the Christian name. A fourth part of the inhabitants are members in regular standing of Protestant Christian churches. The nation recognizes the obligations of the Sabbath. Houses for Christian worship are built by the people, and frequented as among ourselves. So much, indeed, was the blood of the nation polluted by an impure commerce with the world, before our Christian mission, that the people have a strong remaining tendency to licentiousness, which the Gospel will scarcely remove till a more general necessity exists for industry and remaining at home. The weakness of the nation is here. But Christian marriage is enjoined and regulated by the laws, and the number of marriage licenses taken out, in the year 1852, exceeded two thousand. The language is reduced to writing, and is read by nearly a third part of the people. The schools contain the great body of the children and youth. The annual outlay for education, chiefly by the government, exceeds fifty thousand dollars. The Bible, translated by the labors of eight missionaries, was in the hands of the people before the year 1840; and there are elementary books in theology, practical religion, geography, arithmetic, astronomy, and history, — making together a respectable library for a people in the early stages of civilization. Since the press first put forth its efforts in the language on the 7th of January, 1822, there have been issued nearly two hundred millions of pages. Through the blessing of God on these instrumentalities, a beneficent change has occurred in all the departments of the government, in the face of fierce outrages from seamen and traders, and deadly hostility from not a few foreign residents. The very first article in the Constitution, promulgated by the king and chiefs in the year 1840, declares that 'no law shall be enacted which is at variance with the word of the Lord Jehovah, or with the general spirit of his word;' and that 'all the laws of the Islands shall be in consistency with God's law.' What was this but a public, solemn, national profession of the Christian religion, on the high Puritan basis? And the laws and administration of the government since that time have been as consistent with this profession, to say the least, as those of any other Christian government in the world. The statute laws organizing the general government and courts of justice, the criminal code, and reported trials in the courts, printed in the English language, make five octavo volumes in the library of the Board. Court-houses, prisons, roads, bridges, surveys of lands, and their distribution, with secure titles, among the people, are in constant progress.

"Here, then, let us, as a Board of Foreign Missions, in the name of the community for which we act, proclaim with shoutings of, Grace! grace! that the people of the Sandwich Islands are a Christian nation, and may rightfully claim a place among the Protestant Christian nations of the earth!" — pp. 253–255.

We dismiss our subject reluctantly. Peculiar and painful engagements have cut short the treatment which we had designed to give it. At some future time — the Board will never suffer us long to lack a fitting text — we hope to return to it, and, if we fail to do it justice, at least to fall not wholly below our sense of its dignity, magnitude, and blessedness.

SKETCHES OF MISSIONS.

I.—THE ORIGIN OF THE AMERICAN BOARD.

S. C. BARTLETT, D.D., PROFESSOR IN CHICAGO THEOLOGICAL SEMINARY.

In the year of our Lord 1811, the Protestant churches of America had not one missionary laborer, male or female, among the millions of heathen in foreign lands: to-day they have, be sides native helpers, nearly a thousand.

And yet the missionary spirit of the past fifty years is not a new thing in these churches. The same zeal once burned bright in the hearts of our fathers, the old Puritan colonists; and we have but experienced a revival. The heart of the fathers has been turned to the children, and of the children to the fathers. "The first settlers of New England were the first Englishmen who devised and executed a mission to the heathen." Honored be their memory! We come of a missionary stock. No man can rightly apprehend the new dispensation of missions without some knowledge of the old; for the holy zeal of Mills and of Judson stands interlocked with the labors of Brainard and of Eliot.

Have you ever seen the old State Seal of Massachusetts? It still bears the figure of an Indian and of a star. In early times it bore also for its motto, the Macedonian cry, "Come over and help us"; and the star on which the Indian gazes there, is the Star of Bethlehem.

That quaint device was both a history and a prophecy. It records a desire and a purpose for the salvation of the Indian tribes, which not only accompanied, but preceded the coming of the first band of believers to the shores of New England. Governor Bradford tells us how the men of Plymouth discussed this very subject, while in Holland; and among the "weighty and solid reasons" for the voyage, he affirms there was "lastly—and which was not the least—a great hope and inward zeal they had of laying some good foundation, or at least to make some way thereunto, for the propagating and advancing the Gospel of the Kingdom of Christ in those remote parts of the world; *yea, though they should be but as stepping-stones* unto others for the performing of so great a work." Prophetic words were these. Just so it was with the second or Massachusetts Bay colony. John Cradock, the Governor of the Company in England, in 1628 writes to John Endicott, the Governor of Salem, "not to be unmindful of *the main end of our plantation*, by endeavoring to bring the Indians to the knowledge of the Gospel;" and the Company's first general letter of instructions affirms, "that the propagating of the Gospel is the thing we do profess, above all, to be our aim in settling this plantation." The royal charter declares the same "principal end of the plantation"—"to win and incite the natives of that country to the only true God and Saviour of mankind." These facts ought never to be forgotten.

Their practice was true to their profession. A series of historic pictures would well set forth the history of missions from that time to this.

The first scene should be in September, 1622. A little exploring ship lies off the coast of Chatham on Cape Cod. In it there is a dying Indian, and he is asking a white man by his side to pray for him, "that he might go to the Englishman's God in heaven." The little ship is the Swan; the dying Indian is the faithful Squanto; the praying white man is William Bradford, the Governor of Plymouth. And around the scene might well be written the memorable words that came from John Robinson in Holland, a few months later, when he learned of the first collision between Standish and the savages—"O that you had converted some, before you killed any."

The next painting should bring us down to the year 1646. In the town of Newton, the minister of Roxbury is preaching in the barbarous tongue of the natives, to a solemn assembly; and at the close, an aged Indian rises, and asks with tears, whether it is not too late for such an old man as he to repent and seek after God. The Indians are thanking the preacher for his visit, and for the wonderful things they have heard. And again, I see this same John Eliot—for he it is—organizing a little church at Natick, and at several other places, and traveling about among the Indians, from Cape Cod to Worcester county. He fears no threats from the opposing sachems, but tells them, "God is with me, so that I neither fear you nor all the sachems of the country." With a robust body and a dauntless heart, he cheerfully encounters all manner of hardships. "I have not been dry, night or day, from the third day of the week unto the sixth, but so traveled; but at night pull off my boots and wring my stockings, then on with them again, and so continue. But God steps in and helps." Once, even, he preached the Gospel to Philip of Mount Hope, though the fierce savage rejected it with scorn. And that Indian Bible, printed two hundred and three years ago — long in advance of all other Bibles on this continent, though there is no living eye nor ear that takes in its meaning — once found a call for two editions of 1500 and 2000 copies. Thomas Mayhew is already at work on Martha's Vineyard, followed in the labor by his descendants to the fifth generation. Not far from this time, on Herring river, too, Thomas Tupper is founding his Indian church, to be supplied with a succession of pastors that bear his name; and Richard Bourne, at Marshpee, is beginning the labors in which his son, his grandson, and his great-grandson, all are to bear their part. Thomas Fitch meanwhile preaches the gospel to the Mohegan tribe around Norwich, and Abraham Pierson, to the natives on Long Island and in various parts of Connecticut. The names of Cotton, Rawson, Gookin, Thatcher, also, are identified with these early missions. And thus, in 1675, when King Philip's war broke in with its wretched havoc of all these good works, there might be seen on a Sabbath day, some twenty-four regular congregations of "praying Indians," and about the same number of Indian preachers. Twenty years afterwards there were thirty Indian churches in Massachusetts, besides some 1400 praying Indians in Plymouth colony. Their singing, says Cotton Mather, "is most ravishing."

The narratives of these labors and conversions, published from time to time, awakened intense interest in the mother country, and called out collections from the churches of England. About this time, Edward Winslow visits England, and, largely through his influence, the same Puritan Parliament that had just brought Charles the First to the block, incorporates the "Society for the propagation of the Gospel in New England." It was the mother of the organized missionary societies. Even the celebrated Moravian Missions were not begun till 1732.

Pass down a hundred years from the beginning of Eliot's labors, and look again. It is the year 1743. In Rhode Island, under the labors of this society's agent, you may see the tokens of a powerful awakening among the Indians. They are abandoning their dances and drunken revels, and crowding the places of worship. At Westerly and Charlestown ninety of them join the church in a twelvemonth, and the whole community are nominally Christians, while, a few years later, converts are reckoned among all the tribes of that region — Narragansetts, Pequots, Neanticks, Mohegans, Montauks, and Stoningtons. You may see Mr. Horton, on Long Island, in the course of three years, baptizing thirty-five of the natives, and their children with them; and John Sergeant prosecuting his mission at Stockbridge, Mass., and preparing the place where President Edwards will soon preach the Gospel to the Indians, and write his Treatise on the Will. Near Sharon, Connecticut, the Indians may be seen coming from a region twenty-five miles around, to hear Christian Henry Rauch tell them of "God who became man and loved the Indians so much that he gave his life to save them." This very year, 1743, Eleazer Wheelock receives Samson Occum into his family in Lebanon, Connecticut — the germ of the Indian Charity School, and afterwards of Dartmouth College; and David Brainard begins his work at New Lebanon, New York, soon to be followed by that glorious series of spiritual triumphs among the Indians of New Jersey. And his own account of his blessed labors, and Edwards' narrative of his short but glorious life, passed over into England, to rouse the Christian feeling of the mother country, and to help mould the character of Carey, and his coadjutors, for their missionary enterprise. War again breaks the electric chain. The American Revolution, with its long train of excitements and distractions, extending both before and after, interrupts and almost suspends these labors of Christian love. But the good seed had taken root beyond the ocean. Before Brainard's death, a body of Scotch ministers had called for a concert of prayer for the world's conversion; and Brainard's dying charge to his Indian church enjoined upon them to observe that concert of prayer. Our Revolution was followed by the Godless French Revolution — or convulsion; and in the midst of the alarm it occasioned, there was kept up united supplication of Christians on both sides of the Atlantic, for the outpouring of God's Spirit, the overthrow of his enemies, and the extension of his Church to the ends of of the earth. Towards the close of the century, several British societies had begun their labors in Africa, the East Indies, and the Islands of the Pacific.

In this country, God was about interposing to re-unite the chain, and greatly to enlarge its circuit. To heal the desolations of war, and cover the ravages of politics, toward the beginning of the present century, extensive and powerful revivals are preparing the way for the revival, too, of missions to the heathen. Indeed, in the very year when the American Constitution was adopted (1787), the legislature of Massachusetts had incorporated a Society for propagating the Gospel among the Indians and others in North America; and a little later, the Presbyterian Assembly orders collections for a missionary fund. But as revivals begin, the indications grow stronger and wider. In 1797 is formed the Northern Missionary Society of New York; in 1798, the Connecticut Missionary Society; in 1799, the Massachusetts Missionary Society, looking primarily, though not exclusively, to the Indians. The magnetic influence spreads. Next year it stirs itself in the Connecticut Evangelical Magazine, and three years later, in the Massachusetts Missionary Magazine, and the Baptist Magazine, followed, in two years more, by the Panoplist — all pleading the cause of missions. John Norris, of Salem, in 1808, gives 10,000 dollars for a Theological Seminary, "because we must raise up ministers if we would have missionaries." Narratives of eastern missions come over from England. Intelligence and interest are diffused; sermons are preached and prayers are offered; but as yet there are no missionaries in foreign lands. Yet God was providing for the missionaries as soon as ever the Church should be wakened up to send them. He had arranged it before any of these periodicals were started, or sermons preached, or societies formed.

Let us go back and look in upon the little town of Torringford, Connecticut, in the year 1783. Here is a Christian mother naming her son "Samuel." From his early childhood she talks to him of Eliot and Brainard. Once he hears her say to another person, "I have consecrated this child to the service of God as a missionary." He never forgot those words. The first clear indication of his piety, to his father's mind, was his remark that "he could conceive no course of life so pleasant as to go and give the Gospel to the heathen." He longs to go to Africa. At length he broaches the subject to his parents, but it is now too much for his mother's fortitude. "I can not bear to part with you, my son." He tells her what he heard her say of him years ago; and she weeps, but never again objects. And now Samuel J. Mills enters William's College. As he studies the geography of Asia, he broods over its moral darkness, and meditates a mission to that benighted continent. Similar thoughts of missionary labors are already stirring in the minds of James Richards and Gordon Hall, and—far away from them all — of Asahel Nettleton.

Look upon another scene. There is a hay-stack in a meadow not far from William's College, and by the side of it a little group of students. An impending thunderstorm has driven them from their stated place of prayer in the neighboring grove to this place of shelter. And here, says one who was present, "Mills proposed to send the Gospel to that dark and heathen land [of Asia], and said we could do it if we would." The subject was discussed. The storm was passing off. And now, said Mills, "Let us make it a subject of prayer under this hay-stack, while the dark clouds are going and the clear sky is coming." And so they prayed. Thenceforth they deliberated — it was in the north-west lower room of the east college"— till on the 8th of September, 1808, they formed that strangest of secret associations, the "Society of Brethren," the object of which "shall be to effect, in the person of its members, a mission to the heathen." The constitution may still be seen, signed by the names of Mills, Richards, Fisk, Seward, Rice — all written in cipher. It was the first strictly *foreign* missionary Society upon this continent, and was formed on the very year when Rev. Sidney Smith, of England, through the columns of the Edinburgh Review, was pouring in his broadsides upon the "consecrated cobblers," as he called the British missionaries in India. The next year, two of these young men might be found at Andover Seminary — then just opened — where Hall, Judson, Mills, and Nott, agree to establish a mission in some foreign land. In the spring of that year, Dr. Worcester publicly predicts, that, "ere long, God will give the word, and great will be the company of the publishers." Within a twelve-month of that prediction, there are now known to have been some twenty young men pondering this great question of duty.

The time for action draws near. On the 25th of June, 1810, let us go with Rev. John Keep to the parlor of Professor Stuart, in Andover. Here is a little company of eight or nine brethren assembled to confer with these young men. There are Drs. Spring, Worcester, Snell, Griffin, Revs. Sunborn, Reynolds, Keep, Professor Stuart, and Jeremiah Evarts. Samuel Newell states the case. A world lies in ruin, and Christ has said, Go preach the Gospel to every creature. That command has come home powerfully to their hearts, and lain there for years. The sense of duty is so solemn and so strong, that one of them has already said to the call of a most inviting church — "No, I must not settle in any parish of Christendom. God calls me to the heathen. Woe to me if I preach not the Gospel to the heathen." Can they have that privilege? One by one the ministers gave their opinions. To one of the brethren the project savored of "infatuation." But better counsels prevailed, and the conclusion is to go forward, trusting in God. The next day Dr. Spring and Dr. Worcester ride together in a chaise to the General Association at Bradford; and between them, on the way, there grows up the whole conception of the American Board, with its form, its name, and the number of its members.

That General Association was but a little body—eighteen, all told. A paper was presented to them, bearing the names of Judson, Mills, Nott, and Newell. Richards and Rice did not venture to add their names, lest the Association should be alarmed at their number, and the greatness of the burden. Hall's name, also, was not there, although, in his zeal, he was "ready to work his passage to India, and then throw himself on his own resources, to preach the Gospel to the heathen." In that General Association was born the American Board of Commissioners for Foreign Missions. Not altogether in boldness and confidence, but in questionings and solicitudes, and yet prevailing faith. "The attitude of the meeting," says one who was there, "was about this: no direct opposition, a weak faith, a genial hope, rather leaning to a waiting posture." "Never was the value of an intelligent, leading influence more clearly seen," that influence being found in the clear heads and brave hearts of such men as Worcester and Spring. And yet it was the moving of God's Spirit, back of all men and means.

Yea, no man was the ultimate leader. But just as God moved simultaneously on the hearts of Peter and of Cornelius, at Joppa and at Cesarea—and as he often prepares for some great enterprise of his by many diverse and distant agencies at once—so had he now been working silently and separately on the minds of those young missionaries, their wives, the Professors at Andover, the leading ministers, the business men, and, in some degree, the churches at large, till all was ripe, or ripening, for the formation of the American Board. Such is the method of God.

The first meeting of the body that now fills the largest halls with its annual assemblies, occupies two or three churches with the attending communicants, counts its 24,000 living converts from heathenism, and a much larger number now in heaven, was held the same year in the parlor of Dr. Porter, and consisted of five persons. But the work looked formidable. A fund of $60,000 seemed indispensable. The effort failed—fortunately, no doubt; although once, at Salem, the noble Mrs. Norris called out Mr. Bartlett from the committee room to say, "I will give $30,000, if you will,"—and with her dying hand, a few months later, she gave thirty thousand dollars each to Andover Seminary and the American Board. Judson, meanwhile, was sent to England, to negotiate for help. Nothing was effected there. The question was forced back, Will the Board send these young men? When that question first went round, only one member of the Committee ventured to say, Yes. But again God's Spirit led the way, and they finally determined to send them — yet without wives, so far as practicable, and with the reserved alternative of throwing a part of them, if need be, upon the London Missionary Society for support.

One other transaction remains to complete the sketch. It is the sixth of February, 1812, and the old Tabernacle Church of Salem is crowded to its utmost capacity to witness the solemn consecration of five young men to the missionary work. The funds in the treasury are not one quarter enough to pay the first year's expenses; even the great and good Dr. Dwight tells young Nott it is a rash undertaking; but the vessels already lie at the wharves, which are to carry a grander destiny and a surer freight than Cæsar and his fortunes. In the Tabernacle Church are gathered ministers and Christians from many miles around. Students from Andover Seminary and Phillips Academy have walked sixteen miles on that February day, to enjoy the occasion. Ann Hasseltine Judson, and Harriet Atwood Newell—the brides of a day—are there with their husbands, bearing up under many a censure of their "romantic" enterprise. Five of the very chief ministers of New England—Woods, and Spring, and Griffin, and Morse, and Worcester—conduct the impressive services, deepening in pathos to the close. Dr. Woods presents the glorious inducements to labor for the world's conversion, and bids the "dear young men" a tender farewell. Dr. Morse follows with the consecrating prayer, and the five chief ministers of their generation lay their hands upon the five pioneers of all American missions in foreign lands. And as Dr. Spring proceeds with the touching charge, in which he bids them "go, with the tender companions of your bosoms, and lay your bodies by the side of Ziegenbald and Swartz, that you may meet them, and Eliot, and Brainerd, and all other faithful missionaries, in the realms of light, and so be ever with the Lord;" and as Worcester follows with that tenderest of "fellowships," beginning "God is love," and assuring them of the "unspeakable joy" with which the brethren here will read of their labors on "the banks of the Indus, the Ganges, or the Ava," the sound of irrepressible sighing, and even of loud weeping, was heard in that great congregation—and Nettleton weeps, far away in New Haven, that he cannot join that blessed band.

Yea, and what a memorable day was that in the annals of our churches. How it stirred up New England with a great heart-throb of missionary feeling, and vibrated across the waters. Before the vessels left the coast, money came flowing in from all quarters, and all the immediate necessities of the Board were met in advance. How many a parent consecrated his young child to the same good work; and how many a youth then felt our Lord's command pressing on his conscience and thrilling through his heart. The monthly concert of prayer for the world's conversion became an established institution. We read even of children who went away by themselves to pray for the missions, and named each other "Bombay," and "Ceylon." What a freight of holy influence for the world those vessels, the Caravan and Harmony, bore across the ocean. What incalculable springs of missionary labor for the whole church of Christ lay wrapped up in the heroic characters of Hall, and of Judson; what exhaustless fountains of Christian sympathy and holy fortitude in the deep devotion of Harriet Newell, and the queenly soul of Ann Hasseltine Judson!

O, that another such a tide of missionary zeal might flow through the land, and especially through these young, growing churches of the great North-west, to enlist their fervent prayers, to draw out their liberal contributions, and to summon their sons and their daughters to the rescue of the dying heathen!

From Hours at Home, for May, 1866.

KAPIOLANI, THE HEROINE OF HAWAII.

HER EARLY RELIGIOUS HISTORY.

BY RUFUS ANDERSON, D.D., FOREIGN SECRETARY OF THE AMERICAN BOARD OF COMMISSIONERS FOR FOREIGN MISSIONS.

Kapiolani belonged to what may be called the nobility of the Hawaiian Islands. She descended from one of the ancient kings of Hawaii. Her husband Naihe had also a noble descent. They had large landed possessions, which bordered on the quiet and beautiful waters of the Kealakekua Bay, and rose into the woodlands of Maunaloa, with one of the most delightful climates and oceanic prospects in the world. The people inhabiting these lands were in the lowest intellectual and social degradation, and both chiefs and vassals were alike dark-minded and savage pagans, preferring their grass huts down on the heated lava of the shore, to the verdant and temperate regions above.

When first seen, Kapiolani is said to have been sitting on a rock, oiling her naked person. Her habits, at that time, were intemperate and dissolute. This was in the year 1820, when the Rev. Mr. Thurston commenced his mission at Kailua, sixteen miles northward of the place noted for the death of Captain Cook. The name of this place was Kaawaloa, and there was the home of Naihe and Kapiolani. Liholiho, king of the Sandwich Islands, and his young brother, afterward known as Kamehameha III., then resided at Kailua; and these, with several chiefs, old and young, were daily instructed by Mr. and Mrs. Thurston, so far as the king's intemperate habits would permit. The missionaries were an object of curiosity to the people, and many came to see them from distant parts of the island, which has a circuit of nearly three hundred miles. Kapiolani was among the more frequent visitors, coming in her well-manned, double canoe. Her sprightly, inquisitive mind soon seized upon the outlines of the Gospel, and a change came over her morals. She gave herself to study, and to the means of grace.

Near the close of the year 1820, the royal family removed to Honolulu, on the island of Oahu, which soon after became the acknowledged capital of the kingdom; and it was thought prudent for Mr. and Mrs. Thurston, in view of the rude manners of the people, to do the same. Kapiolani and her husband soon followed, and remained at Honolulu till the arrival of the first reinforcement of the mission, in the spring of 1823. In the distribution of the new company, Kapiolani urged the claims of Kailua, and of her own people at Kaawaloa, and great was her joy when it was decided to re-occupy the former place, now under the efficient rule of Kuakini, or (as he was called by American seamen) John Adams. She united with her husband in proffering to Mr. and Mrs. Thurston, and to Mr. and Mrs. Ely, the best accommodations afforded by their own little schooner. Mrs. Ely could not at that time endure the ordeal of such a voyage. And it is distressing, in these days of steamboats, to think of the suffering endured by our missionary brethren and sisters on board those small, ill-ventilated, closely-crowded native vessels, in their protracted voyages, which sometimes were a week and more, only from Honolulu to Lahaina, now occupying only a single night.

The king was at that time cherishing the plan, which he lived to execute in part only, of visiting foreign countries, and seeing in person the King of England and the President of the United States. His departure had the effect to throw the government of the islands into better hands — with Kaahumanu at the centre as regent, and Kuakini as governor of the great island of Hawaii. Mr. Thurston found, on his return to Kailua, that the governor had nearly finished a neatly thatched house of worship, with pulpit, and seats around the walls, and mats neatly spread over the intervening ground. This house, as erected by a heathen ruler, and standing amid the ruins of a *heiau*, wherein human victims had not long before been offered, had a special interest.

Meanwhile, Kapiolani was putting up a similar house of worship at Kaawaloa, and was importunate for a Christian minister, often weeping, it is said, over the unavoidable delay. If Naihe was not yet in thorough sympathy in these matters with his interesting wife, he did not withhold his coöperation; and an old chief, named Kamakau, who is once spoken of as a poet, seems to have been even more advanced than herself in the Christian life.

Mr. and Mrs. Ely arrived at Kailua in February, 1824, and Naihe, Kapiolani, and Kamakau, all united their efforts to secure the new comers for Kaawaloa. They engaged to build them a house, and to furnish them, free of expense, with vegetables, and with fresh water, which had to be brought from a distance. The effort was successful, and the new house of worship was dedicated on the last day of February, Mr. Thurston preaching on the occasion to a large and attentive audience.

In July, Kapiolani had a painful illness. When Mr. Ely expresed anxiety for her recovery, her reply was: "I wish to suffer the will of God patiently. If it be His will, I desire to depart and be with Christ. Then I shall be free from sin. Once I greatly feared death, but Christ has taken away its sting." From this sickness she recovered, to the especial relief of her missionary friends, who expected much from her aid in that part of Hawaii. A Sabbath evening call she made at Mr. Ely's, soon afterward, will illustrate the lively, intelligent character of her piety. She spoke with great interest of the state of man. "The heavens and earth," she said, "the sun, moon, and stars, the birds and fishes, the seas, mountains, valleys, and rocks, all combine to praise the Lord. But where is man, poor, sinful man? He is mute. God has given him a mouth, and knowledge, but man refuses to praise him." As she spoke, she wept. Then she added: "We are dreadfully depraved. We are justly the objects of God's displeasure. We shall stand speechless at the bar of God."

Not long after her recovery, Kapiolani made a visit of a month at Lahaina, on the island of Maui, beautifully situated on a fertile strip of land, adorned with cocoanut trees, with lofty hills in the background. The Rev. William Richards was then residing at Lahaina. Her habit was to make a daily call on him and his wife. Her nature was eminently social, and seems to have been remarkably sanctified by grace. Speaking of public worship, one Sabbath evening, she said: "I love to go to the house of God, for there I forget the world. When among the chiefs, I hear so much about money, and cloth, and land, and ships, and bargains, that I wish to go where I can hear of God, and Christ, and heaven." She continued: "When I hear preaching about Jesus Christ, my spirit goes out to him; and when I hear about God, my spirit goes to God; and when I hear about heaven, my spirit goes up to heaven. It goes, and comes, and then it goes again, and thus it continues to do." She then inquired, with earnestness, whether Mr. Richards did not think she had two souls, saying that it seemed to her she had one good soul and one bad one. "One says, God is very good, and it loves God, prays to him, and loves Jesus Christ, and loves preaching, and loves to talk about good things. The other one says, it does no good to pray to God, and to go to meeting, and keep the Sabbath."

"We shall long remember the last evening that we enjoyed her society," wrote Mr. Richards. "She was expecting soon to return to Hawaii, and I therefore invited her to take tea and spend the evening with us. She came with Keameamahi, who is also one of our best friends. Honorii and Pupuhi joined the circle. The evening was not spent in general conversation. Kapiolani was pleased with nothing that would not come home to the heart. Many enlightened Christians, after leaving a pious circle, would blush at their own coldness, could they but have seen how anxious this chief was to spend her last evening in the best manner possible. At the close of the evening we sung the translation of the hymn, 'Wake, Isles of the South,' and then parted with prayer."

"A few years ago," continues this excellent and beloved missionary—now long since numbered with departed saints—"there was scarcely a more degraded person on the islands than Kapiolani. She gave herself up to intemperance, and every species of degradation. Now she is in every respect perfectly moral. She always appears in a neat dress, has, in many respects, adopted the customs of refined society, and is, in her whole character, raised so far above the generality of the nation, that one can hardly avoid the belief that she was educated among an enlightened people. How gladly would I present this chief to a circle of those who say this people can never be civilized, and let them account for the difference between her former and her present character. There are other similar examples here, but I know of none so striking as this."

KAPIOLANI AT THE GREAT VOLCANO.

Kapiolani is described by one who knew her, as having a portly person, black hair, keen black eyes, an engaging countenance, and a warm heart and leading mind. Her costume at this time was that of a Christian matron; her house was furnished with chairs, tables, and beds, and she "used hospitality" according to the Scriptures. She and her husband were patrons of the schools, and discountenanced vice in all its forms, and their house of worship was thronged with attentive hearers.

It was now the fifth or sixth year since this woman had her first opportunity to hear the Gospel. In that part of Hawaii, numbering then somewhat more than twenty thousand people, the beams of morning light were quite visible upon the retiring night of paganism. It is even probable that some one or more Gospel rays had reached the larger portion of the adult population of seventy-five thousand on that large island. The destruction of idols by the government must needs have awakened some curiosity in respect to the new religion, which had so soon after found its way among them. But there was necessarily a great amount of superstition remaining among the people, especially that which addresses itself to the fears. Indeed, we find not a little of such superstition, even now, in the oldest Christian countries. On Hawaii, this centred in Pele, and the marvelous volcano of Kilauea, of which she was the reputed goddess. It was time for something to be done to break the spell of this superstition, and it could best be done by some native of rank and character. The Lord prepares instruments for his own work, and Kapiolani was the honored instrument in this emergency.

Hearing that missionaries had commenced a station at Hilo, on the opposite side of the island, she resolved to visit them, though it involved a journey on foot of a hundred miles over a rough and most fatiguing way. And as Kilauea was on the route, it was her purpose to brave the wrath of Pele, and give a practical demonstration of her own belief, that the Jehovah of Christianity was the only God of the Volcano. In this act of Christian heroism she rose far above the ideas and sentiments of her countrymen, and, indeed, above those of her own husband, Naihe, who joined with the multitudes of others in endeavoring to dissuade her from so rash an enterprise. The destruction of the idols and of the *tabu* had done nothing toward giving the people a new religion. It was the general sentiment that her presumptuous invasion of the realms of Pele would be attended with fatal consequences. Her response was the same to all — of a calm determination to execute her purpose. When approaching the regions of the volcano, she was met by a priestess of Pele, and warned to stop. The warnings of the pretended prophetess were disregarded, and to a letter from the goddess, which she professed to hold in her hand, Kapiolani responded by quotations from Scripture, read out of one of her printed books.

At the crater she found Mr. Goodrich, one of the youngest missionaries, lately come to Hilo, about thirty miles distant, who had heard of her intended visit, and whom she was glad to see. With her company of about eighty, and Mr. Goodrich, she descended some hundreds of feet to the black ledge, and there, amid some of the most terrible of natural phenomena on the earth's surface, which had ever been appalling to her countrymen, she ate the berries consecrated to Pele, and threw stones into the seething mass. Then she calmly addressed her company. "Jehovah," she said, "is my God. He kindled these fires. I fear not Pele. Should I perish by her anger, then you may fear her power. But if Jehovah save me when breaking through her *tabus*, then must you fear and serve Jehovah. The Gods of Hawaii are vain. Great is the goodness of Jehovah in sending missionaries to turn us from these vanities to the living God." They then united in a hymn of praise, and bowed in prayer to Jehovah, the Creator and Governor of the world.

Was there not a moral heroism in this act of Kapiolani? When, three years ago, the writer himself stood by this greatest and grandest of volcanoes, and saw the mass of molten lava upheaving and surging over the breadth of half a mile, through the agency of an unseen power, and beheld a group of Christian native attendants seated thoughtfully by themselves on the verge of the abyss, he would not have deemed it strange if even they had some lingerings of the old superstitious fears, though it was then almost forty years after the visit of Kapiolani.

KAPIOLANI AT HOME.

Mr. Ely must have exercised a considerable degree of caution in receiving native converts into the church at Kaawaloa, since Kapiolani was not admitted until after her memorable visit to the volcano, near the close of 1825. The reception of Kamakau, the old chief already mentioned, was still later. So late as the close of 1826, Naihe was not an accepted candidate for admission, though believed to be not far from the kingdom of heaven. He was habitually kind to the missionaries, and decidedly favorable to their object. Of Kapiolani, Mr. Ely speaks in strong terms of commendation. "She is, indeed," he says, "a mother in Israel. No woman on the islands, probably, appears better than she; and perhaps there is no one who has so wholly given himself up to the influence and obedience of the Gospel. I am never at a loss where to find her in any difficulty. She has a steady, firm, decided attachment to the Gospel, and a ready adherence to its precepts marks her conduct. Her house is fitted up in a very decent style, and is kept neat and comfortable. And her hands are daily employed in some useful work."

The village of Kaawaloa, where this noble woman so adorned her Christian profession, was situated on a bed of lava forming a plain of from half a mile to a mile and a half in width, south-east of which are the deep and quiet waters of Kealakekua Bay, and south-west the ocean. A precipice of singular appearance rises hundreds of feet on the north-east, and you perceive that it was once a lofty cataract of molten lava, by which the plain was formed. The arable lands are beyond and above the precipice, and a road, of modern construction, now descends along the face of the precipice to the landing below. When Kapiolani built the stone house still standing in the beantiful region two miles above Kaawaloa, near where the house of the Rev. Mr. Paris is now located, is not known to the writer. He only knows that she removed to that place to accommodate Mr. Ruggles, the successor of Mr. Ely, whose health required a milder temperature than could be found on the black lava of the shore.

But it was in the village of Kaawaloa, on the plain below, that Naihe and Kapiolani resided when they entertained Captain Finch, of the U. S. ship Vincennes, and the Rev. Charles Samuel Stewart, in the autumn of 1829; and there we shall see Kapiolani as she was at her own home. The writer imagines that in the year 1863 he saw some of the forsaken remains of her dwelling. Her house, as described by Dr. Stewart, at the time of his visit, was a spacious building, inclosed in a neat court by a palisade fence and painted gate, from whence she issued to meet them with the air of a dignified matron, her amiable and benignant face beaming with joy. We can do no less than quote the expressive language of Dr. Stewart:

"This chief," he says, "more than any other, perhaps, has won our respect and sincere friendship. She is so intelligent, so amiable, so lady-like in her whole character, that no one can become acquainted with her without feelings of more than ordinary interest and respect; and from all we had known of her, we were not surprised to find the establishment she dwells in equal, if not superior, to any we had before seen — handsomely arranged, well furnished, and neatly kept; with a sitting-room, or hall, in which a nobleman, in such a climate, might be happy to lounge; and bed-rooms adjoining, where, in addition to couches which the most fastidious would unhesitatingly occupy, are found mirrors and toilet tables fitted for the dressing-room of a modern belle.

"It was near tea-time; and in the centre of the hall a large table was laid in a handsome service of china; and, after a short stroll in the hamlet, and the rehearsal of the tragedy of Captain Cook's death on the rocks at the edge of the water into which he fell, we surrounded it with greater delight than I had before experienced, in observing the improvement that has taken place in the domestic and social habits of the chiefs. Kapiolani presided at the tea-tray, and poured to us as good a cup of that grateful beverage as would have been furnished in a parlor at home; while her husband, at the opposite end, served to those who chose to partake of them, in an equally easy and gentlemanlike manner, a pork steak and mutton chop, with nicely fried wheaten cakes. A kind of jumble, composed principally of eggs, sugar, and wheat flour, made up the entertainment. After the removal of these, a salver with a bottle of muscadine wine, glasses, and a pitcher of water, was placed on the hospitable board. And every day we remained, similar generous entertainment was spread before various parties from our ship."

The Vincennes remained several days; and when, at the close, Captain Finch requested the Rev. Mr. Bingham, who had come with them from Honolulu, to express to Kapiolani the pleasure his visit had afforded him, and his thanks for her hospitality and kindness, her reply was, that the kindness of the visit had all been to herself, to the king and chiefs, and to the nation; "that he might have had some gratification in the visit, but he could have had no happiness like theirs; *for our happiness*," she exclaimed, clasping her hands and pressing them to her bosom, as she lifted her eyes, glistening with tears, to his, "*our happiness is the joy of a captive just freed from prison!*"

The closing of this domestic scene was beautifully characteristic. Messrs. Stewart and Bingham were to embark in the Vincennes at a late hour in the evening, and Kapiolani had engaged to send them on board in a canoe. Entering the principal house to take leave, they found the family at evening prayers. The parting scene, at midnight, is thus graphically described by Dr. Stewart:

"The paddlers of the canoe had been aroused from their slumbers; other servants had lighted numerous brilliant torches of the candlenut, tied together in leaves, to accompany us to the water; and I was about giving my parting salutation, when not only Naihe, but Kapiolani also, said, 'No, not here, not here, but at the shore;' and, throwing a mantle around her, attended by her husband, she accompanied us to the surf, where, after many a warm grasp of the hand and a tearful blessing, she remained standing on a point of rock, in bold relief amid the glare of torchlight around her, exclaiming, again and again, as we shoved off, 'Love to you, Mr. Stewart! love to Mrs. Stewart! love to the captain, and to the king!' while her handkerchief was waved in repetition of the expression, long after her voice was lost in the dashing of the water, and till her figure was blended, in the distance, with the group by which she was surrounded."

Naihe died of paralysis on the 29th of December, 1831. He was a kind husband, an able counselor, a valuable coadjutor in the support of schools, a decided magistrate, a firm and steady supporter of good morals and religion, and a constant attendant at the house of God on the Sabbath. Though his Christian experience was less demonstrative than that of his wife, he died in the faith of the Gospel; he is believed to have "died in the Lord." Greatly beloved by his people, the loss of his example and authority was much felt.

Mr. Ruggles, after mentioning the death of Naihe, speaks of the bereaved and afflicted wife, as "a precious sister, a burning and shining light in the midst of her benighted countrymen." "The chief desire of her soul," he adds, "seems to be the conversion of sinners, and she is always ready for every good word and work." That the years which intervened between the death of her husband and her own departure, were filled with such acts of usefulness as comported with her state of widowhood, with her advancing years, and (as is probable) with a diminished income, is sufficiently evident in the notice of her death by the Rev. Mr. Forbes, then, and for some years, the missionary in that district. He wrote thus: "Our beloved friend and mother in Christ, Kapiolani, is gone to her rest. She died May 5, 1841. Her end was one of peace, and with decided evidence that your missionaries have not labored in vain. For twenty-four hours and more preceding her death, she was delirious, owing to the violence of the disease, which fell on the brain. This nation has lost one of its brightest ornaments; and speaking thus I disparage no one. Her life was a continual evidence of the elevating and purifying effects of the Gospel. She was confessedly, the most decided Christian, the most civilized in her manners, and the most thoroughly read in her Bible, of all the chiefs this nation ever had; and it is saying no more than truth to assert, that her equal, in those respects, is not left in the nation. There may be those who had more external polish of manner, but none who combined her excellencies. She is gone to her rest, and we at this station will feel her loss the most. We can not see how it can be repaired."

Experienced Christians, on reading this narrative of Kapiolani, will be conscious of fellowship with her, and will feel no disposition to question her piety. They will recognize in her a signal proof and illustration of the genial and beautiful Christianity introduced by the American missionaries into the Sandwich Islands. Other similar instances there were, indeed, and not a few — and the name of Kaahumanu, regent of the Islands, will occur to many — but perhaps in no one case were the graces of Christianity so thoroughly demonstrative as they were in Kapiolani. To set forth the nature of the religion which obtained such hold upon the island people in the last generation, through the blessing of God on the labors of those missionaries, one of their best developed converts was naturally selected; and the writer has aimed to give his narrative a simple form, and avoid exaggeration, and the whole is believed to stand on a firm historic basis. The hand of God is to be acknowledged in the consistent, Christian life for twenty years, of this child of a degraded paganism. Her's was the religion of the Puritans, and would to God that all those Islanders, from the highest to the lowest, were like her. We should then behold a nearer approach to a heaven on earth, than earth has afforded since the fall.

From the Missionary Herald.

TO THE STOCKHOLDERS OF THE NEW "MORNING STAR."

East Boston, Mass., Sept. 14, 1866.

"My Dear Young Friends:—Last May I wrote you a letter, addressed 'to those who love the Morning Star,' in which an appeal was made for a new missionary vessel. To this appeal you have replied by contributions, thankfully received, and to-day I am seated on a joiner's tool-chest, in the captain's stateroom, on board your vessel, with a wish to tell you how the work is progressing, while the joiner is pounding away, putting up 'bulkheads.' You have already been notified, in some of the newspapers, that we are hoping to launch the vessel on Saturday morning, Sept. 22d. Of course she is rapidly approaching completion.

"It has been my privilege to spend many days about her, to watch not a little of the work, and to be comforted as I saw how substantially she was being built. The builders, Messrs. Curtis, Smith & Co., have endeavored to give you a first class vessel, have put in heavier timbers than were asked, and have salted thoroughly, to prevent rotting.

"The hull is a very substantial structure, the model very graceful, the water lines very fine, such as will insure good sailing qualities. The houses on deck are large, airy, and commodious; as large as you would find on a ship of twice her tonnage. Were you on board with me now, though the work is unfinished, it would please me to take you around through the various apartments, through the cabin, in the after house, with its four staterooms, saloon, pantry, linen-closet, wash-closet, &c.; into the little lower cabin, to which we might retreat in case some terrible storm should ever damage our main cabin, of which I have just spoken. Just forward of the lower cabin, and under the main one, is our little store-room ; and in the forward house you will see where the steerage, or mess-room, is to be, and the two staterooms, the galley, and the forecastle. And then in the bows I could show you where we mean to have a sail-room below deck, and a few berths, to be used when we are much crowded for want of room.

"You would like to look at the windlass, and the rudder, and the pumps, and at the bowsprit, which is so firmly put in that we hope we shall experience no difficulty there. You would have liked to see the workmen this morning, when they played into the spaces between the timbers with the Cochituate water, to see whether she would leak anywhere; and then you would have been still more glad to see how tight she was, and how easily they could stop the places where a few drops came through.

"We now hope that she will be all ready for sea by the first of November; and those good people in Boston who have the care of your vessel, are talking of having me take charge of her on the voyage around Cape Horn to Honolulu. Whether I do or not, I can say that if I were to take charge of any vessel, I would rather take that of yours than of any other; and I say this because you, my dear young friends, have built this vessel for our Lord Jesus Christ. May we, one day, meet one another about His throne.

Very sincerely and thankfully, your friend,

Hiram Bingham, Jr."

A later account gives the following:

Launch of the Morning Star.—This missionary vessel was successfully launched from the ship yard of Curtis, Smith & Co., East Boston, on Saturday, the 22d of September. It was estimated that nearly three thousand spectators were present, and the occasion was one of deep interest. Public exercises were held, Rev. S. B. Treat, one of the officers of the American Board, making a brief opening address; after which Mr. L. S. Ward, Treasurer of the Board, detailed the financial condition of the enterprise. It appears that subscription books were opened last May, through the medium of Sabbath Schools, the shares being fixed at ten cents, and a beautiful little book, entitled the "Morning Star," offered to those who subscribed for five shares. The result was that over 50,000 copies of the book, and over 150,000 certificates of stock were taken, realizing $25,092.32. The vessel has cost $20,000. The number of Sabbath Schools which have shared in the work is about 2,000. Hon. Alpheus Hardy addressed the "stockholders,"—the children, and there was a large number in attendance—and after a formal presentation of the vessel to the Committee, by Mr. B. F. Whittemore, of West Newton, in behalf of the children, a prayer of consecration was offered by Rev. Mr. Clark, Secretary of the Board, and Rev. Dr. Anderson gave the command of the vessel to Rev. Hiram Bingham, Jr. The Morning Star is a brig of 200 tons burden, and is in every respect an excellent vessel.

For a figure head she has a full length female figure, with a Bible under her left arm, which she is in the act of taking with the right hand to present to the heathen to whom the vessel is to bear the "glad tidings" of the Gospel.

THE VETERAN EAGLE.

We present a true likeness, from a photograph, of "OLD ABE," the Live Eagle, which was carried through three years of war and many battles, by the brave soldiers of the Eighth Wisconsin Regiment. Every loyal man, woman and child in America feels a glow of enthusiasm when they know the story of this grand old bird. We have not room here for much of his history, and can only give a few words about him. Taken young from the nest by a wild Indian, he finally fell into the hands of the soldiers of the Eighth Wisconsin Regiment. He was carried beside the flag through many sanguinary conflicts, and came home with his regiment to enjoy the peace he had helped to earn.

Every one knows how he helped the sick soldiers' fund at the last Sanitary Fair in Chicago. Mr. Sewell, now publisher of "The Little Corporal," originated and managed, among the children, "the Army of the American Eagle," and by the aid of the twelve thousand loyal children, who rallied to the work all over the nation, raised over sixteen thousand dollars, which he paid over to the Great Sanitary Fair.

Mr. Sewell, in this work, became so much interested in his beautiful children's army, and disliked so much to relinquish the hold he had gained on their affections, that he started "The Little Corporal," so that he might still work with the children whom he loved. "The Little Corporal" is proving himself a most gallant soldier, winning the admiration and praise of many of the best of people and newspapers of the nation. The *New York Tribune*, Forney's *Press*, *The Independent*, and many hundreds of the most respectable secular and religious papers, have given "The Little Corporal" the highest praise. Very many pronounce it the best periodical for juveniles ever published in America, and say that no parent, who knows the value of the paper, will fail to give it to his children.

Mr. Sewell is anxious that not only all the children whose parents are able to pay for his excellent paper shall have it, but that many thousands may have the benefit of it, though they may not be able to pay; and for this purpose, he still offers for sale beautiful colored album pictures of his pet Eagle. To every one who sends him ten cents, he forwards by mail, a short sketch of the life and exploits of the Soldier Bird, and one of the colored pictures above spoken of. *All* the money thus received is used in supplying "The Little Corporal" to orphan children and those who are too poor to pay. Besides this, most magnificent premiums are offered to those who send small or large clubs of subscribers to the paper. All who wish to write to Mr. S., may address him thus:

ALFRED L. SEWELL,
Publisher of "THE LITTLE COPORAL,"
CHICAGO, ILLINOIS.

"THE HEAVENLY CHERUBS," from Raphael's Sistine Madonna.—This is a most superb line engraving, 12 by 16, engraved expressly as a Premium Picture for "The Little Corporal." The pictures will have a very large sale at the regular price of two dollars ($2.00) each. But an easier way to earn one is to send three subscribers to "The Little Corporal," at one dollar each. All who subscribe during the months of October and November, will receive the remaining numbers of The Corporal for this year free, besides the whole of the year 1867.

Address the publisher, ALFRED L. SEWELL, Chicago, Ill.

ORGANS AND MELODEONS GIVEN AWAY.

Alfred L. Sewell, publisher of "The Little Corporal," Chicago, Illinois, is offering great inducements to those who help him in his beautiful work among the children. He offers to give splendid musical instruments, Organs and Melodeons, to those who send him large clubs of subscribers. This affords a good opportunity to young ladies and others to procure, with little effort, fine instruments for their homes, or for their churches or Sabbath school rooms. Send to the publisher for the October number of his paper, which tells all about it.

The price of the "THE LITTLE CORPORAL" is One Dollar a year. Sample copies, Ten Cents. Circulars sent free, on application.

SKETCHES OF MISSIONS — No. II.

Missions of the American Board in India.

S. C. BARTLETT, D.D., PROFESSOR IN CHICAGO THEOLOGICAL SEMINARY.

Henry Martyn, knew the Hindoos well; and he once said, "If ever I see a Hindoo a real believer in Jesus, I shall see something more nearly approaching the resurrection of a dead body than any thing I have yet seen."

But God knows how to raise the dead. And it was on this most hopeless race, under the most discouraging concurrence of circumstances, that he chose to let the first missionaries of the American Board try their fresh zeal.

The movements of commerce, and the history of previous missionary effort naturally pointed to the swarming continent of Asia. It was over this benighted region that Mills brooded at his studies. The British Baptist mission near Calcutta, readily suggested the particular field of India, and the impression was deepened by the ardent imagination of young Judson. His mind had, in 1809, been so "set on fire," by a moderate sermon of Buchanan's "Star of the East," that for some days he was unable to attend to the studies of the class, and at a later period a now forgotten book, Colonel Symes's "Embassy to Ava," full of glowing and overwrought descriptions, stirred him with a fascination for Burmah, which he never lost. The Prudential Committee of the Board, also looked to the Burman Empire because it was beyond the control of British authority, and therefore beyond "the proper province of the British Missionary Society."

Judson did indeed find his way to Burmah, but in a mode how different from what he expected; cut adrift from his associates, and fleeing from British authority. The Board established this mission, but in a place and with a history how diverse fron their intentions. Man proposes but God disposes. Bombay became the first missionary station.

And that choice band of young disciples — God had roused

their several hearts, brought them together from their distant homes, and united their burning zeal to scatter them in the opening of their labor. There was Mills, given to God by his mother, now strengthening her faltering resolution; there was Hall, ready to work his passage, and throw himself on God's Providence, in order to preach the Gospel to the heathen; there was Judson, ardent, bold and strong, and Newell, humble, tender and devoted; there was Nott, with the deep "sense of a duty to be done," and Rice, whose earnest desire to join the mission the committee "did not dare to reject;" and there was the noble Ann Hasseltine, with a heart all alive with missionary zeal before the Lord brought Judson to her father's house in Bradford, and the young Harriet Atwood, gentle and winning and firm, mourning at the age of seventeen over the condition of the heathen, and at eighteen joining heart and hand with Newell, to carry them the gospel. Of all this precious band, two only, Hall and Newell, did God permit to bear a permanent part in that projected mission. Mills was to die on mid-ocean, in the service of Africa; Harriet Newell was to pass away before she found a resting place for the sole of her foot; Nott was to break down with the first year's experience of the climate; Mr. and Mrs. Judson, and Mr. Rice, were to found another great missionary enterprise.

On the 19th of February 1812, the Caravan sailed from Salem, with Judson, and Newell, and their wives on board; and on the 20th, the Harmony, from Philadelphia, with Nott, and Hall, and Rice; the one vessel going forth from the heart of Congregationalism, the other from the center of Presbyterianism, carrying the sympathies of both denominations. They sailed through the midst of the embargo and non-intercourse; and the note of war with England followed their track upon the waters.

Their instructions pointed them to the Burman Empire, but gave them discretionary power to go elsewhere. The Burman Empire could be reached only through the British possessions, and both vessels were accordingly bound for Calcutta. But the British authorities in India at that time were resolutely opposed to christian missions. The East India Company professed to believe that the preaching of the gospel would excite the Hindoos to rebellion, and was meanwhile drawing a large revenue from the protection of idolatry. The Baptist missionaries at Serampore had felt the power of this hostility, but, being British subjects, and having long held the ground, could not be dispossessed.

But the spirit of hostility had of late been kindled up anew. In the very year when Mills and Rice were founding their secret missionary society at Williams College, Rev. Sydney Smith was stirring up the British public through the enginery of the Edinburgh Review, against the British Missions in India. He opened by insinuating that the mutiny at Vellore was connected with a recent increase of the missionary force, he continued with ridicule of "Brother Carey's" and "Brother Thomas'" Journals, and closed with an elaborate argument to show the folly of sending missions to India. He argues, 1st, from the danger of insurrection; 2d, from "want of success," the effort being attended with difficulties which he seems to think "insuperable;" 3d, from "the exposure of the converts to great present misery;" and 4th, he declares conversion to be "no duty at all if it merely destroys the old religion, without really and effectually teaching the new one." In regard to the last point, he argues that making a Christian is only destroying a Hindoo, and remarks that "after all that has been said of the vices of the Hindoos, we believe that a Hindoo is more mild and sober than most Europeans, and as honest and chaste." Such was the tone of feeling he represented, and he returned next year to the task of "routing out" "a nest of consecrated cobblers." The Baptist missionaries are "ferocious Methodists," and "impious coxcombs," and when they complain of intolerance "a weasel might as well complain of intolerance when it is throttled for sucking eggs." He declares that the danger of losing the East India possessions "makes the argument against them conclusive, and shuts up the case;" and he adds, that "our opinion of the missionaries and of their employers, is such that we most firmly believe, in less than twenty years, for the conversion of a few degraded wretches, who would be neither Methodists nor Hindoos, they would infallibly produce the massacre of every European in India." To this hostile feeling toward missionaries in general, was soon added the weight of open warfare between England and America.

The Caravan first reached her destination on the 17th of June. Scarcely had the first warm greetings of christian friends been uttered, when the long series of almost apostolic trials began. Ten days brought an order from government, commanding the return of the missionaries in the Caravan. They asked leave to reside in some other part of India, but were forbidden to settle in any part of the Company's territory, or its dependencies. May they not go to the Isle of France? It was granted. And Mr. and Mrs. Newell took passage in the first vessel, leaving their comrades, for whom there was no room on board. Four days later arrived the Harmony; and Hall, Nott, and Rice also were summoned before the police, and ordered to return in the same vessel. They also applied for permission to go to the Isle of France; and while waiting for the opportunity, another most "trying event" befell them. Mr. and Mrs. Judson, after many weeks of hidden but conscientious investigation, changed their views and joined the Baptists. Four weeks later and another shock; Mr. Rice had followed Judson. "What the Lord means," wrote Hall and Nott, "by thus dividing us in sentiment and separating us from each other, we can not tell." But we can now tell, that the Lord meant another great missionary enterprise with more than a hundred churches and many thousand converts in the Burman Empire.

While the brethren still waited, they gained favorable intelligence of Bombay, and especially of its new governor. They received a general passport to leave in the ship Commerce, paid their passage and got their trunks aboard, when there came a peremptory order to proceed in one of the Company's ships to England, and their names were published in the list of passengers. They, however used their passports, and embarked for Bombay, while the police made a show of searching the city for them, but did not come near the vessel. In a twelvemonth from the time of their ordination, they reached Bombay, to be met there by a government order to send them to England.

While the Commerce was carrying Hall and Nott to Bombay, another sad blow was preparing. Harriet Newell was dying of quick consumption at the Isle of France. Peacefully, and even joyfully she passed away, sending messages of the tenderest love to her distant relatives, comforting her heart-broken husband, and exhibiting a faith serene and unclouded. "Tell them [my dear brothers and sisters,] and also my dear mother, that I have never regretted leaving my native land for the cause of Christ." "I wish to do something for God before I die. But * * * * I long to be perfectly free from sin. God has called me away before we have entered on the work of the Mission, but the case of David affords me comfort. I have had it in my heart to do what I can for the heathen, and I hope God will accept me." She is told she can not live through the day. "Oh, joyful news,

I long to depart." And so she departed, calling with faltering speech, "My dear Mr. Newell, my husband," and ending her utterance on earth with "How long, Oh Lord, how long." And yet God turned this seeming calamity into an unspeakable blessing. Mr. Nott, half a century later, well recounts it as one of the "providential and gracious aids to the establishment of the first foreign Mission," and remembers its influence on our minds in strengthening our missionary purposes. And not only so, but the tale of her youthful consecration, and her faith and purpose, unfaltering in death, thrilled through the land. How many eyes have wept over the touching narration, and how many hearts have throbbed with kindred resolutions. "No long protracted life could have so blessed the church as her early death." On the Isle of France there still is seen a stranger's grave, while another solitary tomb may be seen on the distant Island of St. Helena. The one formerly contained the world's great Captain, the other holds the ashes of a missionary girl. But how infinitely nobler that woman's life and influence, the whole world shall yet with one voice confess.

From February till December, Hall and Nott, at Bombay, were kept in suspense, and even in expectation of defeat. The Governor of that Presidency was personally friendly, but overborne by his official instructions. Twice were they directed to return in the next vessel, their names being once entered on the list of passengers, and at another time their baggage being made ready for the ship, and the Coolies waiting to take it. Again and again were they told there was no alternative, till all hope had passed. Hall had made his final appeal, in a letter of almost Pauline boldness and courtesy, in which he bade the Governor "Adieu, till we meet you face to face at God's tribunal." The very next day, they were informed that they might remain till further instructions were received; and in due time they gained full permission to labor in any part of the Presidency. The Company had yielded to the powerful influence brought to bear, not only from without, but from within their own body at home. When, at the last moment, the Court of Directors were on the point of enforcing their policy, a powerful argument from Sir Charles Grant, founded on the documents of the missionaries, turned the scale. *India was open.*

Hall and Nott were soon joined by Newell, who, bereft as he was, and for a time supposing that his comrades had all been sent back, had yet resolved to labor alone in Ceylon.

Bombay thus became the Plymouth of the American Mission in India: less prominent and influential than other stations, but noted as the door of entrance. Here began the struggle with Hindooism — entrenched as it was for ages in the terrible ramparts of caste, "interwoven throughout with false science, false philosophy, false history, false chronology, false geography," entwined with every habit, feeling and action of daily life, among a people prolific in every form of vice, and demoralized by long inheritance, till the sense of moral rectitude seemed extinct. Hindooism was aided, too, in its recoil, by the dealings of the English nation, who, says Sidney Smith, "have exemplified in our public conduct, every crime of which human nature is capable."

In itself, the Bombay Mission proved one of the most discouraging of all the Missions of the Board. Sickness and death kept sweeping away its laborers, and it was years before the first conversion of a Hindoo. But one missionary now resides at Bombay, and that city is now only one of the nine stations of the Mahratta Mission—numbering some forty-nine out-stations and twenty-two churches, with a membership scattered *through a hundred villages.* The tremendous strength of Hindooism is well exhibited in the fact that up to the year 1856, the total number of conversions in the field was but two hundred and eighty-five; and the sure triumph and accelerating power of the gospel were equally well expressed in the fact that for the next six years the conversions were nearly twice as many as in the previous forty, and that never has there been such depth of interest, and so numerous accessions from the higher castes, as during the last few years. The full harvest-time is not yet come. But Hindooism is felt to be thoroughly undermined; and another generation may witness, if the church is faithful, such revolutions in India as there is not now faith to believe.

It is impossible, in this brief sketch, to follow the course of the several other Indian Missions of the Board. Besides the Mahratta Mission, of which we have sketched the origin, there is the Ceylon Mission, formed fifty-one years ago, by Meigs, Poor and Richards, with a career of comparative prosperity from the outset. It numbers its ten churches, with their five hundred (483) members; has educated five hundred young men in its seminary, and three hundred girls in its boarding-school, and scattered thirty thousand persons through the island, who have read the Bible in the village schools; and, with its kindred laborers, it has made an impression so profound that the heathen extensively admit the final triumph of the gospel. "Yes, Christianity will prevail in our children's time."

There is the Madras Mission, established chiefly as a printing-station, which, besides issuing 450 millions of pages of Bibles, tracts, and other books, has maintained some seventeen schools, and secured a hundred and fifty persons to the church.

Then there is also the Madura Mission, just a generation old, with its fourteen stations, its thirty churches, and its 1160 church members, of twenty different castes, *four-fifths of whom have been received during the last half of the time.* It numbers its seminary and female boarding-school, its eighty village schools, its hundred and fifty village congregations; and during the year 1865–6, by its system of itineracy, preached the gospel in 1200 villages, to 59,000 adult hearers. In this goodly work have been found engaged some of the choicest spirits that the church has seen since apostolic times. The names of Hall and Newell, and Poor and Scudder, and Meigs and Hoisington, and Winslow and Ballantine, and many others now with God, are names of blessed memory and holy fragrance. And where are the like-minded men, by scores, to enter in and finish the work? It was theirs to open the field to the Christian world: who will follow? The task is but begun. "There will probably be," says an intelligent observer, "a long preparatory work in India, and a rapid development."

Hitherto, the enterprise has been carried on amid discouragements, oppositions, bitter persecutions, and even poisonings of converts; but it has steadily gone forward. And when we see the accelerated motion with which the gospel is now pushing its way, when we view men of the higher castes coming in, and the whole fearful enginery of caste giving way, when we see the gathering of the Christian denominations toward India, and listen to the confessions of the Hindoo organs and leaders, we sometimes think the harvest may not be far away.

And to-day, over against the despairing cry of Martyn, and the dogged assertion of Sidney Smith, we will put the admission of the *Indu Prakash*, the native Bombay newspaper: "We daily see Hindoos, of every caste, becoming Christians and devoted 'missionaries of the cross.'" And so far as figures can show the power of a movement that runs deeper than all figures, ponder the following statistics, carefully compiled in 1862. In the three Presidencies of India, there were representatives of thirty-one missionary societies at work, aided by ninety-eight ordained native preachers. They were regularly dispensing the gospel to one thousand one hundred and ninety congregations, besides hundreds of thousands of other hearers; they reckoned a hundred and thirty-eight thousand registered or nominal Christians, of whom thirty-one thousand were communicants; they had ninety thousand children and youth in attendance on their schools.

These facts are to be viewed as only the foundation, long laid in silence below the surface, for vastly greater changes yet to appear. So deep is the hold of the work, not only on the native converts but on the foreign residents, that the churches themselves already contribute twenty-five thousand dollars a year; while British officials in India give a quarter of a million dollars annually to the several missionary societies in that country.

And could the witty writer of the *Edinburgh* now visit the scene, he might incline, in several particulars, to modify his judgment of 1808—that the missionaries "would deliberately, piously and conscientiously expose our whole Eastern empire to destruction, for the sake of converting half-a-dozen Brahmins, who, after stuffing themselves with rum and rice, and borrowing money from the missionaries, would run away, and cover the gospel and its professors with every species of ridicule and abuse." He might be glad, also, to sum up his case a little differently than thus: "Shortly stated, then, our argument is this: We see not the slightest prospect of success; we see much danger in the attempt; and we doubt if the conversion of the Hindoos would ever be more than nominal." It is a marvelous specimen of the folly of this world's wisdom, and a strong showing how God hath chosen the weak things of this world to confound the mighty.

Never was an enterprise begun and prosecuted with a deeper sense of helplessness without God, and of whole-souled trust in His power and His promise. Judson has well expressed the spirit that animated all his comrades. When he had been three years at his post, and had found neither a convert, an inquirer, nor an interested listener, he could write thus: "If any ask, what prospect of ultimate success is there? tell them, as much as that there is an almighty and faithful God.....If a ship was lying in the river, ready to convey me to any part of the world I should choose, and that, too, with the entire approbation of all my

Christian friends, I would prefer dying to embarking." Two years more witnessed but one inquirer—yet the same song of faith and hope: "I have no doubt that God is preparing the way for the conversion of Burmah to His Son. This thought fills me with joy. I know not that I shall live to see a single convert: but, notwithstanding, I feel that I would not leave my present situation to be made a king."

Such was the dauntless, deathless courage that led the first Foreign Mission of the American churches; such the first handful of Christian soldiers that deliberately sat down to the siege of all India—to whom God gave the victory. How sublime that faith! How glorious the reward! "He that goeth forth and weepeth, bearing precious seed, shall doubtless come again with rejoicing, bringing his sheaves with him." Let Christians and churches ponder well the struggle of the gospel for a foot-hold in India, and never again entertain one doubt of the sacred promise, "Lo! I am with you alway, even unto the end of the world."

NEW STORIES FROM AN OLD BOOK — SECOND SERIES.*

THE RUNAWAY MISSIONARY.

"WHICH way bound, Captain?" asked a landsman, tired and dusty with his day's travel, of the master of a vessel all ready for sea.

"She's bound westward," answered the Captain; and seeing at a glance that the questioner was no sailor, he added, in an undertone, "You would not know the port, if I should tell you its name."

"A long voyage?"

"Yes, for a great many days; away across the sea, almost to the end of the world."

"Sail soon?"

"Right away, sir. Any idea of taking passage?"

"Yes—think I will."

"Where do you want to go?"

"Oh, as far west as possible—I don't care much where."

"Pay your fare, then, and come right aboard. We shall be off soon."

The landsman produced his money, stepped aboard and went below to rest, and was soon fast asleep.

"Ho, boys! all hands!" rang over the deck and down into the forecastle; "weigh anchor, get up sail, cast off the lines! We must improve this fair wind."

The ship was speedily under headway, and standing out of harbor, before a strong south-east breeze.

A few hours after, the Captain was walking the deck with an anxious face.

"What's the matter, sir?"

"Don't like the looks of the sky. Never saw such moving clouds; they are flying about up there in all directions! Guess we are going to have a gale. Yes! there it is coming! That cloud is as black as night. See the zigzag lightnings cross it! Hear the thunder! Something besides thunder, too—a roar of wind! Man at the helm! head back to port! All hands ahoy! Reef the sails! Hurry up!"

Too late! The tempest has struck them, and the ship is over. No, she rights again after a little; but one mast is gone, and the mainsail is in shreds. The rudder is broken. How the sea boils and foams around her! The waves dash over her deck every moment. What will the poor Captain and sailors do now? They'll do just what frightened men always do; they will pray. They are down on their knees now, begging for their lives. These men are all idolaters, and of different nations. Each has a god of his own, to whom he is praying. Between their prayers they throw overboard some of the cargo, to lighten the ship—if, perchance, they may save her from foundering. But all seems to do no good. The waves dash higher and higher every minute. The Captain goes below to watch for leaks, and finds there the landsman, fast asleep.

"You land-lubber! what are you here for, asleep? Asleep now, so near death? I am expecting to go to the bottom every minute! Wake up! Pray! If you have any God to call on, now is the time."

The landsman awoke. He saw at a glance the peril, and his own conscience told him that he was the guilty cause of it all.

"Let us draw cuts," cried the sailors, "and find out whose crimes have brought down the wrath of the gods on us!"

The lot fell upon the poor, trembling, self-accusing landsman.

"Who are you? and where did you come from? and what is your business? and what crime have you been committing?" they all asked, in a breath.

"I am a preacher of the true religion, and I know the only true God, who made the sea and the dry land. But I have disobeyed Him."

"How dare you disobey such a God?"

"He sent me on a Foreign Mission. He told me to go to a wicked city, away in the East, and foretell the destruction of all the people because of their wickedness."

"Why didn't you go?"

"I was a popular preacher at home, and I preferred to stay and preach to my own nation. I thought I could do more good at home. I was afraid, too, that the heathen would kill me."

"If your God is so great, He could take care of you well enough."

"Yes; but then, I thought that if the people were all to be destroyed, it would do no good to tell them of it. And, again, I thought that the true God is merciful, and if they should repent and He should spare them, I should be called a liar."

"Well, what did you come to sea for?"

"Oh, I thought if I ran away and went westward over the great sea, I should then be so far off as to have a good excuse, and could get rid of the Foreign Missionary work."

"What a fool you were, to think of getting away from your God on the sea, if, as you say, He made the sea as well as the land!"

"I didn't like his looks," said one sailor, aside, "when he first came aboard."

Said another, "Oh, if it is that great, terrible God that is angry, what will become of us all? He is stronger than all the rest of the gods put together. What shall we do to please him? Tell us, you silly runaway, what is to be done!"

"I know," he answered, "that I am the guilty one. It is all on my account that the storm came."

"He is good to confess it now, and take all the blame. I like that in him."

"Pitch me headlong into the sea," continued the runaway, "and the storm will cease."

"Oh, we can never do that! It is hard enough to see a poor fellow washed overboard, and hear his drowning cries."

"He's our passenger, too," broke in the captain. "He has paid his fare, all right. It wouldn't be honorable to throw him overboard. Pull away again at the oars—pull hearty again—and see if we can not make headway toward the shore!"

The men worked with a will; but it was of no use. The peril was becoming greater and greater all the time.

"All your work will do you no good. You can't contend with the Almighty. You can do nothing with me on board. Fling me out; I deserve it. That will save you, and nothing else will."

They began to reason: "We shall all go to the bottom at this rate, and the stranger with us. He brought the trouble on us. If he can bear it all, he ought to. If we all have to go down, it is better he should go first. And who knows but his own words are true?—that if he is thrown into the sea, the rest of us can escape? His God is angry with him, and wants him punished; and He can't be displeased with us if we do it."

Then, for the first time in their lives, they prayed to the true God: "Oh, let us not all die for this man's sins! Don't blame us for trying to save ourselves as thy own servant has told us to."

And with that prayer on their lips, they threw the runaway overboard. In an instant the storm ceased, and the sea became still. Then the sailors knew certainly that the God of this poor landsman was also the God of the sea; and they worshiped Him.

"But the runaway—now a castaway; what became of him? Of course, though, he was drowned, and made food for the fishes."

No; for he afterward told the story himself.

"How was he saved? Did he swim to land? Did he cling to the rudder chains?"

No, he found the strangest boat man ever was in. A shark, or some great sea monster, swallowed him whole, and carried him under the sea for three days, on such a voyage as no body before or since ever made.

"How did he breathe?"

That is more than I can tell. He thought it was all over with him. But he repented of his sins, and prayed to God earnestly, and promised to obey the next time; and then the Lord made the shark, or whatever it was, carry him back to the shore, and land him there safely. A sorry looking minister I think he must have been after that voyage. He had formerly been the Court preacher; yet I think few of the royal family would have known him when he first landed. But he was cured of his folly, and was now willing to go on the Foreign Mission. He went a long overland journey to the great city. As soon as he reached it, he began to hold open-air meetings, telling the people they were so wicked that the Almighty would destroy their whole city in about six weeks. The people were terrified, and began to fast and pray, and give up their vices. There was a great revival in that city. A merciful God saw their repentance, heard their prayers, and spared their city. And so his missionary tour was wonderfully successful. I am sorry to add that this strange sort of a missionary was less merciful than his God, for he was so afraid that his reputation would suffer, that he was displeased because the Lord spared the city. But the Lord convinced him of his folly, and made him ashamed of himself again.

If any man in these days, whom the Lord is calling to go on a Foreign Mission, is excusing himself because he is a popular preacher at home, or because he does not like to go among the heathen, or because he thinks it will do no good to preach to the heathen, or because he is afraid they will kill him, or because he fears a foreign climate, he had better remember the "Runaway Missionary."

Should the children read this story, they must guess the name of this runaway; his father's name; his nation and his birthplace; where he lived; to what city he was sent, and how large it was; to what sea-port he went; to what port the ship was bound; and whether it is ever safe to disobey God.

LAURENS.

THE MISSIONARY SITUATION.

The financial year of the Board is now drawing to a close. Many of its friends are anxiously inquiring — all who coöperate with it will wish to know — What is the situation? Are there signs of promise abroad? Do any respond to the call for men? How stands the treasury?

To these questions we are able to answer that, for the most part, the omens are auspicious and full of cheer.

(1) The past year has been one of *more than usual religious interest* in the various fields. Awakenings and revivals are reported

from Micronesia and the Sandwich Islands, from all our missions in Turkey, and among the Nestorians. There is a ground-swell of religious inquiry in the hitherto dead masses of India. A special interest in preaching has recently developed itself in China, Mr. Chapin, located in Tientsin, in a recent tour addressing crowds numbering 2,000 or 3,000 persons. The gospel leaven is so working among the Arminians, that a powerful party inside that corrupt church are moving for reform. And the last intelligence from Western, Eastern, and Central Turkey is of a very cheering character. The time has manifestly come for great results, if the church at home will put in the men, properly sustained, to do the work which God is so wonderfully laying to their hands.

(2) *More men and women, here at home, have offered for the work than for any previous year since* 1858. We hope to report for the year ending October 1, the sending out of ten ordained missionaries, two physicians, and eighteen females, married and single. A number of others are under appointment; the names of several more are in the hands of the Prudential Committee; so that at least as many more will be ready for next year.

A remarkable fact in this new development is, that the larger part of these persons come from the Middle and Western States. Four appointments have been made from Wisconsin within a few months. Twelve from the last graduating classes in theological seminaries west of the Hudson — five of them from Chicago — have been received by the Board. One of the physicians under appointment is from Ann Arbor, Michigan; while Iowa sends a representative of its churches to labor in Ceylon.

Putting these facts together, is it not manifest that the promises are hasting to a glorious fulfillment? Very clearly the Spirit of God, which is moving mightily upon the face of the abysses of heathendom, is also brooding over the hearts of many at home, calling them into this high and blessed service.

(3) *The state of the treasury is not so favorable as last year at this time.** The disparity is not large. But should there be *any* at such a time as this? Do we not reasonably expect that the churches which are giving the greater offering, even their choice sons and daughters, should also be more abundant in that which is less — the means to sustain them?

* See statement on second page of cover.

This is a question of special interest to the churches of the North-west. We have surprised the country by our noble gift of men and women. It is not so gratifying that we are responsible, thus far, for our full share of the deficit in the donations.

A letter just received from Secretary Treat says: "The ordination of the five young men at Chicago has made a profound sensation in our churches. It was an unlooked for development of christian large-heartedness, and will long be remembered to the praise of the God of missions." Let us, then, stand by this our offering of men and women, and not in any sort take it back to ourselves by withholding the means to send them to their destined fields of labor. The month of August still remains in which to close up the contributions of the year. Will not all who intend to share in this good work see that their donations reach the treasury as early as the first day of September.

84 Washington Street,
Chicago, *August* 1, 1867.

A WORD TO THE SUNDAY SCHOOLS.

We hear of many schools that are working for mission schools among the heathen children. Quite a number have already sent in their annual offerings, and received the Lithograph of the Morning Star, and the little Photograph Certificates. But some will have to wait till their crops of Missionary Potatoes, and other things which, they have planted come in. A favorite way of earning money this year seems to be by killing potato bugs, at so much a dozen. Bnt we sincerely hope that the opportunity to do this is not large.

There is one month more before the year closes, we shall be glad to have the schools, so far as they can, send in their contributions by the last day of August.

If any superintendent desires to show his school the certificates, with the card photograph on the back of it, a copy will be sent upon application to this office.

S. J. Humphrey,
84 *Washington St., Chicago.*

A PLEA FOR FOREIGN MISSIONS.

PROF. S. C. BARTLETT, D. D.

THE words of Christ and of some Christians are in sharp conflict. "Go and teach all nations," was the solemn charge of the risen Saviour. The gracious promise coupled with it—"Lo, I am with you alway," made that charge perpetual; and the last recorded words of the ascending Saviour pointed away "to the uttermost parts of the earth."

But we often hear a very different voice—sometimes it comes across the waters: "The mission of the American churches is to take care of America." Sometimes it rises from the bosom of the church at home—"We can do no more for the distant nations till the great work is finished here." And the world now asks, more flippantly than ever—"Why send our charities round the earth, when the poor are at our doors?"

Never has the specious plea carried so much plausibility, nor found so many ears half open to receive it. Here is half a continent to be cared for, involving forces unmeasured and destinies untold, still in the critical and the formative hour. Old home charities are coming up with new demands, and new charities are pressing in, full-grown. A half-supported ministry throughout the land must speedily and effectually be relieved. Feeble churches in the older settlements are growing feebler and more dependent; while young churches, by hundreds, in the new settlements and the South, are asking and soon to ask for the help of their infancy. A great company of preachers must be aided into the ministry. Some hundred church edifices are to be erected. A dozen colleges and seminaries are clamoring for endowments. The Union Commission pleads for a whole race of emancipated blacks and an equal number of emancipated whites. The American Missionary Association calls for its quarter of a million of dollars. And while the young Samson is bound with these seven new cords, the cry will also come, "The Philistines be upon thee!" in the influx of Romanists and infidels from Europe.

Is the home work greater and more pressing than it ever was before? Granted;—but the resources of the church also are unprecedented. God has given to these churches the means for such a work as they never yet have done, attempted, or devised. They need not go about to compound with their duties—they need not rob God to save their country, nor harden themselves to the cry of the perishing heathen, because they hear the jubilant song of the rescued slave. In the midst of all these narrow views, *even though their selfishness be continental,* the calm voice of the Master will still be heard—"These things ought ye to have done, and not to leave the other undone." God never yet rolled wealth and power into the hands of a man, or a church, or a nation of churches, that they might sit down and *enjoy it all at home.* Wherever he sends strength, he means work; and while he has undoubtedly increased the urgency of the work at home, he has not abated—he still presses on us the foreign call, and has placed in our hands ample resources for them both.

Dear Christian brother, the Master's solemn words and the Macedonian cry must not be drowned in the din and stir around you. Permit me to recall to your thoughts your obligations to lend a liberal aid to the CAUSE OF FOREIGN MISSIONS.

I. The work of Foreign Missions belongs to the divine economy of Christian labor. The Saviour himself, in the command already quoted, made it the permanent duty of his disciples—their earliest and latest work: "Go ye and teach all nations; and lo, I am with you alway." Repentance and remission of sins were to be preached among all nations, beginning at Jerusalem. Now the disciple is not above his Master, that he should annul his Lord's command. When the young clergyman inquired of the Iron Duke, as to the expediency of Foreign Missions, the curt and decisive answer is said to have been—"Look to your marching orders, sir!" To Christ's follower the motive should be final: HE hath appointed it.

The Saviour, too, in his brief ministry began the work; for while ever hastening on through his native land, to "go into the next towns, that I may preach there also," and while sending forth the twelve and the seventy for its thorough exploration, he yet found time to reap a "harvest" among the despised Samaritans; he let his light shine "beyond the Jordan" unto "Galilee of the Gentiles;" he penetrated the country of the Gadarenes, and he visited the coasts of Tyre and Sidon, to leave there his gracious answer to the prayer of faith.

He took early care to carry out his appointment. While the first disciples lingered around the homestead, the Master let loose upon them the hand of persecution, and they "were scattered abroad every where, preaching the word." The persecutor himself was arrested, to be told by his Lord, "I will send thee far hence, unto the Gentiles;" and in due time the Holy Ghost said, "Separate me Barnabas and Saul, for the work whereunto I have called them," — the Foreign Mission work. That chief apostle gloried in being the apostle to the Gentiles, held himself a debtor to Greek and barbarian, ranged "from Jerusalem round about unto Illyricum," and ever strove to preach the gospel where "Christ was not named." He lived to see Asia Minor and Greece dotted with churches, to visit brethren at Rome, and to send salutations from saints in Nero's palace.

Wherever the spirit of Christ and of Paul has entered an individual or a company, there has been a missionary band. The spirit of religion is none other than the missionary spirit. It is the kindling of a fervent desire that the glorious God may be manifested, and lost men saved. It is the struggling of another light to shine, and to throw its beams far out into the dark. The brighter it burns, the wider it shines—a pure flame, fed by zeal and self-denial, and glowing with the patience of hope and the labor of love.

Accordingly, the best churches in all times have been missionary churches. They have caught the spirit of him who declared himself "the light," not of Jerusalem, nor of Judea, nor of Asia, but "of the world." They have entered heartily into his plan. While the apostolic spirit still lingered on the earth, the early Christians, near the close of the second century, had ascended the Nile, crossed the Euphrates, traversed the Danube and the Rhine, and planted a church on the banks of the Seine. The old Nestorian church, which from the fifth century long resisted the growing idolatries and corruptions of Christianity, became the great missionary church of Asia, and carried the gospel to Persia, Syria, Tartary, India, and even China. That Waldensian martyr church, which handed down a pure gospel through the darkest of the dark ages, began its course as a missionary church. A rich merchant gave his property to the poor, and with a band of pious associates went forth to preach the gospel; numbers of his followers imitated his voluntary poverty, and by their zeal and self-denial spread themselves with amazing rapidity through the countries of Europe. When the great Reformation came, though Europe was ready like tinder for the spark, the fire was kindled by efforts incessant and ubiquitous. The toils of the great Reformer were multiform and overwhelming, and every lighted torch went forth to kindle other lights. On one occasion Bucer and Snepf and Brentz together listened to the words of Luther. Bucer carried the light to Strasburg and to England; Snepf went forth to Marburg, Stuttgard and Jena, and Brentz toiled at Heidelberg, Tübingen and Halle. So the work went on. And not alone by the living voice: books and tracts were scattered broadcast; theology flew abroad among the people, on the wings of sacred song; the poetry and satire of Von Hütten and the prints of Cranach were enlisted in the cause. It was one mighty forth-putting of religion, crowned with proportionate success. The choice vine first planted in New England was preëminently a missionary stock. In the reasons for their voyage, in the presentation of their cause to the King of England, in the memorable "Mayflower" compact, they specify their "inward zeal" to spread the kingdom of God to parts unknown. And their labors confirmed their words. Twenty-four regular Indian congregations bore early witness to their fidelity. And who can say how much the nation is indebted for its late deliverance to the active and aggressive piety descending down the line of those churches, which, like an ever-bubbling spring, has kept the fountain pure at home, and sent its sparkling waters through a thirsty land.

So must it ever be. It was the divine economy that the church, like its Lord, should give itself to the salvation of *the world;* and whenever it ceases to remember the heathen of his inheritance, and the uttermost parts of the earth his possession, then does the Christian church cease to be Christ-like. Shame and woe will be unto it whenever it erects another goal than that to which its Master pointed, or breathes a narrower spirit than that which glowed in the bosom of its Lord. Nothing less than the world's redemption can rightly fill its mind or fire its heart.

II. The work of Foreign Missions is also the true and wise economy of Christian labor. The author of human redemption understood how his own scheme should be carried out. He made no mistake in his plan, to be rectified by his followers. He saw it needful to his churches that their sympathies should be broad, and their labors and charities manifold. He saw it to be needful for the world that its centres of warmth and light should be widely dispersed. All radiant influences, material or moral, intensify their power with their nearness. The little fire that warms a chamber is lost upon the prairie. So God appointed to scatter these feeble flames of warmth and light throughout the world, that each in turn might scintillate new fires, and all might grow and spread till their circles meet. The converted Sandwich Islander must reach forth to the Micronesian, and they together shall not only diffuse the sacred leaven to other islands of the ocean, but they shall react, as they have already done, upon England and America. The Karens of Burmah must extend the gospel to the Karens of Siam, and every mission in time turn missionary.

This world can never be wholly elevated and sanctified by isolated fragments, more than the arctic ice will be thawed in rectangular sections. Every new bond of intercourse between the nations is a new chain of moral action and re-action. In our upward walk we not only carry Ireland and Africa in our arms, but India and China, and the islands of the sea, are clinging to our skirts, and will not let go. It is idle to say we will wait till the pressing work in this land is completed. For the generations to come that work will continue to press — nay, at that rate it will never be done; for the churches, weighed down with the spirit of selfishness, will lose even the power to resist the evil influences rushing in from abroad.

In our own country, even, we find it indispensable to act from numerous diffusive centres. To elevate the negro race, we do not say, "First finish the work in South Carolina." We plant our schools in North Carolina, and Virginia, and Mississippi, and Tennessee—wherever we have the means and find the openings. It is the plainest dictate of common sense. It is not alone the expeditious way—it is, perhaps, the only possible way; and we know well that the general renovation of the South is not to be effected by detachments and at distant intervals, for we have not forgotten how the virus of rebellion quickly spread from little centres through eleven States. We know that at all points there must be a simultaneous invasion, by laws and immigration, by schools and churches, or the renovation will not be wrought.

On the same principle of sound wisdom did the Saviour require the foreign work to keep pace with the home work, and ordain that repentance and remission of sins should be preached "among all nations, beginning at Jerusalem." It was, in fact, because of the bonds which bind the nations together, drawn tighter and stronger at every step of science, art, and commerce, so as to make both the speed and the success of his cause hinge upon the process. For we remember how the lust of the Sandwich Islands not only enwrapped the British sailor at Lahaina Luna, but followed him round the ports of the world, and back to his native home, till at length the wondrous grace of God closed up that pit of abomination, to the joy of good men and the bitter lamentation of the wicked. It was a lesson for all time.

III. The Foreign Mission enterprise is indispensable for its reflex influence upon the churches. It is well for them that the preaching of the everlasting gospel was not literally given to some mighty angel flying through the midst of heaven. A chief privilege and blessing of Christ's followers on earth would thus have been taken away. It was the great Redeemer's purpose to cast out the spirit of self-seeking, whether on the wider or the narrower scale; and in every form to cultivate a philanthropy as broad and high as his own — to infuse a love truly God-like and Christ-like. Therefore, he bade them care and labor, not only for themselves, their family, their church, their neighborhood, their nation, but for the world.

The narrow and self-centering policy has always proved as fatal to churches, as to individuals. It kills out spiritual life and action. Feeble churches have often acted on the principle of caring only for themselves. They have said, "Our burdens are so great that we have nothing to spare. Charity begins at home." And so they have schemed, and toiled, and contributed solely or chiefly for their own wants. All outside efforts get the go-by or the flat refusal, "there is so much to do for ourselves." And the contribution-box goes round on Sundays, and the sewing-circles toil on week days, all for the home want; and meanwhile God curses them with feebleness and barrenness. Sometimes such churches freeze up in their own ice, and perish. And with many a feeble congregation, the day of deliverance and strength has begun when they first began to look out upon the things of others. It is now the settled policy of all wise spiritual guides, that even the beneficiary church must, for its own life and health, turn benefactor. For, however destitute, it can still look forth, in every direction, upon the ruined race, and say, like the wounded Sidney to the dying soldier, "Friend, thy need is greater than mine."

And among all the calls of benevolence that arouse the christian life of the churches, none is so unmingled in its character and claims as that of Foreign Missions. The various schemes at home are enforced by many local and personal considerations. They leave us no option. The purity of the ballot, the wisdom and equality of our laws, the stability of our government, the protection of our own property, persons and privileges, compel us, whether we would or not—whether Christians or unbelievers. And if this be all we do, we may well ask ourselves the question: What do ye more than others?

Enveloped thus by benefactions that touch us close, and press us hard, and clamor in our ears; and beset as we also are on every side by influences and enterprizes that are largely political, material and earthly; peculiarly do these American churches need to throw themselves earnestly and devotedly into some great form of beneficence that cuts loose from all such surroundings, and stands out as *a purely spiritual enterprize.* That great spiritual beneficence is found in the cause of Foreign Missions. It is an unmingled Christian philanthropy. It appeals to the pure love for Christ, and the pure love for dying men, and to nothing else. To carry the gospel to the distant heathen, draws upon those very motives—deepest and highest—which brought the Son of God to this far-off earth. As a means of cultivating and of proving "the mind which was also in Christ Jesus," the great missionary work abroad stands in almost vital relations to the churches of our Lord. It calls upon them to look beyond all their pet schemes and home charities, yea, beyond all the philanthropies of national self-preservation; and, with a benevolence as broad as the ocean that bears their messengers and tokens of christian love, to remember the heathen—their Lord's inheritance, and the uttermost parts of the earth—his possession!

IV. The Foreign Missionary enterprize now presses its claims upon us, by reason of the critical condition of the field. We stir up the churches to the home work because an emergency is on us. And the argument is valid. But there is also an emergency among the nations. I mean not only their general perishing condition, but a special waking up, for good or for ill, that calls for speedy attention.

Fifty years have revolutionized the missionary aspect of the nations. Then the question was, Who will receive us?—now, How can we answer the calls? Many favorable changes are of recent date. The gospel has won at length a foothold in Japan, and the government has given a site for a church and a Mission Institute. China is now thrown wide open for its entrance; and a Baptist missionary writes that, "one year of the present generation is worth twenty of the last." Africa is becoming explored throughout by the traveler, and ready for the missionary. India is said to be "honey-combed" beneath the surface, and the Brahmin is gloomily dreading the future. The old religious foundations in Turkey are becoming so thoroughly undermined that Mohammedanism lifts its feeble hand to strike. In Syria, Mr. Jessup writes, it is "a time of rapid progress and development; but of what avail will it prove unless the gospel keeps pace with civilization?" Great changes are going on in Europe, too, which it is beside our purpose to specify — except that the Papacy is aroused at last to set itself openly against the progress of the world.

And this last fact is significant. Other agencies besides the gospel watch their opportunity, and the posture of the nations is both critical and eventful. A state of society ripe for the gospel is ready to rot without it. The uprooting of an old religion may only make way for a general skepticism, or another false religion. A starving soul will feed on husks. And the departure of one devil, not cast out by the finger of God, may only leave the room swept and garnished for seven others to enter in and take up their abode.

Accordingly the emissaries of evil are seizing the opportunity. A skeptical bishop is teaching another gospel to the Zulus. A political bishop is carrying formalism to the Sandwich Islands. Hostile movements are instigated in Turkey and Persia. The Jesuits are countermining our missions in Syria. The Papacy is struggling to recover its lost hold upon the nations, from China to America. Even worldliness and infidelity are venting their bitterness. And while the grasp of old error is unloosed, to leave the awakened mind unsatisfied, is to harden it for the future.

From almost every mission of the American Board there comes a cry for relief and help. Not only are the missionaries breaking down with over-work, and the places of the dead left vacant, but the wide expanding work opened in God's good providence — that vast whitening harvest of the Lord — is left untouched. From Western Africa again and again have they asked for reinforcements to keep the mission alive. From Syria Mr. Thompson entreats, "If you can get *one* man, send him with the least possible delay." In Eastern Turkey, for four years have those faithful men urged "the pressing need of a reinforcement," till the heart is sick with hope deferred. In Central Turkey, missionaries went home from their annual meeting "as if going home from a funeral," for the lack of helpers; and they "beg and implore the pious young men to come to our assistance." The Western Turkey mission recently sent in its call for six new laborers. Mr. Shedd, of the Nestorian Mission, makes his "most earnest appeal to the servants of Christ to come — to hasten — and enter into the perishing harvest." From Western India comes an appeal "to the Christian young men of America," not alone from living missionaries, but breathed out in the last words of the beloved Chapin, and solemnly emphasized by the death of the noble Ballantyne. The Ahmednugger Mission is on the very verge of disaster. And so the cry echoes and re-echoes from place to place throughout the field. The American Board wants *sixty new missionaries, at once,* for its present missionary stations. And with the men must come the money, followed by the fervent prayers of God's people. And the work ought to break forth beyond its present limits. It is not enough to hold our own.

Never have the people of God in America occupied a position so commanding for this God-like enterprize. The war has taught them what pecuniary burdens they can bear without staggering, and has poured wealth into their hands. They now stand before the world clear of complicity with Slavery. The eyes of the world have been turned hitherward; the cultivators of India have eagerly asked for news of the war, and the Hindoo convert has prayed fervently for the victory of the North. Our missionaries, who have long commanded the respect of Europe for their singular efficiency and fidelity, will now carry such weight of influence among the nations as never before. God has raised up and preëminently qualified this Christian people to be a great light in the world. That is our mission. It is selfish, it is inexcusable, it is wicked, to hide that light at home. All Christendom would deplore it, and God would frown upon it. The Karen and the Sandwich Islander would rise up in judgment and condemn us. What a wretched and heartless return for our wonderful deliverance, to clutch our blessings and hold them fast!

Let us then bring our money and our sons, yea, ourselves,

and offer all as freely unto Christ as we gave to our country. We may cheer ourselves with the thought, that the missionary work is the most economical and effective of human achievements. The very crumbs that fall from the table of our four years' war would feed our present missions for generations to come. The first cost of a "Monitor," or the annual cost of a cavalry regiment * in actual service, has exceeded the present revenue of the American Board.

But let us not linger where we are. God calls for growth. Remember that in the one missionary enterprize are gathered up the support of preaching, ministerial education, the religious press, the Christian schools, and, to a great extent, the Bible and the tract distribution of the heathen world. All these causes, which, in the home field, come each with its separate place and appeal, are massed together under a single name and one chief contribution for the Foreign cause.

And let us not delude ourselves as to the magnitude of our efforts. Through the blessing of God, the results have vastly outstripped the means. Viewed in a business light, the past has been, in the missionary work, but a day of small contributions. Hundreds of business enterprizes in the land are on a larger scale. Fifty-five years' expenditure of the American Board — the organ now of near six thousand churches — is less than the capital stock of either of half a dozen railways leading from Chicago. The churches spend vastly more on their luxuries, their extravagances, and, perhaps, their follies. It is time to disabuse ourselves of the notion that we have done great things; it is God who hath done marvellous things for us. Let this time of our national deliverance mark a new era in our labors for a dying world — an era of true self-denial, and of large and liberal offerings. Let every pastor study the theme till he is full of its power, and then present it to his people; let him keep it before them, and feed them with missionary intelligence; let every church put itself in lively sympathy with the missions by constant reading of their letters and reports, faithfully observe

* The annual cost of a full cavalry regiment, in wages, rations, clothing, forage alone is over $600,000; add to this the loss and destruction of horses, arms and equipments in actual service, and the amount is increased, as I learn from a veteran of the army of the Potomac, by at least another third.

the monthly time of prayer, and take the regular contribution; let every member give, not as others give, but as the Lord hath prospered him: — then should we be amazed at the littleness of our former offerings — we should hear the young men saying, "Here am I, send me,"— and God would pour us out a blessing at home and abroad, that there shall not be room enough to receive it.

AMERICAN BOARD OF COMMISSIONERS FOR FOREIGN MISSIONS,

NORTH-WESTERN DISTRICT,

REV. S. J. HUMPHREY, *District Secretary.*

CHICAGO, *February* 1*st*, 1867.

To the Congregational and Presbyterian (N. S.) Churches of the North-west:

DEAR BRETHREN,—Let me invite your attention to some facts relating to the American Board, which give it a claim to your continued co-operation.

It was created by the churches, and belongs to them. Their best piety and wisdom gave it birth. They designed it to be — and it is — the channel through which they, for the most part, obey the command of Christ, binding on every christian, to carry the gospel into all the world. It has no life, apart from their life. They chose to give it no vested funds, by which it could carry on an independent work. Year by year, nearly all its 1,127 laborers look to the home churches for their daily bread. And thus, in its organic law, these churches have linked it to themselves by a tie of continual dependence.

It is a safe and economical agency. The American Board is financially sound. Its paper is honored at the bank counters of all the world. No dollar of the more than $11,000,000 placed in its hands by the friends of missions has been lost. To collect this large sum has cost about three and one-third per cent. of the receipts. About three per cent. more has been returned to the donors, in the form of missionary publications. And the remaining ninety-three per cent. has gone directly to the work of saving souls in heathen lands.

It is a comprehensive agency. It may not have occurred to you that the American Board contains, in itself, nearly every other form of beneficent working. It is a *Bible Society.* Its missionaries have translated the Scriptures, wholly or in part, into forty-two different languages, spoken by half the population of the globe. Its helpers are all Bible distributors and readers. The native churches, from the first, are put to the work of *Home Missions.* They early organize themselves for this purpose into societies, as in Eastern Turkey, Zulu Land, and the Sandwich Islands. The churches of the latter have their *Foreign Missions.* Indeed, they give more men and means, in proportion to their work, four-fold, than any other christian people in the world save the Moravians. Out of an entire population of sixty thousand, they now have thirty-eight laborers in the dark islands beyond. The Board is a *Tract Society.* It has printed, from the first, over thirteen hundred million pages, comprised in over two thousand different publications; and all its missionaries are, in effect, colporteurs. It is an *Anti-slavery Society.* Barbarism and human bondage go together. But the gospel gives liberty. The Sandwich Islanders were slaves to their chiefs, till our missionaries brought Christ to them. Woman every where, in heathendom, grinds in a miserable servitude. But when the missionary is received, she becomes the light of a christian home. The missionaries are often called to perform the work of a *Sanitary* and *Christian Commission.* More than once they have been the almoners of our bounty in times of famine. A distinguished journal in this country declares that "the single letter of Dr. Hamlin, on the cholera, is likely to be worth, even to this country, this year, all that the Board which sustains him will cost for one year." The Board enforces *Temperance* in all its native christians. There is no genuine reform needed, among the population to which it goes, of which it is not, in the very nature of its work, an earnest patron. It is, necessarily, an *Education and Church Erection Society.* At least two colleges have sprung up under its culture — the Syrian Protestant College at Beirut, and one at the Sandwich Islands. It has sixteen training and theological seminaries, with three hundred and eighteen pupils. In Turkey alone there are more theological students under its care than are in all the seminaries of New England which furnish men for the Board. In the one comprehensive work of preaching the gospel, and planting christian institutions, no real interest of humanity is left uncared for.

It is productive of actual results. Tried by any proper standard, the missions of the Board are a clear and manifest success. Our missionaries plant themselves — often one man to a million — in the midst of populations where barbarism has reigned for centuries; where hatred to foreigners puts up an almost invincible bar to access; where idolatry is woven through all the fabric of social and civil life, stultifying the intellects and embruting the hearts of the people; and yet against this fearful odds, a careful calculation finds that the number of converts to each missionary and native church is greater than in the pastorate at home. In one of our most favored States, the average annual addition by profession, for the twenty-six years from 1839, was, to each acting pastor, about five and a half. During the same time, the accessions to our churches on foreign ground, through the abounding grace of God, was about fourteen and a half to each missionary. See what has been done at one well manned station in Turkey, Kharpoot. Eleven and a half years ago, Dunmore went to this place. He met with little success, and after two or three years, returned home to die in battle for his country. Soon after, three missionaries were sent to the abandoned station, and still remain. And now for the results. Upon a field of fourteen thousand square miles, from a population of about half a million, they have gathered four hundred converts into eleven churches; organized from these a corps of forty-six native helpers, six of whom are pastors, and thirteen others licensed preachers; occupied fifty out-stations; opened thirty-four schools, with nearly one thousand scholars; established a female seminary, with forty pupils, and a theological seminary, where thirty-four young men are now preparing to preach the gospel; received from the people benevolent contributions to the amount of $2,520 in gold; and all this at an expense to the Board, the past year, of the paltry sum of $8,200. And what has been done here could be repeated — it has been, in some cases, with nearly the same results — at many other stations, had we the missionaries and the means to fully occupy the ground.

Here is success. And what shall we say of the 245 churches from the first gathered by the Board? What of the 1,500 souls annually, for the last twenty years, led to Christ? What of the nearly 25,000 native converts now under its training; and what of the more than 40,000 who have already passed from its care, through the gates, into the celestial city?

But to these great results is to be added another fact.

The work of the Board, thus far, is mainly one of seed-sowing for future harvests. The number of its converts is by no means the measure of its success. Outside the little circle of these, multitudes have heard of Christ. The Morning Star has risen upon those dark lands, and many are turning their faces toward the day. Mainly through the labors of our missionaries, there has sprung up, in the midst of the dead and petrified formalism of Turkey, a widely spread hunger for a spiritual religion. India is losing confidence in her idols. An earnest spirit of inquiry is abroad. The expectation that their own systems are soon to give place to the missionaries' religion, is fast gaining ground among the people. There are hundreds of thousands too much enlightened to trust longer in their false gods, and yet too little enlightened to know truly the Christian's God; and already, from the very precincts of heathen fanes, where the old faith is dying out, goes up the agonizing cry, "*Father, Father, give us faith!*" The churches must prepare speedily for appeals from these awakened millions, such as it has never heard before.

The apostolic methods of the Board commend it to your confidence. It accepts with a hearty faith Christ's word, that his kingdom among men is like *leaven* — one soul converted is to be the means of converting other souls. It has fully adopted the policy to send its missionaries, not to be pastors, but apostles; to call out and train a native agency; to establish churches, and place over them pastors raised from among the people themselves; to teach every convert, whether he be preacher or layman, that Christ has a work for him to do. Our missionaries count nothing as really gained till a *self-sup-*

porting and self-propagating Christianity is established; and this is being rapidly accomplished. Although the number of ordained missionaries sent from this country has fallen, during the last six years, from one hundred and sixty to one hundred and forty, yet the preaching outposts occupied have increased from one hundred and fifty to four hundred and twenty-one, and this mainly by the accession of native helpers. In Western Turkey, to twenty-five missionaries, eighty-nine preachers and teachers have been raised up. Nine missionaries in Eastern Turkey have eight native pastors, twenty licensed preachers, twenty-seven teachers, and twenty-nine other native helpers under their charge. With a force from this country of only seven men, one of them an invalid, and two others not yet masters of the language, on the Nestorian field, there has been developed a native corps of one hundred and eleven helpers, sixty-nine of whom are preachers. At Diabekir, out of a church of one hundred and one members, thirty are wont to go out, two by two, to spend Sabbath evening in religious conversation, by appointment, in different houses. The great success at Kharpoot is owing in part to the fact, that scores of unpaid native laymen spend the Sabbath in the whitening harvest fields, gathering sheaves for Christ. Mr. Bruce, of the Mahratta field, multiplies himself thirty-fold, by teaching and superintending that number of preachers and catechists, whom he sends into the surrounding villages; and we just now hear that our beloved brother Bissell, going back to that same field, saddened, because he must return alone, is made glad by laying the hand of ordination upon six native preachers, graduates of this year's theological class. And all this kind of working is still in its infancy. If we can only send out men sufficient to develop and superintend this native agency, it will swell to vast proportions with a continually accelerated speed.

The need which the Board is attempting to meet calls loudly on the churches for help. We have a plenty of work at home; but here it can be shown there is in active service one minister to every thousand souls. How is it abroad? In India, where all Christendom is sending laborers, each missionary, if all were distributed equally, would have an area of more than two thousand seven hundred square miles, and a population of not less than three hundred and fifty thousand. The lamented Walker had a parish of seventeen hundred villages, containing five hundred thousand souls. Parmelee, watching over an invalid wife, at Erzroom, is attempting to hold — he can not occupy — a district as large as all New England. A recent letter from China mentions five large cities on the seaboard, with connected provinces, in some instances containing twenty millions of people, waiting for the first proclamation of the gospel. A full half of the human race have never heard of salvation through a crucified Redeemer. Hundreds of millions more have caught only the faintest rays of the Light of Life. They have been waked up to feel a want which no man comes to satisfy; and from these unnumbered masses what a dark, sad procession of souls is that which disappears every day within the awful shades of another world? We have gone far enough to take away the miserable hope they had. Is it not simply *cruel* to leave them now, with no effectual knowledge of the Christian's hope? Meanwhile Rome is awake; she already boasts of her five hundred priests in China alone, and reckons in her train hundreds of thousands of adherents. Infidelity, too, is active—strewing poison upon the streams of civilization flowing in upon the aroused masses of heathendom. Young India, breaking away from idol worship, is drifting rapidly into blank atheism. At Beirut alone six infidel presses are feeding the newly awaked Arabic mind with the miserable husks of Voltaire and Eugene Sue. The cry for laborers in these perishing harvest-fields was never so imperative as now. It gathers emphasis, in wonderful openings for the gospel, with every new year. The providence of God is saying, in unmistakable accents, to every man redeemed by the blood of Christ: Go to these lost millions with the gospel. Go now. Go yourself with the heavenly message. If this can not be, go by children consecrated to this blessed work. If you have not these to give, go by your money, to sustain those who have the call and the heart to hear it; and go by your prevailing prayers, to make their words the mighty power of God unto salvation.

And now what are our churches doing to meet this call? It is with something more than shame that we turn to the record of the past year. We write it with an unaffected alarm, that from all these more than four thousand churches, but one ordained missionary could be sent, for the first time to "preach among the Gentiles the unsearchable riches of Christ." But we believe that this is the darkness that thickens before day-break. New men are coming forward. There is a prospect that ten or fifteen will be under appointment before the year is closed, and we shall need largely increased contributions to send them out. But what are these few to the vast needs that are pressing upon us? Twenty recruits are not sufficient simply to make good our wasted ranks on foreign shores. The pioneer work already done, the fields already opened and cultivated in part, demand to-day *sixty-five fresh men:* and we could locate them at once to good advantage, did they offer themselves, and the churches furnish the means. Meanwhile the Board is seeking colored men of promise, with whom to open a new mission on the coast of Africa, to be wholly conducted by them; and many wide and effectual doors are inviting us to enter in and possess the nations for our Lord.

There is something of hope in the last year's record of this district. The following comparative table gives the facts in brief:

Illinois	Of	370	churches,	in 1864,	157	churches	contributed	$12,688 70
Michigan ...	"	251	"	"	89	"	"	4,843 28
Wisconsin ..	"	201	"	"	53	"	"	3,270 60
Iowa.......	"	215	"	"	74	"	"	1,358 44
Minnesota ..	"	89	"	"	26	"	"	760 99
Total	"	1,126	"	"	399	"	"	$22,932 01
Miscellaneous contributions								2,009 80
Total..								$24,941 81
Illinois	Of	370	churches,	in 1865,	127	churches	contributed	$10,110 79
Michigan ...	"	251	"	"	106	"	"	5,340 91
Wisconsin ..	"	201	"	"	70	"	"	3,168 93
Iowa.......	"	215	"	"	66	"	"	1,674 66
Minnesota ..	"	89	"	"	30	"	"	693 97
Total	"	1,126	"	"	399	"	"	$20,989 26
Miscellaneous contributions............................								1,657 75
Total								$22,647 01

Illinois	Of	370	churches, in 1866,	159	churches contributed		$11,991 34
Michigan....	"	251	" "	87	" "		5,445 99
Wisconsin ..	"	201	" "	61	" "		2,300 35
Iowa	"	215	" "	81	" "		1,627 13
Minnesota ...	"	89	" "	25	" "		841 21
Total....	"	1,126	" "	413	" "		$22,206 02
Miscellaneous contributions							2,502 39
Total							$24,708 41

The number of churches appearing on our list this year for the first time is 102. But 174 of the churches contributing in 1865 report no collections for 1866. The whole number of churches contributing in 1866 is 417, a gain of 18 over any preceding year. Of the 1,126 churches in these States, 691 have remembered the Board by donations in one or more of the last three years; yet but 163 of these have reported a contribution for each year.

It is encouraging to notice that, while the receipts on the whole field fell off largely, we are able to report a gain in this district of $2,061.40. But the new financial year does not open so auspiciously. The first three months show a falling off from the like period last year of $1,788.47, while in the whole field the receipts about hold their own.

Agencies. The Board has no collecting agents in this field. We desire to save this expense. We are anxious that the largest practicable per cent. should go directly to the purpose for which the donations are given. Do not wait, then, brethren, for the call of an agent. None will come. We entrust the interests of this great cause to your hands.

Very fraternally yours,

S. J. HUMPHREY.

WAS HARRIET NEWELL'S LIFE WASTED?

REV. H. L. HAMMOND.

MORE than half a century ago, in a distant island of the Indian Ocean, a young wife, not twenty years of age, lay down and died. She was a woman of rare talents and accomplishments, who, only a few months previous, had left the cultivated society of New England, to engage in what was then generally thought the chimerical enterprise of a Foreign Mission. She was not allowed to begin her work among the heathen, nor even to reach a permanent missionary field. Those months were mainly spent in sailing from one port to another, to find the heathen.

To all human appearance, that precious life was wasted; and many were disposed to say: "How plain the providential rebuke for her temerity!" The argument then seemed clear, that she made a great mistake in leaving a home-circle she was so well fitted to adorn, where her influence might have won many to Christ, and going abroad to wear herself out in long sea-voyages, and to find a solitary grave among strangers, before she could even learn a language or gather a school.

But the end was not then. Her weeping friends gathered up her letters and journals, and published her memoirs, with her funeral sermon, preached by a distinguished New England divine, thinking, doubtless, that this was the last sad tribute to the memory of Harriet Newell. The book was a very small one. I have lately seen a copy of the first edition, more than fifty years old, in fine print and solid type, humbly bound in sheep. One of these little books found its way to central New York, and fell into the hands of a mother there, in a township that had neither church, minister nor Sunday school. Her womanly sympathies were enlisted, first for the dear young missionary, then for the heathen, and then for the heathen in her own town. She went to her closet and consecrated herself anew to the Saviour. Her husband read the little book, and was reconverted; and then both husband and wife engaged in zealous labors for the salvation of their neighbors. A revival began in their house—the first ever witnessed in that town—and spread with power, till the whole region felt its influence. Scores of young people were converted, who afterward went their several ways to bless the world. Two evangelical churches grew out of that revival. That father and mother never lost the spiritual baptism then received. They came to a western State, as lay missionaries; founded another large and prosperous church, and when they finally, in a good old age, went home to heaven, I doubt not they sought out Harriet Newell, among the heavenly throng, to thank her for that sacrifice of her young life. Their large family of children were all converted—some preceded the parents to heaven, and some still remain to toil in the vineyard. One of them, converted in that first revival, is a layman widely known and honored, in both Church and State; others are pillars of the churches to which they belong; and one, whose privilege it is to preach the gospel, gratefully pens this tribute to the memory of the young Missionary.

And the end is not yet. Doubtless there were similar results in other families and other communities, could they be traced. But if this were all, who could say that the life of Harriet Newell was wasted?

BRIEF ADDRESS AT THE GENERAL CONFERENCE OF MAINE.

Rev. W. Warren, of Gorham, said:—Instead of a speech, or half a speech, Mr. Moderator, I have jotted down with my pencil some questions that have been asked me here, or heretofore, which I will briefly answer.

"How do you get along with the American Missionary Association? Ans.—Finely. We have no trouble. We work together in harmony. They take the freedmen; we, the heathen. They love the Board; we love the Association. Bygones we have given a deep grave.

"How much of the money we give ever goes to the heathen?" Ans.—Ninety-two per cent. It costs only eight per cent. of what is given to work the vast machinery at home.

"But doesn't charity begin at home?" Yes, but it doesn't stay at home. It goes every where, like the great Master. This home-bound, home-sick charity, isn't charity. The real grace seeks the poor and the lost, the world over.

"After all, don't you think the heathen will be saved without the Gospel?" Ans.—Then the way to save the world would be to *blot out* Christianity, rather than to publish it, and incur the risk and consequences of its rejection. Jesus should have stayed in Heaven, and let the world sleep on in ignorance and wake up in bliss. But let me ask, Isn't idolatry named as one of the sins that *exclude* from Heaven? And are the heathen in their pollution *fit* for Heaven? Did not Jesus send Saul of Tarsus to the Gentiles (the heathen) "to turn them from darkness to light; and from the power of Satan unto God?" Will those be saved who die under the power of Satan?

"And yet, what have you accomplished?" Ans.—We have translated the Bible into the languages spoken by half the world; have planted among the heathen every form of institution that we have here; and have put in motion there every civilizing and educating force that we have in this country. Our missions have gathered into churches, from the first, nearly seventy thousand members. They have received some fifteen hundred annually, on an average for the last twenty years. Is not this something?

"But do you expect to convert the world by the few missionaries you send out?" Ans.—No. These are the seed wheat. For every one we send abroad, however, we expect that *several* will be raised up from the heathen to preach the Gospel. We have twice as many native preachers now as we have missionaries, and the ratio is increasing every year. Fifteen years ago there were twice as many missionaries as there were native preachers. There are more students in the

Theological and Training Schools of the Board, than in all the Theological Seminaries of our Order in New England. The Gospel is like the banyan tree; each branch in touching the earth becomes itself a tree, to send forth still other branches. So the tree of life is to cover the earth.

"But can we afford to send half a million of dollars out of the country every year for missions? Why this waste? Ans.—We can afford to do our duty; we can afford to obey Christ. But missions are not a waste. They are profitable pecuniarily. They give safety to our commerce and our men upon the high seas; they open markets for our exports in every quarter of the globe. The gains here far more than cover the cost of missions. For every reason, then, we can not spare them.

"How is your Board coming out this year? In debt?" Ans.—It isn't *our* Board; it is *your* Board, and the church's. It is your institution, your instrument, to act upon the heathen; your highway to go to the nations, and do them good. In debt? The Board was never in debt, and never will be, if it acts economically. It can disburse only what is contributed. No, the debt, if any, will be the *church's*, and not the Board's.

"How much of our money do you want? Ans.—None of it, but some of the *Lord's* money, in your hands, on trust. "Well, then, how much of the Lord's money shall we give?" Ans.—Not any; for how can you *give* what is another's? No, the Gospel idea is—*render:* "Render unto Cæsar the things that are Cæsar's, and unto God the things that are God's."

"How shall we manage this matter of 'rendering;' how regulate our stewardship?" Ans.—Admit the fact of it; feel its reasonableness and binding force. Then resolve to live for Christ; to labor for him; and do business by his rule; and let *His* cause come in for a fixed share of the proceeds.

THE AMERICAN BOARD AT THE UNIVERSAL EXPOSITION, PARIS, 1867.

THE Secretaries have sent to Paris, as the contribution of the American Board to the Mission department of the great Exposition, 1000 different publications, prepared by its Missionaries in thirty-four different languages. This is but half of all that have been issued from the first; but many are out of print, and others are not at command. A few specimens of idols from the Hawaian Islands, and of the various implements once in use, are also forwarded. A brief history of the Board, and its various missions, is printed in pamphlet form for distribution. And the following will be suspended as a placard in conspicuous positions:

AMERICAN BOARD

OF

COMMISSIONERS FOR FOREIGN MISSIONS,

ESTABLISHED IN 1810.

STATISTICS FOR 1866.

Missions..............................18; Stations and Out Stations.... ..525
American Missionaries, ...312; Native Laborers................815
Churches,... ....194; Communicants,..............24,630
Communicants added in 1866,............. 1,119
Training and Theological Schools,..16; Pupils, ...318
Other Boarding Schools,...........16; Pupils, ...526
Free Schools,...................395; Pupils,..................10,057
Appropriation for 1867,......................................$518,000

GENERAL SUMMARY.

Churches from the first,..........245; Communicants, over.........60,000
Missions Closed or Transferred,.. 13
Missionaries from the first, ...1,296
Printing from the first, pages, ...1,368,978,788
Different Publications, over...2,000
Entire Expenditure,...$11,229,013

FOR OTHER PARTICULARS, SEE PAMPHLET.

Missionary House, Boston, United States of America, Dec., 1866.

WILL CHRISTIANITY PREVAIL IN INDIA? *

BY REV. E. BISSELL, OF THE MAHRATTA MISSION.

In one of my tours among the Mahratta villages, I met toward the close of the day, a little company of men at the rest-house. After conversing a while, they asked me to pray, that they might know how christians worshiped God. I assented, and offered a short prayer. They listened in silence, and at the end said, "Well done, that is a good way to pray." Then one of them, a wealthy and influential man, addressed me in the following somewhat remarkable words: "Sahib, your religion is true, and it will prevail in this land. If we do not embrace it our children will—or if *they* do not *their* children will, for it is true and must prevail." He spoke as if in earnest and I have no doubt uttered not only his own convictions but those of a large number of his countrymen.

The prophecy thus finding expression at this man's lips, is confirmed by the promises of God and the experience of the missionaries who labor there. The gospel has entered India and encamped to remain. It is mightily assaulting that stronghold of Satan on many sides. Three thousand years the powers of darkness have been entrenching themselves, and training the people to resist all invasion from the allied hosts of God's elect. But the seemingly impregnable fortress now begins to yield, and the final triumph is sure, for an Almighty arm has undertaken the work.

The place of my own labors for the last twelve or fifteen years, has been on that part of the western coast of India, called the Mahratta country, of which Bombay is the capital. It is the conflict on this field of which I am now to speak.

The Mahratta country embraces some 300 miles of the coast, north and south of Bombay, reaching inland 450 miles, and

* The substance of this address, has been delivered in many churches, East and West. On the eve of Mr. Bissell's return to India he has been persuaded to prepare it, somewhat hastily, for publication. Those who have heard it from his lips will be glad to see it in this form. Others to whom it may come, will find in it a most interesting account of the way of the gospel in that dark land.

contains a population of about eleven millions. This is not one tenth part of India; for, divided into States, Hindostan would make more than thirty of the size of Ohio; and it contains a population nearly six times that of the whole United States.

To know whether the gospel is to prevail in India, we need to understand what obstacles it meets there, and how it overcomes them. I will notice briefly three prominent obstacles: *Ignorance, the Caste System, and Idolatry.*

Ignorance.—It is not easy to give a correct idea of the full import of this word as applied to the Hindoos. As used in this land it is a *comparative* term. An ignorant man or community, means one less intelligent than people generally. But in India it is an *absolute* term. The Hindoo knows nothing that is worth knowing, and what he thinks he knows is but delusion. Only about five per cent. of the people can read at all—few of these intelligently. Their literature, contained in their sacred books, is made up of a little false Geography, a little false Astronomy, and a great deal of false History and Theology. All this, retailed to the people by the Brahmins, the priestly caste, is the foundation of their opinions. False notions of their Creator and themselves—false notions of the world in which they live, and the world to which they are going! The question is sometimes asked, "Why not send Bibles and tracts by the ship-load, and scatter them broadcast over the land?" But books do not dispel ignorance unless they are read. Only five in a hundred of the people *can* read, and most of them *would not* read christian books. The *living missionary* must go with the Bible in his hand to secure its being read. In a village I once visited, a sheriff came to me for a primer for his boy, that he might learn to read. These primers I used to give to the poor, but of the rich asked two pice * each—a mere nominal price. The man refused to buy, but begged one as a gift. Adhering to my rule, I left the place without giving it to him. After going a short distance, I looked back and saw the boy running after me. I thought the man had at last concluded to buy the book, but I was mistaken; he had sent his boy with *one* pice, hoping I would at least remit half the price of the primer. Now this you may take as that man's estimate of the value of an education

* One pice—three-fourths of a cent.

for his son. *Three-fourths of a cent* he would give to buy his son the means of learning to read, but twice that sum he would not expend; and this man, on the occasion of that boy's marriage, would perhaps spend a hundred Rupees † in loading him with ornaments and gay clothing, and feasting the lazy Brahmins. *That* he would think was the proper way of spending money.

"Over the ocean wave, far, far away,
There the poor heathen live, waiting for day,
Groping in ignorance dark as the night,
With no blessed Bible to give them the light;
Pity them, pity them, christians at home,
Haste with the bread of life, hasten and come."

2. *The Caste System* is a great obstacle to the truth. The word caste, means *kind* or *species*. The same word which is used of men is also applied to animals and trees. The orthodox Hindoo theory is, that the Creator in the beginning formed four distinct castes of men. The first of these issued from his mouth, the second from his breast, the third from his loins, and the fourth from his feet. But now, instead of four, probably full fifty distinctions are recognized. When the question "Who are you?" is asked of a Hindoo, he answers it by simply giving his caste. "Who are you?" "I am a *Brahmin*," or, "a *Kunabi*," as the case may be. This is supposed to be the most important item of information respecting a man, and sufficiently defines him. His rights and privileges—where he may go, and where he may not—are then understood. And to maintain this social position intact is one chief aim of his life. The different castes may talk together, buy or sell to each other, etc.; but they may not intermarry, eat or drink together, nor if widely separated, may they touch each other. Between the highest and lowest the chasm is awful. Even the shadow of the Mahar falling upon the Brahmin is polluting. If the low-caste servant brings an official letter, he never places it in the hand of his master, but throws it down at his feet. Oftentimes when I have offered the Brahmin a book, he has refused to receive it unless I would lay it upon the ground—or at least cover my hand with a cloth as I passed it to him, lest some possible pollution might be carried over from me to his sacred person.

† One Rupee—half a dollar.

Now, the gospel gives no place to this caste system. It teaches that "God hath made of one blood all nations of men;" that all are the children of one parent. When a Hindoo becomes a christian he accepts this truth, and hence by his countrymen he is thought to fall out of their social system entirely, and sinks down to the position of an outcast. All his social rights are forfeited. He is an exile in his native land, and an alien in his father's house. When Vishnupunt, originally a Brahmin, now pastor of the second church in Ahmednuggur, became a christian, his parents not only disowned him as an apostate, but they said, "We have no son. Our son is dead:" and they performed the usual funeral rites, as if he were really dead. Such is the ordeal through which the convert from Hindooism must often pass in embracing christianity. To this would be added personal violence, were it not for the protection of civil law, and often it is done in the face of law. What an obstacle to the progress of christianity this system of caste, so tenaciously held, must be, needs no further illustration to show. It drives away inquirers, holds back the timid believer, and sometimes even enters the church, and alienates members from each other.

3. *Idolatry.*—This is an obstacle perhaps even greater than caste. Idol-worship is not only a lie in itself, but it debases and stupefies the man almost beyond the comprehension of moral truth. You have read that description of the idols of the heathen in the 115th Psalm, "Eyes have they, but they see not. They have ears but they hear not, etc.;" and at the close of the description it is added, "they that make them are like unto them, so is every one that trusteth in them." That psalm was penned by one who had lived among the heathen, and seen the degrading effects of a system of idolatry continued through many generations; and he says *the people are just as stupid as the blocks they worship.* The love of truth is gone, the moral sense is blunted, falsehood and delusion are the very atmosphere in which they live. You have read much of the cruelty of the Hindoos—of their widow-burning, hook-swinging, and painful penances—but painful as these things are, this other phase of Hindooism seems to me scarcely less pitiable—its *stupefying, deadening influence*

*upon the intellect and heart.** Religious worship, which should be solemn and impressive, becomes with them, puerile and frivolous. Penance is substituted for repentance, and bodily contortions for heart-homage. Not idols alone are worshiped. They see an imaginary deity in everything. Men and animals, birds and reptiles, stones and trees, in turn become objects of worship. The Mahrattas have one day in the year set apart for the worship of the crows. They prepare a feast and carry it out to these birds, and call it a dinner for the spirits of their fathers. Ask them why the crows rather than other birds, represent their ancestors. and they have no reason to give, only that their fathers regarded it so. Another day in the year is devoted to the worship of the cobra, a poisonous serpent. A third day each year is given to the worship of their oxen. They paint the horns of their dumb beasts, bedeck them with tassels and trinkets, lead them in solemn (!) procession down to a river, bathe and worship them, and the next day yoke them to the plow and whip them. Could anything bearing the name of religious rites be more contemptible! Could any depth of delusion be more pitiable! †

It is sometimes asked, are not these simple notions after all harmless? As an illustration of their influence upon the character and customs of the people, take the following: It is one of the favorite doctrines of the high-caste Hindoos that all life is from God, and is equally sacred. Hence the inference that it is just as great charity to preserve the life of an animal as that of a man. In consistence with this tenet they have built a poor-house at Bombay for diseased and superannuated cows, cats and dogs. There the miserable creatures, which it would be mercy to kill at once, are permitted to drag out a wretched life till nature relieves them. And this is Hindoo charity! And I know not of a poor-house for men and women in all India, built before christianity came there. I have seen the Hindoo take a

* The ignorance, fatalism and mere animality of the devotee of idols defies all description. Discourse on spiritual things to him is, to use one of his own similes—like playing the lute to a buffalo. He is *content* in his physical, mental and moral degradation. "A full stomach is my heaven." "My stomach will soon cry out if I begin to think of any thing beyond my work"—is his language.

† Looking upon such follies, seeing them change the glory of the uncorruptible God into grotesque images of every conceivable thing—and in the absence of the forms their hands have made, bowing down, even to the loathsome reptiles crawling at their feet—how often have we uttered with new emphasis the words of Paul—they "became vain in their imaginations and their foolish heart was darkened. Professing themselves to be wise, they *became fools!*"

handful of sugar or rice, and going out into the field, drop a pinch here and a pinch there over the *ant-holes* to feed these insects. Why not? That handful of sugar would feed a *thousand* ants, and scarcely suffice for *one man*. How much better to feed a thousand living beings than one!

Such are the people, and such the obstacles which the gospel encounters in India. This stolid ignorance, these bulwarks of caste, this dead stupidity induced by the worship of blocks and stones for many centuries, seem well nigh invincible. And now, will the Bible make its way there in the face of such difficulties? Has the gospel power to enter this stronghold of Satan, and dispossess the usurper? I answer unhesitatingly, YES. The work is great—the obstacles immense, but the gospel is a sovereign remedy—the word of God is quick and powerful.

We sometimes see this power illustrated more strikingly in the case of one man, than when we speak of a whole community. I remember on one of my tours, a poor man whose name was Pandu came extending both hands like a suppliant, and supposing him a beggar, I dropped a few pence in his hand and was turning away. He was a victim of that terrible disease, the black leprosy. This scourge, not uncommon in India, begins its work in the joints, the fingers, toes, and organs of the face, and eats them off inch by inch; thus the man may be ten or a dozen years in dying. I have seen the leper, who is generally a beggar, extend a hand for charity which had nothing left but the round palm on which to receive alms. In Pandu the disease was in its first stages, and the catechist who lived at his village told me he was interested in the truth. Said he, "a few weeks ago Pandu was the vilest man in the place. He would abuse with obscene language every one who came near him, and beat his wife cruelly. He seemed to hate every body; no one would let his *dog* go to Pandu's house, the poor animal would be so ill-treated. One day in a rage he seized an old razor and tried to end his miserable existence. The screams of his wife brought a christian neighbor, who wrested the weapon from his hands, and saved his life." While he was suffering from the wound he had inflicted, the catechist visited him, helped him kindly, and read to him from the Bible. This kindness won his heart. He saw there was something in christianity which was not in Hindooism.

As he recovered, he began to attend the meetings of the catechist. He gave up his habit of vile abuse, and his whole life was changed. Even the heathen noticed it with wonder, and acknowledged that christianity had made Pandu a new man. Leaving his home, he came twenty miles to my place of residence, and spent some weeks there attending our daily meetings. He asked to be received into the church, and, after some months of trial, was approved. He was to be received as soon as I could visit his village, and baptize him in the presence of his own people. But a few days after returning home he was taken seriously ill. The catechist told me of his last days. Said he, "he wanted me to read the Bible and pray with him all the time." He said he should not get well, and that he had but one regret; that was, *he had not yet professed Christ and been baptized.* "I am afraid I shall not be received up there, because I have not the seal on me." The catechist comforted him—told him that if he trusted in Christ with all his heart, he would not be rejected because he had not an opportunity of being baptized. He said, "I do believe in Christ, He is my only Saviour." He charged his wife, who was not a christian, to have no heathen rites performed at his funeral. "I am a christian at heart, let the christians bury me." And the christians did bury him, and mourned for him as for a brother. And I verily believe Pandu's name will be found in the Book of Life, though it is not on our church roll here on earth. Now think how low the gospel reached down to save that man! As vile and loathsome as he could make himself—a leper in body and soul—the gospel still found something to take hold of, and lifting him up, transformed him into a humble, trusting believer in Christ. And as he lay down on the bare ground to die, he could sing at heart as you and I hope to do,

> "Jesus can make a dying bed,
> Feel soft as downy pillows are"—

because he had that blessed hope which the gospel gives—that *precious hope which can bridge over the chasm between this world and the next*, and make the transit safe and easy.

I have mentioned the case of Pandu as illustrating how the *gospel can reach even the lowest.* Another example will show what *living christians* the converts often become. *Yesoba* was a man of more than ordinary thought and thrift among his people, and, taking up the business of a cattle-dealer, became comparatively wealthy. One day, when returning from the market with a bag of money, he called upon the missionary whom he had met before, and sat conversing upon the need of a Saviour. As he became convinced of his lost condition, he emptied his bag of rupees on the floor, and said with earnestness to the missionary, "Sahib, take this money and give me salvation." The missionary explained to him that the salvation of the gospel was "without money and without price;" and gathering up his rupees, he went home sad and thoughtful. But it was not long before he found the Saviour, and became his disciple. The enemies of christianity now determined to effect his ruin. His cattle were poisoned, and in this and other ways his property was mostly destroyed. He received hints that if he would renounce christianity his cattle would not die. But his reply was, "there was a man in the land of Uz, whose name was Job, and though my sorrow should equal his, I will not give up my religion." Others became christians, and a little church was organized, of which Yesoba was chosen deacon. He exerted himself to form a missionary society. The monthly concert was observed, and on the first Monday of each month he always put his *rupee* into the missionary box. In his last sickness a high-caste neighbor called, and spoke in a condoling strain of his former prosperity. "I have lost my property, true," said Yesoba, "but I have gained an inheritance in heaven which I shall never lose." Taking the hand of his children he gave each one some last advice. To his eldest son, who would have the homestead, his dying charge was, "on the first Monday never forget to give the rupee—never neglect it."

Such conquests the truth is continually making. The converts come from every caste, the highest as well as the lowest. The proud Brahmin, the high-born Mahratta, and the outcast Mahar meet in the christian church. A few years ago they would not eat in the same house, or draw water from the same well. Now they come together around the Lord's table, eat of one bread, drink of one cup, and acknowledge themselves the children of one Father, the disciples of one Saviour. In the Mahratta mission of the American Board there are now twenty-three organized churches, containing about six hundred and fifty members. And, including baptized children, the christian community numbers nearly twelve hundred. These christians are widely scattered, residing in one hundred and twenty different towns and villages, each a faithful witness for Christ among the heathen by whom he is surrounded. Four or five of these churches have already been supplied with native pastors, and other young men are now studying to prepare themselves for the sacred office. The training school at Ahmednuggur is also sending forth every year young men who labor as catechists and teachers in the surrounding districts.

The native churches are accepting the duty of supporting their pastors, and giving the gospel to their own countrymen. Several of the churches have monthly collections, and employ one of their own members to visit distant villages and preach the gospel to the people. At the anniversary meetings in October, the missionaries from all the stations, and several hundred of the native christians meet at Ahmednuggur. Many of the people bring forward their offerings to the missionary cause on these occasions. At one of these meetings, a native pastor, after making an earnest appeal, took out his purse and emptied it on the table. It contained, as we afterwards learned, twenty-six rupees, or a little more than his monthly salary as pastor of the church. The appeal enforced by the example was electric, and abundant offerings followed; not money alone, ornaments, household articles, animals, grain, etc., were given or pledged, amounting to several hundred rupees. Some gave in silence, others accompanied their offering with a few earnest words. One pastor of a church arose and said, "Last year I met with a loss—sixty-five rupees were stolen from me; I never recovered them. But this year God has kept me and mine, and I will give him the sum which I lost last year." How many would have made the loss a sufficient excuse for diminishing or withholding their contribution, yet this man made it the occasion of giving generously.

A teacher rising, said, "there was one present last year who is not here to-day." He paused a moment from deep emotion. All knew to whom he referred—his own wife, a lovely christian woman who had died within the year. He continued, "She left me a string of gold beads. I would have kept them as a me-

mento of my dear wife; but I think they would better be in the hands of Jesus."

A lad about sixteen years old, a student in the school, who, by diligence and close application, had passed an examination before some English society, and won a prize of twelve rupees, brought—*not half* of it, which would have been a generous gift—but the *whole twelve*, and gave them to the Lord.

A poor illiterate man sat near the table in a scarlet coat, worn for ornament as well as for use. He took it off deliberately, and folding it, laid it on the table—then said, "Begone, my adorning, all beauty belongs to Jesus Christ." How unlike the selfish spirit of the world, which, when it sees a beautiful object, says, "that must be mine." "No," says the Hindoo convert, "that is beautiful, therefore give it to Jesus."

A poor blind woman having taken her seat humbly just inside the door, came groping her way up the aisle, reached out her hand, caught hold first of the leg of the table, and feeling her way to the top, laid a rupee upon it.

Women, and little children even, took off their ornaments from their arms, their necks, their ears, and brought them forward joyfully for the good cause. Now, it may be said, this was an impulsive movement, and hence not so valuable. But it was an impulse in the right direction, and christian principle and the love of Christ were the foundation of it. The Oriental is proverbially impulsive, and what we want is to have all his impulses sanctified, and working for Christ. Then there will be no danger of his doing too much.

Christianity is planted in India, it has taken root, and is already bringing forth fruit. The gospel is a *real power* there. It takes hold of the hearts of men, and transforms them for Christ. If the church will put its hand to this enterprise with an energy and zeal in proportion to its magnitude and importance, India may be converted to Christ before the end of the present century. It is the conviction of many Hindoos that their own system is destined to be swept away. Thousands have lost all confidence in Hindooism, and are halting between Deism and absolute Atheism. Many believe that christianity is true and must prevail. Shall the christian have less confidence in the power of the truth than the unbelieving Hindoo? But one of them, who had expressed the conviction of which I speak, had one question to ask. Said he, "Why is it that so many generations of our people have passed away before the gospel came here?" This was a hard question, and I could not answer it to his satisfaction. But I brought it home for the American churches, and I now give it to you. Eighteen centuries have passed since the command was given, "Preach the gospel to every creature," including the Hindoos. If the church had done its whole duty the heathen would not now be asking us such questions, but would be praising God that they had the gospel. If we have no responsibility for past generations, *we have for the present, and future ones.* Let us meet it faithfully.

On a tour to the south of Ahmednuggur I once saw in nature an illustration of the gospel's progress, which had in my mind almost the force of prophecy. Passing through the village where my tent was pitched for the day, I noticed a large tree, perhaps three feet in diameter, called the "*Bitter Nimb.*" Some twelve feet from the ground where the trunk divided into branches, there came out the top of another tree of an entirely different species—the *sacred Fig-tree.* (*Ficus Religiosa.*) The trunk of the *Nimb* near the ground was decayed on one side, and looking into the cavity I saw that the stock of the fig tree went straight down through the rotten heart of the other into the ground. It was already perhaps a foot in diameter. And there it stood like a young giant in the grasp of some huge monster, in a struggle on which each had staked its life. It was easy to see what would be the issue of the contest. Already on one side the outer trunk had been rift from the branches to the ground, but it had grown over again and the wound was healed. In another place a fresh crack gaped open so that I could thrust in my clenched hand. And by each such split the old Nimb was growing weaker, while the other gained strength and room. The fig tree by its irrepressible growth was slowly but surely bursting open the other, and soon would stand in its place. As I looked on it I thought here is illustrated what the gospel is doing in India. Hindooism is the *Bitter Nimb*—bitter as wormwood. And christianity is the sacred Fig tree. As birds of the air dropped the seed of the fig in the rotten heart of the old Nimb, and it took root there; so heavenly messengers carried the seed of gospel truth and planted it in the midst of the old effete system of Hindooism, and it thrust its roots downward and its branches upward, and now by its vigorous growth, it is rending asunder and uprooting Hindooism, and soon will stand in its place, the beautiful *Ficus religiosa* of Bethlehem. And oh, what precious fruit it bears! A continual harvest of redeemed, sanctified souls, gathered into the garner above.

ILLUSTRATIONS OF HINDOOISM. *

The Vedas.—It is probable that the most ancient parts of the Vedas, or Sacred Books of the Hindoos, were composed as early as the age of Abraham, that is, about 2,000 B.C.

"Without a careful study of these books no real insight into the origin and growth of Hindooism is to be obtained. But to understand them is no easy task. In India itself they are no longer studied in the same sense as the Bible, or Roman and Grecian Classics are studied in Europe; for the present Brahmins care nothing for what the Vedas really contain, but the merely parrot-like utterance of the words of the Vedas according to their time-hallowed accents is deemed quite sufficient for the promotion of their bodily and spiritual welfare. There are hundreds of Brahmins now living, distinguished from the others by the name of Bhatt, who have learned by heart the whole of one of the four Vedas (each of them being, if all its several parts are counted, of a larger bulk than the Bible), without being able to tell the meaning of a single sentence. The mantras or prayers of the Vedas are regarded as a kind of magic formulas, the efficacy of which rests only in the sound and order of the words and syllables. The very words of the text are, therefore, syllable by syllable, learnt by heart with the most scrupulous accuracy, and so much so, that a good professional Bhatt, or repeater of the Vedas, is actually able to repeat by heart, without committing any mistake, even in such apparently trifling matters as accents (but in *their* eyes matter of the utmost importance), the

* From the *Indian Year Book*, 1862.

whole of one of the Vedas. They used to spend twelve to fifteen years in the merely mechanical business of learning the Vedas by heart. This practice still continues. There are some hundreds of young Brahmins at Poona alone who are devoting all their energies, zeal, and industry to this merely mechanical business to earn in after-life, as a poor return for their immense labor and toil, a monthly income of from three to four rupees!"

The following may be taken as a specimen of the contents of the Vedas:

VEDIC HYMN TO FROGS.—The *Times of India* quotes the following from Max Muller's Rig Veda Sanhita:

"The origin of this most curious song is thus related. Vasistha, desiring for a shower of rain, praised Parjanya with a hymn (7,102.) The frogs accompanied his prayer with a joyful chorus. The sage hearing them merrily croak, became extremely pleased, and made a poem on them. We give here a translation of it:

(1.) Just as Brahmins, who, faithful to their sacrificial vow, have been silent all the year, (commence their prayers anew after the vow of initiation has been fulfilled) so the frogs (after having slept for the most part of the year) have found their voice again!

(2.) When the celestial waters fill this (tank), like a leather bag lying in a desert, the frogs croak together just as the cows followed by their calves are lowing together.

(3.) When, on the approach of the rainy season, Parjanya (the god of rain) quenches the thirst of the frogs longing (for water) by a downpour, they merely croak, one following the call of the other, just as a son (follows) his father.

(4.) One (frog) goes to the other, seizing him when the waters pour down in which they both rejoice. Then the frog, wetted by the rain, is jumping to and fro, and the spotted frog mingles his voice with that of the green colored one.

(5.) One responds to the call of the other, just as a pupil is repeating the words of his teacher. You all show signs of happiness in every limb, when you make your sweet voice heard in the waters.

(6.) Among them there is one lowing like a cow; another bleats like a goat; one of them is spotted, another is green. All bear the same character though they differ in form, voice, and color, for in many ways they modulate their voices when croaking.

* * * * * *

(10.) May the frogs give us riches! that one which lows like a cow, and that one which bleats like a goat. May the spotted and the green frogs give us riches! May the frogs which grant us hundreds of cows, prolong our lives in (this) season productive of thousand (herbs)."

In contrast with this, see a hymn of praise from our *Sacred Book*, and then let us be thankful that we live in a land of Bibles.

9. Thou visitest the earth, and waterest it: thou greatly enrichest it with the river of God, *which* is full of water: thou preparest them corn, when thou hast so provided for it.

10. Thou waterest the ridges thereof abundantly: thou settlest the furrows thereof: thou makest it soft with showers: thou blessest the springing thereof.

11. Thou crownest the year with thy goodness; and thy paths drop fatness.

12. They drop *upon* the pastures of the wilderness: and the little hills rejoice on every side.

13. The pastures are clothed with flocks; the valleys also are covered over with corn; they shout for joy, they also sing.*

GODS QUARRELLING.—Miss Cross, of Bellary, writes:

"Near our house live a number of women supposed to possess supernatural power; deluded ones, wishing to know their future history, carry presents, etc., for them to divine them. A boy lives in the same house, who has attended Mr. Macartney's school. This witty little fellow one day, when all were gone out, went into the mysterious room where the gods were, and turned one upon his head, and then took another, and stuck in the feet of the first, leaving them one on the other. This occasioned the greatest consternation, and a grave consultation was held as to what could be the matter with the gods! At last it was concluded that, being left alone, they had quarrelled, and in future some one must stay at home and take care of them!" †

ARRIVAL OF KRISHNA AT AGRA.—The *Delhi Gazette* contains the following:

* Psalm lxv.

† Female Missionary Intelligencer.

"Among some other distinguished arrivals that have lately honored Agra, is that of the god Krishna, who is, we hear, 'putting up' somewhere in the city. He has come in the form of a Brahmin, and passes his time chiefly in a swing, in which he sits while being swung by married women. His presence came to our notice in consequence of one of the ladies, who left her husband to swing the god, not returning to her family. Her husband has laid a complaint before the Magistrate, and the god has been summoned to the Kutcherry to reply to the charge."

TREE WORSHIP.—A correspondent of the *Indian Reformer* writes as follows:

"On the last day of the Bengali month of Bhadra, a very old *Bat* tree, *Ficus India*, situated about three miles from the village of Nadiya, was worshipped by no less than 10,000 people. The worshippers were, of course, ignorant husbandmen for the most part, and women and children. Seven jars of Ganges water were placed under the tree, and two Brahmins busied themselves in collecting pice and sweatmeats from the pilgrims who had come from various parts of the districts of Nadiya and Burdwan. The worship consisted only in sacrificing a large number of animals under the tree. You may wonder, but it is a fact, that, on this occasion, there were sacrificed about 200 lambs, 300 kids, and 500 pigs! A good bit round about the sacred tree the ground ran with blood."

THE STOMACH THE SEAT OF HINDOOISM.—Mr. Purushottam, a wealthy Hindoo, traveling in England, writes thus from London to Madras:

"Before my departure I had fully determined to continue to be a Hindoo, and nothing else, and as this could only be done by a strict adherence to, and performance of, all the injunctions, rites, and ceremonies of my caste and religion, therefore from the moment of my going on board the vessel which was to convey me to England, up to the time that I am now writing, my food has been prepared in a separate kitchen by my Hindoo servant, and the water I drink is pure from the fountain and untouched, and I have my meals apart from strangers, my daily ablutions have been regularly performed, and my prayers recited. Since my arrival in London I have been invited to entertainments given by gentlemen to whom I have been introduced, but all I partake of on such occasions, are grapes, oranges and other kinds of fruit, and a little milk, so that you perceive that nectar and fruits are under any circumstances unobjectionable."

Remarking on this the *Madras Times* says:

"We cannot conceive any person better qualified than Purushottam, by his own showing, appears to be, to support a nationality which depends on the question whether apples are eaten roasted or raw. The model Hindoo dines with English gentlemen, partakes of fruit only, and retains his nationality. But let the fruit appear in the form of a dumpling, and he is a lost Hindoo! Other religions may be seated in the mind and soul—but the stronghold of Hindooism is the stomach. A Hindoo may retain his faith against all argument, and against all violence, but mix a little bit of beef in his food, and his religion is gone! not that he renounces it, but that it repudiates him. In all religions but one, the Almighty is looked to as the protector of the poor against the oppressor: in all religions but one, he who endures to the end will receive his reward. In Hindooism alone man has the power to stand between Heaven and his fellow creatures, and to affect their fate beyond the grave. Let half a dozen Hindoos seize one of their own caste, and forcibly thrust forbidden food down his throat, and (it is a common thing) that man has ceased to have any rights in this world or the next. Is this a faith for which much trouble should be taken in resuscitating?"

EXTENT AND SUCCESS OF MISSIONS IN INDIA.

In India the Missionaries of twenty-three different societies are laboring to give the gospel to these people, sitting in the death shade of Hindooism. Eight of these organizations are in the United States—the remaining seventeen have their seat in England and on the continent.

The following statistics, brought down to the year 1862, will give an idea of the extent and success of their missions.

Area in square miles of India and Ceylon exclusive of Burmah	1,491,279
Population	182,760,764
European and American missionaries	519
Square miles to each missionary	2,734
Population to each missionary	350,397
Native Converts	153,816
Native Catechists and Preachers	1,364
Proportion of Converts to population, ...1 in	1,180
Number of Converts to each missionary	296
Children under christian instruction	90,706
Proportion of pupils to population, ...1 in	2,002
Number of pupils to each missionary	173

ORDINATION OF MISSIONARIES.

In response to Letters Missive issued by the Union Park Congregational Church of Chicago, a council convened April 15th, 1867, to examine, and ordain, if approved, the following persons as Foreign Missionaries: William E. DeRiemer, Samuel E. Evans, Carmi C. Thayer, Spencer R. Wells, and William Henry Atkinson.

These young men were members of the graduating class of Chicago Theological Seminary.

The churches invited to sit in the council, were the Congregational and N. S. Presbyterian Churches of Chicago, Plymouth Congregational Church, Milwaukee, the Congregational Churches of Appleton, Paris and Bristol, Berlin and Delavan, Wisconsin; Farmington, Normal, Harvard, and Jacksonville, Illinois; Dana, Massachusetts; Berkley St. Church, Boston; and the Broadway Church, Chelsea, Massachusetts. The following ministers were also invited: Rev. T. M. Post, D.D., St. Louis, Rev. Prof. Henry Smith, D.D., Lane Seminary, Rev. G. W. Wood, D.D., Secretary A.B.C.F.M., New York, Rev. Profs. J. Haven, D.D., S. C. Bartlett, D.D., and F. W. Fisk, D.D., Revs. H. L. Hammond, G. S. F. Savage, J. E. Roy, and S. J. Humphrey.

The council was organized by choosing Rev. Wm. W. Patton, D.D., Moderator, and Rev. S. J. Humphrey, Scribe.

After a peculiarly interesting relation of their christian experience, by the candidates, and of the motives which had led them to desire the ministry and the missionary work, they were examined in their views of christian doctrine. The council then voted unanimously to proceed to set them apart for the work to which they had been manifestly called.

The ordination took place at the Second Presbyterian Church of Chicago, April 18th. A crowded audience were in attendance, and the services were of the most interesting and impressive character. The principal parts of the ordination service are here published in the confidence that it will subserve the interests of missions, and tend to bind our churches to these their messengers to the heathen, in the helpful bonds of sympathy and prayer.

SERMON.

THE ATTRACTION OF THE CROSS.

PROF. HENRY SMITH, D.D., LANE SEMINARY, WALNUT HILLS, OHIO.

"And I, if I be lifted up from the earth, will draw all men unto me."
JOHN xii. 32.

SOME have interpreted these words as relating to Christ's ascension to heaven. Such does not seem to have been the understanding of the apostle John, for he immediately adds: "This he said, signifying what death he should die." We may say, indeed, that they imply his coming departure to heaven, but their immediate reference is certainly to his crucifixion. In the preceding verse, Satan, the great adversary of Christ and of his kingdom, is presented, and the conflict between them is pictured as approaching the hour of consummation. "*Now* is the judgment of this world." The rival claims of Christ and Satan to the dominion of the world are hastening to the hour of decision. The prince of this world, the king and lord of unbelieving humanity, has staked his empire upon a single cast. He has erected his judgment seat. He has suborned his witnesses. He has summoned his myrmidons to arrest the Lord of Life. They will seize him. In a mock trial they will pass sentence upon him. In derision they will array him in the purple of majesty, and place upon his brow "the likeness of a kingly crown." They will insult him with a caricature of worship. They will lead him away to the place of execution. Stretched upon the ground, they will nail him, hand and foot, to the accursed and ignominious tree. This is their hour and the power of darkness. That prostrate cross they will erect. The Man of Sorrows, agonized, lacerated, bathed in blood, and sinking in the arms of death, they will lift up from the earth. They will complete the tragedy! The lifeless body of Jesus of Nazareth will hang between earth and heaven — a spectacle to the universe! To human eyes, his claims will be annihilated. In the eyes of men and of devils, his empire will be overthrown. Such was the vision before the eye of the Redeemer when he uttered the words of the text. But how different his view of the results of this tragedy, from that entertained by the prince of this world! In *his* view, this apparent triumph of Satan was to be his real defeat. This apparent trial and destruction of himself was to be the real trial and overthrow of the powers of darkness. Now is the judgment of this world. This deed of unheard-of malignity—this master-stroke of hell, by which the fortresses of Satan were to be barred and buttressed to an impregnable strength, and his reign to become supreme and eternal over subdued and universal man, was in reality to expel him from his usurped dominions.

Now shall the prince of this world be cast out; and not only so, but "I, if I be lifted up from the earth, will draw all men unto me." Yes, *all men*—Jew and Gentile, Greek and Scythian, bond and free, shall feel the power of my cross, and multitudes shall submit to my peaceful and happy reign. My kingdom shall be universal. There shall be a great multitude which no man can number, of all nations and kindreds, and people and tongues, who shall stand before the throne, and before the Lamb, clothed with white robes, and palms in their hands, and they shall cry with a loud voice, saying, Salvation to our God, which sitteth upon the throne, and unto the Lamb. The subject presented in this text is—

The Attraction of the Cross of Christ.

I propose this as a theme of meditation, in perfect keeping with the joyful occasion which has assembled us this evening. Having heard the voice of the same Spirit which said to the prophets and teachers of the church of Antioch, "Separate me Barnabas and Saul for the work to which I have called them," we have met to consecrate to the blessed work of Foreign Missions, five young men, the first fruits of this Seminary and of these churches. They have felt in their hearts the power of the Cross of Jesus. We also have felt it. But is this power in its very nature universal and perpetual? May the young brethren count upon its efficacy wherever they go—wherever they find a man in whose ears they may rehearse the story of the Cross? May we count upon it in our efforts and prayers to sustain them? I desire to point out some of the grounds for rendering an affirmative answer to these questions.

Let us for a little time meditate upon this theme—not by looking directly at the Cross, but by looking at that which the Cross is to attract—the heart of man. I desire, at least, to point these young brethren toward the height of their great argument. I desire, if possible, to strengthen my own faith, and the faith of my Christian brethren present, in the final and universal triumph of the kingdom of Christ on earth. I desire to animate their zeal, and my own, in laboring for it, at home and abroad. I desire, if God add his blessing, to persuade some who have not yielded to the power of the Cross, to enlist in the service of our divine Lord. Let me attempt to do this by indicating *some of the universal and controlling principles of human action to which the great truths represented in the tragedy of Calvary make their appeal.*

In pursuing this design, I remark that these truths make a powerful appeal,

First, To the principle of *Curiosity.*

Curiosity has been defined to be, "a desire to see something novel, or to discover something unknown—a desire to gratify the senses with a sight of what is new or unusual, or to gratify the mind with new discoveries." This principle is universal: wherever you find a man, you will find it. It is one of the most restless, vigorous, and unconquerable energies of our nature. It is man's destiny and duty to subdue the earth, to make conquests over nature, to make constant and eternal aggressions upon the territory of the unknown, to extend the sphere of his knowledge upward toward heaven and downward toward the abyss, to penetrate the deserts of arctic ice and the deserts of torrid sand, to bring his food from afar, and the materials which may minister to his development, culture and progress from the ends of the earth. This is the potent activity of his nature which fits him for his work.

Man is a social being. He is to live in society; he is to act upon mind, and he is himself to receive the action of mind. He is to govern and be governed; he is to rule and to obey. He is to move men to good; he is to restrain them from evil. It is his duty and his destiny, therefore, to explore the world within, to become acquainted with the domains of the human mind, and to know its secret springs of action, that he may correct its obliquities, heal its diseases, and fit it to scatter blessings around in that wonderful spiritual interaction of soul upon soul which society presents. This is the powerful principle which is to stimulate and sustain him in sounding the depths and in measuring the capacities and the motive forces of the human spirit.

As a matter of fact, man is immortal. He is to live for ever. His body, indeed, is to crumble into dust, but he himself is to survive the wreck of his body, and to endure in a state of conscious being for ever. This fact, indeed, by his own unaided powers, he is unable to prove; but it is, and ever has been, one of the great problems of his being. With undying interest, which perpetuates itself from generation to generation, he wrestles with the great problem; he gathers up the tokens of its truth within the bosom of his own spirit, and the tokens of its truth without him, in society, in providence, in the unfinished purposes of men, in the unequal distribution of happiness, in the beginnings of moral government broken off, thwarted, left without effect and accomplishment, which he beholds every where in the world; and thus he toils on, age after age, at the mighty question, and wearies himself with endless and perpetually recurring speculations. *This* is the wonderful principle of our nature, whose undying vitality and vigor sustain him in the task.

Now, what relation has this principle to the Cross of Christ, or the Cross of Christ to it? Look a moment at its most obvious and exterior relation. There is something in the death, and especially in the violent death of a human being, which powerfully arrests the attention. We are men, and nothing which appertains to the happiness of a fellow-man, when fairly presented to our mind, can fail to interest us. Especially is it impossible for us to witness the last struggle of a fellow-being with the tyrant of the grave, without feeling a pang of sympathy. When such a struggle takes place in our vicinity, we may brace ourselves against the emotion — we may hide our eyes from the scene, but we are drawn to it, either in body or in spirit, by a mysterious and unconquerable attraction. Behold the operation of this principle attracting the rabble who crowd the precincts within which a felon is to suffer the utmost penalty of the violated law. It is announced to the country that a murderer in Boston, who has stood high in society, is to be executed at a given hour. Guilty though he may be, the striking of that hour smites like a death-knell upon the heart of the nation. Then, if never before, curiosity is awakened; the evidence of his guilt is reëxamined, his character is discussed, his life is investigated, contradictions of witnesses are ferreted out; every circumstance connected with the alleged crime is scrutinized—the possibilities of his innocence are weighed, and if by chance this *post-mortem* trial before the tribunal of his peers in human nature should acquit him of crime, what a sentence of reprobation would smite the guilty court which had adjudged an innocent man to the gallows! How powerful the reaction which would embalm his memory and sanctify his sayings! So Socrates died, and so has posterity reversed and execrated the decree which administered the hemlock to the great teacher of heathen antiquity.

But there has been another death scene, upon a more conspicuous theatre, which has awakened a deeper sympathy, which has aroused a more deathless curiosity in investigating the life and claims of the Sufferer, and which is destined to produce a reaction upon mankind, more profound and universal than any other which has occurred in the annals of the race. The tree upon which that victim died has been called the *central gallows* of the universe. Spoken in scorn, these words are true in fact. They express the wide-spread interest which mankind feel already, and the universal and absorbing interest which they are destined to feel hereafter in the dying throes of the Man of Calvary. The curiosity which that interest has excited has already canvassed every act of his life, from the manger to the cross; and the verdict of mankind, so far as the story of Jesus has been told, has pronounced infamous the decree which doomed him to death. That curiosity has not sated itself with scrutinizing the moralities of his life, and pronouncing him innocent; it has scrutinized his teachings, his miracles and his claims, and pronounced him *divine.* This, then, is the first principle in human nature to which the story of the Cross addresses itself, and which, beyond any other story in the records of the race, it is fitted to arouse. What theme in literature to-day commands the world's ear like the "Life of Jesus?" That which has been will be. The work will go on and on, until the world shall be filled with the doctrines of the Cross.

A second principle in human nature to which the tragedy of Calvary addresses itself is, *the love of the right.*

Fallen as human nature is, the *love of the right* still lingers, an undying principle in the human breast. Men may err in the application of the principle. They may call evil good, and good evil; they may put darkness for light, and light for darkness;

they may put bitter for sweet, and sweet for bitter. But one thing they will not do: you will never bring mankind to admit that they *love* the evil, the dark, or the bitter. It is only when these assume the guise of the good, the light, and the sweet, that they can be brought to approve them. It is with this entire principle of human nature as it is with the love of truth, which, indeed, is only a particular manifestation of it. Men can never be brought to accept and to approve a lie as a lie. In that form their nature rejects and loathes it. They would be ashamed to admit their sympathy with falsehood. They may love the advantage which falsehood brings, and thus pervert the truth, but the false must assume the appearance of the true, the worse must be made to appear the better reason, before men will avow, approve, and defend it. So is it with all wrong. It must be made to appear to be right, before men will accept, and approve it. You will hear no man say, I did this because I knew it to be wrong. I refused to do this because I supposed it to be right. This man is guilty, therefore I will acquit him; he is innocent, therefore I will condemn him to death. Here, then, is a universal principle of human nature, often erring, yet never utterly lost; often obscured and perverted, yet the best basis of our faith in man, that he may yet be recovered to holiness and to God. From the depths of every human soul, there springs forth a profound and eternal veneration for the right. Now there is no specific form which this general principle, the love of the right assumes among men,—truth, courage, fortitude, magnanimity, placability, justice, which the common and universal voice of mankind pronounces to be right and praiseworthy, to which the story of the cross of Christ does not make its appeal. I will refer but to a single one, which, perhaps, is, in some sense, the leading feature of moral right exhibited in the scene of Calvary; I mean the sentiment of *justice.* The curiosity which so strange and awful a spectacle has quickened into unwonted activity, and stimulated to search into the causes which have produced it, is not slow to discover, in the teachings of the victim himself, heralded by prophecy, and succeeded by inspired exposition, the key to the solution of the mystery. It is an exhibition of the justice of God. It is a vindication of the claims of that eternal law, whose inviolable majesty guards the happiness of His universal empire. So teach the prophets of Jehovah. "And one shall say unto him, 'What are these wounds in thy hands?' Then shall he answer: 'Those with which I was wounded in the house of my friends.' Awake, O sword, against my Shepherd, and against the man that is my fellow, saith the Lord of Hosts; smite the Shepherd, and the sheep shall be scattered, and I will turn my hand upon the little ones. And he made his grave with the wicked, and with the rich in his death; because he had done no violence; neither was any deceit in his mouth: Yet it pleased the Lord to bruise him; he hath put him to grief." If any one doubts that in this fearful tragedy,

"The violated law speaks out its thunders,"

let him listen to the words of the victim himself: "Think not that I am come to destroy the law or the prophets; I am not come to destroy, but to fulfill." Let him hear the exposition of their import, as bearing upon the sacrifice of Calvary, in words of apostolic authority: "Without the shedding of blood there is no remssion of sin." Yes, of sin, but whose sin? If the sentiment of justice deeply lodged in every human heart, which responds amen, when the penalty of violated law falls upon the head of the guilty, should begin to lift up a note of remonstrance, when it remembers the spotless life of the Sufferer, and those piteous words of the prophet: "He was oppressed and he was afflicted, yet he opened not his mouth; he is brought as a lamb to the slaughter, and as a sheep before her shearers is dumb, so he opened not his mouth;" its voice will be hushed by the interposition of the Redeemer himself, to vindicate the integrity of the justice of God: "Therefore doth my Father love me, because I lay down my life that I might take it again. No man taketh it from me, but I lay it down of myself; I have power to lay it down, and I have power to take it again." Here, then, is the second great principle of human nature, to which the story of the Cross of Jesus of Nazareth makes its appeal. It is a principle as universal as the race. No system of false religion, no christian creed professing to embody the principles of the Gospel, which erases from the articles of faith, the doctrines which recognize and appeal to man's sentiment of justice, can, by any possibility, become universal. Every such religion, every such creed mistakes the nature of man. That nature will vindicate itself. It will maintain its own claims. It will discard these religions. It will pronounce these creeds a falsehood, a forgery. The sentiment of justice is here, in the heart of man. It must be recognized. The history of society attests it. If human law does not protect and vindicate it, men will rise in rebellion *against* law; they will take justice into their own hands, and vindicate it for themselves. The history of the church attests it; all the creeds which have discarded appeals to this sentiment have been vague, wavering, short-lived, and perpetually changing their form. The history of the heathen world attests it. Under the delusions of false religion, it has heaped heathen altars with hecatombs of human victims; it has swung them on hooks; it has crushed them beneath the wheels of Juggernaut; it has cast their helpless offspring to crocodiles, and beasts of prey. Now, the true doctrine of the cross meets the demands of this principle of our nature. So far forth, at least, it is fitted to become the universal religion, that it vindicates the majesty of the violated law, and presents God to the universe, as a being of eternal and inflexible justice.

A third principle in human nature, to which the tragedy of Calvary addresses itself, is *fear*.

It may seem to be a kind of solecism to speak of fear as among the principles attracted by the cross. A little reflection, however, will remove the seeming incongruity. But is this a principle of human nature? I affirm that it is; and being universal, it gives the lie to the doctrine of the non-existence of evil. Men call fear a base passion, a dastardly emotion, unworthy to be felt by a noble mind, unworthy of recognition as a principle of action. Men sometimes bluster about their courage, and talk of blood and carnage, as if they were child's play. But who ever heard, for the first time, the opening boom of an enemy's battery, scattering its death-hail above and around him, without feeling a tremor throbbing at his heart, and thrilling along his nerves? That throb, and that thrill, were the principle of fear. He may suppress the expression of it; if he is a brave man he will; but it is there, and whoever is true to himself will confess it. Men may bluster, in like manner, about appeals to the fears of men in religion, and talk about the terrors of the Lord as they do about the mythic lightnings of Jupiter.

"The universe," says a magnanimous and courageous spirit of this description, "is made by law; the great soul of the world is just, and not unjust. Rituals, liturgies, creeds, Sinai, thunder — I know more or less of the history of these; of the rise, progress, decline, and fall of these. Can thunder, from all the thirty-two azimuths, repeated daily for centuries of years, make God's laws more godlike to me? Brother, no; perhaps I am grown to be a man now, and do not need the thunder and the terror any longer! Perhaps I am above being frightened; perhaps it is not fear, but reverence alone, that shall now lead me!" Wonderful man! He has escaped, it seems, altogether, from the grasp of fear. He has outgrown human nature, and nothing can now appal him, on earth or in hell. Is this really so? Give Holy Church once more her universal sway in christendom. Reinstate the authority of the Westphalian Vehmgericht. Let the Satellites of the church, or of that secret tribunal, seize this bold talker; hurry him away to their sepulchral dungeons; place him in the red glare of torch-light, before the secret and awful judgment seat, where cowled fanaticism, with stern brow and fierce eye, holds in its hand the awful and imminent issues of life and death; place before him the thumb-screw, the boot, the rack, the molten lead, and then require him, at his utmost peril, instantly to devour his own words. Will he not flinch? Will he feel no sensation of terror creeping around his heart? Ah! he begins to find that he is a man; that life is dear to him; that he quails before that fierce and fanatical gaze; that he shrinks from the terrors of that horrible machinery, which is to rack every nerve in his body with agony. He will consider well whether his words are so very true, and so very important, either to his own happiness, or to the freedom and happiness of the world before he will venture, in this presence at least, to reaffirm them. Behold our heroic orator converted into a man. He feels, it seems, the sentiment of fear. But let him not be ashamed; he has good company, and abundance of it. The truth is, the principle from which he endeavored to escape is a universal principle. It holds in its grasp our entire humanity. It belongs to the race; and more than this, it is base and unworthy only when indulged on base and unworthy grounds.

But what relation now has the tragedy of Calvary to this principle, or this principle to it? That strange and awful spectacle, like the fiery, cloudy pillar, which led the Jewish host in the wilderness, has a two-fold aspect. It embodies, in itself, light and darkness, good and evil, life and death, hope and despair. On the one side it frowns upon the beholder with the dark and lurid terrors of the pit. It speaks of wrath and ruin, unmitigated and eternal. On the other, it is lighted up with the golden splendors of heaven. It speaks of joys, which eye hath not seen, which ear hath not heard, and which have not entered into the heart of man. We are now gazing at its dark and angry side. On this side, it is, as has been shown, an exhibition of the eternal and inflexible justice of God, of his deep and immutable hatred of sin. Think you that sinful man, self-accused, and self-condemned, can believe in the reality of that spectacle, can understand the principles involved in it, and gaze upon it without fear? What! will he shrink appalled before the terrors with which human justice invests a fellow worm, when from an earthly tribunal he speaks the doom of the guilty? And can he gaze, without trembling, upon the quick lightnings of Jehovah? What! will he fear them who kill the body, and are not able to kill the soul, and brave, without fear, him who is able to destroy both soul and body in hell? No; that spectacle believed in, clearly seen and understood, will send a pang of terror to his inmost spirit. Yet that very pang of fear will become his salvation. Instead of driving him from the cross, it will attract and bind him to it. This is precisely what the apostle means when he says, "*Knowing the terror of the Lord, we persuade men.*"

I remark in the last place, that a fourth principle of human nature, to which the tragedy of Calvary addresses itself, is *love.*

Surely I need say nothing to prove the universality and power of this principle. What human heart has not felt it? What human spirit does not leap forth and rejoice to welcome every pure and true-hearted appeal to it? It is the true electric cord which links heart to heart, and family to family, and nation to nation, in the great brotherhood of humanity. Behold it blessing the families of virtue! Husband and wife, parent and children, brother and sister, young man and maiden, friend and friend, from the first tottering footsteps of infancy, to the last flicker of expiring consciousness in age. It greets with kisses, the little wayfarer of life, at his first entrance upon the scenes of human destiny. It supplicates blessings upon his cradle. It watches his footsteps in childhood. In youth it fences him about with the lessons of wisdom, and, as to-day, it girds on his armor for the battle of life. In old age, it ministers, with undying interest, to his infirmities. It bathes his corpse with tears, and plants the funereal cypress, to mark the spot of his final repose.

Behold it redeeming the families of wretchedness and vice! Behold it speeding forth the good Samaritans of humanity upon their missions of charity! Behold it following the footsteps of some wayward and wandering brother man; whispering in his ears words of mingled warning and tenderness, and encouraging him by its sympathy and support to turn his feet once more into the paths of virtue and happiness. Behold it entering the lowest and vilest abodes of wretchedness and guilt; approaching their inmates with the language of kindness, and offering its encouragement and support to every effort put forth to regain the social standing which they have forfeited, and the peace of mind which they have lost. What child of guilt is so degraded, what outcast from society is so utterly depraved as to refuse to listen to its gentle appeal, and to send back from his withered and aching heart a response of thankfulness and joy?

Such, and so universal is the principle of *love.* It is the most precious attribute of the human soul. It is the spiritual magnetism of humanity; sleeping, sometimes, but never extinct; never, at least, on earth, let us believe it, totally and forever annihilated.

What relation now has the tragedy of Calvary to this great principle of our nature?

I have spoken of the two distinct aspects of the scene of Calvary. From the side at which we have been gazing, clouds and darkness gird it round about. It is the side of justice, wrath, fear. But that scene, thank God, has another side, bright with the radiance of heaven; beaming with the smile of God. It is the side of forgiveness, reconciliation, mercy, peace, salvation. If it is true that on the one side,

> "The violated law speaks out its thunders,"

it is equally true that on the other,

> "In accents sweet as angels use,
> The Gospel whispers peace."

Such is the wonderful scheme of redemption, devised in the counsels of eternity. Herein is love. It is the most astonishing exhibition of the depth and power of the principle ever made before the eyes of the world. Herein is love; not that we loved God, but that he loved us, and sent his Son to be the propitiation for our sins. "All things are of God, who hath reconciled us to himself by Jesus Christ; God was in Christ, reconciling the world unto himself; not imputing their trespasses unto them, and hath committed unto us the word of reconciliation. Now, then, we are ambassadors for Christ, as though God did beseech you by us, we pray you, in Christ's stead, be ye reconciled to God. For he hath made him to be sin for us, who knew no sin, that we might be made the righteousness of God in him." This is the great burden of the Gospel message. This is the glad news which we have to proclaim to poor, perishing men, stung by the serpent of sin, writhing under the pangs of conscious guilt, fainting and passing away under the terrors of eternal death. This good news is for you, O dying sinner. As Moses lifted up the serpent in the wilderness, so has the Son of man been lifted up. Look up, O my fainting brother, perishing from the poisoned wounds of sin. Look up and live forever! This good news is for you.

Yea, more; this good news is for all men. In the full faith of this great truth, this school of the prophets, in the midst of most pressing calls from our own country, sends forth to-night, with her blessing, this large delegation to the dark places of the earth.

In the full faith of the power of this blessed Gospel to subdue the world to Christ, Lane sends, through me, her best greetings, her joyful gratulations, her heartiest "All hail" to her sister Seminary of Chicago. Not with envy, but with joy does she behold her sister in one noble gift, reaching one-fourth the entire number, which, during a motherhood of five and thirty years, she herself has been able to consecrate to the work of Foreign Missions. Yet with tears of thanksgiving, she points to her own twenty sons, who have listened to the Macedonian cry of the world of heathen darkness. Some of them, indeed, have fallen asleep in Jesus, but most of them continue to this present.

The beloved young brethren who are to receive our "God speed you" to-night, Lane charges with a commission of love to her own well-remembered sons. To whatever section of the globe, shrouded in heathen darkness, you bend your steps, you will find them there. Bear, then, the salutations—yea, the heartfelt love and benedictions of their theological mother to the Williamsons, father and son, among the red men of the West; to Bushnell and Preston, in Africa; to Smith and Montgomery, in Turkey; to Shedd, in Persia; to Chandler and White, in India; to Williams and Stanley, in China; to Andrews and Pogue, in the islands of the sea; — and especially does she charge you not to pass by without a visit to the sacred mounds which mark the last resting-place of her departed and glorified children. She charges you to drop a tear, and, if Providence permits it, to plant some green and fragrant shrub, in token of her unforgetting love, at the graves of Caswell and Spaulding, and Campbell and Bonney—of Cummings, and Wheeler, and Porter.

Men and brethren, ministers, messengers and members of Christ's churches in the West, whom this unwonted spectacle has drawn together to-night, are you ready for this sacrifice? I know that you are ready, for this act is full of the very spirit of Christ. This good news is for all men. You believe that. It is suited to the nature and to the condition of all men. You believe that. It is to be published in the ears of all men. You believe that. But when, O Christian — when? Gird yourself, I beseech you, in whatever vocation Christ has called you to labor—gird yourself anew and instantly for this work. Christ has laid it upon you; Christ has laid it upon me. Go ye into all the world, and preach the Gospel to every creature. Go in person — go by proxy — go now, for now is the time in which men are perishing for the lack of this Gospel. God has laid this work upon *us*, in whatever form of effort he has called us to serve him.

Let us labor for it—let us pray for it—let us give for it; and as we labor, pray and give, let us have faith in the principles and in the power of the Gospel. It shall triumph — Christ hath promised it: "And I, if I be lifted up from the earth, will draw all men unto me." God hath declared it: "To him every knee shall bow and every tongue confess." It shall prevail, and spread, and prosper, until the kingdom, and the greatness of the kingdom, under the whole heaven, shall be given to the people of the saints of the Most High God. Oh, wonderful scheme of redemption! Oh, love infinite and unsearchable! What heart will not respond to it? What Christian will not rejoice in it? What poor, perishing sinner will not be melted by it into penitence and love?

"Oh, the sweet wonders of that Cross,
Where my Redeemer loved and died!
Her noblest life my spirit draws
From his dear wounds and bleeding side.

"I would for ever speak his name
In sounds to mortal ears unknown;
With angels join to praise the Lamb,
And worship at his Father's throne."

Rev. Truman M. Post, D.D., St. Louis, offered the ordaining prayer, assisted by the following ministers in the laying on of hands: Rev. R. W. Patterson, D.D., Rev. S. B. Treat, Prof. J. Haven, D.D., Rev. P. C. Pettibone, Rev. Z. M. Humphrey, D.D., Rev. C. D. Helmer, Prof. S. C. Bartlett, D.D., Rev. J. Collie, President J. M. Sturtevant, D.D., and Rev. L. Taylor.

CHARGE.

PROF. SAMUEL C. BARTLETT, CHICAGO THEOLOGICAL SEMINARY.

My Dear Young Brethren, — History repeats itself to-night. Fifty-five years ago, in the oldest city of New England, Judson, and Newell, and Mills, and Nott, and Rice, stood up before Spring, and Morse, and Worcester, and Woods, and Griffin, for missionary ordination—the first fruits of America and of Andover. Instead of the fathers, are the sons and the grandsons. And here to-night, on a spot of which the Indian then held long lease, you come to us, another missionary five — only the first fruits, we trust, of these North-western churches, and of this young Seminary. We are here to bid you go. And this council have appointed one who has often spoken to you in the lecture-room, but who will so speak to you no more, to give you their solemn charge.

While I shall not anticipate your particular instructions from the American Board, neither may I forget that we have ordained you specially for the missionary work. Let me then address you with the charge of the great apostle of the Gentiles to his young helper in the work of missions: "Watch thou in all things, endure afflictions, do the work of an evangelist, make full proof of thy ministry."

"Watch" ye; be wakeful and watchful "in all things." And first of all, be watchful over your own hearts. In the delusion that a sacred calling exempts from temptation, you do not share. You know that he who once crawled into Paradise, can linger round the Seminary, can climb the pulpit, or follow on the track of the missionary. You will be encompassed, not alone or chiefly by the ardor of the young convert, but by the low worldliness of the earthen man of China, the gross vices of the out-caste Mahar, by the mummied forms of a dead Christianity. A mission field is not all heaven. Depravity and corruption will be seething around you. Like the sainted Poor, you, too, will get new light on the first chapter of Romans. Now, it was the marvel of Christ's divine humanity that, with a heart day and night in contact with all that was most earthly, that heart beat only of God and heaven. It lay pure as moonlight on a mass of decay. And it is the glory of our missionary band that, from the midst of all that is hard and sensual and hateful, they invariably return to kindle the flame of devotion at home. Such a high spiritual frame, I know, can be maintained only by incessant vigilance. Therefore watch over your hearts with all vigilance, and keep them full of the Holy Ghost.

Be watchful over your lives. I do not warn you against the gravitation of heathen morals, and the poison of the pagan atmosphere all around. I speak of your relations to your missionary brethren. Shut in upon yourselves in fixed relations, specially guard against the friction of a hard and wiry spirit, an unlovely temper, or uncomfortable ways. An uncomfortable man at home, like a live coal, can be hurried along or quietly dropped. *There* he must burn and blister. Even while I am uttering this hint, it seems to me well-nigh superfluous, so wise have commonly been the arrangements of the Board of Missions, and so admirable the spirit of its missionaries. And yet, in view of the infirmities of human nature, and the momentous interests at stake, let me enjoin upon you that heavenly wisdom of practical life which is pure, peaceable, gentle, and easy to be entreated, both toward your missionary brethren and the missionary board.

You must be watchful over your minds. I judge that in all your incessant toils, you shonld not suffer your intellect to rust, nor cease to enlarge your acquisitions. You go to the old homestead of the nations. In spite of his wooden looks, the Chinaman is sharp ; the Brahmin is quick and keen at a sophism ; and even the Turk can propound to you difficult questions on the Trinity. Your intellectual work will not be all play. Henry Martyn carried with him the highest scholarship of Cambridge, and left behind him the name of the man who never was beaten in an argument. Doubt it not, even in those far-off lands, your power for good will be increased by the whole momentum of your intellectual weight. And often with the sword of the Spirit and the helmet of faith, you will need the spear of Ithuriel too.

Be watchful over the body, as well as the heart and the mind. We send you as laborers, and not martyrs or victims ; sacrifices, but living sacrifices. You have spent too many years of preparation to throw away your lives as a thing of naught. Christ's kingdom knows no such economy as that. The Master said: "Occupy till I come." You are to use, and not bury your talent. A late divine once published a sermon entitled "Death a duty." But, brethren, be very sure death is not your duty, so long as you can live to labor. Your sympathies will be sadly, terribly moved by the whiteness of the harvest and the fewness of the reapers. But if you prematurely break yourselves down, you but make the reapers fewer and the harvest sadder. Work, work to the full extent of your powers, but not beyond. Heed the first symptoms of danger, and rescue yourselves for other years of toil. You are too precious an offering to have your heart's blood spilled like water, and every year will add to your value. Remember, at times, the minister who hoped to preach more sermons than Whitefield, but to be longer in doing it. As often, therefore, as you are tempted to destroy yourselves, see that you do it not. But I will tell you what to do. Raise high the signal of distress. Blow long and loud your trumpet to the rescue. Let it echo from the Green Mountains to the Mississippi. Let it reverberate through academy, and college, and seminary, and church. Let it pierce these mothers' hearts; let it stir the young blood in these children's veins; let it disturb the conscience of these sleeping Jonahs and careless Gallios; call louder and louder, till the answer comes. Yea, in all your watching, forget not the church at home. Keep fast hold of the cords of sympathy. Draw on the prayers and interest of your friends. Help us rouse this young North-west. Hold on upon your fellow students and their successors. Suffer not the missionary line—the noblest of apostolic successions—ever to die out in this your *alma mater*. We charge you in all your watching for souls abroad, watch, also, for missionaries and the missionary spirit at home.

"Endure afflictions" or "hardness." The day is indeed gone by when the missionary was said to take his life in his hands, or even when his departure was thought to be returnless. Fifty years have wrought great changes. But the small number of volunteers proves the work to be still distasteful to flesh and blood. Life-long partings, exile from home and native land—sweet words, young brethren,—loss of society, of culture, of institutions, begin the long catalogue. Then comes the time when you will stand tongue-tied in the face of error and sin, like a motionless soldier before the bayonet charge. There is the long drudgery, the halting speech, perhaps the long, fruitless toils, the bitter disappointment, the half-enlightened convert, and the hypocrite. Families are to be reared in moral Saharas; your comrades droop; the harvest whitens, and beckons, and perishes; the churches are dull of hearing, and the young missionaries slow in coming; a money panic sweeps across the mother-land; a complication of troubles arises at your field of labor, which you can neither cure, nor endure, nor escape. You will indeed reap new joys; but such as these, and many more, will be your afflictions. Endure hardness as good soldiers of Christ. You have served, the most of you, and endured well, as soldiers of your country. One of you helped hold Missouri fast in the Union. One marched to put down conspirators in Indiana. One has been under fire at Memphis and at Corinth, and one of you left his right arm at Vicksburg. Be as willing and as faithful soldiers of the cross as of your country, and we ask no more. [Subdued applause.]

"Do the work of an Evangelist." That, brethren, is your calling. You go to preach the Gospel of repentance and faith to the lost. The anguish, and the search, and the joy of the old man Chu have reached your ears from Tientsin; the call of the dying Chapin has been borne to you from India; you have heard the wail that came from Central Turkey, "begging and imploring" for help.

And now you go to the teeming land where the civilization has come down like a frozen mammoth from the ages past; to that other land, where the first family of the great Aryan race found a home and embalmed itself in a marvelous tongue; and to that other region where Homer sung, and Alexander conquered, and the younger Cyrus began his ill-fated march, where Abram left his father, where Paul was born, and the disciples were first called Christians, and the seven churches had their warnings. But it is not your errand to explore the grotesque civilization of China, to delve in the mine of Sanscrit learning, nor to follow the track of Alexander, or Cyrus, or Abram, or Barnabas and Paul, nor to muse by the ruins of Troy, the banks of the Cydnus, the temple of Diana, or the mud-hovels of the old "Queen of the East." You walk in the footsteps of Christ. You go to pour in the rich light and life of God's love. You go to found other sevens of churches in Asia Minor, to call other men *to be* Christians in Antioch. We do not expect you to shut your eyes and steel your hearts to all the scenes and associations around you, as Howard went through Europe and saw nothing but the inside of its prisons. And yet, in the true meaning of the phrase, you, are to know nothing but Christ, and him crucified.

It may be your privilege to add to the mass of obligations with which missions have made science their debtor. Do so if you can. But remember, these things are but the fragrance which religion sheds forth from her vestments, as she walks on her high errand of mercy. Get all the comfort you can, diffuse all the incidental benefits you can, abroad and at home, but evermore do the work of an Evangelist.

And, finally, "make full proof of your ministry." It is the ministry of reconciliation. It rests evermore on those great primal truths — a sin-hating God, a sin-loving world, an atoning Saviour—the only name given under heaven, among men, whereby we must be saved. Remember, we charge you, except as you preach an atoning Saviour, you have no errand to the heathen. They know their sin. They feel God's anger, but they see no hope. The world over, and time through, they have confessed it in penance and sacrifice, in fear and despair. You go to point them to the Lamb of God, that taketh away the sin of the world.

Remember, they are to be sanctified through the truth; and in God's economy the regenerating Spirit follows in the track of the word. Whatever may be our theories as to the possibility that men who know not of Christ, may yet be saved for Christ's sake, if they would but believe in a loving God with a purifying faith; never forget this tremendous and appalling fact, that among the countless millions of our race, the annals of history do not record a dozen cases of such a faith, such a love, and such obedience, except where the word of God has been made known.

Proclaim, then, God's word and not your own speculations. Not merely the milk for babes, but in due time give them the meat for men. Remember you are performing the solemn work of laying the foundations for the far-distant future. Lay them wisely and well. Build on the only foundation, Jesus Christ; build with the gold, silver, and precious stones of divine truth, broad, strong, and high. And, brethren, press home that truth with all its practical, personal power, in the church, in the street, in the house, and by the way. With faith and prayer, urge it home, and then feel, with the noble Judson, that your prospects are "bright." You can trust that truth with the same composure amid the manifold oppositions abroad, as among the infinite scepticisms at home. The living Christ is an ever-living power, and the ministry of Christ a resistless agency. Make but full proof of that ministry, and the end is as sure as the throne and the promise of God.

And now, brethren, go to your work. You are among our jewels, but we lay you on Christ's altar. Would you were more. Sadly but cheerfully we say these parting words. We shall miss your pleasant faces and cheerful voices in our seminary halls. We shall miss you from our festal days, our Alumni gatherings, and convocations of the ministry. We shall miss the warm grasp, and the ever kindly word and look. We shall miss your young enthusiasm and your hearty coöperation in our plans of good for this great North-west. But in Christ's name we bid you go to your distant fields. Only, dear brethren, join hands with us still across the continents; let us feel your warm heart-beat through intervening oceans; from the antipodes let us hear your welcome greeting, and we are content. From the banks of the Ganges, the Yellow Sea, or the old Orontes, and from the shores of Lake Michigan, the paths of duty all converge to the one heavenly home; and there are Woods, and Spring, and Newell, and Judson, with a glorious company and a goodly fellowship, awaiting you and us. Therefore, my dear young brethren, go on your way to the distant nations in the calm and holy confidence of the Master's presence, and in all "the fullness of the blessing of the Gospel of Christ."

PRESENTATION OF THE MISSIONARIES TO THE AMERICAN BOARD.

PROF. J. HAVEN, D.D., CHICAGO THEOLOGICAL SEMINARY.

As the young men who have now been ordained to the ministry of the Gospel, are destined to the special work of Foreign Missions, it seems proper that, in addition to the usual services of ordination, a few words should be spoken more especially consecrating them to that specific work; and so, at their request, in the name, and in behalf of the seminary from which they go forth, and of the churches of the North-west, therein represented, I now present to you, sir, as the representative of the Board, and through you to the cause of missions, these young men, our pupils and our sons.

This Seminary, and the churches which it represents, could give you, sir, no higher proof of their attachment to the American Board, and to the great cause of missions, than the gift which they bring you to-night. For it is not their silver or their gold which they now give you, but that which is dearer and more precious than either — their own sons. And this they do not from their abundance, but of their deep poverty. The value of a gift depends somewhat on the resources of the giver; and whatever, in other respects, may be the resources of the Christian Churches of the North-west, of *men* educated, and fitted for the ministry, they have none to spare. Never was their poverty, in this respect, and their pressing need, greater than now. From the great chain of lakes, on whose border we stand to-night, to the Rocky Mountains, and thence to the far Pacific, hands are outstretched, and voices upraised, saying, *send us men* — men who shall show us the way of salvation, and break unto us the bread of life. Send us those whom you have been educating for the work — those whom we sent to you to be thus instructed. We look upon this field so vast and ready for the harvest, and then upon the little band of Christian students who to-day go forth from our seminary, and say what are these eighteen among so many? Were they multiplied an hundred fold, it would not be enough. And yet from this little band we take out almost one-third the entire number, and set them apart to another destination. We say to our own destitute churches, you can not have all these men. For across the distant ocean other hands are upraised, and other voices are crying out for the bread of life, and in that cry, borne over the seas and mountains of a continent, we recognize the voice of the Master. It comes in at the doors and windows, through the halls of yonder Seminary, and we dare not disregard it. And so to these outstretched Western hands, empty and famishing, we turn and say, touch not the Lord's anointed; touch not those whom the Lord has called to his more distant vineyard; the Master hath need of them. And so, in our poverty, and sad at heart, as we think of our own destitution, yet heartily and joyfully as we look over the field which is the world, we give you these our pupils, our sons, our beloved brethren in Christ, for the work of Foreign Missions.

If ever there was a generous gift, it is this of the churches of the North-west to you to-night. But you have seen something of these Western men, and you know that it is their way to give generously, and to do with all their heart what they do at all. As at the call of their country, they gave generously of their noblest and their best to battle for the true and the right, so now they give of their choicest ones when demanded for Christ and his cause. God's work must not be hindered whatever becomes of us and our little affairs. And so here, O Lord, are we and those whom thou hast given us.

And yet, sir, though we thus speak, I have no fear that we shall be impoverished. These churches, many as they are, and destitute as they are, can well afford to send not these five only, but the whole eighteen if they would go. For is it not the Divine economy that the more we give the more we have? Has it ever been known in the history of missions, that the Christian Church has grown poor by her generosity, and her devotion to the cause of Christ? When the poor widow took from the last remaining handful of meal to make a cake for the prophet, it was not diminished, but *multiplied*, by the taking. And so will it be, sir, with these our treasures. We give but to receive again. In the beautiful vision of Ezekiel, the water that flowed out from beneath the temple, at the south of the altar, and flowed on into the desert and into the east country, rapidly widened and deepened as it flowed, and wherever it went, every thing sprang into new life and beauty. So will it be with this little stream that starts forth from our altar to-night on its way to the desert and the east country. It will widen and deepen as it runs. It will become a mighty river. These five young men are but the first fruits — the earnest — the beginning of what this Western land of ours is yet to do for the work of Foreign Missions. There are not less than thirty students, in various stages of the course, in our colleges, who are already committed to this service. The stream is only to the ankles as yet, but a little farther on it is a river that no man can ford, and the desert through which it passes shall burst into verdure, and blossom as the garden of the Lord.

And what shall I say of these young men whom I now present to you. It was a singular Providence that sent to us from our own New England, from our own Massachusetts, your mother and mine, two of her sons, to receive their theological training, wholly or in part, in this Western world, then to pass on to a still more distant field of labor among the heathen. We would not hold them back, much as we value them. They are not ours, but *His*. Of these five, four have been in the service of their country, and go from the field of material conflict to engage in the sterner strife with a spiritual, but not less real or less dangerous foe. They know what suffering and peril are. That empty sleeve testifies of courage and of patriotism. That arm that bore aloft the flag of his country, and held it firm amid the iron hail at the capture of Vicksburg, was left indeed upon the field; but the arm that remains will hold aloft the standard of the Cross on the plains of India, and never suffer it to be lowered or dishonored.

But I must not speak further. It seems but a little time since we welcomed these our young brethren to the Seminary as students. In the few years that they have been with us, we have come to know them and to love them. And now, as they go out from us, they carry with them our sincere esteem, our high appreciation of their intellectual and moral worth, our affection, and our prayers. We shall not forget them. They will not be forgotten by the churches of the North-west. As the mother of Samuel brought the lad to the temple, so to God's altar we come bringing these our sons to-night. We give them to the God of Samuel and of Jacob. We give them to Christ and His Church. And as the mother of Samuel, in the long and solitary hours, wrought for him with her own hands, the little garment, and brought it to him, year by year, as she came to the temple, so for these whom we bring to-night to the altar, willing hands shall toil, and earnest prayers go up, while they are far away among the heathen.

WELCOME AND RIGHT HAND OF FELLOWSHIP.

REV. S. B. TREAT, SECRETARY AMERICAN BOARD.

It is with great satisfaction that I receive these "first-fruits" of your Seminary as the representative of the Board; for them I desire to express my cordial thanks. When, a few months ago, our hearts were so heavily burdened, we little dreamed that the day-spring would appear in the West. We knew that the "star of empire" was passing by us; but we had not learned to say: "Westward the star of *missions* takes its way." During my connection with the Missionary House (twenty-four years), nothing has occurred in our home operations which has so cheered us as this offering of yours. And not us only: word has gone forth to other lands, "Wait a little longer; the West is coming to the rescue."

But I must be allowed to tender my gratulations as well as my thanks. It seems to me that your Seminary has ceased to be a Western institution, and become a national institution, or rather a world-institution. The setting apart of these young men is not done in a corner. It will be talked about and prayed over by *four thousand* churches. The patriarchs of the East will call to mind the ordaining of the *first five* — that event which sent such a quickened life through all our churches, and they will give you their blessing. Mothers in Israel, who have scarcely heard of you till now, will render thanks for "the grace of God bestowed upon" you, and will invoke in your behalf the choicest benedictions.

I know the value of this offering. I know what it will be for us. I know what it would be for the West. I fully believe, however, that your loss will prove to be your gain. By our earthly arithmetic, *five* from *eighteen* leave *thirteen*. But by the celestial arithmetic, subtraction becomes addition. In this instance, I am sure that *five* from *eighteen* will leave, not *thirteen*, nor even *eighteen*, but many more. No. These young men are not lost to the *United States*, but saved rather.

And now, my dear young brethren, with feelings which I can not describe, I turn to you. I am commissioned by the Prudential Committee to tender you the right hand of fellowship. In their name I welcome you to a self-denying but honored service. I welcome you to a partnership with us, in the work of saving the world. I welcome you to the goodly company of the servants of Christ in heathen lands. I welcome you to the joy of beholding Emmanuel's coming glory, as it touches with silver radiance the high places of paganism, and slowly descends to the deeper shadows below. I welcome you to that peace, like a river, which the Great Missionary always keeps in store for such as truly obey his last command. I welcome you to the ineffable smile which, in the final apocalypse, is sure to rest on those who cordially forsake all for Christ.

I have not come here, you perceive, to speak in the "minor mode." No. I regard you as called by the grace of God to the foremost place among the sons of men. I honor the pastorate. To my apprehension there is in the home field no place like it. But you go up still higher. You have entered the Pauline band. With the great apostle you can say, "Unto me who am less than the least of all saints, is this grace given that I should preach among the Gentiles the unsearchable riches of Christ." Would you prove yourselves worthy of your office? Let these words become "as frontlets between your eyes." Rather, let their spirit, as it were the sweetest perfume, pervade the inmost chambers of your being.

In your meditations thereon, be sure to begin where Paul began. "Unto me, who am less than the least of all saints, is this grace given." Lay the foundation of your missionary life in the truest humility. And when you can take your place beside the Apostle in this respect, you will be ready for those other words, "the unsearchable riches of Christ." You will not expect me to dwell upon this theme. I frankly confess that I have not that knowledge of it which I would fain possess. The more I know of the unsearchable riches, the more unsearchable they appear. The more I study them, the more they seem to transcend all study.

Here then we have two of the chief elements of missionary success, I may say of ministerial success—the lowest views of self, and the highest views of Christ. Charles Simeon revealed unconsciously the secret of his great usefulness, when he said: "There are but two objects that for these forty years I have desired to behold;—one is my own vileness; the other is the glory of God in the face of Jesus Christ."

To what we welcome you, you have already heard. There are some things to which we do not welcome you. We do not welcome you to a tempting salary. What we receive ourselves, we give to you—an economical support—nothing more. We do not welcome you to an untroubled and smoothly-flowing life. How much of joy or sorrow may befall you, we must leave in the hands of the Father. We do not welcome you to length of days. We would gladly do it, if we could; but the Angel of Death is obedient to another will than ours. We do not welcome you to great visible success. If you live to three score years, or three score and ten, you will see important changes, I doubt not; some, perhaps, that you do not anticipate. That noble missionary who has just gone up to his heavenly home (Dr. Goodell) sailed into the Golden Horn in the early summer of 1831. He found himself in a city fitted by its position to be the queen of the earth. But, alas! what intense bigotry did he find! What bitter hatred of the truth! A death penalty, sure to be enforced, hung above the head of every Moslem. "Renounce Islam and die," was the brief formula. He, and those who joined him, toiled on four and twenty years, guiding inquirers to Christ, and gathering churches; when, lo! that which they had not dared to hope for at first, came to pass. That old death penalty was swept away! How? "War did it," says one. "Diplomacy did it," says another. But neither could have done it—both together could not have done it, *without the Missionary.* "The poor wise man saved the city."

At times you may grieve for your poor success, just as pastors do at home. You may bewail, for instance, the shortcomings of your converts. But when the burden is heavy upon you, read Paul's epistles. And remember, especially, that God seeth not as man seeth. Ten years ago, it was the lamentation of missionaries in all parts of India, that their churches had so little of Christian manliness. Just then, however, the Sepoy rebellion burst upon the world. And when the storm had passed by, it was found that these feeble, sickly children of theirs had met the shock with a courage and firmness that became their wonder and delight.

No. We do not welcome you to assured success, but to just so much as the Master shall be pleased to give you, commending his own words to your prayerful study, "According to your faith be it unto you." And there will be single scenes in your history, I doubt not, which will amply repay you for all your toil; as when a missionary of ours stood by a dying Hindoo, and heard him say, feebly, faintly, "Christ has taken all of mine, and given me all of his." "Ah! what has he taken of yours?" "Sin, Sir; death, Sir." "What has he given you of his?" "Heaven, Sir; holiness, Sir."

But I must crave the privilege of saying a few words to these pastors, and these Christian friends. These young men, as you see, are going down to the dark, cold shadows of heathenism. As Carey expressed it, they are *going down into the well.* Will *you* hold on to the ropes? They are entering upon a life-campaign; will you equip them, as you did those regiments which fought so bravely for the stars and stripes, and afterward furnish food and raiment? To put the matter in a definite shape, will you advance your contributions twenty per cent.? I believe you will do it. I do not see how you can help it. Rather, I think you will rejoice in the opportunity.

But I have something more to say. For the last nine months I have felt a weight upon my spirit almost too heavy to be borne. I have asked myself, Oh how many times! "When is the world to be given to Christ? He whose right it is, the Prince of the Kings of the earth, when is He to be enthroned in all the world?"

I have no distrust of present methods. It was after that bloody death, and under the opening heavens, that the command was given, "Preach the gospel to every creature." We are on the right track, therefore; but how slow the train moves! Four thousand churches represented by one hundred and forty ordained missionaries in all the heathen world!

The heathen world! Do we think what this is? Let us suppose it to pass before us—say ten abreast—a living, slow-moving current. From morning to night, from night to morning, the ear is burdened by its heavy, incessant tread. At the pace of one mile an hour, it would consume six years in passing by us, a long, unresting funeral train! At first we are awe-struck and speechless. Myriads upon myriads, millions upon millions; and all traveling, like ourselves, to the judgment seat, and almost all ignorant of the way of life!

Suppose, now, that we should resolve at once to enter, with our whole hearts, upon the work of the world's reconstruction. How appalling would the endeavor seem!

But hopeless as is the undertaking, on the human side, on the divine side, it is perfectly feasible. See what marvels the Providence of God has wrought for missions. A little more than *twenty* years ago, and China was shut against the Christian world — locked, bolted, barred. But we have been told quite recently, that it is now open in all its length and breadth.

With what skill and patience has He exalted the valleys and made low the mountains and hills of Hindoostan. First, papal France was to be excluded from the land, as having no lot or inheritance there. Next the power of the native princes, idolatrous, oppressive and effete, was to be cast down; and then a vast trading company, selfish as the love of pounds, shillings and pence could make it, was to be led along by a hook in the nose, till the set time should come for saying, "Pass on; *your* work is done." And now one of the noblest of Christian men holds the vice regal sceptre over nearly *two hundred millions* of Hindoos.

And look at Madagascar. When the missionaries were expelled thirty years ago, they left a few disciples, without a ministry, with no right to meet for worship, no right to read a book, hated, hunted, in constant danger of a cruel death. But they also left two injunctions, to wit: "Cleave to the Bible, and cleave to one another;" and they did so. They came together, in fear and trembling, and read the Scriptures. After a time it was discovered that some had more skill than others in explaining "the lively oracles;" and they were asked to take upon themselves the ministry of the word. But there were no sacraments. How, for instance, should these persecuted ones commemorate the death of Christ? What else to do, they knew not, and so they asked their teachers to perform this service. When, therefore, Mr. Ellis went there in 1861, he found that a native ministry had sprung up, in spite of all repressing influences, having received its anointing, not from bishops, or presbyters, or councils, but from the Holy Ghost; and the Lord has blessed those servants of His, as also the missionaries who have gone there since, so that the number of communicants is ten times greater than it was in 1861.

What now is the world's chief need? A single word contains the answer. FAITH. *A believing Church might see the speedy triumph of Christ, in all the earth.* Know ye not, my brethren, that God has placed the entire resources of his kingdom at our disposal? Elisha was wroth with the King of Israel because he struck the ground but thrice. "Thou shouldst have smitten five or six times," he said; "then hadst thou smitten Syria till thou hadst consumed it. And that scene by the Mount of transfiguration! "Master, I have brought unto thee my son, which hath a dumb spirit." And then having told his story of suffering and trial, he said: "If thou canst do any thing, have compassion on us and help us." Jesus said unto him, "If thou canst believe, all things are possible to him that believeth."

Were there time, I would gladly say a few words as to *what* we should believe. But I will only glance at two particulars: First, We should believe that *Christ is waiting to see of the travail of his soul, and be satisfied.* He that died for this very end—he is waiting for the tardy movements of his Church. Second, We should believe that *there is soul-travail for us as well as for him.* As by reason of his human nature, he can be touched with a feeling of our infirmities, so we are to share his sorrows and his joys. Remember how he wept over Jerusalem, looking down from Olivet, and then think what it must be for him to look down upon a world lying in wickedness, beholding all the crimes which are committed, thoughts that can not bear the light of the sun, and then glancing through all the ages of the future, knowing perfectly what a lost spirit may become, what a lost spirit must suffer.

It remains for me to give you the right hand of fellowship in behalf of the council. In the name of these pastors and delegates, in the name of the Churches which have sent them hither, as also of all the Churches of the North-west represented in some sort by them, I give you this right hand. It is not a vain ceremony. I have learned that no men have so wide a place, in so many hearts, as those who go to the heathen. In times of trial call this scene to mind, and take comfort and courage therefrom.

A few years ago, a party of missionaries was about to leave Persia for America. They were to travel under a hot sun, over bridgeless rivers, along rough and precipitous ways, pitching their tents in insecure places, till they should take a steamer at Trebizond, and afterward to take a sailing vessel to Smyrna. A Nestorian girl, just as they were setting forth, made a prayer, so simple, so scriptural, and so appropriate to your circumstances, that I will ask the congregation to join me in offering it for you, only changing two or three words in the last sentence: "Dear Father! let not the sun smite them by day, nor the moon by night. Give thine angels charge concerning them, to bear them up in their hands, that they dash not a foot against a stone. When they pass through the deep rivers, let not the waters overflow them. Let the Angel of the Lord encamp round about their moving tabernacle. Spread a table for them in all the long wilderness. When they come to the fire-ship, let not the flames kindle upon them. When they come to the winged vessel, though the waves go up to heaven and down to hell, keep them in the hollow of thy hand, and bear them safely to the desired haven. Let not their dust mingle with the dust of father or the dust of mother; but let it mingle with the dust of their children, with them to hear the last trump, with them to meet the Lord in the air, to be forever with him, all safely home!"

TO THE MORNING STAR BUILDERS.

Dear Children, — The Morning Star—*your* Morning Star—is built.* You remember it was only last May, that the word went out, *we want a new ship!* And the children all over the land heard the call. They sent in money by the hundreds of thousands of dollars, and on Saturday forenoon, September 22d, she was launched upon the sea. A little less than three weeks after, she spread all her sails for the Pacific, and on March 15th, after a very short trip of 122 days — a full month less than the usual time for such a voyage, she cast anchor in the harbor of Honolula. Pretty quick work this, isn't it?

Now, how much money do you suppose the children have given to build this ship? I will tell you. Up to March 1st, the sum had reached $28,085.23. A grand sum this! And what is very pleasant to us to know is, that more than one-sixth of it — $5,746.02 — came from the five States of the North-west.

But children, something more than a ship is necessary. The Morning Star can take food and letters to the missionaries. It can carry them about from island to island, and so help a great deal. But it can not teach school or preach the Gospel. And this is the great end we seek; to lead the heathen to Christ; to save their perishing souls. It takes schools and catechists and preachers, by the grace of God, to do this.

And so we send out another call to the children, not to build a ship this time. The cry is, We want to build schools: we want to train teachers; we want to raise up a great multitude of natives in Turkey and China, in Africa and the islands of the sea, to preach Christ to their countrymen, and turn them from heathen practices to the worship of the true God. Why, children, let me tell you something. In a drawer of the desk where I am writing, is a paper box with a small cord coiled up in it. It is about twelve feet long, and has a loop on its end. What do you think it was for? It was given me only a few weeks since by a venerable man, one of the first missionaries to the Sandwich Islands. He told me that about forty years ago the old high priest of those islands, having been converted, brought it to him, saying, "With this cord I have had *twenty-three human victims* strangled to death for sacrifice."

Now, it is to deliver men from such cruelties and bondage as this that we want to give them schools and preachers. Here, then, is a steady and beautiful work for the boys and girls. It is not new work; ever since the old Morning Star was built, the children of America have been helping to start schools and support students and teachers among the heathen. In this time, they have sent in almost $90,000, enough to build four or five Morning Stars. Add to this what they did to build the old and the new ships, and it makes $150,000 given by the Sunday Schools for missions, in ten years. This is grand! For one, I feel down deep in my heart like thanking the children for it all the time. And I especially thank you to whom I am writing this letter, for what you have done. I was a little afraid that, while the children were lifting so hard at the ship, they would forget the schools. But I am surprised and rejoiced to find that they did more last year, by $381, than ever before.

The whole sum was $2.074.93. This is more than three times as much money as they gave four years ago, and it came from just three times as many schools. We feel very happy about this. But it seems to me we can do a great deal more this year. There are 400 schools that helped at the ship that did nothing for the heathen schools. And there are as many more that did nothing for either. I am sorry for this; but I fully believe that a good many new schools will join to help us in this work.

I am very glad to find from the letters I get, that many of the children are learning to *earn* the money they give. A sturdy little fellow in this State, only four years old, "hoed in the garden for his grandpa, for a dime, to send to help build the ship." He'll be better all his life for doing that.

A letter from a "Busy Bee Society," just received, says: "The inclosed amount ($25.11) has all been either *earned* or *saved* by some act of self-denial."

It is very pleasant to see how many ways children can contrive to get money to do good with, when they have a heart for it. Here is one of them: "Enclosed," writes a lady, "is $1.25, my children's missionary money. Ella wants her dollar — *the price of her turkey* — to go to the India missions. She is eight years old, and feels deeply interested in them.

But now, children, it is time for me to close by telling you a little plan I have about this matter. How many of you would like to see the ship you have been building? Hold up your hands all of you that would like to see *your* ship, the Morning Star. . . Yes, I thought so; a good many. But she's gone to the Pacific, and it will be hardly possible for you to see the real ship. The next best thing, then will be a good picture of her. Now the friends in Boston have had such a picture made — a nice lithograph, twenty by fifteen inches in size, printed in three tints, with colored flags. It gives the ship just as she looked when starting from the wharf with all her sails spread, and the star-spangled banner flying from her mast. What a beautiful thing this will be to hang up in the Sunday School room. I wish all the children in the North-west could see it. But here is the plan. If your school, or any class in your school, will raise $15 or more for the Mission School Enterprise, and forward it here, I will see that you have one of these pictures, free of charge, sent to you from Boston by mail. "But some schools can't raise $15." I know it, and so I have put another thing into the plan. I am having a photograph of this picture made, a small one, card size. There will be a certificate on the back of it where the teacher can write your name and how much you have given. Now I will send to your superintendent one of these photographs for every scholar or class that gives fifty cents or more to these schools, only I shall want him to say in his letter just how many you need. I want all the children to see how their ship looks, and I can think of no better plan than this. I hope it will please you and make you love this work more and more. And now, dear children, may the Lord bless you, giving you new hearts and keeping you from all evil.

Affectionately your friend,

84 Washington St., Chicago, May 1, 1867. S. J. HUMPHREY.

* An admirable description of the Morning Star, with illustrations, may be found in the January *Sabbath at Home*, published by the American Tract Society, Boston.

DR. ANDERSON'S WORK ON THE HAWAIIAN ISLANDS.

BY ANDREW P. PEABODY, D.D., CAMBRIDGE, MASS.

[From the Boston Review for May, 1865.]

The Hawaiian Islands: Their Progress and Condition under Missionary Labors. By RUFUS ANDERSON, D.D., Foreign Secretary of the American Board of Commissioners for Foreign Missions. With Illustrations. Boston: Gould & Lincoln. 1864.

WE may profess implicit faith in the geological theories which adequately account for the condition and contents of the earth's crust; yet our faith in them lacks vividness, simply because no one of the world-forming processes has taken place under our own observation, or under the eye of witnesses who have told us their story. But were there at this moment an unfinished continent or island, still the abode of Saurian reptiles, or the laboratory of fossil coal, the fresh record of explorations in that region would convert our cosmogony from a vague or dead belief into a clearly conceived and intensely realized system of nature.

There has been in the remote past a social, there has been a religious cosmogony, and the greatest difficulty in the way of correct apprehensions as to the origin of civilization, and as to the methods of growth in the primitive church, lies in our lack of realizing and satisfying conceptions of the elements involved in each separate problem. The history of civilization is wrapped in obscurity. The veil of the Dark Ages fell upon certain savage tribes that had the mastery of Europe; it rose upon those tribes, still, indeed, rude in many of the arts of life, but already in an advanced condition of culture and of potential refinement. When we go back to the earlier civilization, we are equally unable to ascend to its cradle and to define the first stages of its growth. Yet birth and source it must have had, heavenly or earthly, and we all have our theories of its genesis;

but we hold them loosely and impassively, because it is so utterly impossible for us to conceive of the transmutation of savage into civilized man. Thus also, there was a creative era of the Christian church, a period when the transition was made, often simultaneously by large numbers of men and women, from Paganism or from Jewish ritualism to a vital faith in the Gospel. Of this era we have numerous memorials in the New Testament. The Epistles are full of the controversies, cases of conscience, weaknesses, scandals, causes of apostasy, incident to this infantile condition. But, though we doubt not the inspiration of the sacred writers, we are apt to enter with but feeble appreciation into the details of their casuistry; many of the topics which they treat seriously seem to us too trivial for grave animadversion; and in not a few cases they recognize as perfectly consistent with a position in the church states of character and modes of conduct which we should regard as incompatible with the Christian name. We thus find it hard to conceive of the earlier portions of Christian history, and while we devoutly acknowledge in them the divine working, we fail to discern the phases of humanity which the record simply describes without interpreting them. But if, after an interval of many centuries, these primitive civilizing and Christianizing processes have been renewed in our own time, even on a comparatively small scale; if even in the least of the nations an organic revolution such as had passed out of human expectation is now nearly consummated, the spectacle has a profound interest equally for the student of history and for the expositor of the Sacred Word.

Such a spectacle is exhibited in the book before us. On merely philosophical grounds it is of unique value. It shows us the means and steps of civilization, the circumstances which favor or check its growth, the action upon it of ideas and institutions respectively, its relations of cause and effect to religious culture. It throws essential light even on the most recondite questions, such as that of the possibility of a nation's becoming civilized except by aid or influence from without, that of man's primitive condition upon the earth, that of his decline or progress from his first estate.

Equally instructive, as we hope to show in the sequel, will this book be found by the biblical scholar. Since reading it, we have understood the Epistles to the Corinthians better than ever before, and have been led, as by no merely critical study, to admire the prudence, sagacity, insight and foresight of the inspired author, no less than his tender forbearance and charity for the newly converted under their liability to the trail and soil of the worship they had abjured. At the same time, we have here full verification of the aggressive power of Christianity in circumstances in no wise favorable for its reception. We learn that it was not as the outgrowth of its own age that the Gospel found reception when first promulgated, but that it is the everlasting Gospel, endowed with like life-giving energy for all times and nations. We especially prize this testimony at a period when naturalism is attempting to sap the foundations of our faith. Other religions have shown themselves the congenial products of their own birthtime by the failure of all attempts to extend their empire, otherwise than by force, in subsequent generations. They grow for a while, rapidly it may be, because they embody and sanction ideas level with the culture of their age; but as the race advances, or changes without advancing, they have no hold, except on the populations which they have educated, and cramped and dwarfed in educating them. A divinely given religion alone can be free from these limitations of time and race, and can work in the eternal freshness of its power on minds of every grade and of every form of culture.

But, most of all, as lovers of mankind, do we rejoice in the evidence here given of a new Pentecost of Christian salvation, in the assurance of the birth into the eternal life of thousands of perishing souls, in the establishment of the reign of Christ upon the ruins of savage fetichism, in the songs of Zion that have replaced the cannibal's war-whoop, in the altars of redemption railed with the broken spears of fierce idolators, in the homes that from beastly dens have become nurseries for heaven.

We should incur the charge of extravagance were we to attempt to convey the impression made upon us by Dr. Anderson's book. His tour among the Hawaiian Islands seems to us the most magnificent progress recorded in history; and his simple, modest narrative, so entirely devoid of egotism and of exaggeration, only makes us feel the more profoundly the greatness of his mission and the preëminent fitness of the agent. Dr.

Anderson in his youth devoted himself in purpose to the career of a foreign missionary, and from the time when he first found the Gospel precious to his own soul, the needs and claims of the unevangelized have never been absent from his thought. In the pendency of arrangements for an Eastern mission, he accepted a temporary clerical appointment on the staff of the American Board. This appointment was soon made permanent; after eight years of service as Assistant Secretary, on the death of Rev. Dr. Cornelius, in 1832, he became one of the three Corresponding Secretaries; and for nearly thirty years he has held the first place in the administration of that noble charity. It is not easy to tell what fertility of resource, what sagacity in the discernment of character, what world-wide knowledge, what executive ability, what hold upon the confidence of good men in all lands, what extended power of influence, have been needed and developed in a life like his. On his prudence, patience, judgment, energy, the entire system has depended, to a degree most fully appreciated by those who have been most intimately conversant with his labors. No statesman or diplomatist has held in his hands so many threads of affairs, often delicate and complicated, often of decisive moment, often involving even grave national interests, demanding with the directness and integrity that befit the servant of the Most High a fully equal measure of the subtile skill and adroit management, in which the children of this world are so apt to surpass the children of the light, and for lack of which a large portion of the philanthropy which has the purest record in heaven leaves no enduring traces of itself on earth.

When Dr. Anderson entered on his official duties, the second instalment of missionaries to the Hawaiian Islands had been despatched, many of the natives were under hopeful training, the language had been reduced to its alphabetic elements, and the first essays at printing had been successfully made. But at that time the mission was a still doubtful experiment. Shortly afterward, the regent and nine of the principal chiefs were gathered into the Christian church, vast multitudes were awakened to a lively interest in the Gospel, and the transformation of institutions, habits, domestic and social life took place so rapidly as to leave no longer room for fear of the reëstablishment of idolatry. During Dr. Anderson's secretaryship more than a hundred missionaries, clerical and lay, male and female, have been sent to the Islands from the United States, under his instruction and direction, while to the Home Board have been constantly referred vital questions of policy and administration, both civil and ecclesiastical, involving difficult relations with the emissaries and officers of foreign governments, and with missionaries, sometimes intrusive, from other religious bodies. Less than the soundest discretion, the most determined vigor, and the most watchful and persistent assiduity on the part of the American Board would at various crises of the mission have placed its interests at fearful hazard, and occasioned disastrous decline in the religious condition of the natives.

In 1862, the Hawaiian people was deemed to hold its rightful place among Christian nations, and the question was raised as to the gradual withdrawal of the support of the Board, with the view of leaving the Islands to sustain their own religious institutions, and to furnish their own Christian teachers. To ascertain data for the safe and judicious settlement of this question it was thought desirable to send an officer of the Board to the Islands, and especially fitting was it to delegate this commission to him who had for nearly forty years identified himself with the work, and who could claim as his "children in the Lord" those thousands of redeemed and converted savages. It was for him an antepast of the blessedness of heaven. Seldom can he who sows in tears count on earth his ranks of ripened sheaves. Even in the ordinary Christian ministry, while the faithful servant of Christ is never without ground for encouragement and gratitude, a collective view of vast results is not often vouchsafed to him; and many there are who have effected so little to the outward eye compared with their longing and endeavor, that they go to their rest feeling that much of their strength has been spent for naught, and only in the day when the secrets of all hearts shall be revealed, will they know their share in the harvest-work. But as Dr. Anderson passed from village to village and from island to island, he was permitted to see in great part the accumulated fruits of his life-toil, multiplied tokens of a regeneration in which his had been the controlling mind, evidences of a work of grace in which he had been the favored instrument, whose magnitude is to be estimated not by past and present converts, but by the unborn multitudes that shall enter on their Christian heritage. He was everywhere received with the love and reverence due to a father in Christ; thanks to God for his visit were sung in that language so strange to his ear; his advent was rapturously welcomed by immense congregations of the natives; he united in the celebration of the Saviour's death with larger bodies of believers than he can often meet in his own land; his words of faith and love, interpreted by his missionary brethren, were listened to with intense earnestness, and met with the most fervent response; and liberal contributions for the distribution of the Scriptures and the furtherance of the Gospel were pressed upon him by those so recently brought from darkness into God's marvellous light. It was, indeed, a triumphal march through this newly conquered province of the Redeemer's empire—how unspeakably blessed to one who felt so profoundly that in all these offerings of affection, gratitude and veneration he was but receiving tribute for the King of kings!

Trusting that most of our readers have sought or will seek for themselves the instruction and edification proffered by the book before us, we shall enter into none of the details of Dr. Anderson's journeyings and personal experiences, but shall confine ourselves to a brief sketch of the former and present condition of the Hawaiian people, and a discussion of a few of the many subjects of interest treated or suggested by the author.

The Hawaiian Islands are ten in number. The native inhabitants bear in color, features and language strong affinities to the Malays, from whom they were probably derived. The population, at the arrival of the first missionaries, was estimated at one hundred and thirty-five thousand, that of Hawaii, the principal island, at eighty thousand. The people were in the lowest condition of savage life. Their genial climate and spontaneously fertile soil had precluded the development of even the rude arts, of which in higher latitudes necessity would have been the teacher. Their dwellings were utterly devoid of comfort; their clothing insufficient for decency. The rights of property were hardly recognized. Extortion on the part of the chiefs, mutual theft and robbery among the people, seem to have been the common law. Polygamy was habitual among all who could obtain and support a plurality of wives, and licentiousness prevailed to the very verge of promiscuous concubinage. Infanticide was so prevalent as to have led to a marked decline of the population, two thirds of the children that were born having been buried barely to avoid the trouble of bringing them up. Murders and crimes of violence were perpetrated almost without restraint; and human sacrifices were offered for the recovery of the king when sick, and as victims at his obsequies. The natural conscience seems to have been obliterated, and there was no trace of a recognized distinction between right and wrong.

The prevalent idolatry was of the coarsest and most senseless type, consisting in the worship of hideous images, with no idea even of their being symbols of unseen powers. This idolatry was extirpated, by a unique combination of circumstances, about the time of the embarkation of the first American missionaries. It was a case in which Satan successfully cast out Satan, through the mysterious working of Him who makes even the wrath and guilt of man to praise him. Among the superstitions inseparable from the national religion was a stringent *tabu* system, extending not only to sacred days, places and persons, but to the domestic habits. Women were forbidden to eat in the presence of their husbands, and were debarred from many of the choicest articles of diet, whether fruit, flesh or fish. The violation of these interdicts was punishable by death, and it was supposed that the offender who escaped human vengeance would be destroyed by the gods. Foreigners had introduced ardent spirits, and to all the other sins of this degraded race was now superadded the habit of beastly drunkenness. The female chiefs, when intoxicated, found courage to indulge in prohibited food. Their rank secured them from punishment at the hand of man, and they were not slow in discovering that no vindictive bolt was launched at their heads by the divinity they had outraged. This *tabu* system seems to have been the fundamental doctrine, the *articulus stantis vel cadentis ecclesiæ* of their creed, and, this proved false, they found themselves atheists. The destruction of their idols, the burning of their temples ensued; and the missionaries discovered, for the first time in the world, an utterly godless people.

It can not be denied that this condition of things offered a vantage-ground for the labors of the earliest Christian teachers, yet less than might seem at first thought. Had the people been far enough advanced in spiritual development to feel the need of worship, or to crave objects of reverence, the *rasa tabula* thus presented would have been easily written over with the holy names of the Christian faith. But these conditions precedent of religious belief seem to have been wanting. The tablet was not there. Yet undoubtedly it was easier, humanly speaking, to create it, than it would have been to make a palimpsest. The resistance presented by the *vis inertiæ* of a race utterly *dead* in trespasses and sins was less than might have been opposed by vital and vigorous misbelief. The seeds of faith lie in the depraved heart, and the dew of the divine grace which alone can make them fruitful is seldom wanting to fervent prayer and faithful endeavor. But, this one feature excepted, the condition of the Hawaiians in 1820 presented as unpromising a field for evangelic culture as lay anywhere beneath the sun, and, compared with the primitive age of the church, an immeasurably less hopeful field than any of the communities to which the apostles carried the word of life.

What are they now? In the arts of civilized life their progress has been at least equal to their conscious needs. While the chiefs and many of the inhabitants of the towns have well-built and well-furnished houses, the squalidness and misery of the rural districts and the poorer classes have given place to habits of decency and self-respect. The government has a written Constitution, with a Bill of Rights as liberal as that of Massachusetts, and with the powers of king, legislature and judiciary carefully defined and limited. The laws are wise, equitable, and preëminently Christian, guarding the religious liberty of the people, but providing against the desecration of the Sabbath and against the renewal of idolatrous superstitions and observances. The courts are admirably organized, and the judicial offices filled by men of competent ability and proved integrity, in part by native citizens, one of the three judges of the Supreme Court being a Hawaiian. There is no country in Christendom, in which life and property are more secure, and none in which the laws against intemperance and licentiousness are more vigilantly and rigidly executed. In the native language there have been published twenty thousand copies of the entire Bible, twelve thousand of the New Testament, and more than two hundred works beside, including school-books, books of religious instruction, and general literature. Three Hawaiian newspapers are issued. The Report of 1849 gives two hundred and eighty nine schools, with eight thousand six hundred and twenty eight scholars. There are several boarding schools, both for boys and girls, at which a superior education is afforded, and a High School, which would bear comparison with our best New England academies, and which has graduated nearly eight hundred pupils, ten of whom have been ordained as ministers of the Gospel. Algebra, Geometry, Trigonometry, Surveying and Political Economy are among the higher branches of learning which have been successfully taught. The people manifest a singular aptness for the acquisition of knowledge, and display an equal susceptibility for the ideas, impressions, tastes and habits which belong of right to advancing intellectual culture.

We can not need to say that this social renovation has been, not only coincident with and incidental to, but commensurate with and dependent upon, the action of Christian truth on individual hearts, and through them on the great heart of the nation. The history of that people for the last forty years has been a multiform commentary on the text: "The entrance of Thy word giveth light." As regards domestic and social habits, we have no evidence that the missionaries have busied themselves especially in the details of improvement. But the Christian consciousness is quick and keen in detecting incongruities and improprieties; the æsthetic nature is stimulated, nourished and instructed by the Divine Spirit, which is the Spirit of beauty no less than of grace; and the consecration of the body and all that pertains to the outward life, by purity, decency, neatness and order, can hardly fail to accompany or follow the consecration of the soul to the service of God. This exterior reformation must needs bear a close proportion, in its extent and thoroughness, to the energy of the work of grace. In these Islands the Gospel had from the first free course among the chiefs and the men and women of commanding influence, and its power was early felt through the whole people. In 1838 there was a great awakening throughout the entire nation, which resulted in the accession of many thousands of genuine converts to the churches. In 1843 more than a fourth part of the entire population were professing Christians; a larger proportion, it is believed, than could be found anywhere else in Christendom. To all these the missionary stations were centres of light, places of familiar resort, seminaries for instruction in things secular no less than in things spiritual. The superior fitness of the habits and appliances of civilized life was promptly perceived and felt; and the disciples, of necessity, became imitators of the teachers and their families in such portions of their mode of living as were applicable to their own condition. This last limitation is essential to a just estimate of the degree of their civilization. Had the missionaries themselves, with all their culture and refinement, belonged to a race for many generations domesticated in that climate, their artificial wants would have been much fewer and more simple; and it would seem to be the tendency of the great mass of their converts to adopt from them just such improvements as they need for decency and comfort, while those who from their position in the state are brought into more intimate relations with the foreign residents conform more fully to foreign tastes and habits. With this essential qualification the Hawaiians already merit a place among civilized nations—a much higher place than would be accorded to the Greeks with their glorious heritage and their little more than nominal Christianity; and they hold this position solely through the transforming power of religious faith and culture.

It is, also, because they have so readily received the divine word, that they have become to so extraordinary a degree an educated and a reading people. The Bible enlarges the mental horizon, suggests themes of thought, subjects of inquiry, gives a sacredness and a zest to knowledge of every kind, stimulates study, and generates mental activity. There evidently exists in this so lately benighted community a higher type of intellectual life, a more genuine love of learning, a surer promise of advanced and extended culture, than can be found in the mass of any people in Europe or America which is debarred free access to the oracles of divine truth.

As for the actual religious condition of these Islands, we have spoken of the proportion of church members in 1843. It is nearly or quite as large at the present time. In the judgment of Dr. Anderson and other equally intelligent witnesses, the evidences of sincere piety are as general and as satisfactory as among professed believers in any portion of Christendom.

Family prayer is almost universal among the converts. The Sabbath is kept sacred to an unusual degree, and its worship is attended by numerous, in some places, by vast congregations. Social prayer meetings are established in connection with every church, and are maintained with constancy, and often with zeal. The average moral character of the church-members is in most respects high, even by the standard of our older civilization, and the sins which have led to frequent ecclesiastical censure and excommunication, though more patent to rebuke, are certainly no more inconsistent with the spirit of our religion than the worldliness, penuriousness and meanness which pass unchallenged among the guests at our communion tabless. Indeed, what indicates, perhaps, more clearly than all things else, the prevalent sincerity of these islanders is their readiness to give largely from their scanty means for the support and propagation of the Gospel. Their contributions average more than twenty thousand dollars annually, and their time and labor are always at the disposal of their teachers for the service of religion. In fine, though they not unfrequently show their still infantile estate as Christians, they at the same time exhibit abundant proof that the religion of the Gospel has wrought in thousands of hearts its regenerating work, and has so far leavened the entire community that there is no ground for apprehending a general apostasy or permanent decline.

We have dwelt on the evidences of their civilization, mainly with reference to the question which it was Dr. Anderson's special purpose to investigate, namely, the expediency of treating them as an integral part of Christendom, and gradually withdrawing from them the special tutelage of the Missionary Board. Their higher or lower degree of civilization or culture may not affect their present condition as Christians; but in their capacity to transmit that condition it is a vital element. The soul of the rudest savage may be converted to God and prepared for heaven; but the light that is in him can shed very little radiance around him. Christian institutions alone can perpetuate the power of the Gospel; and they can be sustained and extended among a population of unsettled habits and undeveloped intellect, only through the agency of a superior race. At most of our flourishing missionary stations the withdrawal of the missionaries would be followed by the speedy extinction of all Christian life. A self-perpetuating church implies the establishment of permanent homes and regular modes of industry, a forethought adequate to provide for future exigencies, mutual confidence among fellow-worshippers, the capacity of combined and organized action, and the existence of means of education and habits of mental industry sufficient to ensure a well-trained ministry and a supply of intelligent office-bearers and leaders in church affairs. A community of which all this could be affirmed is to all intents and purposes civilized, and has within itself resources for further advancement and higher attainment. And in this sense the Hawaiians are civilized. We care not whether they live in houses of grass or of stone, sleep on mats or beds, sit on the ground or on chairs, eat with their fingers or with forks. These matters have no concern with civilization, that is, with the culture which fits men to be citizens and fellow-citizens.

Christianity always tends to civilize a community; but in order to produce this result, it must establish its control over the ruling classes, must permeate the body politic, mould its institutions, preside over its legislation, govern its social intercourse, and, above all, give character to the relations between husband and wife, parent and child, master and servant. Where this work has been in a good measure accomplished, its consummation may be retarded by the prolongation of foreign influence, however beneficent. It is well neither for individual nor collective humanity to remain in tutelage when the period of maturity has been reached. Guardianship beyond its due term cripples and dwarfs the faculties of self-help which it has created. We must, therefore, acknowledge the wisdom of the action of the American Board, in relinquishing the immediate control of the religious interests of these Islands to their native and resident population. The Board still provides for the maintenance of the missionaries already established, most of whom have passed the prime of active usefulness. The counsel and influence of these tried, approved and trusted teachers will be of essential benefit in the transition from pupilage to self-government, while the churches, unburdened by the necessity of contributing to their support, will have no obstacle in the way of securing and compensating the services of native ministers. At the same time those recent heathen are encouraged themselves to enter on the field of missionary enterprise, and this most wisely; for among the means of grace giving is second only to prayer, as the American church has found in its own blessed experience. The superintendence of the Micronesian mission is to be entrusted to an executive board chosen by the Hawaiian Evangelical Association, the American Board continuing its pecuniary aid for such time and in such measure as may be found necessary.

We have thus far presented only the bright and hopeful aspects of the Christian cause on these Islands. Is there not a reverse side? That there is we could not doubt, even were our author silent with regard to it. But, with his perfect candor, Dr. Anderson suppresses nothing, and our readers will miss in his pages not one of the salient facts which have been employed with malign purpose and effect by the calumniators of the mission. We have not referred to these facts in discussing the self-sustaining capacity of the Hawaiian churches, because they are not of sufficient magnitude to have any important bearing on that question, any more than the short-comings, dissensions and corruptions of our New England Christianity have on its power to prolong its own existence, and, by aid from on high, to purify and elevate its own standard of faith and piety. But we will now look at the shades in the picture.

In the first place, it must be admitted that there remains among the Hawaiian Christians a certain proclivity to licentiousness and intemperance. We are grieved, but not surprised or shocked at this. It is what is to be expected in a people separated by hardly a generation from an utterly brutish state of manners and morals. Aside from the theological question of original sin, though casting essential light upon it, there can be no doubt as to the transmission of moral tendencies in families and races. Had one of Herod's children become a disciple of Christ, he would have been a disciple of a very different type from one of the family of Joseph of Arimathea. He might repeatedly, under stress of sudden and intense temptation, have shown his sonship according to the flesh to the vilest of men, yet without losing from his heart the evidence of his spiritual sonship. Just such is the case with a tribe or race of converts from the lower forms of paganism. There is a heritage of evil in their very constitution of body, mind and soul. Ages of slavery to the animal appetites have stimulated those appetites, and given them a natively larger influence over the active powers of the moral nature than they have in a people whose nature has been moulded by centuries of self-control and mental and religious culture. The Christian consciousness may be as genuine and as strong in the recent savage as in the descendant from an ancestry of saints; yet in the former case it will have to contend with a host of the powers of evil, which in the latter were resisted and overcome in the remote past, and have since fought only with blunted weapons and with crippled strength. It must be remembered, too, that the social sentiments and habits of decency and propriety, which are a most essential safeguard and help to the individual Christian, at least in the early stages of the religious life, are of gradual growth and of cumulative efficacy, and that they have but just begun to grow in the Hawaiian people. It is said by the Spirit of God to every subject of renewing grace, as it was said to Abraham, "Get thee out of thine own country, and from thy kindred, and thy father's house, unto a land that I will show thee"; and the reality, intensity and working power of his faith are to be tested, not by the distance yet to be measured to the promised land, but by his distance from his starting point. He who moves on his pilgrimage from an idolatrous country, from kindred steeped in swinish sensuality, from a father's house no better than a kennel, may find himself at the close of a long and faithful pilgrimage below the starting point of natural conscience and conventional morality, at which the child of a consecrated household hears and obeys the same call of God; yet in the eye of heaven he will have fought a good fight, and have finished a noble course, and his children may commence where he closed his career.

As we have intimated, the details in the volume before us at once receive light from, and reflect light upon, the apostolic epistles. In the churches at Corinth and in Asia, St. Paul certainly recognizes as brethren beloved, and praises for their proficiency and good gifts as Christians, persons who needed advice and warning as to the very rudiments of morality. At Corinth there had been gross violations of chastity among the disciples, and it would seem that even the Lord's Supper had been made an occasion of excess and drunkenness. In fine, there was in that church a condition of things incompatible, according to our modern notions, with the lowest concrete form of vital Christianity. Yet in his second epistle we discern manifest traces in these frail novices of a sensitiveness to rebuke, an accessibleness to the movements of contrite sorrow, indicating all that is implied in the apostle's words as to the depth of Christian feeling in their hearts and the reality of their conversion to God. "For behold this self-same thing, that ye sorrowed after a godly sort, what carefulness it wrought in you, yea, what clearing of yourselves, yea, what indignation, yea, what fear, yea, what vehement desire, yea, what zeal"! St. Paul, it must be borne in mind, in view of these moral infirmities of his converts, is slow to condemn, chary of excommunication, prompt and earnest in the restoration of offenders, aware all the while that, though "the iniquity of their heels" — the sins in which they were born and bred, yet which they have in purpose left behind them — may at times "compass them about," there may yet be on their hearts the unobliterated seal of the Spirit. We can not but agree with some of the missionaries, as cited by Dr. Anderson, that among these modern converts excommunication has been too frequent, especially as the excommunicated have in numerous instances passed from a church which would have tolerated, not their sin, but their bitterly repented sin, to the less discriminating mercies of Romanism, which, whatever may be its theories, practically makes the way of transgressors easy.

The same sensitiveness to rebuke, which St. Paul recognizes among the Corinthians, may be remarked among the Hawaiians. Says Dr. Anderson, "I was assured of cases where, after a terrible declension, the return had been with increased humility, experience, watchfulness, and zeal, so that the lapsed recovered ones became at length pillars in the church."

So far from looking upon lapses of this kind, though frequent, as a ground of discouragement, we rather regard them, viewed in all their aspects, as a hopeful omen. It is an immense gain that the community has reached a condition in which such cases of sin are exceptional and abnormal, are not numerous enough to constitute a characteristic feature of the Christian society or to defy its discipline, and are already the objects of unfeigned shame and contrition among the guilty, and of hearty reprobation among their associates. Moreover, this unfortunate liability, so far as it exists, seems to be confined chiefly to those who have been heathen and savages, and is not likely to be transmitted to their children except in a modified and controllable form and degree. The now rising generation, trained under the shadow of the domestic altar and the Christian sanctuary, educated by religious teachers, imbued from their tender years in the morality of the Gospel, and large numbers of them made in their youth hopeful subjects of Divine grace, will grow up under at least as favorable influences as those which surround the young persons in our own land whom we regard as the hope of the church. This future is already beginning to be realized. The pupils of the missionary schools are fast establishing a higher tone of character. Of the native ministers we are told that not one has shown himself unworthy of his sacred trust. The manifest tendency is toward an elevated standard of practical ethics.

In this connection we can not but attach great importance to the laws of the kingdom, not only or chiefly in their prohibitory or punitive function, but as declarative of the collective moral sense, and as educating the general conscience. From all that we can learn, we infer that in the legislation, and at the hands of the judiciary of the Islands, purity and temperance are as carefully guarded as they can be by human authority, and that those who violate them can be protected only by the secrecy of their guilt. The laws against the manufacture of intoxicating drinks and against their sale to native residents are peculiarly stringent and severe, and a very recent attempt to relax the penalty for their sale has been defeated by the vote of nearly three fourths of the legislature — a vote which, as passed after able and thorough discussion, we feel warranted in regarding as an authentic exponent of public opinion.

Does it not appear from these statements that the easily besetting sins of the Hawaiians are treated with greater severity and present better promise of their rapid decline, than the vices that infect the religious communities of older Christendom—the selfishness, avarice and virtual dishonesty, which are "the abomination of desolation" in the church of God, and hold in sordid slavery many who claim to be its very pillars?

A much more serious discouragement to missionary labor on this field might seem to be found in the decline of the native population. On this subject it is not easy to obtain trustworthy data, either as to the extent to which causes of depopulation have operated in former times, or as to the degree in which they are now arrested. Captain Cook estimated the population at four hundred thousand; but this was undoubtedly an over-estimate. The earliest official census, in 1832, gives one hundred and thirty thousand, three hundred and fifteen; the latest, in 1860, sixty nine thousand, eight hundred. But for the first four years of these twenty eight, the decrease was at the rate of more than four per cent. per annum, while for the last seven years it has been less than two thirds of one per cent. per annum. The vices introduced by foreigners held a prominent place among the causes of the rapid decline from the first discovery of the Islands till the arrival of the missionaries. The passion for strong drink made fearful ravages among the people; while the vile lusts of their visitors from civilized lands brought upon them even still more loathsome agencies of disease and death, and undoubtedly weakened the vital stamina of coming generations. There has been also at three different periods since the commencement of the century a visitation of devastating epidemics, though it would seem that the liability to diseases of this class is much less than in regions not lying under the salubrious influence of breezes from the sea. Infanticide and human sacrifices must also account in part for the diminished numbers of the people, and the former of these causes must have ceased very gradually with the progress of Christianity. Then too, though the rude and squalid habits of savage life are not incompatible with a moderate growth of population, improvements in dwellings, dress, food and medical treatment can hardly fail to preserve many lives that would else have been sacrificed in infancy, by needless exposure, or by curable disease. On the whole, we can not but believe that future enumerations will present results of a much more favorable character than the past, and that through the blessing of Providence this mild, gentle, tractable and highly improvable people may maintain its name and place among the nations of the earth, as a monument of Christian philanthropy, as a luculent token of the fulfilment of the promises of God, and as a centre and source of light to populations on the islands and coasts of the Pacific still lying under the shadow of death.

But were the case otherwise, were the gradual extinction of

this people clearly foreseen, would there be any the less reason to rejoice in what has been accomplished, and to extend to the declining remnant of the nation all the offices of Christian love? The salvation of thousands upon thousands of souls will still have rewarded the toil and sacrifice of the church and its agents; the national decline will have been retarded by this ministry of mercy; and there will have been written a chapter of the world's religious history, which we believe will be transcribed in letters of light in the Lamb's book of life.

We refer to this last named contingency, not because we think it probable, but because it may present itself to some of our readers as inevitable. It is undoubtedly a beneficent law of the divine Providence that races of feeble vitality and capacity shall yield place by the operation of natural causes to races of superior physical and intellectual vigor; in fine, that the different regions of the earth shall gradually pass into hands that can subdue it, avail themselves of its resources and enjoy its uses. Under this law, no doubt, the aborigines of North America will ultimately disappear, and the humane policy which ought to have been pursued to them from the first would not have ensured their preservation in the land, though it would have averted the condemnation of blood-guiltiness from the European settlers. But the Hawaiians do not seem to fall necessarily under this law. Their constitution is adapted to their climate; their capacity to their soil. They are amply able to develop the resources of their territory, and to employ for the general benefit the advantages of their position. They thus far show themselves susceptible of cultivation, and have made more rapid progress than has elsewhere left its record in the history of the world. They may not, indeed, have within themselves the elements of a great people; but their cluster of islets can never become the seat of a great people. They could not, indeed, protect themselves by arms against any of the leading powers of Christendom; but we trust that they will guard their modest independence by the arts and virtues that belong to a Christian nation, and by pacific and beneficent relations of intercourse and commerce. Their insular and solitary position may save them from dangerous complications with more powerful states; they can not lie on the track of any future belligerents, or become the victims of wars other than their own; and the time has gone by for aggression or usurpation from abroad, without shadow of reason or pretence of right.

Another danger to which this people is exposed grows out of the influx of foreign residents. Much of the land is peculiarly adapted to the growth of the sugar-cane, while rice, coffee and cotton are successfully cultivated. These commodities are most profitably raised on large plantations, and the soil suited to their production is already furnishing a lucrative investment for the disposable capital of France, England and America; while the commerce of the Islands has of necessity been hitherto conducted to a very great degree by immigrants from the older commercial nations. To these dominant classes of foreigners there have been recently added importations of coolies from China for labor on the sugar-plantations. If enterprise on the one hand and manual labor on the other are to be permanently usurped by immigrants, of course under this double pressure the native population will inevitably decline in resources and in energy, and will be gradually absorbed and obliterated by intermarriage with the intrusive races. But whether this shall be the case or not must depend, we believe, on the thoroughness of the civilizing and Christianizing work which has been wrought upon the natives. If considerable numbers of them are fitted in intelligence and character to hold commanding positions, and to conduct extended operations in agriculture and commerce, they will in the lapse of one or two generations replace the foreign residents; for, with equal ability, they will have the advantage in physical constitution, in attachment to the soil, in the command of the language, and in the confidence of their fellow-countrymen. If, at the other extremity of the social scale, Christian culture develops habits of industry and creates a felt need of the comforts of civilized life, the mass of the people will not suffer the soil to be cultivated by strangers.

The labor of coolies, while on moral grounds little preferable to that of slaves, is not much less costly and wasteful, their nominally low wages being hardly an offset to the expense of importation and the rapid mortality among them; and the Hawaiians, once made aware of the duty and the privilege of toil, will readily demonstrate the superior economy of free labor. Much of the land planted with sugar-cane is now in the hands of small native proprietors; and on these estates free labor is proved to be amply remunerative. On the whole we can not believe that a people that deserves to live can be pressed down and crushed out on its own soil. Foreign enterprise has gained its ascendancy, and foreign labor its foothold in the Hawaiian Islands, only while the natives are in training to take effective possession of their birthright. If they show themselves mentally or morally unfit to retain the heritage, we doubt not that Providence will bestow it on races more worthy of it. But in what God has done for this people, while we may not presume to lift the veil from his decrees, we can not but trust that he has been training, not only souls for heaven, but a nation to serve him in the land which he has given to them.

Another topic, to which we are bound to allude, however unwillingly, in treating of the adverse or discouraging circumstances in connection with Hawaiian Christianity, is that of divided religious interests. In the older portions of Christendom, the phenomenon of rival sects is understood, and their common appeal to the same plenary and divine authority casts the weight of their combined testimony and influence on the side of faith. But those recently converted from heathenism, accustomed to uniformity of belief and worship in their previous estate, and knowing little of the history of the Christian church, are perplexed and often thrown into scepticism by the antagonisms of mutually exclusive sects. They can not comprehend the identity of religion where there is no community of religious interest and feeling. In their view the denial of the doctrines and the contempt of the ritual in which they have been trained are tantamount to the rejection and contempt of Christianity. Even in the age of the apostles, and under the ministry of those who had received their doctrine from the lips or by the revelation of the Lord, it was feared lest different modes of teaching and discipline on the same soil might be fraught with mischief. St. Paul expresses his determination not to enter on other men's labors, and laments and deprecates the consequences of the intrusion on his own ground of teachers not authorized or approved by himself. In the world-wide field open to the philanthropy of the church, modern Protestant missionaries have in general recognized this principle, and have been unwilling to present before heathendom the spectacle of a distracted church and a divided Gospel. When they could not labor side by side without collision or wide dissiliency of aim or action, they have, like Abraham and Lot, fed their flocks apart.

This Christian comity has been violated by the mission of the English church, or, as it styles itself, the "Reformed Catholic Mission." The subject is one which we would gladly omit; but we should do injustice equally to the work under review and to the mission cause, were we to pass it over in silence.

The late king having become interested in the services of the English church, and there being at Honolulu many English residents who had been educated in its worship, application was made by Rev. Dr. Armstrong, once a missionary of the American Board, and then filling the office of President of the Board of Public Instruction, and Mr. Wyllie, an Englishman, Minister of Foreign Affairs, to Rev. William Ellis of London, pledging a moderate salary to some suitable English clergyman, who might consent to assume the pastorate of a church at the capital. The request was made for "a man with evangelical sentiment, of respectable talents, and most exemplary Christian life. A high churchman," added Dr. Armstrong, "or one of loose Christian habits, would not succeed. He would not have the sympathy and support of the other evangelical ministers at all, but rather opposition." This application was in entire accordance with the wishes of the missionaries and their friends. Indeed Dr. Anderson had previously urged a bishop of the American Episcopal church to send out a presbyter of his diocese with reference to such a charge. Mr. Wyllie, who seems to have been playing a double game, had previously entered into correspondence with Mr. Hopkins, the Hawaiian consul in London, and a plan was matured through his agency for sending to the Islands a bishop and three presbyters, under the [high church] auspices of the Society for Propagating the Gospel. When this project became known, the American Board instituted a correspondence with the Archbishop of Canterbury and the Bishop of London, both of whom are understood to have sympathized with the views of the Board, and to have been opposed to intrusion on the field which they had made their own. But the counsels of the high church party prevailed. Bishop Staley was consecrated in 1861, and arrived at Honolulu, accompanied by two of his presbyters, and shortly followed by a third, in October, 1862.

These men of lofty apostolic pretensions have taken precisely the course which might have been anticipated, and will undoubtedly succeed in creating schism and animosity among the native Christians. They ignore the ministerial character and office of the American missionaries. They avail themselves of every opportunity of baptising children, without reference to the ecclesiastical relations of the parents. They have established the most showy and Romeward tending modes of worship, "with surplice and stole, with alb, and cope, and crosier; with rochet, and mitre, and pastoral staff; with Episcopal ring and banner; with pictures, altar-candles, robings, intonations, processions, and attitudes." Meanwhile Bishop Staley has been preaching the most extreme and offensive doctrines of his party in the church, doctrines diametrically opposed to those taught by the missionaries, patristical tradition, baptismal regeneration, the gift of the Holy Spirit in confirmation, confession to the priest, and priestly absolution. At the same time he has stultified himself, while he has no doubt mystified his serious hearers, and encouraged the undevout in the desecration of holy time, by declaring that Sunday is "most falsely and mischievously called the Sabbath," and intimating that the daily service of the church and the observance of its solemn festivals fitly supersede the special reverence with which the people had been taught by the missionaries and required by the law of the land to regard the one day in seven. He has stultified himself, we say; for, unless the high church "has changed all this," the precept, "Remember that thou keep holy the Sabbath day," is read constantly in the ante-communion service, with the response, "Lord, have mercy upon us, and incline our hearts to keep this law." If Sunday is "most falsely and mischievously called the Sabbath," to what observance does this portion of the English liturgy have reference? Or does Bishop Staley require his adherents, in the most sacred service of the altar, to perform an act of solemn mockery, to offer a prayer which is arrant blasphemy, to beg of the divine mercy that they may be inclined to practice "falsehood and mischief"? Candles at noonday are a harmless folly; this is gross impiety.

The success of this mission has as yet been very limited. Its congregations are small. The modes of worship repel the simple tastes of such as have been sincerely attached to the ministrations of their earlier teachers; and those who want to be addressed through the senses, and gravitate toward the old idolatry, can find more that is congenial among the Roman Catholics than among their imitators. Yet under the patronage of the court and of some of the more influential foreign residents, this superstition must needs grow. It can hardly fail to create a diversion from the interests of a simple faith and worship, which is especially to be deprecated at the present crisis, when the autonomy of the native church is just beginning, and needs the combined zeal, effort and liberality of all who love the cause of Christ and seek the prosperity of Zion.

We have spoken freely and warmly of this intrusion; but we believe that we have said no more than candid Episcopalians would readily admit and endorse. For the English church and its American sister we cherish all due reverence, gratitude and affection; and because we feel this, we can not think or write with easy tolerance of the stilted and popinjay caricatures of its solemn order and majestic ritual.

There is also on the Islands a Roman Catholic Mission, numbering as proselytes, (including all baptized persons,) more than twenty thousand souls. The Mormons have, too, a small settlement on the island of Lanai, and reckon, (including children,) not far from four thousand members. It does not appear that either of these forms of belief is making rapid progress, or presents any active hostility to the success of Protestant Christianity.

While we should be gratified to see this new-born people united in faith and worship, we can conceive that this diversity of ministration, these forms of error, these tares growing with the wheat, may be made subservient to their better proficiency in divine things. Inquiry, comparison, mental activity on religious subjects, will be aroused and guided; the native pastors will feel the more intense need of taking heed to themselves, their doctrine and their flocks, because they are in the midst of gainsayers; private Christians will have added inducements to be loyal to the Master who can receive no wounds so deep as in the house of his friends; and thus a more intelligent faith and a more fervent piety may spring from the present division, and may prepare the way for the ultimate triumph of the truth over all obstacles and hinderances.

We have forborne making extracts from the work under review, because we are unwilling that any of our readers should become acquainted with it in scraps or fragments. We have not even given an analysis of it, though our materials have been chiefly derived from it. Besides, there are no *especially* interesting extracts. The whole, from the Preface to the Appendix, is full of intense interest for all who love their Saviour and their race. The narrative flags not for one moment on the eager attention of the reader, nor can it fail to lift the devout heart as with a continuous anthem of praise to Him who has "given such power unto men," as is shown forth in this regenerated people.

One thought suggests itself in conclusion. Much of the science of our day busies itself, with a depraved ingenuity, in detaching man's hold on the ancestral tree by which he traces his descent from God, and of which, among the progeny of the second Adam, he may become a living branch. The true answer to these speculations is not to be found in ethnology or in physiology. No race can make out an unbroken pedigree; nor yet can we deny that there are strong analogies between the higher orders of quadrupeds and the lower members of the human family, not only in physical structure, but in mental capacity. Fifty years ago, the half-reasoning elephant or the tractable and troth-keeping dog might have seemed the peer, or more, of the unreasoning and conscienceless Hawaiian. From that very race, from that very generation, with which the nobler brutes might have scorned to claim kindred, have been developed the peers of saints and angels. Does not the susceptibility of regeneration, the capacity for all that is tender, beautiful and glorious in the humanity of the Lord from heaven — inherent in the lowest types of our race — of itself constitute an impassable line of demarcation between the brute and man? Has physical science a right to leave "the new man in Christ Jesus," which the most squalid savage may become, out of the question in its theories of natural selection or spontaneous development? When the modern Lucretianism can account for the phenomena of Christian salvation, without the intervention of miracle, revelation, or Redeemer, and not till then, can it demand our respect as a tenable theory of the universe.

Personal Piety as Related to the Missionary Work.

A

SERMON

DELIVERED BEFORE THE

FOREIGN MISSIONARY SOCIETY,

OF

NEW-YORK AND BROOKLYN,

APRIL 4 AND 11, 1852.

BY

REV. ASA D. SMITH, D. D.,

PASTOR OF THE FOURTEENTH STREET PRESBYTERIAN CHURCH,
NEW-YORK.

Published by the Society.

NEW-YORK:
ALMON MERWIN, 150 NASSAU-STREET.
1852.

JOHN F. TROW, PRINTER,
49 Ann-street.

SERMON.

PSALM li. 13.

"Do good in thy good pleasure unto Zion: build thou the walls of Jerusalem."

UNIQUE as was the origin of the remarkable lyric from which these words are taken, it is not to be regarded as the outburst, merely, of an individual heart. We pass, as we read it, from the particular to the universal. Here, as in other Psalms, we may, as Luther expresses it, "look into the hearts of *all* good men." Nor are we limited to any single element or aspect of piety. Penitence is, indeed, prominent; but there are linked with it, according to the immutable laws of spiritual affinity, all the other graces. These graces are presented, too, in a most natural order. There is a beautiful climax; the principle of development, the law of growth obtains; there springs up before us, as from the dark germ to the flowery coronal, a perfect organism. Nor is this an incongruous issue of the individual case. The restoration of a lapsed believer is, in its elemental character and its necessary processes, much like a first conversion. Such was David's recovery; with perhaps this difference, that, as not infrequently happens, he was, through abounding grace, brought to a loftier position than ever. He breathes forth, first, the most sincere and profound contrition, that invariable beginning of all true godliness. Under the burden of his guilt, he looks not to any righteousness or strength of his own, but to God's pardoning mercy, and to his sanctifying Spirit. There come before us, then, the conscious purity of the soul divinely cleansed, and the joy and gladness of the forgiven one. Out of the abundance of the heart, we have next the lips speaking. "My mouth," says the Psalmist, "shall show forth thy praise." Nor are his thoughts limited to the narrow circle of his own interests; — into a broader sphere flow forth his quickened affections. He would "teach transgressors;" he would see sinners converted; his earnest desire is, that God's cause may prosper. He pours, at length, the fulness of his soul into the words of the text: — "Do good in thy good pleasure unto Zion; build thou the walls of Jerusalem."

It is with no sufficient reason, that certain critics have regarded this passage as not a part of the original Psalm, but a convenient accretion of later times. We see here, most clearly, David's image and superscription. How natural for the magnanimous man who exclaimed, "These sheep, what have they done?" to beg of God, in this connection, that from the sins he bewailed no harm might come to others. Nay, with all gracious experience — especially with the profound experience here unfolded — the outgoings of benevolence are accordant and homogeneous; they are its necessary consummation. There is in our text no forced or strange transition; the Psalm, without it, were incomplete. That charity which is not only the fulfilling of the law, but the essential element of every Christian grace, though it does in a sense begin at home, yet abides not there. While its centre is the throne of God, its circuit is the universe. In David's time, it is true, the field of active benevolence was comparatively limited; the "middle wall of partition" was not yet broken down. Yet we have in the prayer before us, the vital element of all modern evangelism; we have piety here, going forth from its inner shrine, impelled and animated by the spirit awakened and nourished there, to scatter blessings wherever it may. We have a deep Christian experience developing itself in Christian philanthropy. Were the heart which suggested these words throbbing on earth now, it would be satisfied, we may be sure, with nothing less than the world's conversion. We put no constraint upon this passage, then, when we derive from it, as the subject of discourse on the present occasion, PERSONAL PIETY AS RELATED TO THE MISSIONARY WORK.

We speak of that work in the widest sense, including whatever pertains to it both at home and abroad. And our aim is to show, that as personal piety is its source, so this, under God, is its chief reliance. This is the vital force of the whole movement, the grand motive power of all the machinery. Abstract or weaken it, and sluggishness, inefficiency, and failure ensue; give it depth and strength, and a world-wide evangelism is the natural and even necessary result.

I. For the elucidation of this subject, it may be well to begin, according to a good old method, with a negative view. Certain things there are, unduly trusted in by some, but which are in themselves as a broken reed. Subsidiary in some slight measure they may prove, if the heart be right — nay, important helps; yet without true and deep piety, they are but as a cheat and a mockery. As the trellis-work of the arbor they may be, but not as the living vine, or as the principle of life and growth. Not one of them is to be utterly repudiated; for the whole creation shall be made subservient to God's plan of saving grace. Yet we may not substitute them for the great spiritual motors.

1. I advert first, under this head, to *natural sympathy*. To this many of the aspects and issues of sin in unevangelized regions make a powerful appeal. I need not stop to show how illusory are certain poetical rhapsodies touching the state of nature. Here and there a dreamer may be found, enamored of the blissful ignorance, the charming simplicity, the exemption from corroding care and burdensome conventionalities, the large liberty, the luxurious leisure, the habit of romantic adventure, which, as shaped and colored by his infatuated fancy, pertain to the island or the forest home of the godless savage. Yet Christendom in general is well informed on this subject. To know what

ancient heathenism was, to see clearly its many and varied abominations and miseries, we have only to turn over the pages of Leland or of Tholuck. To see what man still is, without the light of the Gospel—how low he sinks, how the springs even of earthly enjoyment are either dried up or poisoned—we need only look at the beautiful isles of the Pacific as Christianity found them, at the barbarous tribes of Western or of Southern Africa, or at the besotted multitudes of China or of Hindostan. We touch not now on the future consequences of sin, or on the more spiritual evils it here engenders. We advert only to its more palpable inflictions, to the wants and woes quite visible even to the eye of the natural man.

From the broad empire of idolatry, as in one vast moving panorama, what shapes of evil does imagination summon! Behold these motley myriads, squalid and loathsome, the "human face divine" made brutal and fiendlike. Look into that dwelling, the miserable substitute for what we love to call home, and mark not merely the meagreness of its appointments, but the utter absence of all the sweet and gentle fireside charities. Over its forbidding portal you see written, "Without natural affection." Behold the mother, as she issues forth, her heart petrified by superstition, to cast the babe from her bosom to the monsters of the flood. By his own children the aged and enfeebled father is led away to die alone and unheeded. The husband expires, the funeral pile is erected, and the frantic widow casts herself upon it. A group of heathen devotees are before us, with stiffened limbs and lacerated bodies. A pagan altar presents itself, all stained with human gore; and over willing victims roll the ponderous wheels of the idol's car. The bloody Dyak is here, with his vaunted store of human heads; and savage tribes rush to the battle-field, eager not for vengeance alone, but for the profits of the slave-mart.

We object not to showing, by these and other like illustrations, that "the dark places of the earth are full of the habitations of cruelty." It is only thus that the true nature of sin can be set forth. That appeals of this sort, as they have moved the sensibilities of men, have had some influence in urging on the missionary work, we do not doubt. Especially have they been serviceable, when other aspects of heathenism, and considerations of a loftier and more spiritual kind have been the primary incentives. What we insist on is, that we must beware of confiding unduly in such appeals. For this, as for every other form of philanthropy, a slender basis is a mere humanitarianism. Little will be accomplished, if the main fountain of missionary feeling, a true and deep Christian experience, be lacking. The point of sacrifice and self-denial will hardly be reached. It will be but the surface of our being that is stirred; the depths below will be all unmoved. And even the superficial agitation must in the nature of things soon cease. Familiarity with exciting and horrifying scenes, where there is no deeply seated and powerfully operative religious principle, must soon beget comparative indifference.

2. Nor may we lean with greater assurance on what may be called *the æsthetic principle.* God has so made us, that we have a susceptibility to the beautiful and the sublime wherever seen. We are touched by these qualities in external nature, but still more in the province of the intellectual and the moral. As seen in the palpable world, indeed, they are but the types of a higher excellence in the immaterial. A thousand various forms do they assume in the sphere of sentiment and of passion, of natural affection and of moral feeling, of merely secular action and of religious achievement; but nowhere are they more touchingly bodied forth than in the eventful annals of the missionary enterprise. Nay, it were no exaggeration to say, that here may be found their most perfect development. Just here would I look for specimens of whatever is most graceful in emotion, most startling and even romantic in adventure, most lofty and imposing in aim and action. To the broad missionary field would I resort for themes that most effectually stir the poet's soul, or for attitudes and scenes most worthy of the painter's pencil. I would point to Henry Martyn, casting the last look on the white cliffs of England, or sitting alone, as death drew near, in the orchard at Tocat, and thinking of his God, "in solitude his company, his friend, and his comforter." Harriet Newell would rise to my view, receiving the parting kiss of her widowed mother, and bidding fare-

well to the home of her childhood. I should gaze again on that secluded spot in the quiet valley of Williamstown, where a few pious young men, amid their deep self-scrutiny, and falling tears, and solemn vows, laid the corner-stone of our great missionary enterprise. To that first ordination of American missionaries in the old Tabernacle Church would I turn, to the kneeling forms of the pioneer band, and to the venerable men—the sainted Worcester and his compeers—gathered around them for "the laying on of hands." Again would the brig Caravan, with her precious freight, float slowly forth from Salem harbor, while on the strange spectacle many gaze with moistened eyes and heaving bosoms. By that missionary grave would I stand on the Isle of France, or by that other grave beneath the Hopia tree, and think of the sleepers below, as once they walked together on the banks of the Merrimack, and talked of the Saviour whom they loved and would serve unto death. To the death-prison at Ava would I turn, to the blood-stained footsteps of the devoted Judson, and to the loathsome cell at Oung-pen-lay,—to mark not merely the patience in suffering and the holy steadfastness of the man of God, but to note also, and with still higher admiration, the martyr-like heroism of his noble wife. A loftier name than hers, where shall we find in all the glorious "Records of Woman?"

If from the history of missions, crowded with instances like these, we turn to what may be called its literature—to that portion of it especially which is germain to the point in hand—how thickly set do we find it with gems of purest lustre. Among all the lyrics of earth, how few will bear comparison, in respect as well of beauty as of true sublimity, with the oft repeated hymn of Heber! For delicacy of sentiment, and for depth of pathos, what production of the sort in the whole range of our literature, can claim precedence of that letter which announced to the mother of Harriet Newell the death of her daughter? I do not marvel that a beloved laborer in the foreign field, now with us for a season, refers to the perusal of it as the proximate cause—operating, indeed, on a heart already imbued with love to Christ—of his devoting himself to the missionary work. Were I asked to indicate, among all the treasures of English poesy, that one piece, which in the mingling of the sweetest and most touching of the natural affections with the loftiest exercises of the religious sentiment, stands without a rival, I know not what I would sooner name than those well-known lines of Mrs. Judson to her husband.

To particular death-scenes we have already alluded: how replete with æsthetic power is the whole missionary martyrology! In strains at once of classic beauty, and of womanly tenderness, has Mrs. Hemans sung of the perished warriors of her native land:—

> "Wave may not foam, nor wild wind sweep,
> Where sleeps not England's dead."

In like strains, though with more thrilling import, we

might celebrate the dead of the sacramental host. Their requiem comes to us on every breeze. There is hardly a land under heaven but is hallowed by their dust; there is scarce an ocean in whose depths their bones are not reposing. In the green isles of the Pacific they sleep, and amid the spicy groves of Ceylon and Sumatra. In "the land of Sinim" they lie — beneath the waves that wash its coast — and amid the palm-trees and pagodas of India. On the shores of "the great and wide sea," and in the Holy City, are their sepulchres; in ancient Pontus, and beneath the shadow of old Argœus. In the beautiful plain of Oroomiah they slumber, and among the mosques and minarets of the Ottoman metropolis. On the western coast of benighted Africa they rest, and amid the forests and kraals of its southern borders. By the Father of Waters, on our own continent, and "where rolls the Oregon," are their graves; and in more dreary regions, amid "Greenland's icy mountains." Yet there have not been lacking those who were ready to be "baptized for the dead;" and onward still the missionary host have pressed, stayed by no obstacle, daunted by no danger. Nor shall they pause in their glorious career, till

"One song employs all nations."

These and other like aspects of beauty and of moral dignity, we would by no means overlook. In our missionary fabric we rejoice to recognize not only the broad and deep foundations, but the garniture of all manner of precious stones — not the massive and imposing shaft alone, but the curiously chiselled and graceful capital. We would omit, in dealing with man's complex nature, not a single legitimate element of persuasion. Yet in urging to spiritual achievements we must beware of unduly exalting merely natural incentives. A broad distinction is there between the thrills and flights of sentiment, and the martyr-spirit. Not the first was Chalmers to discover "the slender influence of taste and sensibility in matters of religion." Ever since the missionary enterprise began, and especially since it has gained a certain popularity, it has been no strange thing for men to melt into tenderness, or to soar into the loftier moods of thought, as its history and claims have been unfolded, and yet to turn at last from the appeal apparently so effective, to tread as callously as ever the old path of niggardliness and self-indulgence.

3. It may seem strange if we add here — and yet there is reason for adding — that we can base no effectual appeal on the ground of *our own advantage.* The principle of self-love, as held in the grasp of a strict and sharp definition, as properly limited and subordinated, we would not wholly discard. Never perhaps has it safer and wider scope, than as recognizing the reflex influence of the missionary movement. No little benefit of a temporal sort has that movement conferred. How greatly indebted to the research it has required, are science and literature. What discov-

eries have been made in the department of language. Nay, of what creations can we speak. From many a chaos of rude and unsystematized speech, have order, and symmetry, and beauty been evoked. How have the subtle affinities of language been detected. And what light has been shed thus and otherwise, on the broad field — now assuming such interest in the view of the learned — of ethnological inquiry. How many points of geography, of statistical science, and of general history, have been elucidated. On many a topic of this sort, our missionary publications are already regarded as among the most valuable authorities. Some of our missionaries, indeed, may in some important departments of learning, be justly ranked with the best scholars of the age. Not that they have aimed at such distinction; — they have sought first "the kingdom of God and the righteousness thereof," and all these things have been added unto them. By missionary successes commerce has been benefited, and as inseparable from it, the arts and agriculture. When as the result of Christianization, a nation of nude savages, sleeping in miserable huts, are to be civilized from head to foot and in all the appliances and walks of life, no small demand is made on the industrial world. That world is benefited, too, as in many ways intercommunication is promoted. Apart from spiritual religion, moreover, there is, as every thoughtful man must admit, a restraint upon the working of a sordid utilitarianism, an enlarging influence upon the common mind, in holding up before it continually a noble world-wide charity. Many a man who is full of prejudice against the cause we plead, is after all somewhat less of an earth-worm, for the indirect bearing upon his character of that very cause. Taking into view only temporal advantage, it cannot be doubted, that our own land is under great obligation to the missionary enterprise. Were there no eternity, we should as a nation and as individuals sustain great loss were that enterprise blotted out.

We need not hesitate to declare, then, that in this relation as well as others, godliness hath the "promise of the life that now is." We may countervail objections thus, and honor at once God's word and providence. Yet we greatly err, if we regard motives of this sort as of chief importance. The true missionary spirit hath far deeper foundations. It abases self — it goes out of self. Even that most elevated sort of reflex influence, the tendency of missionary effort to advance our own piety — a tendency not to be overlooked by those who hunger and thirst after righteousness — may yet be so regarded as to minister in our hearts to a specious sort of refined selfishness.

4. As truly ineffectual, we remark further, will be found the mere promptings of *conscience*. We speak of this faculty not in the broadest view, as embracing the whole religious nature, but in a narrower aspect, as distinguished from the heart. Appeals to it must be made, and effective they will be, if there lie back of it deep spiritual experiences and sympathies — if the whole renovated soul has joyfully accepted its teaching

and its sway. But quite impotent is it, if the tone of the affections be earthly. Distinctively apprehended, it is not the religious sense — it has no lively susceptibility to the lofty peculiarities of Christianity. To some forms of duty it may address itself, but not to the highest. Or if it essay these at all, it is as with palsied or manacled hand. It may preach, but it is coldly; it may give, but it is sparingly. Amid the shadows of selfishness, it is easily imposed on by the flimsiest subterfuges. It is apt to determine duty by some false measure, instead of weighing it in the balance of the sanctuary. Do what it may, it is slavish, heartless doing, as joyless as it is unavailing. Do what it may, it has no voice of prayer to call to its aid the arm of Omnipotence. Who has not noted the fruitlessness of all appeals to the conscience of the church, whether in regard to sinners here, or to the lost in heathendom, while upon the heart there has rested the paralysis of worldliness. Heart-wise, if at all, the car of salvation is to be moved onward.

5. Nor, finally, is the world to be converted by the mere principle of *association.* Quite accordant is it with the genius of Christianity, that for all good purposes men should be brought to act in concert. And great power, with the needful prerequisites, has this mode of action. There is no little force in the law of sympathy, as thus called into exercise. Broad and deep is the tide of feeling formed by the confluence of many rills. In associated effort, there is economy of strength, and concentration of strength. The indi-

vidual atom has in it but the attraction of cohesion, binding to itself some other atom; the vast aggregate of particles holds to itself some other world. It is one of the happiest auspices of the present age, that combined action is so largely employed for the advancement of Christianity. Beautiful crystallizations of charity have risen before us, all lustrous with the rays of the sun of righteousness. Curious pieces of moral machinery have been constructed, the like of which for perfectness of design and execution, the world has never before seen. Yet in this very perfectness, let it be remembered, there lurks a danger. Very liable are we to forget, that this machinery is not self-acting—that "the spirit of the living creature" must be in the wheels. In our various forms of association we are apt to merge disastrously our proper individuality. We lose sight, too often, of our personal responsibility. By no agglomeration of dead particles, can you produce a living organism. By no enlargement or improvement of machinery, can you accomplish any thing if the motive power be lacking. Multiply as you please forms of benevolent co-operation, you make real progress in the world's conversion only as in each Christian heart is found the ever effective principle of vital godliness.

II. Having glanced thus at the negative aspect of our subject, let us turn now to the positive. Nothing short of deep personal piety we have seen will avail; we proceed to show how necessarily efficacious that must be—how out of its deep fountains in the heart, as naturally as water gushes from the mountain spring, flows out to a lost world the tide of benevolence. Many, indeed, are the connections and correspondences of the world without with the world within. Man has been well called a microcosm. As an old poet quaintly expresses it,

> "Thy mind
> Europe supplies, and Asia thy will,
> And Afric thine affections; and if still
> Thou list to travel further, put thy senses
> For both the Indies."

Little will he do for the outer world's subjugation to God, who has not first subjugated the inner world. That achieved, he is not only irresistibly prompted to all evangelism, but he has the indispensable and most fundamental preparation for it. In illustration of this view, let us advert now to the chief elements of all true piety.

1. First among these I mention the *spirit of contrition.* Very prominent is this grace, not only in the Psalm from which our text is taken, but in all Christian experience. The renewed man, enlightened to behold the beauty of the divine law, perceives in affecting contrast, the hatefulness of sin. He had heard of it before "by the hearing of the ear," but now his eye seeth it, and he abhors himself. Never, indeed, is sin seen as it is, till we see it in ourselves. In the heart are its chief evils, and we cannot inspect the hearts of our fellow men. It is only as we go down into the

"chambers of imagery" in our own bosoms, and mark the defilements and abominations there, that we have any adequate apprehension of what sin hath done in others. Loathing it as revealed in our own consciousness,—sighing for deliverance from it, we are prepared and constrained to pray for other sinners. He only who has lain himself, day after day, on a bed of racking pain, weary of tossings to and fro, has learned duly to sympathize with a like sufferer. None can enter into the case of the imperilled mariner like the man, who has himself felt, on the vessel's deck, amid rocks and quicksands, the pelting of the sleet-laden blast. So in the matter of the soul's maladies and perils, there is nothing like experience to beget compassion. How natural is that outburst of holy feeling, which follows Cowper's allegorical description of his own conversion:—

> "I see that all are wanderers, gone astray,
> Each in his own delusion."

What affecting views of the condition of the unrenewed are commonly taken, by those who have just emerged themselves from the pollutions and glooms of unregeneracy. The history of all revivals shows, that whenever the people of God are brought to see with increased clearness, and to mourn with unwonted grief, their own remaining corruption, then, as by an inevitable sequence, "rivers of waters run down their eyes" because the wicked around them keep not God's law.

Nor does the feeling thus awakened, confine itself to Christian lands. As sin in their own case is the chief of all calamities and burdens—hateful not only in view of its consequences, but in its own nature—so is it, in their apprehension, with all the tribes and nations of the unevangelized. As they long for the deliverance of their own souls from "the body of this death," so do they long and pray for the deliverance of the whole world. The primary element of a true missionary spirit, we hold, is brokenness of heart.

2. Next in order comes *a Christ-exalting spirit.* The renewed heart magnifies Christ as its own glorious portion. All else is felt to be but "vanity and vexation of spirit." "It hath pleased the Father that in him should all fulness dwell." In him is all help; he is a fitting and satisfying object of the soul's affections. "He that cometh to me," he says, "shall never hunger, and he that believeth in me, shall never thirst." Quaffing full draughts from the gushing fountain, the believer would beckon to it the weary and fainting travellers on all the desert. His language is,

> "Oh! for a trumpet voice,
>   On all the world to call,
> To bid their hearts rejoice
>   In him who died for all."

The Saviour, he feels too, is, in his own excellency, and in the glory of his work, worthy to be exalted. His name is "Wonderful, Counsellor, the Mighty God, the Everlasting Father." By him were earth's foundation's laid. It was over his work "the morning stars sang together." In his incarnation "the whole Deity is known." "God, who commanded the light to shine out of darkness," says Paul, "hath shined in our hearts, to give the light of the knowledge of the glory of God in the face of Jesus Christ." In view of the depth of his voluntary humiliation, the ineffable beauty of his earthly example, the matchless love that bore him through the garden to the cross, the might and the majesty with which he vanquished death, and ascended on high "leading captivity captive," the wisdom and benignity with which he wields now the sceptre of universal dominion, how is all finite excellency disparaged and forgotten; how worthy does he seem of "the heathen for his inheritance, and the uttermost parts of the earth for his possession." In his own body, would the true disciple magnify him, "whether it be by life or by death," and earnestly does he desire his promised exaltation in the hearts of all men. He would publish his glory. He would speed the flight of the angel who proclaims it. Day by day, from his full heart he cries,

"Come, then, and added to thy many crowns,
Receive yet one, the crown of all the earth,
Thou who alone art worthy."

2. With all this, I remark further, is intimately connected, in a true Christian experience, the spirit of

self-consecration. This obviously pervades both the text and the context; and much more may we look for it in relation to the fully manifested Messiah. It is an unspeakable privilege, the believer feels, to live for one so glorious. Nay, to live unto him, is, in its principles, its aims, its sympathies, and its achievements, the only true life. All else is but a living death. Thus, moreover, is he bound to live, and that by the strongest as well as the most precious bonds. He is not his own. He is "bought with a price"—"not with corruptible things, as silver and gold, but with the precious blood of Christ." To the advancement of the Saviour's cause, he deeply and joyfully feels, his powers should be all devoted. He imitates the example of those Corinthian believers, of whom Paul testifies, "They first gave themselves to the Lord, and unto us by the will of God." He makes no reserve. Why should he? Can he withhold aught from him who "spared not his own Son," or from him who refused not to give himself for us? As in his person he is the Lord's, so is he in his possessions. A searching inquiry was that of a beloved missionary lately, "Did you see to it, when you yourselves were translated into the kingdom of God's dear Son, that your property was translated also?" Nor is the truly consecrated soul disposed to limit the field of effort. That field, he rejoices to know, is the world. Wherever sin, Christ's foe, may be extirpated, wherever Christ's glory may be made known, thither is he ready, if Christ call him, to go, or if that may not be, to aid by his substance in sending other laborers.

4. As a crowning element, at once of true piety and of the missionary spirit, I subjoin *confidence in God.* For the self-denial and hardness inseparable from the Christian warfare, there is important preparation in the principles already named. Little will he think of privations and sacrifices, who has a due sense of the evil to be overcome, and whose heart is all aglow with love for Christ, and with zeal for his glory. Yet in all his course what formidable obstacles does he meet, and what desponding if not despairing thoughts do they often suggest. In his private conflicts, he has sympathy often with him who said, "I shall one day perish by the hand of Saul." As he sets himself to the work of the world's conversion, what gigantic forms of depravity rise up before him — what towering and overshadowing fabrics of error, what mounds, and ramparts, and battlements of superstition. It is only by that superadded yet homogeneous grace to which we now point, that through all, and over all, he will be borne onward.

In regard to the world's renovation, I know, much account has been made — far too much doubtless — of merely natural forces. Men have descanted on human progress as if there were some other progress in God's kingdom than that of regenerating grace. They have talked of the law of development, as if it were possible out of pure darkness to evolve light. They have enlarged on the diffusion of knowledge, and the improvement of social and political institutions, as if the rays of the sun could change the nature of the granite they fall on, or as if the hue and fashion of the habiliments worn, or of the dwelling occupied, could steal from the frame a mortal malady. As they have diligently shaken the kaleidoscope of their fancy, they have been confidently looking to see the bits of glass in it endued with life, or assuming some other than a most illusory beauty. Even good Christian men, in giving a reason of the hope that is in them for our fallen humanity, have made quite too prominent certain superficial changes. Give men knowledge like that of fiends, and they may still be as malignant. Bring the whole race into the most intimate intercommunion, and it may be, in the enkindling of evil passions, but as the more vehement glow of gathered coals of fire. Helps to the progress of religion may indeed be found — as well as results of that progress — in the changed and changing state of the world. Channels may be opened; highways may be cast up; vehicles may be furnished. But as to the regenerating work, "Not by might, nor by power, but by my Spirit saith the Lord of hosts." The only good hope in this regard, is that which finds no resting place short of the throne of Jehovah.

Now to just this buoyant animating hope is the true Christian led by his own private experience. Whatever obstacles present themselves in the sin-stricken world without, difficulties quite as formidable has he met in the world within. What divine grace and might have done in the one, warrants the largest expectation in regard to the other. If God has changed to flesh my own stony heart, for what heart may I not have hope? If he has cast down the altars reared in my own bosom to a thousand idols, what to his arm is the multitude of pagan fanes? If the darkness of my own soul has been dispelled—the more fearful for its contrast with the light around me—is there not hope even for the midnight of heathenism? Nor is the believer encouraged merely by what God has done. In the same simple faith, with which for himself he cleaves to the divine promise, he rests on that same promise as he labors for the world. The millennial day shall dawn—its noontide shall come—because God hath said it. All other assurances are to him comparatively as the idle wind. It is this which gives wings to prayer. It is this which encourages him to contribute of his treasures, or to go himself to the broad harvest-field. It is this which animates the missionary's heart, as amid the dark places of the earth he struggles with brutal degradation, with hoary prejudice, with cruel and relentless superstition. "Who art thou, O great mountain?" he exclaims, "before Zerubbabel thou shalt become a plain."

We might advert, in the same connection, to other points of Christian experience. But those we have mentioned are not only fundamental and distinctive; in their necessary adjuncts and issues, they embrace whatever is pure and elevated in "the hidden man of the heart." Enough has been said to show, that while all other reliances must prove abortive, deep personal piety is the unfailing spring of all wise and holy evangelism — that heartfelt piety, indeed, and the true missionary spirit, are one and indivisible. We shall be further borne with, as we subjoin briefly certain practical suggestions.

1. It first of all occurs to us, that we have, in our subject, a searching *test of Christian character.* We may ask, on the one hand, whether with some show of the missionary spirit, we have its invariable counterpart, the diligent keeping of our own hearts? It is quite possible to ride in the chariot of Jehu, yet know little or nothing of the tearful vigils of David. True religion is ever symmetrical. But what, on the other hand, must we think of those — or, as it may be better shaped, what should they think of themselves — who, while they profess to be spiritually minded, take little interest in missionary matters? We cast no reflection on the men of another and a different age. The times of that ignorance "God winked at." There were extrinsic causes at work then, to hinder somewhat the normal development of piety. It is of the present day we are speaking, and of persons more or less enlightened as to the subject in hand. If at the monthly concert their places are either constantly or frequently vacant — if the slightest excuse is sufficient to keep them away; if their gifts to the Lord's treasury are few and far between, or, though frequently and regularly made, are yet doled out as from the miser's reluctant grasp; if every point of personal

and domestic convenience and gratification is first amply provided for, and only the mere leavings of luxury, the offerings which in a sense cost them nothing, are laid on God's altar; if they are only aroused to some spasm of zeal, as something new and startling presents itself, as they listen to some strain of sentiment or of romance, as some tale of horror is uttered, or as the galvanic force of a unique and impassioned eloquence is brought to bear on them; how large must be that charity which can refrain from standing in doubt of them? Can they loathe sin in themselves, and yet not loathe it in the world? Can they truly exalt Christ in their own hearts, and yet not fervently desire that all others should exalt him? Can they consecrate themselves and all they have to him, and yet withhold from that cause with which his glory is so intimately connected, either their prayers or their alms, either themselves or their children? Can they confide in Christ for the salvation of their own souls, and yet be paralyzed by doubt and distrust in regard to the world's salvation? Ponder well these queries, ye who stand coldly aloof from the missionary enterprise, or who serve it with but a faint and intermittent zeal.

2. We see, I remark secondly, *why the missionary work has made no greater progress.* We overlook not what has been accomplished. We rejoice in it, and give thanks to God. Yet how much land remaineth to be possessed; how much, after all, has been left undone—how little, compared with the exigencies of

the case, are we now doing! The fault is not, we may be sure, in the heart of him who gave his Son to lay the foundations of our enterprise, or of him who cemented those foundations with his own blood. Nor lies the difficulty in the lack of pecuniary means. There is money enough in the keeping even of the Churches represented in this Association, held by them as the sworn stewards of God—money which might be better spared than retained, the sparing of which would be a gain both for time and eternity—to put the Parent Society beyond the possibility of financial perplexity. It were easy for the churches of our land at once to double its income. Nor need there be a want of laborers. Men enough there are—a superabundance of them—for all the paths and enterprises of worldly ambition. Nor do we lack evidence, as we have seen, of the palpable woes inflicted by heathenism. Nor are appeals wanting to the imaginative faculty, to taste and sensibility, and to our quick perception of reflex advantage. Nor fail the Providence of God, and the Christian press, and the Gospel ministry, to clamor incessantly in the ear of Conscience. Nor has the defect been in the matter of machinery. Machinery enough is already in play to irrigate effectively every desert under heaven. It is the motive power that has been wanting—deep, all-pervading, personal piety,—the power that not only stirs man to effort, but, through the channel of prayer, moves the arm of God. Not with associations, as such, has been the chief fault, or with aught outward and objective, but with individual hearts. Each one of us, my brethren, in his place and his measure, may take home the guilt and the shame to his own bosom.

3. We learn, then, I remark once more, *at what, as friends of the missionary cause, we should prominently aim.* It is the increase of personal godliness. This, as we have seen, is the only hope of our great enterprise; and on this the whole history of the past seems now to cast us. Other motives there are — lawful if subordinate — which appear in a measure to have spent their force. To the miseries and the horrors of paganism — to infanticide and cannibalism, to self-torture and self-immolation, to the offering up of human victims, to all cruel and abominable usages and rites — our thoughts have become accustomed. Little of novelty, indeed, has the cause of missions now to offer. All New-England was moved once — not to say our whole country — at the ordination of five young men to the work of the ministry in heathen lands. Now, a like ordination, with all the consequent scenes of parting and embarkation, is as an every-day occurrence. Once a returned missionary was to the churches almost as an Apostle come back from glory. Now the faces of scores of them are well known to us, and their most startling tales of peril and of suffering have become familiar to our ears as household words. As, when the beautiful vale, or the cloud-capped mountain, is made our abiding place, we soon grow heedless com-

paratively of what once delighted or awed us; so is it, to some extent, with the whole æsthetic element of the missionary enterprise. We have become ingenious, too, it is to be feared, in quieting our consciences. And even on those benevolent organizations which seemed once as the sun for brightness, by keen-sighted gazers spots have been discovered! How obvious, then, that for the carrying onward of our great work, a new impulse must be given to the piety of the Church. A returning to God there must be on the part of the backsliding, and a brokenness of heart such as David exemplified. There must be in us all a deeper Christian experience. A more self-abasing, Christ-exalting spirit must we exercise; more honest and hearty must be our self-consecration, more simple and childlike our confidence in God. To this end, with what earnestness should we seek the outpouring of the Divine Spirit. Who can estimate the blessing that would come to the heathen world from a general revival of religion in our land?

And what we do, I add in closing, it becomes us to do quickly. What urgency is upon us, from the clustering prayers of departed generations, and from the converging lines of a glorious Providence! What preparation for the present, and for the triumphs of the Gospel, do we see in all the past! What a training has the Church had; what admonitory lessons has she been taught! What furniture of knowledge has she gained! And what a highway for salvation has

God been casting up! Inventions and discoveries, which at an earlier day would have been of little avail comparatively — as the mariner's compass, the art of printing, the steam power, the modern applications of the magnetic force, and, chief in its class, the discovery of our own continent — have found their respective places in the divinely appointed concatenation of instrumentalities, just as they might best tell on the work of redemption. In our own times, what a confluence of helps is there to the spread of the Gospel. How, as intercommunication has been facilitated, have new fields been opened, and old ones become better known. As the world has been flowing together, how have barriers of prejudice and custom, of national and international restraint and prohibition, been melting away. How is commerce proffering "its wheel and its wing," to bear to the Gentiles God's word and God's messengers. How has the lightning of heaven come down to earth, that it may flash the Gospel around the globe. The changes among the nations, how coincident are they, in their general scope, whatever temporary reverses may here and there occur, with the great aim of the missionary enterprise. I speak not of these things as themselves to be rested in; how plainly do they reveal to us the Saviour's hand. On island and continent, among the down-trodden masses and on the high places of power, I hear the sound of his footsteps. As he cometh thus, to "set judgment in the earth" — as the valleys are exalted and the mountains are made low, as the crooked is made straight, and the rough places are made plain — how should his people gird themselves for the work he assigns them! Seeing ye behold such things, brethren, and look for such things, "what manner of persons ought ye to be, in all holy conversation and godliness!"

REPORT OF THE SECRETARY.

WE are convened to night to celebrate with sacred services the twenty-fifth anniversary of the Foreign Missionary Society of New-York and Brooklyn. In presenting their report, the Board of Managers, while they gratefully recognize the goodness of God in preserving the lives of so many of their number during the past year, are called upon to record the death of one of their most honored and valued members—the Rev. Erskine Mason, D. D. After a long illness, which he bore with exemplary Christian resignation and fortitude, he departed from us on the 14th of May, 1851. His services in the cause of missions were among his *distinguishing* labors. And this Society has reason to bless God for the monument of his missionary zeal and fidelity which he reared, when about a year before his decease, he preached the first of these annual discourses, and presented to us, and to the churches associated with us, one of the most enlarged and thorough surveys of the condition of the world in its relations to the religion of the Lord Jesus Christ. He, though dead, still speaks to us these words of encouragement. And in his luminous and eloquent reasonings, imparts power and meaning to the prophetic declarations of the Gospel's ultimate triumph.

During the past year the Society has continued its efforts to sustain and advance the missionary spirit in the churches. The meeting held at the Tract House on the Monday of the monthly concert, has, we think, never been better attended or more useful.

During the last fall, a committee was appointed to address a circular letter to each church, on the importance of adopting a *systematic plan* by which to develope more generally the missionary spirit, and enlist the prayers and contributions of as many members as possible in behalf of the cause. This letter was prepared, and sent to every church and pastor, with the request that it be read from the pulpit on the Sabbath. It was also published, at the instance of the Society, in several of the religious papers of the City.

The Board of Managers have also been assiduous in their endeavors to. secure the establishment, in this metropolis, of a Secretary of the A. B. C F. M., who shall be co-ordinate with the Secretaries at Boston. The Parent Society, at its late meeting in Portland, referred the subject to a special committee, which met in this city a few months since. The committee of this Society conferred freely with them, and the hope is confidently cherished that the object, so long and so earnestly sought by them, will ere long be attained.

The receipts from our churches are in advance of those of last year nearly two thousand dollars. In this we rejoice; though when we consider the magnitude and the excellency of the cause of missions, and the number and strength of our churches, we should rather mourn and be ashamed of the result.

The difficulty of awakening and sustaining an interest in a given cause, is very much in proportion to its *spirituality*. The more material and tangible its results—the more conjoined with temporal and national or local interests its appeals, the more immediately successful will an enterprise ordinarily be: while that object, whose promotion is dependent almost entirely upon personal holiness and a *simple faith* in God's Word, will meet with a multitude of appalling difficulties, and be exposed to many reverses and disasters in an unsanctified and unbelieving church. The conquest and subjugation of the millennial Canaan by the church, is not unlike that of the Jewish Canaan by the Israelites. The river Jordan—the sons of Anak—the walled towns—still exist, and are prevalent against the command and promise of the Almighty Himself. Labor, which is mostly in anticipation of results in the distant future, *preliminary* toils and sacrifices, which are attended with very little present and tangible reward, require a simple heroic faith—a self-sacrificing martyr spirit, rare in this age. Hence it is that the grandeur of the missionary enterprise is so feebly appreciated, its appeals are so unimpressive, its enlargement so difficult, its concerts for prayer so thinly attended.

While no cause in the present keeping of the Christian church has so manifestly and abundantly the sanction of Heaven and the co-operation of

God, as has that of Foreign Missions, there is almost no proportionate estimate of its worth and grandeur. With a religion that commands us to love our neighbor as ourselves—to embrace a lost world in our sympathies, how little is done by the Church in this land to evangelize the heathen, compared with what she is doing for religion at home? And has not the reason for this already been intimated? viz., that the work is so eminently spiritual, the labor is to so great an extent preliminary and in anticipation of results. In our home efforts, faith is mixed with sight. Patriotism, temporal interests, denominational rivalries, and immediate results, combine with the purer motives of Christianity: and it is a question, whether we do not deceive ourselves, when we attribute to *piety*, results which the piety alone of the Church never would have accomplished.

During the year 1850, the churches contributed to the various religious benevolent societies, whose operations are almost exclusively in this country, 1,500,000 dollars, while 675,000 was the total of contributions for foreign missions. But this presents a very imperfect view of the case. During that year, Christians in this country paid, at the lowest estimate, 12,300,000 dollars for the support and propagation of the Gospel at home, in salaries, erecting churches, and aiding the societies above referred to, and only 675,000 to the evangelization of the world.*

The missionary enterprise is one almost exclusively of faith. The conversion of 8 or 900,000,000 of depraved, apostate souls, imbedded in ancient idolatries, in ignorance, in despotism, in the pagan customs of centuries, concerning whom it is written that God hath given them up to uncleanness and vile affections, and a reprobate mind—upon whom the influences of an unhallowed civilization are ten thousand fold more abundant and efficient than those of the Gospel of Christ,—the conversion of a world *dead* in sin, is, I say, a work to be prosecuted under the auspices of a living, childlike faith—a principle of action more powerful and more pure than would be the inspiration of the most extensive and brilliant success. When Christians shall look not at difficulties nor disasters, but only at the face of Christ, and shall encourage themselves not upon the favorable indications of a changing empire or state, but in the promises of an unchanging God, and in the glorious issues of futurity,—when Christians shall thus regard the cause of missions, its triumph will commence. For faith can do again what it has done in the past—subdue kingdoms—turn to flight the armies of the

* These statistics are taken from Dr. Baird's "Progress and Prospects of Christianity in the United States."

aliens—obtain promises—overcome the world. The Church will continue her operations amid the shaking and overturning of the nations. And her labors which cannot be shaken—which are never in vain, shall remain the foundation of the world's thorough and lasting regeneration, whereon shall be planted the pillars of the new Heavens, under which shall dwell righteousness.

THOMAS H. SKINNER, Jr.,
Corresponding Secretary.

THE FOREIGN MISSIONARY SOCIETY OF NEW-YORK AND BROOKLYN,

in account current with their Treasurer, J. W. Tracy.

Cr.

From	By Cash, from the following sources:		
April 13,	Allen Street Presbyterian Church, New York,	$129 00	
1851,	Bleecker Street do do " -	875 06	
to	Brainerd do do " -	101 30	
March 31,	Brick do do " -	933 14	
1852.	Broadway Tabernacle do " -	258 01	
	Central Presbyterian do " -	687 40	
	Church of the Puritans do " -	1,252 27	
	Eastern Congregational do " -	19 09	
	Eighth Avenue do " -	25 00	
	Eleventh Presbyterian do " -	88 85	
	Fourteenth Street do do " -	469 73	
	Harlem do do " -	76 60	
	Houston Street do do " -	25 50	
	Madison Avenue do do " -	100 00	
	Mercer Street do do " -	5,139 11	
	Pearl Street do do " -	174 74	
	Presbyterian Ch. on University Place " -	250 00	
	Seventh Presbyterian Church " -	203 77	
	Spring Street do do " -	81 76	
	Tenth do do " -	293 65	
	Thirteenth Street do do " -	38 06	
	West do do " -	406 60	
	Sundry donations in New York and Brooklyn,	1,012 74	
			12,641 38
	Bedford Congregational Church, Brooklyn, -	11 39	
	Central Presbyterian do " -	17 12	
	Church of the Pilgrims, do " -	2,065 23	
	Clinton Avenue Cong. do " -	40 00	
	First Presbyterian do " -	830 58	
	Fulton Avenue Cong. do " -	45 00	
	Plymouth do do " -	452 46	
	Second do do " -	123 68	
	Second Presbyterian do " -	456 28	
	South do do " -	1,219 32	
	Third do do " -	138 63	
			5,399 69
	First Presbyterian Church, Williamsburgh, -		68 75
			$18,109 82

Dr.

From		
April 13,	To Cash paid rent of room for monthly meetings, -	$8 00
1851,	" Expenses of Committees, - -	18 00
to	" for 3000 copies Mr. Storrs' Sermon, -	127 00
March 31,	" A. Merwin agent A. B. C. F. M. at	
1852.	sundry times as per receipts, -	17,956 82
		$18,109 82

E. & O. E.

New York, March 31, 1852.

J. W. Tracy, *Treasurer.*

Examined and Found Correct.

David Hoadley,
Walter S. Griffith, } *Auditors.*

LIST OF OFFICERS

FOR THE YEAR 1852.

PRESIDENT.

JASPER CORNING.

VICE-PRESIDENTS.

ANSON G. PHELPS,	JOHN A. DAVENPORT,
WILLIAM C. GILMAN,	DAVID HOADLEY.

CORRESPONDING SECRETARY.

REV. THOMAS H. SKINNER, JR.

RECORDING SECRETARY.

ALMON MERWIN.

TREASURER.

J. W. TRACY.

DIRECTORS.

Allen Street Presbyterian Church,.... M. T. HEWIT, EDWARD CHAPIN.
Bleecker Street " " .... CHARLES N. TALBOT, CHARLES GOULD.
Fourteenth Street " " .... WM. A. BOOTH, W. E. DODGE.
Brick " " .... A. L. ELY, C. H. MERRY.
Broadway Tabernacle " .... W. G. WEST, DAVID HALE.
Central Presbyterian " .... FREDERICK BULL, A. O. VAN LENNEP.
Church of the Puritans, " .... O. E. WOOD, HOMER MORGAN.
Duane St. Presbyterian Church .... C. E. PIERSON, WM. WALKER.
Eastern Congregational " .... STEPHEN CUTTER, LEWIS CHICHESTER.
Eighth Presbyterian " .... HENRY D. CRANE, R. R. WOOD.
Eleventh " " .... J. E. MARSHALL, E. B. LITTELL.
Harlem " " .... E. KETCHUM, JAMES RIKER, JR.

Houston Street Presb. Church,	....E. H. BURGER, S. DERRICKSON.
Mercer Street " "	....J. B. SHEFFIELD, ANSON G. PHELPS, JR.
Pearl Street " "	....HUGH AIKMAN, F. H. BARTHOLOMEW.
Presb. Church, University Place,	....W. W. STONE, J. K. MYERS.
North Presbyterian Church,	....O. H. LEE, JAMES REEVE.
Seventh " "	....ALEXANDER MILNE, CHARLES MERRILL.
Spring Street " "	....JOSEPH S. HOLT, CHARLES W. FISHER.
Tenth " "	....J. F. JOY, L. E. JACKSON.
Thirteenth Street " "	....J. N. DANFORTH, DAN KNIGHT.
West " "	....A. D. F. RANDOLPH, ABRAM L. EARLE.
Bedford Cong. Church, Brooklyn,	....D. O. CAULKINS, EDWARD T. GOODALL.
Bridge st. " " "	....WM. VAIL, CLARK JACOBS.
Central Presb. " "	....CHARLES C. MUDGE, D. J. LEDYARD.
Clinton Av. Cong. " "	....S. DAVENPORT, MARK H. NEWMAN.
Church of the Pilgrims, "	....CHS. J. STEDMAN, ALFRED S. BARNES.
First Presbyterian Church, "	....ALFRED EDWARDS, R. J. THORNE.
Plymouth Cong. " "	....J. TASKER HOWARD, H. C. BOWEN.
Second Presbyterian " "	....CHARLES CLARKE, LUCIUS HOPKINS.
South " " "	...WALTER S. GRIFFITH, D. W. INGERSOLL.
South Cong. " "	....S. W. GRANT, SOLOMON FREEMAN.
Third Presbyterian " "	....W. W. HURLBUT, JNO. C. HALSEY, M.D.
Fulton Avenue Cong. Ch. "	....F. W. BURKE, ALFRED SMITHERS.
First Presb. Ch., Williamsburgh,	....PAUL J. FISH.

Christianity designed for the World, and the World designed for Christianity.

A

SERMON,

PREACHED AT CINCINNATI, OHIO, OCTOBER 4, 1853,

BEFORE THE

AMERICAN BOARD OF COMMISSIONER
FOR FOREIGN MISSIONS.

AT THEIR

FORTY-FOURTH ANNUAL MEETING.

BY WILLIAM ADAMS, D. D.
OF NEW YORK CITY.

BOSTON:
PRESS OF T. R. MARVIN, 42 CONGRESS ST.
1854.

SERMON.

MATTHEW xiii. 38.

THE FIELD IS THE WORLD.

When Oliver Goldsmith wrote his "Citizen of the World," there is no evidence that he had any comprehension of the religious idea involved in the title chosen for that captivating production. Every Christian is a true cosmopolite. The world is one; and for this large and scattered family God has revealed but one religion. When we assert the imperative claims of the Christian religion to universal faith and obedience, many are disposed to evade the obligation by affirming that Christianity is only one of the many religions of the world; that its historical origin is comparatively recent; its geographical jurisdiction is and always has been very limited; its practical influence, if not a failure, is certainly by no means commensurate with its vast pretensions; and, last of all, that, as politics, the arts and sciences have each their appropriate and distinctive domain, so the gospel of Christ is but one of the many subordinate agencies of the world; a kind of side play, whose proper province is within a certain professional class, and whose field of display is the Sabbath, the church, the house of affliction, and the courts of death; and because of this meagre induction, thousands absolve themselves from all obligation, either to receive or propagate the religion of the Son of God.

Christianity is not a mere afterthought, but an original project; not an episode, but the main plot; it does not belong prescriptively to the small strips of land here and there where its light now shines; its field is the world, and its ultimate jurisdiction will be universal. As our belief on this subject is not a matter of theoretic calculation, or philosophic deduction, but of religious faith, we may expect to find in Christianity itself, its doctrines and its history, the promise and the proof of its universal prevalence. But what is Christianity? Where is Christianity? Not an aroma floating in the air. Not a soft and poetic sentiment playing through the imagination of the philanthropic. It is a historical existence, and is to be examined and judged in its own inspired and infallible records.

Assembled to-day on the beautiful banks of the Ohio, a thousand miles from the place where, forty years ago, this missionary association was organized, and thousands more from the spot where, eighteen hundred years ago, the Author of our religion gave the commission to evangelize the world; cheered by the memory of past successes, and studious still of the methods by which we may bear the gospel of our Lord from river to river and from sea to sea, let us, first of all, go entirely back to the inspired chronicles of our faith, and gather up some of the facts therein contained, bearing on that one sentiment to which we are publicly pledged,—"Christianity designed for the world, and the world designed for Christianity."

The first fact to be mentioned is, that Christianity *asserts* its *own universality;* and this not incidentally, but as inherent in its first and vital principles. There is no authority and there can be no comfort in the Christian Revelation to me, as an individual, if that authority and that comfort extend not equally to all mankind. The gospel addresses us simply as men. It recognizes us only as citizens of the world. It knows no national distinction and no territorial boundaries. Its two central ideas are SIN and SALVATION; man has fallen, and for man has Christ died. The nations are many; but the world is one. Begin your genealogical pedigree where you will, in whatever portion of the earth's surface, among whatever kindred or tribe, all will converge at last towards the first links of the chain which describe the beginning of our race: "who was the son of Adam—who was the Son of God." It is the race of man, the whole race, that have felt the direful visitations of sin; and the offers of pardon and restoration are commensurate with the evils they would remedy. "*To the whole world,*" is the superscription upon the royal proclamation of amnesty and glad tidings. Question this universality in the gospel's own structure and adaptation, and you quench the hopes which brighten your own path; since you are but one of a common race.

The Christian religion, moreover, is the *only* religion which asserts its own universality. The accomplished Reinhard has achieved a goodly service in the analysis which he has given of all the philosophies and religions of the world, in proof of the fact, that, prior to the commission given to the Eleven on the Mount of Ascension, the idea is not to be found of a religious system which claimed to be universal in its adaptation. When the Prophet of Mecca, ignorant of the fact authenticated by modern science, that there are parts of the habitable globe where the sun rises and sets but once for months in succession, incorporated in the Koran the practical precept, that the religious fasts to be observed by men should begin at the very instant the limb of the sun appeared above the horizon, and should be continued strictly until the same disappeared in the western sky, he not only proved the provincialism but the falsity of his religion. Nor was he the only instance in which, through the unconscious adhesions of things absurd and impossible, the ancient fable has found a sober verification; the eagle, purloining meat from the altar of the gods, and perceiving not the coal of fire adhering thereto by which its own nest was to be consumed.

No sooner do we set forth this claim of Christianity to an universal range and authority, than we are met by an objection greatly urged by modern infidelity, — an objection which scoffs at all our religious propagandism, for it affirms the historical fact, that Christianity is only a recent introduction;

that Jesus of Nazareth was not born until two-thirds of the world's age was passed, and that, as good men existed before his advent, under other forms of worship, it is absurd to claim that his religion is the only true and sufficient one for all men and for all times. An objection we admit well put, if we were allowed to forswear the fact recorded by inspiration, that Christianity did not begin in Bethlehem of Judea. It began in Eden; and among the many proofs that it is the one and only true religion which God has revealed is this, that it is the very oldest of all. Long before the Persian adored the sun, or the Chaldean bowed before the hosts of heaven, or the Egyptian framed his colossal altars and idolatries, did Christianity begin its veritable life and progress. Wonder not that the antagonists of the Christian system expend so much time and talent in proving what they affirm, the falsity and absurdity of the Jewish religion. Think not that it is a mere matter of biblical criticism, or philological lore, when so much pains are taken to eject the Epistle to the Hebrews from the inspired canon. Most warily has infidelity chosen its points for attack; and we frankly confess, that were we not fully fortified in the belief of the connection of the Jewish and Christian dispensations as together forming one substantial identity, the one religion revealed to man from heaven, there is no form in which our minds would be so open to skeptical intrusions concerning the necessity of embracing ourselves, and communicating to others, the Christian system as the only hope of man, as that which Neology has assumed in its assaults upon the Jewish system. Therefore it is that inspiration has, to such a degree, exhausted its own skill and explicitness, in explaining to us the appurtenances and forms of the Patriarchal and Levitical worships. Those were not of human origin, like the tripod of the Grecian flamen, the Eleusinian mysteries, or the forms of Druidical worship. They were copied from the pattern shown to Moses in the Mount. Though now obsolete, yet they are not to be classed with the mummeries of false religions. It was Christianity which smoked in the first sacrificial victim that was offered outside the gates of forfeited Paradise. It was Christianity that was enshrined in that sacred ark which was borne across the brilliant sands of Syria, and between the crystal walls of the parted Jordan. It was Christianity that entered the Holy of Holies, in tabernacle and temple, with graven breast-plate and atoning blood. But it was Christianity not yet in its ripeness and readiness; only in its promise and preparation. Christianity was there, just as whole harvests of grain are now included in the husks of that handful of corn which is yet to germinate; just as immense forests were once enclosed within the shell and burr of the seed-nut from whence sprang growth and reproduction.

It is not incumbent on any human wisdom to explain why God appointed such length and slowness to the preparatory stages of revealed redemption. Why should summer insects measure the stupendous revolutions of the stars by the wheelings of their own tiny flights? We, indeed, might refute objections alleged against this progressive development of Christianity, by appealing to all the analogies of nature, "first the blade, then the ear, after that the full corn in the ear." Corn is not fit to be used for planting and reproduction while yet in the blade. And it is quite pertinent to our present argument concerning the universality of the Christian system, to remind ourselves that, though the revelation of Christianity began in the early dawn of history, yet its world-wide diffusion was not authorized until the fullness of time had come.

It is not an admission extorted from us reluctantly, but a patent fact to which, as studious of the ways of God, we call a special attention, that the typical institutions of Christianity were strictly local and stationary. It was not owing to human defects and unfaithfulness, that nothing was done for ages by way of propagating the true faith. This was in accordance with divine direction and interdict. The people chosen to be the depositaries of the one revelation from God, were isolated from the rest of the world by a thousand laws and limitations. Matrimonial alliances, out of their own nation, were strictly prohibited. To convert remote nations to their religion was not their vocation. The admission of proselytes from abroad, though permitted in certain cases, was guarded, according to the structure of their religious system, with the greatest caution. Everything tended to seclusion and concentration, rather than diffusion and extension.

It is of the utmost importance to be understood, that the Jewish system, notwithstanding its relations to the redemption of Christ, was as purely local as our court of common pleas. It was not designed for aggression at all. It had no agencies for propagandism. It was in no sense organized for extension into foreign parts. The high priest was a fixture. No itinerant service had he to perform in Moab or Idumea. No other man on earth was permitted to do what he was ordained of God to perform, and his service was to be rendered only within the solemn precincts of the temple. The sacred scrolls were in the custody of a particular order of men; and the rites of the true religion could only be performed by a certain line of consecrated succession. Everything was arranged to preserve the one revealed faith unmixed and uncontaminated from the profane touch of the heathen.

Observe, at the same time, how the providential condition of the world was suited to this formative and infant state of revealed Christianity. The state of the earth was unfavorable to intercommunication. There were few facilities for travel and commerce. Early in the world's history, men had sought on the plains of Shinar to centralize wealth, population and empire. By a special act, God defeated their purpose, and separated them into distinct tribes and nations, by diversities of language. Everything tended to segregation. A range of mountains, a river, a sea, were sufficient barriers to national intercourse. What an immense trial of faith was it for Abraham, Isaac and Jacob, to pass and repass between the Euphrates, the Jordan and the Nile, where now tourists from this western world find their holiday recreation. Both sacred and profane history abound with proofs of the separateness and solitariness of the nations. Homer is supposed to have lived at the very time that the splendors of the Jewish economy culminated at the court and the temple of Solomon. But the author of the Odyssey was entirely ignorant of countries within a few hours' sail of Greece. The Argonautic expedition is described as sailing up through the Hellespont and the Euxine, and returning by the Pillars of Hercules; as if the sea of Azof were connected with the Atlantic Ocean. The author of the Æneid, describing his hero landing on the shores of Carthage by the inevitable event of shipwreck, relates the consternation which he felt in expectation of losing his life because a stranger and a foreigner.

While typical Christianity, for the sake of its own preservation and purity, was local and stationary, the world itself was retained in a condition suited to the purpose. Time advances, and striking changes occur simultaneously in both. The prophecies of the Hebrew faith are kindling into the morning; all the rays of truth and hope are converging towards the advent of the Son of God; and Christianity is approaching the days of her enlargement and completion. The old walls of partition are broken down. The gorgeous pile of symbolic architecture which crowned the top of Moriah, like an immense mould, was to be broken to pieces; and the spiritual fabric that had been cast therein was to be brought forth to the light. The Kings of the East, the appointed agencies of God, swept down from the Caucasus to the Mediterranean, like birds of prey, and spoiled the sanctities of the Holy City. God's chosen nation, so long preserved in their integrity and separation, are dispersed like the chaff by the whirlwind, and throne and temple vanish from the earth. The nations of the earth become infused and intermixed, passing and repassing in the jostlings and attritions of war, conquering and being conquered,—all in the order of inspired prediction,—until Christianity was ready for the world, when lo! the world is made ready for Christianity!

When the embryo religion was yet in its needful seclusion and quiet, there had been secretly and slowly coming into life a new and masculine power, which was destined to change the face of the world. It began before Isaiah had fallen a victim to the rage of Manasseh; before Nebuchadnezzar had dreamed, and Daniel, interpreting the finger of God, had announced the rise of successive dynasties. It had more than a hundred thousand inhabitants when Xerxes marshaled his hosts on the banks of the Hellespont. Its population had reached a quarter of a million, before Alexander the Great had subjugated the East by his tremendous exploits at Arbela and the Granicus. Rolling through its successive eras, ever tending to aggrandizement, like a swelling river, it at length absorbs in its own vast supremacy all the kingdoms of the world. Sicily, Carthage, Epirus, Macedonia, Pergamos, Bithynia, Galatia, Pontus, Syria, Cappadocia, Egypt, Judea, Gaul and Britain, all became provinces and appendages of the Roman Empire. Never before was any dominion so distinguished by universality. Her consuls and her eagles, at the same time, were on the shores of Wales and the banks of the Tigris; on the summits of the Carpathian mountains, and along the Arabian and Lybian deserts.

In this new phase and condition of the world, in one of the provinces of this universal empire, the Son of God was born, the Lamb of God was slain, and the gospel was ready for the world. For the first time, since the world was made, was the commission given to evangelize all nations. An end had come to everything typical and preparatory; to everything local and exclusive. The Jew, as such, was to be known no more. To MAN is the gospel given. All mankind were now to share in privileges which hitherto had been reserved and restricted to a peculiar people. The early promise made to Abraham, in the dim dawn of the world, "All the nations of the earth shall be blessed in him," found its incipient fulfillment, when, standing on the slope of Olivet, on the morning of his ascension, the Son of God, radiant with the joys of his finished redemption, said to his disciples, "Go ye into all the world, and preach the gospel to every creature." Hard was it for the best and bravest of their number to comprehend this universal quality of the faith they preached. Supernatural methods were put in requisition to convince Peter himself, that the old distinction between clean and unclean was abrogated forever; and when, obedient to the mission, he visited the house of Cornelius, Jewish prejudices were so strong that he was arraigned before a council at Jerusalem for preaching the gospel to a Gentile. One by one, the scales fell; by little and little, the truth prevailed, till at last the glorious conviction was reached, that to be a Christian was more than to be a Jew; and that in the length and breadth, height and depth of one universal faith, all the preceding distinctions of men were to be swallowed up forever. The tiny insects of the Pacific seas, building up the reefs which breast and break the surges of the ocean, the islands and continents on which vegetation rises and cities swarm with life, can have no anticipation of the magnificent results of their subaqueous architecture. No more had the successive emperors of Rome, in the play and passion of personal ambition, in the blind impulses of self-aggrandizement, any knowledge or imagination of the uses of their success; but these arise out of the ocean depths of God's wisdom. Their military roads and bridges were built, their consulates and prefectures were established, and along these 'highways of the Lord' came bounding the footsteps of a free and beneficent Christianity.

With these combinations of the gospel's own nature, history and providential adaptations full in our minds, let us now inquire, for our own practical help and guidance, what were the agencies by which the religion of Christ received its first rapid and general promulgation. These were of three kinds: the *miraculous*, the *organized*, and the *spontaneous*.

The *miraculous* was of temporary necessity, and having subserved this, was suspended. Using the word in its strict rhetorical sense, we say that the *presumption* at first was against the religion of the cross; that is to say, the '*onus probandi*' was with those who first preached it in opposition to long established institutions.* That obligation was not evaded, but met; the author of our religion furnishing his disciples with the power of establishing their proofs through miraculous attestations. But now, after the long and eventful history of the Christian religion, the "burden of proof" is reversed; and if miracles are to be looked for at all, they must be demanded of those who would disprove this ancient, venerable and unshaken faith of the world. If it be retorted that, in other lands than our own, in the presence of the aged superstitions of heathenism, the "burden of proof" rests upon the Christian missionaries who invade them, we admit the fact, rejoicing that such men are deputed for the service as are fully competent and equipped to meet the demands with proofs and arguments, even though the original help of mira-

* According to the most correct use of the term, a "Presumption" in favor of any supposition, means, not (as has been sometimes erroneously imagined) a preponderance of antecedent probability in its favor, but such a *preoccupation* of the ground as implies that it must stand good till some sufficient reason is adduced against it; in short, that the *Burden of proof* lies on the side of him who would dispute it. There is a Presumption in favor of every *existing* institution.—*Whately's Rhetoric*, P. I. ch. iii. § 2.

cles is now entirely withdrawn. Christianity asks and expects no more miraculous assistance in her aggressions; and we dismiss this original agency from our inventory of available forces with the single remark, that the miracles which were wrought by or in connection with the first teachers of Christianity, were all, without an exception, designed to aid and illustrate its universal jurisdiction. The miracle of tongues, the first and most notable of all, is itself a proof that the Christian faith was to be no longer restricted to one time or language,—a miracle needful once only, when men untaught and illiterate were to open communication with the assembled representatives of all nations and languages; but altogether superfluous to-day, when, by the processes of education and the intermingling of men, the acquisition of various languages is an easy and ordinary occurrence.

By the *organized* evangelism of primitive believers, we mean all such human agencies as imply method, plan, system and sagacious adaptation, whether on the part of churches or individuals. Directed to tarry first at Jerusalem, the disciples forgot their world-wide commission till persecution, with its friendly violence, scattered them like a frightened flock. Comprehending, at length, the nature of their trust, we detect wisdom and forethought in the ordination of particular men to particular services. Peter, James and John, "who seemed to be pillars," went unto the circumcision; while Paul and Barnabas were set apart to the ministry of the heathen. What wonders of wisdom are suggested by the bare mention of his name who is known as "the great Apostle to the Gentiles." Lord Lyttelton, fully persuaded that the Bible was an imposture and determined to expose it, selected the conversion of Paul as the subject of hostile criticism, and was himself converted to the truth of Christianity by the very topic chosen for its overthrow. Passing by the phenomena of the Apostle's conversion, it seems to us that an irrefutable argument for the universality of the Christian religion is suggested by the qualities which met in this remarkable man and minister. The service to be accomplished was the widest possible dissemination of the new faith among all nations; the infusion of Christianity into the mind of the world. But what was the mind of the world at that time? Not simple, but complicated. Three forms of civilization there were, distinct yet related, Jewish, Grecian, and Roman. Intermingled were the representatives of each, from farthest East to utmost West. The Jew was ubiquitous, from the Indus to the Tiber, with all the memories of his religion and the pride of his ancestry. The Greek had built his commercial cities and reared his elegant academies in Egypt and Syria. The translation of the Hebrew Scriptures into Greek by the Seventy at Alexandria; Philo, the Jewish philosopher, in the same city, and Josephus, the Jewish courtier at Jerusalem, both ambitiously addicted to Grecian literature, are evidences to what extent the Greek language and philosophy had become diffused; while, as we have seen, over the whole, East, West, North and South, the towering eagle of Imperial Rome was in the ascendancy. How many qualities must be combined in the man who, bearing the august title of "Apostle to the Nations," was to be sent forth to persuade such a heterogeneous civilization of the truth of the Christian religion. A Jew by birth, of the straitest sect, trained in every rite and law pertaining to the religion of his fathers, thoroughly experienced in every prejudice, objection and sympathy of the Pharisee; at the same time, born in Tarsus, a Greek city, the rival of Athens and Alexandria in the zeal of letters; from his childhood a proficient in the Greek language, familiar with the Septuagint as with the Hebrew original, a reader of the Greek drama and a great master of that "mental management" which then was to be learned only within the circle of Grecian dialectics and rhetoric, among his peers on Areopagus, in the presence of Stoic and Epicurean, comprehending perfectly the scorn which sat on the curled lip and gleamed from the half-shut eyes of his erudite auditors when he preached unto them the foolishness of the cross; superadded to all which, he was by birth a free Roman citizen, the highest protection and prerogative of his age, so that in every peril from Jew or Greek he was shielded as by Minerva's ægis, the report that he was a Roman throwing open the jail of Philippi for his egress, delivering him from the scourge and the mob on the castle stairs at Jerusalem, carrying him into the presence of governors and kings; and an appeal to Cæsar, transporting him over the Adriatic to the imperial city, where he had often longed to go, and where, with mingled dignity, heroism and success, he preached the gospel of Christ "at Rome also;" aye, within the very precincts of the palace; Who can study this correspondency of exigencies and qualities in the person of him who leads the long column of Christian evangelists, without admitting the lesson thus taught the Christian church, for all time, concerning the wisdom of preparation, method, adaptation and combination in all her missionary aggression?

Passing from those ordained and official agencies which, as we believe, are perpetual in the church for her edification and enlargement, there remains another, among the earliest instruments of Christian evangelism, which we have called the *spontaneous*, and, as we might have added, the secular and laical; which, however overlooked and suspected now, if we have rightly interpreted the facts of the New Testament, was at the beginning among the most honored and successful of all human instrumentalities, and which is to be revived again, in more than pristine force, as a grand reliance of our modern missions.

It was by no accident that so large a concourse of unofficial persons, from all parts of the world, were assembled at Jerusalem on the day of Pentecost. "Then they that were scattered abroad," so reads the Sacred Record, "went everywhere preaching the word."* Stumble not at the word

* To render it certain that the allusion here is not to the ordained officials of the church, it is added in the same chapter, (Acts viii.) "they were all scattered abroad throughout the regions of Judea and Samaria, *except the Apostles*."

"preaching," because of the official associations which are connected with it by modern usage. It signifies simply, in its original sense, the act of evangelizing or reporting abroad the good news of salvation. The news of a great victory outstrips the official heralds who are sent to announce it. The idea on which we would insist is already before you. Stately apostleships, ordained dignitaries were not the only channels of saving grace. The ceremonial holiness and exclusiveness which, as we have seen, belonged to the official persons, representing the preparatory dispensations of Christianity, were lost forever when Christianity had reached its ripeness and universality. Profanation was it for any mortal, save the anointed son of Levi, to touch the vessels of the local worship; but now that the fountains of life are unsealed, every one who receives of their fullness heralds it abroad in every place. A matter of personal experience, they could not leave it behind them; but bore it with them as an inseparable part of their own life.

The Christian faith was thus propagated in the easiest and most natural of all methods. It was the outbreaking of spontaneous and irrepressible force. It revealed and declared itself, as light shines, without compulsion. Such is our conception of the spontaneity with which the honest self-conviction of the earliest converts to Christ made expression of itself, that it strikes us as something preposterous, to imagine the first company of disciples engaged in urging one another to a more earnest propagation of the faith by that style of arguments, drawn from philanthropy, obligation, expediency, necessity and policy, which make up the persuasion of our modern missionary aggression. There is next to nothing of all this in the New Testament. Possessing, or rather possessed by this one fact of the gospel, that Jesus Christ had died for the world's redemption, they spread the glorious tidings wherever they went.

One of the most pregnant passages in all the New Testament, bearing on Christian missions, is that last chapter of Paul's Epistle to the Romans, which, consisting chiefly of personal salutations to private persons, might strike a superficial eye, as the least promising and instructive, containing nothing but a bare and arid catalogue of names.

There was at this time, Anno Domini 60, a Christian church, that is, a body of Christian believers in the imperial city. It had been in existence for a considerable time. It had grown to such a magnitude as to justify the Apostle in addressing to it the most elaborate of all his Epistles. By whom was that church established? By some, it has been regarded as of prime importance to hold that the Apostle Peter was the founder of that metropolitan church. By itself, the assertion is of very little consequence; correct or incorrect, not worth a tithe of the words which have been expended upon the controversy. But the assertion does not stand by itself. It is the foundation-stone of a vast system of hierarchical pretension. Archbishop Whately has a capital essay on *omissions.* We infer as much, in certain cases, from what is *not* said, as, in others, from what *is* said. The classical reader will remember that it was the mere absence of Cato's statue in the Roman procession, which was so suspicious and suggestive. Here have we, from the pen of "our beloved brother Paul," kindly mention of all the Christians he had ever known, resident in the imperial capital, without a single allusion to him who is now claimed by the Roman primacy to have been the founder, and, at that very time, the resident Bishop of the church at Rome. By whom was it founded? The evidence is before us. Ordinary men and women, engaged in the common occupations of life, merchants, craftsmen, freedmen, who, traveling from one country to another in their professional pursuits, carried in their own bosoms the vital forces of the Christian faith. The first greeting in these apostolical reminiscences is to Aquila, and his wife Priscilla, of whom we have heard before. Five years previously, when the decree of Claudius expelled the Jews from Rome, these unpretending artisans — for they were tent-makers — arrived in Corinth, and Paul wrought with them. Eighteen months afterwards, they accompanied the Apostle to Ephesus, where they stood by him in his perils, and where a church was gathered in their house. Laical and humble in their occupations, their attainments in piety were of no ordinary kind; for when Apollos commenced his brilliant career as an eloquent preacher at Corinth, they received him to their own lodgings and expounded unto him the way of God more perfectly. The death of Claudius removing the interdict by which they were exiled, this pious couple return to Rome, kindle the fires on their own altar, and forthwith Paul sends his greetings to the "church which is in their house." The evangelic prediction of Zechariah is already accomplished.* Every domestic utensil in the houses of men is sanctified more truly than the golden bowl on the ancient altar. Ceremonially, unholy was woman esteemed in relation to the mysteries of the symbolic temple; but no sooner are the blessings of Christianity ready for universal diffusion, than we find the Apostle here making honorable mention of the Marys and Priscillas, of Persis, Tryphena and Tryphosa, godly women, who "labored with him" in the gospel, consecrating the graces and amenities of their sex to the one end of diffusing the savor of Christ's name in every place. Nor was this all. As a beautiful illustration of the ease and readiness with which Christianity adjusts itself to extrinsic necessities, where the vital power is within, instead of being compressed and laced within prescribed and changeless forms, the first personage introduced, in this chapter, is a woman who had an *official* connection with the church at Cenchrea—a deaconess by appointment—because the conventional usages of the times, secluding the female sex by themselves, left them accessible, even when most they needed instruction and hope, only to one of themselves; nor should the church ever forget or forego the right she possesses, of creating or pretermitting many forms of agency

---

* In that day shall there be upon the bells of the horses, Holiness unto the Lord; and the pots in the Lord's house shall be like the bowls before the altar. Yea, every pot in Jerusalem and in Judah shall be holiness unto the Lord of hosts. (Zech. xiv. 20, 21.) Now that the waters of life are for *diffusion*, a cup of horn, or iron, or potter's clay is canonical in the best of all senses, for it is useful.

which necessity and expediency may suggest, as a help to her saving work. We glory in the belief, that in all matters touching the real efficiency of the Christian church, she has received of her Lord the utmost liberty which her largest benevolence could desire. Water, air, light, are not more free in flowing into every opening and filling every cavity, than was the spirit of the primitive church in adapting its action to every exigency. We must go back to the records of Christianity themselves, if we would learn more of what the church is yet to learn much—the power and wisdom of lay-agency. Practical evangelism is not to be confined to Pauls and Peters, Brainerds and Martyns; and in the proper place, it may be well to institute the inquiry, whether among the means and methods of evangelizing the heathen it should not be projected by laymen, of all arts and professions, we do not say to be sent, but to send themselves, in the arrangements of their own trade, toil and traffic, all over the earth, for the express purpose of being succorers of the gospel, rearing churches—as did those men and women whose names inspiration has immortalized in this Roman epistle, above any emblazoned on classic pillar or tablet—in their own homes, and pouring light and love through all the channels of secular intercourse, upon the souls of the benighted.

And now, having considered the relations of Christianity and the world, at the beginning, together with some of the means by which the one was diffused throughout the other, we transport ourselves across intervening centuries and continents, to the spot where we now stand, in the heart of the New World; and from this position, late in time, and remote in space from the point where Christianity began its flight, we are to ask whether the relations of these two objects, Christianity and the World, are such as will justify the sentiment to which we are pledged.

And here, the first fact which stretches itself entirely across our vision, is the astounding verity that eighteen centuries have entirely passed away since the ascension of our Lord, and yet so limited is the territorial domain of Christianity, that not one whole nation under heaven can be found entirely and thoroughly pervaded by its presence and power. Scoffing skepticism would bid us answer, what else than a chimera it can be, for us to set forth the notion that the world and Christianity were made one for another, when, after so long an experiment, Christianity has not even retained its own, but has been diluted by error, subject to monstrous abuses and perversions, and has lent itself to the most long-lived and tyrannical of all superstitions, cursing the nations it should have blessed, and diverted out of its course by a thousand obstacles.

We volunteer no explanation of the mysteries of Providence, in the history of the Christian religion. The life of God is eternal; and his plans extend through thousands of years. Speak of delays and disappointments, of long ages of darkness and of barbarism! Tell us of the centuries in which the Christian faith was wrapped up in the mummy cerements of formalism and superstition! The very mistakes of men, in reference to religion, are instructive; and the experiments of human folly, though they consume ages, are a real economy of time; for men, when they are bent on making trial of their own expedients, in place of the blessed gospel, emerge on the hither side of the experiment with more of wisdom, more of self-conviction, because the lesson has been burned into them by centuries of suffering and shame. Multiply your objections to any degree, as drawn from the delays and corruptions of the Christian faith, the one fact remains, and this is all which we are concerned now to state, that Christianity has been a gainer at every stage and epoch of its eventful life. It has not merely survived opposition, but actually drawn lustre from reproach, and developed strength in every conflict, so that its practical power is greater now than ever it was before. Its power is greater to-day than when it was first preached at Jerusalem. It is greater now than when the labarum of Constantine blazoned the cross in courts and camps. It is greater now than when Britain was converted to the Christian faith; greater by far than at the era of the Reformation. It possesses a wider territorial jurisdiction than when the Puritans landed in the new world. Who can doubt that it has a stronger hold on the intelligent convictions of the world, than it had before Lord Herbert wrote his work, "De Veritate," Toland his "Christianity without Mystery," Lord Shaftesbury his "Characteristics," Collins his essay on "Free Thinking," Bolingbroke his "Essays and Fragments," Tindal his "Christianity as old as the Creation," Hume his "Dialogues on Nature and Religion," or Paine his "Age of Reason."

If we have been instructed in observing the adaptations of Christianity and the world, one to another, at the beginning of the Christian era, who can doubt that both have proceeded from the same authorship, and have obeyed the same direction, in subsequent stages and developments?

We have spoken of *the world* as being ready for Christianity, when Christianity was ready for it. We mean the world *as it then was.* We have reason to believe that the feet of the Apostles and their contemporaries traversed the then known world, from Arabia to Britain. But how large a portion of the world we inhabit, was entirely concealed from their knowledge and approach. The roads surveyed by the last imperial decree before the advent of Christ, were less than four thousand miles in extent. The most westerly land known to the "mistress of the world" was one of the Canary Islands; the most northerly, called Ultima Thule, one of the Shetlands. Africa was supposed to be joined to Asia on the south, and was not circumnavigated till the fifteenth century after Christ. In the geography which was compiled by Ptolemy in the second century, we have embodied all the knowledge which then existed of the earth. From this we learn that the portion of land belonging to the globe, of which anything was known to Ptolemy and his contemporaries, was scarcely one-third of that which is known to us; while of the one hundred and fifty-five millions of square miles of water covering the rest of the globe, they knew absolutely nothing. How scanty the knowledge possessed by them of the globe, appears from the belief then prevalent, that none but the temperate zone was habitable ; both the torrid and the frigid zones being supposed to be destructive of animal life.

Plainly it was the intention of Providence, that Christianity should pass through various trials before, in its highest and latest sense, it should be fitted for the literal occupancy of the whole world. The mystery of the sea hid one entire hemisphere from human sight. These broad rivers were running their long way silently and wondrously to the sea. These forests grew and decayed, and grew again in their endless reproduction. These wide and western prairies lay beneath the eye of God, in patient and beautiful trust in the future uses of the Almighty. No Tyrian ship, no Egyptian barge, no Grecian argosy, no Roman galley, no Saracen flotilla was suffered to pass the "pillars of Hercules," and break the silence and mystery of the Western ocean, and plant on these shores the irradicable seeds of their varied and mighty superstitions. The time was not yet for the widest possible dissemination of the Christian faith.

Observe the changes to which Christianity itself was subject; trials and changes for which *time* was needful, and each and all of which were developing more and more of the universal qualities of the true faith.

The first great trial to which it was subject, was in the presence of Jewish intolerance and heathen hate. The one question was, whether it should be suffered to live. World-wide the persecution rages against the church. The Neros, the Caligulas, the Domitians of the earth resolved to drown the spreading "superstition" in blood. The more violently the storm rages, the deeper are the roots which the Christian faith strikes into the ground, and the broader the growth which it spreads into the air.

Next, Christianity was corrupted and perverted. The very power which before had assaulted the religion of Christ, now treacherously assumes the name, the crown, the robe and the sceptre of Christ, and the world became enslaved to an aged and colossal tyranny. The next advance of Christianity was to divest herself of all these falsehoods and enslavements, and come forth free and reformed.

The Protestant Reformation was a great event, marvelous in its nature and effects. But it was not an event complete and ultimate. It was only one of the demiurgic days of the world's creation. It was not the Sabbath of the world's finishing and repose. It was a movement in the right direction; but it implied the necessity and the promise of greater changes to come.

Protestantism itself crystalized into icy forms, and Christianity was lulled to sleep in the arms of political establishments. It had its rituals, its injunctions, its forced conformities; at length its lifeless ceremonies. It was needful that reformed,

Protestant Christianity, should have a second resurrection. At last it came. When truth had taken root, when it had become incorporated into church creeds, and had become an admitted element of national faith, then came the Puritans and the Non-conformists, an order of men whose sole desire was for spiritual life ; and now it was that Christianity, invested with all the accumulated experience of ages, crosses the ocean, and finds, in a new world, the theatre for a new and higher development.

Observe, this country was not settled, not at all in the proper sense of the term, until after the Protestant Reformation. The men who gave a soul to our history were Protestants in a double sense ; reformers of the reformation. Yet were they called of God to a service which, while it was needful and manly, was not the most favorable to spiritual extension. Times of resistance to ecclesiastical despotism are not the most auspicious for true evangelism. Those who are summoned to do vigorous battle against positive wrongs, are not always the best prepared or the most successful in making glad the wilderness with the verdure and bloom of the gospel. This accounts for the fact that, at the Reformation, Christianity, though liberated by the struggles of Truth, was not largely extended by the power and impulses of Love.

A century was allowed the new church to strike its roots deep into our soil ; a century of unmolested freedom, with just trial enough to make root and fibre tough and strong. The ocean rolled between it and ecclesiastical despotism. Here was Protestantism, and Protestantism free, unshackled, with none to dictate or circumscribe, and a new and boundless continent for its expansion. She planted her churches, established her schools and colleges, educated her children, reared her ministers, and with occasional follies and mistakes, such as will mar all things human, the thing attained was a community of free and thoughtful men, born and bred in the faith of God's own word.

When all this was accomplished, there occurred, throughout the Christian world, but chiefly on our own continent, an event, now little more than a century ago, which, if we rightly understand it, must be regarded as the most significant and important, and, in its relations to the future, suggestive and prophetic, of all which has taken place thus far in the history of the Christian church since the ascension of our Lord and the wonders of Pentecost. We refer to that great revival of religion, which, like the breath of spring, passed over the face of Christendom, the focal point of which was in the central parts of Massachusetts. Time enough has now elapsed for generalizing into one, events which, at the time, appeared distinct and unrelated. Methodism, as it arose in the English church, a thing, not a name, so ably analyzed and described by Isaac Taylor, and the revivals of religion in Scotland and New England, may be regarded as one historic development. The peculiarities were local and formal; the essential was the same in all. The substantial features of that great religious movement, were the waking up of personal consciousness, a new sense of individual relationship to God, of intense life and earnest zeal for the conversion of souls. Men were converted to the truth of Christ in unusual numbers, with unusual rapidity and with unusual distinctness. The effect of that event has been felt in every part of the civilized world. The "missionary spirit," as the common expression is, that is, *active evangelism*, carrying and applying the gospel in every direction, at home and abroad, is the legitimate result, or rather the best description of that general movement. To mark the progress which has since been made by the Christian church, it must be observed that events, which once were extraordinary, are esteemed so no longer. The minds of men are already become familiar with occurrences and expectations which once were regarded as very uncommon. Many of the striking conversions recorded by Edwards, the pious historiographer of the earlier stages of this movement, would awaken no sense of surprise to-day. In the year 1820, Dr. Worcester, then Secretary of this Board of Foreign Missions, in an address to Christians of all denominations in this country, uses the following language: "By means of these establishments, [missionary,] and mostly since our last address to you, more than *thirty* persons, belonging to five or six different heathen nations, have, in the judgment of charity, been brought to the spiritual knowledge of the truth." The announcement is made as of a great event, and in very guarded phrase, as if it must meet with incredulity. Yet such advances have been made since then that, without any surprise, we hear that *thousands*, in a single year, have been converted to God in the Pacific Isles. Should it be announced before this our annual session is closed, that twenty thousand among the Tamil and Armenian population of the East were truly converted to Christ, it would not appear half so wonderful as the conversion of the first ten or twenty at the beginning of that era of evangelism from which we measure our latest progress. We have been moving with a great current, of the swiftness and force of which, as of our Mississippi, we have but little conception while borne upon its mighty tide. The Christian sentiment of the country has deepened in its flow. There is more of active philanthropy now than ever before; more of organized effort to relieve misery, reclaim vice, inform ignorance; more, in a word, than at any previous epoch, to diffuse the gospel with its light and charities. Added to all which, those revivals of religion, which have given a peculiarity to this latest period of Christian development, have not disappeared; fewer in number, feebler in power, more limited in extent than we could desire, yet sufficient in well-attested effects to keep it fresh in our minds to what period of time we belong, and always prophetic of the greater disclosures of the future.

Turning to the future, we expect and believe that the gospel, diffused and extended, by appropriate instrumentalities, throughout the world, will be accompanied by a power from on high, producing effects on the minds of men, compared with which all that has preceded is but the shadow of the sun. We predict no smooth current of undisputed and uninterrupted prosperity. Fallings away, heresies, infidelities, strugglings, like the heathenish signs of the zodiac, may be in the path of our sun. Nevertheless, the pure truth of God will receive the widest circulation. Copies of the word of God will be multiplied, and the Christian ministry reinforced in adequate numbers. All the appliances of modern invention and enterprise, the new stimulus given to commerce, and all the facilities for international communication, will find their true dignity and use in diffusing the truth of God with ever-increasing rapidity and extent. In this service of disseminating truth, there will be a place for every kind of instrumentality. Lay-agency, introduced so efficiently by Wesley and Whitefield in the last awakening of the church, was only prophetic of that universal life and activity which are hereafter to characterize the membership of the Christian church. Here then is one definite expectation for the future. Here is an appropriate place for every good work. As God converts men by truth, it is an indispensable work. "The *knowledge* of the Lord is to cover the earth, as the waters cover the sea."

Nor is this a service to be finished, by itself, before we are to expect yet greater things. Simultaneously with the diffusion of truth, we may expect those applications of the Divine Spirit, which will subdue opposition, conquer unbelief, and bring mankind into a personal acceptance of the gospel in numbers, rapidity and decision, such as never yet have been seen. The great harvest, of which all preceding gatherings are but the first fruits, is yet to come. We have had, as yet, only the type and the shadow. The substantial reality is still future. Nothing yet has occurred worthy to be regarded as a fulfillment of the great promises of Scripture relative to the universal outpouring of the Holy Spirit. What occurred at Pentecost, "signs and wonders in the heavens, sun and moon changed, the heavens and the earth shaken," was only the beginning in the verification of the tropical language of Joel, the first in that long series of events which are to mark the triumphs of the Spirit of God. We rejoice over the conversion of a few, here and there; one from a family, and two from a neighborhood; but accessions are not always to be made to the church of Christ after this manner. The church will never overtake the growth of this world's population, according to such an arithmetic. We have as yet but a glimpse,—enough to bear up and guide our faith, but a prophecy still,—of the *number* of those who will be made willing in the day of God's power. They are likened unto the drops of the morning dew. The church is yet to be the joy of the whole earth; and men will flock into it as "CLOUDS AND AS DOVES TO THEIR WINDOWS."

Nor is it of numbers only that we speak. A new epoch is coming as to the character of those converted, and the nature of a religious life. We talk of men converted now; but, oh, how little do we know of spiritual life! We are like corpses galvanized into partial vitality. We talk about the spiritual world. But how little does the strongest faith apprehend, as yet, of the powers of the world to come! Sense still holds the ascendancy. This is not to be so always. We have reason to anticipate such a new power, applied by the Holy Ghost to the souls of men, that the life, the love, the faith, the joy, the sanctity of men renewed will be so much in advance of all we now experience, that our life, compared with theirs, will appear like a sleep. Those great words, GOD, CHRIST, MAN, SIN, SALVATION, HEAVEN, HELL, over which men now slumber, even when they admit them into their intellectual convictions, will be as if illuminated with flame. We do not comprehend the gospel at all, in its richness and glory, as it will be comprehended in the future effusions of the Spirit. We see men as trees walking. We are purblind, groping our way among shadows. The time is coming when men will be as if endowed with new senses, so vivid, so intense will be their consciousness of spiritual things. God will no more be thought of as afar off, but nigh unto all who call upon him. Heaven will no more appear as a distant and dreamy world of the imagination. Its fragrant odors will be inhaled, and its happy songs will be heard by those who dwell upon the earth. Love to Christ will be no more a frozen compound of obligation and self-interest; but a well of gratitude and joy, springing up to everlasting life. Then property will all be consecrated to the best uses.

What is now extorted reluctantly, by the pressure of duty and the commands of conscience, will then be the spontaneous promptings of an ever-cheerful and ever-living love. Holiness to the Lord will be upon the bells of the horses; and commerce, and art, and enterprise, will flow on musically and joyfully in the channels of justice, love and mercy. The half-and-half life of the best Christians is only prophetic of that future power of the Spirit, when renewed man shall once more be a LIVING SOUL. The most godly men, of these modern times of revived evangelism, are but the shadows of that approaching form of the Christian man, who is to be "filled with the Spirit." Primitive Christianity did not fulfill that great promise. Beautiful was the simplicity of the early disciples of Christ. That quality is to be regained, copied and surpassed. In stature, we are children but once. But when we have outgrown infancy, and the body has reached its maturity, and the intellect its strength, the glory of our nature is in becoming little children again in simplicity of spirit. Even so the church, led through the discipline of ages, adult in strength, clothed with the sun for knowledge and power, will find her highest perfection and exaltation in superadding to all these gifts and graces the simplicity and love of those who first followed Christ as "dear children." Literally may it be true, in a sense, never imagined by ancient piety, that, as the lightning cometh out of the east and shineth even unto the west, even so will the coming of the Son of Man be. These electric nerves, which make the air to throb with thought and life, not always to be the heralds of mere political and mercantile tidings, will be the vehicles of religious news and religious love. Nor is it any freak of our imagination, to suppose the time may come when, as the people of God are assembled at the rising of the sun for praise and prayer, the lightning shall report it from the east, '*The Lord is here;*' and the lightning shall flash it back from the west, '*The Lord is here,*' and so the "tabernacle of God shall be with men. He shall be their God, and they shall be his people."

Long before that time shall fully come, we, fathers and brethren, will have passed from the earth. What then? Have we no relation to it? Verily, we are living in the dispensation of the Spirit. Ours is the day of preparation; in some regards more privileged, since faith, patience and labor are the instruments of future success. Better are our times than those of our fathers. For their fidelity, for their quick discernment of the ways and work of God, we may well be thankful; but the future is all bright with promise for us and our children. Our fathers are still with us. Their grateful spirits are over us and among us, when we meet to prosecute the work which they began. As the martial hero, whom poetry has described on the eve of battle as new-strung with life, when, at the tap of his drum, the shades of his ancestors came thronging around him, in the dusky air; so do we feel ourselves cheered, ennobled and exalted, by the memory of the good and the great, whose faces smile on us from the past and from heaven; the serene and hopeful Worcester, the sagacious Chapin, the devout Lyman, the generous Phillips, the manly Huntington. We knew not how to spare them when Evarts, Cornelius, Wisner and Armstrong were taken from the world; but we have found that they are not lost to us and our cause, now that the heavens have touched them. In the inventory of available means by which the church is to conduct her conquests, we could not afford to subtract the influence of those who have already died in the service. Our dead missionaries are as eloquent as the living. The brave soldier who was bearing home the heart of his King, in an urn, to be entombed in his native land, when sorely pressed and in danger of defeat, rose in his stirrups, and, before the eyes of his troops, threw the precious treasure far in advance, into the very thickest of the enemy; knowing that this would be the surest method of inciting his countrymen to press forward to the rescue. The church has thrown many precious hearts into Heathenism, as the pledge and the motive for further advancement. Those who have sent their Newells, Lathrops and Huntingtons, their Fiskes, their Halls and their Grants, their own sons, daughters, brothers and sisters to die in Asia, Africa and the islands of the sea, have never so much as thought of abandoning a cause already endeared to them by so many precious associations. A thousand living hearts and homes in America are drawn towards the lands in which are the graves of our deceased missionaries. As

Abraham bought a cave in the field of Machpelah, as a burying-place for his household, a pledge of his faith in the divine promise, that the whole land should one day belong to his posterity, so is every missionary grave, in every heathen country, a similar proof of our belief that the lands in which they lie will hereafter be converted unto Christ. Tocat will not be Mohammedan, when Henry Martyn shall rise in the last day; nor will Aleppo, nor Ceylon, nor the Isle of France, nor China, be lands of delusion, when those who have gone from our homes and our churches to sleep therein, shall greet the light of the promised resurrection. Towards that vast result everything advances. There are eddies and back currents in our largest rivers; but the main course is on and on, resistless and magnificent towards the ocean. The quiet Merrimac, on whose peaceful banks this missionary organization had its inception, beareth greetings to-day to the broader and deeper Ohio; and both clap their hands together, as they flow on to meet the Ganges and the Euphrates. These mighty valleys, covered with corn, laugh with gladness, in prospect of that spiritual affluence which they are yet to distribute over all the earth. The churches which have sprung up on the edge of the wilderness, fast as the forest has dropped before the march of civilization, instead of being themselves beneficiaries, in need of assistance, have, many of them, already become, and more will yet become, the most munificent almoners in a service which is destined to endless growth and reproduction. The footsteps of our children are already on the shores of the Pacific. Before their fathers have left the world, from the "Golden Gates" which God has given us, they look out upon those Christian islands, which sparkle like gems in the sea, converted, in our own life-time, from barbarism to the dignity of an intelligent, self-governed and religious people. Our language and our religion already encircle the globe.

We pledge ourselves, therefore, to no doubtful issue. This world was not only made *by* Christ, but FOR Christ. Every loyal thought, every pious act, is auxiliary to that kingdom of the Redeemer which has the oath of God, and the decree of eternity for the certainty of its triumph. For that result, Faith waiteth with calm serenity; her hand upon her anchor. Christian calmness is not the offspring of doubt, but of conscious strength. God has anointed his king on his holy hill of Zion. Clouds may hang around its top, and billows may break at its feet, but that mountain standeth on its eternal foundations. Oppose in heart or life the dominion of Christ, and the wheels of the prophet's vision roll over us and grind us to powder. Acquiesce therein, and we become identified with that numberless throng who will swell the train of His triumphs and reflect and share the glories of His reign. We shall die; but Christ liveth. Because He liveth, we shall live also. Good and faithful men shall be jewels in the diadem of our God, which will sparkle when the stars are dead.

MOTIVES TO THE MISSIONARY WORK.

A

SERMON,

BEFORE THE

AMERICAN BOARD OF COMMISSIONERS FOR FOREIGN MISSIONS,

AT THEIR

MEETING IN ROCHESTER, N. Y.

OCTOBER 6, 1863.

BY

ELISHA L. CLEAVELAND, D. D.
Pastor of the Third Congregational Church, New Haven, Ct.

BOSTON:
PRESS OF T. R. MARVIN & SON, 42 CONGRESS STREET.
1863.

AMERICAN BOARD OF COMMISSIONERS FOR FOREIGN MISSIONS.

ROCHESTER, N. Y., OCTOBER, 1863.

Resolved, That the thanks of the Board be presented to the Rev. Dr. CLEAVELAND for his Sermon, preached on Tuesday evening, and that he be requested to furnish a copy for publication.

Attest,

SAMUEL M. WORCESTER, *Rec. Secretary.*

SERMON.

LUKE xxiv. 45–47.

THEN OPENED HE THEIR UNDERSTANDING, THAT THEY MIGHT UNDERSTAND THE SCRIPTURES, AND SAID UNTO THEM, THUS IT IS WRITTEN, AND THUS IT BEHOOVED CHRIST TO SUFFER, AND TO RISE FROM THE DEAD THE THIRD DAY; AND THAT REPENTANCE AND REMISSION OF SINS SHOULD BE PREACHED IN HIS NAME AMONG ALL NATIONS, BEGINNING AT JERUSALEM.

THIS is the first great commission ever received by the church from her risen Lord, for the evangelization of the world. Forty days after, it was repeated in still more emphatic terms, as he stood ready to depart. That was the day of his ascension; this was the day of his resurrection. That reveals the thought last on his mind before he disappeared from mortal sight; this discloses the thought first in his heart when he rose from the dead and entered on his new career of triumph. It was the same great thought that filled his soul from the first to the last moment of his resurrection-life on earth. So that in the deliverance of the text, we have the very inauguration of the work of missions. Here are the first principles, the very roots from which the entire growth has sprung, and on a vital connection with which, depend its vigor and fruitfulness. All the value, all the efficiency, and all the grandeur of our cause, lie in the simple, but fundamental truths which gave it birth. Higher than these we never can rise — beyond them we never can pass. Happy will it be for us, and for our success, if we can keep mind and heart in intelligent and loving sympathy with them.

As, then, lost Christian zeal can only be recovered by a renewed touch of the great magnet from which all its electric force is derived, let us go back to the hour and the spot from whence this sublime movement broke forth upon the world,—back to the first Great Missionary, and his first great words, as, with lips just released from the seal of death, he commissions his Apostles for the ministry of reconciliation: and in that august Presence, let us charge ourselves anew with the momentous work we have in hand, and open our souls to the glowing pulsations of his infinite heart.

The first thing that arrests attention in the account of this original missionary meeting, is the change wrought by our Lord on the Apostles themselves, by way of qualification for their work. He "opened their understanding, that they might understand the Scriptures." He not only expounded the Word to them, but he opened their minds to comprehend the exposition. He imparted to them that inward, spiritual illumination, without which the Scriptures are, at best, but a dead letter. When Christ performed this service for his disciples, they saw at once, as they had never seen before, that it was incumbent on him to suffer death, and rise again; and that since the atonement now made is the only ground of salvation, it became their highest duty and privilege to proclaim repentance and remission of sins in his name, among all nations. If any man, therefore, fails to discern the true relations of Christ's death and resurrection to the salvation of souls, or the true relations of the church to impenitent sinners and the unevangelized world, it is certain that his understanding has not yet been opened by the Lord Jesus to the real meaning of the Scriptures. In other words, the work of missions is a fruit of the Spirit of Christ. Till he opens the heart, there is no generous outflow of love to souls, no quenchless zeal for the honor of God, no vital force to outlast and overcome all discouragement and opposition. It is this that gives reality to things unseen and eternal; that discloses the exalted nature and priceless worth of the soul; that lifts the curtain of the world to come, and reveals an empire, vast as immensity, peopled with the countless generations of countless worlds, and governed by one Infinite Being whose presence and glory fill it. This it is that uncovers the pit of woe, and shows the sinner's doom; this too, brings near the home of the blessed, and the rewards of the righteous. And it is when, with an eye of faith, we look down into the horrors of the one, or up to the glories of the other, that the spirit of missions comes upon us, and we feel that we cannot labor too earnestly to spread that gospel, which alone rescues man from perdition and raises him to heaven.

In commissioning his Apostles, our Lord, you will observe, enjoins it upon them, to begin their work of love at Jerusalem. And why begin at Jerusalem? Was it not here that he had encountered the boldest, the deadliest, the most unrelenting opposition? Was it not here that a malignant persecution had been set on foot against him? Was not this the prolific fountain that had poisoned the whole nation of the Jews with enmity to God? Was it not in Jerusalem that a conspiracy had been formed against the life of Christ? Had she not just murdered her own Messiah? And does he now offer to Jerusalem the first benefits of that redeeming blood which Jerusalem had shed? Does he extend the first overtures of mercy to that very multitude who cried, "Not this man, but Barrabas;"—"Away with him, crucify him"? Does he seek out the very men whose hands are still reeking with his blood, and invite them to share the blessings of his grace? Yes, it is even so! Such is the sublime elevation, the illimitable range, and the quenchless fire of Christ's love, that it yearns toward his worst enemies, and selects his murderers as the first objects of his compassionate regard. The fact that a man is peculiarly wicked and inimical to God, so far from repelling the Saviour, excites his pity, and moves him to acts of kindness and offers of mercy. It was on this principle that Christ would have his disciples begin their mission at Jerusalem. This was to be the starting-point of the missionary work; from this centre the field was to be swept with a radius equal to the earth's diameter. Here, too, we have the key-note of the enterprise,—*love to the bitterest foes*,—love which makes its first advances to the most ill-deserving! A love which could begin at Jerusalem, would surely never stop till it had encompassed the whole world:—if it could overleap this first and highest obstacle, it is certain that nothing else would arrest its progress. In the fulfillment of our mission, therefore, we may carry this gospel to the ends of the earth, assured that we shall find no people so corrupt that the love of Christ will not reach and reform them; we shall find no case of depravity so desperate as to preclude the application of this all-sufficient remedy.

Such, then, is the great work committed to the church by her ascended Lord. Let us now look at the motives by which it is enforced upon our hearts and consciences. I name

1. *The command of Christ.*

Co-operation in the work of missions is not left to our discretion, or to our good-will; it is imposed as a duty. The command emanates from the highest authority, and can neither be resisted or neglected without sin. The majesty of a sovereign is impressed on every word,—"Go ye into all the world, and preach the gospel to every creature." No ingenuity can torture this into mere advice; no ignorance or dullness can fail to understand it; on no pretext can it be evaded, which would not be equally good against every other precept of the Bible.

It is the command of *the newly risen* Saviour. When he first uttered it, he had but just come forth from the grave. It is not the requirement of a sovereign reposing amid the peaceful glories of his heavenly throne and kingdom, and enjoining labors in which himself had no share. It comes from one still standing, in humble form, on the earth, bearing on his person the scars of that mighty conflict in which he had vanquished the powers of death and hell, leading captivity captive: it is the command of Him who had just come up from treading the wine-press alone, in the greatness of his strength, his garments dyed in blood, and whose own arm had brought him salvation. In this precept there breathes the memory of a fearful struggle, an unknown distress, a mysterious weight of woe, an agony that must have conquered the most heroic fortitude, had it not been sustained by the whole strength of his Godhead. Had he possessed no right in virtue of his divinity, he would have fairly purchased it by the battle he had fought, and the victory he had won. The work he requires *of* us, is nothing to the work he has done *for* us. On the field where he bids us toil, he had wrought himself, with incessant and exhausting labor. He had borne every burden we are to bear, and infinitely more. But for what he endured, our burdens would have been insupportable, our duties impracticable. By his patient obedience and sufferings, a path has been opened for us, not of salvation only, but of usefulness. And now, when he closes his laborious mission by commanding us to enter on that path, and co-operate with him in carrying out the work he had begun, preaching repentance and remission of sins in his name among all nations, shall we not obey? Need we any thing more than this simple injunction? When the crucified one, just descended from the cross, just risen from the grave, tells us to proclaim to every nation, every soul, what he has done and suffered for man's salvation, shall we not do it? Shall we not fly on the wings of the wind to fulfill the great commission? But again —

It is our Saviour's *last* command. The last words of expiring greatness, — how precious, how weighty! The last words of departing goodness, — how sacred, how heavenly! Is there any duty you are more careful to perform than the dying command of a sainted father or mother? Jesus, the loftiest, saintliest being that ever trod this earth, left a farewell commission with his bereaved church. His great work finished, — all things ready, — the moment at hand when he was to be received up to glory, — yet had he one parting command, one farewell injunction, before he could leave them. Had the world understood that scene as it is now understood, had it been publicly known that the King of Zion then stood on Mount Olivet, ready to ascend into heaven, and that he waited but to utter one last command to his disciples, — what multitudes would have covered the summit and declivities of the mount, and filled the valleys below, and hung upon every elevated point commanding a view of the scene, — with what solemn hush and reverence would they have listened to catch those last words, that final charge! Nothing less than the weight of eternity would have seemed impressed on the farewell utterance of the world's Redeemer. And so, in truth, it was. Although the millions were not there, and only a few persecuted disciples gathered with affectionate reverence about the person of their Lord, the occasion was none the less august, the words none the less momentous. They wax greater with the roll of ages, gathering a more awful sacredness as the web of history unfolds to the gaze of the church. Uttered so near to the moment of his final disappearance, no other deliverance of Christ is clothed with an emphasis so sublime. It breathes of mercy and of majesty, of grace and of justice, of goodness and of severity. It peals out on the ear of startled nations, and down on the stream of coming ages, with a voice which arrests the careless, and rebukes the disobedient. And can *we* neglect *such* a command? While the heavens are opening over the spot, and angels are hovering, and countless worlds are looking on in silent wonder, and the eternal Father himself is waiting to receive his victorious Son, do we not hear the imperial mandate thunder as from the excellent glory, "*Go ye into all the world, and preach the gospel to every creature: he that believeth, and is baptized, shall be saved; but he that believeth not shall be damned*"?

2. We are urged to earnest efforts in behalf of this great cause, *by the immense work that yet remains to be done.*

Fifty years ago, the heathen were estimated, in round numbers, at six hundred millions. You remember how those terrific figures, — emblazoned before the eyes of Christendom, — trumpeted in startling appeals from land to land, — were employed by the Holy Ghost as one of the grand arguments that first roused the church to the work of modern missions. Now let me ask, What, after a half century of missionary labor, is the present number of the heathen? Can we report any material diminution in those dreadful figures? Can we reduce them by so much as one million, or even half a million? No. Thousands, and tens of thousands, have been brought to Christ, but there are the six hundred millions still! The banner of the cross has been planted in almost every pagan land, and many are the witnesses for Jesus among those idolaters; still there are the countless masses of India, the untrodden depths of Africa, and the unexplored regions of China. As if in defiance of all our efforts, heathenism still glories in her proud temples, still whitens the earth with the bones of her victims, and darkens the sky with the smoke of her idolatrous sacrifices. Who can look at the hoary heights and massive fortresses of this ancient empire of sin, and see how firm and strong it stands, and not feel the stupendous nature of the work? Think of its *antiquity!* dating back thousands of years before Christ. Think of its *origin!* from the father of lies, who, having set himself up as the god of this world, invented this system of idolatrous worship, that he might bind the apostate millions of earth to his cruel sceptre; — "for the things which the Gentiles sacrifice," says Paul, "they sacrifice to devils, and not to God."

But what is the lesson we are to gather from these moral wastes which still stretch out their interminable spaces before the missionaries of the cross? Is it a lesson of despair, or even of despondency? No; it is a lesson of rebuke, of repentance, of faith, of duty, of increased effort, but not of despair. Despair is for those who believe in no God, no Saviour, no Holy Ghost, no gospel, no atonement, no covenant, no promise, no invincible grace;—but co-workers with Omnipotence, know nothing of despair. We have great reason, however, for shame. Much, indeed, has been done, but nothing to what ought to have been done, and might have been done. Had the laborers been tenfold more numerous, the faith and love tenfold stronger, and the prayer tenfold more abundant and energetic, the success might have been a hundredfold greater. Glorious things have been achieved, it is true. But after all, there are the six hundred millions, still groping in the shadow of death, and perishing, twenty millions a year! And as long as those dense, dark columns present their unthinned ranks to the gaze of Christendom and the world, how can we feel that Christians are doing their whole duty? Is this a fulfillment of the great commission? Do we not hear a voice from the solemn past, saying with an emphasis, never so loud or awful as now,—'Church of God, how long—O how long, shall "darkness cover the earth, and gross darkness, the people?" How long shall more than three-fourths of the race be left in heathen blindness? How many more generations shall perish before they hear of Jesus and the resurrection? How many centuries shall roll on, before the church is willing to spare her silver and gold, her sons and daughters, until the wants of all mankind are met? When, O when *will* she go into all the world, and preach the gospel to every creature?'

3. We are constrained to this work by the *love of Christ.*

The love of Christ! who can measure it? We ascend in thought above the earth, above these visible heavens—we pass onward and upward, from star to star, from system to system, until,—suns and systems, far beneath us,—we raise our eyes, within the pearly gates, through towering hierarchies of angels and arch-angels, to a throne, high and lifted up, standing in massive and immutable strength against a background of infinite light. No mortal vision can bear the look of Him who sits thereon;—no mortal tongue can describe the surrounding scene of angelic beauty and glory,—the solemn bowing down, the ravishing minstrelsy, the grand choral song, rising in lofty praise to the mysterious Being who reigns in awful majesty over the universe of worlds.

Now, from this elevation, take the distance to the manger in Bethlehem:—from Godhead, to humanity;—from heaven's throne, to a malefactor's cross;—from the music of celestial voices, to the execrations and curses of an infuriated populace;—from the blissful life of his own glorious home in the bosom of the Father, to the agonies of death by crucifixion;—from his seat of pre-eminent authority, with the created universe for his foot-stool, to the narrow confines, intense darkness, and unbroken silence of the tomb! Can you fathom the descent? Have you a plummet to sound the infinite depth? Can you comprehend how it is, that He who bore so easily the weight of countless worlds, now faints and dies beneath the burden of sin? More than all, can your intelligence grasp the awful problem of a divine being standing in your place, and dying in your behalf? If this is too high for human, even for angelic powers, it still remains true that what you cannot *understand*, you may at least *feel*. Your thoughts may plunge in unfathomed depths, and find no shore, no foothold on which to rest; yet all the more will your soul be filled with the fragrant mystery of Christ's love. Incompetent as you are to penetrate the whole philosophy of the crucifixion, yet this you may know, (and to know it is life eternal!) that all this humiliation and agony was for *you*,—for your deliverance from sin and perdition. And just here lies the main-spring of the missionary enterprise. This it was that roused the Apostles to those untiring labors which ceased not but with life. The process by which they arrived at this mightiest argument for Christian effort, was simple, natural, and as open to us as it was to them. They had looked on their suffering, dying Master, merely as the unhappy victim of Jewish malice; but when he told them that it was necessary, as a part of the divine plan, that he should suffer, and rise from the dead the third day, in order that repentance and remission of sins should be preached among all nations, the inference flashed at once through their minds, as a surprising and joyful discovery,—'Then it was for *our sakes* he endured the horrors of crucifixion!—in all that scene of shame and agony, it seems, he was working out our redemption from sin and hell! And was it *then* that we forsook him and fled? Is *this* the love we have requited with unmanly cowardice and desertion?' Think of the effect of this discovery on the broken-hearted Peter! Crushed under a remorseful sense of his great crime, and doubtful whether he was ever again to be recognized as a disciple, how must the glorious truth have amazed and melted him! 'What! did my blessed Master die for *me?* Did my injured Lord go from the judgment-hall, where I so wickedly denied him, to pour out his blood for *my* guilty soul?—to wash away *my* damning sins? O, was there ever such love as this?—so pure, so deep, so self-sacrificing! Shall I ever deny him again? Can I ever love him enough? Is there any thing I will not do or suffer for so kind a Saviour?'

The love of Christ in dying for lost sinners was the one thought which, more than any and all others, burned in the hearts and inspired the labors of the first missionaries. Ask the great Apostle to the Gentiles what moves him to the perilous undertaking? He answers, "The love of Christ constraineth me." But, Paul, why persevere in the face of such tremendous obstacles and dangers? 'Because of the great love wherewith he hath loved us.' But think of the sacrifices you are making, of fortune, position and fame! "I count all things but loss for the excellency of the knowledge of Christ Jesus my Lord." But why wear out your strength, and rush upon certain martyrdom? "He loved me! he gave himself to die for me!" But what do you expect to gain by this course? To "comprehend, with all saints, what is the breadth and length, the height and depth, and to know the love of Christ, which passeth knowledge." Well, then, if you will identify yourself with the despised Nazarene, you must share his reproach. "God forbid that *I should glory*, save in the cross of our Lord Jesus Christ; by whom the world is crucified unto me, and I unto the world!"

And will any lower motive, think you, suffice for us, in prosecuting the work of modern missions? Is it not to speak the Saviour's precious name — to make known his matchless worth — to set forth his dying love — to publish the glad tidings of redemption to a perishing world — to win lost souls to his cross, and add star after star to his crown, — is not this the grand motive-power of the missionary enterprise? Other considerations, doubtless, may have their legitimate influence; but only as they emanate from, and are articulated with, this master-principle, are they acceptable to God, or valuable to Christianity. Our natural sympathies may be strongly excited by the temporal miseries of the heathen, we may take pleasure in sending them the gospel as the necessary means of improving their condition in time, and even their prospects for eternity. We may be drawn into the missionary movement by the air of romance with which some minds invest it. There is the fascination of heroic self-sacrifice in leaving home and kindred and country, for an exile in distant climes; there are the charms of foreign travel and residence in lands made classic by ancient story and song, or made sacred by the footsteps of Patriarchs and Prophets, of Apostles and the Son of God himself. There, too, is the elevated field of toil, lifting the humblest of its laborers into the view of a great spectatorship; the tempting opportunity of acquiring a general, perhaps a national, possibly a world-wide reputation for scholarship or discovery. We may be drawn into active co-operation with this enterprise by the imposing aspect of a powerful organization, wielding an immense influence, receiving the confidence and support of millions, and carrying forward a system of missions which commands the admiration of the world. There is something, moreover, in these annual convocations, with their crowded meetings, impressive solemnities, exciting discussions, and thrilling associations, which magnetizes the mind to an unwonted fervor. In an atmosphere so electric, vivid imaginations, and sympathetic natures, may easily kindle into a glow of excitement, under which high resolves are taken, eloquent words are spoken, and generous deeds are performed.

All these influences may indeed be sanctified and exalted by Christian principle. It is equally true, however, that they may stand apart from it entirely. It is quite possible that the man who, under these circumstances, warms towards the cause of missions, would be altogether indifferent to it, if the circumstances had no existence. If the Board held its annual meetings now, as it did fifty years ago, in private parlors, encompassed by an atmosphere of chilling incredulity, neglect and unfriendliness, — with nearly the whole heathen world closed against its missionaries, — with a scanty treasury, — with no starred names of martyred heroes on its catalogue, — with no illustrious record of conquests achieved, — with, as yet, only unpromising experiments to reward its courageous venture on the word and faithfulness of God; — few, I imagine, would, under such circumstances, be drawn to the cause by any attraction of romance, or of distinction, or of visible grandeur, or of popular excitement. Nothing less than the love of Christ, and of souls for which Christ died, would ordinarily avail to identify a man with an undertaking so forlorn in the public view. No feebler motive, I am confident, could successfully encounter the stern realities of the mission field.

And we may rest assured that what was necessary to success in that "day of small things,"— that period of inception and experiment,—is no less requisite now that the work has swelled to such vast dimensions, has impressed into its service so many auxiliary forces, and is moving on with such prodigious momentum. The God of missions accepts no man in this cause, who is not inspired by gratitude for the love of Christ. The money and the influence we offer in his service, he may use for his own gracious purposes; but we ourselves will not be accepted, unless prompted thereto by the same high consideration that constrained the first missionaries. Natural philanthropy may kindle up a feeble and transient blaze of compassion for heathen wretchedness; but Christ's love for lost souls no man may feel, but by the Holy Ghost. Flesh and blood never reveal that to us: it can only come by an illumination from on high. It is a fruit of renewing grace — it is a peculiar and essential element of experimental Christianity. Hence its power with God; hence its depth of feeling, the tenacity of its hold, and the energy of its operation. Nor has the experience of eighteen centuries taken any thing from the original freshness, and the sweet surprise with which the convert of our time makes his first discovery of Christ's love. Not more suddenly did it flash as a strange light from heaven on the astonished Apostles, than it breaks to-day on the quickened soul in the moment of its spiritual baptism. Nor will the eyes once opened to the glory of that sight, ever wholly lose the vision. Thenceforth a new life will breathe, a new fire will burn, a new power will work in the soul. It is a principle of unequaled moral leverage, lifting the Christian into a purer atmosphere, introducing him to a more exquisite experience, and putting him upon a loftier course of action than he had ever deemed possible. No other motive can impart such a grateful sense of freedom, and generous enthusiasm, — can stimulate to such noble endeavors, and give such support under hardship and peril. If this fails, every thing will fail. Should the time ever come when the love of Christ shall cease to be the animating principle, the main impulse of the missionary enterprise, then the work of missions will itself die out. Organizations may survive, but only to show that vitality is extinct. The usual movements may be gone through with, but without spirit, force, or effect. Annual meetings may be held, but to glorify man rather than

God. Christ will not be there; and the love of souls — the love of the heathen — will give place to the love of this present world.

I have exhibited some of the great motives which urge the people of God to an energetic prosecution of the work of missions; — the perishing state of the heathen; the command of Christ that the gospel shall be preached to them; and the constraining power of his own love for sinners. To what practical results, let me now ask, in conclusion, should we be led by these weighty considerations? What specific forms of action do they press upon us, as the imperative duty of the present time?

The first and most important duty suggested by the foregoing arguments, is *the entire consecration of ourselves to the Lord Jesus.*

Consecration is the simple and legitimate consequence of a real discovery of Christ's love. It results from no selfish calculation — no cold, iron chain of logic — no frothy rhetoric — no shallow, transient impulse — no vapid sentimentalism — no artificial lashing up of the soul to feeling. It is purely the effect of faith's direct look at the Lamb of God. One believing glance at that sacrifice of love, and the soul takes fire. There may be no conscious process of argument, yet argument there is, the most potent. The philosophy is unperceived, yet instant and irresistible. It is the philosophy of the heart. It is the result of that swift "chemistry of thought" which, under given conditions, spontaneously combines in results as exquisite, as they are surprising. Ask me not to demonstrate it by logical process. If you need an elaborate argument to persuade you to this consecration; if a simple look at the cross, and at Him who hung there, — at the love which triumphed there, and at the redemption which was wrought out there, — does not of itself reveal to you the secret attraction of that great magnet of hearts, then, alas, how far do you stand from that glorious centre of loyalty and love!

Calvary, then, is the place for reconsecration. It is when standing around the cross of Christ,—with its atoning blood sprinkled on our consciences; with its mingled glories of justice and mercy streaming over us; with its flood of love bathing our souls, and its touching memories subduing our hearts,—that we may most fitly renew our oath of allegiance to the Head of the church. This self-consecration is indeed the noblest and most needed offering we can present to the cause of missions. The great want of that cause at the present moment is an increase of piety in the churches. There is, indeed, a pressing demand for more money, and more missionaries; but the most urgent necessity of all is a larger measure of the spirit of Christ in the members of his body. However godly, or faithful, the laborers on mission ground, it is impossible but that their success should be affected by the state of the spiritual atmosphere among ourselves. As the head and pressure at the reservoir, determines the elevation to which the water may be thrown from the pipes in the distant city, so the degree of piety in the constituent churches must exert an influence, for good or evil, on the missions supported. Not to speak of the likelihood that the men who go out from year to year will share the general tone and spirit of the community which sends them,—there is the powerful influence of prayer, by which Christians at home may mightily co-operate with the workmen abroad. And how efficiently may the earnest intercessions of a godly people be followed up by the silent argument of a holy life, and of a tender yearning of soul over the mission field. An habitual and deep-toned godliness pervading the churches, would react on our missionary operations with overwhelming effect. Gifts bestowed, would be consecrated by a simplicity of faith, enriched by a wealth of love, and winged to their designation by a power of prayer, which would tell in glorious results on the hearts of the heathen. Alas, how far do we fall short of this desirable condition! The type of piety, on the breath of which this Board rose into existence, is certainly undergoing serious modifications, and who will say, for the better? Who does not feel that the glory of that light is fading,—that the power of that early faith and love is wanting? Who does not acknowledge that the grand necessity of the church in these days is a new baptism of the Holy Ghost? What we need is an unction from on high, that shall lift our actual life to the full level of our principles and professions; — nay, that shall raise us into the atmosphere of the cross; that shall make every Christian a witness and a missionary for Jesus, whatever his sphere; — willing to perform any service, to labor in any place, and encounter any hardship, suffering or peril, at the call, and for the sake of his Master. He who has this spirit is a missionary of the cross, whether he exercise his ministry among the savages of Africa, or the churches of this favored land. It is a common, but a great mistake, as it is a great evil, to regard the spirit of missions as a peculiar kind of Christianity, not to be expected, perhaps not required, of Christians generally. So far from being something superadded to, or different from, what is usually understood as the Christian spirit, it is precisely the same thing. The true spirit of missions is, simply and emphatically, the *spirit of Christ*. It is love for the perishing souls of men — such love as prompts to personal effort and sacrifice in their behalf. It is not predicated on locality or condition at all; it is compassion for lost sinners wherever found. There may be just as much of a missionary spirit in laboring to save souls in Christian as in heathen lands. Indeed, to be a Christian at all, one must have something of the missionary spirit. No pity for the souls of the heathen argues no pity for any man's soul. It is a contradiction in terms, for a man claiming to be a disciple of Christ to excuse himself from service among the heathen, on the ground that he never had the spirit of missions. It is tantamount to a confession that he has no sympathy with the Great Missionary himself — no part or lot in his salvation. Away with such unworthy, fatal misconceptions of Christianity! Suppose, in our great army of patriotic volunteers, a part should beg to be excused from marching to the front, and encountering the sterner hardships and perils of active hostilities, on the ground that they never had a patriotic spirit! Never had a patriotic spirit! Then why did you enlist? What business have you in the army? You, a soldier, and not ready to go, at the word of command, wherever your country sends you! And what, think you, will our great Captain say to those who claim to be soldiers of the cross, and yet shrink from toil and danger because they lack the missionary or Christian spirit? It is time we were done with such holiday soldiering as this. Let us at least be consistent; and either renounce all pretensions to a calling for which we acknowledge our unfitness, or else manfully accept the high responsibilities we have assumed, come squarely up to the spirit of the position, and courageously undertake the duties it involves. If we *are* what we profess to be, we have enlisted, not for the home guard, nor for camp duty, but to go wherever we are ordered, to do whatever we are required. Be the field near at hand or far away; be the service easy or hard, safe or dangerous; we must hold ourselves ready to obey the will of our Master. A thorough consecration makes no reserves, stipulates no conditions, and asks no privilege, except that of being permitted to serve and suffer for the Lord Jesus, wherever and however he may appoint.

The next duty connected with our subject, is that of *Christian liberality in the supply of funds for the prosecution of our work.*

This is closely connected with the matter of consecration. For when a man gives himself to Christ, does he not give his property also? Can he give the greater, and not the less? The love which can bestow so precious a gift as the heart's deepest affection, could not at the same time tolerate any reserves in regard to things of inferior value. The consecration that does not embrace every thing, is essentially defective. Our charities should be conducted on the principle that self-denial is an essential element of personal sanctification. Almsgiving is enjoined in Scripture, quite as much for the spiritual benefit of the donor, as for the temporal relief of the recipient. It is prescribed as a means of grace, because it exercises both our benevolence and our self-denial. And the more we deny ourselves for Christ's sake, provided we are sincere and cheerful in it, the richer will be the blessing on our own souls. It is a great mistake, therefore, to give to benevolent objects, only what we can easily spare, and never know it. Even if that reaches the wants of the destitute, it does not reach our own case. Such a rule of charity indicates excessive self-indulgence,—a surfeit of worldly good, symptomatic of spiritual apoplexy. The case is alarming, and demands a bold and resolute effort at depletion. The lancet must be applied freely and without delay. Let the charities be at once doubled, quadrupled, tenfolded. Let us give that which we shall miss when it is gone, in some cherished, but now restrained indulgence. Let us make some actual and costly sacrifice, that shall put our love to the proof. Let us apply an intrepid surgery to the spirit that would hoard wealth on earth, lest it impoverish our souls, and prove a sad reversion in the world to come.

It is no part of my purpose to determine the delicate question as to personal and family expenditures. Nor is it needful. If the principle of supreme love has passed over from self to Christ, this question can, and will, be easily settled by each individual. If self reigns, we shall be concerned to know how much we can do for our own temporal interest, and how little will answer for Christ. If Jesus reigns in our hearts, we shall only care to ask how little will serve for ourselves, and how much can be spared for our Master. Place the question under the burning focus of supreme love to the Redeemer, and the ligatures with which selfishness has bound up the heart will be consumed, and leave the soul to the generous impulses of Christian gratitude. To a man whose breast dilates with such pure and blissful emotions, what are the pleasures, the elegancies, the glories of wealth, but

> "Snow that falls upon a river,
> A moment white, then gone forever."

Instead of using his wealth to pamper the lusts of the flesh, he will account it his honor and happiness to use it for the glory of God in the conversion of sinners. Alas, how often are these poor vanities with which men regale the passing moment balanced,—in the souls of lost heathen,—by the weight of eternal woe! O, could that professed Christian, who lavishes upon his princely establishment, and his habitual luxuries, an uncounted and ungrudged expenditure, while he doles out, with apparent reluctance, a few scores, or at most, a few hundreds of dollars for the salvation of the world, have his eyes opened to the true relations of things,—could he look upon his possessions in the light of eternal realities, and with a vision quickened, like that of Elisha's servant,—he would see them spotted with the blood of souls. The guilty proof of his neglect of lost immortals, would cry out against him from all his beautiful things.

It is a fearful thought, that property, which God intended for his own glory, will be avenged on those who have compelled it to serve their selfish lusts. Every dollar thus perverted will become a swift witness before God, of all the base uses to which it has been degraded. Alas, how hard are some men toiling to accumulate the testimony which is to strike them dumb with guilt in the day of judgment! Be it our care to make friends of this mammon, by a faithful consecration of it to the cause of Christ, so that in Jesus' name, it may plead for us before the throne, in many an act of faith, in many a deed of kindness, in many a soul saved, in many an idolater brought out of darkness into marvelous light.

Finally, all our gifts and consecrations to the cause of missions will be in vain, unless God makes them effectual by the almighty co-operation of the Holy Spirit. This work began with a dispensation of the Spirit. At that first missionary meeting, already referred to, Jesus breathed on his assembled disciples, and said, "Receive ye the Holy Ghost." On the very day they commenced their ministry, a still more affluent outpouring of the Spirit fell upon them, like a mighty, rushing wind, with cloven tongues of fire. From that day to this, the work has prospered only as the same omnipotent agency has attended the labors of the church. If that is withdrawn, the missions languish and die. It is the great rain of God's strength, without which all spiritual vegetation ceases.

But this indispensable blessing is usually bestowed only in answer to prayer. The Apostles were praying and waiting for it when it descended on the day of Pentecost. When Christians feel the chill and darkness caused by the partial suspension of the Spirit's influence, and begin to sigh and yearn after him, lifting up penitent hands in earnest prayer, for his return, then the time of visitation draws nigh. Just here, then, lies a special and most important duty. The American Board of Missions was prayed into existence, by Judson and Hall, Mills and Newell, and other devoted spirits, whose hearts the Lord had touched. It has been borne up, ever since, on the breath of prayer. Prayer has planted every mission, and wrestled into the kingdom every heathen convert. Let us not dream of success without prayer. If deserted monthly concerts indicate that the churches are growing weary of intercession, the effects will surely be seen in some new check of the missionary work, and in some deeper decline of piety at home. What need we more than this decay of prayer, to account for the religious declension which now afflicts the land? Why else this cessation of revivals—this falling off of religious activities—this lull of the breeze that kept every thing astir—this spiritual languor and stagnation? Yet it is not, we trust, an absolute and final departure. The Holy Spirit hovers near, and prayer may call him forth again, to breathe fresh vitality into this scene of religious inaction. This moral torpor by no means forbids the hope of revival. Such moments have we seen in nature, when motion sleeps, and life itself holds its breath. You stand upon the hill-top on a summer's day. It is an hour of calm repose; the elements are still; each leaf motionless; smokes rise perpendicularly; the sail drops idly against the mast; the ship becalmed waits for the propelling force; clouds rest on their beds of ether, solid and immovable as castles of marble, or mountains of snow; and the "mute, still air" lays upon the earth like

"Music slumbering on her instrument."

Presently, you perceive a change in the outline of yon marble castle. Its turrets and towers begin to dissolve; the mountains are flowing down, and the whole vast pile is on the move; like some immense fleet, it has weighed anchor, and is sailing over the etherial ocean. You drop your eye to earth, and observe that the smokes are deflected now, and swayed in the same direction as the moving cloud; the tree-tops, too, are in motion; every leaf is lifted, and pointed in the direction of the flying vapor. The ripe fields of grass and grain are roughened into rolling waves. And commerce, rousing from her temporary sleep, lifts up her glad pennons, shakes out her idle canvas, and, ploughing her way through the deep, soon whitens the sea with her wings, and hastens to enrich all lands with her treasures.

What the wind is to this scene of joyous life and activity, the breath of the Holy Spirit will be to the church and the world, when he visits them with his reviving grace. Waited for, longed for, prayed for, by devout souls, he at length moves on the face of the great deep, and awakes life from apparent death. Wherever his influence passes over a community, it gives a common impulse to all hearts that feel it. It turns every quickened soul towards God, as the breeze points every leaf of the forest in one direction. It sweeps over states and nations, and whatsoever it touches, springs into life. It leaves the impress of holiness on every heart, and in every home it visits. Following the track of its progress over the earth and through the ages, a spirit of praise and thanksgiving rises to God with the choral grandeur of the great Reformation; it ascends from beneath the majestic arches and fretted vaults of old cathedrals, from within the walls of humble conventicles, and from under the roofs of private dwellings; it reverberates from the rocks of Switzerland, from the glens and caves of Scotland, and from the wilds of America. And as the sublime movement rolls on, the same sweet song comes up from heathen lands, from the homes of idolaters, from amid scenes dark with the blood of human sacrifices,—until at last the whole world is vocal with its resounding echoes.

Why should it be thought a thing incredible that God should do this? Is it more than he has promised? Is it more than he is able to perform? Is it more than he will certainly do, at some future period? Has not his Spirit often given assurance both of his power and of his purpose to fill the whole earth with the knowledge of the Lord? And at this present crisis,—by these rough and stormy winds, tearing up old institutions of oppression and cruelty, driving the ploughshare of his judgments under the roots of ancient and mighty wrongs which obstruct the progress of his course, and shaking the nations of the earth,—does he not indicate that the 'Desire of all flesh is coming,' to make "new heavens and a new earth wherein dwelleth righteousness"? May we not accept this tremendous overturning, as one of those grand steps in the historic march of divine Providence, which signalize great eras of religious advancement? The contrast between our own peaceful work of love and the present scene of civil war, is indeed painfully impressive; but it were disregarding the most instructive lessons of history, to deny that, bloody as it is, this conflict may be working out results of happy omen to the kingdom of Christ in general, and to the cause of missions in paritcular.

Yes, our work shall yet be accomplished! The cause shall triumph! The kingdom of Christ shall overspread the earth! "He shall see of the travail of his soul, and be satisfied." We are toiling for no uncertain end. "He that goeth forth and weepeth, bearing precious seed, shall doubtless come again rejoicing, bringing his sheaves with him." It is the faithful laborer who will shout the harvest home. His will be the crowning joy of that hour, when the ransomed of the Lord shall come up in countless millions,—from Greenland and China, from India and Africa, and the far-distant islands of the sea,—washed in the blood of the Lamb, radiant with the beauty of holiness, to receive their immortal crowns. And as they "pass through glory's morning gate," the whole host of the redeemed will hail the returning conquerors in the rapturous strains of the victor's song,—

> "The soft peace-march, beating, Home, brothers, Home"!

And welcoming angels respond,—

> "Home, brothers, Home"!

The Missionary Enterprise a True Development of the Life of the Church.

A

SERMON,

BEFORE THE

AMERICAN BOARD OF COMMISSIONERS FOR FOREIGN MISSIONS,

AT THEIR

MEETING IN WORCESTER, MASS.

OCTOBER 4, 1864.

BY

JONATHAN B. CONDIT, D. D.
Professor of Sacred Rhetoric and Pastoral Theology, in Auburn Theological Seminary.

BOSTON:
PRESS OF T. R. MARVIN & SON, 42 CONGRESS STREET.
1864.

AMERICAN BOARD OF COMMISSIONERS FOR FOREIGN MISSIONS.

WORCESTER, MASS., OCTOBER, 1864.

Resolved, That the thanks of the Board be presented to the Rev. Dr. CONDIT, for his Sermon preached on Tuesday evening, and that he be requested to furnish a copy for publication.

Attest,

SAMUEL M. WORCESTER, *Rec. Secretary.*

SERMON.

PHILIPPIANS II. 15, 16.

AMONG WHOM YE SHINE AS LIGHTS IN THE WORLD; HOLDING FORTH THE WORD OF LIFE.

THE responsibility of this hour is of no ordinary kind. The cause of missions in its eventful history, in its wide reach—looking to the restoration of a world to the allegiance of Christ, in its present posture, necessitous yet hopeful, makes a demand on him who pleads it, in view of which he may well tremble. What words shall he speak, so that something may be added to the power of the church in this work of love? His duty is plain. Let him take his position on the foundation which Christ has laid, and exalt the unchanging principles of his kingdom. Then under the blended light of providence and promise, let him shape his plea in harmony with the process by which God is working for the conversion of the world. The text will be an appropriate guide to such a plea. "Among whom ye shine as lights in the world; holding forth the word of life."

Light and darkness represent two opposite states in which men are found. One is known by its intellectual and moral elevation; the other by its prevalent ignorance and corruption. Christ is the source of light. "In him was life, and the life was the light of men." From the era of its rising to the present time, it has been struggling with the darkness. "It shineth in darkness, but the darkness comprehendeth it not." As the struggle goes on, the lines which bound it are pierced here and there by its rays—the presage of a fuller shining. Indeed it has already "touched and glanced" on many lands not long since wrapped in darkness; and faith anticipates the day when it shall become an all-pervading radiance.

The provision for extending this light is a beautiful example of divine wisdom. In one form of it, it depends on the principle of reflection. Character, moulded by Christianity, embodies its lessons and virtues, and becomes a living expression of the truth. It is a source of light all around; in its full power "like the disk of the sun sending out a ray of light from every point in its surface." Another method is by the inculcation of truth, to show unto men the way of salvation. In both modes, the experience of the power of the word is an essential condition, and will be a guide to us in this attempt to unfold the true philosophy of the missionary enterprise. They, to whom the light has come with a saving influence, are not only invested with the commission, but with the spiritual endowment, for spreading it over the whole earth. The truth, therefore, to which I ask your attention is this,—

The missionary enterprise is a true development of the life of the church.

False views are often entertained of the relation of this work to the church. Some regard it as a scheme which has its origin, like that of many worldly enterprises, in the invention of ambitious minds; sustained by a passion for achievement, and therefore destined to a short existence. Others treat it as the fruit of an enthusiasm, in which there is no fair estimate of the power of Christianity, or of the power of the church to spread it; and having no intelligent principle as its basis: a scheme appended to the church, so morally significant as for a time to arrest attention; but economically unsound, and hence must ere long be a failure.

A system of effort for the renovation of the world must stand or fall by this test—Has it a foundation in that which is true, effective, and permanent? Is it the result of deep spiritual convictions? Has it an inner spring that can originate and sustain a steady movement against the powers of darkness? Life in the church seeks a development. This is true of all life. The nature of the life determines the form of its development. There is the never ceasing process in nature, from the germ to the stately tree, with its growing stock and branches. Life in man is the spring of growth and varied activity. A nation's life is manifested under the operation of some one or more grand principles. It may give the supremacy to a single principle. This determines the form of its institutions, the efficiency and direction of its forces. It exemplifies this principle to all the world. According to its resources, and the devotion with which this idea is cherished, it is executing a mission to spread it among other nations. Its code defines it; its diplomacy is based on it; its flag is a symbol of it; its whole economy is its out-growth.

The life of the church is spiritual. The church is not a device of human policy; nor the product of circumstances in a given age. Neither is it a mere corporation, with its constitution, by-laws, and varied machinery, to perpetuate a privileged rank in its membership, and issue edicts against error and sin. It has its organization, its forms of worship, and modes of action; but it is a divine creation, deriving its life from God, and living on, because it is imbued with his life-giving Spirit. The development of its life is not a contest for supremacy in ecclesiastical power; nor a splendid frame-work of offices and titled dignities, guarding the sacred enclosure. Neither is it simply a zeal and courage in the maintenance of theological dogmas. As the spiritual body of Christ, it has holy principles, sympathies and aims, which exalt it as a great moral power, with a mission of mercy to the race. This its character indicates its true development in the missionary enterprise. This will appear as we consider some of the *essential elements of a spiritual, living church.*

I. The life of the church has its foundation in faith, or a deep, spiritual conviction of truth. Philosophy speaks of a "connection between the various forces of nature," suggesting that they have a "common root, or that they form a circle whose links are connected." We note a corresponding fact in the spiritual forces of the church. They have a common root in its inner life. They come forth in intimate union, and combine their strength in every department of service. In this circle of spiritual forces faith is the primary one, because it is the instrument of the interior working of truth, by which it becomes spirit and life. It appropriates the provisions of atoning mercy, and secures the needed culture for all the graces.

Christianity is directly connected with piety by its doctrines. Truth is called the "word of life" in the text, not merely because it reveals a life to come, but because it is the means used by the Spirit in the production of spiritual life. It pervades all genuine, Christian experience, and is ever a source of growth in holiness. It is not merely a creed, embalmed as a venerated symbol, to be handed down through successive generations—a monument in the history of religious opinions; but an inworking force through all the powers and affections. There must be more than an intellectual conviction of it. Spiritual life begins when the heart is opened to the entrance of the word, so that it penetrates with light and energy. Here we have the primary, impelling force to the dissemination of truth. Philosophy and the Bible agree on this point. The language of an eminent philosopher is, "If a man makes a mental advance, some mental discovery. . . what is the desire that takes possession of him at the very moment he makes it? It is the desire to promulgate his sentiment to the exterior world—to publish and realize his thought. When a man acquires a new truth, has acquired a new gift, immediately there becomes joined to this acquirement the notion of a mission." The Bible says, as the language of Christian experience, "We believe and therefore speak"—'we cannot suppress the truth which faith has accepted. Having this new discovery of the beauty and excellence of divine realities, we desire in every possible way to make them known to all people.'

Great power is vested in the truths of the Gospel; as they unfold the character and government of God; the glory of the Redeemer and his work of mercy for our lost race; and the character and condition of man, by nature a child of wrath, with no hope of restoration to holiness and bliss, but through the atonement of Christ. We may set our seal to them in a public confession; analyze and defend them with dialectic skill; and they may have no more effect upon us than the common places of any familiar science. But they cannot be inwrought in the man by the power of the Holy Spirit, and be powerless. Can the soul come into fellowship with these divine thoughts in all their celestial power and heat, given to guide us to heaven, without being aroused to publish them in the hearing of all men? Can they who have made such spiritual discoveries as faith imparts, and who, after the test of a blessed experiment, can say, 'We know whom we have believed,' have no care to put the world in possession of such knowledge? If the philosopher, who has found a theory in science, which overthrows a prevalent error, hastens to the work of convincing the world of the truth of it; not less urgent will be the experience of the power of divine truth to lift others into the light of it. An eminent Christian scholar, tracing the history of doctrine in successive periods of the church, has recently said, "The scientific expansion of a single doctrine results in the formation of a particular type of morality or piety; which again shows itself in active missionary enterprises, and the spread of Christianity through great masses of heathen population." What then must be the effect, when all these great truths of the Gospel dwell in the very heart of the church, the spring of its joy and strength? When Luther received the doctrine of justification by faith, it became the master of his heart and all his powers, chartering them for the work of propagating the truth through all Germany. There is nothing mysterious in the fact, that the disciple of mere natural religion has no care to disturb Pagan mind in its moral death; that he has no longing of soul, no spirit of self-sacrifice prompting him to go forth on a mission. But faith embodies in the believer's life truths of such import and value, that the heart is deeply moved toward such an engagement. As it is a realization of these in respect to man's eternal destiny, what can suppress its tendency as a living force within, to give them extension?

Faith acts too in the light of the promise that "the earth shall be full of the knowledge of the

Lord." Accepting the promise as that which cannot fail, it expands to the compass of the promised achievement. This is no romantic idea of a golden era in the future, luring men by baseless visions to a certain disappointment. Faith rests on the unchangeable word of Jehovah, who has authority and power to subject all agencies to his service. The desire for the propagation of the word is not left to fall back on itself because there is no answer to the question, How can it be done? Faith gives the answer. Directing the soul to God as the author of its own light and peace, it associates every conquest of truth with his power and faithfulness. It receives the announcement that this world shall be converted to righteousness, not as a possibility, not as an event subject to circumstances which often cause a failure in human projects, but as a glorious certainty; keeping before the heart, especially in every adverse hour, the promise of the Master, "And, lo, I am with you alway, even to the end of the world." Paul appreciated this development of faith in the direction of missionary effort, when he said to the church in Corinth, "Having hope when your faith is increased, that we shall be enlarged by you, according to our rule abundantly, to preach the Gospel in the regions beyond you."

This then is the power of a deep spiritual conviction of truth. And when men in darkness are now crying, Who will give us light? Where is the tablet from heaven, on which we can read the lessons of truth adapted to the immortal spirit? Will not the faith of the church spring with augmented energy to embrace the auspicious moment? Surely those who hear this voice, having proved the efficacy of truth, will be prompted to go forth, announcing to the benighted multitude, 'We have found him of whom Moses in the law, and the prophets did write, Jesus of Nazareth. Come and see. Come and read the lines of mercy, written by the finger of God. Look up, for the day-star has risen in the heavens. Listen, for a voice comes from the excellent glory, This is my beloved Son, in whom I am well pleased; hear ye him.'

II. The sympathy of the church with Christ in the purpose of his life and death, has its direct development in the work of extending the Gospel. As the life of the church has its origin and support in him, there is implied an intimate union with him. It is such a union that he comes into sympathy with his people; manifesting it in kind watching, effectual protection, and holy intercession. They also come into sympathy with him, adopt his cause, and respond in the heart's deepest voice to the language of his heart. As each can say, "I am crucified with Christ; nevertheless, I live; yet not I, but Christ liveth in me;" so he becomes identified with the work of him whose great purpose was to seek and to save that which was lost. By the very law of the new life, this sympathetic element must have expression in the pursuit of the object to which the Saviour consecrated himself. Believers must determine its claims upon them, according to the position to which he exalted it, by the costliest sacrifice infinite love could make. They cannot live in intimate fellowship with him, and fail to catch the fire of his heart. As they see him filled with his high purpose, and pressing on to its accomplishment amid determined opposition; and then hear his memorable words, 'And I, if I be lifted up on the cross, will draw all men unto me;' can they help coming with "hearts warm from the cross," into the work of bringing all men under its attractions?

Let not this sympathy be regarded as a mere emotion, and not an element of character. It has the force and permanence of a principle. If it imparts tenderness to the spirit, so also courage and decision. The gentleness which it begets is a reflection of the spirit of the Lamb of God, which blends with, and gives dignity and charm to the earnest purpose—"I must work the works of him that sent me while it is day." While Paul is passing his imprisonment at Rome, waiting the decision of his destiny for life or death, he sends his sympathizing words to his former flock at Philippi—all self-forgetful, with no defiant spirit towards his enemies, with no complaining appeal to his friends. But at the same moment, with his heart leaning on the bosom of his Lord, his sympathy with him flows out in the calm, majestic purpose of one whose "taste it was, to believe, to suffer, and to love,"—"For me to live is Christ,"—'I have nothing to recall of past devotion to him. If I live, it shall be to exemplify his spirit, and spread abroad the knowledge of his name. I am bound in my life's best energies, and to my latest breath, to the object of his life.' When the modern missionary says, contemplating a violent death at the hands of his enemies, 'My life is given to Christ; he will take care of it, if it is his will that I live; I am set here to work, and, if need be, to die for him;' we find the spring of such heroism in this warm sympathy with Christ. Indeed you cannot separate it from the hopes and obligations of believers. We have traced its root in the gracious life within. It grows under the culture of the Spirit, and adds strength to the bond which unites the soul with Christ. It is on this as a principle of action Gospel arguments for duty and sacrifice fix their grasp. It is an ever-living power, forming the character after Christ as the model. When he said, "My meat is to do the will of him that sent me and to finish his work," he declared the fixed purpose of his life. It awaked with every morning light; each day teemed with some new manifestation of his heart of love. It bore him onward till the last blow was struck, which was needful to turn out the invasion of sin, and restore this world to the service of its Maker. This was the mind of Christ. Sympathy with him is the mind of the man; not a temporary emotion to be started into being at every new phase of the necessities of the world. It underlies that career of consecrated living, in which the object of the Saviour's heart is embraced in its commanding attitude and claims.

III. Another element of the life of the church which gives the same direction to its efforts, is love to man. This is inseparable from sympathy with

Christ. Faith and love are also combined in the union of believers to him. If one is the instrument that forms it, the other seals and binds it. If faith accepts the privilege, it works by love to manifest the union when formed; not only love to Christ, but also to man for whom he died. Love to man has indeed a foundation in what he is, and in the relation of one to another. He possesses marks wherever you meet him, which assure you that he is your brother. He has an intelligent spirit, giving out a spark, when you touch it with truth, which indicates its alliance with immortality. He has hopes and fears and cravings like your own. The millions without the Gospel, bowing down to their "gods many," are your brethren. But looking at man in the light of Jesus' love to him, and in sympathy with his manifestation of it, love assumes a new tone and vigor. You have pondered such questions as these—What does the law of love to a brother enjoin us to do for him? Have we that which will make these dead men live again? Have we that which will restore their debased natures, so that they shall shine in the likeness of God? Go, sit beneath the cross, and let the heart kindle under its power; and you will give a right practical answer to these questions. It will put every sinner of the race in the position of one who has a common right with you to the blessings of the Gospel. It will show that the mercy seat where you go for pardon was built for him as well as for you; and that the atonement of Christ is ample for all, in all their guilt. The cross not only reveals the depth and corruption of the sepulchre in which men are buried, but also the possibility of a resurrection to moral beauty and happiness. It defines the way in which we may pour light into their dark hearts, make them awake from their spiritual death, throw off their grave-clothes, and put on the vestments of purity and love.

Here is light concerning man in his ruin, and the method of his deliverance, which no Grecian sage, no Confucius, nor "Doctors of eternal reason" have furnished—the source and nourisher of that love which is another name for the religion of the Bible. It has no true definition in any other professed system of truth. It has had no lodgment in human hearts under the teachings of human wisdom. Here it is, at once the child of the cross, and the inspiration of the infinite heart. When the missionary stands the representative of this principle amid the narrow, selfish systems of religion which cover the heathen world, it is in this he is a mystery to their disciples. What wonder is it, that at first they count him a selfish schemer? That they suspect him of concealing some mercenary design under a profession of love to their souls? And I may add, what wonder is it, that, at length, the power with which this love invests him, is the means of opening their hearts to his message? What more reasonable interpretation of such a mission to save them, than that the religion he brings to them is divine? The message itself—the reasonings, the appeals, the tone and tear, with which he enforces it, all bespeak the origin of that love in him who first exemplified it in a mission from heaven to save sinners.

The work of evangelizing the world by the system of Christian missions, carries with it its own explanation. It is the love of Christ to man, reproducing itself in his followers. It is in every converted soul a power for the conversion of other souls. When you say, that the law of love to man is founded in my constitution, I respond to it. But expound it as the Saviour breathed it; stamp it with the signet of his heart; publish it, not only arrayed in the majesty of Sinai, but also in the glories of Calvary; it comes with an incomparably stronger force. Love then becomes the passion of a heart enlarged to embrace a world. It kindles an energy that breaks down the wall of selfishness, that cannot be baffled by the forces of evil, nor discouraged before any degree of corruption and misery. It seeks to get the ear of every wanderer from God, and tell him of the way to eternal life. It craves the privilege of going into every jungle, of traversing every mountain and valley, where man in his wretchedness dwells, to minister to his soul the balm of the Gospel. It longs to stop before every altar of heathenism, where deluded worshippers are offering their sacrifices, and point them to the one great sacrifice for sin, saying, "Behold the Lamb of God, which taketh away the sin of the world." It would make the circuit of the globe, spreading the knowledge of Jesus "wide as sunshine."

IV. But with this faith in God, sympathy with Christ, and love to man, is combined a desire for the glory of God, as a principle of church-life. God established and has preserved the church for his own glory. When his Son came down to redeem the world, angels ushered in his coming with the ascription, Glory to God in the highest. When he was about to leave the world, he said, "Father, I have glorified thee on the earth." Then he identified his followers with this end. "Herein is my Father glorified, that ye bear much fruit; so shall ye be my disciples." 'Ye have received the truths of my Gospel; they have become to you the elements of a new life; now manifest that inward power to the glory of its divine Author.' "Let your light so shine before men, that they may see your good works, and glorify your Father who is in heaven." They come under the power of this principle of action. The grace that made them new creatures, gives this direction to their spiritual activity. Their first act of self-consecration is a declaration of this desire—let God be glorified. Such a desire, united with a sense of obligation, never dies, but grows with every new discovery of the riches of Christ. As the new life becomes deeper and stronger, the tide of gratitude rises, bearing the soul upward in an ever-increasing devotion to the honor of God.

This principle has its fit expression in the work of missions. This appears in view of the origin of the enterprise. God's hand was in it at the beginning. Some have seen in it so much of human wisdom and calculation, that they have forgotten it was no device of man. Its charter came from the lips of Christ just before he left the world. The first action under that charter had the broad seal of his authority and power. It was the unfolding of spiritual life under the striking manifestations of his providence and spirit. In respect to the origin of missions in this land, we may challenge the world to give any other explanation of it than this—it was the result of a direct and wonderful movement of God. In it was heard his "still small voice." It was no conventional plan to match the powers of evil. It was no scheme of youthful ambition to get a name. No messengers came from the heathen world with a warm appeal to Christian sensibility. There was no assurance of an open door to the Gentiles. What then was the spring of that movement? There was a waking up of spiritual life in a few faithful servants of Christ, under a special, divine influence—a development of faith, Christlike sympathy and love, which demanded the consecration of themselves to the missionary work. The hand of God was there. When he touched the hearts of those noble men, they rose to a position of faith and hope, to a sublimity of purpose, far in advance of the church. Thence a power went forth, which has been steadily spreading till the present moment. As we now turn the eye back to the scene of its remarkable beginning, more than half a century ago, is not every heart ready to ascribe the glory to God?

The relation of the enterprise to this end appears also in the fact, that God is the source of power in its execution. A master-spirit may infuse into it an inventive skill, and the energy of an indomitable purpose, which will command admiration; but God gives it success and thus connects it with his own glory. What has been the import of all the despatches that have come to us, reporting the triumphs of truth by our missionary forces? What is the voice of that "nation born in a day" in the Sandwich Islands, coming to us from its churches, schools, and household altars? What is the testimony of the infant churches in Turkey and Ceylon? Or that which reaches us so often in gladdening tones from revival scenes in the Nestorian mission? Should I ask a representative from some mission field, now with us, he would stand up and cry, "Not by might, nor by power, but by my Spirit, saith the Lord of Hosts." This truth which shines out amid Apostolic successes, is prolonged in the achievements of the Reformation, and in the victories of the Gospel to-day. You see the church in battle, then rejoicing in victory; in darkness, then emerging into light; moving on with an inextinguishable life; kings coming to its fold, and kingdoms regenerated; but at each successive step all are prepared to join in the doxology, "Not unto us, O Lord, not unto us, but unto thy name, give glory, for thy mercy and thy truth's sake."

At length, in the universal extension of the Gospel, the church will have its complete development; and every part of the work done will reflect the glory of God. The church will be made up of a redeemed multitude which no man can number, of all nations, and kindreds, and people and tongues. They will gather in throngs from China. India will add her long procession. From the land of the patriarchs and prophets accessions will be made to the vast company. The children of Africa will come in redeemed from their bondage, and made free in Christ. The dwellers on every continent and island will swell the host, to meet the Lord, when he comes to be glorified in his saints and to be admired in all them that believe. They will stand clothed in white robes, each having a harp and a song. As they look at the wrath they merited, and the grace that rescued them; at what they were, and at what they now are; wearing the seal of a gracious adoption; heirs of a kingdom prepared for them; they will sing with one voice—"Blessing, and honor, and glory, and power, be unto him that sitteth upon the throne, and unto the Lamb, forever and ever." This is the end of the perfectly developed life of the church. "When the Lord shall build up Zion, he shall appear in his glory." In Christ, all the building fitly framed together, has grown to a holy temple in the Lord. Glorious temple of Zion! An eternal monument of grace to the honor of God! In every one of its "lively stones" his image shines; and the blended radiance of every part is the manifested glory of the builder. This is the consummation to which the power of the church in the missionary enterprise is directed.

Is it said that the voice of history is not in harmony with the truth which I have aimed to establish? Though the energy of a living church has not always been put forth in missionary effort, it is not difficult to trace the influences that have prevented it. Some may suggest an explanation derived from the process of nature. As the life of the tree in winter is not discernible in the blossom and the fruit, so spiritual life in God's people must have its winter season, when its ordinary fruits are not brought forth. We do not recognize any such established law in the kingdom of grace. The primitive development of the church was, in an eminent degree, of the missionary type. The early disciples, if not at first appreciating the diffusive spirit of the Gospel, soon accepted the token from heaven to give it extension. But the life of the church was ere long impaired by the prevalence of an unholy ambition and a worldly policy. Formalism took the place of spiritual devotion. The awakenings of the Reformation were marked by the outflowing of sympathy with the cause of Christ. But the reasons are obvious to all why no system of effort was adopted for the extension of truth to other lands. The spirit of the Reformation, if it had not been perverted, would have led forth an emancipated church to teach the nations. But the direction given to the learning and energy of the age, by some controlling minds, checked that development which the springing life of the church indicated. A missionary zeal was not characteristic of the piety of the seventeenth century in England. Extension beyond its own sphere was not a quality of the sanctified intellect of that period, distinguished as it was for effort and sacrifices in behalf of the truth. The consciences of good men were educated in another direction. They believed they were doing the work of their generation in contending for the faith. While we acknowledge the value of their labors, we cannot fail to see that the secular and ecclesiastical influences of the age prevented the wealth of intellectual and moral power vested in it, from being consecrated to the work of evangelizing the nations. Richard Baxter, almost if not quite alone, among ruling minds of the time, looked out with a sympathizing heart over a benighted world. We are not surprised that this holy man, who wrought with burning zeal for the salvation of men around him, had such sympathy with the condition of the heathen world, and a longing heart to do something to save it. We are not surprised, that as he stood among two thousand ministers ejected from their pulpits by the arm of power, he saw little to regret if they could but go forth, a missionary band, to preach the Gospel to "Tartars, Turks, and heathens." Let God be praised that he has put the church in this land in such a posture, and under such a ministration of the Spirit, that its life may have its true development in the spread of the truth. It is not ours to question the ways of God in the trust assigned to good men at different periods. But it becomes us to accept the spiritual emancipation which he has wrought for us; opening to us the wide field of the world, and enlarging the faith of many to go up and take possession of it for Christ. It now shines out, as at "the beginning of the Gospel," that the life of the church demands the form of aggressive action, instead of that which is chiefly self-protective. Not merely the erection of defences to resist attack; aiming at little more than to preserve the order and prestige of the church. Not the forces of the church in an encampment, answering at roll-call for an occasional drill; most of the time with armor off, satisfied with a secure resting place; but enlisted and organized for one long campaign; pushing out on every side to make conquests for Christ, and binding conquered foes to his standard.

We are now prepared to see the value of God's discipline of his church, as adapted to develop its life in the missionary work. It is first in the form of *conflict*. Opposition began with the Apostolic missions, and is still continued. Not always in the form of bloody persecution; sometimes it is by the agency of wealth, philosophy and learning, designed to crush the truth and strengthen false systems of religion. Then it is the discipline of *loss*. The work of missions has put on such magnitude and responsibility, in its various departments, that it calls most earnestly for the consecration of men of the highest culture, as well as those of most ardent devotion. Such sons of the church are its great necessity. But, as in the past, so recently, noble men have been stricken down, while still strong and "valiant in fight" for the Lord of hosts. As Stoddard, Bridgman, and Dwight have fallen, we have been ready to say, the cause of missions cannot spare them. It has also been the discipline of *delay*. We have heard of the "quickness with which the barrenness of some northern regions is turned into a paradise, so that there appears to be no interval between the frost and the flowers;" and some have indulged the hope that thus quickly the moral desert would be made to rejoice and blossom as the rose. They have found it easy in theory to leap into results, and gather them speedily around the beating heart of the church. They forget that God may have important ends to accomplish by leaving them to sow the seed and then wait long for the harvest. I believe that a more rapid progress awaits this enterprise. If the "day of the preparation" is not yet ended, the universal Sabbath of the church is hastening on. But the burden of the labor is yet upon us. God's command is—'Go work in my vineyard to-day, and whatsoever is right I will give you. Cast up, cast up the highway; gather out the stones; go through the step and the beat of the sower; drop the seed in the valleys and on the tops of the mountains; then like the husbandman, have long patience.' But now God's discipline is in another form. Never before has the church in this land felt his hand as it does to-day, when the nation is reeling under the shock of his fearful judgment. If this war is putting to the test the existence of our admirable Government, and taxing the wisdom and courage of our strongest men; is it not, in a special sense, a trial of the faith and devotion of the church?

Let us mark the connection of such varied discipline with the development of church-life. Uninterrupted success has tended to relaxation and forgetfulness of dependence on God. We cannot measure the growth of the church by its external prosperity. Its energies have been brought out in proportion to the demand—working most effectively under pressure. Put to the test in reverses, they have been nerved to bolder action. Let principle as the basis of action be supplanted by motives which are semi-secular, or founded in popular sympathy; let corruption take its seat in high places, and the names of men be exalted as bulwarks of the cause; let covetousness and worldly conformity prevail; then we may look for God's hand to be laid upon his people in some form of discipline, if he would recover them to a spiritual vitality and devotion. Obstacles to success multiply; helpers fail; defeat after defeat attends the forces of Zion. In such a time, no temporizing expediency will avail. It is soon felt that success can only come, by falling back on that element of strength, unyielding Christian principle. That principle now assumes new power. We have marked the wisdom of God in training men to meet the "moment to which heaven has joined great issues." The form of his providence was effective in developing individual life and energy. It is the spirit rocked in the storm, that is nurtured for doing great things. The same is true of national life. The principle of its life may be dormant. God puts the nation through a process of trial; when that principle strikes its roots deeper, and comes forth in a more vigorous manifestation. It demands emphatic expression. It begets an upheaving of mind to throw off corruption. It obeys the summons to the protection of endangered interests. That which is true of individual and national development, is a law in the church. One season of stern trial, like that through which we are now passing, may be worth a thousand fold more to the church, than many years without check or strait. We give thanks to-day that the churches have practically endorsed the recommendation to put five hundred thousand dollars into the treasury of the Board during the year now closed. Is it a mistake to interpret it as the fruit of an expanding spirit of benevolence under God's disciplinary providence? His hand is touching the heart of the church. Lessons of duty are now invested with unwonted solemnity. The sanctions of conscience put on a more impressive power. Motives derived from the peculiar displays of God's character and purposes, are arrayed with a penetrating force. Trust, love, sympathy, and a desire for the glory of God, are invigorated. Submission and patience are made to blend with a steadfast faith in prayer, and an energetic purpose in action. The church has sometimes been reduced to a feeble band, in the presence of enemies strong and defiant; so that some were led to say, its end is near. Yet, at that moment, it was drawing strength from a divine source, with which to go forward. Though scarred in battle, it came forth radiant with the light of promise, joyful in its leader, and loving the cause better by reason of the trial to which it was subjected. Discipline and development go together.

In conclusion, we ought to note the importance of the present moment for bringing out the strength of the church in the work committed to our hands. This is the point where there is reason for deep solicitude. God has opened the way for the church, but the inward, propelling power is wanting. If he binds us to this cause by his authority, so also by the very life he has imparted to us. The necessity of the hour is this—that the Spirit be poured upon us from on high, to produce a full exhibition of the principles of this inner life. The past admonishes us against retreat. The present reveals most impressively the necessity of multiplied resources. The future invites with all the attractions of promise—promise of needed aid and of ultimate success. In view of embarrassments, unbelief may prompt some to say, stop—wait for more decided tokens that God bids us advance, and make conquest of new territory for Christ. Shall we stop, when we have such proof of the power of the Gospel? Shall we stop, when we have such evidence of the capacity of the church to do the work, and of the faithfulness of God to give success to our efforts? Shall we stop, when voices come from the graves of those who have fallen in the fight, bidding us not to faint? When voices come from the more than one hundred and fifty churches gathered on heathen ground, calling us to help them in the onset against the powers of darkness? When voices come from myriads yet in bondage, sighing for deliverance? Stop? No, not till "great voices are heard in heaven, saying, The kingdoms of this world are become the kingdoms of our Lord and of his Christ; and he shall reign for ever and ever." We cannot stop. For what was this new life begotten within us? For what are we kept in this world? For what, if not to be the "light of the world and the salt of the earth?" We want no further sign of the Master's will. He gave it just before he ascended to his Father—"Go ye therefore and teach all nations." It is hung out to-day on the banner of the cross. No reverse shall take it down. The struggles of truth are not over. It has yet to meet mighty foes. But as in the past, when depressed, its friends few, and its enemies boasted that it was buried forever, it rose again and appeared unto many with a spiritual presence and power; has since lifted its voice on many a Pentecost, assailed many a strong-hold and gained the victory; so, as God is true, it shall live through every coming conflict, till it shall take the throne of universal empire. Blessed day, when the people of every land, lifted out of darkness and corruption, shall put on the "beautiful apparel" of truth and righteousness; and earth and heaven unite to celebrate the final victory of him who rose to conquer and to reign.

HOME MISSIONS.

A

SERMON

IN BEHALF OF THE

AMERICAN HOME MISSIONARY SOCIETY;

PREACHED IN THE CITIES OF NEW YORK AND PHILADELPHIA,

MAY, 1849;

BY

ALBERT BARNES.

NEW YORK:

PRINTED FOR THE AMERICAN HOME MISSIONARY SOCIETY,

BY WILLIAM OSBORN, SPRUCE STREET, CORNER OF NASSAU.

1849.

SERMON.

DEUTERONOMY I. 21.

BEHOLD, THE LORD THY GOD HATH SET THE LAND BEFORE THEE: GO UP AND POSSESS IT, AS THE LORD GOD OF THY FATHERS HATH SAID UNTO THEE; FEAR NOT, NEITHER BE DISCOURAGED.

I HAVE been requested to lay before you the cause of Home Missions in this country, as conducted by the "American Home Missionary Society." I use the text not as having reference originally to a subject like this, but as containing a principle which it is proper to apply on this occasion. It is this:—that when we are manifestly called by divine Providence to engage in an arduous and important enterprise, we are not to be discouraged or to fear. It may be added, also, in regard to the text, that the *language* is singularly appropriate to the object aimed at by this Society. If the text had been originally penned with reference to the train of thought which I wish to submit to you, I do not know that better language could have been chosen to indicate the main points in the argument. It would be entirely appropriate to say, respecting the field on which the Home Missionary Societies propose to operate in this country, that 'the land is set before us;' that we may regard ourselves as called upon by 'the Lord God of our fathers' to 'go up and possess it'—for we are in fact but carrying out the work which he conveyed them to these shores to accomplish; and that, in doing this, there is no reason why we should 'fear,' or be 'discouraged.' In a sense that is not merely constructive and figurative, we think that the God of our fathers summons the people of the present generation to take possession of this land for the cause of evangelical religion; and that great as is the labor of doing this, and formidable as are the obstacles in the undertaking, he commands us neither to fear nor be discouraged. It is my duty to make as clear and impressive a statement on this subject as I can, and to do this rather on the ground of what is proper to be said in order to place the subject fairly before you, than with reference to the inquiry whether the same things have not been as well, or better, said by those who have gone before me. Believing, as I do, that the salvation of the West, and consequently of our whole country, depends on the successful prosecution of this, and of kindred enterprises, I shall endeavor to set forth the reasons for this opinion in the most simple and direct way in my power.

In order to give some degree of lucid arrangement to my thoughts, I propose to arrange what I have to say under these three heads:—The field to be occupied; the contending elements in that field for the mastery; and the practicability of securing the ascendency of evangelical religion there. The last head will involve an inquiry as to the adaptedness of this Society to be one of the instrumentalities to secure that end. These points will bring out all that I wish to say on this occasion.

I. *The field.* Our Saviour, when speaking of the spread of his gospel, said, "the field is the world." As a subordinate, but essential, part of that greater work, we may say of the enterprise in which we are engaged, 'the field is our own country'—our whole country. Whatever in the original limits of the republic, or by voluntary or forced accession from time to time, is a part of our country, comes fairly within the field of our labors. Wherever, within these vast boundaries, there is a destitution of the preached gospel, whether we find it in some neglected spot in the older States of the Union; among the masses congregated in our cities; on the vast prairies of the West; or in the new and yet unexplored regions of Oregon, New Mexico, or California, there is the appropriate field of this Society's labors, and to that place it stands pledged before the world to convey the pure gospel, if the means are placed at its disposal. Yet, it will be no disparagement to the general argument, and it may serve to make a more definite impression, if, instead of directing our attention to that great field in general, embracing such a vast extent of territory, and such a variety in the degrees of civilization, refinement and religion, we endeavor to bring before us a single portion of this territory, and confine our attention to that. I refer now to what has been familiarly known as the Great West—that portion of our country to which the attention of this Society has been more particularly directed. To limit our view to this, will accord with the object before us on this occasion, because if *that* is secured, our country is safe; if that is lost, our liberties and our religion are at an end. I shall, therefore, confine my remarks in the main to that great Western Valley whose waters find their way to the "Father of Rivers." When speaking of this as the field of our labors, we naturally speak of the country itself, and of the character of the population.

Any number of men having resided in that country, or having, though in the most cursory manner, travelled over it, would be likely, in describing it, to bring up a different report in regard to it. Men look at objects from different points of view. They have different powers of observation, and different qualifications for judging accurately. Of so vast a land they would see different portions, and those with different degrees of advantage. Their conclusions would be determined much by their tastes; by their professions; by their education; by their purposes in residing there, or travelling there. The farmer would look at it from one point of view; the mechanic from another; the professional man from another; the statesman from another; the minister of the gospel from another. He who had expected to find only barbarism there, would be surprised at the cities, villages and towns, that, in magnificence, beauty and refinement, begin to rival those of the East; the man of over-refined sensibilities, or in a certain state of mind, would be mainly struck with the evidences of rapid degradation and a tendency to barbarism. When, in journeying through the wilderness, Moses sent out spies to search the land of Canaan, every man on his return seemed to be influenced in his report, by his idiosyncrasy, or by his previous habits of thought, or by the degree of his physical courage, or by something peculiar in his point of observation. All agreed, indeed, in the report that it was an exceedingly rich land—"flowing with milk and honey"—for, a proof of its amazing fertility they carried with them on their return. But a part, and the larger part, too, saw only giants, and walled towns, and barbarians, and cannibals. "Surely," said they, "it floweth with milk and honey. Nevertheless, the people be strong that dwell in the land, and the cities are walled and very great; and moreover we saw the children of Anak there. The land through which we have gone to search it, is a land that eateth up the inhabitants thereof; and all the people that we saw in it are men of a great stature. And there we saw the giants, the sons of Anak, which come of the giants; and we were in our own sight as grasshoppers, and so we were in their sight." It was only a small minority of that company that saw things in a more favorable light. "Caleb stilled the people before Moses, and said, Let us go up at once and possess it; for we be well able to overcome it." Numb. xiii.

In like manner, the reports which men bring up from the West to influence the Eastern mind, are as various as the points of view from which they contemplate it; as their own professions and callings; as their own temperaments—sanguine, choleric, melancholy, or phlegmatic; as the portions which they have traversed; as the time during which they have resided there:—perhaps as the season of the year in which they were there, or as the state of their bodies, whether bilious or well. All agree, indeed, that it is a vast land; and a land of surpassing fertility. But one sees there only the evidences of a worldly spirit, and reports that all the institutions of learning and religion are forgotten or trampled down. Another sees only evidence that infidelity abounds, and that it is to spread inevitably all over that land. Another comes back with the report that Romanism is destined to prevail there, and that nothing can save it from the projects of spiritual ambition that are formed in regard to it at Rome and Vienna. Another reports that that is not the first danger, but that the way to it is through a progressive and almost certain barbarism. Another is struck only with the countless numbers of emigrants there from the old world, transplanting the institutions of foreign lands, corrupting and diluting the principles of liberty, and constituting elements for the demagogue or the military chieftain. Another, amidst many things to excite solicitude, sees safe and salutary influences silently operating in all the discordant elements there, and reports that it will be easy to secure all that land for the cause of liberty, learning and religion.

I have had fewer advantages by which to judge on this subject than many who have spoken, but it is my duty to state the impressions which I entertain, and the reasons for those impressions.

The country has been often described; its extent has been set forth in figures; its fertility has been spoken of; its beauties have been dwelt upon, and yet no one has obtained a correct view of it by mere description, nor, probably, is it possible to convey to Eastern minds any adequate idea of what the West is destined to be. The "growth of the West," indeed, has become a familiar topic. "The West begins, in the apprehension of Eastern people, to represent a complex idea, embracing not one State or territory, but many States and territories. Eleven great States now enter into that idea, and, without including an acre of Minnesota, of the Missouri, Nebraska and Indian territories, of Oregon and California, it covers more ground, and is capable of sustaining a larger population, than England, Scotland, Ireland, Denmark, Belgium, France, Holland, and Portugal, united. Embraced within these limits are now six or eight millions of people, urging on the various forms of activity—ploughing, reaping, building, mining, forging—vexing the earth and water with incessant motion, under the most powerful stimulus, and with unprecedented success." Within those same limits, will soon be twenty millions, then fifty, then a hundred, then three hundred—and within a period not remote, according to the present law of progress, that land will contain a population larger than China has now:—and a population with all the advantages for effecting changes, and drawing forth the fertility of the richest soil in the world, and navigating the noblest rivers, and establishing churches and schools, and communicating with the rest of the world, which the press, and the power of steam, and the telegraph, and the best systems of education, can furnish. The arm which is to control this nation is to be there; the power which is to determine the question, whether this land is to enjoy the blessings of liberty, civilization and Christianity, is indubitably now developing itself beyond the mountains. "Every paper that comes to us tells us of the mighty energies of the West. 'A few years since,' said a gentleman at a public meeting, 'I was paddled in a birchen canoe all along the shores of Wisconsin, from Chicago to Green Bay, a distance of several hundred miles, seeing scarcly a white man.' Now, overlooking those waters stand the goodly towns of Sheboygan, Milwaukie, Southport and Racine—the market outlets of a hundred and fifty thousand people, lying at convenient distances behind them. On those upper lakes, the first steamboat was launched in 1818; now more than a hundred of the largest class are fully occupied with a commerce estimated at one hundred and fifty millions of dollars per annum. On those Western lakes and rivers, the number of steamboats, as reported to the 'River and Harbor Convention' at Chicago in 1847, was no less than twelve hundred, employing seventeen thousand persons in their navigation, besides four thousand keel and flat boats with their crews. And it was stated on the same occasion, that the total value of the commerce afloat on those inland waters, was $439,000,000; being double the amount of the whole *foreign* commerce of the nation."

Of the *extent* of the West, or of those portions of our country on which the effort is to be particularly made to spread evangelical religion, we may perhaps form the most just idea by procuring a map, and cutting out one of the older States, and seeing how often we can lay it down on some of the new States or territories. Let Massachusetts, for example, a State among the most influential in the Union, be such a divider. "Ohio and Kentucky could each be divided into *five* such States. Michigan, Illinois, Iowa, Wisconsin, are each equal in territory to *seven* such States. Missouri could be divided into *nine*. Texas alone could be divided into *forty-four* such States.

The territory ceded by the late treaty with Mexico, exclusive of that which is claimed by Texas, would make *seventy-two* States of the same dimensions. Our whole country could be apportioned into *four hundred and forty-eight* such States as Massachusetts." What a country! What a field for Christian enterprise!

No one from the East gets any just idea of the vastness of the West, from any mere description. No figures give any adequate conception of it. And even when one from the East has visited the West, and has passed along the ordinary lines of travel, or has struck out new and unfrequented paths for himself, while he feels that he had before no proper conception of the magnitude and resources of that land, he will also have this feeling, that he seems to himself to know less of it than he supposed he did before; that the older portions of his country dwindle into comparative insignificance; and that no one is in danger of over-estimating the importance of the efforts put forth to plant schools and colleges there, and to bring to bear upon it all the appliances of evangelical Christianity.

I visited the Falls of St. Anthony. I know not how other men feel when standing there, nor how men will feel a century hence when standing there—then not in the *West*, but almost in the centre of our great nation. But when I stood there, and reflected on the distance between that and the place of my birth and my home; on the prairies over which I had passed, and the stream—the "Father of Rivers"—up which I had sailed some five hundred miles into a new and unsettled land—where the children of the forest still live and roam—I had views of the greatness of my country such as I have never had in the crowded capitals, and the smiling villages of the East. Far in the distance did they then seem to be, and there came over the soul the idea of greatness, and vastness, which no figures, no description, had ever conveyed to my mind. To an inexperienced traveller, too, how strange is the appearance of all that land! Those boundless prairies seem as if they had been cleared by the patient labor of another race of men—removing all the forests, and roots, and stumps, and brambles, and smoothing them down as if with mighty rollers, and sowing them with grass and flowers—a race which then passed away, having built no houses of their own, and made no fences, and set out no trees, and established no landmarks, to lay the foundation of any future claim. The mounds which you here and there see, look, indeed, as if a portion of them had died, and had been buried there: but those mounds, and those boundless fields had been forsaken together. You ascend the Mississippi amidst scenery unsurpassed in beauty probably in the world. You see the waters making their way along an interval of from two to four miles in width—between bluffs of from a hundred to five hundred feet in height. Now the river makes its way along the eastern range of bluffs, and now the western, and now in the centre, and now it divides itself into numerous channels, forming thousands of beautiful islands—covered with long grass, ready for the scythe of the mower. Those bluffs, rounded with taste and skill such as could be imitated by no art of man, and set out with trees here and there gracefully arranged like orchards, seem to have been sown with grain to the summit, and are clothed with beautiful green. You look out instinctively for the house and barn; for flocks, and herds; for men, and women, and children—but they are not there. A race that is gone seems to have cultivated those fields, and then to have silently disappeared—leaving them for the first man that should come from the older parts of our own country, or from foreign lands, to take possession of them. It is only by a process of reflection, that you are convinced that it is not so. But it is not the work of man. It is God who has done it, when there was no man there—save the wandering savage, alike ignorant and unconcerned as to the design of the great processes in the land where he roamed;—God who did all this, that he might prepare it for the abode of a civilized and Christian people.

The population that is spreading over that Western world, is as remarkable in its character as are the natural features of the land. That that country has been reserved and prepared for some mighty development in the purposes of divine Providence, is too plain to need any proof; and the people whom he is summoning there from all parts of the world are a people, who, if right influences are brought to bear upon them, will make it hereafter as eminent in moral beauty as it is now in the richness of its scenery, and the fertility of its soil. God prepared the Pilgrims to make New England what it now is; he has put it in the power of this generation to make the West what it ever onward should be. That it is not *now* what it should be, may be admitted. That there are evils existing, and evils to be apprehended, may be also admitted. In our attempts to make the Western mind what it should be, and to plant there the institutions of learning and religion, it is important to have a distinct view of what that Western mind *is*, that we may see more clearly what is the work to be done, and may have a more just view of what are likely to be the ultimate results.

The Western mind is, in its elements, capable of great energy and power. I refer now to it as it appears in its original composition, and before it is brought under any of the peculiar influences existing there. This results from the fact that it is always that kind of mind that goes out to explore unknown regions; to visit distant lands; to navigate dangerous seas. We look for energy, therefore, for enterprise, for hardihood, for determination, for a power and a purpose to overcome difficulties. Were that mind homogeneous, and under the right kind of influence, it would be just the mind adapted to the West. But it is not homogeneous. For the world itself is not homogeneous; and nearly all the world has its representatives there. It is a strange and mighty intermingling of minds of great power, under different propensities and views—constituting such a population as the world has never before seen on the settlement of a new land. The colonies that went out from Phenicia, and that laid the foundations of empire on the shores of the Mediterranean, had a homogeneousness of character, and transferred the principles and feelings of the mother country at once to the new lands where they took up their abode. The colonies that went out from Greece to occupy the maritime regions of Asia Minor, carried with them the love of the arts, of literature, and of liberty, which distinguished Corinth and Athens; and Ionia became merely a reflected image of what Attica, and Achaia, and Argolis had been. The colonies which landed on Plymouth rock, at Salem, and at Boston, were the same people, with no intermingling of foreign elements contemplated or permitted. Substantially so it was in Pennsylvania, in Virginia and in Maryland. We see at first in each of them homogeneousness of character; sameness of views in religion, in literature, and in the principles of government; and these views and principles were allowed to develop themselves long before there was any foreign ingredient that could tinge or modify them—like a river that long runs pure amidst the wild rocks, and over the wild plains, working a deep and permanent channel for itself, before any other stream mingles with the waters.

When we turn our eyes, however, to the Great West, we discern an entirely different state of things. There is no homogeneousness of character, of origin, of language. There are elements already struggling for the mastery, any one of which, if alone, would have vital and expansive power enough to diffuse itself all over that great valley.

There is a large infusion of the Puritan mind, as modified by the institutions of New England. That mind at the West, as elsewhere, is one of great energy, perseverance, determination, ability to conquer difficulties, and to make all circumstances bend to the promotion of its own objects. It is a mind strongly imbued with the love of civil and religious liberty; with hatred of oppression and wrong; with the value of the simplest and purest forms of the Protestant religion; and with a desire to promote the cause of sound learning. Of that mind, however, it should be said that it appears at the West, mainly in one of its modifications, and that perhaps not in all respects its most desirable and best one. It is rather the *active* than the *contemplative* form of that mind that is there; rather the portion of the Puritan mind that would be represented by Pym, and Cromwell, and Hampden, than that which would be represented by Selden, and Owen, and Milton. It is not always the best educated, or the most religious, or the most literary in its tendencies, but that which is most bold and enterprising. The roving and the unsettled migrate there.

Those who would not be contented on a small farm, with slow gains, and with the staid and settled habits of New England, go there. Those who fail at the East, often go there to better their circumstances. Those who have less of the "home" feeling, in whom the ties which bind them to the scenes of childhood and youth are feebler, and the love of new scenes stronger, go there. Intermingled with these, there are not a few also who go with settled principles of morals and religion; men whose power *would* be felt any where, and *will* be felt there; men who go with a determination to attempt to mould the public mind, and to make the West what it should be. And it should be added also as a painful and sad truth, but which has a special bearing on the designs of this Society, and which should not be withheld, that not a few go there who are professors of religion in the East, attracted by the love of gain, who seem to rejoice in the opportunity of detaching themselves entirely from the Christian church; who soon forget the Sabbath and the sanctuary; who erect no family altar; who are unknown as professors of religion; whose lives are useful, so far as religion is concerned, only as they show how often religion is the creature of circumstances in the East, and how proper it is to distrust the reality of that piety which has never been tried. Among these, it cannot be denied, are sometimes found the most bold and open opposers of the doctrines of the Cross.

Intermingled with these, there is a large infusion of a *foreign* mind, with little homogeneousness of character and views, except in the single reason which has precipitated it on our western shores. It is the foreign mind which in its own country most feels the weight of oppression; which has the greatest desire of liberty; which possesses in the highest degree the spirit of adventure; which is most ready to brave difficulties; which is most imbued with the desire of rapid gains. There are different languages; different manners and customs; different modes of faith and worship. It is, however, alike in this—that it is a mind mostly bred up under monarchical forms of government; little acquainted with our republican institutions; restrained at home less by an intelligent public sentiment than by the bayonet; tenacious of the forms of religion in which it was trained; and, to a large extent, having little sympathy with the principles of the Protestant faith.

Intermingled with these, too, I need not add, there are representatives from all portions of our own country. They who at the South have become dissatisfied with the evils of slavery, are there—whether they have been impoverished by the system, or whether they have learned conscientiously to abhor it as a wrong in itself, or whether they dread its influence on their children. Often with indolent habits themselves, as the result of slavery; with that remarkable disregard of the appearances of economy, thrift, and neatness, which is always the result of that system, and yet with high notions of personal honor; men more frequently poor than well off, as the result of slavery, they mingle with the great population of the West as one of the elements to make that land what it is to be.

In that vast valley, therefore, in which we seek to establish and maintain the influence of evangelical Christianity, there are representatives from nearly all the nations of Europe, and all the older portions of our own country. Ireland, and France, and England, and Germany, and Holland, and Norway—all the States of New England, and all the South, have their representatives there; and they appear there, not yet as amalgamated, but, to a great extent, as still embodying the sentiments which they cherished in the lands where they were born. "The shrewd New Englander, the luxurious Southerner, the positive Englishman, the metaphysical Scotchman, the jovial Irishman, the excitable Frenchman, the passionate Spaniard, the voluptuous Italian, the plodding German, the debased African"—the Polander, the Norwegian, the Hollander, and the Dane, are all there, flung into this "mighty crucible," each with his own language, his own plans, his own prejudices, his own religion. The antagonist elements are in contact, but refuse to unite; and, as yet, no agent has been found sufficiently potent to reduce them to unity. "The iron is mixed with miry clay," and so repellant are the elements of society there, that they "cannot cleave one to another, even as iron is not mixed with clay." "As yet no common sympathy binds them together; no great heart sends its generous blood throughout the system, to impart to each member a healthful and a generous vitality."

As a consequence of this, the permanent character of the Western mind is as yet undetermined. Society is there, as far as it can be, a resolution into its original elements; and as, in ancient chaos, there was a struggling and commingling of the various elements before beauty and order appeared, so it is there. It is, to a great extent, broken off from old fixtures and associations, and new affinities and attachments are not yet formed. In the language of one who has preceded me in this service, "Society transplanted, in a case of emigration, cannot carry its roots with it; for society is a vital creature, having roots of antiquity, which inhere in the very soil—in the spots consecrated by valor, by genius, by religion. Transplanted to a new field, the emigrant race lose, of necessity, a considerable portion of that vital force which is the organic and conserving power of society. All the old roots of local love, and historic feeling—the joints and bands that minister nourishment—are left behind; and nothing remains to organize a living growth, but the two unimportant incidents, proximity and a common interest." In the settled and fixed opinions of an old country—as, for example, in the older portions of our own land; amidst the permanent influences derived from early associations, and an established public sentiment, it is comparatively easy to adhere to the lessons of virtue; comparatively easy to preserve the ascendency of religion. For here is the sanctuary, where we have been accustomed to worship from childhood. Here is the Sabbath-bell, reminding us of the return of the day of holy rest. Here are our fathers' sepulchres, faithful though silent mementos of the value of the principles which they held, and of the worth of religion in life and in death. Here is the school-house, a reminder of the lessons learned in early years. Here is a well-formed, vigorous, decided public sentiment, from which it is always difficult and perilous for a man to break away. But, in a new country, the power of these things is, of course, as yet unknown. There is no ancient sanctuary, or Sabbath-bell, or sepulchre of the dead, or school-house, or established public sentiment on which we can rely, or whose aid may be invoked in the cause of virtue and religion. The power of virtue as derived from association, and from reminiscences of the past, was broken the moment the emigrant turned his face toward the setting sun; and when he crosses the mountains he is in a new world, and is dissociated from the old things which bound him to fixed principles and opinions, and open to any new influences that may meet him there. Tens of thousands of minds thus detached from all that was fixed and settled in their native lands, are thus thrown together without order, in interminable forests, or on boundless prairies, with commingled and unsettled views, prepared for any new influences that may meet them there. This feature of the Western mind, I cannot better describe than in the language of one who has long resided there, and who has had an opportunity of extensive observation: "In consequence of the incoherency of this element, in a population thus heterogeneous, and broken off from the fixtures of old communities, without time to form new ones, all the social forces are shifting and mutable, and yield like the particles of liquid to the least force impressed. This quality of Western society, combined with the bold, prompt, energetic, and adventurous temperament impressed generally on it by common influences in the life of the emigrant, exposes it to vehement and brief excitement, to epidemic delusion and agitation. Upon this sea of incoherent and vehement mind, every wind of opinion has been let loose, and is struggling for the mastery; and the mass heaves restlessly to and fro, under the thousand different forces impressed. The West is, therefore, peculiarly perturbed with demagoguism and popular agitation, not only in politics, but in religion, and in all social interests. Amid these shifting social elements, we want principles of stability; we want a system of permanent forces; we want deep, strong, and constant influences, that shall take from the changefulness and excitability of the Western mind, by giving it the tranquillity of depth, and shall protect it from delusive and fitful impulses, by enduing it with a calm, profound, and pure reason."

This condition of things, however, has its advantages, as a relief to what might be otherwise too dark a picture.

One of those advantages is, that while there may be much that is perilous in breaking away from associations whose tendency is favorable to virtue, there is much that is desirable in breaking away from those that are evil. It is true that the emigrant from the older States of this Union goes away from the school-house, and from the sanctuary, and from his fathers' sepulchres, and from a thousand things that bound him to virtue and religion; but it is *also* true that the emigrant from the old world, by the fact of his crossing the deep, and making the new world his home, has broken away from a thousand influences in favor of a false religion, and bad principles of government, in his own land. All the influence under which he grew up adapted to foster error and superstition—in the moss-grown cathedral, the consecrated relics of the saints, the pompous ceremonial, the imposing procession, the trappings of royalty—is unseen, and will be soon forgotten, by himself or his children, when a man makes a western prairie his home. If these ever exist there, they are to be reproduced, and it will be with diminished venerableness and splendor, and only after a lapse of years, and when his own mind, and the minds of his children, in spite of all efforts to the contrary, shall have been open to the better influence of our Protestant and Republican institutions.

And another benefit is, that, if in these things there is much in regard to a forming mind that is undesirable, there is much also that, from the same circumstances, has a tendency to produce that which is manly and noble. The boy that leaves his home and becomes a seaman, is exposed indeed to numerous bad influences; but there will be developed in his mind, when he becomes a sailor, some of the noblest qualities of human nature. He will be open, frank, liberal, generous, forgiving, and ever ready to do you good. So the emigrant at the West. You naturally look there, for what you are sure to find, noble and magnanimous feeling; large and liberal hospitality; a readiness to aid those who are in distress and want; a purpose to take part with the oppressed, the wronged, and the defenceless; the absence of a penurious spirit, and a courtesy, often expressed indeed with roughness, that yields the tribute of respect to those who are in any way entitled to it. A minister of the gospel may be certain that he may travel there any where without being insulted; or, if he is insulted by *one*, there will be a *dozen* who will defend him simply because he *is* a minister—though possibly it might be with many modes of expression that would not fall mellifluously on the ear; and an unprotected female in the West, in public conveyances, may be sure of a defence from insult which could not have been enjoyed in the best days of chivalry. No wayfaring man will want a home for a night; no one who is sick will lack those who, without fee or reward, will watch the live-long night at his bedside; no one will suffer for bread, while the humble stores of the log-cabin will furnish it.

Another thing that is to be said of the western mind, is, that it will be developed. There are none of the causes operating there to produce imbecility and inaction which exist in many of the older portions of the world. There is all that can exist in the purposes for which the emigrant seeks a new home; all that there was in his native character and habits which led him to break away from the ties of kindred, and to brave the toils and perils of a new land; all that there is in the fact that others are intensely active, in the enjoyment of the most ample freedom, in the prospects of rapid and vast gains, in the hope of rising to honor and office, or in the possibility of swaying by eloquence the popular mind, to develop whatever slumbering vigor may exist in the soul. And there is all that there can be in a society composed of such elements, to produce intellectual strife, earnest conflict in debate, impassioned eloquence, the struggle of mind with mind:—for, if you place "a New Englander, proud to stand as the representative of some stern Puritan ancestor, in contact with an Irish Jesuit; or a positive English monarchist, with as positive an American republican; or a reckless Italian, with a conscientious, law-abiding Scotchman;" or an apologist for slavery—all his life long trained to think that the best institution—with one who in the depths of his soul abhors the whole system, and let the questions arise which *will* arise when such minds come in collision, there will be fierce intellectual conflicts, and if mind has any hidden resources, they will be developed. And there is all in the natural scenery, too, which is fitted to develop mind. It is on a scale so vast and grand:—the majestic rivers, the boundless prairies, the deep forest, the immensity of the rich domain spread out there, cannot but make man vast in his schemes, gigantic in his purposes, large in his aspirations, boundless in his ambition.

Such are some of the characteristics of the western mind. The *religious* tendencies of that mind will be more appropriately noticed under another head of this discourse.

II. I have considered the field on which this Society, in common with many others, proposes to operate. I proposed, in the second place, to consider the *contending elements* in that field for the mastery. This opens before us the inquiry, What is probably to be the form of society that is to exist there? and What is the practicability of arresting existing tendencies, and of diffusing there the principles which, at the East, we have been accustomed to regard as essential to the perpetuity of our civil and religious institutions?

The first thing that is to be said on this point is, that the West may now be regarded as the great battle-field of the world—the place where probably, more than any where else, the destinies of the world are to be decided. The struggle which is going on there for the mastery is to be more important in its issue than that of any battle ever fought in the plain of Esdraelon—more important than the result of the strife at Marathon, at Cannæ, at Bunker Hill, at Waterloo. More individuals are now, and are to be, engaged in the struggle; more interests are at stake; more powerful minds will be engaged; more talent will be developed; and more momentous results will follow. The eye of the world is, and should be, fixed with a more intense interest on that struggle than any which has ever occurred on the earth, for the ultimate issue will be more far-reaching and mighty. The centre of power in this nation has already gone from Plymouth, from New York, from Philadelphia, from *Washington,* over the Alleghanies, and is moving with fearful rapidity to the centre of that Great Valley—perhaps soon will have passed Cincinnati, and reached St. Louis.* If this nation is to be free, the population of that valley is to preserve and perpetuate our freedom; if it is to be enslaved, the chains that are to fetter us are to be forged beyond the mountains. When Fisher Ames wished to raise the note of alarm at what he deemed a measure of most dangerous policy, he said that, if he had the power, he would lift his voice so that it would reach every log-house beyond the mountains. He who now seeks to rouse his country to a sense of her danger, must seek so to speak that his voice may be heard in all the cities, towns, and villages of the East—in those places where the battles for freedom have been fought, and where there is still power to send out an influence that shall determine the scale of victory in the great conflicts of the West. The struggle there is for the rule. It is to determine what shall be the governing mind of that vast land. Shall it be barbarism? Shall it be infidelity? Shall it be the Roman Catholic system? Shall it be evangelical religion? Never were there so many passions and powers contending in any other conflict; never was a field so large; never was the prospective crown of victory so dazzling.

In the visions of the Apocalypse, the banished John saw four angels standing on the four corners of the earth,

* The exact position and course of the moving centre of Representative Population in this country, will be seen from the following table, calculated by Dr. Patterson, of the United States M nt at Philadelphia:

"In 1790, the centre of representative population was in Baltimore co., Md., 46 miles N. and 22 E. from Washington.

In 1800, it was in Carroll co., Md., 52 miles N. and 9 E. from Washington.

In 1810, it was in Adams co., Pa., 64 miles N. and 30 W. from Washington.

In 1820, it was in Morgan co., Va., 47 miles N. and 71 W. from Washington.

In 1830, it was in Hampshire co., Va., 43 miles N. and 108 W. from Washington.

In 1840, it was in Marion co., Va., 36 miles N. and 160 W. from Washington."

"Thus, it appears that the centre of representative population has moved westward with accelerated velocity; the last ten years, between 50 and 60 miles. It 'is just now about the Ohio river, and in 1850 will be in Washington or Monroe co., Ohio.'

"An interesting feature of this calculation is seen in the fact, that this moving centre of population has kept very nearly on the same parallel of latitude for fifty years, viz.: about 39° 30. It now *passes out of the slave States*, and should it preserve the same direction, it must continue on free soil until it shall cross the Mississippi. Before it shall enter Missouri, that State also will probably have long been a free State."—*Home Missionary for May*, 1849.

holding the four winds of heaven, that the wind should not blow on the earth, nor on the sea, nor on any tree. Then he saw another angel ascending from the East, having the seal of the living God; and he cried with a loud voice to the four angels to whom it was given to hurt the earth and the sea, saying, Hurt not the earth, neither the sea, nor the trees, till we have sealed the servants of our God in their foreheads. Rev. vii. 1–3. We may not fancy to ourselves that there will be any miraculous suspense—any holding back of the winds that are to sweep over that Western valley; but as those winds are beginning to blow, and before they sweep over those regions with their full blast, and mingle all in wild confusion and ruin, the angel of peace may go and seal the servants of God, and perhaps the threatening blasts may yet be stayed.

The question of ascendency or mastery there lies essentially between four things:—barbarism, infidelity, Romanism, evangelical religion. There is but one other thing conceivable as pertaining to this land—for the question about Paganism and Islamism can have no place here—and that one thing would be a civilized and enlightened state of society, without *any* form of religion, or any reference to religion. But such a community never has been found; there is no tendency in our nature to the formation of any such community; there is none especially in our own land.

(1.) First, then, barbarism. Is that the form in which Western society will develop itself, either if left to itself, or in spite of all we can do to prevent it? So many fear; so some would persuade us; so some of those who have gone out over that land and have returned, report to us. They speak of the prevailing ignorance, and of the want of churches, and of the diminished reverence for the Sabbath, and of coarse, rough, blunt manners, and of profaneness, and disgusting habits, and uneducated children, and of long tracts and regions where the sound of the church-going bell is never heard. They dwell on the fact, that 'society, transplanted, cannot carry its roots with it; on the fact, that education must, for a long time, be imperfect in degree, and partial in extent; on the fact, that, as men's tastes grow wild, their resentments grow violent and their enjoyments coarse; on the fact, that, in religion, their views will be narrow and crude, and their animosities bitter; and on the fact, that, in respect to civil order, the old common law of the race is not transplanted as a vital power, but only as a recollection that refuses to live.' And they dwell on the character of those who have emigrated in former times, and seek an argument from those results to prove that, in all emigration, there must be a tendency to deterioration.

One cannot deny that there is enough in these things to excite deep thought; and the apprehension of these things has had much to do with the formation of this and kindred societies. Nor can it be denied that one may pursue such lines of travel in the West, on the rivers or over the prairies; that he may visit such destitute and semi-barbarous places; or, perhaps, still more important than all, that he may travel under such moods of mind, or under the influence of such feelings generated by a bilious state of the body, that he shall see around him only such ignorance, and coarseness of manners, and inconveniences of life, as to mark a descent far towards barbarism.

But, in regard to the essential character of *emigration*, such prophets must have forgotten Ionia—beautiful, classic Ionia—colonized from Greece; they must have forgotten Carthage, the Rival of Rome, and its origin in Phenicia; they must have forgotten Palestine, settled by colonists from Mesopotamia; they must have forgotten England—the Anglo-Saxon race and blood; they must have forgotten our own land—a land settled every where by colonists and emigrants—and yet, not a land that has deteriorated from what our fathers were; nay, they must have forgotten Australia, a land colonized under the worst auspices that the world ever saw, and yet promising soon to take its place among civilized and Christian nations. Such things might teach us, at least, that there is no *essential* tendency to barbarism in emigration; or, that there might be some spirit infused to counteract these tendencies, and that it is possible for a people who 'change their sky *not* to change their principles' for the worse, but to grow better.

But, barbarism at the West. Is there no 'salt' there to

preserve it? Is there nothing on which the eye of cheerful faith may repose? Is there no ground of hope that it will be a land of refinement and of civilization? Is there danger that the dwellers there will go back to the condition of savage tribes, and that all the change produced has been to expel the aboriginal barbarians to make way for barbarians made out of the degenerate descendants of a Christian people—more formidable because they have more power and more skill?

Perhaps a western man would hardly consider it courteous to have this question argued at all, but since there is an apprehension of this in some minds, and since this is one of the conceivable types of society any where, it may be proper to make a remark or two on it. (*a*) It is well, then, to reflect on the origin of a considerable portion of that western people. The dwellers there are not those who have come out of the recesses of deep forests; nor are they like the swarms that came out of the northern hive—the followers of Alaric, Attila, Genseric, and Odoacer—and that overspread the territories of the Roman empire; nor is the mass made up of those who have been trained amidst the institutions of despotism, or debased by a grovelling superstition. The ruling mind at the West, is the *American* mind: and there is not a college or an academy at the East; not a theological seminary, a law school, or a school of medicine; not a church, a county, or a town, that has not a representative there—and there with all the notions of liberty, and with all the impressions of the value of learning and religion in which he was trained, deeply engraven on his heart. (*b*) Again: They are united with us as one people, and that not in a sense that is constructive and metaphorical, but in a sense that is in the highest degree literally true—in a sense far more literally true than could have been said of the inhabitants of the old thirteen colonies. If we have any arts at the East, they are their arts also; if an invention is struck out here, it becomes theirs as soon as it does ours; if there is any thing that essentially tends to refine and elevate us, it tends to refine and elevate them also. In the time of the old thirteen colonies, it was impossible to strike a chord that would vibrate instantaneously from Massachusetts to

Georgia, and if a note of freedom was sounded by Patrick Henry in Virginia, or by John Adams in Faneuil Hall, it was long before it would vibrate to the extremities of the country. If there was an invention in the arts, the knowledge of it moved slowly over the land, and if a newspaper was published, it was borne slowly along from place to place. Now, at St. Louis, and New Orleans, and Chicago, and Dubuque, the arrival of a steamer at Halifax is known simultaneously, and intelligence that is to wake up thought, and direct enterprise, is spread in a moment all over the land. On the very morning after the late Presidential election, the results of that election in Western New York, and Maine, and Massachusetts, and Rhode Island, and Connecticut, and Vermont, and Ohio, and Michigan, and Illinois, and South Carolina, and Virginia, and Kentucky, were sufficiently known to determine the question, and to calm down the public mind every where to a state of rest. (*c*) Again: There is much in existing circumstances in the West, to counteract all the tendencies to deterioration. True, there is a most exuberant soil, and in the exhaustless luxuriance of the country it would seem that there was a temptation to indolence, and to the vices which indolence engenders. And so there might be, if it were not for the stimulus of enterprise and industry just adverted to, and by the fact that the world is open for the productions of the West. What the world elsewhere produces, may be soon theirs; what they produce, may be soon in the market competing with all which is produced on the sea-board. (*d*) And again: He who argues that barbarism is to be the type of society in the West, must have forgotten the schools and colleges already established there. That vast land is now better supplied with colleges than New England was a hundred years after the landing of the Pilgrims, when Harvard and Yale furnished all the facilities for the education of their sons: better supplied in number, and in the character of the institutions—for a comparison between what the Western Reserve, and Marietta, and Illinois, and Wabash, and Galesburg colleges are now, and what Harvard and Yale were then, would be any thing but flattering to the latter. But, I need not argue this point farther. He who has travelled over the

West, and seen only evidences of deterioration, or had his mind troubled with the apprehensions of barbarism, must have selected not the ordinary routes of travel, or must have discerned the process of it in something that would not strike an ordinary traveller, or must have gone with erroneous anticipations, or must have been in a discomposed and melancholy state of mind. That the traveller *may* find things sad and alarming, may be true; that he may find things unlike what he may have been accustomed to, is more than probable; but he will not wander among savage hordes, or find that he has gone beyond the abodes of civilized men. I confess that a man must have travelled with far different feelings than mine, and must have looked at things from a different point of view, to have seen the evidences of barbarism there. Villages of beauty that will compare with any at the East; cities of more bustling activity than most of those on the Atlantic slope; colleges much in advance of what our most venerated institutions were a hundred years after they were founded, and that will compare favorably with them now; churches that will vie with those at the East—and the latest inventions in agriculture, in navigation, in the arts as familiar there as here, argue any thing but deterioration and barbarism.

(2.) Is infidelity to be the characteristic of the West? There can be no doubt that the hopes of infidels have been much concentrated there. It was natural that they should be. The *argument* on the subject of the divine origin of Christianity, may be regarded as well-nigh complete; and the hope of extinguishing Christianity by *persecution* is at an end. Whatever laurels there were to be won in the field of argument by infidelity, have been gained; whatever glory there was in persecution, has been secured; whatever honor was in reserve for men like Nero and the Duke of Alva, has been conferred; and whatever triumph there was in attempting to prove that miracles could not be wrought, or in sneering at Christianity, has been already achieved. If infidelity is to make progress in the world, it is to be by the heart rather than by the understanding; by secret influences rather than by open controversy; by detaching men silently from the faith, rather than by driving them from it by force. For that great and last experiment, if that was contemplated, it cannot be denied that the great West in our own country offered the most inviting field that could be desired. Vast almost without limit; rich in its soil beyond comparison with any other portion of the world; inspiring hopes of wealth such as the world has never seen, except when the Spaniard came formerly to the new world, and now when the gold of California has inspired still more brilliant hopes; society torn from its roots; multitudes detached from all the old associations of religion, and released from what were galling restraints of piety and virtue in the place of their birth; great numbers from all parts of the world thrown into a land without churches or schools, and extensively without the restraints and the sacred influences of the Sabbath; society to be reorganized of such materials as might happen to be collected in any particular place; a population outstripping all the means of grace—in such a state of things, it was natural that infidelity should hope there might be found at last the field of its triumph.

But the result—what is it thus far? What is it likely to be? That there are causes of solicitude enough to awaken the mind to watchfulness and prayer, I shall not deny; but he must have looked at the West with a different method of reading its destiny from mine, if he believes that open infidelity, either in the form of Atheism, or Deism, or Pantheism, is to be the prevailing form of society there. For (*a*) The mass of those who go there are men whose minds have been strongly imbued with some sentiments of religion on their native soil; and, whatever those sentiments are, there is no part of the world where they will be likely to be developed with greater vigor or power of growth. They are not colonies of Atheists and infidels, who go to people the Western world. Most of those who have gone, and are going, have been trained up in connexion with those forms of religion which take the deepest hold on the human soul, and which are the last to die out by neglect, or by any counteracting influence. The Puritan sentiment, as an element of conduct, never soon dies away, and is the least likely of all the principles which influence men to yield to opposition; to be displaced by counteracting influences; to detach itself from the minds of advancing generations. The mass of Germans who emigrate to the West, are religionists, and are in their original temperament too immovable to be organized into new associations of professed infidels. The Hollander is a friend of religion, and of that form of it that has been most identified with liberty. The Romanist retains his religion as an active principle wherever he goes. 'He changes his sky, but not his mind, when he crosses the ocean,' and the power of the priest lives and lingers long after he leaves the cathedrals, and relics, and consecrated burial-places of the old world; and more than one generation must pass away before his mind will be wholly prepared for the purposes of infidelity. (*b*) Again: One of the most striking things at the West is the *religious* development, in some form. There is not there one great denomination of *infidels;* there are many sects of *Christians*, with all the old opinions ever held in any age of orthodoxy or heresy, mingled with all the new forms of opinions to which crossing and re-crossing those sentiments will give rise; with all the ancient names known in history, and numberless names unknown to the rest of the ecclesiastical world;—a spirit of *sect-making* where there is the slightest difference of opinion, and a carrying out of the spirit of independence in apapointing a preacher in every place for each one of these sects, and organizing a church on the principle that there is to be as little as possible of a spirit of generalization. A traveller finds the small village to be the seat of a dozen such sects;—amidst them all he would probably not find even a pretended organization of infidels. (*c*) Again: The books that are read there are not infidel books; the books that are sought are not infidel books; the books that can be most readily circulated are not infidel books. With all the corrupt and unbelieving tendencies of the natural heart of man, and with all that has ever grown up in the West hostile to evangelical religion, no organization of infidelity at the East could vie with the Bible Society, and the Tract Society, and the Sunday School Union in circulating books; no amount of wealth embarked in such a 'book concern' could give a distribution to Paine and Volney equal to that which can be given to the Pilgrim's

Progress, and the Saints' Everlasting Rest. And (*d*) as a matter of fact, the organizations that have been formed for establishing infidelity at the West, have had so little vitality; have found so little to sustain them there; and have impinged on so many fixed principles, or so many forming opinions, that not one of them lives. Infidelity never found a place more favorable for developing its nature, than New Harmony. If a new country, and an unformed state of society, and an ample field, and a land of richness, fertility and beauty, and talent in the founder of such an association, could ensure success, that was the place where it might be anticipated that there would be the permanent centre of a vast organization of men without God. It is 'situated on a broad and beautiful plateau, overlooking the beautiful Wabash, surrounded by a fertile and heavily-timbered country, and blessed with an atmosphere of health.' It had been prepared by a colony calling themselves *Economists*, who had erected substantial edifices, who had laid out their grounds with beautiful regularity, and who had established there a botanic garden. It was cultivated by them for ten years—and then, by purchase, passed into the hands of infidels—to be a model school of unbelief; a better Eden than the first—where men might live in a community without the Bible, and without a Sabbath, and without God. It was proclaimed that the 'promise of never-ending love in marriage was an absurdity; that children should become no impediment to separation, as they were to be considered members of the community from their second year; that the Society should have no professed religion, and that all temporal possessions should be held in common. On one night of every week, the whole community met and danced; on another, they united in a concert of music; the Sabbath was devoted to philosophical Lectures.' But all in vain. Dissension insinuated itself among the members; one after another dropped off from the community, and the scheme was abandoned. The plan had failed, for there was no sympathy for such an enterprise, and the failure of the scheme was a proclamation to the world that infidelity is not the type of society which is to prevail at the West. So the last of the Mormons is disappearing there.

Their beautiful temple is in ruins. The enterprise has failed, because the people of the West do not choose to have their land studded over with infidel institutions.

(3.) Is Romanism to be the prevailing religion of the West? So, many travellers there report to us; so one large portion of the world hopes; se another fears. And these reports, and hopes, and fears, are not unnatural. From the eyes of even the most faithful and sanguine of the Papal Church it cannot be concealed that in the old world its days are numbered, and that the ancient institution is tumbling to ruin. It has aspired to universal conquest; it early saw that this land must be secured or that its hopes would be at an end; and the events of the last few years have not diminished its sense of the importance of subjecting our country to its sway. The plan was early laid, and there *was* a time when the issue might have been doubtful. When, long before the Alleghanies had been crossed by moving masses of Protestant emigrants, they had formed their *cordon* of ecclesiastical posts, and had seated themselves at Du Quesne, and Detroit, and Prairie du Chien, and Dubuque, and Kaskaskia, and St. Louis, and Gallipolis, and St. Genevieve—designing to secure all that land as subject to the Papal power, who then could have doubted that their plans were laid with wisdom? Who could have failed to admire the sagacious policy of the Jesuit? There are those that feel that the danger is not passed, and it is not to be denied that there is enough to awaken apprehension; just enough to be a healthful stimulus to arouse the friends of evangelical religion to do their duty. But he must read the destiny of the West different from what I have ever been able to do, if he supposes that that expiring power is to renew the vigor of its youth in our land. I look at such facts as these—which your patience will not allow me to enlarge upon: (*a.*) The character of the priesthood of that denomination, for learning, for public enterprise, and for the other needful qualifications to affect the *American* mind. A clergy to have power in this land, must be of the people; must have a large share of American feeling; must enter into all our notions of civil liberty, and mental freedom; must fall in with all that can be properly called the *devel-*

opment of the principles of the declaration of Independence—with all that was properly represented at Jamestown, on the Rock at Plymouth, or when the great Quaker laid the foundation of Pennsylvania. But a foreign clergy; educated with foreign notions; never assimilating with the American mind; never making books to affect the American mind as such, what can they be expected to do? Beyond the limits of their own denomination, what Catholic priest makes a book that tells on the American mind; what one preaches so as to affect the American mind; what one expects to make his way except as the religion sustains itself in Italy and Spain? What man will point me to an elementary book in education, in morals, in jurisprudence, in history, in theology, in the exposition of the Scriptures, from the multitudes of the Catholic priesthood in this land, that is adapted to mould the American mind? Where, beyond the limits of those who come to us from abroad, do they make any impression? (*b*) I look at the relative position which they now occupy, compared with what they once did in our own land. We are astonished at their growth. We forget that the Protestant growth is vastly greater. We are alarmed at their numbers when we are told, in their almanac, that they amount to a million and a quarter. We forget the twenty millions of Protestants. We are alarmed when we are told of the number of their churches. They report nine hundred and sixty-six. Protestants number theirs by thousands. We are frightened by the number of their priests. They report eight hundred and seventy-three 'in the ministry,' and one hundred and fifty-three 'otherwise employed.' Protestants number some twenty thousand. Once, the strong towns were theirs—Pittsburg, and St. Louis, and Baltimore, and the whole West where to choose. A few years since, in a popular vote in St. Louis, they could poll two to one to the Protestant population; now two Protestants could cast their votes where one Roman Catholic could. The traveller at the West finds already a few decaying or dilapidated towns. They are strange anomalies in that new world—but there they are—seats of former Catholic power—selected to control the nation—and proofs, after all, of a singular want of sagacity. There are Cahokia, and Kaskaskia, and Gallipolis, and St. Genevieve, and Prairie du Chien, bearing French names, and indicating their origin, standing in strange contrast with the smiling villages, and the splendid cities around them. Meantime there have sprung up Cincinnati, and Louisville, and Chicago, and Milwaukie, and Galena, and Peoria, and Quincy, and Madison, and—a thousand other places where the Catholic religion never had the ascendency, and never will. It is, also, a significant and instructive fact, that according to the Catholic Almanac of the present year—a work generally recognized as safe authority in the statistics of its Church—there has been no increase in the dioceses of Baltimore, New Orleans, Louisville, Boston, Philadelphia, New York, Charleston, Mobile, Detroit, Vincennes, Natchez, Pittsburg, Little Rock, Milwaukie, Albany, Galveston, and Buffalo. 'The only green spots in this wide-spread desert,' to use the language of the Freeman's Journal, 'are the Dioceses of Cincinnati, Dubuque, Nashville, Chicago, and Oregon.' According to the same authority, the total *decrease* of Catholics during the year, has been one hundred and nine thousand and four hundred:—and that in a country where during the year ending Sept. 30, 1847, the number of foreigners arriving in the U. States was more than two hundred and thirty thousand (239,270). (*c*) I look at their colleges and schools. They report indeed, in the whole land, thirty-four literary institutions for young men, seventeen of which are colleges; eighty-six female academies, twenty-three male religious institutions, and fifty-eight female religious institutions. But there is a question lying back of all the estimates of the *numbers* of such schools and colleges, of material bearing on the final result. It is, whether such schools are adapted to form the American mind, or, which is of as much importance, whether they will long be *regarded* as adapted to that end. Success in these schools, beyond the limits of their own denomination, or as designed to act on the public mind at large, must depend on their being able to keep up the impression that their schools are *superior* to Protestant schools. Now, whatever may be the cause, and whatever may be the truth on the subject, there is, undoubtedly, a great change taking place in the public mind in regard to those schools. There is an impression gradually and firmly gaining ground, that the instruction in those schools, as mere literary training, is less thorough than in Protestant schools; that foreign priests, Jesuits, and nuns, are not the best qualified to train American youth; that the design of all these establishments is to make converts to the Catholic faith; that there are branches of knowledge of great importance for an American youth, which cannot be imparted in those schools; that a Catholic teacher cannot consistently give a correct history of our own country, explain the principles which brought our fathers to these shores, or defend those which have gone into our freedom; and that there is no branch of science or morals that will be taught in those schools, that will not be so taught as to be made designedly subservient to the Roman Catholic faith. In a memorial, addressed by the Roman Catholic archbishops and bishops of Ireland to the British government, on the proposal of the government to establish in Ireland a certain number of colleges for education in the various branches of secular learning, to be open indiscriminately to young men of whatever church or denomination, they say in so many words: 'That the Roman Catholic pupils could not attend the lectures in history, logic, metaphysics, moral philosophy, geology, or anatomy, without exposing their faith or morals to imminent danger, unless a Roman Catholic professor should be appointed for each of the chairs.' It *is* so, whether in Ireland or in the United States. As these sciences would be taught, if taught as they should be, they could not be made to support the Roman Catholic faith:—and this being so, the conclusion is coming rapidly to be reached by American minds that these sciences will *not* be taught in their true nature and thoroughness in Roman Catholic schools. There is no conclusion which the public mind is more *likely* to reach, than that, for all the purposes of an education adapted to the wants of an American citizen, the schools taught by these foreigners are inferior to those taught by the Protestants of our own land. Where is there a Jesuit institution in the United States, or a Roman Catholic institution any where, that dares to give to its pupils a true history, or a true account of the condition of North and South America; or that dares go back and trace the history of New England and Mexico? In what Catholic seminary has it ever been told, or will it ever be told, why the one smiles in beauty, intelligence, and peace, and the other is sunk in ignorance, and shrouded in gloomy superstition? (*d*) I look again at the obvious and palpable mistakes which the Roman Catholics are making every where in their attempts to spread their religion in this land, and the vast waste of monies in their plans. There are two methods of attempting to spread religion in a country like this. The one is, by building magnificent and costly cathedrals; by erecting convents; by fitting up public places of worship in a manner adapted to make an impression on the outward senses of mankind:—the other is, by taking the money which would thus be expended, and sending out living teachers of religion, and distributing tracts and books, and seeking to rear the temples of religion in the hearts of men. The one is that pursued by the Roman Catholics; the other by this, and by kindred Protestant societies. The one may be adapted to perpetuate a form of religion in Spain or Portugal; the other is that which is fitted to free, thinking, intelligent mind. The Jesuit deposits a hundred thousand dollars in the walls of a cathedral—and there it remains, happily, without use, for ever; the Protestant commissions a host of missionaries, sends out an army of colporteurs, establishes a large number of Sunday schools, and distributes the word of God in the families of a new state of the Union. As we love Protestantism, and as we would rejoice in all the indications that the days of the Papacy are numbered, and that it is not to spread over our land, we should rejoice at the laying of the foundation of any costly pile by the hands of Jesuits—for we may be sure that *that* money at least will not make converts to the faith which it is designed to support, and is a new indication that this religion is not to spread over this land. For we may be certain in regard to this and to all other forms of religion in this land, that *none* will succeed here which does not make its primary ground of appeal the reason, the conscience, and the sober sense of mankind; that the way to spread religion here is not by processions, or genuflexions, or pomp and show; that mitres and crosiers lose their charms when men leave the old world; that there are elements in our national character and principles which will not be met by what is adapted to Portugal or Spain; and that the victory here is to be awarded to those who can do most to enlighten the public mind, diffuse farthest the word of God, maintain most steadfastly the right to the free exercise of opinion, and do most to make men feel that they are directly responsible to their Maker. Strange indeed would it be, if with our Protestant eighteen or twenty millions of people; with our eighteen or twenty thousand Protestant clergy; with our common schools all over the land; with the universal sentiment that the Bible is to be read by every man that chooses; with the whole system of Sunday schools; with a Protestant population increasing in a ratio with which no immigration can compete, and with all the probability that the foreigner or his children will amalgamate with us, and silently lay aside his reverence for institutions based on ignorance, and adapted to despotism, we cannot compete with a priesthood of a thousand in number, and with all the appliances that they can use to move the American mind.

III. I proposed, in the third place, to consider the *practicability of securing the ascendency of evangelical religion in the field which we have surveyed.*

The object aimed at by this Society, in connexion with other similar associations, is, to bring that western mind under the influence of evangelical religion, primarily, and mainly by *preaching*. But to see more distinctly the purposes aimed at by this Society, and the ground of its claims to the public confidence which it now enjoys, and the much higher public confidence which it desires, and which it seems to me it deserves, there are two or three remarks which it is proper to make here.

Christianity, in its power over a people, may be contemplated in the following respects, and in reference to each of them some peculiar measures or organizations are to be adopted. (*a*) One is in respect to places where it is already established; where it has the popular belief in its favor; where it has long prevailed, moulding the public mind, giving shape to the public taste, controlling colleges and schools, recognized in the laws, and in popular feeling associated with the intercourse of social life, with marriage customs, and with funeral solemnities—as in New England, Scotland, England, Germany. Religion there is not a tree just transplanted, or the germ of the acorn that has just sprung up, it is an ancient oak that has struck its roots deep, and that has stood through many winters, and that defies the storm. In such cases it requires the education of pastors that shall be fitted to secure these advantages, and to transmit these institutions unimpaired, to future times. Or (*b*) the effort to extend and perpetuate religion in the world, may be contemplated in its reference to heathen mind—whether that mind be partially civilized, and connected with semi-civilized institutions, as in China or India; or as migratory and wandering, as among the Tartars, and many of the Indian tribes of America, or many of the tribes of Africa; or as sunk in indolence, effeminacy, and stupidity, as in many of the tropical islands. Here, it is evident that peculiar organizations are demanded, requiring a wisdom in conducting the enterprise of Foreign Missions, which would, in other spheres, be fitted to manage the affairs of state. Or (*c*) it may be contemplated in its application to mind in a colonial state; forming new states or empires; detached from old fixtures and associations, and forming new combinations.

It is this last, to which the American Home Missionary Society has reference:—mind, such as I have endeavored to describe in the former part of this discourse. To see what is to be done, it is necessary to have a clear view of what that mind would be, and do, if nothing were done from abroad—if it were left to develop itself under the influences in which it is found in the great West in our own land. And to see this it would be necessary to be able—what perhaps no human sagacity could do—to see what in a course of years, or of centuries, would spring up as the result of the elements assembled there. It is with reference to the modifications of old opinions which would be the result if thrown together in those circumstances; to the new combinations of ancient thought and opinion which would be formed there; to the effect of being detached from the safeguards of virtue and religion in the older portions of the world; to the probable success of demagogues and ambitious teachers of religion; to the effect of a prevailing and controlling desire of gain in the richest part of the world; to the effect of the circumstances in producing relaxation from wholesome restraints, and a casting off of the bonds of virtue; to the effect of transplanting society without its roots; to the effect of excitement from the new schemes of gain that might be presented; to the effect of a very scanty supply of schools, and colleges, and books; to the effect produced by a great amount of leisure time, to be spent in idleness, amusement, or dissipation; and, perhaps more than all, to the effect which would exist among a people where, at the start, the results of the highest discoveries in science, and inventions in the arts were at their disposal, abridging human labor, making communication easy and rapid, and opening access to an amount of productions which no other land ever produced, to a ready market.

It is such a population, in such circumstances, that this Society proposes to influence by *preaching*. But, there are some things also, which I wish to say in regard to this preaching.

The first is, that it is not every *kind* of preaching that is contemplated. The kind of preaching is as definite as any other part of the work to be done. There are preachers enough in the West, such as they are; there are Buddhist priests enough in China, and Brahmins in India; there are Popish priests enough in Spain, and in Italy—and there will soon be enough of them in all the new states of our Republic, if their coming is not forestalled by a better ministry. It is not a question, then, in regard to that land, or any other, whether there shall be an abundance of ministers of religion or none; it is, whether there shall be just enough and not more than enough, whether they shall be intelligent or ignorant, whether they shall depend on preaching for success, or on processions and genuflexions, whether they shall nourish an intelligent Christianity, or a miserable and debasing superstition. You have only to make any people debased, ignorant, and superstitious in any part of the world, to cause a certain class of ministers of religion to be multiplied like the frogs of Egypt. It is intelligent Protestantism only which diminishes the number of the ministers of religion, and the expense of maintaining them. I said that there are preachers enough at the West, such as they are. In twenty counties of the southern part of the State of Illinois, a few years since, it was ascertained that, embracing preachers of all orders, there was one for every three hundred of the entire population. I need not say that it is not such men as most of those preachers are, that this Society seeks to send forth. A Home Missionary of this Society is, or should be, and usually is, a man of a strongly-marked character. He is an educated man, having enjoyed the best advantages of our literary and theological Seminaries. He is himself a friend of education, and will be a patron of colleges and schools. He is a man who will himself possess a library, if he can, and who will aim that there shall be a library in every neighborhood. He is a man who will be an advocate of temperance, and a patron of every institution of benevolence. He is a man who will make his appeals to the reason and consciences of men, rather than to excited feelings. He is a man qualified to guide public opinion, and to grapple with thinking minds, and to show them that Christians are not necessarily fools. This Society regards western mind as needing a high order of educated intellect as really as that in the East, and would feel that of two men, one of whom should have a strong and well-cultivated intellect, and the other of whom should sink below mediocrity, he of humbler endowments should find his place in some city or country parish in the East;—his more gifted brother should receive a commission to go beyond the mountains.

Another remark which I take the liberty to make, under this head, has respect to the class of mind that the Society expects mainly to affect at the West. The patrons of this Society are not without their own views of what constitutes truth, and of the doctrines which are to be promulgated. It does not expect to occupy the whole field, nor does it expect to exclude other denominations of Christians. It aims, indeed, to send the gospel, as it understands the gospel, as far as in its power, to all; and would preach it, if it could, in every log-house beyond the mountains. It cannot be denied, it need not be denied, that the form of Christianity which it seeks and expects to propagate, is that which has been much spoken against in this world, and known now as the Calvinistic form, and that it expects to make its way because there are minds in every community that are likely to embrace Christianity in that form, and because it is presumed that the more mind is elevated, and cultivated, and brought into connexion with colleges and schools, the more likely it will be to embrace that form. There is a class of minds in every community which will be disposed to look with favor on those views; which will be influenced by the arguments by which those views are defended; which will, of themselves, so interpret the Scriptures, and which will be led to those conclusions by their own reflections. Whether the different theological systems in the world are, or are not, the result of some original peculiarity in certain classes of minds, it is undeniable that there *are* certain classes of minds more disposed to certain views than to others, and that in certain systems they find what is congenial to their modes of thinking, and to the views which they take from the points where they stand. In the Roman Catholic communion, it has always been presumed that there would be a great variety of opinion, and that if there were minds disposed to the doctrines of the Jesuits, there would be also a class disposed to those of the Jansenists, and the boasted 'unity' of the Church is preserved by yielding to this diversity of view, and by conceding, in fact, as great a diversity as there is in the contending sects of Protestants. Among Protestants, with no greater violation of real union, the same thing has occurred by the fact that a great variety of denominations has sprung up, and that men of peculiar views will be likely to unite together, while, at the same time they yield this liberty to others, and maintain a common Christianity, and a common charity. We think that the class that will favor the Calvinistic views—the essentially ***Puritan*** views—is never a small class, and that it will be likely to be increased just in proportion as we can send forth an educated ministry, and can promote the cause of sound education and true mental philosophy in the land. We will not undertake to say whether John Wesley could ever have been a Calvinist, but we can say that Jonathan Edwards could never have been any thing else, and if there be a mind in any community formed like that of Edwards, we anticipate that it will embrace those views. Further: To a large extent, the colleges in the land are, and will be, Calvinistic institutions, and the educated mind of the nation will be in a considerable measure imbued with those views. The first college in our country, and the third, and the fourth, were such institutions, and a large portion of all in the land maintain the same character now.* And further, to a great extent thus far in the world, the friends of Calvinism have been found among the educated and thinking part of mankind, and among the sternest and firmest friends of liberty. Whatever may or may not be true of other modes of belief, it is not true that the system of faith which we seek to propagate, has been diffused by attempts to excite the passions of men, or by appeals to the authority of the Fathers, or by leading men to confide in their own goodness, or by veneration for the relics of saints, or by forms and ceremonies, or by tradition, or that it has shown any particular propensity to attach itself to the State as an established religion. The appeal, in maintaining its doctrines, has been to argument, and men have been convinced because they could no more help being convinced, than they could of the truth of a proposition in geometry; and we expect that the same thing will still occur. We anticipate, whatever may be the cause, that just in proportion as we can found schools and colleges; establish Sunday schools; send out an intelligent and educated ministry, and diffuse copies of the Bible, there will be found a class of minds disposed to adopt and maintain those views—and that the ratio will be increased as we multiply these means. We anticipate, in making our appeals to the sober sense, the reason, the conscience of

* Twenty-six of the whole number.

mankind, that such appeals will be followed by the establishment of churches of the Presbyterian and Congregational orders, doing for the West what the same kind of churches have done for the East.

We are not so presumptuous, nor do we take such views of human nature, as to suppose that the *entire* mind of the West, or of any other portion of our country, will be found to embrace these views. There are reasons which could easily be stated, why no such result is to be anticipated. But we *do* expect that a considerable portion of the educated and ruling mind will embrace these views; and we do believe that the right way to attempt to influence the heterogeneous mind of the West, as of all other mind, is to carry forward our efforts by making *preaching*, of as high an order as possible, the primary thing; and by connecting with that the influence of colleges and schools—the diffusion of the Bible and of the best books that sanctified mind has produced in all the languages spoken at the West. And we do anticipate that this plan, in connexion with other evangelical efforts, will, with the blessing of God, yet save the West.

There is not time to state the grounds of this opinion at length now. It would be found partly in the arguments already submitted that there is no reason why barbarism, infidelity, or Romanism, should reign there. It would be found partly in the fact that a great portion of what is now the ruling mind of the West has been trained under the best Christian auspices, and is favorable to the best influence of religion. It would be found partly in the fact that all the colleges in the West are Christian colleges—not one of them having been founded to maintain or propagate infidelity. It would be found partly in the remarkable success which has attended all the efforts to spread evangelical religion there—a success unequalled by any amount of similar efforts in any other age or portion of the world. It would be found in the facilities for affecting the public mind in this age—in the power of the press—the power of steam—the power of the telegraph—the power of business ties binding all that West to the East—making our land one, and all tending to make the West what the

East is. It would be found mainly in what we believe to be the designs of God.

As one of those means for securing the ascendency of evangelical religion at the West—more important, in my apprehension, than any other—the American Home Missionary Society stands before the American people, presenting itself for their patronage and prayers. We need not undervalue any other agency, but we know what the influence of the missionary of this society will be. We are in no doubt as to what he will attempt to do; we have no doubt of what he will do. On the prairie, in the almost unbroken forest, in the village of log cabins, or in the city, we know what will spring up around him. There will be, as soon as possible, a neat house of worship. There will be a Sunday school. There will be a common school. There will be a Temperance Society, and an effort to supply every family with a Bible, and with a Christian literature. There will be preaching that will gradually more and more, though perhaps repelled at first, attract and hold the educated and the thinking portions of the community, and that will not be unattractive or unconvincing to the masses of men. Associated with others, the missionary will be found engaged in laying the foundation of academies and colleges, destined to send forth healing streams long, long after he himself, worn out with many toils, shall have gone down to the grave.

The Home Missionary Society is one of the most *comprehensive* of all agencies ever employed to affect and benefit mankind. Without undervaluing any other means of influence, and without seeking a comparison with any other society, yet it secures within itself what *all* other benevolent societies are endeavoring to do; and though it does not wish to operate without them, yet it embodies within itself the *germ* of them all, and no one of them could live and accomplish its ends, without that which is primary in the purposes of this Society. It relies on *preaching*—preaching as the first thing, and the second thing, and the third thing:—preaching, Christ's great ordinance for the conversion of men, and the means of redeeming the world—for the great commission of the Church is, 'Go into all the world and *preach*.' Mark xvi. 15. Around the devoted and intelligent preacher every thing else that is good will spring up; without him no other agencies that men can employ will secure the end in view. It is a glorious thing to circulate the Bible; it is noble to send out Tract distributors; it is a great and good work to establish Sunday schools, and to commission temperance agents, but all these things are embodied and expressed in the purpose to fill the land with pastors 'after God's own heart,' and all will find in the success of this Society, the most certain pledge of their own.

The work contemplated by this Society, in unison with others, is among the grandest undertakings ever conceived by man. It pertains to the future—the far distant future. It has respect to our country—our whole country. It looks out on all this broad land—this rich inheritance which the God of our fathers has committed to this generation, with a purpose to make it what it should be. It spreads its wing over all those vast prairies—over all those now almost unbroken forests—over all those places where will soon be busy marts of commerce, and bustling cities and towns;—over all that territory which our fathers secured by their perils and their sufferings, and all that which in our own times has come into our possession by conquest and by purchase. It seeks to make this a Christian land throughout—such a country that it can be, and ought to be, loved by God and man; to make it, as it is destined to be a leading power among the nations of the earth, a power whose influence shall be always peaceful and pure; to show to other people the spectacle of one Christian nation stretching from ocean to ocean; to dot it over with churches, and colleges, and schools; to exhibit to the world its hundreds of millions of freemen, governed by law, and with no armed men to restrain them; to create such a public conscience that the decisions of courts shall be always acquiesced in, though millions of capital should be involved; to form a nation concentrating in its institutions the results of all the struggles for liberty in the world, covering the sea with their fleets, and the land with rich and abundant harvests;—a nation where there shall be the best application of the principles of Christianity to society, whose voice shall be heard and respected in putting an end to war, and to oppression, and to wrong every where. This Society has undertaken to do a leading part in this great work. By the blessing of heaven it will accomplish it, if the Christian citizens of this land can be made to understand their duty, and to appreciate their privilege.

The missionary that we send out, needs a little temporary aid. And it is not much that he needs; it is not much, compared with the value of the work which he does, which he receives. I make no comparison between this Society and any other institution of benevolence in this respect; but this I will say, that no cheaper method of doing the same amount of good has been devised, and that none who value our religion or our liberties, can believe that the amount bestowed on these missionaries is either beyond a just recompense for their toils, or is wasted or lost. The average expense to the Society, during a period of twenty-three years, of supporting a missionary, exclusive of what he receives from the people to whom he ministers, is one hundred and sixty-six dollars a year—including in this average all the expenses of the Society.* The mis-

* The exact average expense for each year may be seen in the following table, prepared by one of the Secretaries of the Society. The tenth column is obtained, by dividing the sum total of the expenditures of each year by the years of labor performed.

Society's Year.	Receipts.	Expenditures.	No. of Missionaries.	Not in commis. the preceding year.	No. of Cong. and Mission. Districts.	Years of Labor.	Additions to Churches.	Sabbath Schools and Bible Classes.	Aver. expen. for a year's labor.	Aver. expen. for ea. Mis-s'y.
1—1826-27	$18,140,76	$13,984,17	169	68	196	110	not rep.	not rep.	$127	$83
2—1827-28	20,035,78	17,849,22	201	89	244	133	1,000	306	134	89
3—1828-29	26,997,31	26,814,96	304	169	401	186	1,678	423	144	88
4—1829-30	33,929,44	42,429,50	392	166	500	274	1,959	572	155	108
5—1830-31	48,124,73	47,247,60	463	164	577	294	2,532	700	160	102
6—1831-32	49,422,12	52,808,39	509	158	745	361	6,126	783	146	104
7—1832-33	68,627,17	66,277,96	606	209	801	417	4,284	1,148	159	109
8—1833-34	78,911,44	80,015,76	676	200	899	463	2,736	Pupils.	172	118
9—1834-35	88,863,22	83,394,28	719	204	1,050	490	3,300	52,000	170	116
10—1835-36	101,565,15	92,108,94	755	249	1,000	545	3,750	65,000	169	122
11—1836-37	85,701,59	99,529,72	810	232	1,025	554	3,752	80,000	180	123
12—1837-38	86,522,45	85,066,26	684	123	840	438	3,376	67,000	194	124
13—1838-39	82,564,63	82,655,64	665	201	794	473	3,920	58,500	175	124
14—1839-40	78,345,20	78,533.89	680	194	842	486	4,750	60,000	162	115
15—1840-41	85,413,34	84,864,06	690	178	862	501	4,618	54,100	169	123
16—1841-42	92,463,64	94,300,14	791	248	987	594	5,514	64,300	159	119
17—1842-43	99,812,24	98,215,11	848	225	1,047	657	8,223	68,400	149	116
18—1843-44	101,904,99	104,276,47	907	237	1,245	665	7,693	60,300	157	115
19—1844-45	121,946,28	118,360,12	943	209	1,285	736	4,929	60,000	160	126
20—1845-46	125,124,70	126,193,15	971	223	1,453	760	5,311	76,700	166	130
21—1846-47	116,717,94	119,170,40	972	189	1,470	713	4,400	73,000	167	123
22—1847-48	140,197,10	139,233,34	1,006	205	1,447	773	5,020	77,000	180	138
23—1848-49	145,925,91	143,771,67	1,019	192	1,510	808	5,550	83,500	178	141

sionary that we send goes often among a poor people, who have their lands to buy, and their forests to fell, and their prairies to break up, and their houses to build, and their wells to dig, and their fences, and bridges, and roads to make, and their school houses and humble sanctuaries yet to rear. He goes often to fields where, as in all new countries, for successive seasons, he, and his family, and his people, may be prostrated with temporary sickness. He goes where it is difficult to procure books, and where for a time he must be deprived of the comforts associated with the idea of an eastern home. We send him too, often, among a people with many prejudices, a people who have as yet much to say against learning in the ministry, and more against Calvinism. Give him time, and he will live all this down. Sustain him a little while, and these prejudices will disappear, and the principles which he holds will diffuse themselves through the community. Lend him for a few years a helping hand, and he will gather around him a people who will build their own churches, and sustain their own pastor, and be in their turn a light and a helper in spreading the gospel abroad:—and as the wilderness and the solitary place where he has gone is made glad, and the desert blossoms as the rose, so on a more distant portion of the wilderness and the solitary place the same blessing diffused shall descend, until the whole land becomes the garden of the Lord.

The Society is constantly appealing to men for their aid. It designs by this service to make an appeal—to avail itself of this method of making its purposes and its wants known. It appeals to those who believe that a vast fertile land like this should not be left without morals and without religion; to those who believe in the downward tendency of human nature, and who would save the land from barbarism; to those who, warned of the evils of infidelity in the old world, would save this beautiful country from its desolating influence; to those who believe that there was occasion for the glorious reformation under Luther, and who would save this fair land from what Spain in the Old world is, and what Mexico is in the New; to those who remember what an intelligent ministry did for New England, when our fathers were driven to these

Western Shores; to those who remember what Harvard, and Yale, and Nassau Hall have done for our country; to those who appreciate in respect to their own hearts and hopes, and in respect to the peace and refinement and intelligence of their own firesides, the value of the evangelical doctrines; to those who have felt the power of the promises of the gospel in opening before themselves the bright visions of immortality, and who would wish that these same blessings should be diffused all over this beloved land.

THE END.

Man's Duty, in Relation to the Lord's Work.

A

SEMI-CENTENNIAL DISCOURSE,

DELIVERED BEFORE THE

MASSACHUSETTS HOME MISSIONARY SOCIETY,

IN BOSTON, MAY 29, 1849.

BY RICHARD S. STORRS, D. D.,
Pastor of the First Church, Braintree.

Published by order of the Executive Committee.

BOSTON:
PRESS OF T. R. MARVIN, 24 CONGRESS STREET.
1849.

DISCOURSE.

ACTS IX. 6.

LORD, WHAT WILT THOU HAVE ME TO DO?

THE conversion of Saul of Tarsus, whèther we regard its attendant circumstances, or its immediate and remote effects on the course of the church and the world, is an event of surpassing interest. Jealous of the honor of his ancestral religion, breathing out threatening and slaughter, and hurrying on to scenes of anticipated triumph over the defenceless disciples of Jesus, he is suddenly arrested by a brilliant light from heaven, and an unearthly voice of tender remonstrance. Overwhelmed by the vision, he falls to the earth. The power of the Highest subdues and transforms him. His spiritual eye enlightened, and his heart changed, his life takes a new direction; the church rejoices in a fresh auxiliary to her works of faith and labors of love; and the wide world thenceforth becomes the object of his solicitude, and the theatre of his hallowed toils and conflicts.

The elements of this great event enter into every instance of conversion over which the angels of heaven rejoice. It has God for its author, truth for its instrument, and the turning of the strong current of man's thoughts, emotions and movements from the carnal to the spiritual, for its effect.

"Trembling and astonished," Paul's heart prompts the inquiry, "Lord, what wilt thou have me to do?" thus revealing the first convictions and resolves of every renovated man; it is the spontaneous and uniform expression of piety, whether new born or matured. We are now concerned, however, only with a single topic of instruction, suggested by the text, viz:

GOD HAS A WORK TO BE DONE BY MAN.

Powerless and dependent as we are, unable to retain our lives or direct our steps by wisdom of our own, it is an undeserved honor to be admitted into the field of God's highest labors, and made sharers of the toils involved in securing the noblest ends of an intelligent existence.

Whatever God would accomplish in this world, he might clearly bring to pass, by that simple energy of Will, that speaks, and it is done—or, commands, and it stands fast. Had it been God's pleasure, who dare say, that man might not have lived without carefulness—the fields supplying him food, the skies dropping honey as the dew, the fowls of the air, the fish of the sea, and every living thing contributing to his comfort, leaving no demand to be enforced on his physical energies, nor the *ennui* of the sluggard to be relieved by unfitting indulgence? So, in the arrangements of the moral world, who dare say, that man might not have been exempted from the necessity of ceaseless intellectual and spiritual discipline, of untiring resistance to the downward tendencies of society, and constant effort to elevate the world to its destined condition of purity and love? If we look to the power of God alone, all this is obviously possible. But Infinite Wisdom has determined, after having incorporated the indestructible elements of activity in man's constitution, that they have scope for their development; that he be placed in circumstances where happiness and labor are identified; where all the faculties gather strength by judicious exercise; and where assimilation to God is proportioned to the constancy of active obedience.

That God has a work for man to do in his relations to the material world, will not however be questioned. The indications of the fact are clear in his entire physical organization; every bone, muscle and tendon of his frame declare him to be made for activity; and his earliest developed propensities demonstrate the same truth, no less than the pressing necessities of his nature, and the testimony of universal experience to the connection between happiness and well regulated action.

Nor are the indications less clear, that God has work for man to do in the *moral* world. The mind never sleeps. Its repose is found in action. Whether it receive impressions or produce them, it feels and acts agreeably to the necessity of its nature; and these impressions correspond in character with the action of the law written on the heart. If that law operate according to its original design, the whole course of life will be marked by beneficence—and love, order, peace and joy will prevail against their antagonistic principles; but if its original design be perverted, and the law in the members triumph, confusion and tears will permeate the whole sweep of its authority.

The great work that God has for man to do, is none other than that begun by Christ, in pursuance of the gracious counsels of eternity. So far as it relates to the magnifying of the law by the shedding of blood, it is already accomplished. In the fearful scenes of Gethsemane and Calvary was the foundation laid for the sinner's restoration to his Maker's favor, by the vindication of Jehovah's truth, and of the majesty and perfectness of his law. Here, God in Christ acted alone, "and of the people there was none with him." But the living structure destined to rise on this foundation, demands human workmanship in connection with the divine; the lively stones composing the spiritual house, are not hewn and brought to their places without man's instrumentality; the world is not to be recovered from sin's dominion, nor the hold of the fallen angel on the race to be broken, nor the clouds of gloomy darkness to be rolled away, and the true Light to be comprehended, without the sustained activities of regenerated humanity. Spiritual ignorance is every where settled and profound. Men know not God as they ought to know him, nor the extent and spirituality of his law; they know not even themselves, nor the principles that control their conduct; they know not Christ, nor apprehend the grand design of his mission to the world; they know not the Holy Spirit, nor receive his reproofs of sin, of righteousness and judgment; they understand not their duties one to another as subjects of a common guilt, and heirs of a common destiny; and, of heaven, the habitation of the pure in heart, as of hell, the eternal home of the wicked, they have no definite conceptions. And, upon these subjects, knowledge is to be diffused;—the Bible is to be sent abroad on the wings of every wind; its doctrines and precepts are to be expounded and fast bound on the conscience; the gospel is to be proclaimed in all its fulness and glory; its paramount authority is to be urged, and its spirit exemplified, while its rewards and punishments are to be displayed in all the vividness and force appropriate to eternal verities; the life giving influences of the Holy Spirit also are to be secured by prayer, with corresponding activity in preparing the hearts of men to receive them. The teachings of the gospel, inefficient in themselves, are mighty only through God, to the pulling down of strongholds, and casting down lofty imaginations; "not by might, nor by power, but by my Spirit, saith the Lord of hosts," is the heart subdued, and the eye turned away from earth to heaven.

The work given man to do, demands faith in God, as the author of every good and perfect gift. Believing, man can do all things; unbelieving, he can do nothing. It demands self-denial, or, the sacrifice of ease and gain—

the doing with all the might, whatsoever the hands find to do, to persuade men to be reconciled to God. It demands practical wisdom ; we are to become all things to all men, that their prejudices may be obviated, their passions quelled, and their attention gained ; and then, every appliance of argument and motive is to be discreetly made. It demands patience and perseverance too ; for ignorance is not to be banished, nor perverseness conquered, nor the regeneration of the individual or the community effected, in a day.

The field of these labors is the WORLD. Divide it as you will, and rear the walls of separation between the nations high as heaven ; let configuration and color, social customs and education, language and religion, hereditary strifes and belligerent dispositions interpose as many barriers between them as the bitterest foe of human equality can desire, yet, as by heaven's ordinance all men are brethren, so by Christ's command, all are to be evangelized. Nor are there wanting on record facts innumerable demonstrative of the power of the Gospel to break the stout heart of the savage warrior, dispel the dark-mindedness of the stubborn idolater, constrain the infidel to hang his hopes on the cross, and subdue the wildest sons of profligacy to the obedience of the faith. The labor demanded therefore is practicable. The end contemplated is attainable.

It is not to be attained however suddenly, by isolated or even united effort. As no possible combination of the energies of man can at once bring every mountain low and exalt every valley, or create lines of communication spanning the earth, and connecting every country, city and hamlet by iron bands ; yet as mountains are giving way and valleys rising, and communications are passing with lightning speed from land to land, and intelligence extending beyond all the conceptions of other years, by the application of newly awaked intellectual energies to the eternal principles of science ; and as the pickaxe and the spade, the drill and the lever, the wheel and the steam in the hands of persevering industry, are tearing down the Alps and the Andes, and circumambulating the world with the precision of the diurnal sun;—so the idolatries and superstitions of the nations, though too deeply imbedded in the corruptions of fallen nature, and of too mountainous height and strength to be swept away at once by any conceivable combination of the moral forces of Christendom, yet "by little and little" may they be subdued and extirpated, as were the Hivite and Canaanite and Hittite of old. If faithful laborers are employed, and furnished with appropriate instruments of operation, and if time be allowed them, and the electric wires of fraternal love and high resolve connect all hearts and hands devoted to Christ and his church, then shall the cloud-capt towers and gorgeous palaces of Pope and Pagan be overturned, and the way cleared for the triumphant march of pure and undefiled religion over the entire moral world. But, as in subduing the elements of nature to human purposes, and levelling the inequalities of the earth's surface, and preparing the way for the freest intercommunication between the several kindreds of the earth, there are various processes to be carried out, and instruments to be used—as the labor involved must be divided into distinct departments, and each department supplied with laborers of appropriate qualifications; so in the conquest of the world to the authority of Jesus, and in the diffusion of the light and love which are to bind all nations in a common brotherhood, a corresponding division of labor and diversity of laborers is demanded. And for this Heaven has made provision in the distribution of its gifts throughout the church, giving to one, as in apostolic days, the word of wisdom, to another the word of knowledge, to another faith, to another the discerning of spirits, to another divers kinds of tongues, and to another the interpretation of tongues. The principle of adaptation, so visible every where in the material creation, is maintained with equal force and clearness throughout the moral world. As the husbandman and the mechanic, the professional man and the merchant, the ship builder and the mariner, in their different departments of labor, each contribute according to their industry and skill to the attainment of the great end proposed by human enterprise and toil—the amelioration of each other's condition, and the increase of the comforts of the great family of man ; so the minister at the altar and the subordinate officer of the church, the theological professor and the Sabbath school teacher, the author of the tract and its distributer, the evangelist at home and the foreign missionary, have each their distinct spheres of action, to be occupied with mutual benefit and a common success, proportioned to the humility and zeal with which their respective duties are performed. The comparative importance of one department or another is scarce a subject of pertinent inquiry ; all of them are marked out in the economy of Providence with like reference to one grand result ; and if filled with faithful laborers, that result will be secured—souls will be saved from death, the earth will be blessed, and God will be glorified.

Thus are we instructed, that to make our influence felt over the world, and accomplish what the Lord would have us do, it is not necessary that we individually traverse and explore each continent and isle of the sea, nor that we become familiar with all languages, and fix the eye with equal directness and intensity on all the various tribes of men. Providence assigns us a field of labor to which our circumstances, abilities and dispositions adapt us, without foreclosing other fields, by such an assignment, against those whose capabilities and desires qualify them for their occupancy. If Paul go to the Gentiles, and Peter remain with the circumcision ; if Edwards labor at Northampton, Stockbridge or Princeton, and Brainerd station himself at Kaunameek ; if Dwight and Griffin trim the midnight lamp for the education of the greater lights of our country, or the edification of our largest churches, and lay their bones in the land of their fathers; so with equal propriety and acceptance Fisk and Parsons explore the desolations of Palestine; Hall and Newell expend their strength on the shores of India; Mills and Ashmun consecrate their energies to the redemption of Africa; and Munson and Lyman lay down their lives in answering calls from the islands of the sea, for emancipation from bloody thraldom. The inquiry, "Lord! what wilt thou have me to do?" is thus answered by the Providence that assigns the field and the species of labor to one and another, in correspondence with their tastes, habits of mental discipline, physical and moral developments, and the "necessity laid upon them."

As to the comparative claims of Home and Foreign missions, it may be said confidently, that they admit of settlement by no rules of man's arithmetic. The imprimatur of heaven is on them both. They are "twins, tied by nature." Each demands the whole-souled support of every friend of Christ. If churches at home languish, missions abroad pine away. If desolations increase here, and thorns of the wilderness spring up in the once blooming garden of the Lord, never will the fragrance of the Rose of Sharon be diffused over the world's wide wilderness. So thought our fathers. So let their children think, and act accordingly.

On the twenty-eighth day of May, 1799, a few friends of Christ from the central and eastern counties of the Commonwealth, assembled by previous agreement in this city of our solemnities, for the organization of a Missionary Society, on the same scriptural principles that have formed the basis of every evangelical association for the world's conversion since Christ went home to heaven. Among them were the honored names of EMMONS, AUSTIN, SIMPKINS, SANFORD, HOPKINS, WELD, SPRING, BARKER, NILES, CRANE and STRONG, who were selected from their compeers to bear the responsibility of carrying out the purpose deliberately formed; of "diffusing the knowledge of the gospel among the heathens as well as other people, in the remote parts of our country, where Christ is seldom or never preached." And, to this movement were they led by the response of Heaven to their prayer, "Lord! what wilt thou have us to do?"

Five years later, when increasing familiarity with the spiritual wants of the world had expanded their views, they so amended the article of the constitution just recited, as to make it embrace the whole family of man. "To diffuse the gospel among the people of the newly settled and remote parts of our country, among the Indians of the country, and through the more distant regions of the earth, as circumstances shall invite, and the ability of the Society shall admit," became thenceforward their all-comprehensive object. Neither a nobler nor a more single one ever presented itself to the human mind. It is large and indivisible as the great command of the ascending Redeemer. Embracing at once the home and foreign fields as equally the Lord's and alike cursed by the usurpations of Satan, and calling for deliverance in tones of unutterable agony—they contemplated nothing less than the moral emancipation of the WORLD, and the shivering of the dark sceptre under which it had "groaned and travailed in pain," for almost six thousand years. Their efforts, it is true, were feeble, and their immediate success small; but their reach of mind commands admiration, and their perseverance amid untold discouragements proves their hearts to have been attempered amid the fires that glow on heaven's altars. To them, the Saviour's life of toil and death of woe illustrated the magnitude and value of the work; the labors and sufferings of Apostles threw around it a quenchless glory; the priceless worth of the gem of immortality concealed in every bosom—its rescue from destruction in the persons of uncounted millions—the redemption of the ground from its entailed curse, and the ineffable splendors of heaven, overspreading eternal ages of blissful occupation—all opened on the eye of their faith the unsearchable riches garnered up in the results of the work the Lord gave them to do—a work as fresh and glorious in the hands of apostles of the nineteenth century as in those of the first.

I have alluded to the feebleness of their early efforts, and the embarrassments that crowded the incipient stages of their enterprise. And this will be understood, by allusion to the fact that during the first year of the organization, one thousand forty-five dollars and eight cents only, were received into their treasury ; and, that no man could be persuaded to enter the missionary field, though appointments were made, and pressed with much entreaty. The second year added but about two hundred dollars to the funds, though four missionaries were obtained ;—one of them for three months, to labor in Vermont, another for several months in Maine, and the others ten months each, in "the new settlements, between Whitestown and the Genesee river, and among the neighboring tribes of Indians." It was a day of small things ; but still it was the birth-day of a system of operations, which now carries joy and gladness into ten thousand habitations of our own land, and makes known the wonderful works of the Lord far and wide throughout the world. I speak advisedly. Wherever were the birth-place of Foreign Missions, and whatever their aliment in their infancy, they were dandled on the knees of the Massachusetts and Connecticut Missionary Societies while they themselves were yet feeble. The Directors and executive officers of "the Board" were chosen from among those whose wisdom and experience had ripened into maturity under the teachings of the Home Missionary spirit ; its plans and movements were devised by those who, like Worcester and Evarts, had taken their lessons in the Home Missionary school ; and its successful labors have been accomplished by men whose earliest philanthropic emotions were inspired by the genius of Home Missions. In this we rejoice as Heaven's arrangement, and the seal of its approbation; and, "as the truth of Christ is in us, no man shall stop us of this boasting in all the regions of Achaia." But with this branch of the Society's early operations in reference to "the Indians of the country and the more distant parts of the earth," we are no farther concerned, since its separation from the parent stock in 1810, and its able management by "the American Board."

Till 1827, the Society struggled for enlargement, and scattered its laborers, sparsely indeed, from Maine to Louisiana, aiming to execute its commission faithfully "among the people of the newly settled and remote parts of our country." The correctness of its policy may fairly be questioned, while the largeness of its desires cannot be too earnestly emulated. Its aims were high, but its energies were crippled by the scantiness of its resources. A little more than fifty thousand dollars, making an average of eighteen hundred per annum, formed the total amount of its receipts during the first twenty-eight years of its existence, exclusive of small donations of Bibles and tracts committed to its missionaries by liberal friends, for gratuitous distribution. During this period, however, experience taught knowledge, the spirit of piety increased, the tokens of future accomplishment multiplied, and the foundations of ultimate success were deeply and broadly laid.

While the Society's charter allowed free course to its movements in all other parts of the land, Massachusetts herself seemed to be regarded as a palace of silver built on a wall, and inclosed with boards of cedar, liable to no decay, requiring no repairs, rich in heavenly treasures, and consequently shut out from the reach of the beneficence that scattered the blessings of the gospel broadcast over "the remote parts of our country." An investigation of facts, however, revealed the mistake. From various causes, some churches had become extinct, others were enfeebled to a degree that rendered their continued existence doubtful, and others still were violently assailed by the adversary who spread out his hand on all their pleasant things, and the area of wasteness and desolation was found to be rapidly extending. This state of things demanded attention. The eye affected the heart, because of the daughters of Zion. And in 1818, the General Association of the State resolved on the organization of the Domestic Missionary Society of Massachusetts, and appointed a Board of Directors, whose labors and successes in raising up fallen churches, strengthening the feeble, relieving the oppressed, and furnishing means of grace to the destitute, admit not of recital here. But after fulfilling its commission for nine years, without being known in law, and with no other funds than the freewill offerings of the people, but with highly gratifying results, it became united with the Society whose semi-centennial we celebrate to-night, in consequence of a change effected in its charter, authorizing and empowering it to employ its funds in Massachusetts or elsewhere, at its discretion. This union long desired, was thus happily consummated.

In the mean time, the American Home Missionary Society had risen into life, as the offspring of that wisdom which is from above, the representative of the Home Missionary spirit of the whole land, and the heaven-ordained agent of accomplishing a stupendous moral revolution in the religious aspects of the country. Its felicitous organization in 1826, its central position, catholic principles and promised efficiency, at once secured confidence. The necessity of such a bond of union as its constitution offered, between the scattered elements of Home evangelization—a necessity arising from our rapidly expanding population, with its heterogeneousness of character, and strong tendencies to unbelief and viciousness, had become extensively felt. As was natural, and even indispensable to the carrying out of the original designs of the Massachusetts Missionary Society, an auxiliary relation was established between them without delay, which has hitherto been maintained, with ever-increasing harmony of sentiment, and mutual advantage.

It is hardly possible to do less, and quite needless to attempt more on an occasion like this, than to "stir up your pure minds by way of remembrance." The enterprise in which we are engaged is not new. The principles on which it rests, are familiar. The spirit that crowns it with success is not a stranger to your hearts; and it is only the cumulative argument, impelling to re-invigorated action, that need be urged. And even this is so often presented, in such variety of phase, and with such cogency of appeal, as well nigh to discourage all attempted utterance of the heart's convictions, that our country, if saved at all, must be saved by the gospel's power. Let me say, however,—

It is a grand moral achievement that is contemplated by Home Missionary Associations—nothing less than the spiritual regeneration of the whole land. Value as we may, intellectual enlightenment, purity of morals, refinement of manners, the peace of neighborhoods, the success of agriculture, manufactures, commerce, or the mechanic arts,—the maintenance of our civil institutions, —the perpetuity of immunities handed down to us from our fathers, and our defences against foreign aggression; —yet all are but the small dust of the balance in comparison with the renewal of the mind in the image of God, and the possession of an incorruptible inheritance in the heavens;—a renewal effected only by God's truth in the hand of the Spirit, and forming the basis of all that is lovely and of good report in each relationship of life, as well as of peace in death, and glory beyond the grave.

1. Through God's favor we have a pleasant land, of whose extent and capabilities no mind but faintly conceives. Exclusive of the late acquisitions from Mexico, the area of the United States admits of division into 376

States as large as Massachusetts; and, including the territories ceded by Mexico, the number of such States rises to 448.* Three millions two hundred and fifty thousand square miles form a broader field than twenty-six kingdoms like Great Britain would cover, and is exceeded only in 500,000 square miles, by all Europe, embracing three empires, sixteen kingdoms, and more than forty other independent states. And it has been said, less accurately, perhaps, than elegantly, that "plains here open to our view as boundless as the ocean; mountains that look down upon the clouds; slopes that cover thousands of miles in extent, and rivers co-extensive. Nature paints on her largest scale; all her figures are colossal; all her features bold and strongly marked." If perchance, loftier mountains, broader streams, or more extensive plains be found elsewhere, there are yet none richer in their productions, more accommodating to the demands of commercial enterprise, nor more abundant in their returns to the hand of industry. Its mineral, vegetable and animal resources are proved exhaustless, by the developments of advancing years. Its ten thousand miles of continuous coal field, its iron mountains, and newly discovered mines of lead and copper, of silver and gold; its numberless lakes and rivers; its verdant hill tops, fruitful vallies and beautiful prairies rolling like the sea, baffle description, while they indicate the purpose of high Heaven to make it forever the glory of all lands. That ancient land whose "brooks of water, fountains and depths springing out of vallies and hills," are celebrated in inspired song—"a land of wheat and barley, and vines and fig trees and pomegranates, a land of oil olive and honey—whose stones were iron, and out of whose hills brass was dug"—was rich indeed, salubrious, and blessed of Heaven; but our own country is richer still, as healthful too, sharing more largely in all that ministers to human welfare.

* See Twelfth Annual Report of Hon. H. Mann to the Board of Education, page 33.

2. Already a population of more than twenty millions spreads itself over this broad land. The Anglo-Saxon race, elevated and vitalized by the influences of a pure Christianity, forms the substratum of the wonderful combination, into which enters in various proportions the imperturbable spirit of the Dutchman, the vivaciousness of the Frenchman, the pride of the Castilian, the hardiness of the Norwegian, and the perseverance of the German. All nations have their representatives among us. And it is more than possible, that after the inevitable effervescing process of these discordant elements shall have passed, the singular compound will receive a deeper impress of whatever is noble in human character than has yet been made on any nation under heaven ; it may be confidently anticipated indeed, if faith shall work by love, and pour into the fused mass a copious mixture of the Apostolic spirit.

3. The unexampled rapidity with which this population increases—in the ratio of three per cent, or eight hundred thousand souls a year—unless it shall be interrupted by unforeseen interpositions of Providence, will give to the country within a hundred years, a larger population than China boasts, and double the amount of that of Europe ; nor in this fact is there anything to excite apprehension, if the knowledge of the Lord shall keep pace with the advancing numbers of the people; for then will there be ever increasing harmony of sentiment and warmth of patriotic emotion, combined with earnestness of effort to extend the blessings of civilized and intellectual life over the broad expanse of the nations. But the mass of ignorance that now exists and accumulates from year to year, through the addition of five hundred thousand foreign immigrants, is not to be removed nor even neutralized in its influence on succeeding generations, apart from systematic and persevering missionary effort.

4. We claim to be a Christian nation ; and the claim is just, in so far as dissent from the faith of Jews, Moham-

3

medans, and Pagans confirms it. The Bible is among us, as a commonly recognized revelation from heaven. The Sabbath to some extent is honored. The sanctuary opens its doors to them that fear God ; and an efficient ministry commands respect extensively and holds the evil tendencies of society in abeyance. Still, infidelity occupies high places, and diffuses itself far and wide. Godlessness abounds. Vice forgets to blush. Crime escapes unpunished. Oppression and violence triumph over the weakness of humanity. Principles of licentiousness take root, and bring forth luxuriantly the grapes of Sodom and the clusters of Gomorrah. Even religion itself is wounded in the house of its friends; and, betrayed into the hands of its enemies, or else clothed in the attire of an harlot, is employed by the great seducer to bind over multitudes to destruction.

But of the varieties of religious faith, and observance, and of the feuds of rival sects, I need only say, that as the legitimate offspring of combined imbecility and corruption, they will vanish before the advancing light of the Sun of righteousness, as offensive reptiles and beasts of prey disappear before the manly enterprise that converts their hiding-places into blooming fields and cultivated gardens. Formalism may assert its title to the heavenly inheritance, but meek spirituality successfully confronts it. Fanaticism may boast of new revelations and of intercourse with disembodied spirits, but an intelligent and whole-souled piety confounds it. Rationalism claims a higher divinity than it allows to the Word of God, but cowers in the presence of the unsophisticated faith that "knows the Bible true, and knows no more." Romanism, dark-minded, jesuitical and destructive in all its bearings on civil and religious liberty, may arrogate the honors that belong to God alone, but in the evangelism that pervades the Protestant community, it finds an invincible antagonist. So happily has Heaven adjusted the checks and balances of truth and error, that we have nothing to fear from the prevalence of the latter, if we fall not from our steadfastness in maintaining the former.

The world is a wide battle-field of conflicting principles and opinions. In far the largest part of it, a servile subjection to hierarchical establishments and traditionary records is gloried in. Freedom of thought and independence of judgment are unknown. The mind quietly submits to vassalage. Ignorance is the mother of idolatrous and superstitious worship, and corruption is its father. Largeness of mind, purity of heart, and integrity of conduct are sacrificed to the lusts of the flesh, and the baser passions of the moral nature. But nowhere is the field of conflict so clear, nor an active contest so warmly waged, or so promising in its issue, as in our own country; for no consolidated superstitions are here—no ecclesiastical establishments frown defiance on the spirit of open inquiry; no powerful priesthood throws into prison the offending preacher of God's truth, nor maintains the right of dictating terms of admission to the privileges of citizenship and offices of State; nor does any civil power interfere with the rights of conscience, and impose "pains and penalties" for non-adherence to prescribed forms of faith; but every man worships when and where he chooses, or *nowhere* if he dare, and adopts and defends opinions, under responsibilities to none but Jehovah! And if, as a consequence of this unrestricted liberty, repulsive errors come in like a flood, and proselytism run rampant, and "confusion worse confounded" temporarily prevail, so that "truth falls in the streets, and equity cannot enter"—yet have we nothing to fear, while the field of argument is open to all, and while with spiritual weapons in our hands, we faithfully follow the leadership of the Lord, mighty in battle. Truth is mightier than the mightiest, as God is higher than the highest among the children of men. Further,

5. True it is, that the moral desolations of the land are wide and appalling, and thousands of communities, and

millions of individuals are groping their way in darkness, to the judgment seat of Christ. And it is clear that these moral wastes are most numerous in portions of the country, where the foundations of society are not yet laid in just and commonly understood principles, and cemented by mutual acquaintance and love;—where the forest slowly yields to the woodman's axe, and the plow-share is driven with difficulty through soil undisturbed for centuries, except by the tramp of the buffalo, and the swift-footed hunter. Physical wants there press heavily; every energy is tasked for the supply of food and raiment; and the cravings of the intellectual and moral nature for appropriate aliment are unheeded. Error and dissipation too, are widely triumphant amid these scenes of desolation. The arm of civil authority is weak, and imposes few restraints. Educational influences, however strong in the happier circumstances of childhood, operate but feebly on neglected manhood. The sound of the church-going bell is rarely heard; the solemn assembly is forsaken; and the Sabbath, stripped of its sacredness, is devoted to recreation or vicious indulgence. Even where the institutions of religion languish in happy New England, the bands of social order break asunder, the youth grow up to ignorance, the spirit of honorable enterprise fails, and hard griping avarice, or low-lived cunning, and filthy pleasures absorb the mind's wakefulness, uprooting honest industry, banishing domestic confidence, and laying open the whole community to the ingress of the foulest spirits of the pit; but, far more broadly true is this of other sections of the country, where religious institutions have never yet laid strong hold on the public mind—where thousands on thousands of children and youth are untaught the first rudiments of human and divine knowledge, where half the adult population cannot read the oracles of God, and nine-tenths of the remaining half prefer the instruction that causeth to err from the words of knowledge! Caterers to sensuality are never wanting there; preachers of another gospel than that which Paul proclaimed, are ever at hand to do their master's work ; edition after edition, of the doctrine taught in Eden, revised and amended, bound and gilded after the latest fashion, is thrown off, caught up, and greedily devoured by such of the community as have threaded the mazes of the spelling-book, and become thereby wiser than Moses or Solomon. They scatter around them a moral pestilence, breaking forth in boils and blains more grievous and fatal than those which covered the Egyptians—issuing in death eternal. Besides,

6. The heterogeneousness of the population involves a thousand diversities of intellectual habits and social customs, as well as of religious and political opinions. From these, spring prejudices and strifes, whose inveteracy and violence, time only, in combination with evangelical instruction, can undermine and destroy. The sentiments and habitudes of early life, yield but slowly, in the most auspicious circumstances, to later influences ; and nothing short of the power from on high, operating through the truth of Revelation laid upon the conscience, can thoroughly subdue them. The Sandwich Islander may be Americanized—the enslaved African may become an independent and honored citizen—the oppressed Irishman may be transformed into an intelligent freeman—and the Russian serf may learn to appreciate the blessings of liberty ; but years must roll on, and intellectual and moral appliances must be wisely and perseveringly used before homogeneity of feeling and action will be produced between them. Bring all classes into the same daily pupilage, and under a common system of evangelical instruction—and their social customs, religious and political opinions, with the prejudices and passions nourished by them, will ultimately be melted down like mingled ores in a common crucible, and prepared for harmonious action in all that concerns the interests of Zion and the world.

Such a result demands varied labors for its accomplishment, and an energy of faith, indomitable as that which coursed through the veins of the Puritan fathers two hundred years ago. The Bible must be put within the reach of all ; the colporteur must explore the dormitories of ignorance and the dens of iniquity ; the schoolmaster must be abroad ; the Sabbath school must be sustained on the basis of a broad evangelical Catholicism ; and no effort may be spared to furnish every family with the productions of the religious press. But an instrumentality high above all this, and to which all else is subsidiary, is the holy MINISTRY, ordained of heaven to command all men every where to repent,—to establish churches, administer ordinances, and supervise the auxiliary movements of the spirit of benevolence. Aside of this, every other instrumentality is as powerless to subdue and bind the man of sin, as the green withes and flaxen cords of the Philistines to conquer the son of Manoah. It is the word preached, that becomes the power of God, and the wisdom of God unto salvation. "Faith cometh by hearing ;"—and, "how shall they hear without a preacher!"

7. We have a paramount duty to discharge to our country. Here are the sepulchres of our fathers. Here are our homes, and the homes of our posterity ; and here must our bones rest till the dawn of the resurrection morning. Not only so, but it is the LORD's land, committed to us, for cultivation and the ingathering of his harvest ; and if the vine be dried up, and the fig tree languish ; the pomegranate tree, the palm tree also, and the apple tree, even all trees of the field wither, and the wheat and the barley of the field perish, then shall shame cover us. This work is committed to us alone. No other nation can share it. And we have abundant *means* to accomplish it. If we speak of wealth, it is here ; or of laborers, they are here ; or of faith and prayer and energy, they are all here. These are the Lord's TREASURES, to be freely poured forth at the call of his providence ; and, whatever other channels are prepared for their outflow, Home Mis-

sions is second to none. "Go! preach my Gospel, saith the Lord;" the living voice, the speaking eye, the strong inward emotion gaining utterance through every limb and muscle of the frame, have mightier power over the spirits of men, and bring them into closer contact with the Spirit of God, than all other means combined; apart from them, indeed, all else is powerless as moon-beams on the ice of the polar circles.

8. And then—if the extremities of the earth are to be reached, and all nations are to be brought to the feet of Jesus, it must be done by the instrumentality of the fifty millions of the Anglo-Saxon race, spread over this and our fatherland. Piety and zeal certainly exist in some other portions of Christendom, but the labors and sacrifices to which they prompt, however great, cannot be commensurate with the home demand. The Anglican and American families have a special commission, clear as the sun shining in his strength, to give the knowledge of Christ to every people under heaven. To fulfil this commission, the flame of love must burn brightly on our own altars; religion pure and undefiled must be vigorously maintained in our own bosoms. None of our churches may be left to decay, nor our fields to grow over to thorns and briars; but the gospel must be proclaimed in all its richness and power throughout the land, that converts to righteousness may be multiplied, the friends of truth strengthened, and every desolate waste transformed into a garden of the Lord!

Brethren! Can you doubt what the Lord would have you to do? Your country is before you. Its wants are known to you. Its dangers are seen; its calls are heard; its destiny is yet undecided.

Would you swell the amount of its industry, wealth and beneficence? Evangelize it throughout.

Would you confirm and perpetuate its admirable civil institutions, and political privileges? Proclaim in every part of it the Gospel.

Would you give activity to mind, increase its acquisitions, and render the common school, the college and the higher seminary, nurseries of intelligence and virtue? Establish every where the authority of the Bible!

Would you refresh the hearts of thousands who are waiting for the consolation of Israel, and ready to perish through lack of the crumbs that fall from your Father's table? Send them the pastor, who will break to them the bread of life.

Would you turn back upon its source the strong current of licentiousness, and save the bulwarks of freedom and the temples of God from threatened overthrow? Make the voice of Jehovah Jesus heard—"hitherto shalt thou come, but no farther."

Would you increase the moral influence of the country on the destinies of the world, and through the ten thousand filaments connecting it with other nations create the vibrations of love and good will in all human bosoms? Then echo the glad tidings in the ear of every American from the Aroostook to Mexico, and from the Atlantic to the Pacific. Or,

Would you multiply your own consolations, and send your treasures before you into heaven, and secure friends who will receive you to everlasting habitations? Then devote the gracious gifts of God to your country's evangelization. Spare not. Grudge not. Labor earnestly. You have hold on the same enterprise sustained by him who commanded the Apostles to "begin at Jerusalem." Prosecute it to the end. Heaven hallows it. The world feels its impulse. And ere long, its results will blend in the completion of that temple whose top stone will be brought forth with shoutings of Grace, grace unto it.

A word more in conclusion. "Give me a place where to stand, and I will throw the world from its orbit," was the vain boast of the ancient philosopher. "Twelve men were sufficient to establish Christianity," says the so-called philosopher of modern days, "but one shall suffice to overthrow it." Presumptuous boasting! Blood and carnage, desolation and war follow its utterance; but Christianity lives, escapes unharmed the flood of waters poured forth to swallow her up, and multiplies her bloodless victories. SHE has a place to stand, hard by the throne of God, and in her hand a lever that lifts the world. She plants her three thousand missionaries on pagan ground, and sustains other thousands amid her own waste places; she pours forth the light of truth from hundreds of presses, and gathers millions of her sons and daughters into Sabbath schools; she disperses the oracles of God by tens of millions among the rich and the poor, and scatters the leaves that are for the healing of the nations, by hundreds of millions; forswearing unchaste alliances with the principalities and powers of the world, she arrays herself calmly against war and oppression, undermines thrones of despotism, and compels tyranny to bite the dust.

Still, says the enemy in his wrath, "I will pursue, I will overtake, and divide the spoil;"—but, the wind of heaven blows, the sea returns, he sinks like lead in the mighty waters.

Oceans shall be drained, the strong foundations of the earth loosed, the sun turned into darkness and the moon into blood, and all the elements of nature thrown back into their primitive chaos, sooner than the moral kingdom of Jehovah shall be shaken. Omnipotence must be dethroned before the triumphs of Zion can be confounded. When I see the church of God borne safely in an ark of gopher-wood over floods that drown a world filled with violence, and again, wending its way on dry ground through the channels of the deep; when I see the hearts of kings turned as the rivers of water are turned, the mouths of lions stopped, the violence of fire quenched, and armies of aliens turned to flight, and then listen to the great voice out of heaven, saying, "Behold! the tabernacle of God is with men, and he will dwell with them, and wipe away all tears from their eyes," I cannot doubt the continued triumphs of the church over the boundless craft and furious opposition of earth and hell. What persecution has she not endured in by-gone days, what tortures has she not been subjected to, at what time has she not been compelled to wade, step by step, through blood flowing from her own veins, constantly inquiring, "Lord! what wilt thou have me to do?" All this has humbled, but not conquered her. Nay, the sword and the faggot, the dungeon and the rack have proved her life. Her foundations are laid too deep, and her top-stone is reared too high to be reached by the arms of man or of fallen angels. Never have the heathen raged, nor the kings of the earth set themselves, nor the rulers taken counsel together, nor the angel of the bottomless pit sent forth his armies like scorpions, nor the great red dragon fought with Michael and his angels for the mastery over the world, when the Lord God has not spoken to them in his wrath, and vexed them in his sore displeasure, and finally broken them with a rod of iron, and dashed them in pieces as a potter's vessel. And ere long, when the trump of the seventh angel shall sound, great voices shall be heard in heaven, saying, "The kingdoms of this world are become the kingdoms of our Lord and his Christ, and He shall reign forever and ever."

In the prospect of such a consummation, who rejoices not! But to hasten it in its time we have much to do. The relations and claims of our country determine the sphere of our activity. The vastness of its extent and capabilities, the peculiar character of its present and prospective population, its wide destitutions, its multiform religions, its Gorgon infidelity and blaspheming atheism, with its rampant vices, and atrocious crimes, its intimate connections with other nations, and its mighty influence for good or ill over the world, according to the spirit that pervades its bosom, through the channels of learning, commerce, and quenchless enterprise—all distinctly announce our duty to "publish salvation," and say to every city, hamlet and individual of the land, "Jehovah reigns."

Would you then, brethren, bless your country and the world? Rise to labor, and lead forth the streams of salvation, and invite every man who claims a common birthright here, to come to the waters—to come, and drink, and drink again, without money and without price. So shall our American Zion become an eternal excellency—joy shall fill her sanctuaries, glory shall cover her palaces, and her righteousness shall spring forth before all nations.

"O thou,
Whose kingdom shall extend,
Till earth like heaven, thy name shall fill,
And men like angels do thy will;
Shine on our path, in mercy shine,
Prosper our work, and make it thine."

OUR COUNTRY FOR THE SAKE OF THE WORLD.

A

SERMON

IN BEHALF OF THE

AMERICAN HOME MISSIONARY SOCIETY,

PREACHED IN THE CITIES OF NEW YORK AND BROOKLYN,

MAY, 1851,

BY

REV. DAVID H. RIDDLE, D.D.,

PITTSBURGH, PA.

NEW YORK:

PRINTED FOR THE AMERICAN HOME MISSIONARY SOCIETY,

BY BAKER, GODWIN & CO.,

No. 1 Spruce Street.

1851.

SERMON.

PSALM 67: 1, 2.

GOD BE MERCIFUL UNTO US, AND BLESS US, AND CAUSE HIS FACE TO SHINE UPON US.

THAT THY WAY MAY BE KNOWN UPON EARTH, THY SAVING HEALTH AMONG ALL NATIONS.

The beautiful principle embodied in these words, we propose, on this occasion, to apply to the subject of Home Missions; for rightly understood, we think it places that enterprise in its most attractive and sublime relations. This principle, if we have apprehended it, is, that the establishment and prevalence of right religious influences and institutions in our own land, is the surest and speediest method of securing the evangelization of the world. The principle originally applied, of course, to those who lived under the Old Testament dispensation. This Psalm belonged to the liturgical service of the Jewish church; and was a portion, therefore, not merely of the private devotional reading of that people, but of their public religious education. It was designed and adapted to develop a proper spirit in the mass of the people, and to shape the genius of the ancient church.

The peculiar structure of the passage shows the close relation existing between the spiritual prosperity of God's ancient people, and the salvation of the nations of the earth. "God be merciful unto us, and bless us, and cause his face to shine upon us." In these words is acknowledged God's blessing as the true source of national excellence and prosperity, and the only security of their glorious institutions. But why did they so earnestly desire this blessing and the perpetuity of their national institutions? "That thy way"—God's revealed method of salvation—"may be known on earth, thy saving health"—God's means of curing the moral maladies of man—"among all nations." "God shall bless us, and all the ends of the earth shall fear him." This view of the passage, which accords, we think, with all just principles of philosophy, exhibits the ancient church in a lovely, to some, possibly in a novel aspect. Even in the ancient church, when under tutors and governors, till the times appointed by the Father, there was cultivated an expansive benevolence, which embraced the wants and wretchedness of the race—a spirit which taught them to esteem themselves trustees of the blessings of God's salvation for "all nations." To every child of Abraham his native land was peculiarly lovely, associated as it was in every hill and valley with so many glorious recollections of the past; the land of promise, where the battles of the Lord had been fought by the heroes of faith; where the bones of the Patriarchs reposed; where the Ark of the Covenant dwelt, and the Shekinah appeared. In their jubilees piety and patriotism blended in the rapturous cry, "He hath not dealt so with any nation." But when the true spirit of the dispensation of types and shadows was imbibed, their country, the glory of all lands, was most glorious in its destined relations to God's plans towards the world,—loveliest, as the chosen centre whence the "lines" of "saving health" should "go forth through all the earth," and bless and beautify "all nations." A genuine patriotism baptized with the spirit of religion, became, as it always must, a blessed and world-wide philanthropy. In his nation and country was embosomed, and afterwards manifested, "a light" which was to lighten the Gentiles, as well as be "the glory of his people Israel." When the church should obey the voice of her Lord, "Arise, shine, for thy light is come, and the glory of the Lord is risen upon thee," then nations would come to her light, and kings to the brightness of her rising. The forces of the Gentiles, the abundance of the sea, the flocks of Kedar, the rams of Nebaioth, gold and incense, the fir-tree, the pine-tree, and the box together,—the peculiar products of every clime and the glory of every kindred, were to beautify his sanctuary, and make the place of his feet glorious. And for this purpose, to them were intrusted the Oracles of God, and to them pertained the adoption, and the glory, and the covenants, and the giving of the Law, and the service of God, and the promises. Theirs were the fathers, of whom, as concerning the flesh, Christ came, who is over all, God blessed forever.

A Jew, rightly trained by the inner spirit and genius of this dispensation, would therefore prize his institutions, and pray for their continuance; would most earnestly of all desire God's blessing, the sunshine of his face and favor on his native land, for the sake and salvation of others, yea of "*all nations.*" "God be merciful unto us, and bless us, and cause his face to shine upon us, that thy way may be known upon earth, thy saving health among all nations." "As the new wine is found in the cluster," potentially and in purpose, and one saith, "destroy it not, for a blessing is in it," the Jew would rejoice that one whose word was omnipotent for preservation, had said this of his land and nation, because in it, to God's eye and the eye of faith, was found an element, not yet indeed matured, the new wine of the kingdom of God, which yet all nations were to drink for refreshment and salvation—the prelibation of a nobler cup at the marriage supper of the Lamb.

Brethren, as Americans, and especially as American Christians, we are privileged as was the ancient Jew, and for analogous reasons, to love our country, and to pray for God's blessing and the sunshine of his favor on our native land! Patriotism, without boastful presumption, may say, "He hath not dealt so with any nation." God never made such another country as ours. The sun, as he goes careering and rejoicing as a strong man to run his race, from the one end of heaven to the other, does not shine on another land like this. Yes! we may, and for good and substantial reasons, LOVE OUR COUNTRY. But there is a nobler sentiment which should be enkindled in every soul, and incorporated with every passion, and refine and ennoble every thought and feeling and action of all our mighty population—OUR COUNTRY FOR THE SAKE AND SALVATION OF OUR WORLD. If we are true to our mission, and imbibe the spirit of our Master, and walk worthy of the manhood of the church, and be not rebuked by the manifestations even of its pupilage; American patriotism, baptized by piety, must become a blessed world-embracing—world-benefiting—world-saving philanthropy!

We should seek the blessing of God on our country, and labor for its spiritual prosperity, and the universal establishment, in all our borders, of christian institutions and their collateral and consequent influences. And he is not a Christian, in deed and in truth, who does not do this to the full extent of his ability and opportunity, by his wealth, example and influence. But Oh! what an increment of motive and energy will be added to all, if we do this, as the willing instruments and conscious trustees of the great God, for the speedy and universal evangelization of our race.

On this high ground, we desire to place the enterprise, and obligations, and glory of Home Missions. We plead and labor for the establishment and extension of a sound ministry, and the evangelical influences which invariably cluster around it, beneficent to man and conservative of his interests in all his relations. By the enlargement of Home Missions, correspondently with our unparalleled enlargement of territory, and increase of population, we desire to secure the prevalence of true piety and christian principles at home; but in so doing, we are pleading and laboring for a world's redemption, for the good of a race for which Christ died, and over which he is set to reign; and thus, indirectly, indeed, but effectually and practically, we are fulfilling the injunction of the Master, "Go ye into all the world, and preach the Gospel to every creature." We try to fulfil this intensive dispensation of christianity in our land as represented by David, that so "the mustard seed," the symbol of its extension, may grow to its destined proportions, and happy spirits from all nations may sing amidst its branches, thence to take their flight, in joyous myriads, and nestle amidst the branches of the tree of life in the midst of the paradise of God, where all at last, of every tribe, and kingdom, and clime, will sing together the new song of Moses and the Lamb.

Let our whole land be leavened, our country thoroughly evangelized—let all our institutions be brought under the sanctifying influences of christian principles; let all our population, high and low, rich and poor, learned and rude, from the President who occupies the people's house, to the peasant who inhabits the lowliest hamlet or hovel of our Western wilds, be baptized with the spirit of Jesus Christ; let Christianity of a pure apostolic type, reign without a rival in all our councils, modify all our legislation, be the inspiring genius of all our commercial, agricultural, and manufacturing interests ; let its precepts direct the application of our increasing and superfluous wealth, and the grace of its author guide us in projecting and prosecuting our schemes of philanthropy ; let America, in a word, as the result of God's blessing on her institutions of religion and organs of benevolent action, once fully realize her responsibility to God, and see aright her mission to mankind, and the way of God would soon be known on earth, and his *saving health* would soon be experienced among all nations. Right institutions, civil and religious—the common heritage of man, and which appertain equally and inalienably to all nations, and which we hold in trust for the rest of the race, would soon be enjoyed by this dark and troubled world, tossed so long by tempests on the surges of unavailing change. The prayer of the great American church of all denominations, caught from the ancient oracle, should be, "God be merciful unto us, and bless us, and cause his face to shine upon us, that thy way may be known upon earth, thy saving health among all nations." And every one who has a heart to love God, his country and his kind, should say, Amen ! For it is the prayer and response of enlightened patriotism, enlarged philanthropy, and true Christianity.

This position of Home Missions is based on the assumption of the immense influence of our country, for good or evil, on the other nations of the earth,—a postulate which we presume will be questioned by no intelligent Christian or citizen who has allowed his mind at all, or intelligently at least, to dwell upon the subject. The providence and past dealings of God seem to say to our country, "Who knoweth whether thou art come to the kingdom for such a time as this?" In the arrangements of that Being who "setteth up one and putteth down another," whether it be spoken of a nation or a man only, we have come to a position of peculiar, at least, if we cannot say peerless eminence, amongst existing nations; to the possession of extensive, if not incomparable influence, giving us incalculable power over the rest of the world. With a gladness of gratitude, not unmingled with solicitude for the fearful responsibilities involved, we gather evidences of this, alike from the acknowledgment of friends, and the unwilling but not less unequivocal admissions of our enemies; from the hopes of the struggling masses, and the fears of the dominant and oppressive minorities of the earth. And was there ever "such a time as this," when so many elements derived from the intimations of prophecy and occurrent events, combined to constitute and justify the expectations of a crisis, and when the possession of power involved such mighty responsibilities? Granting that there is to be an end, as unquestionably there is an expectation, that God—who has allowed these anticipations to be gradually formed in the great heart of humanity, deepening and becoming more definite from age to age—means to meet and fulfil them; that the scoff of an atheistic age, "all things are to continue as they were from the beginning of the creation," in never-ending cycles of expectation and disappointment, is unphilosophical, as well as untrue; do not the signs and the tendencies of the times, the voice of prophecy, the wants of the world, the deep cry of our baffled race "made subject to vanity," all seem to indicate, that soon God's "way is to be known on earth, and his saving health among all nations?" and that our country, for this purpose has been raised up, and trained, and disciplined, and preserved through all our past vicissitudes and perils as a nation?

Surely God has a purpose in so ordering events, that elements of power, at particular periods, should come into the possession of particular nations, so that they may exert a decisive influence on the destinies of the age and the fate of the world. "If thou hadst known, even thou, at least in this thy day, the things which belong unto thy peace," said the Saviour, to a nation of old; "but now they are hid from thine eyes." Thus it has been often in the past history of the world. If nations could have seen their dispensation, as we now see it—could our light have been thrown back on their path, or the issues thundered in trumpet tones, how different would have been their consciousness of their mission, and possibly, the course of their conduct.

At one period, had one more onward step been taken, Carthage, the representative of African, instead of Rome, the representative of European civilization, might have triumphed, and been mistress of the world: and at another, had some other general, instead of Grouchy, been selected, who would have scorned to taint his itching palm with gold, the tide of battle might have been turned at Waterloo, and with it, the fate of the world. God, who "hath determined the times, and the bounds of our habitations before appointed," seems to have purposed that our country, if conscious of her mission and prepared to meet it, may exert a mighty, possibly a decisive influence on the destinies of the earth, and have a glorious part assigned her amidst the last acts of the long drama of time. And shall it be said of us, "Oh! if thou hadst known in this thy day?" Or shall we try to realize our true mission, and come to the consciousness of God's kind intentions before it is too late? There is danger indeed of unduly modifying the interests and probable results of our own period, and of exaggerating every present crisis, and of glorifying our own particular mission. Many such a presumed crisis has passed, and the world abideth still. Heaven and earth have been invoked, in regard to the perils or prospects, now forgotten, or remembered by the thoughtful student or antiquary with the smile of pity or contempt. But surely "the end cometh."

There is a great temptation, also, to exaggeration among Americans. But aside from all these self-exalting exaggerations, in the sober and solemn light of facts and statistics, and the deep responsibilities they involve, we can hardly adequately measure the present, and especially the prospective greatness and consequent influence of our country. This impression is deepened by every view we can take of our country.

Look at the extent of territory, embraced in our present limits, immensely enlarged by recent annexations and acquisitions, requiring new editions of geography and alterations of maps every year to keep pace with our progress. Stretching already from the Atlantic to the Pacific, from wintry Maine to golden California! What a country! What an immense sea coast! And then a northern boundary of glorious inland seas—God's highways of commerce and communication from one extremity to the other!

The same impression is made, if we look at the *physical resources of our country*—the almost immeasurable capacity of sustaining population, and the almost infinitely varied productions of her soil. The natural resources of the American continent, it is computed, would afford sustenance to 3,600,000,000 inhabitants—four times the estimated present population of the globe. The Western country alone, could supply the whole world with bread-stuffs! I remember to have seen at one time, years ago, on the levee at St. Louis, a pile of such, half a mile long, and nine feet high!

Again, this impression is deepened, if we think of the *prospective population of our country*. It is conjectured, that fifty years from this time, we shall have a population of 75,000,000; and 100 years hence, of 275,000,000. In other words, where there is now one person, 50 years hence there will be 5, and 100 years from this time 16. And these will not be serfs or paupers, but American freemen, enlightened by education, conscious of their rights, and privileges, and powers, whether moulded and restrained by religion or not. Long before this latter period, our people, reinforced from the effete nations of the old world, will have filled up the vast basin of the Mississippi, and stretched across the Rocky Mountains to the shores of the Pacific, and be occupying centres of commercial wealth and of moral power, in close proximity to China and the East; and thus, empire and civilization, completing the mystic cycle, will reach the point whence they began their march westward round the world! Recent developments prove how speedily their centres can be moved half across a continent. Long before that time, too, the appliances of locomotion and transportation, now going forward, will be completed. Intelligence will be transmitted, with lightning speed, from one end of the continent to the other. From Boston and New-York, to San Francisco and Oregon City, dispatches can be sent in a few seconds, to hasten vessels of steam across to China, or Japan; and men may travel continuously from Maine to California without breaking the Sabbath.

Again, the same view is confirmed if we think of the *enterprise of our country*. How many hundreds of thousands of square miles of territory have we settled already; and how many tens of thousands of miles of canals and railroads have we constructed, and are now constructing and projecting! What immense primeval forests have given place, as by enchantment, to villages and towns and cities! See how agriculture, and commerce, and manufactures, and schools, and churches spring up along the path of American enterprise! In virtue of this characteristic the United States have already become the third, if not the second in the rank of commercial nations. The rapidity of our growth in this respect, throws Tyre, and Venice, and Holland, and England altogether into the shade. We now compete successfully with England in furnishing ships, engines and machinery for other nations. We excel and undersell her, in almost every market of the world; and by superior diplomacy, share with her in the results of her conquests in India and China. At the wharves of Pittsburg we fit out vessels for the trade of the Orinoco. American artisans build railroads for the Autocrat of Russia. They construct steamers for the Sultan of Turkey, and build and drive coaches across the desert for the Pacha of Egypt. We shall soon have lines of communication across the Isthmus of Darien, and a continuous communication to the Pacific, across the continent. But a few years ago, we carried on a war with one nation of the New World, and without inconvenience, fed at the same time the starving nations of the Old. Go where you will over the globe, and you will find Americans—amidst the icebergs of the Northern and Southern Poles, in the ports of China, India and Japan, in the Bosphorus and the Baltic, at the foot of the Himalayas and the Caucasus, at the World's Fair in London, and in search of Sir John Franklin!

In the same connection we may notice the element of power involved in *our unity*. With this immense population, and almost measureless resources, we shall have, unless evil counsels and sectional animosities prevail—which God in his mercy forbid—the influence of a united people. There is nothing like this in Europe. The ten toes of the great image, part iron and part clay, have no common principle of cohesion. European influence is frittered, from the fact that it has had no unity since the age of Charlemagne. Europe is but a congregation of nations of different languages, habits, and religions; and the traveller feels it as he passes from Britain to France, Spain, Germany, and Italy. But power, as it passes into our hands, comes to one people, speaking the same language, the language of Milton, Shakspeare, and the English Bible, having one literature, and one great common soul. Amidst all other ominous aspects, it is cheering to see how soon the process of homogeneity and nationalization is perfected here. Contrary to all antecedent reasoning, and in face of the Latin adage, "*Cælum, non animum mutant qui trans mare currunt,*" it is a fixed fact, that men of all nations and languages, are here unified and Americanized! It seems as if the great God meant of all these materials to "make one new man," a type of humanity embracing the separate excellencies of all other forms. The element of power, for good or evil, involved in this unity and nationality, is immense. Already the name of America, embodying our institutions and the weight of our example, to the hope of millions, is strangely magical, in the ears and hearts of the savage and civilized portions of the Old World. What will it be, if fifty years hence finds us as now, "E PLURIBUS UNUM;" when the new man, now comparatively in childhood, shall have grown to the measure of the stature of his destined proportions? What will be the influence of such a united and immense people, for good or evil, to scatter christianity and its temporal accompaniments and eternal consequences, or circulate pestilence and death over our world ? In this view especially, the problem of perpetuated union, to the christian philanthropist, presents reflections of unparalleled intensity and interest. It is especially in the light of the the great idea, our country for the sake of the world, that the question of division and secession should be contemplated ; and that Christians are concerned to know whether the centrifugal forces must necessarily be predominant, or whether one national life cannot be made to pervade this great land, notwithstanding differences of sentiment, and interests, and peculiar institutions.

If we look at these elements separately, especially if we combine them together on the most obvious principles, it must be allowed that our influence will be great ; the weight of our example must be felt, the spirit of our institutions will be copied, and the type of our christianity or infidelity will be reproduced over the globe. We are set for the rise or the fall of many in our world. Nations unborn will rise up and call us blessed, if we become their benefactors, or load us with their heaviest curses, if we disappoint their rightful expectations. Oh ! my country, after traversing thy beautiful prairies, and vast rivers, and inland seas, and viewing thy growing territory, and population, and future prospects, especially these elements of power ; who that has a heart to love God, or his race, can refrain from praying, " God be merciful unto us, and bless us, and cause his face to shine upon us, that thy way may be known upon earth, thy saving health among all nations !"

We do believe—who can indeed help believing ?—that if these elements of power are christianized and consecrated to the glory of God, and the spiritual good of men; if in our voyages and circumnavigations to every port where we traffic, and to every people where we transport our fabrics, we take the Bible, and a beautiful exemplification of its precepts in our own lives and principles; if American enterprise becomes synonymous with christian activity, and the love of Christ—the noblest and sweetest passion—comes to constrain commercial men, with a power and constancy equal to the love of money, which is the meanest; the way of God will soon be known on earth, and his saving health among all nations. On the other hand, if these elements be left to flow forth in selfish and vainglorious channels, unregulated by conscience and a sense of accountability; if the American name becomes identified in the apprehensions of the nations of the earth, with cunning, covetousness, and accumulation; then, no tongue can tell or heart conceive the influence for evil which will be exerted all over the earth, by our country.

We try to abound in hope; but we cannot altogether repress our fears, when we study the history of the spirit of trade in past ages, and trace, with facts before us, the premonitory symptoms of the decline and fall of the ancient centres of commercial greatness, which have successively figured and faded on the tableau of time. It is sad to muse on the elements of the glory of ancient Tyre; it is a solemn study, in view of the portraiture of the prophet Ezekiel, and the accomplished fact, to remember the late prediction of the Secretary of the Treasury in regard to this city, that "*soon the balance sheet of nations will be adjusted in New-York.*" We are a great people, indeed, and our greatness is increased on every side, and is increasing every decade. While traversing the mighty West, a man finds himself saying, "This is a great country—great for good or evil, for Christ or Antichrist!" Which shall it be? Whose shall be these prairies and cities, and this stalwart yeomanry? What part will they take in the great battle of principle? Whose forces will they swell in the last conflict? There is one reply every Christian would love to make, but there is an alternative also, in which all this enginery will be for evil—part of "the sublime mechanics of depravity," more potent, because more polished instruments of perdition.

Yes! American Christians, in the nature of the case and from the analogies of the past, it is safe to conclude that we must be a great people, but not necessarily or universally a holy people. This, with the blessing of God, depends on the efforts and sacrifices of those who have pledged themselves, and covenanted with God, to make the world's salvation their paramount concern, and every thing else subservient thereunto; and who, understanding aright the relations of our country to the world, as we have tried to depict them, have resolved to do their part under this stirring idea, "at such a time as this." For, let no man delude himself with the dream, alike contrary to fact and philosophy, that without evangelical influences and institutions, any thing else, however excellent, will preserve us as a people from ruin. There is no absolute warrant of safety in the peerlessness of our position, the grandeur of our mission, or the awful results of our failure; no promise of God, to prevent the most terrible catastrophe which fancy can conceive, or past history enables us to realize, provided we do not use the means which God has put in our power. Unless Christians, by their efforts and self-sacrificing zeal, make christian institutions, and their collateral evangelical influences commensurate with our widening population; unless we send the educated christian missionary along with the emigrant, and plant churches and Sabbath schools where the hand of enterprise has felled the forest or dotted the prairies with farms and villages ; our country, the star of hope and guidance to bewildered nations, will itself wander, and we shall lose an opportunity of blessing mankind, such as God never gave to any people since the world was created. Nothing but the power of the Gospel, made effectual in the hearts of men, and influencing them in all their relations, can save a free country like ours from destruction—a country where no despot in church or state does or dares force outward conformity to religious requirements; where the people rule, and make their own laws ; where public opinion is well nigh omnipotent, and independence of all control, human and divine, is the most striking and characteristic natural tendency. Here, the alternatives are moral principle,—making every man a law unto himself, without which outward law is a cobweb—the wildest anarchy, or military despotism. The Gospel planted these colonies with "seed sifted from three kingdoms." Gospel institutions have made us what we are, and nothing but the Gospel can preserve us from destruction, or enable us to fulfil our high destiny towards the race. It is not enterprise, or physical improvements, or a glorious constitution and good laws, or free trade, or a tariff, or railroads and steamships, or philosophy, or science, or taste ; but the grace of God, that bringeth salvation, appearing to every man, and inwrought into the heart of every man, that can save us from the fate of former republics, and make us a blessing to all nations.

The issues involved in this question depend very much, too, in our apprehension, on the character assumed and influence exerted by the West—on the fact, in other words, whether we supply its wastes and build there in a few years "the foundation of many generations." Religious institutions do not rise spontaneously, or necessarily keep pace with the growth of population. The human heart naturally does not value or secure evangelical influences. Its uncounteracted tendencies, if not to barbarism, are certainly to irreligion. Men every where, and in all ages, love darkness rather than light; especially the men who go out from the influences of churches and pastors, to seek their fortunes and dig for golden ore, and build them towers whose top will reach unto heaven. And such is the character of much of the population crowding the West. Scorched by the revivals, and restive under the restraints of other States, they go like Cain of old to found or find a city of repose. The restless spirit of change, the feeling of Daniel Boone, drives men from New England or New-York, to Illinois or Iowa, and then to Wisconsin and Minnesota, and then to Oregon and California. The outward wave is rolling onward, without regurgitation, till it meets the Pacific, where next to dash, God only knows! No one who has not travelled in the West can conceive aright of this subject, and the momentous issues involved in it. In the absorbing cares of business, the multiplicity of outward incitements and ever-recurring pageants, the uniform flow of affairs year after year, in older States and cities, we are prone to think that all is well, and the West will take care of itself. But to be able to pray the prayer of the text aright, every Christian ought, if possible, to see the West for himself. Good old deacons from New England, staid divines from churches where order and orthodoxy are triumphant, New-York merchants, retired civilians, and philanthropists, in order to realize their obligations, should go and survey the land where their children or children's children are to dwell—to be blessed or cursed, be blessings or curses, according as we do, or neglect to do our duty. This rapid transfer of population from the older settlements to the new, and the unparalleled tide of emigration from the Old World, to which recent events there will only give additional momentum, is a new development in the economy of nations, giving rise to new duties and responsibilities, and adjusting Christian obligation on a new scale of projection altogether.

> "No pent up Utica contracts our powers,
> But the whole boundless continent is ours,"

to care for, and to christianize. It is hard, after all we have read, to conceive with what rapidity the West is filling up with population. In some parts, "a nation is born in a day." Fifty years ago, a line drawn from Pittsburg north to Lake Erie, and southward along the Alleghany and Cumberland Mountains, to the Gulf of Mexico, would have embraced a white population of less than 500,000; now the State of Ohio alone contains a small fraction less than 2,000,000; Indiana little less than 1,000,000; Illinois 850,000. The total population of the States and Territories west of the Mississippi and north of the Ohio River, in 1830, was 1,840,000, less than Ohio alone at this time; while the entire population of Wisconsin amounting to upwards of 300,000, and of Iowa a little below 200,000, has been received since 1838. The city of St. Louis has regularly doubled its population every six years since 1831, when it numbered 6,000; at which time Chicago, Milwaukie and others, now young giants, had no existence. A brother in the Convention in Chicago, a few years ago, said, "In June you see one cabin on a prairie, passing along in September, you see forty."

It need not and ought not to be concealed, that in the West there is a singular "energy of error," and tendency to extremes of opinion on all subjects. Every thing there is on a large scale—rivers, forests, prairies. However philosophically accounted for, the same is true of their errors also. Errors, like weeds, grow rank in the human heart; without constant cultivation; while truth, like the valuable productions of the husbandman, requires constant, patient and diligent cultivation. The errors of the West are of gigantic proportions. Their leaders are bold, reckless and revolutionary. One of the most striking characteristics of the West, too, is the spirit of self-reliance, not to term it self-assurance, which manifests itself in church and state, among saints and sinners. They pronounce judgment on subjects which have perplexed the wisest heads of all time, with a self-satisfaction absolutely thrilling. They have, beyond all doubt, "the spirit of power," whether blended or not with the elements of "love and a sound mind." They are like their steamboats of high pressure, which have vast propelling power, whether they have prudent captains and sober crews or not. Like one of their representatives in Congress, many of them feel themselves head and shoulders above the rest of mankind. Every variety of human opinion, too, every heresy ever conceived in the human heart, or studied in the silent chamber in past ages, every plunge of radicalism, and every grade of infidelity is there. The errorist and revolutionist, from the older States and the other hemisphere, there find the material all plastic to their hand. The extremes of opinion, represented in our most sober communities, and trying in vain to work themselves into the religious and social structure, may there be carried out to the full extent, without regard to consequences. The mighty West seems like a great caldron, where every heterogeneous element is fermenting, foaming, and every now and then overflowing. Far off in these wilds you may meet travelling agencies for

New York books, a certain kind of literature, there known as the "Yellow Cover Literature," the miserable trash of paid scribblers—the staple productions of some large and flourishing eastern establishments. Whether we sleep over this subject, or wake up to a proper sense of duty and danger, while some ecclesiastics are fearing lest colportage will trench on their official prerogatives, there are bold and strong men there, "not afraid to speak evil of dignities," night and day sowing tares, scattering broadcast over the land their pestilent errors, loosening the bonds of morality, sapping the foundations of society, and baptizing the young with their baleful influences. What we do in this matter, we must do quickly, if at all—with our might, or the crisis is past. The preponderating political and religious influence of our country will soon be found, if it does not exist already, in the West. If we wait, if we trust these matters to chance, or please ourselves with dreamy anticipations, and do not rise and build, other hands will be found to give shape and character to this region, and seize these elements of power, and use them for their own purposes. There is a tide in human things, moments when the light dust may turn the balance of a nation's destiny one way or the other. And what but an educated, orthodox ministry, a ministry acquiring influence by intellectual superiority, and retaining it by intelligent piety and persevering efforts—just such a ministry as the Home Missionary Society proposes to send out—will meet the exigency created by these circumstances? What other conservative principles, than evangelical piety and institutions, can we trust amidst the tempests of passion and error which threaten to ingulf all that is dear to us as patriots and Christians, and all that is embosomed for our world, in the purity and perpetuity of American Christianity?

In addition to all we have said, you are aware that systematic overtures are making to bring our country, through the predominating power of the West, and thus our world, under Roman Catholic influence; to fight in that arena the battle of Popish or Protestant supremacy! On this point we are not, and never have been alarmists. We do not blame the Roman Catholics for their zeal. We honor them, on the contrary, for their consistency. They believe there is no salvation out of the church—meaning the Romish church; that the best temporal and civil interests of man are identified with the possession and prevalence of the true religion; and that every interest must be subordinated to the establishment and extension of Christ's kingdom on earth. With these principles, what else could we expect than the most vigorous and well-directed exertions to gain preponderance of power in our country, whose institutions are destined ultimately to spread over the world? They are fully cognizant of the facts and principles we have been stating. They know that our country must have immense influence, one way or the other, on the nations of the earth, and that the West is the destined seat of power. They lay their plans, and plant their institutions accordingly. They project their cathedrals, schools and colleges, on a scale of magnificence commensurate with our loftiest anticipations of the future. They build for future ages. They believe in perpetuity. They take hold of human nature by every handle to turn it to their purposes, and despise no avenues to human affection, or instrumentalities of human confidence. It is by no means uncommon to meet large Catholic churches where there are, now, scarcely any Catholic hearers; and female seminaries where there are scarcely any other than Protestant patrons. Verily, the prize is worth contending for—the privilege of a preponderating influence over this land, and thus over the world. As was said in the ancient games—" *Detur dignissimo*" —the prize to him that wins it. In this matter, God will not reverse the great principle of his economy, " The hand of the diligent maketh rich." It will not do for us to be forever quarreling with the Catholics, calling them bad names, accusing them of ambition, conspiracies, and what not, while we are doing nothing to establish Protestant institutions. It is pitiable to be groaning perpetually over Catholic progress and encroachments, while we lavish our wealth in schemes of self-glorification, without equaling, or at least emulating the zeal and benevolence of those whom we dread. We must rear better schools, give a better education to youth of both sexes, found libraries, sustain a learned and orthodox ministry so liberally, that they can cope successfully with the Jesuit. We must scatter evangelical books and a christian literature, over the whole field. Yea, we must personally labor in our respective posts, learn the luxury of making money to give away in large-hearted schemes of benevolence, if we would not see another generation, seduced by the gorgeous ceremonies and splendid pageants of Popery, forsaking the religion of their forefathers, and surrendering the institutions of America to the power of Antichrist.

Roman Catholics are in earnest. They say, " We must make haste; the moments are precious. America will one day be the centre of civilization, and shall truth or error establish there its empire? If Protestants are beforehand with us, it will be difficult to destroy their influence." Such is their avowed policy, and its expected results. Are we prepared to contemplate such a policy, and such results, with composure? Is it nothing to us whether truth, in their sense of the term, that is, Popery, or error, by which they mean the Protestant faith, Protestant morals, and Protestant institutions, shall be established in our land, and thus reign over the earth?

Catholics are united too, as well as earnest. Would to God, Protestants were also. We want a blessed evangelical alliance, with the spirit of the text for its motto, *Our country for the sake and salvation of our world.* Whatever denominational distinctions and lines of operation our imperfect sanctification and absorption in non-essentials may render still necessary or unavoidable, this great idea should outmaster and control every other, and make every one who loves Christ and labors for the salvation of our country, our brother beloved and honored, whether he casts out devils by our formularies, and follows with us or not.

A village in the West, for one half its population, which is Catholic, has one church and pastor, one Lord, one faith, one baptism; the other half, which is Protestant, has five or six pastors and churches, and each has his separate "Psalm, doctrine, tongue, revelation and interpretation!" Yet, "God is not the author of confusion," but of peace, in all the churches of the saints.

Brethren, the mission of our country, and the alternative it involves, has not been conjured up for the occasion, but it is placed upon us by Providence, and grows necessarily out of the facts, principles and statistics we have been contemplating. In the light of the idea we have endeavored to elucidate and incorporate with your heart's deepest feelings, we can best see the reason and meaning of all God's past dealings with our country. In this aspect, our country must ever appear, to all capable of apprehending her position and relations, most lovely and glorious—as the signet in the right hand of God Almighty, by which he purposes to seal upon our fallen humanity its last type of beauty and blessedness. In the light of this purpose, we read with peculiar interest the facts of our antecedent history, civil and religious, from the beginning, hitherto. We can see why he planted these colonies; why he has preserved them; why he has interposed in answer to prayer in our darkest perils; why he has kept alive the spirit of piety, and granted us so many seasons of revivals; why he suggested the idea of voluntary associations; why he originated the Tract Society, and the glorious appendage of colportage; why, when the career of emigration first began, he put into the hearts of good men to form the Plan of Union; why, in advance of that unexampled career of expansion in recent times, which finds limits only by stretching from ocean to ocean, he originated this glorious Association of Home Missions, with its collateral blessings, to keep pace, if possible, with the march of an almost incalculable multiplication. Yes! it does seem as if God, our Heavenly Father, had prepared us, has been teaching us, for something great, and good, and glorious,—as Joseph was trained in youth, and then raised out of prison, to save much people alive in time of famine; and as David was called from tending sheep to lead the armies of the living God; and Hadassah was advanced from orphanage to the side of royalty to save her people, at an awful crisis.

Oh! my country! "Who knoweth whether thou"—lone orphan, cast out from thy fatherland and cut off from a mother's kindness in thy youth, and now Queen regnant, imperial and peerless—"hast not come to the kingdom for such a time," and for such a purpose "as this?" And after all, wilt thou fail to understand thy mission, and fall in with God's obvious purpose, and appreciate aright thy privilege and responsibility? In schemes of self-glorification or aggrandizement, wilt thou lose the glorious opportunity of impressing thine image, as God's signet, on the rest of the earth? O, holy brethren, partakers of the heavenly calling, American Christians of this generation! "Shall our country be the home of piety and virtue, or the mighty reservoir of irreligion and vice? Shall the voice of prayer and praise, or of cursing and blasphemy be heard throughout her borders? Shall our literature and science, and commerce and agriculture pay their tribute to the King of kings, or serve to foster to giant growth the worst passions of the human heart? Shall this great nation be rent with sectional jealousies and scarred with the judgments of the Most High, or shall its future millions, as they rise in successive generations, walk in the light of his countenance, and, appreciating themselves the value of civil and religious liberty, extend their blessings to every land illumed by the sun or laved by the sea?"

GOD BE MERCIFUL UNTO US, AND BLESS US, AND CAUSE HIS FACE TO SHINE UPON US; THAT THY WAY MAY BE KNOWN UPON EARTH, THY SAVING HEALTH AMONG ALL NATIONS.

AMERICAN HOME MISSIONARY SOCIETY.

The object of this Society is to assist congregations that are unable to support the Gospel ministry, and to send the Gospel to the destitute. It seeks and sends forth missionaries; by counsel and pecuniary aid, it encourages the people to help themselves; strengthens feeble churches, gathers new ones, settles pastors; and thus renders *permanent* the institutions of the Gospel.

The Society was organized in 1826, by delegates from the Presbyterian, Congregational, Associate Reformed, and Reformed Dutch denominations, and had then in its service 169 missionaries. The fifth year, the number of missionaries was 463—the eighth, 676—the sixteenth, 791—the twenty-fourth, 1,032. The first year's expenditure was $13,984—the fifth, $47,247—the eighth, $80,015—the sixteenth, $94,300—the twenty-fourth, $153,817 90.

The *twenty-fifth* year of its operations is briefly noticed in the following abstract from the last Annual Report, presented May 7th, 1851:

SUMMARY OF RESULTS.

More than one-third of those who were present at the organization of the Society a quarter of a century since, have ceased from their labors. Death has also removed, the last year, Rev. CALVIN CHAPIN, D. D., and Rev. DAVID PORTER, D. D., Vice-Presidents of the Society; Rev. HENRY WHITE, D. D., one of its Directors; KNOWLES TAYLOR, Esq., its former Treasurer; and Rev. WASHINGTON THACHER, the Agent of the Society in Central New-York.

The Society has had in its service the last year, 1,065 ministers of the Gospel, in 26 different States and Territories: in the New England States, 311; the Middle States, 224; the Southern States, 15; the Western States and Territories, 515.

Of these, 640 have been the *pastors* or *stated supplies* of single congregations; and 425 have occupied larger fields. *Four* have ministered to congregations of *colored people;* and 41 have preached in foreign languages—10 to *Welsh*, and 29 to *German* congregations; and *two* to congregations of *Norwegians* and *Swedes*.

The *number of congregations* supplied, in whole or in part, is 1,820; and the aggregate of *ministerial service* performed is equal to 853 years.

The pupils in Sabbath schools and Bible classes amount to 70,000.

There have been *added to the Churches* 6,678, viz.: 3,855 by profession; and 2,823 by letter. Many of the Western Churches have been visited with the special effusions of the Spirit. *Seventy-seven* missionaries make mention in their reports of revivals of religion in their congregations; and 366 report 3,096 hopeful conversions.

THE TREASURY.

Resources.—The balance in the Treasury, April 1st, 1850, was $15,553 69. The *receipts* of the succeeding twelve months have been $150,940 25; making the resources of the year, $166,493 94.

Liabilities.—There was due to missionaries, at the date of the last report, $11,935 77. There has since become due, $151,515 41; making the total of liabilities $163,451 18.

Payments.—Of this sum, $153,817 90 have been *paid.* The remainder—$9,633 28—is still due to missionaries for labor performed. Towards liquidating these claims and redeeming the additional pledges on commissions which have not yet expired—making in all, $64,906 49—there is a balance in the Treasury of $12,676 04—the greater part of which was received near the close of the year, and is available only as a means of cancelling the present indebtedness of the Society to its missionaries.

PROGRESS.

Thirty-three more missionaries have been in commission than in any preceding year, and this increase has been mainly in the Western States and Territories; *forty-one more years of ministerial labor* have been performed; and *two hundred and forty-five* more congregations blessed with the preaching of the Gospel.

Forty-three churches have passed from a condition of dependence to that of *self-support; sixty houses of worship* have been completed; *fifty-five* others repaired; and the building of *forty* others commenced.

During the twenty-five years of the Society's labors, not far from 800 *churches,* which had been reared and nurtured by its instrumentality, have passed from the list of beneficiaries, and are now supporting their own Gospel institutions; some of which are among the strongest and most influential churches in the land.

AUXILIARIES AND AGENCIES.

The Report gives detailed statements of the prompt and liberal manner in which the views of the Executive Committee have been seconded by the local Boards of Agency, and by the State and other Auxiliaries,

While nearly all evince their activity by an increased number of Missionaries and of Churches assisted, they all report a larger number than in any previous year as having become independent of foreign aid. The sound and healthful growth of the missions is seen in the number and value of the houses of worship erected, in the increasing energy of measures to promote temperance, in the establishment of Sunday and Week-day schools, and in general, in the yearly progress of whatever promotes the stability of the churches and the order of society.

GENERAL VIEW.

The favor which God has shown to the Society during the past year, in preserving the lives of its officers and missionaries, and crowning their labors with such a measure of success, furnishes fresh occasion of gratitude, and new ground of encouragement. This record of the labors of the year, completes the history of this Society for a *quarter of a century.* Within this period, how has the field of its operations extended, and its work increased. Our frontier has receded from the banks of the Ohio to the shores of the Pacific. Seven States have been added to our confederacy, and 12,000,000 to our population. In all the elements of national importance, we have made unparalleled progress; and the work appropriate to this Society has increased in like proportion. And, though it has not accomplished all that with greater resources it might have accomplished, yet the wide fields where it has gathered rich harvests for Christ—the multitude to whom it has distributed the bread of life—the 3,000 churches it has aided, and the 100,000 souls it has gathered into the fold of the Great Shepherd, testify that it has not labored in vain.

In the prospective growth of our country for another quarter of a century, we foresee the accumulating responsibilities of this Society.—While, in the older States, it must "be watchful and strengthen the things that remain that are ready to die," it must also go forth "bearing precious seed," with the advancing tide of emigration, as it rolls toward the setting sun. In planting Gospel institutions in our great central valley, and on the shores of the Pacific, a work is to be done for Christ, such as he has intrusted to no other people. *It must not be delayed.* To this work let the friends of the Redeemer gird themselves anew.—Encouraged by his past favor and the promise of his presence and aid, let them prosecute this enterprise with increasing zeal and on a more extended scale.

THE AMERICAN CHURCH.

A

DISCOURSE

IN BEHALF OF THE

American Home Missionary Society,

PREACHED IN THE CITIES OF NEW YORK AND BROOKLYN,

MAY, 1852.

BY

REV. LEONARD BACON, D.D.,

PASTOR OF THE FIRST CHURCH IN NEW HAVEN, CONN.

NEW YORK:

PRINTED FOR THE AMERICAN HOME MISSIONARY SOCIETY,

BY BAKER, GODWIN & CO., NO. 1 SPRUCE STREET.

1852.

DISCOURSE.

TITUS 1: 5.

THAT THOU SHOULDST SET IN ORDER THE THINGS THAT ARE WANTING, AND ORDAIN ELDERS IN EVERY CITY, AS I HAD APPOINTED THEE.

THIS, and some other passages of the same sort, describe one essential point in the primitive propagation of the Gospel. The Apostles and their associates went everywhere, preaching the word, reasoning out of the Scriptures in the synagogues of Judaism, and disputing, if they had opportunity, in the schools of Gentile philosophy. But this was not all. They baptized individuals and households, on a profession of faith in Jesus Christ as the Son of God and the Savior of the world—thus marking a line of distinction between the holy commonwealth of the redeemed and the world of the unbelieving. But this was not all. They wrote books and tracts, giving them such publication and currency as was then practicable; thus putting upon record, for all nations and for all ages, the great facts and elementary principles which they were commissioned to promulgate. But this was not all. There was another step to be taken, without which Christianity would hardly have had a place in history. Up to this point, if their work be regarded as ending at this point, all their results are incomplete—the half-collected materials of a structure—

the dissevered parts and members, on the one hand, but not compacted into symmetry and strength; the living spirit, on the other hand, but not embodied as an organic force, with a local habitation and a name. "For this cause," says Paul the Apostle to Titus the Evangelist, "left I thee in Crete, that thou shouldst set in order the things that are wanting, and ordain elders in every city, as I had appointed thee."

In the great island of Crete, Paul seems to have labored in person, and he seems to have been interrupted and called away before the ordinary plan of his operations had been carried out. Some arrangements were still wanting, which Titus was expected to supply. In every town or local community where converts had been made, he was to organize the Christian fellowship by instituting elders, the proper officers of a stated worshiping assembly. In other words, the work for which the Apostle had left him in Crete was that of constituting local churches, and so completing the introduction of the Gospel there. The same thing was done wherever the Apostles performed their office. By the establishment of churches—local Christian societies for worship and for religious instruction and discipline—Christianity became something more than a matter of individual opinion, conviction and experience; something more than a merely domestic influence, hallowing in God's name the relations of household love and duty; something more than a new element infused into literature and philosophy, and taking effect upon the progress of human intelligence from age to age. It became an incorporated and organized religion, with its own arrangements and institutions for self-perpetuation, and for aggressive influence. Christianity establishing itself in local churches, became a new social institute within the State, yet not of it; a new order and form of human association, with an independent life of its own and yet connected by a relation of constant action and reaction with that old order of things into which it had been cast.

The American Home Missionary Society devotes itself to a work of the same kind with that for which Titus was left in Crete. It has for its own special department of effort, on the broad field of Christian activity in our country, not merely the work of diffusing Christian knowledge, not merely the work of winning individuals to personal faith in Christ, not merely the work of multiplying and sending abroad the living preachers of the Gospel, but the work of planting Christianity as an organized religion and an organizing power. Books, however excellent, and however profusely distributed; the itinerant and desultory preaching of the Gospel, whether by book-venders and tract distributors, or by professional and authenticated ministers of the word; Sunday-schools, with their apparatus of libraries, teachers and traveling missionaries, may co-operate powerfully for the advancement of Christian knowledge and experience; but such efforts, if they are all, work no organic change in society. Another kind of effort must accompany them, or follow them, to "set in order the things that are wanting," or else, so far as permanent influence is concerned, their labor is in vain.

Allow me to say, in this place, that, in respect to ecclesiastical arrangements, the Home Missionary enterprise, as represented by the Society for which this service is performed, is not a sectarian undertaking. It attempts nothing more than to establish local churches —churches in the New Testament sense of the word—

organized parochial societies of Christian people, for the support of public worship, and for the various duties of Christian neighborhood and communion. With the internal arrangements of these churches for the management of their own ecclesiastical affairs, with the relations which associated churches may see fit to establish among themselves for the sake of mutual recognition and intercourse, or of mutual helpfulness and authority, it does not intermeddle. The particular church may or may not conduct its own affairs on purely democratic principles; it may or may not incorporate itself with some larger and more comprehensive organization; the Home Missionary Society does not concern itself with such questions. The plan of our great charity is essentially opposed to the denominational or sectarian spirit. So long as the churches which it plants, or which it aids in the period of their weakness, are evangelical in worship and doctrine, holding that view of the Christian system of which the word *evangelical* has become, in modern times, the recognized and current designation; so long as they are essentially self-governed, and not priest-governed; so long as they do not formally exclude from fellowship with them the great body of churches on which this charity depends for its resources, so long it cares not what regulations and arrangements, or what denominational standards may be adopted by any particular congregation. It has to do, not with the extension of organized sects or denominations, but only with single churches, local churches. As a purely American institution, called into existence by an exigency in the growth of this great American people, and operating to extend the dominion of Christ over all the territory of our Union, it devotes itself to the one work of setting up Christianity in the form of local Christian churches, that shall operate from age to age upon the character and destiny of the countless millions of our population.

Thus there opens before us, at this point, a great subject of thought and inquiry:

THE CHRISTIAN INSTITUTION OF LOCAL CHURCHES AS RELATED TO OUR AMERICAN CIVILIZATION.

I feel that the subject has its difficulties. I am fully conscious that I shall not succeed in giving it such illustration as it deserves. But I am sure that even an imperfect illustration of it will help us to some new views of the position which this Home Missionary work ought to have in our affections and in our plans of patriotic and Christian beneficence.

I. Let me remind you, then, that religion, embodied in religious institutions, is an essential and potent element in every form of civilization. Religion, in the generic sense of the word—the consciousness of dependence on an invisible and infinite Power—is not only an inseparable part of our human nature, belonging, like reason and the faculty of moral perception, to the constitution of every individual mind; it is also, like them, essential to the constitution of society. It has to do with all human relations, but most of all with those complicated relations of man to man which constitute the conscious unity of the commonwealth, and by virtue of which the life of the State runs on in undying and uninterrupted identity through successive generations of individual mortal existence. Though religion is in one sense wholly individual; though true religion, considered as a religious experience, is the awakening of the individual man to a just view of the relations between himself and his Maker; it is none the less true, that the religious instincts and sensibilities are developed in society. They have their place and their activity in connection with every social affection and every social duty, giving a sanction from the Infinite to all the complicated relationships which hold society together, and connecting the visible and transient, at every point of human life, with the invisible and the eternal. They are eminently sympathetic, yearning after communion, unfolding and strengthening themselves in the consciousness of fellowship; so that some form of religion, not merely as a private personal conviction, but as a social institution, with public or social worship, is a necessity of human nature. Thus they take their shape and direction from social influences; and in one form and another they are incorporated into the character and historic life of nations and races. Thus all history is full of the influence of religion as a leading element of civilization. Of this it may be a sufficient illustration to say that in every land that ever had a history, the great architectural remains and monuments, from which, more perhaps than from any historic records, we learn the extent and the distinctive character of the civilization which once flourished there, are remains of religious architecture. The colossal structures of Egypt; the august colonnades of Baalbec and Palmyra; the disinhumed remains of Assyria; the stupendous excavations and sculptured mountains of India; the old, rude columns on Salisbury Plain; the fantastic mounds reared by an unknown race upon the soil which now we call our own, all testify to the power of the religious principle in human nature, and to the invariableness of its presence as an element in every form of civilization. And how plainly does history, in its records, teach us that the introduction of a new religion, into any country, carries into the civilization of that country a consequent and proportionate change.

II. Turning now to recollect for a moment the distinctive characteristics of our American civilization, and to inquire how it differs from the civilization of other ages, and from the existing civilization of other countries, we find, at the first glance, certain great outlines sufficiently definite for our present use. We see an entire separation of religion from the jurisdiction of the civil magistrate, and an absolute freedom of voluntary association for worship, and for all religious purposes. We see the religious element everywhere at work; the people everywhere organizing and sustaining their religious institutions altogether independent of the civil government, which also they organize and sustain. We see the principle of local and municipal self-government carried to the greatest practicable extent, in opposition to the centralization of power. We see an equality of personal and political rights, such as has never existed elsewhere, and, growing out of it, a constantly counteracted but ever elastic tendency to equality of condition. We see an unparalleled diffusion of intelligence and of the spirit of inquiry and free thought, stimulated continually by the genius and the working of our political institutions. We see twenty-five millions of people, spread over a territory of various and boundless resources, and trained to the habit of relying on themselves rather than on the government for guidance and control, and of exercising their own faculties of thought and judgment on matters of public, not less than of private interest. We see this teeming population increasing every year by a stupendous immigration from all regions of the ancient world; the immigrant myriads bringing with them from beyond the ocean their own languages and fashions, and their own forms of religion or of irreligion, yet mingling with the mighty mass, unable to resist its tendencies, and slowly but surely losing their foreign peculiarities,—as the waters of the Mississippi, poured into the Gulf and the Atlantic, and slowly mingling with the rolling tides, lose their freshness, deposit the soil that they have brought from distant plains and mountains, and are gradually lost and undistinguishable in the world-embracing ocean, without discoloring by one shade or turbid stain its boundless azure.

III. And now, with these views of religion as a necessary element in every form of civilization, and with these views of the peculiarities by which our American civilization is distinguished, we may take the position that in our country, and under our social and civil organization, the strength of free and Protestant Christianity, considered as an organized religion and an organizing power, must reside in local and self-governed churches. To illustrate this, let me point out to your attention certain facts and views, which show what local churches have been in the progress of our history to the present moment, and what they are likely to be in the future.

1. It is worthy of notice that the history of the origin and progress of Christian institutions in this country, hitherto, is almost wholly bound up in the history of the origin and growth of local churches. In New England, as you are well aware,—which has had by its religious and political institutions, and by the character which those institutions have wrought into its

people, so wide an influence upon the political and religious organization of the country as a whole—the institution of local churches, self-constituted and self-governed, was at first the end for which every thing else was instituted. The Puritan emigration from old England was an emigration for the express purpose of founding in the wilderness local, separate, independent churches, which should control the founding of every thing else; and around which, as so many distinct centers of vital power, there should arise the laws and magistracies, the order, the industry, the justice, the popular virtue, the universal education and intelligence, the frugal plenty, and all the stern and saintly beauty of a Puritan civilization. Whatever there is in New England that warms the heart of the New Englander with glad and reverent affection at the thought of her gray rocks and her green hillsides, when his filial regards turn eastward from the prairies, or from beyond the Rocky Mountains,—is most intimately associated with the influence of those New England churches. Whatever errors there may have been in the ancient legislation there, whatever violations of the principle of religious liberty, whatever unwise attempts to make men religious, and to keep them in right ways of thinking by the force of law, there was never in those Puritan commonwealths a centralization of ecclesiastical power; never a priestly corporation independent of the people; never any religious organization higher or stronger than that of local churches; and at this moment all the embodied and organized religious influence there is summed up in the fact, that in every township, and in every parochial district, the local church is present, the organized congregation of free Christian men, the self-governed Christian society, with its stated worship, with its house of prayer, with its teaching ministry, and with all its apparatus of instruction and influence.

But I would not be understood as speaking of that particular form of church-order which is called Congregationalism, or as claiming for the churches thus denominated a special advantage, in this respect, over churches bearing other names. What was the origin of Presbyterianism on our soil? It did not begin here, as it began under the hands of the Reformers in Scotland, in a General Assembly, distributing and parceling itself out into synods and presbyteries, and ending in the organization of parochial arrangements. On the contrary, it began in local, separate, Presbyterian congregations, each with its own arrangements for worship, discipline, and the ministry of the word; and it was the voluntary confederation of congregations previously independent of each other, which gave being to presbyteries, synods, and general assemblies. So with other churches of similar faith and order, but of a different genealogy—the Reformed Dutch, the German Reformed, the Lutheran,—trace their history back to its earliest sources, and, in each instance, you find a particular congregation in one place, and another particular congregation in another place, and then another and another, till at last these many congregations, drawn together by special affinities of faith and order, of ancestral feeling and perhaps of language, are confederated for mutual helpfulness in classical and synodical assemblies. But in all these instances, and even in others which are very unlike to these in some respects, but of which I could not speak without entering into explanations which the limits of this discourse preclude, the strength of the organization, its efficiency in maintaining and extending the kingdom of Christ, and especially the efficiency with which it dispenses the Gospel, as a vital and organizing force in society, molding the character of the people; the efficacy with which it works to carry into households, and into the experience of individual souls, the light and life of holiness, must be found, not in its supposed or attempted centralization of power, but in the strength, the number, and the spiritual health and activity of its local churches. And to a thinking, generous, Christian mind, the value of all these ecclesiastical confederations, by whatever name they may be called, and whatever may be the theory on which they are constituted, lies in their ability to subserve the true interests, and to promote the legitimate efficiency, of parochial churches, and to provide for the multiplication of such churches in a just proportion to the wants of the population. The presbytery, the consociation, the classis, the convention, the synod, is for the churches; not the churches for it. Its strength is not in itself, but in the churches whose confederation has created it. Its value is measured exactly by what it contributes to their edification and efficiency. If the churches which it includes are, by virtue of their relation to it, more peaceful, more prosperous, more potent in their local influence, then it answers a legitimate and important purpose, and deserves to be honored accordingly. But if, instead of this, the churches gather from it only a thorny harvest of strife and debate; or if it becomes a mere arena for feats of logical and theological gladiatorship, then, let Diotrephes admire it and rejoice in it as he may, it answers no good end, and forfeits its right to existence.

Pardon the desultory character of these remarks. They are intended to illustrate, and, if I mistake not, they do illustrate the position that Protestant Evangelical Christianity upon this American soil is identified, in its beginning and growth, and in its present position and influence, with the origin and progress, the prosperity and efficiency of local churches. Perhaps I have said more than enough; and yet I cannot refrain from adding, that if any intelligent and impartial man will set himself to study the institutions of this great metropolis, he will find that not the colleges, nor even the public schools, not the learned academies, nor the charitable institutions, nor even the diversified apparatus of extra-ecclesiastical religious enterprise, can be compared in importance with the churches, the natural depositaries, the legitimate conservators and dispensers of all Christian influence. And when he takes his census of the churches, and sums up their power, and makes his estimate of their capabilities, he will think of them only as so many organized congregations of Christian worshipers, with their pastors and other officers, their sabbaths, their places of public worship, their lecture-rooms, their Sunday-schools, their meetings for edification and brotherly communion, their arrangements for aggressive action on the masses of ignorance and impiety that lie around them; and he will take no account of presbyteries or associations, of classes or synods, unless it be for convenience in the prosecution of his inquiries, and the summing up of his results. This very church, for example, in whose consecrated edifice we are this evening assembled, how shall we estimate its importance as one of the institutions of this metropolis? This house of prayer, these Sabbath assemblies, the sacred tie that binds these congregated households to each other, the covenant of baptism, the remembered blood that bought our pardon, the eloquence on themes of infinite grandeur that has here distilled from lips touched with the fire of God's own altar, the impressions and experiences that have taken place within these walls, the decisions that have been formed here for eternity, the consolation that, in connection with these ministrations, has been poured into the bosom of affliction, the rainbow-splendor with which hope here nurtured has so often overarched the river of death, the great thoughts and emotions that have here been born and cherished in believing souls and that have gone out hence to be translated into godlike action, the mischievous influences that have been counteracted from this center, the wanderers that have been reclaimed, the outcasts that have been saved, the miseries that have been alleviated,—Oh how can we conceive of the infinite history! And all this influence is the influence of—what? A single, organized, local congregation, taken by itself. Who, when he attempts to estimate this influence, and when his heart swells with the thought that there is such an institution, and that this is only a specimen of what churches are doing for the moral welfare of this great metropolis, can think of asking to which presbytery the church belongs, or whether it belongs to any? How completely would any such question let us down from the altitude at which we see the church itself in its legitimate and blessed influence!

2. And now, though we begin to feel the narrowness of our limits as to time, let me lead you to inquire whether it is not a fact, that in all ecclesiastical organizations within the scope of our American civilization, there is a steady tendency toward the increase of what we may call the parochial element in ecclesiastical order, as opposed to the element of consolidation. I have called your attention to the fact that the history of

Protestant Evangelical Christianity among us is to a great extent, when rightly viewed, the history of local churches, as local centers of evangelical influence upon the people; but now I wish to lead you to a wider view. The tendency to the increase of this parochial element of church-order, cannot be easily measured by a reference to those religious bodies in which the parochial element has always been predominant. There is, however, a powerful evangelical body, the history of which is in some respects singularly contrasted with that of the various churches to which I have already made particular allusion. I speak of that body here with no sentiment that is not consistent with the profoundest respect for its Christian and evangelical character. I thank God for the Methodist Episcopal Church in these United States. I thank God for that wonderful system of evangelism which has done so much for the advancement of our common Christianity, and which gives promise of so glorious an usefulness in the future. But what is it which that great itineracy is everywhere accomplishing? What are its achievements as a permanent and organizing influence in society? How is its usefulness to be measured upon the scale of history? Wherever it works, it is working to form permanent congregations, local, organized churches, as fixed centers of local influence. And do we not see that the Methodist house of worship, after a little while, is no longer a mere preaching station? The benches are displaced by pews; the original division of the assembly is superseded by a distribution into households; the itinerant preacher, who hastened from one station to another, has become a temporary pastor; and presently the congregation, trained from the first to an intense religious activity, begins to be conscious of its corporate unity, and of its duties, and its rights too, as a local, Christian church. It is not for me to prognosticate the issue of a pending debate. It is not for us in this place to intermeddle with affairs that are not our own. But may we not confidently expect, from the deep sagacity that has characterized the progress of that religious body heretofore, and from the evident blessing with which God has attended it, that whatever may be the immediate result, the end will be, not conflict, not disorganization and confusion, but such an adjustment as shall provide more adequately for the development of the parochial element of church-order, without impairing the aggressive force of that system of evangelism?

We might take a still wider view. The Roman Catholic system has long been struggling to establish itself in this country. Having to do almost exclusively with the foreign element in our population, as distinguished from the people that have been born and trained under purely American influences, it has hardly begun to feel, as yet, the forces that are destined ere long to act upon it. But is there any intelligent observer who is not aware that in the bosom of that great system of spiritual despotism, as it exists among us, there are already some movements significant of what will be hereafter. A Roman Catholic congregation of American citizens, born and nurtured on the soil, and in the atmosphere of our national life,—nay, a Roman Catholic congregation with only an infusion of the true spirit of American civilization,—when once it begins to be conscious of something like a corporate unity, begins to be strangely conscious of corporate rights and corporate duties.

There is meaning in this. Wherever it appears, it is a phenomenon which invites an inquiry into the reason of it. And the reason of it is found in the congruity between the parochial principle of religious organization, and that principle of local and municipal self-government which is the grand distinction of our political system, and which is most thoroughly carried out where our political system exists in its most perfect and compacted form; which is where the territory of the State, after having been divided into counties, is again divided into townships, and where the inhabitants of every town are a complete local democracy, enacting their own by-laws in popular assemblies, choosing their own magistrates, taking care of their own free roads and free schools, and having a part by their own town-representative in the legislation of the State.

IV. May we not come, then, to this conclusion: That which we have seen to be the Protestant Evangelical form of church-order, the system of parochial churches, each a local center of all Christian influences, is essential to the right and successful working of our great principle of local self-government in the civil state. Our entire system of social organization—the entire genius of our people expressing itself in political institutions—dreads and abhors the centralization of power, refuses to collect the majesty of government into any one imperial locality, sets up everywhere the municipal, local democracy, and insists that the people, at every point at which a political body can be constituted, shall attend to their own business of governing themselves. In such a structure and system of society, the only religious principle, so far as order and organization are concerned—the only principle, I mean, that is in harmony with the genius of the people, or that can adjust itself without conflict or collision to all the machinery of their political life—is the principle of parochial and self-governed churches. This is the distinctively American method of religious organization. The people—a Christian people in their descent and history, in their language and literature, in their recognized standards of morality, and in their ideas of God, and of the worship which men owe to their Creator—are the State; as such they organize themselves for political and civil purposes under the forms of a free self-government, resting on the basis of municipal institutions universally distributed; and this is the American political system. The same people, acting in reference to their religious wants and sympathies, organize themselves everywhere, voluntarily and according to a Christian freedom, in stated assemblies for worship and religious instruction; and this is *the American church system.* The Church and the State are everywhere present to each other, and everywhere mutually dependent. Each system is complete in itself, yet each is intimately related to the other, and to the living whole of which they are the living parts. There is no rivalry between them, no clashing of jurisdictions, no conflict of powers, no subordination of one to the other. The State everywhere protects the Church from outrage, recognizes its rights by recognizing and maintaining the right of free association for religious purposes, guards every worshiping assembly against disturbance, hallows by law the Christian Sabbath as the people's day of rest, inaugurates its own proceedings in legislative assemblies, and often in courts of justice, with religious services, conducted according to the order of the local churches. So, in return, the Church everywhere gives life to the State; everywhere it penetrates with its vital force all the municipal divisions and arrangements of the commonwealth,—as the nervous system in the human frame is spread through every limb and organ, every muscle, every fibre, the vehicle of life and sense and motion; everywhere, if adequately developed, it works upon the common mind and life of the people, keeping alive the sense of relations to the invisible and the remembrance of truths that reach beyond the sphere of sense and time. And this parochial, self-organizing principle of evangelical Christianity, everywhere present; everywhere building the house of prayer; everywhere providing the ministry of the life-giving word; everywhere touching the most sacred springs of human sympathy, by exhibiting the simple symbolic rites of Christian faith and worship; everywhere establishing its order, its discipline, its multiform activity; and thus acting everywhere with a steady, molding influence on the sentiments and habits of the people, trains the people into the capacity of self-government. It deals with them from their childhood as intelligent and reasonable beings, and as capable of acting under the excitement and guidance of the sublimest motives. It holds them to the duty of exercising their own faculties of thought and judgment on themes of infinite reach and grandeur. It makes them familiar with the consciousness of a responsibility to God, which rises far above all other responsibilities, and includes them all, and from which no considerations of personal or worldly expediency can absolve them. It teaches them in these methods the grand lesson of free and manly thoughtfulness, and of free and manly self-control. Accustoming them in their various religious communities to discuss and regulate, under one form or another, and in one degree or another, their own religious affairs, by yielding a generous deference to the judgment and the choice of the majority, it trains them for political freedom and for self-government, as members of the civil commonwealth. How happy the lot, how beautiful the aspect, of a great people whose institutions, thus organized in Church and State, spring as it were spontaneously from the tendencies and yearnings of the popular mind, and are adapted to the ends for which the Church and State exist in their harmonious co-operation—the Church and the State each resting on the basis of local self-government, and each the complement but neither the servant of the other—the people, self-governed in all their communities, free because they are Christian, and Christian because they are free!

But if we reverse this view, and instead of Protestant Evangelical Christianity establishing itself in those institutions of local self-government which are so congruous to its nature, suppose the ascendency of a different system, establishing itself, according to its nature, in the form of a consolidated spiritual despotism, how different will be the result! Look at that system, with the gigantic efforts which it is making to achieve for itself dominion on this hallowed soil. What if it shall gain in these broad realms of freedom the ascendency at which it aims, and for which it is drawing, as it were, to one center all the forces of fraud, cunning, wealth and organization, that can be wielded by the rulers of the darkness of this world? Let that system conquer; let its institutions, with no local self-governed Christian assemblies, become the predominant religious organization throughout our country; let it have, undisputed, the religious training of the people; let it teach the American citizen everywhere to bow in awe before the divine authority of the priesthood, to forego the *keeping of his own* conscience, to renounce his right of judging for himself under the guidance of God's word and Spirit, and in the discharge of his personal responsibility to God; let it succeed in molding the hearts and habits of the people, by the action of its institutions, into accordance with its own despotic genius, and how completely will it counteract all the better tendencies, and extinguish the characteristic spirit of our existing American civilization.

With such an enemy working against us—an enemy so powerful in his resources, so unwearied in his diligence, and so deadly in his hostility to all that we value for ourselves, or hope for in behalf of our children, and our country, and the world—we are to "set in order the things that are wanting," and to spread the organized form and organizing spirit of free and pure Christianity, from beautiful New England, from this imperial New York, from the Atlantic shore adorned with cities to which the commerce of the world brings riches, westward through the disappearing forests, westward over the prairies, westward still, beyond the mountains so soon to be pierced and threaded by the iron path of commerce, westward, even to where our remotest west, in its golden pride, looking forth upon the Pacific, confronts the farthest and eldest orient, and is already making China and India tributary to the greatness of its future. How inspiring is the thought of effort and achievement in such a field! "Time's noblest empire," with resources that shame the riches of the world, with capabilities of power and progress that defy all calculation, and with a position of pre-eminent grandeur, in relation to the destinies of the human race, is to be saved from the dominion of darkness and of sin, and is to be filled with the freedom of the sons of God!

This, then, is the work of the American Home Missionary Society. It undertakes to carry the Gospel with all its quickening and sanctifying influences, the Gospel, with its institutions and social order, the Gospel, not only as the offer of Divine grace to the individual soul, but also as an organizing power in the commonwealth, through all the length and breadth of this great empire. Wherever it goes, it puts its hand to the foundation, and helps to shape the structure of society. It does not merely scatter the seed of the word here and there in the wide and tangled wilderness; its work is to subdue the wilderness, to spread new order over its neglected vastness, to change its gloomy waste into the garden of the Lord. Where various currents of population, from the north and from the south, from the old world and from the new, with habits and tendencies as diverse as their origin, meet to mingle and be confounded, it sets up in that confusion of influences an organic self-perpetuating force that shall act upon unborn generations; and where the pioneer might, perhaps, have left to his posterity an inheritance of barbarism, it spreads over the subdued and renovated soil the light, the bloom, the living and perennial beauty of a Christian civilization.

THE CATALYTIC POWER OF THE GOSPEL.

A

DISCOURSE,

DELIVERED BEFORE THE

Massachusetts Home Missionary Society,

AT ITS ANNIVERSARY, IN LOWELL INSTITUTE, BOSTON,

MAY 25, 1852.

BY EDWARD HITCHCOCK, D. D.

PRESIDENT OF AMHERST COLLEGE.

BOSTON:

PRESS OF T. R. MARVIN, 42 CONGRESS STREET.

1852.

At a regular Quarterly Meeting of the Executive Committee of the Massachusetts Home Missionary Society, held on the 8th June, 1852:

"*Voted, unanimously,* That the thanks of the Society be tendered to the Rev. Dr. HITCHCOCK, for his Sermon delivered at their late Anniversary Meeting in Boston, and that he be requested to furnish a copy of the same for publication."

Attest,

J. S. CLARK, *Secretary.*

DISCOURSE.

MATTHEW XIII. 33.

THE KINGDOM OF HEAVEN IS LIKE UNTO LEAVEN, WHICH A WOMAN TOOK, AND HID IN THREE MEASURES OF MEAL, TILL THE WHOLE WAS LEAVENED.

It is not often that the discoveries of modern science elucidate and make more impressive the language of Scripture. The text, however, is one of these rare instances. It describes, indeed, a very familiar process,—that of bread-making,—which, as a practical matter, has been known from very early times. But the principles on which some parts of the operation depend, are even yet among the most recondite in chemical science. Something is known of them, however; and although the person who is acquainted only with the process of leavening bread, must be struck with the peculiar force and appropriateness of this illustration; yet the man acquainted with its rationale, cannot but realize it more deeply. I shall feel justified, therefore, in spending a few moments in scientific details, which would be appropriate to the chemical lecture room; nay, I should feel condemned, if I did not take this course, because I am confident that I can thus make the beauty and force of this passage more obvious and impressive. And in doing this, and introducing a few technical phrases, I hope my hearers will not charge me with pedantry, till they have heard me through. Gladly would I avoid these scientific details, could I in any other way bring out the full strength and appropriateness of the text.

The phrase, *kingdom of heaven*, in this passage, demands a passing exegetical notice. The radical idea contained in it, as well as in the cognate expression, *kingdom of God*, is that of dominion or government. Even when it means heaven itself, as it sometimes does, this original idea clings to it; for in heaven the most prominent manifestation of the Deity will be through his government. In the New Testament, however, this phrase often designates the reign of the gospel dispensation; and hence it very naturally is sometimes put for the principles of the gospel. Such seems to be its precise meaning in the text. Christ evidently meant to say, that the truths of the gospel, when brought into contact with society, operate like the leaven of the bread-maker, when mingled with the dough.

And how, precisely, does this operate? Chemistry, to some extent, informs us. It is an example of those changes in bodies, which, for the want of a better name, is called *Catalysis*. This term embraces a great variety of decompositions and recompositions, which are not explained by the common principles of analysis and synthesis. In catalysis, the mere presence of a certain body, among the particles of another, produces the most extensive changes among those particles; and yet the body thus operating, is itself unaffected. Thus, a stream of hydrogen poured upon a piece of platinum will take fire, that is, unite with the oxygen of the atmosphere through the influence of the platinum; and yet that metal will remain unaltered.

In cases of catalysis, more analogous to the example referred to in the text, the substance itself, which is the agent of the change, is in a decomposing condition. This is the case with leaven, or, as it is sometimes called, ferment or yeast. One sees, from the commotion among its particles, that a change is going on in its internal condition, and that new compounds are forming out of its elements. Introduced in that state into the meal, it communicates a change to the whole mass, analogous to that which it is itself experiencing. This is called fermentation. In bread it is not allowed to proceed very far, but is arrested by the heat of the oven.

It is found that the remarkable power of leaven to change the character of compounds, depends on a peculiar principle which it contains, called *Diastaste.* This substance is so powerful in its action, that one part of it, mixed with two thousand parts of starch, will change the whole into sugar in a few hours.

How it is that so small a quantity of one substance should be able to produce such extensive changes in another, thousands of times larger, it may not be easy in all instances to see. But in the case of leaven, we have a probable theory; for, as the particles of the leaven, themselves in the act of change, come in contact with some of the particles of the body into which it is introduced, they start a similar change there; and this, communicated from particle to particle, pervades the mass until the whole is leavened. This view is certainly a statement of what takes place; but if asked *why* such effects should be propagated through bodies by mere contact, I confess myself unable to see.

The history of catalytic changes, then, furnishes us with two principles of importance in elucidating the text. The first is, that it needs but a very small quantity of leaven to produce a complete change in a very large amount of farinaceous matter. The second is, that it is only necessary to start the process of change in one or a few spots in the mass, where the particles of the leaven happen to be, in order to have it permeate the entire heap. It is not necessary that a particle of the leaven should actually come in contact with every particle of the mass. It need only commence a process in one spot, which will spread of itself through the whole, or at least to a great extent.

To return now to my text,—such a power does Christ declare the gospel to possess. *The kingdom of heaven is like unto leaven, which a woman took, and hid in three measures of meal, till the whole was leavened.* Hence I take for my subject on this occasion, *The Catalytic Power of the Gospel.* I wish to show that wherever that is cast into the dead and inert mass of human society, it shows a quickening, expanding and multiplying power possessed by no other human institution.

In order to avoid misapprehension, let me premise one or two remarks. Because I shall attempt to show that gospel truth has a mighty power over the human heart, let no one imagine me a disbeliever in the necessity of a special divine influence to give that truth success. In that doctrine, most cordially do I acquiesce; and when I speak of a peculiar efficacy of the truth, I assume that the conversion of men is *not by might, nor by power, but by the Spirit of the Lord of hosts.* My only object is to show that the truth, in itself, possesses a peculiar adaptedness to win its way and transform society. And surely it will encourage our efforts, as well as make us feel more deeply our obligations, to learn what an admirable instrument God has put into our hands with which to labor.

Let us now look at the evidence of the catalytic power of the gospel.

In the first place, such a power is derived from the adaptedness of the gospel to human wants.

How well adapted it is to promote the temporal welfare and happiness of man, may be seen by comparing the condition of society in Christian lands with that of heathen and Mohammedan countries. So striking is the contrast, that truly and literally we may say of Christianity, it has *the promise of the life that now is, as well as of that which is to come.* But it is mainly of man's spiritual wants, that I speak at this time. For though felt more or less by all, and by many with great intensity, they are met and satisfied nowhere save in the gospel. Yet how purblind men are to this panacea! They search for remedies every where else. They run the whole round of sensual gratification in the vain expectation of relief; but they find only a bitter aggravation of their sufferings. They toil for wealth, for honor, for power, and perhaps are eminently successful. But the void in their hearts is only made larger and more painful. They resort to social enjoyments, or to learning, or to splendid worldly enterprises; but all in vain; the terrible craving of their nature continues, and, like the cast-out unclean spirit, they *go through dry places, seeking rest, yet finding none.* They resort finally to deeds of charity, to self-mortifications, and to the rites of a religion of forms; and here they fancy they must find peace. But if they do, it is only a false and a transient peace; the peace of self-delusion, not the peace of God. And when some trying exigency of life overtakes them, the visor drops from their eyes, and the cheated soul within cries out in anguish for something to lean upon in the hour of suffering and of death.

Such are the vain phantoms which most men pursue through all their days, urged on by the deep, restless, unsatisfied wants of their nature. Nor does one in a thousand fancy that he is walking in a vain show, until God's Spirit open his eyes to see the plague of his own heart. He is amazed and overwhelmed by the view. Such deep and dreadful depravity, pervading his whole nature, he never once suspected. He can live with such a heart no longer. Ah, he sees now what he wants, and prostrate in the dust he cries out, *Create in me a clean heart, O God, and renew a right spirit within me.* His prayer prevails. He rises a new creature in Christ Jesus. The aching void in his heart is filled,—filled with divine love and divine peace. He is saved by the washing of regeneration and the renewing of the Holy Ghost. He has found, at last, the grand panacea which nature could never discover.

> "This remedy did wisdom find,
> To heal diseases of the mind,
> The sovereign balm, whose virtues can
> Restore the ruined creature, man."

During the preparatory process that goes before regeneration, as well as in the act, the peculiar adaptedness of another great doctrine of the gospel to human wants is made most manifest. The man is deeply conscious of having broken the law of God; and when he is made to feel how reasonable that law is, and how holy, he does not see how he can be pardoned. The law only condemns him, but discloses not one gleam of hope. He looks around solicitously for some way of escape. He inquires whether he can, himself, make any offerings to God that will be a ground of pardon. Especially may not the sacrifice of animal life avail? To such sacrifices have men in all ages and countries resorted, either by the promptings of instinct or revelation. And it shows, at least, how general is the conviction of men, that sin cannot be pardoned without some expiation made by a substitute. But a voice from the Scriptures replies, *It is not possible that the blood of bulls and of goats should take away sin.* The sinner sinks down in despair, at this announcement. How well prepared, then, to receive another, issuing from the same inspired record,—*The blood of Jesus Christ cleanseth us from all sin,*

Christ being come, a high priest of good things to come, not by the blood of goats and calves, but by his own blood, he entered in once into the holy place, having obtained eternal redemption for us. The great central truth of a vicarious atonement gradually opens upon his agitated mind. At first, he sees it only dimly and doubtingly. But, ere long, his heart perceives that here is the divine remedy for its otherwise hopeless case. Here, mercy and truth meet together; righteousness and peace embrace each other. Thus *God can be just, while he justifies the believer.* Faith can doubt no longer. It rushes to the cross, and pardon, peace and holy joy succeed to anguish and despair. The most pressing want man ever experiences,—the desire of forgiveness,—is thus fully met; and ever after the pardoned sinner, addressing his Saviour, exclaims,

" E'er since by faith I saw the stream
Thy flowing wounds supply,
Redeeming love has been my theme,
And shall be till I die.

" Then in a nobler, sweeter song,
I'll sing thy power to save,
When this poor lisping, stammering tongue,
Lies silent in the grave."

The character of the Being who made the atonement, is another doctrinal point most wisely adapted to the wants of man. Whatever may be said as to those engaged in intellectual pursuits and accustomed to abstractions, the great body of men have ever associated some material or human characteristic in their idea of God. And the Old Testament, out of regard to this want of human nature, has made most of its representations of the Deity quite anthropomorphous. But it is in the character of Jesus Christ, that this want is most fully met. In that character the divine and the human are so beautifully blended, as to invite confidence without destroying veneration. Had it been said only that the *Word was with God and was God*, man would feel as if there were an infinite gulf between him and his Saviour. But when it is added, that the *Word was made flesh and dwelt among us*, the idea of a common nature draws us to him, and especially when he calls us his brethren, and declares that he was tempted in all points as we are, for the very purpose of affording succor to them that are tempted, and to stand as our daysman, our Advocate and Intercessor, our hearts can no longer resist the appeal, and we approach the throne of grace boldly, because we know that we have a sympathizing friend to plead our cause. And yet he is an almighty friend, and what more can we ask? No wonder that the heart cleaves to such a Saviour with a supreme and undying love.

"Clothed with our nature still, he knows
The weakness of our frame,
And how to shield us from the foes
Whom he himself o'ercame.

"Nor time, nor distance e'er shall quench
The fervor of his love;
For us he died in kindness here,
For us he lives above."

It is hardly strange that to the acutest minds, unenlightened by revelation, this world should seem to be a hopeless enigma; or that it should be looked upon as a state of retribution, and that the half Christian Manichee should imagine two supreme principles, one of good and the other of evil, holding with each other an everlasting war. But there are two doctrines of revelation that solve the dark riddle, and show to the eye of faith the full-orbed glories of the Divine Benevolence behind the thickest clouds. One of these doctrines is, that the world is in a fallen condition, and because sin has entered it, suffering has followed; so that, in fact, *the whole creation groaneth and travaileth together in pain.* The other is, that God's providence sits watchfully above the whole scene, and so controls every event, that the final result shall be happiness and glory. It is wonderful how these truths resolve the most agitating doubts, and anchor the soul to a rock amid the fiercest tempests of life. Faith does not fear but that infinite power, wisdom and benevolence, will bring order out of confusion, peace out of discord, holiness out of pollution, and everlasting happiness out of temporary misery. She can see how wisely adapted even the evils of life are to the moral discipline essential to a fallen being. And when the tempests howl around, and the billows come pouring over her, it is enough for her to *know that all things work together for good, to them that love God.* She has reached that happiest condition of human existence, unreserved submission to the will of God.

Springing from such a system of doctrines, cordially embraced, there are hopes and consolations such as nothing else can give. All other hopes and consolations fail to satisfy; but these leave nothing to be desired. The man does not cease to be interested in this world, but he is more interested in another. The consciousness that his eternal future is safe, makes every blessing the sweeter which he receives on his way thither. And it also lightens every labor and neutralizes every trial. So near to immortal and unalloyed happiness, of how little consequence to him are the short-lived inconveniences he meets in his brief sojourn below; especially when he knows how necessary his trials and labors are to prepare him for eternal joy! Oh, if such a man has not within him the elements of happiness, they cannot be found on earth. Daily the manna falls from heaven around him; and even in the thirsty desert, he can smite the rock, and the cool and refreshing waters will gush out. And he knows that when he comes to the banks of Jordan, the waters, touched by the wand of faith, will divide for his passage.

Such is the wonderful adaptation of the gospel system to human wants. How could it do more to fill and satisfy them. Now my argument is, that whenever men are made conscious of their spiritual wants, and such a gospel is made known to them, it will be eagerly embraced. And if embraced by a few, they cannot but make it known to others; and thus, if no untoward influences prevent, will the whole mass at length be leavened. It does, indeed, meet with a powerful obstruction in human depravity; and were it unadapted to the necessities of man, it could make no progress; but now it has a catalytic power which enables it to find its way through the sluggish mass.

In the second place, man's conscience testifies to the truth of the gospel system, and thus prepares the way for its admission to the heart.

Of all the powers of the human soul, conscience has suffered least from the blasting influence of the apostacy of the race. The corrupt heart is able to make every other faculty its pander and slave ; but conscience always stands erect and unsubdued, ready to lift her voice in defence of the right and to rebuke the wrong. Her mouth may, indeed, for a time, be forcibly closed, and her sensibilities blunted, by the hot-searing iron of iniquity, but her internal vitality remains unaffected ; and when, at length, her liberty and vigor are restored, her retributions will be terrible.

Now it is an interesting fact, that unperverted conscience is a stern advocate for evangelical religion. Tell an unconverted man that his heart is deceitful above all things and desperately wicked, and his pride and self-sufficiency will resent the charge; but his conscience knows it to be true. Tell him that with such a heart he could not be happy in heaven, and that, therefore, he must be created anew in Christ Jesus, and his corrupt inclinations will muster a stout defiance against the mortifying truth; yet the faithful inward monitor often compels him to acknowledge its reality. Hence you will often see the strange anomaly, of a man confessing his utterly lost condition by nature, and his entire unfitness for heaven without a new heart, and yet so bolstered up by pride and self-sufficiency, that he feels little anxiety and makes no efficient efforts to change his condition.

Again, in spite of all the struggles of perverted reason, conscience often compels men to acknowledge the justice of the penalty annexed to sin. Sophistry may enable them to make out a very clear demonstration of the inconsistency between divine benevolence and eternal punishment. But conscience compels them to acknowledge that they deserve it. They know that with such wicked hearts, they could never experience any thing else but punishment, and they are conscious of having done nothing to lay God under obligation to give them a better heart; so that, without his interposition, eternal misery follows as a natural consequence.

But though thus dependent upon God's grace, conscience will not release them from their obligations to love and serve Him; for that faithful and keen-eyed observer testifies that their inability arises from a perversion of the powers which God has given them, and not from any natural defect; and, therefore, they are as much bound to love and obey their Father in heaven, as a perverse child is to exercise filial affection and do service to his earthly father.

In this dilemma, how strenuous an advocate for the doctrine of special grace does conscience become. Instead of pleading the sinner's apology on the ground of inability, and striving to release him from obligation, she charges him with having crippled himself, and therefore as lying under the full weight of responsibility to the divine law. Yet how certain to perish, if the special power of God do not interpose!

In the human conscience, then, we have a powerful instrumentality for the diffusion of the gospel. Once let the leaven of its great principles be brought into close contact with that conscience, and in spite of the hostile influence of pride, selfishness and passion, it will rouse and transform the torpid soul, and make it henceforth alive to duty and to God. That soul will in fact *become a new creature in Christ Jesus, old things having passed away and all things become new.* But such a perfect network of sympathies is human society, that you cannot change the feelings and character of one individual, and not send a like influence into the hearts of those around him. Let one man's conscience be roused to do its office, and his neighbor's conscience cannot be wholly quiet. So numerous are the points of contact between men, that no one can remain long wholly ignorant of a moral change in his neighbor, nor unaffected by it when known. Thus, through the force of conscience, a self-propagating power is imparted to religious reformations. Once start the process in a particular spot, and conscience will become the catalytic agency to transmit it from individual to individual, we cannot tell how widely.

In the third place, the history of Christianity shows it to be possessed of an extraordinary catalytic power. Recall to mind the circumstances under which the gospel was first introduced. Its Author, a poor, persecuted wanderer, chose twelve illiterate fishermen for his council, his heralds, his body-guard, and his successors in propagating his system of truth among men. The whole world, too, stood armed to the teeth to resist its introduction. All its prejudices, its social, political, religious, and even its military power, was ready to be arrayed against the gospel; and, in fact, all these forces were employed to arrest its progress and to root it out of the world. Ten times, within three hundred years, did the mighty emperors of Rome assail Christianity with fire and sword. And they felt sure of a triumph; for how could a few feeble, contemptible fanatics, without wealth, power, or influence, resist an array that had conquered the world. But how little did these worldly wise rulers know of the inherent vitality, the self-sustaining, and self-propagating power of the gospel! So that, in fact, while they supposed they were giving the finishing blow to the system, it was silently and irresistibly working its way into the hearts and affections of all classes of the community, till at length, in the beginning of the fourth century, it became the established religion of the empire.

Perhaps you will say this was the effect of the miraculous agency that was manifested in the church in apostolic times. This might have had some influence, in the first introduction of Christianity; yet far less, even then, I apprehend, than is generally supposed; for it is usually quite easy to get rid of the influence of a miracle by imputing it to imposture, jugglery and delusion, as we know was done in those days. But it is not settled whether the power of working miracles was possessed by any after the days of the Apostles; certainly that power was withdrawn a century or two before the days of Constantine. Nor have we evidence that there was any thing peculiar in the Divine Influence which was exerted upon the hearts of men in primitive times. It seems to have operated then, as now, according to the established laws of mind, and in proportion to the means employed. Furthermore, we have the testimony of the Bible to the position, that men are no more apt to be convinced by miracles than by the ordinary truths of the gospel; for *if they hear not Moses and the Prophets, neither would they be persuaded though one rose from the dead.* We must, therefore, impute the extraordinary success of the gospel in early times, and in the midst of fiery persecution, mainly to its adaptation to human wants and the human conscience.

In subsequent periods of the world's history, this same experiment has been often repeated. And it has ever been true, that the kingdom of heaven cometh not with observation. No loud trumpets have sounded its advent; no powerful array of means has ushered it in. A few obscure men, without money or influence, and perhaps with little of worldly wisdom or policy, unarmed, save by the Bible and faith, have gone into the arena of conflict, like David to meet Goliath. And so inadequate have the champions and their weapons seemed, that the world have looked upon them with as much contempt and derision as Philistia's giant did upon David. And yet the despised pebble has found its way to the giant's forehead, and the Galilean has conquered.

Take Great Britain, for an example. The conquests of that kingdom by Julius Cæsar, by the

Saxons, the Danes and the Normans, are all on record, and constitute distinctly marked epochs of history. But who can tell us when and how Christianity won its more thorough and enduring conquest, penetrating where the arms of the Roman, the Dane, and the Saxon, could not reach, and converting tribes of the rudest heathen into civilized and Christian men? It is indeed said, that Augustine and a few other monks were once sent as missionaries to Britain; but how feeble an instrumentality to accomplish a work a thousand times more extensive and important than all the conquests to which Britain has ever been subject, or which she has made by her arms since her political existence began. Had there not been an unseen, self-propagating power to carry forward the work, begun only in here and there a spot by humble missionaries, the whole mass could never have been so thoroughly permeated.

The same fact exhibits itself when we compare Christian with Pagan or Mohammedan nations. In the latter, you meet with much more of the external manifestations of religion than in the former. Temples, images, processions, public prayers, and other rites, are rife every where; but, after all, you perceive that little influence, save an injurious one, is exerted in such countries upon the public morals, manners or welfare; yet, in Christian lands, it is manifest that an influence has gone deeper into the public heart and conscience; and hence you find more kindness, amenity and decency, more of civilization and respect for morality and piety. The rude and ferocious elements of human nature are more tamed and moulded by Christian influences, than by Pagan or Mohammedan.

I believe this is true of all nominally Christian lands, although we must confess that, in many of them, the gospel has been well nigh deprived of its vitality, and little more than its external covering remains. But even there, Christianity exerts a decidedly better influence than the most refined system of human invention. Moreover, we may impute whatever of good moral influence is exerted by Mohammedanism to the principles,—and these are not few and unimportant,—which it has purloined from the Bible.

Again, you will find that just in proportion as Christianity has been corrupted and the Bible is withheld from circulation among the people, will the literary, civil, social and moral condition of a nation be degraded. Suppose you had the power to pass suddenly from such a country as New England, or Old England, or Scotland, into Austria, Russia, Spain, or France. Would you need a geographer to tell you that you were in a land where a withering blight had come over the pure gospel? While you would meet crucifixes, oratories, cathedrals, chapels, and confessionals every where, you would find the Bible nowhere. And while you would hear te deums and chanted prayers, and the praises of the virgin and the saints in all places of worship, and on all days and hours, you would listen in vain for unadulterated gospel truth at any time. And while the antiquated walls of monasteries and convents would meet you in every place, the academy and the school-house would be wanting in all places. And when you became acquainted with the character of the great body of the population in those lands, you could not doubt that the gospel, which you had seen doing so much in the country from which you came, to elevate, enlighten and bless, was here shorn of the lock of its strength, and had been moulded and trimmed to adapt it to systems of superstition, ignorance, intolerance and despotism.

The whole history of the missionary enterprise, foreign and domestic, affords decisive proof of the leavening influence of the gospel. To mere worldly wisdom, the most striking feature of that enterprise is the total inadequacy between the means employed and the expected results. When a man, who has been accustomed to estimate the amount of outlay and preparation requisite in any successful undertaking in commerce, manufactures or agriculture, or who knows the amount of effort necessary in a successful political campaign,—when such a man looks at the very slender instrumentality which the ablest missionary societies employ for the conversion of the world, it seems to him a want of wisdom amounting to infatuation, to go forward. Why, men are more tenacious of their false systems of religion than of any thing else ; and yet you send one, or two, or half-a-dozen, plain, powerless men, among twenty or fifty millions, and are disappointed if, in a few years, you do not hear of numerous conversions.

Alike inefficacious do such feeble instrumentalities appear to the heathen and the Mohammedans themselves. And this is one of the grounds on which missionaries are allowed to pursue their work, unmolested, in countries most hostile to their plans. Imagine, for instance, that the Emperor of China, or the Shah of Persia, or the Sultan of Turkey, should learn that one, or two, or even half-a-dozen, unarmed, inoffensive men, had taken up their abode in Canton, or Oroomiah, or Constantinople, with a view to preach the doctrines of Christianity, and to teach the principles of human science and literature to the young. Do you think that either of these despots would have any fears excited that the established religion of the country was in danger? Would he not treat the suggestion with contempt, and look on the missionaries as deluded men, whose efforts to proselyte would be harmless, and whose literary instructions would be valuable to the empire, and therefore their residence might be tolerated? And if a British minister would be gratified by having these teachers protected, how ready would he be to issue the decree which should place them and their followers on a footing with their other Christian subjects. But let these rulers learn something of the catalytic power of the gospel, by seeing multitudes converted, as if by a mysterious influence, and you would see the sword of persecution unsheathed and martyrs multiplied. And it is mainly because such conversions have not been in general extensive enough to arrest the attention of rulers, that persecutions by the government are so infrequent. I fear that they are yet to put the faith and courage of the church severely to the test. For by and by, heathen and Mohammedan nations will learn that the leaven of the gospel, hid in the community by the humble missionary, has, unperceived, sent its transforming power through the whole torpid mass, and that their false systems are crumbling into ruins.

A still more manifest example of this mighty though unnoticed influence, is often seen in our own land, when the Domestic Missionary Society sends its benevolent agencies into some waste place where iniquity is triumphant. In such a place are found, it may be, a few humble Christians, but the wealth, the fashion, and worldly influence, are all hostile to the truth; and when the missionary calls around him the few followers of Christ at the prayer meeting and in the church, it only makes matter for amusement and ridicule among others, who, in view of the apparent feebleness of the instrumentality, exclaim, with Sanballat and Tobiah of old, *What do these feeble Christians? Will they revive the stones out of the heaps of the rubbish which are burned? Even that which they build, if a fox go up, he shall even break down their stone wall.* But the despised leaven silently operates; God's Spirit comes down to urge the movement forward, and the great mountain that seemed so strong, crumbles down and becomes a plain. The gospel triumphs; decency and refinement of manners takes the place of obscenity and vulgarity; temperance succeeds to drunkenness; peace to discord; thrift and enterprise to decay and poverty; and spiritual religion to errors of every name. Yet so quietly was the change effected, through the gospel's catalytic power, that opposition and skepticism stand amazed.

From this principle of the self-propagating power of the gospel, thus established, we may derive inferences of great importance, and eminently adapted to encourage and strengthen those engaged in the missionary enterprise, whether domestic or foreign. Indeed, since the recent rapid expansion of our population across this broad continent, these terms, domestic and foreign, have become nearly synonymous.

In the first place, this subject should inspire us with strong confidence in the power of divine truth.

The current of worldliness often sets so strongly against the truth, and the means appointed for its diffusion seem so simple and inadequate, that we are apt to be disheartened, and to forget the mighty power which the doctrines of the gospel possess to work their way amid obstacles, and become mighty through God to the pulling down of strong holds. But when we recollect what that truth has done in time past, how it has transformed whole nations as if by magic, how at this moment, abused and perverted as we know it to be, it makes Christian nations stand out on the world's panorama so conspicuously, and when we think of its wonderful adaptation to the deepest wants of man, and what a stern advocate it finds in the human conscience, and especially how thorough is the renovation of the individual who gives himself up entirely to its influence, we ought to be ashamed of our distrust of its power, and to feel that we have in our hands an instrument which, by God's blessing, can and will create anew and sanctify our lost world. So that wherever we have an opportunity to bring the gospel in contact with the human conscience and reason, we ought to urge its claims with as undoubted an assurance of its efficacy as a woman exercises when she hides only a modicum of leaven in three measures of meal.

Secondly, the subject is full of encouragement to those who are laboring in weakness with great obstacles and discouragements, in the dissemination of the truths of the gospel

Let them remember that the leaven, when mixed with the meal, seems to be lost, and little or no visible effect is produced, until at length it is found that the whole loaf is thoroughly leavened. Let them remember, too, that the pure gospel, when brought in contact with men's consciences, is as sure to commence a catalytic process there, as good leaven is in the meal, although without special grace it will not result in conversion. Nor will the laborer, perhaps, perceive any good effect produced for a long time, and possibly not while he lives. But moral reformations usually move very slowly onward. It needs time for the leaven to work. And in many cases the sower is not permitted to gather the sheaves. But if they are finally reaped, *he that soweth and he that reapeth will rejoice together*. Let him who is faithful in doing his duty in some barren field of labor, be assured that the truth has never yet failed to manifest, sooner or later, its transforming power. His field of labor may be narrow, and his discouragements many; but let him bear in mind that he has a mighty instrument to work with, and an almighty God pledged to sustain him.

In the third place, the subject shows the fallacy of the doctrine, that the world is growing worse, and will continue to grow worse, in spite of all efforts to spread the gospel.

The world does indeed abound with wickedness, and often the success of the truth in a place is the occasion of a grosser development of iniquity. But the truth has the advantage, because it meets and satisfies man's highest wants so completely, and enlists in its favor the human conscience. And whence arises this want of confidence in the truth, as an instrument of the world's conversion, among these our brethren, some of whom are missionaries, and yet they do not believe the world can be converted by the gospel, but will continue to grow worse till the Saviour makes a visible display of his power? Have they not felt the power of truth in their own souls? and have they not seen its mighty efficacy upon the souls of others? Do they doubt its ability, when applied by God's Spirit, to convert the world? If the world is growing worse, how happens it that all Christian nations, even where the gospel is dreadfully perverted, are so far superior in character and condition to Pagan and Mohammedan nations? Surely these men forget the catalytic power of the gospel, as developed in history. True, the improved physical, social and intellectual condition of a nation, is far from being its conversion to God. But it is an important prerequisite to that conversion. And it does imply that some in that nation are truly converted; and why is not all this an earnest of the final and complete triumph of pure religion, if its comparatively few genuine disciples do their duty? For every accession to their number increases their power; and why may not that leavening influence go on till it has reached the world's entire population?

In the gospel, then, you have an agency abundantly adequate to the work; and why then call in miraculous power? for we know that it is a settled principle of the Divine Government, not to work a miracle when established agencies are sufficient.

Finally, this subject should greatly encourage and animate the hopes and efforts of those engaged in the work of missions.

They learn from it that they need not be discouraged, though the common principles by which men judge of the probable success of their enterprises, should show their chance to be small. The fact that they are following a divine command, to go into all the world and preach the gospel to every creature, may, indeed, be sufficient to give them courage and perseverance amid powerful difficulties. But it is important, also, to know what an extraordinary instrument they possess for carrying on the enterprise; how it works its way into the hearts of men and silently changes their characters, and the whole aspect of society; and sends down an influence, they cannot tell how far, into generations unborn. *It is, indeed, quick and powerful, sharper than a two-edged sword, piercing even to the dividing asunder of soul and spirit, and of the joints and marrow, and is a discerner of the thoughts and intents of the heart.* It takes a stronger hold of society than all other influences, and abides longer. Its secret energy rouses human society into action, and propagates the catalytic change from individual to individual, from family to family, from community to community, and sometimes from kingdom to kingdom. Nor can the missionary tell, when he deposits the leaven of the gospel in one spot, even though scarcely heeded there, but he has started a process which shall go radiating outwards over a whole continent; for thus it has often done.

But though thus adapted to cheer the missionary in every land, this principle affords much more encouragement in some countries than in others; and most of all, on American soil; to the home missionary here. To prove and illustrate this from the analogies of my text, let us recur to certain facts respecting catalytic operations in nature, which I neglected at the commencement of this discourse.

The essential principle to which I mainly refer, is this: that in order to make leaven, or any other catalytic agent operate, it is necessary that the mass to be leavened should be in a certain state, as to consistency, temperature and permeability. The baker well knows, that it is of no use to hide leaven in a mass of frozen dough, nor unless its temperature is a good deal above the freezing point. So if from any other cause it has become condensed and rigid, the leaven cannot spread itself among the particles, and little or no effect will be produced, even though the leaven be in the best condition.

Apply now these principles to the dissemination of the gospel. Attempt to propagate its truths in a country where Heathenism, or Mohammedanism, or corrupt Christianity, is firmly established, is sustained by the learned few, and the ignorant and superstitious many, and by wealth and influence ; is linked inseparably to the government, and can show a long list of illustrious defenders. By such causes the false system has been knit firmly together, and is settled down into a hard, impenetrable mass, which resists all change. Without a miracle, you would expect that if the truth should make any headway, it would be slow and difficult. Whereas in a nation where a false religious system sets loose upon the people, and has little social or governmental support, and especially where commerce, education and free principles are breaking up the torpid and indurated mass, the way is prepared for the gospel's catalytic power to show its mighty transforming energy.

Facts now corroborate the truth of these principles. For never has the gospel made rapid progress in any country where a false system of religion has entrenched itself behind the prejudices, the social habits, the pecuniary interests, the splendor of rites and forms, and governmental favor ; and its most signal triumphs have been witnessed where the false system has but a feeble hold upon the public mind, or men have begun to think for themselves. Certain conditions seem necessary, in order that the leaven may work ; nor where these are wanting are we to expect success, any more than that the laws of chemistry will be set aside in the process of bread-making. God does sometimes, indeed, give unexpected success by the power of his Spirit, to show that, after all, the efficiency lies with him. But such cases are exceptions, which we cannot calculate upon, and are not our rule of judgment or of duty.

From these principles we should confidently infer, that Mohammedanism, and especially Popery, would offer more powerful obstructions to the spread of the gospel than any other systems of error. Hence it is, that while missionary stations are multiplied among the heathen, they are yet so few in the great centres of Mohammedan and Papal influence in Asia and Europe. Nor can we doubt, that long after every heathen pagoda has been converted into a Christian temple,—nay, long after the Bible shall have supplanted the Koran in every mosque and minaret,—will the perverted Christianity of forms, propped up by leagues and bayonets, present its yet unbroken front, to be breached only in the *battle of that great day of God Almighty.*

On the other hand, from these same principles, we infer that nowhere on earth is there such a preparation for the spread of pure Christianity as in our own land. Here we have no inert and indurated mass of dead formalism to break up; no frozen and petrified system of rites and ceremonies to arrest the leavening process; no iron arm of government to check the onward movement. But the genial light and warmth of free institutions and of general education, have brought the community into a state most favorable for receiving the gospel and giving it free course. Wherever faithfully planted, it is sure to communicate and spread its vitalizing influence outward and onward; and if

Christians will only do their duty, they may be sure that the whole land will be leavened.

And here I ought to mention another chemical principle that has a parallel in the condition of our country. Chemists tell us that elements in their *nascent* state, that is, when first produced, unite far more readily than they do afterwards. Now the elements of our social condition are as yet, in a great measure, in a nascent state; and therefore more ready to be operated upon and form valuable combinations than in the old world, where every thing has long since become immovably fixed, either by affinities within or pressure without. Oh how important that the gospel exert its catalytic power upon our population, before that same binding and paralyzing process pass upon them! The wide world does not furnish another field of missionary labor so promising. I mean not by this, that other countries are not open to the gospel, and that missionary efforts should be limited to our own land. God bless these efforts and increase them a hundred fold in every land. But I do mean, that our country preëminently invites and demands efforts for its evangelization. I do mean, that it is a more promising and a more important field than any other on the globe, and therefore calls for every heart and every hand to engage in it.

Do I seem to any to be taking too strong ground? Let me propose to them an experiment, which I sincerely wish all my hearers could try, to test this opinion. Let them take the next steamer across the Atlantic, and in one fortnight they would find themselves on ground very favorable for a comparison. They would be traversing lands where state religions exist, with all their pompous and imposing rites and ceremonies, with their exclusive and intolerant spirit, and their hostility to freedom of opinion, and to all that is vital in personal piety. Religion there, is sustained by governmental decrees and by bayonets. Throttled in the embraces of the state, its lifeless form is made use of as a speaking-trumpet, through which are proclaimed, not the doctrines of God, but of man; such as the divine right of kings, the duty of unreserved submission to the government and the church; the infallibility of the church, not of the Bible. The sweet countenance of gospel charity has been changed into that of a persecuting fiend; and the snaky locks of a gorgon cover her head, freezing and petrifying all around. All places are full of religious forms, but alas, to find its power you must search long and deep. The very highways are studded with crosses and crucified Christs, with oratories and images of the virgin, while the towns abound with vast and venerable cathedrals and chapels, full of golden images, splendid paintings, and sacred relics; and the magnificent organ peals along the sounding arches and thrills the wondering soul, as the gilded priests chant their te deums, their pater nosters, and their ave marias. You enter the convent at the sound of the vesper bell, and a thousand white veiled nuns are kneeling around you, and gorgeous music lends enchantment to the vesper hymn. Every where in the streets you meet the cassocked priest, and often the imposing procession, while the multitudes uncover their heads as it passes. In short, to an American, accustomed to the simplicity of our modes of worship, the most prominent feature in European lands, save in the glorious fast-anchored isle,—and even there to great extent,—is, that in spite of the most imposing externals, the whole is little more than heartless formality,—a wretched substitute for the bread of life. Yet when he sees how firmly rooted is this system in the pride and prejudice, the worldly interest, the interests of despotic governments, and a swarming priesthood, and how it is woven into the very texture of society, he cannot but feel that little short of a miracle will be required for effecting a revolution. With what deep interest, then, after only a few weeks of such observation in those lands, will the heart of the Christian American turn towards his own country. In the hallowed language of our gubernatorial proclamations he will exclaim, "God save the Commonwealth of Massachusetts!" Save her religion from the base alloy of formalism, superstition and intolerance. Save her system of education from the blighting touch of aristocracy and priestcraft. Save her free institutions from the savage ferocity of the ignorant and unprincipled many, and the grinding oppression of the despotic few. Save her, for the sake of the country. And God save that whole country for her own sake, and the sake of the world. For to save her, is to save the world; and to lose her, is to lose the world.

It needs only a short pilgrimage through the old world to excite such sentiments as these in the heart of a Massachusetts American. And his prayer to God will be, that he may live to go back and labor harder than he has ever done, to build up the cause of pure religion, of learning, and of freedom, in that land which he has now learnt to be the only one on earth where, for the present, this indissoluble trio of noble institutions has any chance of wide-spread success. And if this man learns only this lesson by his foreign tour, it is worth all the sacrifice and expense of ten thousand miles of voyage and travel.

What a noble work, then, is committed to our hands! What an inviting field has the Home Missionary Society before it! The man who enters it finds society not only in a state more favorable for casting in the leaven of the gospel, but that the influence of his labors is felt almost to the ends of the earth. Let him be laboring to build up some obscure waste place, say in Massachusetts. He may seem to be unnoticed and neglected. But he is doing his part towards sustaining and perpetuating the free and the religious institutions of the country, and therefore, in fact, the eyes of many millions in Europe are watching his labors with deep interest, and with earnest prayers for his fidelity: for their chief hope of the world's emancipation rests on the success of civil and religious liberty here. And if the true gospel be not preached and received among us, free institutions must for the present fail. In preaching the gospel, therefore, in the obscurest nook of the land, a man may feel that he is working for the whole country, nay, for the whole world. Indeed, Providence is sending representations from the whole world to our doors. By multitudes they pour in upon us from every European land, and swarms of Asiatics are crowding into the valleys of California. So that in fact we may become missionaries to Papists, Mohammedans, Boodists and other heathen, without leaving our own shores.

What responsibility, then, attaches to the name and position of an American. When, in foreign lands, I have met kings and queens, dukes and marquises, counts and viscounts, they appeared to be men and women of only the ordinary stature; but when I first set my foot again upon our own shores, and met free-born Christian Americans, it seemed to me that I was looking upon giants, because God has given them the power of giants to bear up the pillars of freedom, of education, and of religion, and to cast down the pillars of ignorance, superstition and despotism.

If your patience is not quite exhausted, allow me to add one or two further suggestions, growing out of a scientific view of the text.

In order that leaven should operate effectually, or even operate at all, it must itself be in an active condition and of a proper temperature. In proportion as its thermometric state is too high or too low, or if there be an admixture of inert substances, or its own decomposition be slow or partial, will its catalytic power be diminished.

So it is with the moral leaven of the gospel. If its purity be marred by an admixture of error and vain speculation, or if it be cast into the community distorted by ignorance, or disfigured and blackened by the fires of fanaticism, or enveloped in the ice of formalism, feeble will be its influence, if indeed it do not become a nuisance. Instead of proving the wisdom of God and the power of God unto salvation, men will see in it only the weakness of human wisdom and strength, overpowered by the superior might of human depravity.

Now it is this perverted and deficient gospel, that too often finds its way into our waste places, into our new settlements, and among the floating population of our cities. It has the name of Christianity, and usually contains some truth, but a larger proportion of error; so that while it produces traces of religion, it shows more of fanaticism, or bigotry, or self-righteousness and formalism. How important then, that into fields, thus grown over with briars and weeds, a pure and holy gospel should be carried by pure and holy men. Those engaged in sending this gospel abroad, through our Home Missionary Societies, should have their piety in that active condition, without which their prayers, example and efforts, will only deepen the spiritual slumbers of ignorance and sin. And still more important is it, that the direct agents in this work should preach an unadulterated gospel, not only by their voices but by their lives.

Finally, astonishing as is the power of leaven to change the mass into which it is cast, there is a limit to that power. One part may, indeed, transform two thousand parts of the meal; but if the latter be increased much beyond that proportion, not only will all the excess remain unaffected, but it will operate to prevent the leaven from producing its full effect. Nay, it may nearly or quite destroy that effect. Hence if the leaven and the mass to be leavened be enormously disproportionate, the best leaven may become powerless.

Now to apply this principle to Home Missionary efforts, I fear, my brethren, that this is just what we are doing in our country. The mass to be leavened by the gospel is out of all proportion to the means employed. In 1850 we built between four and five thousand miles of railroad at an average cost of $50,000 per mile. During that same year we expended only enough upon domestic missions, to construct five miles of railway. And railways are only one branch of American enterprise out of many. How exceedingly small, then, must be the proportion of our pecuniary means devoted to an enterprise which transcends all others in our country in importance. For if that fail, all others will be smitten with a deadly blight. Irreligion cannot triumph without trampling in the dust our systems of general education, of public enterprise and freedom, and crushing the hopes of liberty through the earth. Our hopes, therefore, must centre in the Home Missionary cause. We make enormous outlays, and labor without weariness to advance our worldly schemes, and that, too, where the means employed have little or none of the catalytic power inherent in the gospel; and where the results bear no proportion in importance to the work of Home Missions. God has committed to American Christians the noblest enterprise which he has given to the present generation in any part of the world. And he has put into our hands an instrument with which to accomplish it, a thousand times more efficacious than those employed in commerce, in manufactures, in agriculture, or indeed any ordinary art or pursuit. How dwarfed must be our piety, how low our standard of patriotism, how contemptible our philanthropy, if we do not supply the means necessary to prevent the leaven of the gospel from being overpowered and neutralized by ignorance and depravity. Ought we to be satisfied to expend $50,000,000 annually for railways, and only one thousandth part as much in working out the grandest problem in politics, in education and religion, of this generation! Oh, if any cause has motives powerful enough to rouse men to action, it is this. If we enter into the work resolutely and cheerfully, with humble reliance on God's help, we are sure of success. And success will bring such a day of brightness and blessing to this wide continent, as never yet has visited any other. Though the deluge of ignorance, despotism and false religion, should engulf every other land, ours shall stand high above the flood and beat back its angry waves; and, ere the close of the present century, one hundred millions of Christian freemen shall here be found richly enjoying those social, political, educational, and religious rights and privileges, which God originally gave, but which man has hitherto unrighteously withheld.

A NATION SAVED FROM ITS PROSPERITY ONLY BY THE GOSPEL.

A DISCOURSE

IN BEHALF OF THE

American Home Missionary Society,

PREACHED IN THE CITIES OF NEW YORK AND BROOKLYN,

MAY, 1853,

BY

REV. LAURENS P. HICKOK, D. D.,

OF UNION COLLEGE, SCHENECTADY, N. Y.

NEW YORK:
PUBLISHED BY THE AMERICAN HOME MISSIONARY SOCIETY.
1853.

BAKER, GODWIN & Co., Printers,
Tribune Buildings, N. Y.

DISCOURSE.

MARK X. 23 to 27.

"And Jesus looked around, and saith to his disciples, How hardly shall they that have riches enter into the kingdom of God! And all the disciples were astonished at his words. But Jesus answereth again, and saith unto them, Children, how hard is it for them that trust in riches to enter into the kingdom of God! It is easier for a camel to go through the eye of a needle, than for a rich man to enter into the kingdom of God. And they were astonished beyond measure, saying among themselves, Who then can be saved? And Jesus, looking upon them, saith, With men it is impossible, but not with God; for with God all things are possible."

A young man, with natural qualities so amiable that Jesus loved him, and yet with a heart so worldly that he could not give up his great possessions, had just gone away from the Savior, grieved at the strictness of his requisitions. From this incident, Jesus Christ took occasion to give to his disciples the very impressive instruction in the text. Riches exclude from heaven. The inclination to trust in them is so strong that they effectually shut the way of life from their possessor. Leaving human nature to its own course, the rich man would no more pass the strait gate than the camel would go through the eye of a needle. And yet the salvation of a rich man is not utterly hopeless. God, to whom all things are possible, has a way to save even those who have great possessions.

This striking truth is not applicable merely to rich men. Great nations stand in the same relation to it, and are in the same way concluded by it, as single persons. The natural course of a rich nation is to destruction. It will trust in its prosperity, and boast of its destiny, and lose its integrity, and bring upon itself its own ruin. It will not open its eyes to its dangers till too late. Its wise men and great statesmen will not save it. Its very abundance will corrupt its own members, and if left only to its own resources it will go on to its dissolution.

But with God there is power to restrain and save a nation from the consequences of its own prosperity. His method of doing it is by the preaching of the Gospel, establishing christian churches and maintaining christian ordinances, and then pouring out his Spirit and kindling up pure revivals of religion over the land; and in this manner he so sanctifies the people and gives such elevated and vigorous spiritual life to public sentiment, that the nation can bear its growing greatness, and even pass on in its prosperity, making continually, physical and moral improvements. God can so save rich men, and rich nations; but, as fallen human nature is, it is impossible to save either in any other manner.

The general proposition, therefore, which I deduce from the text is this—THAT IT IS IMPOSSIBLE TO SAVE A NATION FROM THE DESTRUCTIVE CONSEQUENCES OF ITS OWN PROSPERITY, EXCEPT BY THE GOSPEL.

The truth of this proposition may be seen *in apprehending precisely what a nation is.* The state cannot be a mere aggregate of individuals. The choices of each man in a community fix upon their respective objects, and the agency of each goes out to attain possession; and thus the whole community is put in motion. But these choices and their execution will be perpetually clashing and colliding with each other, and the free action of one will make the free action of many impossible. If one have his choice, many others cannot have theirs. Individual freedom must be public oppression. Each person, therefore, must be restrained by what is due to the whole, and particular freedom be controlled by a regard to public freedom.

This interest in each, that others should be restrained by that which is due to the freedom of all, at once knits the community together, and makes the whole an organized unity. No one may live to himself. The whole have a right to restrain each, for the highest freedom of all. Thus the state *is* from the very activities of society, and has the right to make its own constitution and form of government.

It is thus manifest that nothing can be vital in the state, which does not come up into it from the life of its individual members. The laws of a nation are mere dead forms, except as the popular sentiment breathes its own life into them. A constitution will not create national life ; it is the state which puts its own life into the constitution. The liberty and virtue of a nation must live and grow in the hearts of the people, or as a nation it has no liberty nor virtue. Its wise men cannot preserve its integrity by legislation; for although its laws were inspired, yet if they did not meet an answering sympathy in the public bosom, the whole statute-book would be a dead letter. Yea, were the state thus corrupt in its own members, its wise men, if there were any, would not be its legislators. The public will bring out of its bosom that which expresses its own sentiments, and the law-giver and the law will conform to the feeling, beating heart of the nation. Whether despotism or democracy, it will ultimately become *like* people *like* law—an administration which expresses the very life and soul of the social community.

Such is the state; and the Bible and long experience tell us what is man, of whom the state is made. Such an organization, with such elements, cannot bear perpetual prosperity. There is an inherent native depravity in mankind, tending constantly to excessive gratification. The possession of wealth stimulates avarice; the presence of power kindles ambition; the allurement of pleasure induces voluptuousness. Where opportunity is given and restraint removed, indulgence follows. Solicitation brings consent, and vice grows in enormity as temptations multiply. The corruption of one generation perpetuates itself into the next, increasing crime with greater violence and familiarity with wickedness. Every man is intent upon his own pleasure or interest, and the public welfare is disregarded. Political peculation and venality are witnessed by only careless and listless observers; society has lost the moral energy which enspirits heroism and cheers patriotism; the virtue which frowns down selfishness and baseness, is gone; and every thing hastens rapidly to dissolution. The magistracy become perjured; the judges are bribed; witnesses are suborned; favoritism tramples over law; the moral life of the people, and thus the vital energy of the state, has died out; and national extinction is near at hand. Exclude anywhere the influence of the Gospel from man, and open the opportunities of great national wealth and power, and, no matter what may be the form of government over the people, it will be impossible to save their virtue or their liberty.

The same truth is also equally manifest *in the history of nations.* The lesson of warning is on every page, that the prosperity of kingdoms destroys them. They grow populous and powerful, their prosperity begets corruption, and they perish. Egypt was; but Egypt, in her power, and wealth, and numbers, is no more. Nineveh extended her walls on the banks of the Tigris, inclosing a population of millions, and spreading her power wide over Asia; but her luxury and drunkenness has long since made her a heap of rubbish. Babylon, once ruled the world; but she, too, has fallen from the excesses her riches had occasioned; and wild beasts roam and satyrs dance, over the ground where once her walls and palaces stood. The very monuments of these kingdoms tell of their debauchery and effeminacy, as plainly as of their wealth and power, which induced their voluptuousness and perdition.

And so, also, the Persian Empire followed, proud in great armies, and splendid with riches; but her effeminate population became an easy prey to the Greek; and this mighty Grecian monarchy also fell in pieces from its own weight, so soon as Alexander's short life was over. And then Rome arose, holding law in its sternness and severity everywhere dominant, and grew slowly to universal empire. But her wealth was also her ruin. Luxury and venality and anarchy prepared the way, and the great metropolis of the world was sacked by hordes of northern barbarians. The richest and the strongest of modern European nations have had their prosperity but for few centuries; and the evidence accumulates among them, that great prosperity is incompatible with national integrity and security. One nation may destroy another by violence, before its own iniquity destroys itself; but wherever the trial has been fairly made, the prosperity of the nation has proved its downfall.

An Asiatic despotism may hold its sway over torpid millions for an indefinite duration, but this is no exception to the universal truth, inasmuch as these Pagan kingdoms cannot be said ever to have had national prosperity. Political liberty has never been theirs, to enjoy or to lose; and national wealth has never been diffused, to induce popular corruption.

From the great facts which history teaches, we thus confirm the truth, that to take man as he is, and as he makes states to be, and give him wealth and power, and let him take his own course, and he will dig the grave of any nation. It will be as impossible to keep him in the strict paths of virtuous patriotism, as to drive the camel through the needle's eye. One may be a natural and the other a moral impossibility, but both alike an infallible certainty. God alone, by the interposition of Gospel grace, can hold a prospered people back from destruction.

And now, with this truth thus stated and established, the design is to apply it, in some special cases, to OUR OWN NATION, and show how our own prosperity is inducing most alarming dangers, which nothing but the Gospel can remove.

It is quite obvious, here, to remark, that so far as any nation has been endangered by its prosperity, ours is so preëminently. Never was such progress made, in the attainment of all that ministers to the material greatness of a nation, among any other people as in our country. Territory, population, industry, enterprise, wealth, power, all have accumulated beyond all former precedent. However other nations have been endangered by rapid growth, we more. And still another remark is quite as obvious—that we seem to be endangered by nothing but our prosperity. There is no external enemy for us to fear. There are no inward constitutional weaknesses, nor causes of national decay: our danger of death is only from plethora. Should our grand experiment of free self-government ultimately fail, it will doubtless be because our prosperity is greater than our virtue can bear. Not a cloud appears above our political horizon, that is not gathering and condensing itself from the full moisture of our own atmosphere.

The importance of this whole subject, also furthermore appears, in that whatever danger menaces a state, the great interest involved makes those dangers of momentous concern to every citizen. With this is so connected all that concerns the welfare of man, so interwoven is his weal with the state's safety, that whatever threatens his country puts also in jeopardy his own dearest interests. And with this consideration, I may ask a continued attention while I proceed to state—

Some of our national dangers from our very prosperity, and from which only God through his Gospel can save us.

I pass by those obvious and common evils which are the immediate results from the depraved abuse of wealth and power in all human history, since my design is particularly to consider some of our own peculiar dangers. An increase of luxury, dissipation, prodigality, inducing popular effeminacy and frivolity; a growth of ambition, ostentation, vain-glory, begetting national self-conceit, arrogance and insolence; all bringing in venality and corruption to elections, legislation, and judicial decisions, destroying the very life of all patriotism and public liberty,—this is common everywhere to the rapid acquisition of national wealth. We are as really and as imminently exposed to all these dangers as were any of the old kingdoms and republics which have gone down into the grave of nations, and from which the Spirit of God and the Gospel can alone save us. But, to notice more specially *American* dangers from *American* prosperity, I call attention—

1. *To the increase of Crime.*—This, perhaps, may be said to be the natural attendant of growing wealth in any nation; but there are circumstances which give to this evil peculiar significancy in our country.

Our political prosperity is in connection with, and helps directly to induce, great commercial and mercantile prosperity. The inducements to fraud, theft, robbery, midnight burglary, and murder, which thus increasingly abound, are thrown not only upon our native population, but upon such as an unprecedented foreign immigration is pouring upon our shores. Of the many thousands who come to us annually from abroad, most are from the poor and many are from the vicious population of the old countries which they leave, and are thus of character or condition the most open to temptation, and the most liable to become criminal with their first introduction among us. Many of them are already adepts in crime and wickedness before they leave their own country; and in the loss of old restraints, and the as yet unappreciated force of our laws and the working of our systems of municipal police, it is not otherwise than to be expected that crimes and misdemeanors will multiply in the midst of us.

This need not be a topic for remark, as if it were something surprising; the wonder rather is, in our circumstances, that the increase is not greater. There is not another nation on the earth which could bear such an influx of foreign pauper and vicious population within it, and yet get so much control over it, as we have. The openings to honest industry, employment on the public works, and the cheap new lands of the West, are really taking up the great proportion of all this fresh material for violence and criminality, and employing it safely, usefully, and even virtuously, as it comes to hand. Still, our growing wealth and power and political freedom, vastly augment our danger from this one evil. The foreign criminal comes, and not only practices his own iniquities, but is most fearfully educating our own juvenile delinquents to the perpetration of the most dreadful enormities.

Add to all this the peculiarity of our own elective government, the tendency to wink at immoralities, and even crimes, for the sake of political suffrage; and especially the difficulties on this account in shutting up the frightfully deepening stream of intemperance, engendering more crime in the midst of us than all which is imported, and it is impossible but that offenses will come, and greatly multiply among us. All this is the natural result of our growth, and that restraining influences are not coming spontaneously up to check it. Leave it to its own way, and the end is destruction.

But we only say here, that to the power of God in the Gospel all things are possible. You have only to look at what christian kindness and christian faithfulness have already done in a few short months, even in the most abandoned portion of this very city, and the evidence is as clear as that from old miracles, that the Gospel is the mighty power of God. We have only faithfully and promptly and perseveringly to apply it, and no sinner is so hardened that it cannot fit him for and take him into heaven.

2. *The influx of Foreigners.*—This is here adduced as having its dangers in another direction besides the increase of crime. With our national prosperity, and the poverty and oppression of the masses in European governments, the flow of emigration to our shores is as natural as the currents of air towards the points of highest rarification. Nothing indicates a check, but many things may probably even accelerate it for years to come. The current will flow, and left to its own course will work out its own changes. They may not so certainly and necessarily work destruction as the tendencies of some other agencies. The blending of Celt and Saxon, Dane and Norman, gave the world the Anglo-Saxon race; and perhaps this commingling of blood and crossing of races may greatly invigorate the stamina of even the American stock. But this cannot work itself out in the preservation of our free institutions, except under

an influence which shall assimilate the discordant parts, and so prepare them "as kindred drops to mingle into one."

To such a combination, natural causes are only slowly tending, giving long occasion for discordant interests and chafing animosities, under any coming aggravations, to ripen perhaps into incorrigible alienations. National habits and prejudices work themselves out very tardily from the exotic, and assimilate it very gradually to the indigenous stock; and these peculiarities become the more unyielding, when counter religious creeds and rituals come into perpetual collision; and more especially so, if the foreign creed be constantly receiving fresh vigor from new infusions of its native spirit. Romanism cannot naturally become republicanism. Very pressing and stringent circumstances must make it so in spite of its inherent antagonism, if it come at length to work harmoniously and cordially in the order of our free civil polity. Its constant struggle is against it, and the influence and accessions it receives from its old home keep it rigid and reluctant to any democratic changes. It will work its modifications into American Protestantism, while that shall be working its assimilations into Romanism. The changes will not be all on one side; and how far that from Rome may prevail, and yet leave our political liberty and free institutions safe, is truly a problem of vital importance to American freedom. Leave these conflicting forces to their natural action, and they will not safely adjust themselves. Watchful patriotism will not be so prompt nor so constant as selfish ambition. The aspiring demagogue will pay the price of liberty for the combined vote of priestly followers; and hostile elements will soon be at work in our republican administration, which will require quite another adjusting balance than popular elections.

This variety of race and religion is already operating powerfully through our whole social and political community; it is a natural result of our national prosperity, and will doubtless very much extend itself for many years to come. It must modify, and left to its own course it might completely revolutionize, our whole civil polity. The political wisdom and skill of no statesman is about to bring and keep such discordant materials harmoniously together. This is only possible to God, and his revealed method for it is the Gospel of his Son.

There is power in the Gospel to bring different races and opposing religions into one. The effort must be in this direction, to make them all study the Book of God together. Frank and friendly discussion, the preaching of Protestant truth in its purity, and full permission to the Catholic to preach Romanism as he will, but to meet him in candor and love, in faithfulness and firmness, at all times and in all places of the land,—this will ultimately assimilate all on the right basis. If the Protestant has a wrong spirit, and where the Catholic has a wrong sentiment, this will correct both. Perpetual dropping of divine truth never yet fell, in faith and prayer, on human heart so hard, that at length it did not wear the stone away.

3. *The growth of Slavery.*—If the slave himself is property, then is the increase of slavery an augmentation of national wealth; and if we exclude all right of property as claimed in the slave, still the profit of slavery is the grand motive for its perpetuation. And this grows more profitable as the state grows more wealthy. The increase of the quantity and value of slave products is an aggravation of all the evils and dangers of slavery itself. That would soon die in the pros-

tration of national credit and business; and thus here, as before, our prosperity is the occasion of all our danger.

And how great this danger is, may be partially estimated from the recent convulsions and present irritation and sectional jealousy through the land. I am not called, by my present design, to dwell upon the immorality of this institution, nor upon the wickedness and cruelty incident to its perpetuation; nor again, upon any imprudences that may have characterized the opposition to it; but some of the prominent facts connected with it show, even to the blindest, our imminent danger as a nation from it.

The public sentiment of the civilized world, not involved in the practice of slavery, is every year growing stronger and deeper in reprobation of it. The pulse of humanity beats fuller and quicker, and indicates that the public heart swells in tenderer sympathy for the slave, and in sterner abhorrence of his wrongs; and such sympathies and repugnances will manifest themselves in corresponding remonstrances and expostulations. On the other hand, growing national prosperity, accumulation of interest in slave property, and the augmented profits of slave labor, are calling out more strenuous defences of the institution, and enlisting greater numbers in upholding it, and its wider business connections raise up new apologists for it. As the abhorrence and remonstrance increases, so grows the defence and the determination to perpetuate it. Political ambition uses both sides as occasion offers, and greatly increases the rancor of the strife and aggravates the danger.

It may not well be said what the onward movements of Providence may do, in bringing in the competition of pauper free-labor, or supplying the products of present slave labor from other sources, or introducing other products which shall drive these from the market; but, for years to come, there is no other prospect but a deeper interest in this strife and a sterner feeling among the antagonists. In the prosperity of the nation slavery will grow with it, and its defenders and their tenacity of purpose will increase; and so also the growing philanthropy of the nation and the world will augment the abhorrence and intolerance of the evils of slavery. These antagonisms of interest and kindness are as deep in humanity, under the circumstances, as the law of the tides or the ordinances of day and night in nature.

Very wise men may have fondly hoped to avert the coming threatened explosion by political expedients, and laboriously arranged their balanced interests and established compromises. Resolute affirmations of "finality," and denunciation of all further agitation may occur; but he who knows how deeply to read human nature, very well understands that such elements in such antagonisms are not about to remain quiet. The truce is broken on both sides; from one comes the fierce denunciation, and from the other the fiery defiance. This volcano is not so capped over. These materials for an explosion would shake down far mightier mountain-barriers than any political compromises. The rich man may enter heaven as well as the rich nation pass through these storms safely. God alone can help; and verily I look for no other miracle of deliverance, than the application of the plain truth of the Gospel to both sides, with the blessing of the Holy Ghost sent down from heaven.

That Gospel will tell the slave "to obey his master;" and it must so be preached to him. Even in "fear and trembling," he must be obedient; and this not only to "the good and gentle" master, "but also to the froward," yea, when so froward that the master "buffets" the slave for "doing well." But this very stress and extremity of obedience determines unanswerably the principle on which the Gospel puts it. Not at all because the master has any righteous authority to so command; not that the Apostle was here defending the froward master's right against the right of his trembling slave; but solely because this was most expedient for the slave himself. You are in the power of a tiger, provoke him not. Soften his froward temper and quicken his conscience to tenderness, and make him to blush at every recollection of his cruelty and baseness, by showing the very spirit of your divine Master, who, when the insult and the scourging came, "opened not his mouth."

And so also to the other party, the same Gospel has the same doctrine to be preached. "Ye masters do the same things to them." If you have a froward and turbulent slave, "forbear threatening" him; do nothing to provoke him; "give to him that which is just and equal;" remember what terrible inducement the assumed authority you exert over him gives to him, to manifest the deepest repugnance and revulsion to your service. If you keep him in the family, do the duty of the head of a family to him; baptize him; religiously instruct him; train him up for the state and for heaven. Do this with the same ends of freedom and of piety as in the nurture of your child; and as long as such is due, you will have the approbation of your conscience and your God.

Such a Gospel, so preached, will save the nation even from the growing dangers of slavery. The missionary is to be sent with this Gospel, not only where slavery is not, but more urgently where slavery is. He may not slur over the plain message to the master, nor may he teach the slave to take violently his own rights. This is not so well for the general freedom or the piety of the slave. It is not the Gospel. It will not so readily bring about universal emancipation. If the slave "may be free," teach him, by all means, "to use it rather." It is his right. There is great wrong in keeping in bondage, and not be every day educating for freedom, and fully giving it as soon as prepared for it. But if you are thus wronged, and are "called" of God, being a slave, "care not for it." Your title to heavenly liberty, as "God's freeman," makes your earthly bondage as nothing. I say again, such a Gospel, so preached, will save the nation. Like the rod of God it will work its miracles through the land, and no enchantments of the politician or the philanthropist can imitate it.

4. *The practice of annexation.*—Perhaps the genius of our government is such, that new territory and new States, to an indefinite extent, may be added to our republic; but in order that it may be done safely, the circumstances must be most carefully and wisely estimated. As the rich man prospers, he adds house to house and field to field; and if it be in the spirit of honest enterprise and prudent regard to family wants and public claims, his increased wealth and purchased acres may not injure him. But if he be moved only by selfish ambition and greedy avarice, this will certainly grow by that on which it is permitted to feed. The magnitude of the area he acquires, makes also the adjacent exterior so much the larger, and the stimulant to his covetousness so much the stronger. But such covetousness, "which is idolatry," will no more certainly destroy the rich man's soul, than the like greedy lust of territorial acquisition will destroy a republic's liberty.

We may not, in the case of our country, confine our view to the common evils flowing from national avarice or a lust for conquest. There are other things with us which make a national passion for annexation specially hazardous. Whatever different opinions there may have been about the constitutionality of the purchase and annexation of Louisiana, a strong national interest urged towards that measure, particularly in securing the mouth of the Mississippi and free access to the Gulf of Mexico. And when the Floridas were obtained and annexed, universal patriotism might find its grounds of approbation. The Governments of France and Spain voluntarily ceded, the discordant population was comparatively inconsiderable, and the advantages universal to the country. But the next great accession of Texas, brought in many evils. The guilt of a war of great suffering and bloodshed rests upon the nation, and, from this, the further annexation of New Mexico and California; greatly augmented jealousy, acerbity, and sectional animosity, have been created by it; and while the public conscience has been made less sensitive to injustice, the popular appetite has been sharpened for spoil and conquest; and that high national character for honesty and integrity, which would give weight to our reproof of European plunder and rapine, has been lost.

Besides, such is the condition of all outlying territory now, that the interests of annexation are determined almost solely by the interests of slavery. Cuba and Hayti, and the neighboring states of Mexico, and even the distant Sandwich Islands, are all viewed through this medium, and are coveted or rejected according to their supposed bearing upon this institution, the most dangerous of all others to our Union. None of these countries could be annexed without bringing in a large population, unfitted by race and habit, education and religion, from very soon and safely participating in the franchises of our government. We cannot, in our present condition, make another stride in annexation without fearfully augmenting our most imminent and threatening dangers.

And yet, who does not see that our national progress, as the spirit and ambition of the country is, will push these questions upon us, both from the South and the North, in only a few years more of our prosperity; and if sectional and party interests are to mingle in the strife, and add their perils to the trial, what man, wisely on the lookout, does not foresee dangers from which nothing but God can save us?

But, we say again, let the Gospel be everywhere preached and prevail; through this let party spirit and sectional interest be lost in enlarged patriotism and benevolence, and let ambition and avarice give place to righteousness, and the nation will patiently wait until the providence of God has ripened events for wise decision and safe action; and thus a few years will do that beneficially for all, which an earlier rashness and violence would have made everywhere disastrous. This Gospel only can hold the nation steady till the time comes; this only carry us steady through the destiny which opens upon us; and this only assimilate and incorporate in us that which the tide of providential events is steadily bringing to us. I have no more hope that our republic will pass this coming crisis safely without a wide diffusion of the christian spirit, than I have that we can drive camels through the eyes of needles.

5. *The selfishness of Party.*—There is always occasion for different opinions upon important measures, and in reference to broad political principles, even among the most wise and patriotic; and such differences of opinion may induce and perpetuate, for a long time, opposite po-

litical parties. Each side may fully express and strenuously advocate their own principles and measures, and strive to carry an election in favor of its own candidate at the polls. Such parties contending earnestly for sincerely adopted principles, will not be likely to work any mischief in the State. They are the natural result of free opinion, and quite incidental to the working of all intelligent free governments, and, in their wholesome and legitimate counterworking, will tend to the conservation of popular liberty rather than endanger it. Like the composition of forces in mechanics, a balanced movement and a determined progress may thus be attained, which single powers could not accomplish.

But political partizanship has manifestly removed itself very much from the ground of steadfast principle to that of personal interest. The party is not so much for the expression of opinion, as for the constraining and coercing it. It keeps itself together by studied tactics and coercive drill, and manufactures principles and platforms to suit the exigency, and proscribes and denounces all bolters. The real freeman cannot permit himself to belong to any modern political party, without sacrificing personal liberty for party trammels.

Legitimate party action, in the free combination of numbers under honestly adopted opposing opinions, is now scarcely known in the land. The maxim has become as practically prevalent in politics as in war, that "to the victors belong the spoils;" and as the national power and wealth increases, these spoils become the more tempting and their distribution the more corrupting. The emoluments of office control the entire canvass, and the selfishness of the office-seeker drives the public elections to violence and riot. He calculates the economy of so much time and money spent on the election over against the salary and the perquisites, and goes deliberately at work, as if the sacred suffrages of freemen were only things of barter in the market. Even the farmer from his plough, and the artisan from his shop, begin to say, "We cannot afford to lose our day at the polls for nothing;" and they put their votes in the ballot-box for that party which has paid them the most for it.

When the popular current sets so strongly in such a direction, and is drawing into it the very heart and life of the state in its working population, where have we any safe-guards for freedom? What human arm is about to arrest this venality and profligacy, and save to posterity our free institutions? The purifying influence of the Gospel, and the general prevalence of genuine revivals of religion, can do it; but beside this nothing can. Make men truly pious, and you will make them watchful and consistent freemen. Growing temptation in growing national prosperity will, of itself, make party politics more corrupt and unscrupulous; but fill the land with bibles and churches and pastors, and it is at once bringing in God's method for saving the nation.

6. *Home Missionary Sectarianism.*—I put this last, because I think there may be seen in it some of the most serious indications of danger. Should sectarianism be allowed to prevail extensively in Home Missionary operations, it must very much weaken, or perhaps break up, this most effective instrumentality for the nation's deliverance. If the many elements of ruin which national prosperity is setting loose among the people be left to work on to their natural issue, we have seen that they must end in national destruction. God has provided for himself but one way to turn the current and arrest the disastrous result; and that is by the diffusion of gospel truth, which it is the direct design of Home Missions to

accomplish. How like the malicious subtilty of the arch-enemy will it be, if we should see his last master-stroke of policy to be the destruction of the most effective instrumentality for spreading the Gospel, just then when the national prosperity is most thickening its dangers around us! How bitter his taunt and scorn if he can blind Christians to the end he seeks, by their denominational sympathies and sectarian prejudices!

Through great national prosperity our wide territory is rapidly filling up with an active, enterprising population. In addition to our native increase, there comes in annually nearly half a million of foreigners. The aggressive movements of the Church upon these western new settlements have been most eminently successful. New churches have been formed; the ordinances of the Gospel established; precious revival seasons have occurred; family altars have been erected; and all the discordant elements of a new settlement have been wrought into the order, harmony and piety of a christian society. All this has been done best where there has been the least manifestation of sectarian interest and zeal. The closest union of effort and prayer has hitherto had the most signal success. But this great success of our united operation becomes the occasion of a new danger. Prosperity in the Church is now speaking out the same warnings as in the nation. Alas! if it must prove true, that the Church of God cannot bear prosperity any better than the state, and that the piety of the age is not pure enough to carry out her plans of union!

The great evangelical divisions of the Church are at work in the same field, and preaching substantially the same Gospel. Each has its eye very much directed and intent upon its own denominational enlargement; and in this attitude it is very liable not to see, that a course of policy seemingly wise for the sect may yet be very unwise for the Church catholic. The general cause may be much hindered, by that which is for a time rapidly building up a particular denomination. This makes it incumbent upon all evangelical denominations to be jealous and fearful of their own spirit, lest it be working injury to the grand cause of Christ, which is common to all. No denomination may so work for itself as to overlook the higher interests of their common Christianity.

But more especially is this incumbent upon those kindred and active denominations who from the first have labored together in the cause of Home Missions, and have collected and expended their charities through one organization. In the fullness of their general success, sectarian zeal has recently become greatly excited; and both have manifestly begun to calculate their own separate gains, and to be jealous of rival interests, and are thus very likely to look with prejudice upon measures really best for the whole, because they are thought not to be so directly subservient to the wants and wishes of the particular denomination. The minds of many good men have very decidedly assumed this position; and some of our best and ablest brethren both east and west, are already acting towards each other under such alienating influences. This spirit has not yet very extensively diffused itself through the churches, and it may perhaps be hoped that their steady piety and fraternal unity will at length resist and check its onward progress; but the action of public ecclesiastical bodies, and the opening of the discussion in our weekly papers and quarterly reviews, is doing what it may to call out any dormant prejudices, and latent antipathies. The current of denominational feeling is already rapidly drifting many brethren apart; and a little broader stream and further progress, and we can work in the same cause through the same organ no longer. If we stand side by side any more, it will be because the same field, and not the old, kindred sympathy, brings us together.

And here, Brethren, I will make no unkind imputations; but, loud as my voice may utter, I would sound the word of caution. Such a rupture of fraternal bonds, and determined future distinctive action, will not leave either denomination any more harmonious or homogeneous. On the one side, there will still remain invincible and active repugnances to strict and stringent ecclesiastical jurisdiction; and on the other, there will come the occasion for a more fierce and bitter doctrinal contention. While neither will probably have gained very much in denominational efficiency, and nothing in ecclesiastical harmony; very much will have been lost in the progress of a common Christianity to save our own nation, and to evangelize the world. The violent sundering of ecclesiastical ties has already done too much evil for this generation; and there should not now be added the action of a sectarian zeal, which will greatly paralyze, if not effectually break down, the most effective voluntary organizations which the world has ever known for her conversion to Christianity.

Strenuously would I urge, that in the pressing duty of church extension by each denomination, there be carefully excluded the uncalled for zeal of sectarian prejudices and partialities. Our separate interests, at the most, are trifling, and really sink to nothing when held in comparison with the universal triumph of the general cause. No advantages to either should have any force in shaping measures, if they do not directly bear upon the complete evangelization of the entire country. A tried organization has been long and most successfully prosecuting the work of Home Missions; and it is now of far less moment that either denomination operating through it should advance its own church order, than that both together should still hold on united, and thereby most successfully and rapidly convert the nation and the world to God. The perpetuation of such joint action, and the steady example of such liberal and benevolent operations, will do more honor to Christianity than any zeal which both may show in rival competition. It is far more like the spirit of the apostolic age. Most thorough is my conviction, whether the *fact* shall prove to be such or not, that the *obligation* upon both of these denominations, from patriotism and Christianity, now is, that they magnanimously bend sectarian interests to harmonious coöperation, and not push them out to fraternal disruption.

I conclude, by emphatically urging a preached Gospel as the effective and the only cure for all our dangers. I have only alluded to this, in connection with the national dangers I have specified, as the one medium instituted by God, through which it is possible for him to save rich men and prosperous nations. There never was a people to whom this truth so manifestly applied, as to us; for there has never been a government so dependent upon that political integrity which the Gospel inspires, as our own; nor has there ever been a government, which so invites and encourages the friends of the Gospel to establish its ordinances everywhere, as ours. America, with its present millions, and its unborn hundreds of millions, cannot be saved without the Gospel; but eminently, above all people the world has yet known, Americans can be saved by the Gospel. Where such aland, since the Savior's commission and ascension for "the word of the Lord to have free course and be glorified," as ours! Such an ancestry; such an education and training in national habits from the first, as to make the house of God, the Bible and the preacher, as much a want as the hall of legislation, the statute book, and the justice of the peace. The institution of the Sabbath, though in many places most sadly desecrated, yet still acknowledged and giving to the evangelist, through all our newly settled territory, the opportunity of gathering the people to worship God, who have already given up for that day the secular business of the world. Not a rapidly rising village or city of the West so preöccupied by irreligion and infidelity, but the preacher of the Gospel may go and take up his abode among them; and so soon as the faithful labor begins, the blessing of the Holy Spirit may be expected, and revival seasons are enjoyed, the vicious reclaimed, and the ordinances of religion become established. These are the common, the regularly anticipated results, of stated prayer and faithful preaching of the word, all through the land. What has been, evinces plainly enough what can be done. The church of God can thus spread her power over all the country, and perpetuate her saving influence through coming generations. So can we, under God, save this nation; and in saving the American church and nation, there is ultimately secured the salvation of the world.

Let us thus unitedly and courageously prosecute this work. Let us give to this nobly proved Society, whose anniversary brings us now together, a more prompt and liberal support. When the seventh angel shall sound his trumpet and say, "The kingdoms of this world are become the kingdoms of our Lord, and of his Christ, and he will reign for ever and ever," I anticipate that America will be among the most conspicuous of those saved nations of the Lord; and I as confidently anticipate that our American Home Missionary Society will, that day, be known and honored as one of God's most conspicuous instrumentalities in effecting so blessed a consummation. AMEN!

American Home Missionary Society.

THE object of this Society is to assist congregations that are unable to support the gospel ministry, and to send the Gospel to the destitute. It seeks and sends forth missionaries; by counsel and pecuniary aid, it encourages the people to help themselves; strengthens feeble churches, gathers new ones, settles pastors, and thus renders *permanent* the institutions of the Gospel.

The Society was organized in 1826, by delegates from the Presbyterian, Congregational, Associate Reformed, and Reformed Dutch denominations, and had then in its service 169 missionaries. The sixth year, the number of missionaries was 509; the twelfth, 684; the eighteenth, 907; the twenty seventh, 1,087. The first year's expenditures were $13,984 17; the sixth, $52,808 39; the twelfth, $85,066 26; the eighteenth, $104,276 47; the twenty seventh, $174,439 24. The total of receipts for the twenty seven years, is $2,537,154 64; the total of years of labor, 14,836; the whole number of additions to the churches, 120,680.

During the twenty seven years since the organization of this Society, the Gospel has been preached by its missionaries at not less than *four thousand* stations; and not far from *nine hundred* churches, which had been gathered or nurtured through its instrumentality, have passed from the list of beneficiaries, and are now supporting their own gospel institutions; and not a few of these are among the strongest and most influential churches in the land. They are to be found in the chief places of social and commercial power—on the lines of our canals and lakes and rivers—along all our great thoroughfares of commerce and travel—at almost every gateway into the distant interior.

The *twenty seventh* year of its operations is briefly noticed in the following abstract from the last Annual Report, presented May 11th, 1853:

SUMMARY OF RESULTS.

The Society has had in its service the last year, 1,087 ministers of the Gospel, in twenty seven different States and Territories: in the New England States, 313; the Middle States, 215; the Southern States, 12; and the Western States and Territories, 547.

Of these, 584 have been the *pastors* or *stated supplies* of single congregations; 288 have ministered to two or three congregations each; and 215 have extended their labors over still wider fields.

Ten missionaries have preached to congregations of *colored* people; and 71 in foreign languages—17 to *Welsh*, and 46 to *German* congregations; and others to congregations of *Norwegians*, *Swedes*, *Swiss*, *Hollanders* and *Frenchmen*.

The *number of congregations and missionary stations* supplied, in whole or in part, is 2,160.

The *aggregate of ministerial labor* performed, is equal to 878 years.

The number of *pupils in Sabbath Schools*, is 72,500.

There have been added to the churches, 6,079, viz. 3,362 on profession, and 2,717 by letter. *Fifty six* missionaries make mention in their reports of *revivals* of religion in their congregations; and 426 missionaries report 2,888 hopeful conversions.

Forty seven churches have been *organized* by the missionaries during the year; and 39, that had been dependent, have assumed the support of their own ministry.

Fifty four houses of worship have been *completed;* 50 *repaired;* and 66 others are in the *process of erection.*

Eighty nine young men, in connection with the missionary churches, are in preparation for the gospel ministry.

THE TREASURY.

Receipts.—$171,734 24.

Liabilities.—$185,184 01.

Payments.—$174,439 24—leaving $10,744 77 still due to missionaries, for labor performed; toward canceling which, there is a balance in the Treasury of $7,202 15.

PROGRESS.

The *receipts* exceed those of the preceding year, by $11,671 99; 22 *more missionaries* have been in commission; 16 *more years of ministerial labor* have been performed; 212 *more congregations* have been blessed with the preaching of the Gospel; and 6,000 more children instructed in *Sabbath Schools*. The large reinforcement sent out to the Society's missions on the Pacific coast constitutes, also, a grateful as it is a most important feature in the advances of the year. The work which the Society has undertaken in this field is one of peculiar difficulty, and involves much pecuniary expense; but if its claims are promptly and liberally met; if the fountains of influence which have been opened among these mountains are made pure; if the church, like the prophet at the streams of Jericho, shall go forth to the spring of the waters and cast the salt in there, the streams that will issue thence shall clothe those distant shores with moral verdure and beauty, and bear the ark of salvation to the perishing of other lands.

Officers of the Society.

PRESIDENT.

HENRY DWIGHT, ESQ.

SECRETARIES FOR CORRESPONDENCE.

MILTON BADGER, D. D.
CHARLES HALL, D. D.
REV. DAVID B. COE.

RECORDING SECRETARY.

MR. CHRISTOPHER R. ROBERT.

TREASURER.

MR. JASPER CORNING.

AUDITOR.

MR. CALEB O. HALSTED.

EXECUTIVE COMMITTEE.

Mr. Abijah Fisher.
William Patton, D. D.
Charles Butler, Esq.
Dr. Alfred C. Post.
Edwin F. Hatfield, D. D.
Mr. Simeon B. Chittenden.
Asa D. Smith, D. D.
Mr. William C. Gilman.
Rev. Richard S. Storrs, Jr.

MEMBERS EX OFFICIO.

Mr. Jasper Corning, *Treasurer.*
Milton Badger, D. D.,
Charles Hall, D. D., } *Secretaries for Correspondence.*
Rev. David B. Coe,
Mr. Christopher R. Robert, *Recording Secretary.*

ASSISTANT TREASURER.

MR. H. W. RIPLEY.

HOME MISSIONS: AS CONNECTED WITH CHRIST'S DOMINION.

A

DISCOURSE

IN BEHALF OF THE

American Home Missionary Society,

PREACHED IN THE CITIES OF NEW YORK AND BROOKLYN,

MAY, 1855.

BY

RICHARD S. STORRS, D. D.

PASTOR OF THE FIRST CHURCH IN BRAINTREE, MASS.

NEW YORK:
PUBLISHED BY THE AMERICAN HOME MISSIONARY SOCIETY,
BIBLE HOUSE, ASTOR PLACE.
1855.

BAKER, GODWIN CO., PRINTERS,
COR. NASSAU AND SPRUCE STS.
NEW YORK.

DISCOURSE.

REVELATION, XIX: 12.

"And on his head were many crowns."

The crown is an emblem of dignity and glory; also, of victory, and supreme authority. "Many crowns" denote an accumulation of honors, and a succession of victorious achievements.

Jesus wears them. "The Faithful and True" in righteousness doth judge, and make war. Clothed with a vesture dipped in blood, and followed by the armies of heaven, he hath a name written, "King of kings, and Lord of lords."

When the Man of sorrows bowed his head on Calvary, though nature sublimely expressed her sympathies, and the tears of loved ones testified their affection, it was little understood, by friends or foes, that to the victim, bleeding at the point of the Roman spear, belonged the sovereignty of worlds. Soon afterwards, seen in vision by the beloved disciple, he has eyes as a flame of fire; many crowns are on his head; and a name is written that no man knoweth but himself, "The Word of God!" Wonderful transformation, of the babe that was cradled in the manger, and the sufferer who cried upon the cross, "My God! My God! why hast thou forsaken me!"

The Lord Jesus Christ has a wide and glorious Dominion. We may contemplate it in three aspects, viz.: its extent, his title to it, and the principles on which he exercises it.

I.—THE EXTENT OF HIS DOMINION.

1. It extends over the CHURCH.

Those redeemed by his blood, whether before his incarnation or after it, and whether on earth or in heaven, form a distinct and 'holy nation.' Each trembling penitent below, and each triumphant victor on Mount Zion, is alike the subject of his government, and the object of his tender care. Widely separated, and mutually unknown as they may be, diverse as are their circumstances, elevated their joys, or overwhelming their sorrows, yet the laws that bind them, the hopes that sustain them, and the rewards that await them, are common to all. They are one family, of which he is the Head; one nation, of which he is the Ruler; a world within worlds, of which he is Proprietor; and though thrown into numerous divisions, each distinguished by peculiarities of faith or of practice, they yet hold "one Lord, one Faith, and one Baptism." If through infirmity individuals contend, and churches divide, on questions of ritual observance and ministerial authority, all yet harmoniously defer to the will of Christ, as they apprehend it; and whether earth or heaven be their present home, Christ is their acknowledged Prophet, Priest, and King. Now, and for ever, is he to them "for a crown of glory, and for a diadem of beauty."

2. It extends over the WORLD.

There is given unto him dominion and glory, that

all people, and nations, and languages, should serve him; "the government is on his shoulders," and every spring, wheel, and movement of its ordered machinery is regulated by his agency. Is there evil in the city, and he hath not done it? or joy and gladness, and he hath not ordained it? The king's heart is in his hand, and he turneth it as the rivers of water are turned. The obdurate Pharoah yields, and lets the people go; Cyrus, who knows him not, sets at liberty his captives; the cross surmounts the eagle, on the banners of the ambitious Constantine; all, in fulfilment of his purpose. The heathen may rage, and the people imagine vain things, but the Lord's Christ hath them in derision. What though the nations be convulsed, and blood flow till it reach the horses' bridles, it is but for the dethronement of idolatry and superstition, or the overthrow of infidelity and licentiousness, that the way may be prepared for the universal reign of righteousness. The heathen are given to him for an inheritance, and the uttermost parts of the earth for a possession.

> "Kings shall fall down before him,
> And gold and incense bring;
> All nations shall adore him,
> His praise all people sing."

3. It extends over Heaven.

Exalted far above all principalities and powers, all might and dominion, Heaven's hosts pay him homage. As, in his humiliation, angels ministered to his wants, so, in his glory, they cast their crowns at his feet, and fly to execute his will. Whether Elijah needs to be strengthened, or Peter to be brought out of prison; whether the Assyrian is to be despoiled of his prey, or the great Deceiver of the nations to be bound; these glorious spirits are commissioned to do it. Equally employed for him are ransomed saints, gathered from earth about his throne; and the song of Moses and the Lamb flows forever from their lips, into the ear of their Lord and Redeemer.

4. It extends over the WORLD OF WOE.

Hell is the prison-house of his empire. He hath spoiled principalities and powers, triumphing over them, and binding them in chains of darkness. And if, when loosed for a little season, they rule the darkness of this world, he yet destroys their works, and from 'confusion, worse confounded,' brings forth the final peace and order. Every blow they aim at Zion, recoils upon themselves.

5. It extends over the MATERIAL UNIVERSE.

He hath stretched out the heavens as a curtain, and hung the earth upon nothing. He alone doth bind the sweet influences of Pleiades, and loose the bands of Orion, and bring forth Mazzaroth in his season, and guide Arcturus with his sons. He numbers the clouds in wisdom, and stays the bottles of heaven; provides the raven his food, and hunts the prey for the lion. Famine and pestilence are his ministers; earthquake and storm, elemental war and desolation, as well as the peaceful series of the seasons, go forth at his bidding. As by his power all things were created, so by his providence are all upheld, and by his authority are all controlled. "He is "All in all."

II.—HIS TITLE TO THIS DOMINION.

This is two-fold, and lies:

1. In the absolute perfectness of his CHARACTER.—He is the "Holy One," who loveth righteousness and

hateth iniquity. With him are the treasures of wisdom and of knowledge. His goings forth have been from of old, even from everlasting. His understanding is infinite, his greatness unsearchable, and his goodness unbounded. Hence his right to hold the throne, as "God over all, blessed forever."

2. In his relation to the universe as Redeemer.—Because he humbled himself, and became obedient unto death, God hath highly exalted him, and given him a name which is above every name; that at the name of Jesus every knee should bow, of things in heaven and things in earth. Other orders of intelligence are scarcely less interested in the world's redemption than man, because it displays the manifold wisdom of God beyond any other of his works. Angels desire to look into this, as an exhibition of mercy and truth meeting together, of righteousness and peace embracing each other; God's law being magnified by it, his truth vindicated, yet salvation proffered to the condemned sinner. In no other department of the Divine administration are the fundamental principles of moral government, with their glorious results, so fully and sublimely disclosed. Well, then, may angels be required to worship Christ, and all creatures that have breath to praise him, as the Alpha and Omega in the kingdoms of Nature, Providence, and Grace! And well may the Lamb, standing on Mount Zion, surrounded by the hundred forty and four thousand, be honored by a new song, flowing as "the voice of many waters, and as the voice of a great thunder, and as the voice of harpers harping with their harps"—for He is worthy!

III.—THE PRINCIPLES ON WHICH HE EXERCISES THIS DOMINION.

1. That he may manifest THE INFINITE GLORY.

Leaving the world to go to the Father, he said: "I have glorified thee on the earth; I have finished the work which thou gavest me to do." The principle thus developed lies at the foundation of all his administration, for it all has reference to the one work of Redemption. The essential glory of the Father admits neither of addition nor diminution; because his perfections are the same yesterday, to-day, and forever. "He is a Rock; his work is perfect."

But this essential glory admits of increased or diminished manifestation. As created minds are susceptible of indefinite expansion, and of ever-increasing knowledge, and as the heart may be enlarged to worship God according to his excellent greatness, and the spirit be strengthened in its faith, quickened in its obedience, and made more clearly to reflect the lustre of heaven, through the wonder-working power of Christ—so, 'herein is the Father glorified.'

2. That he may promote THE HAPPINESS OF THE INTELLIGENT CREATION.

Two provinces under his sceptre are in revolt: the world in which we live, and the world of fallen spirits. From the silence of Revelation, and the assurance of the Saviour that he has other sheep which are not of this fold, we are justified in the inference that inhabitants of other worlds are happy in uninterrupted communion with God; and that, numerous as human sinners and fallen angels are, they are inconceivably outnumbered by the myriads of intelligences who worship God without ceasing. And even of human sinners, thousands of thousands, and ten thousand times ten thousand, shall reign as kings and priests before God forever.

Still, it is not to be denied that within the dominions of Christ there not only is, but will continue to be, misery without end. He himself affirms it. Nor is this a greater mystery than the existence of sin itself; than which, nothing is more baffling to the understanding of man, when searching into the wondrous elements and movements of the Divine administration.

It is enough, however, to know, that sin is a voluntary matter; that no man is compelled to its commission, by any power beyond himself; that Christ appears its mighty antagonist, and urges not only authority, but motives of infinite weight against it; that man has an understanding fitting him to weigh these motives, and a law written on the heart to enforce them, and is therefore without excuse for his transgression.

Still aside from this, too, and above it all, is the fact, that sin's entrance into the world lies at the foundation of Christ's dominion, as the God-man, Mediator. It was to *destroy* the works of the devil, and to advance Jehovah's glory in the salvation of men, that he ascended the mediatorial throne. He took the kingdom, after sin and death had entered it; and he still maintains those Divine operations by which men become partakers of the blessings of holiness, and prepared for its final consummation. And, to use the eloquent language of another, a divine of a former generation in this very city,* when speaking of this kingdom of Christ, "when it rises up before us, in all its grandeur of design, collecting and conducting to the heavens of God, millions of immortals, in comparison with the least of

* Dr. John M. Mason.

whom the destruction of the material universe were a thing of naught—whatever the carnal mind calls vast and magnificent, shrinks away into nothing!"

Can a doubt then remain, that the character of the Supreme will be more perfectly unfolded, the purity of his law more fully vindicated, and the holy in heart be forever strengthened in their love, by the admission of sin into the universe, and the conquest of it by Christ; through the revelation of its deformity and shame, as contrasted with the beauty and glory of holiness, shining in the person of him who weareth many crowns? God will be glorified, even through him who leaves the bar of judgment speechless; much more, then, through the songs of those delivered from so great a death, and shouting, in their triumph, "Worthy the Lamb that was slain!"

REFLECTIONS.

1. Opposition to Christ is unavailing.

The pillars of heaven are not more immovable than his purpose to subdue all things unto himself. And when thrones and dominions, principalities and powers, fall before him, can he whose habitation is in the dust withstand him? Let the fool say in his heart, "No God!" Let him yield to the tempter, sear his conscience, and add drunkenness to thirst; nay, let the whole world rally beneath the banner of Satan, and draw the sword, light the fagot, and deal out destruction and death on those that fear the Lord; their defeat is as sure as the word of Jehovah! Righteousness will be maintained. The designs of Mercy will be accomplished. Indignation will fall on the head of the wicked; while glory, honor, and immortality will reward the just. But, why do the claims of Christ meet such resistance? He doeth all things well! He is holy, harmless, undefiled, separate from sinners, and made higher than the heavens! O that Earth, throughout her whole domain, would bow to his sceptre, and join with Heaven, to crown him Lord of all!

2. Indifference to Christ's glory, becomes none who love him.

For them, he drank deep of the cup of sorrows; and for them, he hath ascended up on high, to make intercession, to regulate the movements of other worlds, and to provide for his children everlasting mansions. Beyond this, voluntary obligations bind them to glorify him; for they have sworn to present themselves, with all they have and are, forever, a sacrifice upon his altar. Such engagements stand on heaven's record. Indifference to his cause, then, is neither fitting nor blameless. 'Here, Lord, am I! replenish me with thy grace! unveil to me thy glory! do with me whatsoever thou wilt!' Surely this should be the cry of every believer!

3. Nothing great and good can be accomplished, within the earthly dominions of Jesus, without earnest labor.

Aside from this, neither can the individual mind be enlightened, nor the conscience aroused, nor the heart subdued, nor the life regulated as God would have it. Much less, can the world be transformed into a quiet resting place of the saints, and all its sorrowings be converted into rejoicings. Let revolted man be found where he may, on continent or isle of the sea, on the throne or in the lazaretto, compassion must follow him, the voice of persuasion must reach him, and the arm of love be thrown around him, to bring him to Christ.

But this involves all-absorbing labor, performed in the spirit of prophets and apostles, nay, of the Redeemer himself. And, only when this is done, throughout the church, shall earth assume its true character. Then there will be joy in the presence of angels, and the Lord God will rejoice over his people with joy!

4. A large revenue of glory is due to Christ, from that province in his dominions which we occupy.

On no people under heaven hath he stronger claims. Were another prophet to arise, having his eyes open upon the land given to us, he would exclaim, "How goodly are thy tents, O Jacob, and thy tabernacles, O Israel!" We are made to ride on the high places of the earth, that we may eat the increase of our fields, and suck honey out of the rock, and oil out of the flinty rock. Nations have been driven out before us, greater and mightier than we, that we might enter in, and take the land for an inheritance, as it is this day.

You hardly need to be reminded of its extent; embracing, as it does, an area larger than that held by the five controlling powers of Europe, and, excepting Russia, more than twice as large as all the European states and kingdoms combined. Nor need you be told of its rapidly increasing population; of its remoteness from the battle-fields of the old world; of its mild and popular government; of its civil and religious freedom; of its wide spread intellectual privileges; of its abundant contributions to individual wealth, and to national prosperity; of its commercial advantages, and its boundless resources for promoting the moral improvement of the world—to be convinced that He, on whose head are many crowns, justly expects from it a large revenue of glory.

Three millions of square miles of that soil redeemed unto God by his blood, and partially enlightened by his Spirit, is too much to be relinquished to the sway of the powers of darkness without a struggle. And a population shooting forth in such strength that, in the language of Burke, "state the numbers high as we will, while the dispute continues, the exaggeration ends," a population that doubles every five-and-twenty years, may not be quietly surrendered to the deadly embraces of infidelity and vice; a population which, though affected but indirectly by the intrigues and violence of other nations, is yet sufficiently so affected, through the intermixture of foreign elements in the body politic, to require the putting forth of every energy, for the hastening of the conversion of its masses unto God! Government interposes no obstacles to the universal diffusion of Truth and Love here, through the combined learning, piety and wealth of Zion. Mind, untrammeled by state authority and hierarchical institutions, asks not 'Fathers,' nor 'Bishops,' more than civil rulers, for permission to select its field of action, and to prosecute its inquiries; and the heart bows to the God of heaven, or to the gods of earth, irrespective of all constraint. And where in the wide world is to be found a more perfect garden of nature—a land superior in its mountains and vallies, its lakes and streams—a land more teeming with riches on its surface and in its depths, more prolific in animal, vegetable and mineral productions, under the hand of industry and skill, and more exempt from the malaria that scatters pestilence and death broadcast over other regions of the earth?

Then, whether from the eminence we occupy, we turn our eyes Northward or Southward, immense territories open on our view, from Baffin's Bay to the Straits of Magellan, more or less inhabited throughout, and capable of sustaining dense and happy populations, whenever the Sun of Righteousness shall penetrate their tangled forests and uncultivated plains. The loftiest mountains, the most luxuriant intervales, the most majestic rivers are there, all at present desecrated by the fanes of superstition, degraded by stolid ignorance, and involved in ceaseless strife, under the weight of despotism's iron arm, or the withering breath of anarchy. Amid these sad influences, millions on millions urge their way to eternity ; and other swelling millions are to follow them in future years,—whether to enjoy the radiations of a purer light, or to continue blinded like their fathers, is a point to be determined by the pervading spirit of the American Zion. This spirit alone can arouse them to a just appreciation of their intellectual and moral dignity, and of the inalienable rights with which Heaven has invested them, and inspire the purpose of their vindication. Schlegel, a few years since, referring to 'the contagious disorders' then threatening the quiet of European monarchies, declared " the true nursery of all these destructive principles, of the revolutionary school of France and the rest of Europe, to be North America." Nor did he mistake the fact. The principles of civil and religious liberty, that have disquieted European despots, shaken their thrones, and claimed recognition in tones of thunder, *are* those which form the basis of our country's preëminence. And these principles have their origin in the Bible, and draw their life-blood from the Cross. As surely as they are understood and cherished, in the modern "Land shadowing with wings," so surely will they extend, wherever the wind and waves waft our merchandise, or the venturous explorer, the earnest philanthropist, or the minister of religion, plant their feet. Their progress cannot be arrested, nor their influences be resisted. The question is, *Shall they be sanctified?*

Let the moral character of our country be what it should be,—let our learning, statesmanship, and enterprise be baptized in the waters of Siloa, ere they go abroad to proclaim the worth of our laws and institutions,—and not a nation under heaven shall remain unblessed by them! But the Gospel alone, diffused in purity over the length and breadth of the land, and permeating in its influence the whole population, will give us that character, and render us the benefactors of the world. Let our people swell to scores of millions, and be pervaded by the spirit of wisdom and piety breathing from the oracles of God, and then every ship that leaves our shores, every civil or religious embassy to foreign lands, shall carry abroad an influence grateful to oppressed humanity. Thus, in a few short years, religious and civil emancipation shall crown the aspirings of all people; the dove of peace shall spread her wings over all lands; and earth, throughout, shall bow to Heaven's authority! Abundant, then, the revenue of glory flowing in upon Him who "weareth many crowns."

5. Since the Church especially reflects the glory of Christ, her prosperity is to be sought with invincible energy and perseverance.

Christ's glory is upon her; her birth-place is in heaven; her Father and protector is the eternal God; angels are her ministering servants; the armies of heaven throw their shields over her, and fight her battles. As the stone cut out of the mountain without hands, she smites all kingdoms in her progress, abolishes idols, and compels the great men of the earth to do her homage, and lay their tribute at her feet.

"If I forget thee, O Jerusalem, let my right hand forget her cunning!" In the same spirit did the Apostle to the Gentiles seek the salvation of Israel, and of the world, undaunted by perils, and glorying in stripes, imprisonments and death. To remove from deathless man the curse of God's violated law, to purify the fountain of the moral affections, shut up the open gateway of death, and lead the sanctified spirit into the presence of God, where is fullness of joy—what else so worthy of a seraph's zeal and effort!

"Salvation! O the joyful sound!"

Heaven, only, will reveal its preciousness and grandeur; when love and glory, beaming from the throne, shall entrance the ransomed spirit, and impart a happiness that eye hath not seen, nor ear heard, nor the heart of man understood! And who, that justly appreciates the soul's worth, and knows the sacred fellowship of saints and angels—who that has the mind which was in Christ, and looks joyfully onward to his ultimate triumph—must not rejoice in the reflection of his glory, through the prosperity of the church!

Moreover, the Church is man's only safeguard against exterminating judgments, this side the grave. The little church of the old world is no sooner shut up in the ark of gopher-wood, than the wheels of nature leave their track, and plunge man and beast, mountain and field, beneath the ocean wave! So long as one heir of heaven dwells in Sodom, the city is safe; the moment he departs, the people of the curse meet their doom. And when true Religion, as incorporated in the Church, shall have finally left the habitations of men, the Angel of God, standing on the earth and on the sea, will lift his hand to heaven, and swear that time shall be no longer! Annihilate the Church, and you extinguish the light of the world. Lay her inclosures waste, let infidelity plant its foot amid the hills and vallies of a nation, and pour its streams of deadly pollution through her mountain gorges—let the dark banner of the god of this world float over the dismantled towers, and down-broken walls of the Church—then the Holy Spirit no longer humbles the pride nor subdues the unbelief, that bend not beneath the thunders nor melt before the flames of Sinai; but turning tearfully away, he leaves the fearful sentence pealing upon the ear, "Let the despisers wonder and perish!"

'Peace and good will' to suffering humanity, breathe only from lips that invite the weary and heavy-laden to Christ for rest. The relief of the disordered mind and the wounded spirit, supplies for the sons of want and for the stranger in distress, forgiveness to the enemy, equity to the oppressed, are promptings of the same authority that converts the sword into the plough-share, the spear into the pruning-hook, and that secures to every man the shadow of his own vine and fig-tree. Irreligion and superstition, infidelity and delusion, are equally powerless of good and prolific of evil, wherever they prevail.

And then, where are the powers of the human mind most fully developed? Whence, but from the bosom of the church, have sprung the Newtons and Lockes, the Bacons and Edwardses, who have extended the boundaries of human knowledge, and carried us up to its first principles? And where are the lights of education so diffused that the rich and the poor, the high and the low, are taught alike to reason justly, and to act worthily of their immortal destiny? Where, but in lands that bow to the authority, and reflect the glory, of Christ! On the other hand, where are the flood-gates of depravity thrown wide open, where are vice and crime of every name palliated by a corrupt public sentiment, and perpetrated without hazard to reputation, and without danger of inflictions from civil law, except where the Gospel and its ministrations have lost their power, or have never made their influence felt? So unquestionable is this, that often has the unbeliever himself demanded the very ministry he scorned, and urged the necessity of its support, in defence of the endangered morals of community. "Their rock is not as our rock, our enemies themselves being judges."

When the evils and perils of spiritual destitution thus meet the eye, can we turn from them with the inquiry, What is all this to us? Oh, never! Let the elements of nature come in conflict, let the earth quake, and the lightnings play; let the noon-day destruction, or the noiseless pestilence, affright our cities; or let the clashing of arms, and the groans of thousands weltering in their blood, on the fields of Borodino or Inkermann, meet us on the highway of life; and we are not unmoved! How, then, without emotion and countervailing effort, can we witness the conflict of these moral elements; and the impetuous rush of millions, bone of our bone, and flesh of our flesh, to the world of death, where the redemption of the soul ceaseth forever! Yet if such a catastrophe is to be avoided, the Gospel must be sent over the whole vast extent of the land; the cross must be planted on every hill top; the living water must be conducted through every valley; and the invitation must be poured on every ear, "Look unto me, and be ye saved!"

6. Fearful destitutions exist in our country, demanding immediate recognition and relief.

Twenty-four hundred years ago Israel saw the spot in ruins over which the Shekinah had hovered, where prophets had proclaimed the will of God, where priests had made atonement for the sins of the people, and where assembled congregations had long offered incense to the Most High. Desolation marched over it, and the enemies possessed it. The holy prophet wept for this, while the elders, in sack-cloth, sat upon the ground, and cast dust on their heads. Nor is Christendom a stranger to such destitutions and mournings. Many a child of God hangs his harp on the willows, because his pleasant things are taken away, and few are left to respond to the tears of his penitence, or the raptures of his praise.

Need I say that, in our own land, communities by thousands exist, where no church has been planted; or where, if planted, it has become powerless; and where religion, if existing at all, has retired into corners, and surrendered the field to ungodliness? where scattered churches, deserted tables of the Lord, dilapidated sanctuaries, faithless and immoral professors, or graceless zealots exulting in their vain triumphs over reason and conscience, meet the beholder on every side? Millions there are, not even nominally connected with any Christian denomination; not taught the existence of God, or a mediator, of heaven or hell; filling up large districts, whole counties indeed, abandoned to every untoward influence, and well-nigh loosed from all salutary restraint.

That the destitutions of our country are extensive and appalling—that ministers intellectually and morally qualified to guide men are few, compared with the urgency of the demand—and that calls for holy ministrations are pressing, beyond the ability of the almoners of our bounty to meet them—are facts, both sorrowful and undeniable. Here and there, amid these destitutions, are gems that shall deck the crown of Zion's King; but scarcely are they recognized, for the rubbish that surrounds them, dim is their lustre, and the darkness comprehendeth them not. Jesus commands that these be gathered up, cleansed, and polished for his use, in the day of his approaching glory.

Living and faithful men only can do this. If revivals are to be enjoyed, and disciples multiplied, if law and order are to be maintained, vice and crime to be suppressed, and the bonds of society to be strengthened—then must the heralds of salvation lift up their voice like a trumpet, and proclaim through the land "Thy God, O Zion, reigneth!" Amid these wide-spread desolations, infidelity knows no shame; the supremacy of Christ, and the retributions of eternity, are laughed to scorn; ignorance and depravity engender every species of delusion, and nourish into maturity heresies the most fatal.

Think you there lurks no *danger* in the prevalence of such delusions and heresies among the spreading millions of our country? Is there no danger to the stability of divine institutions, and to the souls of men, when the oracles of God are unheeded? when the great commands, on which hang all the law and the prophets, are practically disavowed as the rule of life? when the national conscience is defiled by contact with oppression, and our country, as one expresses it, 'still drags after it Slavery, that fatal heritage of another age, as the convict drags his chain and ball'? when this immense and enduring system of legalized oppression overshadows us with a cloud dark and portentous as Egypt's night, pregnant with storm and tempest, and threatening righteous retribution for injuries inflicted on God's image in the form of humanity ? when the pretensions of an apostate church to the exclusive possession of Heaven's grace are treated with respect, and her schools and colleges share Protestant patronage ? when the disciples of Loyola swarm like locusts in the land, and the peculiar treasures of kings are sent from abroad to sustain them ? and when ghostly prelates, sworn to the extermination of heresy, control the action of individuals, of legislative bodies even, at their pleasure ? I repeat the question—Is there no danger in this ? If, even now, we be not sleeping on the crater's edge, whose fiery floods threaten an overthrow of our civil and religious liberties more terrible than was felt by Pompeii or Herculaneum, the signs of the times and the interpretations of prophecy deceive us !

Vainly do we flatter ourselves with expectations of safety, on the ground that light is abroad, that the spirit of piety is in action, and that the world is too far advanced in years to be again seduced into folly by the mother of harlots ! Though we cry "peace, peace," war is kindling, and the battles of Romanism and of Slavery are to be fought to their end, on our own soil. And, however quiet our slumbers and delicious our dreamings the flames, working up their way beneath us, may burst forth ere we are aware, and unless God prevent, end our dreams and liberties together ! Well may we fear the Antichrist, who pronounces the Bible an insufficient guide to heaven ; who proposes other mediators than the Lord Jesus Christ ; and who proclaims plenary indulgence to sin, on payment of the price ! Well may we fear the ecclesiastical despotism that bound all Europe in chains for more than a thousand years; dethroning kings, overturning kingdoms, and shedding blood enough for navies to swim in; and that still holds in its remorseless grasp the liberties of every Christian nation, not emancipated by the word of God! I say, well may we fear this, so long as sin reigns in human hearts, and ambition, covetousness, and a reckless disregard for Heaven's authority, maintain their ascendency in high places.

Nor are these dangers to be successfully met, till the public eye is more widely opened, and the pulse of the great community beats more harmoniously with the spirit of prophecy, assuring the downfall of whatever opposeth and exalteth itself against God. Then will the heralds of salvation, clothed in full Christian panoply, go forth to the conflict in vastly increased numbers; and, sustained by the combined energies of Zion, their courage and high resolve shall never fail, while they 'play the man for God' against principalities and powers, and spiritual wickedness in high places.

Nor can it be that in a land filled with plenty, like our own, 'sucking of the abundance of the seas and of treasures hid in the sand,' there should be a want of MEANS to sustain the self-denying missionary. If he be not thus sustained, it is because the churches do not understand their obligations, or are not prepared by the love of God to meet them. Two things are certain, as the ordinances of Heaven: viz. More *may* be done than has ever yet been attempted, to make this land the land of Immanuel; and, More *must* be done, if that end is to be attained.

The recent additions to our original domain,—the fertile hills and vales of Oregon, the rich bottom and table lands of Texas, the auriferous sands and streams of California, with its mountain steeps and smiling bays, no less than the recently opened prairies and luxuriant valleys of Kansas and Nebraska—are rapidly filling with an enterprising yet heterogeneous population, which demands immediate and large ministration to its spiritual necessities. Few of the hardy pioneers in those outstretching regions of the West, feel the pressure of their spiritual wants, or are prepared to provide for themselves, or to ask of others those supplies of the bread of life, without which they perish. But such supplies Heaven demands for them; and only the open hand of Christian beneficence can meet that demand.

If these just claims of the advancing multitudes, destined soon to cover every acre between the Atlantic and the Pacific, are to be honored, the standard of pious liberality in our churches must be elevated far above its present stand-point. The claims of Jehovah Jesus, the relations of man to time and to eternity, the riches of heaven, and all the hopes that centre there, demand a higher appreciation, and a nobler response from the bosom of Zion, than has yet been given. Tell me: What else has the Christian to live or to die for, but the glory of Him who "weareth many crowns!" And shall he ever hesitate to meet the sacrifice to which heaven calls him, and to which his own vows pledge him? Shall not the rich man's gifts, and the widow's mites, flow onward together, in ever-deepening streams, that shall at length overpass their banks, and fertilize every arid waste and every rocky promontory between the seas, till they become the lovely adornments of the garden of the Lord?

Fain would I see every where displayed the spirit

of one, who supports herself and her aged parents, and still, by economy, saves ten dollars a year to send the Gospel to the perishing! Or of another, who quits the rich and attractive home of her childhood, for the toils of a factory, that she may personally instruct the ignorant, and sustain the missionary abroad! Or of the revolutionary soldier, who, crutch in hand, deposits annually nine-tenths of his pension in the Lord's treasury! Or of the enfeebled day-laborer, who lays aside a fifth of his earnings, as a benefaction to the cause of missions! Or of Richard Baxter, who first contrived to need as little as possible; then, to lay out nothing on things unnecessary; then, to profit others by whatever he used himself; and, finally, to do all the good possible with whatever he could save, of the competency God gave him! And more than all, the spirit of Him who, though he was rich, for our sakes became poor, that we, through his poverty, might become rich!

When such offerings are made, and are sanctified by prayer and Heaven's blessing, neither will Paul plant, nor Apollos water, in vain. The missionary will go forth armed, like Bunyan's Great-heart, with sword, helmet, and shield. The house of the Lord will arise here and there, wherever needed, in simple majesty; new congregations will be gathered, and churches organized; schools will be established, benevolent associations be formed, and converts to Jesus be multiplied. And then, the voice of thanksgiving and praise, flowing from ten thousand hearts, will ascend to the throne of God, and meeting the joyous response of ten thousand times ten thousand, will bring down blessings, in endless variety and infinite profusion, on all who have freely given, as they have freely received!

7. The liberal support of Home Missions brings immediate glory to Christ.

No churches in the land are more ready to deny themselves, and to identify the interests of the church universal with their own, than those planted and nurtured by Missionary labor. Their piety is indeed often warmer, and their active devotedness greater, than that of churches long nursed in the lap of ease and plenty.

Well did I know a feeble church in New England, gone so far down the valley of the shadow of death a few years since, that when one of the most eminent of our foreign Missionaries, previous to leaving his country, offered them three months' service, if they would simply *board* him, they declined the overture, through inability to meet the terms. The Missionary Society, like the good Samaritan, passing by and seeing their distress, had compassion upon them, took them up, and cared for them. A few years only elapsed, when religion revived, strength returned, they rose up in the name of the Lord, disclaimed further dependence on man, and, beyond their expenditures at home, cast four hundred dollars at once into heaven's treasury for distribution abroad; and they have increased their contributions, till now no country church exceeds them in liberality! Only a specimen this, of what is in the course of accomplishment throughout the land, by the action of the American Home Missionary Society.

A large proportion of the youthful talent, directed to the ministry, and to other benevolent agencies, is drawn from Home Missionary fields. "God has blessed my labors," says one, "to the conversion of FIVE YOUNG MEN, well prepared by nature and grace to preach the gospel. What shall I do with them?" "I have sent three young men to college to-day, who I expect will be ministers," says another; "and my church is not only giving the dew of her youth to the Lord, but has this year returned more than an hundred dollars into the treasury."

Then, if the interests of common school education, if habits of industry, the cultivation of a noble public spirit, the advance of temperance, and the maintenance of just law, and of true social order, are better sustained in one portion of Zion than in another, it is where the laborious Home Missionary is established and at work. Beyond other men, he feels the presence of "a great cloud of witnesses." Not the eyes of his people only, but of his brethren abroad, and of the churches at large, as well as the eye of Heaven, are upon him, constraining him to lay aside every weight, and to run with patience the race set before him. And many of the loveliest spots amid New England communities are those, where the heart and hand of the Missionary have nurtured trees of righteousness, for transplantation into the Paradise above.

And now, dear brethren, let me ask you, in the presence of Him who "weareth many crowns,"—for He is in the midst of us!—*What will ye do*, beyond what ye have already done, to raise from the dust some hundreds of feeble churches, long since planted by the hand of God? and for the younger churches, struggling against difficulties for a precarious existence? What will ye do for the planting of other churches, by scores and hundreds, to form radiating points of Immanuel's glory? and for the restoring of Sabbaths and sanctuaries to the destitute HALF of your country's population? In a word: *What will ye do*, to give "the kingdom, and the greatness of the kingdom, and the dominion under the whole heaven," into the hand of the

Great God your Saviour? More effectively you cannot labor for this end, than in multiplying and sending abroad heralds of salvation, over the whole reach of our moral desolations, following them with your 'prayers and alms,' like the Roman centurion.

Nor is the encouragement of Providence small, to those who heartily labor in this work. When the Society whose anniversary we celebrate has sustained laborers in the field, whose aggregate services, for twenty-nine years, exceed sixteen thousand five hundred years of missionary labor; who have been instrumental in adding to the churches more than a hundred and thirty-two thousand souls; and who have established thousands of Sabbath Schools and Bible Classes, elevating the moral character of hundreds of thousands not yet brought to Jesus' feet,—the smiles of Heaven on this enterprise, and the Divine influence accompanying these preachers of righteousness, cannot be doubted. And when we add the salutary reforms they have started and sustained in their respective localities; their direct and indirect influence in the establishment of the Common School, the High School, and the College, amid the prairies and forests so lately tenanted by the deer and the buffalo, or the wolf and the Indian hunter; when we know that they have broken up a thousand leagues of fallow ground, gathered out the stones, turned the desert into a fruitful field, and cast up a highway for the return of future generations to God—have we not the marked encouragement of Providence to persevere in these labors of love?

What, then, I ask again, will ye do in the future, beyond what ye have done in the past, in this work? Surely, you will not for a moment forget that the foundations of an empire, of unsurpassed extent and glory, are here being laid! and that it will require but the lapse of a century or two to cover the broad area of our country with hundreds of millions, who shall extend a resistless influence over the world's destinies! And is it not wise—nay, is it not imperative on us, as God's authority can make it—to plant the gospel in its purity, at the earliest hour, in every part of this domain? and then to sustain it, by every required sacrifice, till its principles of love and meekness shall be firmly grounded, as the everlasting hills, in the nation's heart?

Brethren! make up your minds for increased labor and sacrifice, and take hold on the enterprise with larger heart and stronger hand than ever before! Some of us must soon pass away to the judgment, for our work is well nigh finished in this world of death; but, we hope then, through rich and boundless grace, to look back from the heavenly hills, sympathetically and joyously, on the spirit of devotion that shall animate the bosoms of our sons and younger brethren, urging them onward in the work devolved on them by Heaven;—a work surpassingly great, if you will allow credit to individual convictions, matured into certainty by thoughtfulness and action extended over scores of years; or rather, if you admit the supreme authority that binds to its prosecution, and apprehend the 'exceeding great and eternal weight of glory' to be secured by its accomplishment! Heaven, earth, and hell, unite in urging you onward. In the language of another, "the heavenly hosts are looking down to see in what estimation the commands of Christ are held; millions stretch out their hands, and implore your aid; and, methinks, I hear ten thousand of the Lost, lifting up their voices, and saying, 'Send, O send, the preachers of the gospel, lest they also come to this place of torment!" Who, indeed, that claims to love Christ and his country, can withhold for a moment his whole influence from a cause that aims to turn back the dark river of moral death upon its source, and to conduct the streams of salvation, through each heaven-prepared channel, to every hamlet of the land! Rich or poor, learned or unlearned, all may freely share the labors and partake the honors of those who turn many to righteousness and to God!

Labors and honors these, splendid as those which invest the life and encircle the head of Him who "weareth many crowns;" ravishing as the song of the hundred forty and four thousand; and pure as the great white throne, on which the Eternal sits for judgment! Brethren! shall they be yours? Your own hearts will decide; your deeds will tell! Let that decision and testimony be entered on the records above, in characters of light, at this auspicious hour! Then shall the full fruition of earth's labors, and of heaven's honors, be learned by you, in the presence of Him whose many crowns fill the upper world with joys that mortal eye hath not seen, nor ear heard, nor heart conceived!

And now, "Awake, O north wind, and come thou south, and blow upon this garden of the Lord, that the spices thereof may flow out!"

American Home Missionary Society.

PRESIDENT.

HENRY DWIGHT, Esq.

SECRETARIES FOR CORRESPONDENCE.

MILTON BADGER, D. D.
Rev. DAVID B. COE.
Rev. DANIEL P. NOYES.

RECORDING SECRETARY.

Mr. WILLIAM C. GILMAN.

TREASURER.

Mr. CHRISTOPHER R. ROBERT.

AUDITOR.

Mr. CALEB O. HALSTED.

EXECUTIVE COMMITTEE.

Mr. Abijah Fisher.
William Patton, D. D.
Charles Butler, Esq.
Alfred C. Post, M. D.
Edwin F. Hatfield, D. D.
Mr. Simeon B. Chittenden.
Asa D. Smith, D. D.
Richard S. Storrs, Jr., D. D.
Rev. Joseph P. Thompson.

Ex-Officio.
Mr. Christopher R. Robert, *Treasurer.*
Milton Badger, D. D., Rev. David B. Coe, Rev. Daniel P. Noyes, *Secretaries for Correspondence.*
Mr. William C. Gilman, *Recording Secretary.*

ASSISTANT TREASURER.

Mr. Hezekiah W. Ripley.

ABSTRACT OF THE ANNUAL REPORT,

MAY 9, 1855.

THE number of ministers of the Gospel in the service of the Society, in 27 different States and Territories, during the year, has been 1,032.

Of the whole number, 528 have been the *pastors* or *stated supplies* of single congregations; 328 have ministered to two or three congregations each; and 176 have extended their labors over still wider fields.

Ten missionaries have preached to congregations of *colored* people; and 60 in foreign languages—19 to *Welsh*, and 34 to *German* congregations; and 7 to congregations of *Norwegians*, *Swedes*, *Swiss*, *Frenchmen* and *Hollanders.*

The *number of congregations and missonary stations* supplied, in whole or in part, is 2,124.

The *aggregate of ministerial labor* performed, is equal to 815 years.

The number of *pupils in Sabbath schools*, is 64,800.

There have been added to the churches, 5,634, viz. : 2,948 on profession, and 2,686 by letter. *Forty eight* missionaries make mention, in their reports, of *revivals* of religion in their congregations; and 366 missionaries report 2,434 hopeful conversions.

Sixty six churches have been *organized* by the missionaries during the year; and 40, that had been dependent, have assumed the support of their own ministry.

Sixty one houses of worship have been *completed ;* 38 *repaired ;* and 52 others are in *process of erection.*

Eighty nine young men, in connection with the missionary churches, are in preparation for the gospel ministry.

RECEIPTS.—$180,136 69.

LIABILITIES.—$190,206 08.

PAYMENTS.—$177,717 34—leaving $12,488 74 still due to missionaries for labor performed ; towards canceling which, and meeting the further claims on commissions not yet expired—amounting in all to $96,518 40—there is a balance in the Treasury of $16,804 31—the greater part of it received in payment of legacies near the close of the year.

The pledges of the Society are now greater by $10,289 06 than at the date of the last Report. If these pledges are to be redeemed ; if the work, which has been commenced in our new Territories and on the Pacific coast, is to be prosecuted as its exigencies require ; if every well-qualified laborer is to be sent forth into the harvest-field, with the assurance that he shall not want ; if this work of Home Evangelization, which has been borne upon the hearts of God's people so long, and with results so glorious, is to be carried forward another year without faltering ; if it is to be extended, in any measure, as opportunities invite, and the necessities of our fellow-countrymen and the hope of the world and the exceeding great and precious promises of God imperiously demand, a great enlargement of pecuniary resources is indispensable.

AMERICAN EMIGRATION.

A

DISCOURSE

IN BEHALF OF THE

American Home Missionary Society,

PREACHED IN THE CITIES OF NEW YORK AND BROOKLYN,

MAY, 1857.

BY

REV. J. M. STURTEVANT, D. D.,

PRESIDENT OF ILLINOIS COLLEGE.

NEW YORK:

PUBLISHED BY THE AMERICAN HOME MISSIONARY SOCIETY,

BIBLE HOUSE, ASTOR PLACE.

1857.

John A. Gray, *Printer and Stereotyper*,
16 and 18 Jacob St., Fire-Proof Buildings.

DISCOURSE.

Matt. 10 : 5, 6. "These twelve Jesus sent forth, and commanded them, saying: Go not into the way of the Gentiles, and into any city of the Samaritans enter ye not: but go rather to the lost sheep of the house of Israel."

If I mistake not, the superficial reader of the Bible often greatly misapprehends these words; perhaps some have even felt themselves shocked at the sentiment supposed to be expressed in them. If we will not have the candor or take the trouble, to infer their true spirit from the general tenor of our Lord's life and teachings, and especially from the relations of his then present labors to the establishing of the kingdom of heaven among men, these words will seem to have been uttered in that spirit of Jewish exclusiveness, which would forever confine the knowledge and the blessings of the true religion to the Jewish people, and deprive all the rest of the world of any participation in them. Nothing, however, could be farther from the true spirit of the text.

Many persons seem to consider the Jewish dispensation as a perfect failure. Their conception of the subject is, that God raised up the Jewish nation to be his peculiar people, disciplined it by a series of miraculous interpositions through a period of fifteen hundred years, and then broke it in pieces and cast it off, because nothing could be done with it; that it did indeed receive in trust those lively oracles of God, the Old Testament

Scriptures, and hand them over to the Christian Church, and that a Jewish mother did indeed give birth to the Messiah; but that from this point the influence and usefulness of the Jewish dispensation ceased.

This is certainly a very shallow and inadequate view of the subject. It was the object of that ancient economy to raise up and qualify one people to receive the promised Messiah, to appreciate that fullness of divine revelation which he should make, and to become his missionaries to publish his glad tidings to the nations, and found the Christian Church in many lands.

And with this design of the Jewish Church the result corresponded. True, the Jewish state rejected the Son of God, and instigated his crucifixion, and thus doomed itself to speedy and terrible destruction. But there were thousands of humble and devout persons among the Jews, who were prepared to receive the promised Saviour, and to appreciate his spiritual doctrines and his divine mission; while the most refined philosophy of Greece mocked and said, What will this babbler say? Jewish men did first receive the Gospel; Jewish men became its first preachers and missionaries; Jerusalem became the very centre and citadel of the christian mission; and from Jerusalem Jewish men carried the Gospel to the Euphrates and to the Pillars of Hercules, to the banks of the Nile, and the Rhine, and the Danube. Jewish men did, in a single generation, fill the vast Roman Empire with christian teaching and christian churches.

Hence, in establishing his kingdom on earth, our Lord's first work was with the Jewish mind. The ripe harvest of fifteen hundred years was to be gathered in. The men who, as the product of the long history of God's chosen people, were trained for the solemn crisis, now at hand, were to be, by the voice of the Master and his chosen band, called out from among the Jewish people, and prepared to go abroad on their mission to mankind. The chosen people of God were to be summoned to come up to the help of the Lord against the mighty. The Pentecost was to be ushered in; the church of Jerusalem was to be founded, from which the beams of salvation would shine on the remotest nations of the known world, before the men then living were in their graves. And time pressed—the hour of destiny was near. In a few months the great expiatory sacrifice would have been offered, the veil of the temple have been rent, and the time for proclaiming the kingdom of heaven to all nations have come. To the Jews then—to the JEW, was the first message. Well might the Lord say, "Go not into the way of the Gentiles," they are not prepared for this crisis of the ages; "into any city of the Samaritans enter ye not," their time is not yet. "Go rather to the lost sheep of the house of Israel," and summon them to their glorious national destiny, as the missionaries of these glad tidings to every people, and kindred, and nation. This is, I am persuaded, the true spirit of our text. There is no national narrowness, no Jewish exclusiveness here.

There are several analogies between the age in which the Christian religion was first propagated in the world and that in which we live, which are full of interest both to the philosopher and the Christian, and which must be regarded as invested with very great practical significancy. In that age a general expectation had been awakened by the prophecies of the Old Testament, that the Messiah was about to appear, and establish the kingdom of God among men. The meaning of the prophecies foretelling those great events, was then but ill understood; but we know that they implied that the blessings of the revealed religion were to overleap those national boundaries, which had hitherto confined them, and to be freely imparted to the Gentile world. In our age, the prophecies of that same ancient Book of God have awakened a like expectation, that the Gospel of Jesus Christ is to overleap the boundaries which have long confined it, and to be given to all nations. In that age, there was a providential preparation for the planting and wide dissemination of the Gospel in the world, such as had never existed before, and did not exist again for more than fifteen hundred years. In our age, there is an equally providential preparation, the work of many ages, for the fulfillment of the prophecies which point to our time; the giving of this same Gospel of salvation to every nation under heaven. In that age, there was one people, a rebellious and stiff-necked people indeed, and yet trained by ages of providential discipline to be the messengers of Christ to the millions of the Roman Empire, and that people placed by their wide dispersion, —which had already been going on for ages,—in such relations to the mighty mass, as to give them peculiar and unrivaled facilities for accomplishing the work assigned them. The converts on the day of Pentecost were devout Jews, from every nation under heaven, assembled at Jerusalem to worship. In that assembly, was the nucleus of a christian church in almost every city of the Roman Empire. Wherever the Apostles went, they found Jews and a Jewish synagogue, and in that synagogue they preached their first sermon, and made their first converts. Dispersed Jews formed the line of electric conduction, along which the Gospel flashed from Jerusalem to the extremities of the empire. This is Providence—this is God's work.

But in this particular, our analogy does not fail us. In our age, there is a people no less distinctly marked than the Jew in the age of Augustus—prepared by a providential training no less peculiar, for achieving this work of Christian propagation, now indicated alike by the index finger of prophecy and Providence. As Abraham was called by the voice of God, to go out from his kindred and country to seek an unknown land for the inheritance of his posterity, so was that modern people, to which I refer, driven out by the fierce persecutions of the seventeenth century from kindred and country, to seek for themselves and their children a home across an almost unknown ocean, and in the great and terrible American wilderness—a home where they might worship God according to the dictates of their conscience, and construct the Church and the State after the model which had already been shown them. It is due to the simple historic truth, to recognize the fact, that all which is most characteristic and most valuable in American history and American society, is due to the influence of that portion of our original population, which was brought to our shores by the pressure of such circumstances, and the influence of such motives. This is all which is intended by the statement just made. And I give no other preëminence to New England, than results from the undeniable fact that its settlement was almost wholly the result of the causes alluded to. It is enough for my purpose that it be borne in mind, that God did separate from all the elements of the old world, a very peculiar people; that he let loose the fires of persecution to drive them from their homes, and led them by his providence, to this good land of ours, to lay the foundations of a free religious republic, which, though it had no model in the past, was to be the hope of the future.

The proposition which I assert, and which I wish to confirm and apply is, that *as God in the apostolic age, committed the work of propagation to Jewish hands, so, in this age of universal Christian propagandism, he hath preëminently committed it to this people*, which he thus providentially planted in the American wilderness; and that, consequently, this American people should enlist the prayerful solicitude of all who in our day labor for the conversion of the world to Christ—just as the Jewish people were regarded with most peculiar interest by Christ and his Apostles.

It will at once be apparent to every thoughtful hearer, that the subject thus indicated is of vast extent, and that in order to have any hope of handling it successfully in a single discourse, I must pass by a very large portion of the material of instructive thought which it suggests, and present it only in a single aspect. And there is a single view of the subject which is peculiarly appropriate to this occasion. *What is the function of the American Home Missionary Society*, in whose behalf we are met this evening? It is, to *follow the American emigrant, in all his migrations, and to plant the permanent institutions of the Christian faith wherever he builds his cabin.* That religious stock from which, as I have said, all the best peculiarities of American society originated, have ever regarded it as a cardinal article of their creed, that religious instruction must keep pace with the migrations of the emigrant, and that ample provisions for religious culture must be made coëxtensive with the tillage of the soil. The American Home Missionary Society has been, now for these many years, the principal agency by which this article of their religious faith has been carried into practice. With American emigration, then, has this noble Society to do.

I risk nothing in the assertion, that it is through this same emigration that the American people is to exert, beyond comparison, its most powerful influence upon the religious destinies of the world. It is this very emigration which, more than any other peculiarity of our history, constitutes us the missionary people of the nineteenth century.

Let us, then, for a few moments contemplate this phenomenon of *American emigration*, and try, if possible, to grasp its import and its relations to the future religious condition of mankind, and endeavor to derive from thence those motives to greater efficiency in the cause of Home Missions, which a true view of this subject will certainly furnish. The Jew converted the Roman Empire to Christianity, by the occasion of his forced dispersions. The American people shall yet convert the world to Christ, by their voluntary and spontaneous migrations.

Since the introduction of Christianity into the world, perhaps the most striking feature in history is the steady and irresistible progress of population from the East towards the West. It is as steady as the flow of our own Mississippi towards the Gulf, and almost equally dates from immemorial antiquity. What is modern Europe but one of the products of this migration, which overhung in dense and threatening clouds of barbarism the frontiers of Greece and Rome in the palmiest days of their power, which trampled them in the dust, in the days of their decrepitude, and overspread all Europe. And when Europe was full, and these barbarous hordes had been for ages subjected to civilizing influences, borne over that deluge of barbarism in the ark which God had provided—the Christian Church—then America was discovered, and laid open by an improved art of navigation to the colonial enterprises of Europe. The ocean was bridged, and the mighty human stream rolled on towards the West without obstruction. An unpeopled continent opened its bosom to the coming emigrant. It is now more than three hundred years since emigrants from all the principal nations of Europe have been taking possession of this new home of the human race in the West. Nearly all the principal nations of Christendom have participated, in greater or less degree, in the movement; and the Atlantic Ocean, before unvisited by the most adventurous mariner—except along its eastern shores—has become the great highway of the world.

In the early part of the seventeenth century, the eastern shores of the United States began to receive an European population, mostly from England, and from these beginnings originated a series of providential developments unprecedented in the history of the world. The emigrants were largely the descendants of those same Saxons, who, more than a thousand years ago, invaded England as a band of barbarian pirates. But when they reach our shores they are barbarians and pirates no longer. They bring to the inhospitable wilderness, the highest culture of the age and the purest religious faith on earth. Here they form a community in the wilderness. Soon, the wilderness disappears before them. The Atlantic slope of the continent is a garden, the Alleghanies are crossed, and a multitudinous emigration from the older settlements spreads itself over the magnificent central valley of North America. Here the most adventurous emigrant imagined that the ultimate destination of this wondrous human flood was reached, that to fill all this great valley with a civilized and almost numberless population, was all that remained to be done. But how great the mistake! The very men, who began the settlement of the Mississippi, lived to see the barriers of the

Rocky Mountains crossed, and the same human deluge, spreading itself along the shores of the Pacific; and American emigration can now as easily fill our whole national domain, from ocean to ocean, as, in their season, it could people Vermont or Western New York. The Anglo American emigrant holds North America in his grasp. And is this the end? Have we at last reached the final results of European, and especially of English and American emigration? If with a population of twenty three millions we seize with such vigor on the unpeopled lands of the earth, what should we not achieve with a population of two hundred millions, extending from the Atlantic to the Pacific? Are we not dealing, then, with a world phenomenon rather than with one which belongs alone to North America?

In order to do any justice to this theme, I must be indulged in a few numerical calculations. It is with unfeigned sorrow, that I perceive that I can not, in accordance with truth, found these calculations on the actual population of our whole country. But I am compelled to acknowledge, that there could be no appropriateness to my subject in any estimates founded on such a basis. I can not shut my eyes to the fact that the cruel and unchristian system of oppression, which has gained possession of fifteen States of our beloved confederation, has, to a great extent, disqualified them to take their part in this missionary work, which the Lord hath allotted to the American people. Instead of aiding in planting Christian churches in regions beyond, they have need, even now, of an expensive system of missionary effort, to rebuild those which this abomination hath made desolate in generations past, and is making desolate in the present. Their migrations are, to a wonderful extent, not the migrations of intelligence, but of ignorance; the wilderness is seldom made glad by their coming; the institutions of free instruction and free worship spring up but very sparsely along their pathway. With few and rare, though noble exceptions—with some of whom it has been my own privilege to coöperate—they do not carry abroad either religion or freedom. The greatest danger of our country is, that vast regions of our virgin soil, now enjoying Nature's freedom, will be overrun by that dark system of slavery, which this portion of our country nurtures at home, and disseminates abroad. I say not these things because I love to say them, but because truthfulness to my subject requires it; and this I will not violate in a vain attempt to conceal that shame of my own dear country, which has already fixed the gaze of an astonished world. If these States of our Union ever bear their part in fulfilling our great religious destiny, it will be after that system of oppression, so fatally in conflict with our origin, our history, and our religion, shall have been completely swept away. Such a day, I trust, is coming. The Lord hasten it in his time!

We must, therefore, confine our view to the sixteen non-slaveholding States. For obvious reasons, unnecessary to be particularized, we shall also leave out of our estimate the colored population of the Free States. It is, in them all, too small to be a very influential element, and in many of them, is rather diminishing than increasing.

The free white population of the Free States was by the census of 1850, in round numbers, 13,000,000. The population of the same States in 1790 was, 1,900,000. One may easily satisfy himself from these data, that the rate of increase for this period of sixty years was more than 38 per cent, for each ten years. It is also worthy of remark, that from 1830 to 1840, the ratio was above 39 per cent; and from 1840 to 1850, almost 40 per cent; showing, thus, an increasing rather than a diminishing rate of progress. There is no reason to doubt, that nearly the same ratio of increase extends far back into the colonial period—probably to the very founding of the colonies; but there are no data for ascertaining this point with accuracy.

From the date of the last census to the year two thousand, is a period of one hundred and fifty years. Let us, therefore, assume as a basis of calculation 13,000,000, as the free white population of the Free States, in 1850. Let us take as the ratio of increase, not 38 per cent, which is the actual ratio of the last sixty years, but $33\frac{1}{8}$ per cent, which is less than the ratio of increase of our whole population, certainly since the Revolution, and probably from the very founding of the Colonies. With these data, let us carry our estimate forward for a period of one hundred and fifty years, or till A.D. 2,000. The time is short. There may be those sitting on these seats to-night who will behold the faces of some who will witness its completion; and yet the result is overwhelming. We are almost afraid to announce it. It is very little short of *one thousand millions*—equal to the present estimated population of the whole earth. This is not given as a prophecy of the future, or even as a proximate prophecy. But it is given as showing the magnitude of that force with which we are dealing, in our Home Missionary enterprise. I wish also to show, that in our ordinary conceptions of this subject we set much too narrow limits for the probable future expansion of this amazing force.

The supposed counteracting causes which would, on a superficial view of this subject, lead us to set aside the astounding result just given, as of no practical value, are three, and only three—want of room, failure of foreign immigration, and a gradual deterioration of the average character of our people.

As to the *first* of these causes of limitation, it is to be remembered that our question is not how far the American Union will extend, or how great a nation the United States will become. That is a question which no human sagacity can decide; and with which our present subject and this occasion have nothing at all to do. In regard to this matter, we are engaged in a political experiment which has no precedent in the past; and the world, philosophers and all, will be obliged patiently to wait for the issue. But our inquiry relates to the extension of a population having certain religious and social characteristics, and bearing the moral lineage of the Pilgrims of the Mayflower.

It is also to be remembered, that our question is to be judged of, not in view of the tardy movements of bygone ages, but in view of the quickened and constantly quickening movement of the nineteenth century. Our instruments of locomotion and communication are commensurate with the resources of our planet. While I am speaking, preparations are in progress for uniting Europe and America in marriage, by the telegraph wire. The iron track of the steam chariot will soon be continuous, from the Hudson to the Columbia, and from the English Channel to the Yellow Sea. With the control of such instruments of locomotion, it is in the power of a people such as now inhabits these States, to expand itself upon any unoccupied lands on the face of the whole earth. Our question then is not what unoccupied room there is in our country, or in North America, or even in all America, but on the globe! How little danger there is, then, that any people having the will and the power to expand itself over an unpeopled world, will be restrained by want of room. What untold millions may yet find room in our own national domain. The wildest enthusiast who has spoken on this subject after his first tour in the West, has never half reached the truth. One will be much more likely, indeed, to appear as an enthusiast, after a sober residence of a quarter of a century in the great valley, than after a single autumnal tour. Of the capabilities of our great central valley for affording the materials of human subsistence and wealth, the half has never yet been told, and never will be, till we are all in our graves. And what of all our Pacific slope? And what of all the rest of North America, so far as now unoccupied—or held by peoples utterly incapable of retaining it for a moment, against the competition of an energetic, free, and highly civilized people? And what of all South America, either in the wildness of nature, or held by peoples who have not the energy, the civilization, or the arts, to subdue and use it, in five centuries? There is no occupancy of South America, which can present any obstacles to an energetic and free people, invading it, not by the barbarous battalions of the fillibuster, but by the arts of peaceful industry. Let us take, as an illustration, the empire of Brazil. Considered in respect to its territory, its climate, and its soil, it is perhaps the most magnificent national domain on earth. Its territory exceeds in extent the whole present territory of the United States, by 37,000 square miles. Its settlement dates nearly one hundred years prior to the settlement of the United States. And yet, its present population is only about six millions. And of these six millions, three millions are Negro slaves; two millions more are of the various cross races, of the Portuguese, the Negro, and the Indian; and only one million are of full European blood. The increase of its population is scarcely greater than that of the overgrown and decaying monarchies of Europe.

What is the probability that such a nation can hold that vast territory against the peaceful spread, and healthful, natural growth of a free and enlightened people, armed with all the appliances of art, industry, and instruction, and taking possession of the earth, not in the name of any earthly majesty, but in the name of freedom, of religion, and of God? And yet, this is but a specimen of every inch of American soil, not already occupied by men who speak the English tongue, and love English-born freedom, and the faith of English Protestantism.

America, then, from the Arctic seas to Cape Horn, is open to the growth of a free religious people, such as our fathers planted on these Atlantic shores. I deem it no exaggeration to say, that if we are looking for room into which to expand our growth, for a hundred and fifty years to come, America alone, will afford accommodations, and a magnificent home, for more than one thousand millions—the result of our numerical calculation. And what of all the thousand islands of the Pacific, whose native population, in the loveliest climate of the earth, is slowly melting away, before the vices of barbarism, and leaving them almost vacant to the hand of the civilized and christian emigrant? And what of the almost continental group, which divides the Pacific from the Indian Ocean, with all their vast resources of agricultural and mineral wealth? And what of all Africa, just beginning to be opened to the geographer, still almost a wilderness? And what of vast regions of Asia herself, once swarming with uncounted millions, now almost as desolate as the American wilds?

I know, much of this unoccupied land is desert—much of it unfit for the home of a civilized and enterprising people, on account of a malarious atmosphere. But when you have made all these allowances, and every other which the case requires, it seems to me, that the limit which will check the increase of a people, full of the vital energy of freedom and pure religion, is too remote to create much present apprehension, or much to modify our estimates of the future, for a period not longer than one hundred and fifty years.

The truth on this subject is not to be seen in the experience of the past, but in the clear prophecy of the future. In the past, man has never been able to people the earth. The causes which have prevented, though full of interest, would open too vast a field for this occasion. The fact is obvious. Here and there have been found spots of limited extent, enjoying what is called civilization, and with a dense population; while nine tenths of the whole world has been, in all past time, peopled by a few scattered barbarians, or lying in desolation, untrodden by human feet. This will not last forever. God will yet raise up a generation strong enough to grasp and use this earth, which he hath given to man. We are not without our hopes that he has already done so. If so, we need have no fear that there is not ample room for its expansion.

But perhaps it will seem to some, that though there is ample room in the unpeopled earth for all these millions, yet the phenomenon of Anglo American increase and *expansion is necessarily temporary* and transient, because due to causes which must soon cease to act, and that the progress of our population will then only be such as has been exhibited by other lands, and in other times. Let us then inquire:

What are the *causes* of this wonderful growth?

It is obvious, in the first place, that it is not caused solely by the mere abundance of cheap and fertile land. Thomas Carlyle is reported to have said, in conversation with an American: "The secret of your prosperity is plenty of cheap and fertile land." The remark may be worthy of the transcendental mystic, but certainly is not worthy of the sound practical philosopher. Many other modern nations have been, or are now in circumstances as favorable in this respect as ourselves, and yet in our case only has this result followed.

Of the maritime powers of Europe, England was almost the last in the race of discovery, and that in an age when discovery gave little to the lands discovered; yet England alone has succeeded in transplanting civilization into the wilderness. One hundred years ago, France had a far better prospect of planting a mighty empire in America than England. From the mouth of the St. Lawrence to the mouth of the Mississppi, all was hers. The French mind was full of the conception of a vast Gallic empire in America, and was exerting its best energies for its realization. But where is the French empire in America now? How few the foot-prints of the French colonist! The very language of France, with all its power to fascinate, is perishing from the Continent. It furnished, indeed, a considerable portion of our geographical nomenclature; but the names derived from that source are now so Anglicized, both in form and sound, that a Frenchman would seldom recognize them.

And the failure of French colonization in America is not the mere fortune of war. Notwithstanding the transfer of Canada to the British crown, the large French population of that colony have had unlimited freedom of growth and expansion. But where are their colonies? The French philosopher, De Tocqueville, says of them: "Wherever the French settlers were numerically weak and partially established, they have disappeared. Those who remain are collected on a small extent of country, and are now subject to other laws. The 400,000 French of Lower Canada constitute at the present time, the remnant of an old nation, lost in the midst of a new people. A foreign population is increasing around them unceasingly on all sides, and already penetrates among the ancient masters of the country, predominates in their cities, and corrupts their language." He elsewhere states that this remnant of the old French colony is already experiencing the evils of an overgrown population, almost as much as the old nations of Europe; yet nothing can quicken their enterprise to spread themselves abroad over an open continent, after the manner of their English and American neighbors.

Russia has no lack of cheap and fertile land; but the increase of her population, except by annexation, is scarcely, if at all, more rapid than that of England herself. Spain had possession of Mexico a century, and of Peru three quarters of a century, before the Pilgrims set their feet on Plymouth Rock; yet the Mexico of the year 1850 is not more civilized, and scarcely more populous, than the Mexico of Montezuma; and the Peru of our day has no reason to exult in a comparison with the Peru of the Incas. Brazil has been longer under the hand of the European colonist than the United States. Yet, with a territory larger and more magnificent in its natural features than ours, it has only one million of European inhabitants.

There is, then, something here besides "plenty of fertile and cheap land." What is it that has given to the English settlements everywhere, and to the United States in particular, this amazing preponderance over all the other colonial enterprises of modern times, I may say with equal truth, of all times. For the phenomena of American emigration are entirely unprecedented in the history of the world, ancient or modern. What then are its causes? Are they permanent or transient? If they are transient, the results would be of great interest. But if they are permanent, the destiny of an unpeopled world is in them. I claim that they are, or, by the blessing of God on our endeavors, may be, as permanent as our mountains and our rivers. What, then, are they?

Though to a superficial view the causes appear to be various, yet when traced back by a careful analysis to their source, they are all found to be emanations from one single moral force—*the characteristic religious system of the English dissenters of the seventeenth century.* Despotism could not endure these principles, and drove them out with fire and faggot from the Old World, and in so doing, planted the seeds of a world-wide freedom in the New. The Church of God could not be planted in Egypt; and therefore God suffered Pharaoh to drive out Israel by intolerable oppression, that he might plant it in the promised land.

The causes of American growth which strike the eye are chiefly three.

1. The moral dignity and purity of the christian family. It is the complaint of the philosophic and candid De Tocqueville, that wherever Frenchmen have formed settlements in the neighborhood of barbarous native tribes, they have uniformly intermarried with them, and instead of making Frenchmen of these natives, they have themselves become savages. The same language may be applied, with equal force and justice, to the colonial settlements which have emanated from all Catholic Europe. De Tocqueville could discern this fact and its sorrowful consequences; but he does not appear to discern its cause. That cause is found in the Roman Catholic doctrine of the superior sanctity of a state of celibacy. According to that doctrine, the family

is not indeed exactly a state of sin; but it is a degradation. No father, no mother can compare in dignity with the unmarried priest and nun. There can be no holiness in the family altar. If one wishes to worship at a holy altar, he must go where unmarried priests officiate in robes canonical. Who does not see that such a religion degrades the family?—places it on the very borders of a vicious life, shorn of all its moral dignity and glory? No wonder, that one whose views of domestic life are thus vitiated and degraded should choose for a wife a heathen or a savage. And accordingly, wherever men of this faith have formed colonies in the wilderness, this result has followed; and it will follow in the future. Society is thus rotten at its heart, and what can it do but languish and die, as it does in all the colonial settlements of Catholic Europe? This is the sickness of which it languishes.

How different the influence of our fathers' faith! With them the family is the holiest thing on earth. They knew nothing of an altar holier than the family altar. They knew no priest of greater sanctity than the father, priest of his own house. Oh! how improbable that a man of such a faith would choose, to preside around his fire-side, a heathen and a savage! No! he will choose a cultivated being, a Christ-like spirit, a blessed heir of heaven. Ah! thanks to God, the family constituted according to that faith, is a germ of christian civilization, which never can die. Place such a family in any remote wild of the earth, and it has life in itself; it will send out the roots, and the branches, and the seeds of a christian civilization, which will cover the hills, and make glad the valleys all around it. And here is found one of the principal sources of the vital power of the Anglo American emigrant. Wherever such a family is planted in the American wilderness, there is the Church of Christ, there is freedom, there is christian civilization.

And God be forever praised for the *American Home Missionary Society*. Its function is to follow such families to the heart of the Western wilderness, to the banks of the Columbia, and the gold fields of California, and cheer, and encourage, and help them to plant the Church of Christ in those primeval solitudes.

2. Another and most potent cause of the wonderful characteristics of American emigration, is the fact that with us the laborer is an educated, civilized man. It is with us almost alone, that the thinking, independent, self-poised, and self-responsible mind, is united in the same person with the brawny arm and hard hand of the laborer. Yet this is a condition without the fulfillment of which the phenomena of our emigration are quite impossible. The wealthy, the high-born, the ruling classes will not emigrate to the wilderness. They enjoy far greater advantages at home, than the wilderness, however fertile in resources, can afford them. If the unpeopled waste is to be reclaimed and made the home of man, it must be by those, whose lot is comparatively a hard one, by the laboring classes. But if the laboring classes are uneducated barbarians, as has been the fact in most other countries, they will be destitute of that skill, that knowledge, that self-reliance, without which men will seldom undertake the task of seeking a new home in the wilds. The very conception of a migration to Kansas, or Minnesota, or Oregon implies knowledge, resources, self-reliance in a very high degree. And then, again, if an uncultivated, uneducated, laboring population does emigrate, it will not carry civilization with it. It has it not to carry. Its colonies will languish for ages in ignorance and barbarism.

It is precisely for this reason, that the civilization of

Greece and Rome did not cover Europe and Asia, and fill them with light, and leave no barbarians to destroy them, and thus render the dark ages impossible. The laborer, the only man who would emigrate to the wilderness, was too ignorant to know that there was any wilderness, and too barbarous to transplant civilization. This is the only reason why Egypt did not explore and subdue the banks of the Nile, as rapidly as we do those of the Mississippi and its branches. Talk not of malaria—there is malaria enough in the dark, damp, primeval forests that overhang the Mississippi, the Missouri, and the Illinois; but it is no barrier to the progress of the civilized laborer, seeking a magnificent home for himself and his posterity.

The same consideration furnishes the only explanation of the fact that, though Europe is at this day swarming with emigrants from almost every nation, none of those nationalities, except the English, are at all reproducing themselves by their colonies. Their emigrants are all mingled, absorbed, and lost in the English speaking deluge, which is encircling the globe. The reason is, that, for the most part, their laborers are uncultivated men, quite incapable of carrying civilization and freedom into the wilderness. They are therefore glad to avail themselves of those foundations, which our emigrants lay. They are absorbed into our new settlements, and rapidly lose their language and nationality.

It is then perfectly obvious, that we owe our power of multiplying civilized communities in every unpeopled spot to the fact, that our laboring classes are educated, thinking, self-reliant men—as De Tocqueville says of them: "the product of eighteen centuries." Whence, then, this characteristic of our people? Clearly, from the religion of our fathers. That religion is the only moral force, which ever has educated men in masses as men, individually responsible to God, and having individual, inalienable rights. Take your stand in that religious faith, and knowledge—knowledge of God through his word and his works, knowledge of rights, and knowledge of duties to God and man—becomes the first want of every human soul. No child will grow up in ignorance in any family which heartily adopts that faith. A community which is pervaded by it, will effectively provide for the education of every child within its limits. Education, culture, become as necessary and as universal, as air, water, or sunlight. This faith it is, which has educated the American laborer, and given him his power to make the wilderness to rejoice and blossom as the rose. And he will never lose this power, till he loses his religion, and, therefore, the educating force which it exerts.

3. The only remaining cause which I shall mention of the characteristic results of American emigration is, the peculiar public spirit, or, if I may so call it, the social constructiveness, which characterizes the American emigrant. This results directly from what has been said, and therefore need not detain us long. It would be difficult, adequately to describe the rude and unsightly figure, often presented by a company of American emigrants on their way to their new home in the wilds. It has often excited the derision of the gay, the pleasure-loving, and the proud. But any one who well knows that group, and has a heart to appreciate it, will look on with veneration. Æneas is said to have carried the Trojan household gods to Italy. Those unsightly wagons are bearing a nobler and more enduring treasure, more worthy to be celebrated in the immortal epic, than the Trojan Penates. They carry no material image, no external emblem, but in their very minds and hearts they bear along, through forest and prairie, all the in-

stitutions of a ripe christian civilization. The school-house, the college, the church, the teaching ministry, are all traveling in those rude wagons to their new home in the wilderness. At Harvard and Yale, college halls stood beneath the shade of the primeval forest; and to this day it is the peculiarity of the American emigrant, that he mingles in one concert, the tolling of the college bell, the howling of the wolf, and the crack of the huntsman's rifle.

Nor is it needful to spend time to prove, that this peculiarity is the result of the same religious system, or that all other colonizations in the New World have utterly failed, for the want of this very social constructiveness. Among the colonies of France, of Spain, of Portugal, you look for it in vain; and for the want of it, weakness and premature old age and decay, mark all their settlements.

I think now, that any candid man will admit, that the peculiar and wonderful success of American colonization, is to be ascribed, almost wholly, to these three causes—the purity and moral dignity of the family, the education and culture of the great mass of our industrious population, and the public spirit, the social constructiveness, which distinguishes us from all other peoples; and that these three causes run up into one—the religious system of our Puritan fathers. Then must such a man grant all which I claim, on this occasion, that, *so far as that religious system prevails, so far will this American people retain their power of expanding themselves over the earth.* So far as this system prevails, it will cause that "every one that is feeble among the people shall be as David, and the house of David as God, as the angel of the Lord before them."

Let us suppose that the whole present territory of the United States were filled with such a people, numbering, as it inevitably must, not less than three hundred millions—every family a fortress of social strength, every laborer an educated, civilized, relf-reliant man, conscious of his duties and his rights, every community rejoicing in those institutions, which provide for universal culture—with what power would such a people extend its arms to the North and the South, to the East and the West, to take hold of and subdue an unpeopled world. Its colonial settlements would be found on every unoccupied spot, where a furrow could be turned on a tillable soil, wherever there was a water-fall to turn machinery. Every wilderness and solitary place would be glad for them, every desert would bud and blossom as the rose.

And why should we despair, that this grand conception may be, in some good degree, realized? To a result so sublime, the settlement of our religious fathers on these shores evidently looked. If I may so speak, it seems evidently to have been God's plan. And shall we be like the faithless one of old, who said, if there were windows in heaven, then might this thing be? Shall we not rather believe that God can and will accomplish what he has undertaken? True, *slavery* now holds half our States in bondage. But may we not believe that this giant iniquity will be swept away, before this inevitable current of Christian freedom? The time is near—it will perhaps be in the days of some child in this house — when every foot of our national domain will be wanted for the free laborer; and slave labor can not long hold it against such a competition. Already, are there unmistakable signs, that freedom is dawning upon the fertile plains and iron hills of Missouri. It is not alone to recent political events that I allude; though these are of a character to enlist the sympathies of the patriot, and the prayers of the Christian; but I refer still more especially to the amazing relative increase of her free population, resulting from causes so deep and permanent, so entirely providential, that her politicians have little power, either to accelerate or retard it.

Nor can slavery long protect itself from destruction, by the same cause—the inevitable inroads of free labor, all along its northern border. Virginia—glorious old Virginia, amid whose sunny hill-sides holy Mount Vernon nestles, must yet again be free, and extend, as of old, the unshackled hand to her brothers of the North, in carrying religion and freedom over the continent. Time would fail me, to discuss this subject. Let us trust in God and take courage. I can not believe, that God has doomed one half the soil of this home of the free to perpetual slavery. There is ground for hope—the time of deliverance may be near. Room for expansion is as much a necessity of our free laboring population, as air or sunlight. The days of plenty of cheap fertile land, easily accessible and protected from the curse of slavery by national *faith* and national law, are drawing to an end. Nothing will then remain, but the living stream which for half a century, has been rolling on towards the North West must flow down upon the border Slave States, and spread itself over lands which slavery can never cultivate. The free laborers will not leave three fourths of the lands of the adjacent slaveholding States to lie forever uncultivated. Freedom will want those lands; and it will have them: for in this country, no law can hinder, that the owner of unoccupied land should enrich himself by its sale. Whenever, therefore, the free laborer wants those lands, he can have them. This seems to me a providential cause which dooms slavery.

It may, however, be thought by some, that the rapidity of our growth and expansion must soon be greatly diminished by the *failure of foreign immigration.* I shall not devote much time to this part of the subject, but only make two or three brief suggestions.

It may seem to some, that the sooner it fails, the better for our hopes. But I think we may safely leave this point in the hands of the Divine Architect of our national destiny. He has, evidently, designs much more comprehensive, than merely to build up a great free religious nation out of the direct descendants of our pious ancestry. The leaven of their principles is about being mingled with a mass almost as mighty and heterogeneous as that through which Christianity was diffused, in the ages that succeeded that of the Apostles. And God knows best, with how much meal it is safe to mingle it. The leaven shall not be lost; it shall not lose its power; the whole shall be leavened. Nor can I see anywhere the indication, that the religious character of the American people, is to be materially modified by the accession of these foreign elements. There is evidence, on the other hand, that they are themselves undergoing a process of assimilation, unequalled in all the past. Scarcely any portion of the social structure, is so sensitive to foreign influence, as its language. Where, then, is the evidence that the English language is to be either supplanted among us by foreign influence, or permanently corrupted? Assimilation in language, is a type, and only a type, of the universal assimilation that is going on. Nor can I forbear remarking, that the influence of foreign immigration in increasing the rapidity of our growth, is, in my opinion, greatly overrated. The ratio of our increase has, as a matter of fact, been but little greater, when foreign immigration was greatest, than when it was least. And whilst these ever-increasing American communities continue, as now, to present to the needy and oppressed populations of Europe, inviting prospects of freedom, wealth, and plenty, it may be expected that foreign immigration will increase, rather than diminish. I see no reason to apprehend, either that we are to be relieved of foreign immigration, if it is an evil, or to be deprived of it, if a benefit. This topic is one of great interest and great importance, but want of time forbids my dwelling upon it now.

I do not, then, pretend to set any definite limits to the growth of our population, or to utter any definite prediction. But I do say that, on the supposition that the religious principles of our Fathers can be made to prevail coëxtensively with the migrations of our free population, I can see no cause which is likely, in any great degree, to impair the rapidity of our increase for the next one hundred and fifty years. There is no fear of want of room—an unpeopled earth affords room enough. All the causes of our unparalleled growth hitherto, originated only in the pervading influence of a pure Christianity; and provided the prevalence of these principles be made coëxtensive with our growth, may act with just as much energy upon hundreds of millions as upon a few thousands.

With these things in view, I can not help regarding this power of the American people, to extend itself over unpeopled wilds and multiply with such amazing rapidity christian communities and nations, as a cause which looks quite beyond all our vast national domain, with all the hundreds of millions it is capable of sustaining, and as promising to exert a controlling influence on the religious destinies of the globe.

The depth and solemnity of this conviction is greatly enhanced, when I take in the additional fact, that our own dear mother England, (she ought to be called the mother of nations,) is spreading abroad her own colonial settlements, largely composed of materials kindred to our own, in almost every quarter of the globe. English and American emigration is sweeping over North America in parallel lines. If the population of British America is less than our own, it is probably increasing with no less rapidity; and evidently has open before it a most magnificent future. In the Indian Archipelago, New Zealand, and the thousand islands of the Pacific, the English human current from the west, and the American from the east, are soon to meet, and mingle their kindred waters.

It is true, then, beyond controversy or doubt, that the migrations of the English language, the spread of the old English stock, by peaceful colonization, over the unpeopled world, is the grandest phenomenon now visible on earth: it is the mightiest visible agency, which God is now employing, to change the religious and social condition of the human race, and plant the Christian religion over the world. To make England and America thoroughly Christian, is to fill the world with the knowledge of the Lord. It is to plant the Gospel of Jesus Christ in every land, before the year of our Lord, 2000.

When I have reached this stand-point, I seem almost audibly to hear the same voice, that said: "Go not into the way of the Gentiles, into any city of the Samaritans enter ye not;" and urging in our ears, go teach, *teach*, TEACH, the English and American emigrant. Let every emigrant's wagon that crosses the prairie, be a sanctuary of God; let the voice of christian prayer and praise ascend from the cabin of every steamer on the Western waters; let the christian minister and christian teacher accompany the woodman, the hunter, and the gold-digger, to the wilderness; build the church and the school-house, wherever the squatter builds his cabin; and the earth shall soon be the Lord's, and the fullness thereof. Before our grandchildren go to their graves, the triumphant song shall go up: "The kingdoms of this world are become kingdoms of our Lord and his Christ."

But let us remember, that this is not the hour of triumph and victory, but of mighty, and, to human eyes, dubious conflict. There is no doctrine of manifest destiny here. The Jews had a manifest destiny; but of that destiny, as a nation, they failed. We may fail too; and if so, our failure will be the most signal in history. The passer-by will exclaim: "O Lucifer! son of the morning, how art thou fallen!" Worldliness may invade our churches, and set up the altar of Mammon, in the temple of God. Our migrations may become entirely divested of the religious element. Our emigrants may go to the wilderness only for gain, and leave their Penates behind them. Our ministers may be too fond of ease and comfort and refined literary leisure, to follow the emigrant to his wild home. The members of our churches may become too covetous and too fond of the ostentations of fashionable life, to sustain the cause of Home Missions, along our ever-receding border. Our frontier may thus be inhabited by a people knowing no God but money, and no freedom but that of licentiousness. And no man well acquainted with our recent new settlements, can help feeling a sickness of heart, at the symptoms of such moral disease seizing on these extremities of the body politic. Let us not deceive ourselves. If such a day ever comes, our glory will have departed.

We can no more subdue a continent by an emigrant population without religion, without the Church, the school, the ministry, than Rome could hold on in her career of conquest, with the enervated legions of the latter years of the Empire. If such a day ever comes, we shall stand before the other nations of the world, despite our boasted Anglo Saxon blood, like Samson before the Philistines, when his locks were shorn.

This effort to plant the institutions of free christian society upon the borders of the ever receding wilderness demands the united and earnest coöperation of *all*, in every portion of this land, who love and cherish the faith of our fathers. It is sometimes asked, when are the churches of the old States to be relieved from these demands for aid to the new settlements? *When? Never*—till either these churches shall have utterly apostatized from Christ, or there shall be no more unpeopled wilderness on earth, to which the American emigrant can penetrate ; NEVER, till this living stream shall have flowed round the earth, and planted the Church of Christ on every sunny hill-side, and in every fertile valley. The *American Home Missionary Society*, in prospect of the immediately coming future, has as truly the *world* for its field, as the American Board of Commissioners for Foreign Missions. And if any who have put their hand to the plow are disposed now to look back, they are unworthy of any part in this work. The missionaries of this Society shall yet follow the American emigrant, not only to all the fertile valleys which nestle among the snowy peaks of Oregon, and to all the gold fields of California, but to the table lands of Mexico, to the banks of the Amazon, the Orinoco, and the La Plata, and to all the thousand islands of the Pacific. This is the time for girding on the harness, not for putting it off.

And I can not forbear saying, in conclusion, that our Home Missionary enterprise ought to be a great deal more comprehensive than it is. The work we have in hand has no particular relations to the political boundaries which separate nations. It is an effort, by means of the colonization of an English speaking people, to propagate the religious faith and the religious institutions of English Puritanism over the world. In those principles only lies the whole strength of the movement. These are the seven locks of this modern Samson. And there should be, there might be, a combined effort of all in every land, not only in these States, but in England and Scotland, in Canada, Australia, and New Zealand, of all, I say, who read the English Bible, and adhere to this faith, and love these institutions, to plant them in every spot, where an English speaking emigrant makes a home. Exeter Hall should annually resound with eloquent appeals in behalf of this greatest enterprise of the English race. Every church in the British Isles, which adheres to our principles and institutions, should be annually summoned to its aid; and the desire to plant the Church of Christ in the wilderness, should become the universal passion of English and American Christians; as the desire of conquest was in the Roman mind. This, and nothing short of this, would be a ruling passion corresponding with our God-appointed Mission. To this ruling passion, we must attain, or utterly fail of our manifest destiny, and hear the awful curse of the Master at last, because we "knew not the time of our visitation."

Let us never forget, that all turns on the preservation and universal diffusion of those religious principles, which have been the seeds of our national growth, thus far. It is in those principles only, that our strength lies. We have no occasion to lay any flattering unction to our hearts, because we have Abraham for our father. God is now as of old, able of these stones to raise up children to Abraham. We do well to revere our fathers; but if we mean to finish what they began to build, and thus be truly and morally their children, we must carry their principles to the extremest limits of our national domain. We must diffuse them through all this multitudinous population, from ocean to ocean. We must represent them in institutions, as permanent as our everlasting mountains, as pure as the springs that gush out from our hills. We must never rest, till, as often as Sabbath morning returns to visit our lands, the church-going bell shall be heard on every foot of our domain, and summon every dweller on our soil to the place consecrated to spiritual worship and free christian instruction.

Then, and only then, shall our strength be irresistible. Then shall every spot which the soles of our feet tread upon, be ours. Then "shall our days be multiplied, and the days of our children, in this good land which the Lord gave unto our fathers, as the days of heaven upon earth."

The Missionary a Witness for Christ.

A

DISCOURSE

IN BEHALF OF THE

American Home Missionary Society,

PREACHED IN THE CITIES OF NEW YORK AND
BROOKLYN, MAY, 1858.

BY

REV. JAMES B. SHAW, D.D.,

PASTOR OF THE BRICK PRESBYTERIAN CHURCH, ROCHESTER, N. Y.

NEW YORK:
PUBLISHED BY THE AMERICAN HOME MISSIONARY SOCIETY,
BIBLE HOUSE, ASTOR PLACE.
1858.

JOHN A. GRAY, *Printer and Stereotyper*,
16 and 18 Jacob St., Fire-Proof Buildings.

DISCOURSE.

Mark 5 : 19. "Go home to thy friends and tell them how great things the Lord hath done for thee."

Two things concerning Christ are incidentally suggested by the text, which ought not to be overlooked. Home seems to have been as dear to the Saviour as to us. Most of his earthly life was spent with Joseph and Mary in their humble home at Nazareth. Humble it must have been, for they were poor; and holy it must also have been, for they were pious. Joseph and Mary were "both righteous before God, walking in all the ordinances and commandments of the Lord blameless." There was an altar in that house, and the morning incense, and the evening oblation. No outward sign distinguished it from the other houses in Nazareth—no cloud hovering above, no angel standing by the door. We must pass the threshold, join the little circle, and tarry until the dawn, if we would know what makes the place so dear to Jesus. We think he tarried there so many years, because that earthly home was more like the heaven which he had just left, than any other spot.

And if we need further proof that home was as dear to Jesus as to us—that he was not indifferent to its sweet attractions—we have only to recollect that about the last thing he did, and that, too, on the cross, and in his agony, was to provide a home for his mother. "When Jesus, therefore, saw his mother, and the disciple standing by whom he loved, he saith unto his mother, Woman, behold thy son! Then saith he to the disciple, Behold thy mother! And from that hour that disciple took her unto his own home." Let me remind you before leaving this thought, for we shall have it in mind during the discourse, that home is an expansive word. It may be so expanded as to include the community in which we dwell, and so expanded, still further, as to include our country, our dear fatherland. It is only extending the walls, throwing up a higher and broader roof, and spreading a little larger table.

The other thing incidentally suggested by the text, is the fact that our Lord owned and honored all the lawful relations of life. He honored these relations *directly* by assuming and fullfilling them. He became a son, and as such he was subject to his parents. He consented to be a citizen, and as such paid tribute to Cæsar—fullfilled all righteousness. And if a man would know whether patriotism is a virtue, and to be commended, let him think how Jesus loved Judea, and never left it—how his heart went out after the lost sheep of the house of Israel, and how he wept over Jerusalem when he could not save it. No man can be like Jesus, and not love his country. And so he *indirectly* honored the relations of life. He honored them when he gave the son of the widow of Nain back to his mother; and he honored them when he sent this man, who had his dwelling among the tombs, to his home and his friends. This fact is very distinctly brought out by the Evangelist, and no man should pass it with a careless glance. "And when he (Christ) was come into the ship, he that had been possessed with the devil, prayed him that he might be with him." But this was a request which *even Jesus* could not grant. "Howbeit Jesus suffered him not, but saith unto him, Go home to thy friends and tell them how great things the Lord hath done for thee." The devil had taken this man away from home, had compelled him to leave his own, and have his dwelling among the tombs. And the Saviour sent him back—commanded him to take up his duties just where he left off, and show that he was no longer possessed, by fullfilling those relations which God had ordained, and he voluntarily assumed. It is the devil who takes a man from home, and Christ who sends him back. These men who can not live with their wives, these wives who can not tarry with their husbands, these fathers and mothers who have cast their own children out of their hearts—we know by whom they are possessed. "Let no one think," says the great Reformer, "that the devil is dead, for as he that keepeth Israel, so he that hateth Israel, neither slumbers nor sleeps." Let me ask you to notice here, that this man seems to have understood as well as you and I, that home is an expansive word. He put a liberal construction on the Saviour's command. He did not consider himself as bound never to pass his own door-sill, nor cross the confines of his native town. As all throughout the region had seen him among the tombs, so all should see him clothed in his right mind—nothing but meekness, and gentleness, and love—the tears falling faster than two hands could wipe them away. "And he departed and began to publish in Decapolis, how great things Jesus had done for him, and all men did marvel." We shall see, before we close, why they marveled—why his story created such a sensation, and filled every heart with wonder, if nothing more.

As I am to speak this evening of Christ, I could not

refrain from alluding to these two things incidentally suggested by the text; and now I will call your attention to some things which have a more intimate relation to the Saviour's words. What I have to say, will be in the following order: *Christ is ready to do all for his disciples which he consistently can do. Christians are bound to tell all which Christ has done for them. Christians should seek to know more of Christ, that they may have more to tell. The reason why Christ does no more for many of his disciples. If Christians had more to tell of their Master's wonderful works in them, and were more faithful in telling it, our country would sooner be brought to Christ. It is the work of the American Home Missionary Society to send forth men to tell what great things the Lord hath done for them. The men sent forth and sustained by this Society, of all men, have most to tell.*

Let me say, in the outset, that in this discussion I include the whole work of Christ, his objective, as well as subjective work. Before the Lord touched your heart, or mine, he laid aside his glory, took on him the form of a servant, and became obedient unto death. His humiliation, and death, and resurrection, and ascension preceded our peace. And yet while the whole work of Christ is included, I have special reference to his work in us.

1. WE WERE TO SHOW IN THE FIRST PLACE, THAT CHRIST IS READY TO DO ALL FOR HIS PEOPLE THAT HE CONSISTENTLY CAN DO.

That Christ is *able* to do great things for his people, exceeding "abundantly above all that we ask or think," we can not deny without taking the crown from his head. Who shall limit his power, who "stretched the north over the empty place and hung the world upon nothing." And that Christ is *inclined* to use this great power in behalf of his people, is evident enough, from what he has already done—done for them. We send the doubter to Bethlehem, to Gethsemane, to the judgment hall, to Calvary, and to the sepulcher in the garden. He who left a throne, and such a throne, and endured all this for his disciples, is there any thing that he will not do for them—do for them unless their unbelief interpose a barrier? And if the man has been to the manger, and the cross, and the tomb, and come away a doubter still, then we would remind him of the *relations* which Christ's people sustain to their Lord; and ask him whether in these he can not find more evidence than even he may need? We are Christ's sheep—will not a man do all that he can for his sheep? We are Christ's friends—will not a man do all that he can for his friends? We are Christ's brethren—will not a man do all that he can for his brethren? We are Christ's body—will not a man do all that he can for his body? Would he have, with his own consent, a halting limb, or a withered arm, or a blemished eye—willingly wear a deformity through life? Beloved in the Lord, we will not tarry here; we will take it for granted that Christ is ready to do all for his people that he consistently can do, that, if they are ever straitened or stinted, we must not look to the right hand of the Father for the reason. The last thing to impeach is that heart which the spear pierced, and from which the water and the blood flowed forth. We pass to show,

2. THAT CHRISTIANS ARE BOUND TO TELL ALL THAT CHRIST HAS DONE FOR THEM.

And here some may remind me of the leper, who met Jesus as he came down from the mount. This leper is a favorite character with the silent disciple, and must not be passed unnoticed. "And behold there came a leper and worshiped him, saying, Lord, if thou wilt, thou canst make me clean. And Jesus put forth his hand, and touched him, saying, I will, be thou clean; and immediately his leprosy was cleansed; and Jesus saith unto him, See thou tell no man; but go thy way, show thyself unto the priest, and offer the gift that Moses commanded for a testimony unto them." And what do I learn from this—what, but that a man is bound to tell what Christ has done for him, unless Christ himself forbids? If a man has received a positive prohibition, a "Thou shalt *not*," then let him hold his peace; then let him pass among the multitude with a silent tongue, as if before he met Jesus, he were not a tainted thing whom no man would touch, not daring to enter his own house, or put his hand on the head of his own child. Besides this, we know that the Saviour then had a reason for commanding silence which he can not have now. A premature publication of his wonderful works, would have hastened the end; and he was not ready for the end. He had much to say and do before he reached Calvary. The leper can not help the silent believer. He must go in another direction to find an excuse for silence; and whither to go I can not say.

The rulers of the people thought it very unbecoming in the apostles, to tell what the Lord had done for them. They tried to silence them, and might as well have tried to silence the sea or the sky. "And they called them, and commanded them not to speak at all, nor teach in the name of Jesus. But Peter and John answered, and said unto them, Whether it be right in the sight of God, to hearken unto you more than unto God, judge ye. For we can not but speak the things which we have seen and heard." This was Peter's reason for speaking; he could not help it. It was just as natural, and almost as necessary for him to speak as for the sea or the sky to utter their voice. Had the Messiah lived and died and risen again—had the desire of all nations come and finished his work, and returned to the Father, and could they keep it all to themselves?

There was a time, brother, when you had something to say for Christ. Will you ever forget that morning when you awoke with a new hope in your heart, and a new song in your mouth? "Old things have passed away, behold all things have become new." What a bright day it was! Your heart was so full of joy and joyful anticipations, that if an angel had appeared suddenly by your side, you would hardly have been surprised; and had the firmament parted, and through the broken sky you had seen the land which is very far off, it would have seemed quite natural. You were looking for something great. When you went abroad into the city, you thought that all the bells ought to be ringing, that all the children ought to be out with palm branches in their hands, and that every man should be spreading his garment in the way; for you felt, oh! you felt that the Son of David had come. And the next Sabbath as you went to the house of God, your mother leaning on your arm; she so happy, and you so happy; it seemed as if the very stones were singing under your feet. Then you could not hold your peace; then you must speak. Nothing but a command—a command from God, and that straight and clear as the light—could have sealed your mouth. And if your heart—will you allow me, in all kindness to say it?—if your heart were as full of love now, as then, you would not ask me to prove that a man should tell what great things the Lord hath done for him. And if any one should forbid, you would answer with Peter before the Sanhedrim, "I can not but speak the things which I have seen and heard;" or with

Luther before the Diet at Worms, " Here I stand, I can not do otherwise. God help me. Amen." For one, if I had no tongue, I would talk with my fingers; and if I had no fingers, I would manage to make my features, inexpressive as they may be, say something for Christ.

3. Christians should seek to know more of Christ, that is, more experimentally, that they may have more to tell.

It is enough to state this proposition; it carries its own evidence, and no man who believes that the love of Christ is worth knowing and worth telling, will question it. It is important that, just here, I should drop a word of caution. There is a wide difference between seeking for ourselves and seeking for others—between gathering to hoard, and gathering to give; and Christ's disciples oftentimes make the sad mistake of seeking for themselves, and gathering to hoard. They would have more faith, more love, more peace, more joy, a brighter hope and a stronger assurance, and have them to keep, not to impart. It is not of the multitude passing by their door, on the way to death, nor of the world lying in the wicked one, that they think. They are engrossed with their own doubts, and fears, and forebodings. *They* would be delivered—they would be comforted and arrive at the last station on the celestial highway ahead of time. And this is one reason—we shall look at another in a moment—why Christ does so little for them. They seek grace just as the miser seeks gold, the one to put it in his chest, and the other to hide it in his heart.

And as we are urging you here to know more of Christ, that you may have more to tell, perhaps this is the place to say, that a man never speaks so effectively as when he speaks from experience. When the demoniac told his story they all marveled, because it was his story. This is the man who dwelt among the tombs; this the man whom no chains could bind; this the man whose frantic wail "awoke the echoes of the mountain, and startled the fishermen in their lonely night watch on the sea." Yes, I am the man; and among the tombs, and with the dead, and frantic as ever I should have been, had I not met the Son of David.

Yes, they all marveled, for this was the demoniac himself, and he told his own story. Would you convince me that Christ can heal, bring hither the man who had a withered hand, a hand that before he met Jesus, could not lift to the mouth the food which the other hand earned. Would you convince me that Christ can open the eyes of the blind, bring hither Bartimeus who sat by the wayside begging; let me look on the eyeballs that had searched so long for the light, and would have been searching still, had not some good friend said, Jesus of Nazareth passeth by. Would you convince me that Christ can raise the dead, bring hither the man who had been in the grave four days; let me see the head that was bound about with a napkin, and hear the tongue that could not answer a sister's call; and, oh! would you convince me that Christ can do a still greater work—that he can raise such as are dead in trespasses and sins—that he can open the sepulcher of the soul and awake it to newness of life—find some man who has heard the life-giving call—some man who has laid aside his grave clothes, and come forth. Conduct me into the prison-house, and let me see Manasseh; lead me through the street called Straight, into the house of Judas, and let me see Saul. We want the man who can show his broken fetters, who can point to his discarded burthen, and let us look into his empty sepulcher.

Perhaps we should not leave this part of our subject without guarding against another misapprehension.

We are pleading with men, not to tell what they have done for Christ, but what Christ hath done for them. It is not what we have said, but he hath said—not what we have given, but he hath given—not what we have wrought, but he hath wrought. Pride prompts a man to speak of himself; gratitude and love urge him to speak of Christ; and it is to gratitude and love that the Christian should give heed.

4. LET US NOW LOOK AT THE REASON WHY CHRIST DOES NO MORE FOR MANY OF HIS DISCIPLES.

It will not be denied, I think, that Christ does far more for some of his disciples than for others. Some of God's children seem to have attained "unto the measure of the stature of the fullness of Christ;" they are full-grown men, can bear a man's burthen, and do a man's work. These favored ones look down on the storm; they have pitched their tent higher than the clouds can climb, and live on that sunny summit where the darkness and the light no more divide the day. Others of God's children seem to be stunted from their birth. If they grow at all, it is so slowly as not to be perceptible to an ordinary eye. I have seen a child nearly twenty years old, in a cradle; and I have seen a Christian who numbered as many years of the new life, in a cradle. He never leaves the cradle—eating only as he is fed, and sleeping only as he is rocked—living for no purpose, unless it be that others may have something to do—*cradle Christians*—the Church of God is full of them. Now whence this difference? Why do some receive so much more than others? The chief reason—not by any means the only one—but the chief reason is, that we do not make an honest surrender of ourselves and ours to the Lord; and are not willing to be brought into those exigencies where alone he can do great things for us. Are we in his hands as the clay in the hands of the potter? Can he make any thing of us that he pleases? The clay never resists, never protests. He may make it a vessel unto honor or dishonor, and the clay interposes no objection. He may take the lump and form an article sacred as the urn which contains the ashes of the dead, or common as the bowl from which the poor man takes his mid-day meal, and the clay never asks why. "Shall the clay say to him that fashioneth it, What makest thou?" Are we the clay? May he make us any thing that he pleases, and put us to any use that his glory demands? Perhaps an honest scrutiny would show that no one thing, in our inventory, is entirely at God's disposal—no one thing, unless it should be "the torn, and the lame, and the sick." Alas! some bring nothing to the altar except what the shamble rejects. If our self-surrender were sincere—if according to the motto on Calvin's seal, we have "given all to God—kept nothing for ourselves," how is it that there is never a demand on God's part without a struggle on ours? How is it that we shrink, as if by a sinful instinct, from every strait where the arm of the Lord might be made bare? And thus struggling, and thus shrinking, we still ask, Why hath not the Lord done greater things for us? We want Joseph's patience, without going into the pit. We want Daniel's faith, without entering the lions' den. We want Paul's joy, without passing into the inner prison. We want John's raptures, without an exile in Patmos. We sigh for Abraham's faith, pray for it, wonder that it is not given, when the voice and the vision of God could not bring us one step towards Moriah. We would have the waters part, without approaching the sea—eat the manna and drink of the water which comes from the rock, without entering the desert; and feast on the clusters of Canaan, without foregoing the flesh-pots of Egypt.

5. We are to show, in the next place, that if Christians had more to tell of the Saviour's wonderful works in them, and were more faithful in telling it, our country would sooner be brought to Christ.

And we believe that this country is to be brought to Christ. We can not deny that there are many omens of evil, clouds in the sky, voices in the air, and sounds under our feet, which foretell any thing but peace. And yet we can also discover omens of good. If there are clouds in the firmament, there are also broader patches of clear sky; and the sounds over head and under foot are not all portentous. God "has not forgotten to be gracious, nor hath he in anger shut up his tender mercies," as this great awakening shows. The altars are not all cold, nor the intercessors all dead, nor has the Shekinah departed from our sanctuaries. Until the Lord shall forsake his own house, disown his own word, and deny his own child; until he refuses to hear, and forbears to help, we will not despair for the republic, although the sun should become black as sackcloth of hair, and the moon wade in blood. We can not believe that, in digging these channels, and constructing these roads—in redeeming these waste places, and founding these cities—in planting these institutions of learning, and erecting these houses of mercy, and these houses of prayer, we have only been extending the dominion of sin—only been adding another province to the empire of Satan. Our fathers took possession of this land for God, and when they died left it to God; and will not God take care of his own? If Jonah is on board, Jonah must be cast into the sea. If Judas is in the company, Judas must go to his own place; and if the name of these traitors to truth, and these fugitives from God should be legion, yet our text will not suffer us to forget that there is One who can cast the legion out. We do not then despair for the republic. We can not believe that the loom of destiny is weaving our shroud. Others think that they can hear the sound of the shuttle, but we suspect it is only a ringing in their ears.

To bring our country to Christ will involve much work, and many conflicts; blood may be shed, lives lost, and some win a martyr's crown. But we have tried weapons and trusty allies—God is on our side, and legions of angels about our banner; nay, the very stones of the field are in league with us, and the stars that fought against Sisera will not stand aloof from the battle. And, our country safe, the world is safe. Allured by our example, and guided by our light, people after people will join the smiling brotherhood of christian nations, and swell the hosannas that welcome the returning King.

Now if our country is to be brought to Christ, would not the work be sooner done if every disciple of our ascended Lord had more to tell, and were more faithful in telling it? Malachi, in speaking of the latter day, the day which ought to be here, says: "Then they that feared the Lord spake often one to another, and the Lord hearkened and heard." It seems *he* was interested in the conversation, and most deeply interested, too, "for a book of remembrance was written before him, for them that feared the Lord and that thought upon his name." Oh! if we spake often one to another—if we had more to tell, and told it—if our hearts were so full of the love of Christ that we could not hold our peace—if we went every where, like the scattered disciples, preaching the word—if every christian man were, what every christian man ought to be, a witness for God, how much longer would that morning without clouds delay, or that chariot which is to bring the King, tarry? Oh! it is a sin and a shame—and you and I must come in for a share—that Christ has been kept so long out of his rightful possessions, and especially that he is not now the undisputed Lord of this favored, but faithless, and yet we hope, not forsaken land.

6. WE HASTEN TO SHOW, IN THE NEXT PLACE, THAT IT IS THE WORK OF THE AMERICAN HOME MISSIONARY SOCIETY, TO SEND FORTH MEN TO TELL WHAT GREAT THINGS THE LORD HATH DONE FOR THEM.

They send forth *men*, and that is something not to be overlooked; and not men merely, but men whom God has called, whom God has qualified, and who have spared no cost or pains, to fit themselves for the work.

I believe in the tract. Although but a leaf from the tree of life, yet it is from the tree of life, and must have healing virtue. But a man is better than a tract. I believe in a book, a good book; for although it can not open itself, nor get into a man's hand whether he will or no, yet it has its work to do, and does it well; but a man is better than a book. And I believe in *the* book, the book which God gave, which he hangs as a light in my tabernacle, and holds before my feet as I walk the highway; but inasmuch as there is more power in the spoken than the written word, I believe that a man with the Bible in his heart, and the Bible in his mouth, is the best edition of the book. Then I have great faith in the colporteur. I believe that the colporteur is one of our grand discoveries; and that we shall have the millennium here the sooner, because he has harnessed himself so willingly to the chariot of the King. But an ordained minister of Christ—one who can baptize the children, bury the dead, spead the table of the Lord in the wilderness, and be a shepherd to the scattered sheep, must be better than a colporteur.

And this Society sends forth these men to tell what great things the Lord hath done for them. They are not sent forth to preach denominational peculiarities, the things which keep us apart, and which never, since the tried stone, the precious stone on which all must build, was laid in Zion, brought one sinner to Christ. They are not sent forth to run dividing lines and build separating walls—and build probably with stones stolen from another man's foundation. They go to tell what the Lord hath done for them, and is ready to do for all who will believe on his name. They take the attitude of the first disciples: "Verily, verily, I say unto thee, we speak that we do know, and testify that we have seen." The forgiveness on which they dwell is a forgiveness which they feel. The peace which they offer is a peace which they possess; and the joy of which they beg every man to partake, is a joy which came from God, and has made their hearts its earthly home. Oh! it is not so much Christ in the manger whom they preach, or Christ in the garden, or Christ on the cross, or Christ in the grave, or even Christ in glory, but Christ in them. And it is surprising what a sympathy such men as these seem to have with the Saviour. As a humble disciple of the Lord Jesus once said to me: "I have followed my Saviour all the way through. I have been with him every where." Others read how Jesus wrestled in the garden—they wrestle with him. Others read how he was set at naught at the judgment-seat—they are set at naught with him, put on the purple robe, and wear the crown of thorns. Others read how Jesus was crucified—they are crucified with him. Others read how he was buried in the sepulcher which no mortal relics had profaned—they are buried with him. Others read how he rose again—they arise with him; with him endure the humiliation of the grave, and with him share the glory of the resurrection.

We would not imply that these men do nothing but tell what great things the Lord hath done for them. This is their chief, but not their sole mission. They have a hand and a heart for every good work. No opportunity is missed, no opening neglected. Never too disheartened to toil, nor too weary to pray, like the Lord they go from the multitude to the mountain, and then back again from the mountain to the multitude. They lay the foundations of society, and put in the braces which bind the superstructure together. Nor is there a thing in the community, which time will spare and God guard, that does not bear the imprint of their hands.

7. But this brings us to our last thought: the men sent forth and sustained by this Society, of all men, have most to tell.

The Apostle to the Gentiles speaks of the Lord Jesus as the "finisher of our faith." There is such a thing as a finished faith—a faith which never wavers, never hesitates; a faith which asks no questions, and seeks no supports; a faith which looks the calmest when the sky lowers, and walks the steadiest when the earth reels; the faith of Noah when he laid down the keel of the ark; the faith of Abraham when he bound the unresisting victim to the wood; the faith of Jacob, when he wrestled all night with the angel, and prevailed; the faith of Joshua, when he called on the sun and moon to stand still, and they obeyed; the faith of Elijah, when he raised the windows of heaven, and let the willing water come; the faith of our Lord Jesus, when he opened the door of the grave, and brought his friend Lazarus back.

Faith, beloved in the Lord, is a strange plant. It

does best in darkness, grows strongest in a chilly air and under a wintry sky, and never looks so fresh and green as when every thing beside is withering with the frost. Nothing like the vigor of an arctic winter for faith. It is the balmy air, the transparent atmosphere, the summer's sun, that are most fatal to faith. This is the reason why the cup comes round so often to the believer, why he must take deeper draughts from the bitter bowl, than his neighbor; this is the reason why he must be planted on the north side of the wall, in the shade and the cold, away from the sun. Faith requires a northern exposure. Long droughts, hard winters, and such skies as Paul found in the stormy Adriatic, when "neither sun nor stars appeared for many days;" these are the things which make faith thrive, which "finish" faith.

Now, no men are so favorably situated for securing a finished faith as our Home Missionaries. They live, emphatically, on the north side of the wall. What hardships they undergo; what privations they endure—the wolf outside the door, and perhaps something more dreadful than the wolf within. Alas!—is that the word to use?—alas! they must trust or die. And yet, and for this very reason, these are the men who know most of the loving kindness, and the everlasting faithfulness of the Lord. Christ always does most for those who do least for themselves. "Whosoever shall seek to save his life, shall lose it; and whosoever shall lose his life shall save it." That is the law of the kingdom. Would we know what Christ is—I am afraid that many who call him Lord, do not know what he is—would we know what Christ is, we must start for the West; we must press on to the outposts of civilization; we must enter that cabin, free alike to the rain, and the snow, and the wayfarer's foot, and the angel's wing, and find the man who has suffered most for the Master. He can tell you what Christ is. Perhaps he is on a bed of sickness; perhaps he is watching by the side of his dying wife; now feeling at the wrist, if the pulse still beats; now bending down to the lips, if the lungs still heave. Perhaps he has just closed the eyes of his last child, and is kneeling down by the cold clay, to ask the Lord for a shroud and a coffin. Oh! how can he deny the dust so dear a decent burial? Brother, did you ever go to the mercy-seat on an errand like that? This man can tell you what Christ is. Oh! he can tell you what Christ is! Not an angel before the throne knows so much, it may be, of the Saviour—has tasted so much of his goodness, or gazed so often on his glory. Many a time has he left toil, and care, and sorrow behind, ascended Tabor and seen the Lord transfigured. Such a man has been under my own roof; and it seemed better, even, than entertaining an angel—it was a little like a visit from the Lord himself. No, I am not going back to the past, nor speaking of the dead. Such men are now in the land; and that is one reason why the land is yet above the waters.

And shall not these men be sustained—sustained whatever the cost? They ask only food and raiment, nothing more than the day-laborer's wages, just enough to keep the lamp from going out. And shall they not be sustained? What could we do which would better please the Lord, who loves us all, and would more certainly secure his blessing? Nor let any say that it can not be done. Have we parted with our last luxury? Do we carry our whole wardrobe on our backs? Have we been brought to one meal a day? Have we nothing left but hope? Let us stand by these men of God so long as one undivided loaf remains. If we neglect them, if we suffer them to be brought into still greater straits how can we meet that Judge who, although he was rich, yet for our sakes became poor—so rich and so poor that he had not where to lay the head, which but for us, would never have needed a place to rest.

And should we not also sustain that *Society*, which has sent these men forth, and, in our behalf, assumed the responsibility of their support? My interest in the American Home Missionary Society, is not of recent origin. Living, then, in this my native city, I may say that I was by when it was born. I knew it when it wore its swaddling clothes; and a goodly child it was. I was present, I think, when, for the first time, it celebrated its birth-day; and since, I have been more familiar than most persons with its operations. It has been my privilege, in various ways, to coöperate with it; and my whole ministry has been spent in a region of our country for which it has done great things. Western New York, it is my heartfelt conviction, would never have been Western New York, but for the American Home Missionary Society. This, I know, will in some quarters be regarded as questionable praise. Some associate nothing but evil with our name. And it can not be denied that, in more senses than one, we have a prolific soil, a soil that abhors barrenness, as nature abhors a vacuum. It *will* bring forth. No one knows this better than the adversary. He hath sowed tares, and gathered, as every one who sows there does, a large increase. And many think that we grow nothing but tares. They overlook the wheat—the wheat, I mean, which goes to God's garner. They forget the great husbandman. We have schools in Western New York, schools of the humbler and higher grades, and we have as many churches as schools. We have asylums and hospitals, homes for the friendless, and homes for the fatherless. We have two colleges, two universities, and two theological seminaries, which it will be glory enough for the metropolis to excel; and we have one State prison, which we are enabled to keep full only by *importation.* Are there any churches in the land which, according to their ability, do more or give more than ours?—any churches where there is so much activity, with so little extravagance? so much freedom of opinion, with so little error?—churches which God has more significantly owned and honored? It is true, we believe that any form of life is preferable to death; that the heart had better beat too fast than not beat at all; and we have no partiality for a religion laid out, no matter how fine the shroud or costly the coffin. That we have had things to lament and put away, we will not deny. We have experienced the evils incidental to new settlements, to society in its infancy. But we have outgrown these things. When we became men, we put away childish things; and yet some will still upbraid us with the tottering, and stumbling, and occasional falls of our childhood. We wonder if our brethren, who are so dissatisfied with us, are themselves enjoying a millennial state? Instead of their standing aloof and warning others to beware, let them come and see us. We give them a cordial invitation, begging them only not to leave their eyes behind. A blind man will find nothing but darkness. There are some, estimable men too, that we never expect to convince. Nor could we convince them of error if they were pleased to believe that our fertile valleys are salt plains, and our beautiful lakes dead seas; that nothing can grow in the one, or live in the other.

Now, as I believe in Western New York, so do I believe in the Home Missionary Society; for this Society has done more than any other agency in making us what we are. The first missionaries who came among us — Seth Williston, Jedediah Bushnell, and Amasa Jerome, now in glory—were sent by New England Missionary Societies, and as early as the year 1799. So that we, with all the world, owe something to New England; and we are not ashamed to acknowledge it, nor do we mean to forget it. Not that New England needs any man's patronage or praise. Her patron is on the throne, her glory God will guard. While, however, we are indebted to other institutions, our heaviest debt is due to the Society whose anniversary has called us together. This Society fed us, when too weak to feed ourselves, and even now scatters the morning manna about many a tent. And we mean to stand by it, for the best of all reasons, because it stood by us. To forsake the American Home Missionary Society, or even cleave to it with a divided heart, would seem like treason to the memory of our fathers; and as to rending it, we would as soon rend the shroud that wraps our dead.

This allusion to the dead reminds us of that dispensation by which, during the year past, Western New York and this Society have been both bereaved. Our honored and revered President, one of the founders of this Society, ever its fast friend, and who loved it unto the end, is with us no more. Henry Dwight, the bearer of an illustrious name, which he received and transmitted untarnished, was a man of refinement and culture, of a sound judgment, a far-seeing eye, a conciliating spirit, and a heart true to Christ as the needle to the north. Our brother and father died "in a good old age, an old man and full of years, and was gathered unto his people." The angel of the Lord found him sleeping in this world-wide prison house, and said unto him: "Arise up quickly and follow me." As the angel spoke, his fleshy fetters fell, and "the gate which leadeth unto the city opened unto him of his own accord." To find him we have only to follow his foot-prints; and the same foot-prints will lead us to the Lamb. *Here*, our brother was a light on the headlands overlooking the sea of life; *there*, he is a star in one of the constellations which burn about the throne of God.

In conclusion, let me say, that I never loved this Society better than to-night. It has done nothing for me to forgive. Of all our benevolent Societies, it has always had the first place in my heart; and that place it shall hold, until it changes its Constitution, ignores its history, and denies itself. And is this the time to stand aloof, cast suspicious looks, and utter distrustful words? Now, when its work, and its responsibility, and its need, are greater than ever, shall we tie its hands, muzzle its mouth, and repress the pulsations of its mighty heart? Let us rally around our own Home Missionary Society, yield it a heartier support, give it a larger income, and thus enable it to fulfill its three-fold mission—bless the people, save the republic, and welcome the coming generation to a land of light, and love, and liberty, and life—a land whose walls shall be salvation, and whose gates shall be praise, GOD HER GLORY, THE LORD HER EVERLASTING LIGHT.

THE WORK; AND THE WORKMEN.

A

DISCOURSE

IN BEHALF OF THE

American Home Missionary Society,

PREACHED IN THE CITY OF NEW YORK,

MAY 8, 1859.

BY

WILLIAM T. DWIGHT, D.D.,

PASTOR OF THE THIRD CONGREGATIONAL CHURCH IN PORTLAND, ME.

NEW YORK:

PUBLISHED BY THE AMERICAN HOME MISSIONARY SOCIETY,

BIBLE HOUSE, ASTOR PLACE.

1859.

John A. Gray, *Printer and Stereotyper*,
16 & 18 Jacob St., Fire-Proof Buildings.

DISCOURSE.

Luke 24 : 47. "And that repentance and remission of sins should be preached in his name among all nations, beginning at Jerusalem."

From the connection of thought which exists beween this verse and the forty ninth, and also the fourth verse of Acts, 1st, it would seem that they must have been all uttered by our Lord on the same occasion; and that, but a brief season before his ascension. But however this may have been, the text prescribes to his apostles the great course of duty on which they were to enter so soon after his departure, and which they were to prosecute during life. They were to proclaim among all nations repentance and remission of sins in the name of the once crucified, but now enthroned Mediator. Greek and Roman, Scythian and barbarian, nay, the remotest dwellers on the earth, were to hear from the lips of these witnesses of their Master's death and resurrection, the good tidings of great joy. Whither, after their hallowed course of journeying and preaching should have fully commenced, it was to be subsequently directed, the passage gives no intimation; but the point, the place of its commencement, was announced as fixed. "Beginning at Jerusalem," was the sovereign charge. Their work was to be the greatest ever to be performed by mortals; for all the labors of patriarchs and prophets like those of John the Baptist, were to possess but little dignity and to accomplish but little benefit for the race in comparison; but that work could have no commencement other than at Jerusalem. Ephesus and Smyrna and Sardis, Athens and Corinth and Philippi, nay, Rome, the mistress of the world, were all to welcome the mystery of the Gospel. But to none of them might an apostle journey, to none might messenger or message of salvation be ever speeded, until after repentance and remission of sins had been effectually proclaimed in Jerusalem.

Such was the high command of the Saviour, given in anticipation of his ascension. The narrative of the Book of Acts informs us that it was strictly obeyed. The apostles left not Jerusalem, but continued with the one hundred and twenty disciples in prayer and supplication until the day of Pentecost was fully come; when the miracles of tongues was wrought, when Peter first preached repentance and remission of sins in the name of Jesus, and when three thousand converts attested their faith in him as the Messiah, by receiving baptism. They left not Jerusalem, but continued to preach and to bear witness to their Master, until, after thousands of additional converts had been made, and a great company of priests had become obedient to the faith, the martyrdom of Stephen took place, and this army of converts became scattered throughout Palestine and into other regions. The apostles still left not Jerusalem, except for brief visits to other towns in Judea, or in Samiara and in Galilee, until after eight years had elapsed from Christ's resurrection, when Peter was sent to Cornelius. Then, after the Gospel had been published, and churches had been established "throughout all Judea and Galilee and Samaria," churches which were "walking in the fear of the Lord and in the comfort of the Holy Ghost," and "were multiplied," then the beginning of the great work had been made, and then that work was to be pursued among other nations. That the line of separation which the Saviour's hand had thus drawn, might now be crossed, the visit to Cornelius was the announcement; yet that announcement was preliminary only, for four additional years must also elapse before it was crossed a second time. Then Barnabas and Saul were sent forth by the Holy Ghost, from Antioch in Syria; and then, ere their return, they preached to the Gentiles in Antioch in Pisidia, salvation through the one effectual name.

"Beginning at Jerusalem," was thus the law of that vast missionary enterprise which dates back more than eighteen centuries, which in subsequent ages was seemingly suspended for long intervals, but whose rapid progress during the last fifty years has given such vigor to faith and ardor to hope. It needs not be here added that the entire ministry of Christ himself, whether prosecuted in person, or by successive missions of the twelve and of the seventy, was controlled by the same principle. Neither he nor they went into the way of the Gentiles, but to the lost sheep of the house of Israel. The Greek inhabitants of the Decapolis were not indeed forbidden to intermingle with the Jews, to whom, when journeying through that region, he preached the advent of the kingdom of heaven: the Syro-Phœnician woman might also implore, and successfully, his healing aid in behalf of her demoniac daughter. But such cases were not even exceptions. To the seed of Abraham as such, to his own people and kindred according to the flesh, he came preaching peace; while the Gentile from other lands who was occasionally numbered among his hearers, though never personally addressed, was permitted to remain.

The text and these great historical facts which the

sacred narrative proclaims to us as a practical commentary upon its true import, affirm a most important principle: That the great work of making known the Gospel of salvation which Christ has assigned to his followers in all ages and countries, is to be first effectually commenced by them at home. While they are never to overlook the similar need of other nations, while the unconverted world demands their efforts and their prayers, the claims of their own country are to be ever esteemed prior in the order of nature, and often also in that of time. "Beginning at Jerusalem," is to be the motto and the law, at the present day and in our own beloved country. The duty is as absolute now as it was on the day of Pentecost, for the principle is unchangeable.

Views such as these originated, thirty three years since, THE AMERICAN HOME MISSIONARY SOCIETY. Many of its founders had been previously connected with similar Societies in different States, and especially in New England. Good men who deeply felt the power of our Lord's command in this passage, had been for many years coöperating in assisting needy churches in their own neighborhood to secure the stated ministrations of the Gospel; and also in sending forth pioneer missionaries to the scattered settlements in Western New York and Pennsylvania, and to the frontier border of Lake Erie. The work which these good men then undertook and gradually accomplished, was indeed a "work of faith and labor of love," and it was done in much "patience of hope." But when in the fullness of time, this National Society was formed, they gladly transferred to its vastly superior efficiency the great trust which they had previously assumed of sending the Gospel to the widely increasing and distant settlements; while they still sustained, in whole or in part, the work of assisting the needy congregations within their respective States. Such has continued to be the relative sphere of duty until the present time. Thirty three years, as just remarked, have passed away, and the American Home Missionary Society has been steadily growing, until it has taken deep root and filled the land. It has sent out its boughs unto the sea, and its branches unto the river, and the hills are covered with its shadow.

The second article of its Constitution is as follows: "The object of this Society shall be to assist congregations that are unable to support the gospel ministry, and to send the Gospel to the destitute, within the United States; also to coöperate with evangelical Christians in the support of Home Missions in nominally christian countries, to such an extent as the funds of the Institution may justify." Confining myself to the first half of this article, which includes what has long constituted its entire sphere of operation, I would observe that it specifies the appropriate work of the Society; and that it also names the agents whom the Society commissions to perform that work. We shall proceed to notice with some particularity THE WORK and THE WORKMEN of the American Home Missionary Society.

Its appropriate work is, in the words of the article: "To assist congregations that are unable to support the gospel ministry, and to send the Gospel to the destitute, within the United States." This is, in its essence, the same with that which is specified in our passage: that of making known to multitudes who would otherwise remain in ignorance, the Gospel of salvation by the Lord Jesus Christ. The language of the article is more particular than that of the text; for the article speaks of local churches, while the text does not name them. Local churches were not gathered until after the Saviour's ascension, but within the first five years they were planted throughout Palestine. Let us notice this work in several of its distinct aspects.

The work is that of *Home* Missions: The Society's sphere of operation is "the United States." It is one among many great kindred institutions, through all of which Christians are steadily laboring to extend the kingdom of their Master. But while some of these are confined to foreign countries, as their appropriate sphere of effort, while others may operate in all foreign lands and in our own, this Society, as its name denotes, is practically restricted to our own country. Its work, we repeat it, is that of Home Missions; and except in the contingency which is named in the latter part of the article, it can embark in none other. Our whole country, all our respective States and Territories, constitute the Jerusalem where only its work is to begin; and unlike the literal city of that name, they are the Jerusalem where only is its work to be perpetually prosecuted. We would cherish not the slightest jealousy toward one of these kindred associations; the kingdom of Christ needs them all; we bid "God speed" to them all, and pray that all may be trebled in their efficiency. We would name here particularly that noble institution, the American Board; while we would at the same time rejoice that this Society is, in all its length and breath of survey and operation, a Home Missionary body. Its existence was originally dictated by sympathies, interests, principles, which are sanctioned alike by nature and by grace; and the same sympathies, interests, principles have augmented its power for a third of a century, until now its broad stream wafts health and gladness to a thousand churches of our God. Man has not been formed to survey the near and the remote, either in space or duration, with an equal eye. Angels, we have no reason to believe, are elevated either intellectually or morally, above the necessity of these discriminations. Nay, there can be but one Being to whom the scenes of earth's last morning and of this evening can be alike vivid, to whose ear the young convert's first hymn is now rising as distinctly as the seraph's raptures before the throne; because he fills all time—all immensity. As creatures, and therefore as human beings and as Christians, the circle of which each of us is made to himself the centre, gradually fades as it widens; so that none but the half-crazed cosmopolite will be moving professedly in a circle whose centre is every where and its circumference no where. We begin existence, we advance to consciousness, we then enter on voluntary action, within a circuit of relations how narrow; and how slowly is that circuit enlarged, that it may include the friends, the acquaintances of childhood and early youth. From the family to the neighborhood, to another quarter of the village, to the adjoining town, thence in time—it may be—to the neighboring city, and thence beyond the circuit of the State, and thence still more distant, is the transit, until at length we grasp with some little energy the conception of country, of our nation and native land. Man may in time receive the one great complex idea of country, his natural sympathies—his moral and sanctified emotions may become proportionally diffusive; but the whole process of transition and enlargement only illustrates the principle that his sphere of duty and efficiency is primarily at home. The child practically comprehends this no less than the philosopher, the nomadic Tartar as truly as the inhabitant of London. The family, the Church, the State, were otherwise unmeaning terms, nay our entire race were but an immense aggregate of individuals, as unconnected as the sands on the sea-shore. What a testimony to this principle was once given by the Jewish captives, who wept by the rivers of Babylon when they remembered Zion, and then exclaimed: "How shall we sing the Lord's song in a strange land? If I forget thee, O Jerusalem! let my right hand forget her cunning!" What a testimony was also given by the Apostle of the Gentiles, when he exclaimed: "I could wish that myself were accursed from Christ for my brethren, my kinsmen, according to the flesh!"

The sphere of action of this Society, we say again, has been chosen in direct conformity to this principle: its great work is to diffuse the Gospel at home. It interferes not in act or purpose with institutions that bear the Gospel to other nations; it is a co-worker with them all in that vast field which includes the world, but its efforts are concentrated and engrossed by one portion of that field—our own country. The moral wastes of our own land can not be cultivated and changed into the garden of the Lord by the scattered, or the associated efforts of separate local churches and of benevolent individuals; great national institutions are also indispensable, and among them as the very foremost has ever stood this Society. As a home institution, its efficiency is immensely augmented: this is, necessarily, the universal law. As the prosperity of the family, of the local church, of the city, the state, or the nation, can in the same circumstances be tenfold better promoted by its own action than by that of any other similar body, so the Home Missionary enterprise is necessarily conducted with vastly greater advantage than the Foreign. Broad as may be the region which it embraces, although stretching from the western slope of the Alleghanies to the Pacific, and from the fountains of the Mississippi to the Gulf, it is still one country, it is our own land, in distinction from all other lands. No three months' or six months' wearisome voyage must precede the missionary's arrival at his destined field of effort; no tedious season of acclimation—a process scarce ever effectual in its safeguard — must then extend through successive years. He needs no preliminary study of a foreign language, civilized or barbarous, the whole structure of which is so dissimilar to his own that years elapse before it becomes the familiar, the fit expression of his thoughts. The gift of tongues, were he to receive it as largely as did Paul, would be but a disservice, for even inspired Paul could write and speak only in Hellenistic Greek; while he addresses his countrymen from the Ohio to the mouth of the Columbia in one common language, whose idiomatic transparency not a dialect disturbs. This Society needs no diplomatic agents, American or foreign, to secure protection for its missionaries or for the converts whom they make. The idea of persecution, or of toleration by the government as a boon, or of interference in their work of publishing the Gospel by a human being, never enters the mind. The work in all its magnitude and ever continuing, is still performed wholly at home; in our own healthful climate; under the protection of our own constitution and laws; in the midst of our own homogeneous population; and at a vastly reduced expenditure of money. What an augmented efficiency is thus possessed by this Society! Other nations must also receive from us the Gospel, the whole earth is in time to become the kingdom of Immanuel, but what an argument for our hearty coöperation in its efforts is urged in the consideration that its work is that of *Home* Missions!

Such is the work in its region of operation: We should also notice *its magnitude.* This is sufficient to call for all the resources of this Society and for all other kindred agencies, were they trebled. Secure, were it practicable, all that could be justly demanded for the foreign missionary work; suppose that the whole world east of the Atlantic and west of the Pacific were to be converted to God; the work to be done here at home, would still transcend estimate. Let us limit the region of labor to what is proper missionary ground, excluding wholly New England and the eastern half of New York, New Jersey, and Pennsylvania; and the region remaining which the missionaries of this Society are now traversing and are in time to traverse, exceeds a million and a half of square miles. True, other agencies will be also imperatively summoned; true, large portions of this vast area will be preöccupied by them or will continue unoccupied, from the utter inability of this Society or of any single institution to enter on them. Still the congregations which prefer the Presbyterian or the Congregational polity are already so numerous, such mutitudes of congregations are so rapidly forming wherever American emigration moves westward, and each coming year assures us of so vast an increase hereafter, that sobriety of estimate is scarcely practicable. The buffalo and the savage alike retreat instinctively, as the tide of civilization moves steadily, ceaselessly onward, with no ebbing wave: a tide not like that which rushed forth from Germany and Gaul over the waning empire of Rome, and then swept back in alternate desolations, but wafting enterprise, thrift, strength on all its advancing waves. Like an eruption from Etna or Mauna Loa, the flood moves irresistibly onward; and it is the work of this Society and of all other available agencies under God so to direct it, that it shall waft life and salvation instead of destruction. The statesmen and political economists of Europe look amazed and aghast at our unprecedented growth as a nation, for their own history and experience afford them no standards of calculation.

The approaching census will announce that our population exceeds that of the British isles: the census of 1870, that we shall at that time outnumber the population of France: the census of 1880, that we shall then, probably outnumber the population of Russia in Europe, and be far the most powerful nation on the globe: the census of 1900, that we shall all but equal, if not exceed a hundred millions. Nothing human can arrest this prodigious increase, its causes are as fixed as those which produce the ascent of flame or the reverberation of thunder, so that the practical question for living American patriots and Christians, is, How is this vast population which is so speedily to take our places, to be made a moral, religious people? It is not the question, How shall we continue till the next century to be one people; for it is impossible that we should be disunited. Slavery or no slavery, the manufacturing against the cotton and tobacco interests, increased jealousies and variances ending for the time in civil war—all can not long divide us: the community of descent of language, laws, religion, historical renown, and the natural features of our country, all proclaim that what God has thus joined together, man can not put asunder. But how are the one hundred millions of the year 1900 to enter on that century a moral and religious people; instead of being then a nation, which, inflated by its resistless strength, and steeped in luxury, shall neither fear God nor regard man? This Society undertakes, relying on God's omnipotent grace, to answer this fearful question to the full measure of its own responsibility, and that answer we have given in the language of its Constitution. It will "assist congregations that are unable to support the Gospel ministry, and will send the Gospel to the destitute, within the United States." It purposes and promises to do this, and it neither promises nor purposes to do any thing more. This it has been actually doing from its very organization for thirty-three years; and its friends—to use Scriptural language, are "shut up" to this single mode of operation by its Constitution, by God's economy of grace, and by the very structure of society. This already immense population, swollen every year, in addition to its own rapid natural increase, by streams of emigrants from New England and the Middle States and by the twenty or thirty myriads who seek a better home than Europe affords them, consists not of Scythian or Tartar nomads, it can never sink into Asiatic or European barbarism. But such a population, breaking through the restraints imposed by our constitution and laws, may in time become a military republic, as maddened by the lust for universal dominion as was that of revolutionary France; and such a republic, after British America and Mexico had been acquired either by conquest or annexation, would then hasten on to reduce the different countries of South America into as many submissive provinces. The work then of the Society is of no less magnitude than this: With its many coädjutors, it is to plant and cherish the institutions of the Gospel wherever they are needed—especially through our entire Western States and Territories, and thus to preserve to the remotest generations our national freedom and happiness. In the accomplishment of this vast work two difficulties more formidable than all others, are to be surmounted: two hostile forces are to be encountered and vanquished.

One of these is Romanism. Perhaps three fourths of the emigrants from Europe since the year 1800 have been Romanists, and these have consisted mainly of natives of Ireland and of Roman Catholic Germany. This portion of our population, which is steadily augmenting by natural increase, is not only becoming a substantial element in our great cities and in our Atlantic States, but is rapidly diffusing itself over the West; and it is in the West that Romanism is specially to be dreaded, where the hetrogeneous and repellent elements are constantly intermingling, and often seemingly without the possibility of fusion. To what multitudes from our Atlantic States, who leave all their religion behind them, will Romanism — as it gradually gathers its myriads here and there, and erects its cathedrals and chapels, and appeals to their refined or coarse taste by the pomp of its architecture, its solemn processions, its ministering priesthood, its matins and vespers, and its gorgeous ritual—will it find for the time a not unwelcome access? Transforming itself so far as its wiles are successful, into an angel of light; and assuming relations of a persecuted faith with those who are ignorant of its history from the beginning, both as the the oppressor of its own votaries whenever daring to question its supremacy, and as the steady enemy of Protestantism; it will then advance its claims to an antiquity coëval with Christianity, to an infallibility ever centered in its popes and councils, to a supremacy—opposition to which is rebellion against God. To the sentimental or rapt votary, and to those leaning in either direction, it furnishes its imaginative worship, its biographies of saints, its conventual dreams and mysticism. For the sensualist or the libertine who would drown all recollections of his Puritan faith, it can supply indulgences and the absolution of the confessional: his penances will form a sufficient expiation for all but deadly sins, and he needs but intrust the keeping of his conscience to his priest to be freed from burdensome remorse. Such is Romanism, unchanged, unchangeable, but wearing every needed disguise where not allied to the state; and as all sects, however true or false their faith, possess the same civil rights in this country, her disguise in the United States is as complete as it can be rendered. Yet even here, where Protestantism has triumphed for more than two hundred years, her attempts to expel the Bible from our schools, not only in this city but in two of the States of New England, announce—what Romanism would do if she had the power; and what she will do, the moment that she possesses the power: crush the supporters of every faith but her own, and destroy our free institutions; because freedom and liberty of conscience are inseparable. But her spiritual guides, for these are ever her leaders, well know that the power which they covet—if ever acquired—must be acquired at the West; and they can afford to wear disguises, to plot, to toil on, and toil on unwearied half a century longer, for should they even then succeed, the recompense will a hundred fold exceed the toil. We say then again, that the magnitude of the work of this Society is not to be estimated simply by the hostility or indifference which irreligious Protestants may constantly manifest. That indeed is truly formidable, and requires every effort for its overthrow. But a power working under a disciplined and most compact organization, inherently an enemy to the free institutions which protect its followers, and never abandoning its purposes of conquest, is also to be encountered at a hundred and a thousand points over these vast western regions: and how long, how long, think you, is the warfare to continue before we shall exult in the victory!

The other of these hostile forces is Infidelity. There seem to be but two great forms of opposition under which, in countries self-styled Christian, man's depravity arrrays itself against the religion of Christ. In one of these, the professed reception of that religion is but the credulous obedience which the ignorant and deluded masses render to the instructions of their spiritual guides. A superstitious and blind credulity receives, not what the Bible teaches, but what the priest teaches. This is the religion of ignorance; and the religion of the vast majority in every country in Europe of real, as distinguished from professed, Romanists. In the other form, Christ's religion in its true spirituality and life, is directly rejected. No belief of its revelations, intelligent or unintelligent, is either cherished or pretended, it receives no conscious nor unconscious homage. It is treated either as the work of imposture, or as a non-entity. This other form is Infidelity; and infidelity in our own country becomes in most cases—not in all, but in most—but another term for blank unbelief, for what is tantamount to speculative atheism. A moral necessity leads to this result; for wherever the Bible, with all the evidences of its divine origin as we possess them, and especially that of its transforming energy in the hearts and lives of men, is absolutely rejected, natural religion becomes divested of all its power. The man sees not the sun, and he has made himself blind to every lesser light. American Infidelity is, accordingly, more to be dreaded than European infidelity: its skepticism is not that of ignorance but of comparative knowledge, its descent is into deeper caverns, its spirit is more utterly godless. Nor can we specify the different classes which it threatens to allure, and peculiarly in the Western States, to its standard—secretly if not openly. Among these is the great multitude of emigrants from the Eastern and Middle States, who, as has been already said, have left all their religion behind them, and who at the same time can not be won over to Romanism; men, not a few of whom were once professed disciples, but have hopelessly apostatized, and have thenceforth sought to destroy the faith in which they once professedly gloried. Among them also are men of broken fortunes; the entire class of ruined speculators, the men who prey on the honest industry and enterprise of the community, the gamblers, the swindlers, the thieves, and all the men of violence and crime who hang upon the skirts of our great cities, and who, when driven from the East, flee to the West. And among them are the myriads, for whom life is but the gratification of the coarser appetites with their kindred amusements; to whom inordinate eating, and drinking, and smoking, the dance, the horse-race, and the theater, constitute the only joys to be desired in paradise. And among them, for we can name but another class, are those, who, chafing under the restraints of law and order at home, but hopeless of release while here, are ever ready to pounce upon any feeble State or territory abroad; the fillibusters, the armed brigands and cut-throats, who proclaim liberty at their landing, and then hasten on to fight, to plunder, and destroy. The men of these and other classes, and the "name" of each is rapidly becoming not one only, but many "Legions," constitute the serried ranks of infidelity as it is now growing at the West: and infidelity, which at one time will fight single-handed under its own standard, and at another will combine, if necessary, with Romanism, as did Herod with Pilate; for each discerns that our Protestant faith must be overthrown, before either can hope to triumph.

These two great hostile forces, we repeat it, are every where to be encountered by this Society while sending the Gospel to the destitute, and assisting feeble congregations to support the gospel ministry, throughout the West. Its own proper work is great indeed: for were that vast region all prepared for the immortal seed, what a labor of generations would be that of planting and sowing, and watering and weeding, of still planting and sowing and watering and weeding, and then of duly reaping and gathering in the harvest, as it should ripen under the dews of the Spirit and the beams of the Sun of Righteousness! But where thorns and briers are ever springing up, and stony places or the rocky bed beneath so often denies that depth which prevents the germ from withering, where the boar out of the wood is ever ready to waste the ripening grain, and the wild beast of the field to devour it, what a magnitude does the work assume!

While the work is to be thus performed at home, and its magnitude can be scarcely exaggerated, there is still another aspect to be momently noticed: *its necessary influence* on other nations. Just as easily can a *cordon sanitaire* shut out the cholera from crossing over an imaginary boundary line of two nations, as different forms of government or language can resist the influence of our great country from vitally swaying every bordering people. We will not cross the vast Pacific and ask—What is to be the power of our free institutions and of our religion, when the United States shall contain a hundred millions, on China and Japan and all Eastern Asia—God's Providence now visibly beginning to remove every obstacle to their full efficiency on these great civilized races at no distant day: an efficiency, be it remembered, which is to go forth from our country westward, and not eastward. This particular topic, momentous as it is, we can not notice. But we do ask: What, as this Society continues its work for twenty years and forty years to come through our wide Western population, will be, must be, the influence of our country, on the British provinces at the North, and on Mexico at the South; or on the whole of the rest of North America? Does any discreet observer doubt that our fifty five millions in 1880, and our one hundred millions in 1900, whatever then our national character, will sweep these two inferior nations onward in the same course, as the central orb controls its satellites? Should all schemes of foreign conquest be forever abandoned, should our whole intercourse with these two border nations be henceforth that of justice and good will alone, can all physical and moral causes united arrest this overwhelming current, when in 1900 our population shall be, as it is now, tenfold that of British North America; and when poor priest-ridden, superannuated Mexico, shall have, a quarter of a century previous, to preserve herself from dismemberment and extinction by internecine wars, implored her own annexation to our republic? We ask—What can avert this issue, whatever is to be then our national character? But we would anticipate here, as if God's whole past guidance of our nation were but the prediction of a far more glorious future, the steady and commensurate growth of true religion over our Western States to the Pacific; we are gladdened by the belief that this Society and all kindred agencies are to become relatively far more effective through these coming years of destiny; and we therefore affirm, that its work will be as really vital in these other immense regions as it is to be through God's blessing in our own. But we can linger over these brightening scenes no longer.

Such is the work. This Society sends forth its appropriate *workmen* to perform it. We say its workmen, for vast as is the enterprise, and assured as are its friends from the Word and the Providence of God that his Spirit's power and truth are indispensable to its successful prosecution for a single day; they are also assured, that the great spiritual harvest will not be gathered in without human coöperation. The Infinite

One is pleased to employ those whom the Apostle styles—his co-workers, and the Society's entire system of operations has been directed by this principle. We learn who are its workmen, by resorting again to its second article. "The object of this Society shall be, to assist congregations that are unable to support the gospel ministry, and to send the Gospel to the destitute, in the United States." How simple, nay, how crude, would the mere man of the world exclaim, is this whole scheme! To assist, where otherwise there would be an inability, in supporting the Gospel ministry, and to send the Gospel to the destitute—this, then, is the narrow platform on which itself and its supporters all stand! Its workmen are to be all taken from the ranks of the gospel ministry, they are to be ministers and preachers only! Yes, these are the workmen, simple, if any choose to apply to them the epithet—simple ministers and preachers: the Society commissions none other. They are commissioned exclusively, not because they seek not and enlist not, as far as may be, the coöperation of all the friends of religion and of human happiness around them; but because Christ has assigned to the ministry which himself instituted peculiar duties and relations. The most important of these are included in the brief passage which has given direction to our thoughts: "And that repentance and remission of sins should be preached in his name among all nations." In this passage the grand yet simple principle is announced by the Saviour, which this Society has ever made the basis of its system of working. When he purposed to evangelize the world, he also purposed to accomplish the mighty object, *primarily*, through an Agency which, deriving all its efficiency from the Holy Spirit, should be unlike any which mere human wisdom has originated. This agency is that of ministers of the Gospel. The Apostles went forth as the leaders in this great enterprise, while at the same time their special agency in advancing it consisted, not in their labors as Apostles, but as ministers. They indeed were inspired, they wrought miracles, to them was delegated the work of organizing the Church; but what efficiency would have attended all these peculiar powers, had they not, in the language of the text, preached repentance and remission of sins in Christ's name to the nations? It was Paul's preaching, which accomplished the wondrous results at Antioch, at Philippi, at Thessalonica, at Corinth and at Ephesus: miracles and the speaking with tongues and all his other apostolical gifts would otherwise have been as powerless to convert the Gentiles, as were the miracles attending the giving of the law from Mount Sinai to convert the sensual and slavish Israelites. Our Society, we say, acts systematically on the grand yet simple principle here established by our Saviour—that of employing an Agency to do its appropriate Work, unlike any which human wisdom has originated. When he determined to extend that kingdom of which himself is the head, throughout the nations, how many systems of operation might he not have adopted; what diverse classes of agents might he not have employed! Had his kingdom been of this world, as even the Apostles fondly imagined it until the Day of Pentecost, he would have employed military force: each of the Twelve would have headed a conquering army against the legions of imperial Rome, and the fanaticism of the Crescent would have been antedated six centuries by the fanaticism of the Cross. Or had he chosen to propagate Christianity (then, indeed, how diverse a system from the Christianity of the New Testament!) by the more peaceful triumphs of Philosophy, he might have established Eclectic schools to send forth bands of teachers over the civilized world, each of them imbued with all that was renowned in Indian and Grecian and Jewish lore. Or, instead of abolishing the Mosaic ritual with its priesthood, he might have added to the one all that was venerable and gorgeous in the ceremonial rites of Egypt and Babylon, of Persia and Hindostan; and to the other a reputed infallibility, surpassing tenfold that of papal Rome. We may make the suppositions for the sake of illustrating the immediate topic, and proceed to say that, had all these modes of swaying the minds of men to the acknowledgment of his supremacy been rejected; Christ, as the author of a new religion, might have anticipated by eighteen hundred years the political science of our own days, and have established free institutions over Palestine or some other country, as affording the grand expedient for securing the unobstructed and triumphant propagation of the Gospel. Or, to speak here with greater definiteness, instead of bestowing on his disciples after his ascension the gift of tongues alone, he might have added—what to philosopher and peasant would have seemed as wonderful, and what to modern missions is immeasurably more important—the art of printing, as we now possess it. But had it been possible for Christ to have adopted any of these systems of operation, any of these agencies, could he have continued to be *the* Christ any longer? What assistance can a kingdom which is built on the Truth, ask, either in its foundation or its advancement, from the sword and the bayonet; from the dogmas of oriental and occidental philosophy; from an ancient or a modern ceremonial which aims to captivate the senses; or from free institutions, and particularly from a free press, as the necessary partner of its triumphs? No. Christ, while absolutely discerning the power of each of these instrumentalities for good or for evil, rejected them, all, and he sent forth primarily but one class of agents —ministers of the Gospel. We repeat it, that he requires, as indispensable to the great result, the coöperation of his disciples universally in every age; that ministers always seek this coöperation; that the Society in whose name I speak ever looks to this coöperation as vital; whilst we say once more, that in the text and throughout the New Testament, Christ has named but one class of *official* agents for the extension of his kingdom on earth, and that these are ministers. They are to preach repentance and remission of sins in his name: they are to proclaim his gospel fearlessly, faithfully, fully, as the power of God unto salvation to the believer, in the sanctuary and by the wayside, on the deck of the lonely ship or in the depths of the forest, because Christ has appointed it; because it has pleased God, by what men term, "the foolishness of preaching," to save them that believe. We say then again, that the workmen whom the Society commissions, are ministers of the Gospel; and we shall now proceed very briefly to notice their fitness for the performance of its great work. This is necessary to the proper elucidation of the subject, while it will also exhibit the wisdom of Christ as the Head of the Church in his institution of the christian ministry.

Let me specify as one element of their fitness, that they are *converted men.* In scriptural language, they have been born again, they have been sanctified by the truth. It is intended here, not only that Christ requires evangelical piety as a vital qualification of every minister, and that his own assumption of the office is an implicit affirmation that he deems himself the subject of such piety; but that in our own country, and particularly among the two great denominations of which this Society has the entire confidence, such is almost universally the admitted fact. I speak not of the priesthood of the apostate Romish Church, although the word church, in its true scriptural sense, is an utter misnomer as applied to that body ; and as little of any other merely human ecclesiastical organization which, in Protestant countries, has been established by the state ; but of the christian ministry, as the New Testament and particularly as the Epistles of Paul describe its character, and as we personally behold it sustained among ourselves. The men who constitute it, are converted men. They are neither men of loose morals, nor hypocrites, nor decent worldlings, nor self-righteous fanatics ; they care not for the fleece rather than the flock, their chief object has not been a life of quiet indolence or of literary culture or of official influence and power. They have first personally experienced the transforming energy of the Gospel, and have thus made "partakers of the divine nature ;" and they have subsequently, overlooking the prizes of wealth, high station and power which draw such numbers elsewhere, selected the ministry as the sphere of their most effectively honoring the Saviour and benefit, ing their fellow men. How immense the advantage which the christian minister thus possesses ! Place him in any region, whether at the East or the West, where the controlling object shall be, not to heap up money till the pile rivals the pyramid of Cheops, not to kindle the furnace of party politics, not to lead silly women and men of a disturbed brain to swallow the inanities of Spiritualism, or of any similar delusion ; but to produce those great moral changes which are decisive here and endure forever ; changes in which the drunkard becomes rigidly abstemious, the libertine pure, the swindler an honest man, the blasphemer reverential, the infidel a believer—changes where God's authority as the basis and the measure of all human authority shall be generally acknowledged: and what other laborer's efficiency will equal his own? Place him by the side of the moralist, whether refined like some of the British essayists, or uttering the strong and homely maxims of Franklin: place him by that of the metaphysician, who shall enlighten the educated as to the interaction of the intellect, the feelings and the will, while "the school-master shall go every where abroad," among the ignorant: let the Press in its daily and weekly issues disclose the selfishness of every mere party measure, municipal, state and national, and expose every crime and its perpetrators to public abhorrence: while at the same time in our large cities a strong police shall stand forth as an active coädjutor: and we ask again—Which of them will be the most efficient workmen? Nay, will not the minister be more effective than all the others? The experiment has been too often tried, to admit of doubt: in the hamlet, in the scattered population of the town, in the village, the city, the metropolis, in Europe amid Romanism and Protestantism, and in the United States. The man of no religion and no faith, if he possesses property which is to be secure from theft, will uphold the minister as the best of all peace officers: the lover of private and public order admits that *his* teachings are necessary to the prevention of private brawls and the outrages of mobs: the true Christian esteems the office and the men who worthily sustain it, as inspiration directs that they shall be esteemed. This is one element of the fitness of the workmen; they are converted, godly men.

They are also *Educated Men.* Their office is that of religious teachers, and to qualify them for its duties they have received the very best training which our country affords. With exceptions so few as scarcely to be counted, all of them have passed through a preparatory course of ten years' study; three at the classical school, four at the college, and then three at the theological seminary. Two thirds of our physicians have never entered a college, and probably two fifths of our lawyers; while not more than one fifth, or one sixth, of the ministry have failed to receive these ten years' preliminary training—the best, we say again, which our country affords. Thus trained, they enter on their life work as preachers of the Gospel, a course necessitating an amount of reading and of patient discriminating thought, giving a play and energy to feeling, and securing a comprehensiveness and elevation of views such as no other life work produces or requires. They are not educated to be agriculturists nor merchants, neither for the bar, nor for the healing art: but do I err when affirming that, as a profession, they are better acquainted with husbandry than merchants, and with the principles and practical course of trade than agriculturists; that they have a superior knowledge of the physiology and pathology of the human frame than lawyers, and of constitutional and common law than physicians? Let it not be said that this is the language of mere professional sympathy, the same in spirit with that of Demetrius of Ephesus. Christ's commission to the ministry can not generally be fitly held, its solemn trusts can not generally be rightly executed, where the preacher of the Gospel is not thus trained: the work of this Society can not be performed, either at the East or the West, unless such are the workmen. It is not claimed for them that, as a body, they are either profound scholars or popular authors, that they are artists or statesmen. While they have more true scholarship than any other educated class, still the Pulpit and the Pastorate are too engrossing to permit them to be mere scholars, or artists, or little statesmen, or great statesmen. The minister, in the relations of his labors to eternity, is ever constrained to adopt the language of Nehemiah: "I am doing a great work, so that I can not come down; why should the work cease, whilst I leave it and come down to you?" What is claimed for them is simply this: that the ministry of the two great denominations which sustain this Society, have received the most thorough preparatory training in all its stages which our country can give; and that the subsequent studies and labors of life are but the completion of such a training. Place them, then, where you will, in the quiet villages or crowded cities of the East, along the margin of mouldering forests or of vast lakes, or on the prairies, or in the swarming cities, at the West, and you have workmen rightly educated for their work. The minister belongs to no priestly caste, severed like the Brahmin of Hindostan and the Romish ecclesiastic from fraternal sympathy with his fellow man. He claims no official sanctity, he proclaims neither the infallibility of his Church nor his own power to dispense or withhold pardon. But as one who consciously knows the Gospel to be the power of God unto salvation, and assured that others will perish unless they also shall become possessed of that blessed consciousness; a man of like passions, habits, wants, of one country and language and faith with those whom he addresses; he will seek to win, and with the divine aid he will win, them to the side of order, of private and public virtue, of Christ and of God, as no other man will win them. He can meet the cloistered Romish priest with weapons furnished by the armory of God, and drive him from the field.

He can meet the infidel on the ground of natural religion, and constrain him to surrender. Does not the history of Presbyterianism and Congregationalism, does not the existing state of the churches and the ministry, justify these affirmations?

They are *the firm friends of Liberty*, and *of Law*. Where the Spirit of the Lord has once released the mind from its bondage to sin, to superstition, to the fear of man, and where free institutions, as the Northern and Middle States enjoy them, purify our air and gladden our very heavens, from our cradles—I ask not, what must be the man, but what must be the minister, who loves not Liberty as he loves life! First, the Gospel; and then Liberty, that he may enjoy the Gospel and all things else most dear. Such are the converted and educated men whom we are contemplating, such that portion of them whom the Society commissions. Their love of Liberty is their birthright, their ancient inheritance. It has been transmitted to them from the signing of the Declaration of Independence, from the fight at Lexington, from the embarking at Delft Haven, from the flight of Robinson and his flock to Leyden. It has been strengthened in them by every fresh reading of the histories of the English Puritans, of the Scottish Presbyterians and Covenanters, and of those earlier champions for freedom—the men of the seven United Provinces of Holland. Thus generated and strengthened and sanctified, their love of Liberty can never be divorced from their love of the Gospel: their religion purifies and exalts their freedom, their freedom is the minister and the protector of their religion. Are not such men needed to do the work of this Society at the West, where, and where only, Southern Slavery can hope to gain an entrance? Who shall then stand in the breach, and drive back this foul spirit, if not the men who are armed with the sword of God's Spirit, even his quick and powerful Word? And who among them save the few descendants of John Bunyan's *Feeble Mind*, and of *Mr. Despondency*, and of his daughter, *Mrs. Much afraid*, will falter wherever this contest is to be carried on; whoever may revile them, or attempt to crush them! They love liberty too well, and know their duty too clearly, to be found wanting here.

Nor are they less the friends of Law, the twin sister of Liberty. It is irreligion that renders men lawless, and despotism digs a common grave for liberty and law. Where has a freedom comparable to that of the Israelites under the ancient theocracy been seen on earth, except among ourselves: and where has law in its manifold limitations and restraints, been more truly honored? Our intermingling and slowly fusing population at the West, will need for half a century, as the flood moves onward to the Rocky Mountains and the Pacific, the inculcation of obedience to Law, of reverence for civil government as the institution of God, of respect by every man for the rights of his fellow as equally sacred with his own. Liberty accompanies the emigrant from the Atlantic States each step of his far westward progress, she threads with him the forest, she crosses the prairies, she drinks with him at the sources of the Missouri; while Law follows on slowly, and often far behind. Though not a slave nor a slaveholder were ever to be seen beyond the limits within which they have now a legal existence, a fierce licentiousness of spirit, equally impatient of the restraints of human law and of God's law might easily and rapidly become general. The two must bear sway in equal measure together, or they must unitedly totter and fall. While then the ministers sustained by this Society will preach the Gospel as the remedy for all sin and suffering, while they will proclaim its condemnation of all injustice and oppression, particularly of that Slavery which would spread its sooty wings over our remotest States and Territories, they will also, as men who have been found faithful, set forth wherever they go the supremacy of Law. Liberty, or the right to think and speak and act, when, where, how each man's own reason and choice may guide him: Law, or those restraints and none others, which shall protect his neighbor from the abuse of that liberty. Liberty, as essential to that exalted state of earthly good which ancient prophets assure us awaits our race in coming years, and as an element of the higher bliss of heaven: Law, or that control of rightful authority here, which fits him for blessed subjection to infinite authority forever.

We have done. This Society commenced existence at the beginning of the second quarter of the century, and its thirty third Anniversary is now at hand. The Annual Report will then announce the rich measures of prosperity with which God has favored it. Its treasury enlarged, its missionaries prosecuting their labor of love with undiminished patience of hope, large showers of grace ripening the seed which they have sown into harvests of salvation, God's voice thus proclaiming that its course is to be ever onward. The same simple but grand object, that of extending Christ's kingdom as a Society for Home Missions, will continue to give wisdom to its counsels and vigor to their execution. Its officers, its friends, should then anew thank God and take courage. He has summoned it from the beginning to its great WORK: May He in all coming years, prosper the more abundantly the labors of its WORKMEN.

THE HOME MISSIONARY.

Go, ... PREACH the GOSPEL, ... *Mark* xvi. 15.
How shall they preach except they be SENT? . . . *Rom.* x. 15.

Vol. XXXVII. FEBRUARY, 1865. No. 10.

THE PULPIT'S PLACE AND POWER.

[THE question discussed in the following discourse is of great practical importance, and is now awakening much attention among the churches. The able and, as we think, conclusive, argument which we present to our readers, is from the pen of Rev. JOHN TODD, D.D., of Pittsfield, Mass.]

"*It pleased God by the foolishness of preaching to save them that believed.*"—1 COR. 1: 21.

WE are not to suppose that the apostle in our text intended to teach us that the plan of making "preaching" the great instrument in converting men was a foolish plan—or that foolish preaching is just as good as wise preaching; but that, what to "the wisdom of this world" would seem foolish, is God's plan. In all the arrangements of God's plans in nature, in providence, and in grace, we constantly meet with what to us seems unwise—else we should not complain of the weather, envy our neighbor's lot, worry about the future, doubt his providences, disbelieve his word, or reject his authority.

A thousand experiments are made to discover some method of saving men, quicker, wiser, and more efficient than the old way of preaching the Gospel by the living voice of the living preacher. Men forget that God used Moses to "speak" unto the children of Israel; the prophets to "proclaim" his instructions, his advice, and his warnings; that Nineveh and Babylon had no other means than the "voice" of prophets; that Christ entered his ministry by "declaring" God's name, "proclaiming" his kingdom, and calling upon men to repent; that his great charge was that his disciples should go into all the world "and preach the Gospel to every creature;" that the day of Pentecost was made powerful through preaching; that the great work of the apostles was "to preach" the Gospel. And the experience of the church is, that this instrumentality is greater than all others. No enlightened Christian would ever think of naming any other instrumentality in comparison with it, any more than he would think of lighting the world by any thing besides the sun. For this reason, our fathers and their children, up to this day, have been anxious to have an educated, a pious, and a powerful preaching ministry. What was the practice, even of inspired men? Nehemiah says, "Thou hast appointed prophets to *preach* of thee." Isaiah—"The Lord anointed me to *preach* good tidings." Jonah—"*Preach* to it (Nineveh) the preaching that I bid thee." Matthew—"From that time Jesus began to *preach*"—"He (Christ) departed to *preach* in their cities." Luke—"That he might send them forth to *preach* the Gospel." And so through the New Testament, the great work of the apostles was to "preach" the Gospel.

At the present day there is an effort made to set aside *preaching*—at least half the time—and substitute something else; to have but *one* sermon on the Sabbath, and to have the afternoon service given up to the Sabbath school; and to make this the custom of all our churches and congregations. Some churches and pastors have fallen into the practice, and the subject has been gravely and solemnly discussed in Conventions and Conferences. I have tried to give this subject some thought, anxious thought, for, if the custom prevail, it must revolutionize our whole system of means of grace. Now let us look candidly and solemnly at the subject, and first,

THE ARGUMENTS IN FAVOR OF THE CHANGE.

Better Attendance.

1. It is said that if we have but *one* service on the Sabbath for preaching, *it will be better attended.*

Perhaps it may be so in some one church. But we can't plan for particular churches—such perhaps as are in cities. We must look at the good of the whole. It may be that for a time the congregation *would* be larger—and so it might be larger still, if we had but one sermon in a month. But we must remember that in all our rural towns at least, there are some who can not go to church but half of the day. I mean mothers with little children, families in which are sickness and watchings. A part of such families go one half of the day, and a part the other half. If you have but one service, you cut them off from public worship entirely, every other week. Is this right or wise? Does not the mother who is shut up in her little family need to have her weary spirit bathed in the waters of the sanctuary, at least oftener than once in a fortnight? So of the faithful watcher over the sick bed. Then there is our domestic help, they often can not attend worship but a part of the day. Shall they hear but twenty-six sermons in a year? My impression and belief is, that in a short time actual experience would demonstrate that the congregation would not be as large as it now is; and I reason from the fact that in places where they have preaching but half the day, or once in two weeks, in our thinly-populated towns, the people are very little interested in the service, and not at all anxious to attend. Experience has as yet been too limited to throw much light on this new experiment.

Better Sermons.

2. It is said that if you have but one sermon on the Sabbath *you will have better sermons;* more study, more thought, more instructive, and more powerful. Is this so? Does not every minister know that he is made up of nerves, and glands, and flesh, and blood, and that more depends on the state of his system than upon the time that he has? Does he not know too, that the excitement of the morning preaching—both on his part and on that of the audience—carries him along so that the afternoon service is more effective than the morning? Don't he know that the morning service is more for the rousing the intellect, and that the afternoon sermon is by far the most powerful on the conscience? Do the Bishops in the English Church who preach but once in six months, preach with power in proportion?

Or are they truly "visitation" sermons, for which the hearer is thankful that the "visitation" comes but twice a year? I may not doubt that if we had to prepare but one sermon a week, we should try to gather more thought; but would there be warmth, unction, earnestness, in proportion? Would it meet the last charge of Paul to Timothy, "Preach the word, be instant in season, out of season?" What has been the experience and practice of the most successful and godly ministers that have ever preached Christ? Did they not "abound" in preaching the word?

Easier for the Ministry.

3. It is said that by having but one sermon *we should make it easier for the ministry*, that ministers are wearing out, and breaking down, and so if they should be permitted to preach but one sermon a week, it would be easier for them.

So it would, and easier still if we preached but once a month! Now, the fact is, the ministry don't expect, and don't want, to have their work easy. Most of them were educated by the church—at the expense of the church; and all men, merchants, physicians, lawyers, mechanics, all classes, work hard and so must ministers. We don't expect, or want, to be an exception. It is a necessity of the age to work hard. All classes want more comforts and more luxuries than their fathers had, and they know that they must work hard in proportion. And if we have to work hard and fast, we have great facilities. We have warm studies, we have better books, we have more thought on the wing, than ministers once had. Our congregations, most of them, are willing that we have an annual vacation—they are willing that we should favor ourselves, and are always glad to see us taking measures to preserve our health; and I am very slow to believe that it is *work* that kills ministers, though I am willing to confess to some hard and constant work. But we lack the knowledge or the self-denial required, to take care of our health. It requires a vast deal more self-denial to take regular exercise and obey the laws of health, than it does to groan and die with dyspepsia. And if a minister finds that he must break down, he can change his field of labor without any loss of character, (though he must for a time feel a loss of influence). Now I have no belief that the ministry want to be released from hard work, or that they can be, without a great loss of moral power. If a minister finds that two written sermons are too much for his strength, and he *will* find it so—let him preach one sermon expository. This he will soon find easy and delightful to himself; and no preaching will be so acceptable and useful to his people as expository preaching, *after they have become accustomed to it.* In no other way can the congregation be so well instructed in the Scriptures as in this.

Easier for Sabbath School Teachers.

4. It is claimed that it would make it easier for the Sabbath school teachers to have but one sermon, and so have the Sabbath school take the place of the present afternoon service.

I reply, the Sabbath school teachers are usually the young and the healthy and the vigorous of the church. They can work hard, and do work amazingly hard on the week days. They feel that they *must*, or Mammon won't give them even the crumbs that drop from his table, or the dust which sticks to his fingers. They understand, too, that this is an age of hard work, and that in the church as out of it, they must work hard. If, however, out of the fifty in each congregation who are teachers, (and they won't average so many)—there are *ten* who can not attend both services, let these attend one besides the school. I don't believe that our teachers, if they rightly understood the thing, would wish to have one half of the services of the sanctuary given up *for their ease.* I feel that I should do them wrong to believe any such thing. Nor do I believe we are so destitute of self-denying disciples that we must make a great and hazardous experiment in order to make the work of Sabbath school teaching easy.

Congregational Bible Class.

5. It is said that if we have our Sabbath school in the afternoon *we can get the whole congregation together to study the Bible.*

A very beautiful theory; but in practice a thing out of the question. Ask a congregation to do it, and what would they say if they *spake* as they thought? Those who *now* come but half a day to church, would say nothing, but they *certainly would not come.* Many would say, "I have no time to study the lesson so as to be questioned on it. I read my Bible in my humble way and enjoy it, but neither my failing eyes, nor my family duties, nor my discipline of mind will allow me to meet the teacher and recite, and be catechized, and have my ignorance exposed!" And besides, they would say, "we have all been through the Sabbath school in childhood, and we feel that childhood is the season in which to attend the school, and we can not consent to be in the place of childhood all our lives." Now we know that the complaint is almost universal in our Sabbath-schools that when a boy is grown up, he leaves the school. The reason is, he feels that he is no longer a child, to be numbered with children. There are, and will be, exceptions to this, but as a general rule, our congregations will either have the preacher prepare and come and pour instruction in upon them, or they will not have any. As for making and keeping a whole congregation in the Sabbath-school a very long time, I have no belief—from what I have seen of such experiments.

After all, there is a heavier objection to the change, which comes in here; and that is, that however valuable the Sabbath school may be, it is yet, in a certain sense, certainly an experiment in the church. *It is not a divine appointment* as the preaching of the Gospel is. I have no doubt that great alterations in the system have yet to be made. And, though I will yield to no one in my estimation of the importance of instructing our children, and beginning early, nor yet of my estimation of the Sabbath school as an auxiliary instrumentality; yet I do not believe that the children (who are not a fourth part of the community) should have half of the Sabbath, and half of the sanctuary given up to them. It seems out of all reasonable proportion; for, though we are commanded to feed Christ's lambs, we are also commanded to feed his sheep. That a man who is thus led through a Sabbath school occupying one half of the Sabbath, would in comparison with one who was trained in the old way, at the age of fifty, be a stronger, more balanced Christian, I have no faith. Human nature, and especially American human nature, delights to run to extremes, and to feel that almost any change must, of course, be an improvement, and in proportion to the greatness of the change.

So far I have attempted merely to answer the reasons urged for this giving up one half of the Sabbath to the Sabbath school and having but one sermon.

ARGUMENTS AGAINST THE CHANGE.

I now wish to advance a little *and urge my reasons against the change.*

A Feeble Ministry.

1. I think it would result in having *a feeble ministry.* Now, as things are, when the young man, say at eighteen, makes up his mind to enter the ministry, he looks forward to years of confinement and hard study—years of privation and self-denial. But he looks forward to a great work: that of being an ambassador from God to men! He looks forward to preaching the Gospel as the great work of life—and a

hard work of course. His mind is filled with the magnitude of the work. He knows that our fathers never preached less than twice on the Sabbath, and most of them much more than this. But suppose he knows that when he gets through all this preparation, he is to preach but one sermon on the Sabbath, that the pulpit is on a level with the Sabbath school, that he is not expected to preach more than about thirty or thirty five sermons in a year—taking out his vacation and the calls of agents, and exchanges, he probably can have opportunity for not more than thirty or thirty five sermons annually to his own flock; that if his ministry last twenty years he will have preached actually not over about six hundred regular sermons, and to a part of his people only half that number! Is *this* the way to encourage men to give the strength of life to the pulpit? Is this the way to make strong men, and give our churches a powerful ministry? If you want strong men you must make them lift heavy burdens. Even gun-cotton, the most powerful of all material agencies, is six times as strong as gunpowder only as you compress it. Why, you have told the man that he is a dwarf in comparison with his fathers. And the result inevitably will be, if I read human nature aright, that instead of raising up *strong* men, you will train up very weak men. If the pulpit is no more important than the Sabbath school, then the man who can fill the office of superintendent can also fill the pulpit.

Destruction of Church Music.

2. *The plan will destroy our church music.*

All who have been in the ministry for years know that this part of worship is a *very* important part, and a very difficult one also. My own experience is, that you can't have a good choir, any more than you can have any thing else that is good, without great labor and painstaking, on their part. They *must* meet for rehearsal and practice once a week the year round. They want also, an organ, and eventually all our churches will have organs, of some kind or other. Now suppose you tell the choir that you don't want their services but half a day, to sing twice, or at most, three times a week! Are they to have zeal enough to meet weekly just for that preparation? Is the congregation to be at the expense of an organ and to procure somebody with skill to play it, merely for a half-day service? It is not in human nature to do it. Very few in a congregation have any conception of the labor required, in order to have good church music: and if you belittle that service as the proposed plan will, how are you to have good church music?

Allow me to say, too, to those who have no ear for music, and hardly know one tune from another, that they would run away from a church which had no music; and if the music is poor, they feel it and complain. Let any minister preach even in a school house where they can not sing, and he will tell you the meeting was a failure. He could not preach nor could they hear.

Perhaps you will say, "Give up the choir and have congregational singing!" Were this the time and place I think I could convince you that this can never prevail in our churches. I have no hobby to ride, but my observation teaches me that in *this* part of the country there is too much cultivation, and too much refinement of taste ever to be long satisfied with congregational singing. A good choir and good music are indispensable to profitable public worship—and this I do not believe you could have if you cut the Sabbath in two, and give half to preaching and the other half to class teaching.

Spiritual and Intellectual Leanness.

3. The plan would result in having *our church lean in spirituality and our congregations in intelligence.*

It is claimed that if you hear but one sermon on the Sabbath, you will remember it better, digest it better, and improve more by it. Perhaps if you were to inquire of those who now come to the house of God but once on the Sabbath, you might get some light on this point. I shall not say that they are *not* of all the congregation the most benefited, and I am sure you will not expect me to say that they are! The observation of my life leads me to say that very few of our congregations *remember* much of what they hear from the pulpit. If the best Christians remember enough to make any allusion to a sermon in the Sabbath evening prayer meeting, I always feel abundantly satisfied! But Christians grow in spirituality, and a congregation grows in intelligence, not by memory, but by the *impressions* they receive. Instruction goes into character, as food into the body. We don't know that we are to-day using the food eaten yesterday, or last week. We only know that we feel vigorous. The mind forgets what it reads, but it grows in strength and power by reading. You come to the house of God and hear a sermon, and it mostly fades from the memory, but the soul retains the *impressions* received, and these become a part of your character. You may tell me that the afternoon sermon covers up the morning discourse, and makes it faint on the memory. Undoubtedly. And if we depended on the memory for the good received, we should esteem this a great calamity. If a man received no good from reading his Bible in the morning except as he remembered it, his reading would do him but little good. It is the *effects* of bathing his soul in the river of God, and not the water that remains on him that does him good. So, if you can not remember the morning sermon as well after hearing the afternoon discourse, you gain in continued deepening impression, which eternal truth makes on the spirit. Take away one half of this impression, and this kindling the intellect, and you inevitably dwarf the soul; and as to the *intellect*, the benefit of the pulpit is not so much that it communicates great or original thoughts, as that it puts the hearer's own thoughts in motion; he may not *remember*, but he *must think*, if the preacher be a "workman rightly dividing the word." Remember that this age is not one of meditation and solitary thought. Character is formed now by *impressions* made on the soul in public. Those who attend public worship are no exception to the rest. The reason why we multiply meetings and preaching in a revival is, not that men then *remember* any better than at other times, but *impressions* are made and repeated, and we never have any fear lest one sermon shall destroy the previous one. And so, if you take one half, at least, of all the impressions which the pulpit makes, you leave the heart and the intellect to be dwarfed. I put it to your common sense, and ask if you do not believe that the church and congregation who have two discourses from the pulpit would be stronger in faith and in intellect, at the end of ten years, than if they had but one sermon? You may say that the Sabbath school is a service—and so it is, but it is a *school service.* Out of the whole day, your two sermons, with the worship, occupy perhaps three hours. Is that too much for the adult portion of the community in which to worship and to receive instruction from the man of God? And you know that men will look up to the pulpit and to the true minister of Christ, as they will to no other teacher, and I, for one, should not dare lay my hand on this influence and diminish it at least one half.

Indifference to our Church.

4. *The plan would be likely to destroy attachment to our own church.*

From the very nature of the case, you can not expect to induce all churches and congregations to come into the plan. Well, then, suppose my church has but one sermon; the result will be, that all those who do not like the plan, will take seats in other churches which *do* have an afternoon service. They will go there, and in proportion as they do, their attachments to their own church and form of worship will be weakened. This result is certain, and it would not take a long time so to weaken this feeling of attachment, that we should be indifferent where we went, or whether a part of our families went to one church and a part to another—and the idea of the Puritan churches will exist only in the past. I do not dwell on this point, simply because you can all see that it *must* be so.

Sabbath Desecration.

5. *The plan would result in having the Sabbath desecrated.*

It is perfectly idle to think that we shall get our congregations into the Sabbath school whenever we have it. By efforts, and by the presence of the pastor, doubtless we could enlarge it and make it more efficient than it now is; but what of the great number who would only attend but one service, because there *is* but one? To them, the Sabbath will terminate with the forenoon, and they not only will have the opportunity to walk and ride and visit in the afternoon, but they will *take* it. They are tempted to it. They are not to be shut up in the house one half of the day, because you virtually shut them out of the church—unless they attend the catechetical service—to which they will not submit. They will go somewhere else. And my belief is that in a few years, the Sabbath would lose its sanctity and be desecrated as it is in Europe, where almost universally, they have but *one* service, and the Sabbath becomes a holiday. If you put guns in the hands of men they will want to shoot them; if you put half of the Sabbath into vacancy, it will be occupied for pleasure and amusement. Even now the Sabbath is in danger of being injured if not buried up by the world. The world has taken from us the good old Saturday night preparation season, and the world now votes the Sabbath ended at dark, so that all kinds of visiting are proper, and now if the world takes one half of the day, how small a portion have we left for God and for the soul! I put it to you—and ask, if the change would not be hailed with joy by those who are now troubled by the sanctity of the Sabbath? Would not the moral instincts of all who want to live without submitting to the bonds of the Gospel, hail the change with great joy?

We know that the Jewish worship was in the morning and in the afternoon; and we know that the apostles made preaching the great business, end and aim of life, and we know that God has appointed it as the great means of saving men, and we know that hitherto it has been more efficient than all other instrumentalities united—and so I believe it will be; and I have no fear that our churches, should they throw away one half of the pulpit's opportunity and power, would long adhere to the plan—for the church would soon see that she must go back to the old paths or she is ruined. But I don't want our churches agitated and troubled by the question, or heated by the change; and I feel confident that the sound judgment of New England will go against it. The change would inaugurate the commencement of future experiments which would lead—we know not where. Certainly I have no interest in the question except as I believe it makes for or against the cause of Christ, the good of our churches, and the salvation of men. I am not ready to throw aside the experience of our fathers ever since New England was settled, and what we know is in the line of God's own appointment, for the sake of an experiment. I want new church edifices, and new organs, and new hymn books, now and then, and will never object to changes that affect not the great plan of God; but when you come to take away half the altar of God that you may have need of less fire, or that you may make it the teachers' platform, I must have reasons for the change, such as have not yet been advanced. "It pleases God by the foolishness of preaching to save them that believe!" And it is his own wisdom that selected this instrumentality! Is it wise, then, to make a doubtful experiment? "I speak as unto wise men, judge ye what I say."

MISSIONARY INTELLIGENCE.

CALIFORNIA.

From Rev. J. H. Warren, Agent.

A MONTH'S WORK.

Clayton.

My work for the month may be summed up thus.—The first Sabbath, I spent with the Congregational Church in Clayton, Contra Costa county. This church was organized two years ago, with ten or twelve members, under the labors of Rev. J. J. Powell, who now preaches as your missionary in Somersville, five miles from Clayton. It now numbers twenty seven members. It has been without a minister about a year. Occasional visits from neighboring clergymen have given them a few sermons. I found the church in very good condition, spiritually. They keep up weekly prayer meetings, and these meetings are well attended and most always interesting. When they have no minister, instead of doing as many churches—have no meetings—they come together on the Sabbath and one of them reads a sermon. The Sabbath school is very flourishing, embracing about all the children of the neighborhood. Within the last year, this little church has enjoyed a precious revival, and from the fruits of it the membership was more than doubled. Oh, how they long for a minister—a man of God, to break to them the word of life. The members of the church are poor, as to this world's goods: there is not *one rich man* among them. They have figured up, for the support of a minister, $400; and with a man on the ground, reckoning what can be collected at the outstations, the amount may swell up to $500 or upwards. They seemed to be doubtful and anxious about receiving any aid from the Home Missionary Society, because they could do so little themselves. I told them, that it was for just such churches as they were that the Society was organized.

Clayton is but a small town, as yet, and will probably never be a large place. It is most charmingly situated at the base of Mount Diablo, in the midst of a rich pastoral and agricultural region, and also in the neighborhood of coal and copper mines. From Clayton, as a center, a minister could strike out into three other places, where he could hold regular services. Two of those places, Pacheco and Antioch, are central points and really important.

The church in Clayton are moving for a parsonage. With some assistance from San Francisco, they hope to complete one, by spring. Here, then, is a field open for a good man. The man particularly needed for this place, is one of ardent piety and devotion, warm heart and fresh experience. This must come first. They are a people that can appreciate an able sermon and all that, but they want, first of all, the spirit of the Gospel, then ability, and the rest. They have the good sense to know, that they can not command the first class talent; but they feel that they can not be without the Holy Spirit. Would that this were true of all our churches.

If, therefore, you can find a man who has had some experience as pastor or preacher, and is willing to go to Clayton and share with the people their poverty and their graces, I do not hesitate to say, that in one or two years, the burden of support will be taken off your hands.

From Clayton I went to

Dutch Flat.

Dutch Flat is the largest town in Placer county, and is situated on the route of the great Pacific Central Railroad. It contains about 1,200 to 1,500 inhabitants. Its mines are extensive, rich, and will not be exhausted for eight or ten years.

On my arrival, I found an Old School Presbyterian minister on the ground. He had been there some weeks, and expected to remain permanently—provided the people voted in favor of a Presbyterian church. The community to whom the church would be obliged to look for support of a minister, was mainly of New England origin, and the money held by christian people was in the hands of Congregationalists. When the matter came up for decision, the vote was unanimous, with a single exception, for a Congregational church.

The reasons assigned were two. 1st. The Congregationalists were out and out loyal to the country. 2d. A Congregational church could be better supported there, than any other. Two first rate reasons certainly. Accordingly, on the Sabbath I was there, I assisted them, according to request, in organizing a church, which they call "The *Plymouth Church.*" A council is to meet, in two or three weeks, to complete the good work.

Sierra Valley.

I went to Downieville and supplied Rev. Mr. Pond's place, while he went to Sierra Valley. This valley, he had visited before, as county superintendent of schools, and made an extensive acquaintance. Much was said, at the time, about a Congregational minister for the Valley. On his second visit, he succeeded in organizing an ecclesiastical society, and brought back with him an application for a missionary. Such are the present wants and prospective importance of that large and rich Valley, that we should have felt authorized in sending Rev. Mr. —— right to that place, had he made his appearance with the others.

Sierra Valley is on the eastern boundary of the State — thirty miles from Downieville. It is about thirty miles in length and twenty in breadth—a very rich and productive valley, while its proximity to the Washoe market adds much to its value. It is all taken up, and the whole valley is fenced. The assessor of the State taxes has assessed the property, this season, at $350,000. It is largely settled by New England families, and a Congregational minister is needed there, very much. The place will be kept open for B., provided he comes on by spring.

So much, for the month: One church (self-supporting) organized; one ecclesiastical society formed; and an endeavor to comfort and encourage one of the Lord's own churches. There is more of the same kind of work, needing immediate attention.

NEBRASKA.

From Rev. R. Gaylord, Omaha City, Douglas Co.

A Nine Years' Retrospect.

Yesterday closed the labors of another missionary year; closed, too, my special labors with this church, as their spiritual teacher. Nine years since, I made my way, with my wife and three children, in the midst of winter exposure and peril, by a land journey of three hundred miles, to this place; where, till the present time, I have endeavored to hold up the light of a pure, gospel Christianity. Our first experience in a frontier city, where, fifteen months before, but one cabin marked the spot, was severe in the extreme. The first year brought sickness and death to the family circle. It was ours, to begin the work of organization, to lay the foundations of a church, to make provision for a house of worship, and to put in operation all the appliances of the Gospel. Regular preaching, a weekly prayer meeting, and a Sabbath school constantly maintained, have been steadily exerting their silent but salutary influence, in a place where worldliness and wickedness abound.

A Visit to Old Friends and the Old Home.

The constantly increasing burden of labor for years, without any rest, at last wrought its legitimate result, in impaired strength and wasted energy. In consequence of this, on the 23d of May last, we left Omaha for the East, and availed ourselves of the opportunity thus afforded, of enjoying intercourse with christian friends in a region of country where the institutions of the Gospel were established long ago.

Very pleasant was the cordial greeting of old friends and acquaintances, and their heartfelt sympathy in the pioneer Home Missionary work. It was refreshing, after so long a period of isolation, to come in contact with, and feel the warm pulse-beat of christian hearts; and to be permitted to awaken their interest, as opportunity presented, by recounting what the Lord had done in the great Northwest, and the providential movements, tending to settle the wider region, westward still.

It was a rare privilege that I enjoyed, and one not soon to be forgotten, of listening to the preaching of such men as Dr. Storrs, Dr. Budington, and Rev. H. W. Beecher, of Brooklyn, and Dr. Thompson and Dr. Adams, of New York, as well as of others, and of mingling in the deliberations of the venerable ecclesiastical bodies of Connecticut and Massachusetts, with the more youthful one of New York, and of representing there the great and growing interests of Nebraska and the region beyond.

But most precious and tender of all was my visit to Norfolk, my birthplace, the home of my mother, who still lives to pray and labor, at the advanced age of ninety. We wept, and rejoiced, and prayed together. She is full of patriotism, and spends much of her time in knitting and sewing for the soldiers. With memory perfect, her first sight restored, and all her faculties unimpaired, having outlived all of her eight children but two, she waits joyfully the coming of her Savior, to take her to himself.

At Work Again.

We reached home on the tenth day of October, much improved in health, and strengthened to enter upon the work to which the Executive Committee of the American Home Missionary Society has seen fit to appoint me. The field assigned to me is new, and yet one of immediate prospective importance. The valley of the Missouri stretching through it, from North to South, and the valley of the Platte, from its western border to the Missouri river, both of them affording rare attractions for settlers.

During the five weeks since I reached home, I have been very busy. Besides the preparation and the preaching of sermons on the Sabbath, I have written a large number of letters, attended a meeting of our Association at Nebraska City, fifty miles from here, and a meeting of the trustees of our institution at Fontenelle, forty miles distant.

KANSAS.

From Rev. D. Ellex, (colored,) Lawrence, Douglas Co., by Rev. R. Cordley.

Rev. Mr. Ellex desires me to report to you for him, for the past two quarters. The progress of his church seems to be steady. No additions have been made to its numbers, but it is gaining otherwise. The other denominations (Methodists and Baptists) have about suspended. His service is the only regular one held in town, among colored people. The congregation is growing, and often fills the house to its utmost capacity. There is a good degree of interest in their meetings. The Sabbath school is very full and encouraging. The children are learning very fast, and some of them are becoming quite good scholars.

The Freedmen and the Invasion.

All our interests have suffered, the past month, from Price's invasion. The militia were all called out, all business was stopped, and every man compelled to enter the ranks. The colored people did their part well. Brother Ellex shouldered his musket and started for the border with his company. Over a hundred of them went down with the militia, and as many more were enlisted for home defense. When on the border, not one flinched. They got no chances to fight; for Price kept out of range of their muskets, never coming nearer than four miles. The cavalry and artillery only could reach him. The "iron-clads" came back in good spirits. Government furnished them with the best arms in the service—Enfield rifles. We hope now that the danger is over. A few guerillas remain in Missouri, but they are trying to get out before the leaves fall. We trust that our people can now settle down to the pursuits of peace, and that they will be able to give attention to the interests of another world.

Services among the Colored People.

Rev. Mr. Ellex preaches twice, every Sabbath, and holds prayer meetings, on Friday evenings. Besides these meetings, they have a meeting on Sabbath afternoon. This is a general meeting; at which they sing for practice, and at which the Sabbath superintendent tells them the news of the week, especially in its bearings on the colored race. It is a meeting for general information. It may seem a little out of place, for the Sabbath; but when we remember that these people can not read, and are dependent on some such medium for all they know of passing events, it will not seem so much out of the way. A religious impression is always left, and many valuable lessons are impressed on their minds. I regard them as among the most useful meetings.

MINNESOTA.

From Rev. C. Seccombe, St. Anthony, Hennepin Co.

The Home Field and the Foreign.

Our collection for the Home Missionary Society has been forwarded to Rev. Mr. Hall. We have also made a donation to the American Board, during the last quarter; not, however, altogether in the shape of dollars and cents. We have furnished from our church a *wife* for Rev. J. N. Ball, who is soon to sail for Adrianople in Western Turkey. The lady whom he married was Miss Martha A. Haines, a teacher in one of our public schools, who united with us on profession of faith one year ago, last March. She took a very decided stand when she gave herself to Christ, and became a very devoted Christian. They were married on Sabbath afternoon, in church. The house was crowded; and the other exercises were those of the monthly concert, Rev. Mr. Ball occupying most of the time. The ladies of our church did what they could in helping to furnish an outfit; and a collection was taken up at the concert for the benefit of our missionary friends.

It gives us great pleasure, to feel that we have sent one laborer into the Foreign field. We have, before this, furnished one or two wives for the Home Missionary field; and one young man who united with us on profession, has since been through the Seminary, and is now preaching in Maine. In our weakness, we feel the loss of such persons very much; and yet we should be glad to give half of what remains, if they could be so well employed.

IOWA.

From Rev. L. Jones, Bellevue, Jackson Co.

Mode of Conducting a Sunday School.

I came here at the urgent request of your Agent. After a few weeks, I made direct efforts to get the church into working order, but found this and no more—that they were willing that *I* should work, and do all the good I could. I saw that I could hope to do but little, and that slowly, in this way; and therefore bestowed a large part of my attention upon the children and young people of the village, who were not reached by any of the churches. I took charge of the Sabbath school. By the use of various means, the attendance soon increased; and now it averages one hundred and twenty. The greater part of these are between the ages of fifteen and twenty years. We have fourteen classes. I have used as teachers any adults who would act. That the school should not fail in its objects on account of inefficiency on the part of teachers, I have conducted it as follows: *Twenty minutes* are given to singing, prayer, recitation by the school, in concert, of the Sabbath school rules (which are: 1st. Be regular. 2d. Be punctual. 3d. Keep order. 4th. Give attention. 5th. Remember what is said. 6th. Practice the good we learn). *Twenty five minutes*, for class exercises. *Five minutes* for class book accounts. Then, *thirty minutes*, for the consideration of a subject given out, the previous Sabbath.

I prepare, each week, a subject, and announce it as the one for consideration on the following Sabbath. Each class furnishes one Bible text, as near as they can to the point; and I select such verses as I think they may not find, and arrange them, if the subject admits it, topically. During the time of the class exercises, I visit the classes, to see that they have a passage. They seldom need assistance. When the time comes, after insisting upon obedience to our 4th rule (which, now, is seldom needed), I ask for the subject; then call upon the classes, in order, for their verses; refer them to other verses when necessary; put the subject before them in proper shape; and, when I can, illustrate each point, with one or more short stories. In this, I am very much aided by The "Cyclopedia of Moral and Religious Anecdotes." Sabbath before last the subject was, "What does the Bible say of the punishment of the wicked?" With a few verses added to those of the classes, I put the subject thus: Does *God say* he will punish the wicked? Verses. *Where* and *when* will it be inflicted? Verses. What will be its *character?* Verses. *How long* will it last? Verses.

Our last subject was, What does the Bible say of our hearts? Are they good or bad? The verses from the classes were all to the point, and the best. I endeavored to show the *difference* between one's heart and one's actions. I spoke of the conduct of wicked kings who had done as they pleased, there being nothing to restrain them; also of the probable conduct of all persons, if there were no laws; and as to their own probable conduct, if they were to do always as they desired, or thought of doing. I then tried to show them that God is a *searcher of hearts;* he looks not only on the conduct but also, and chiefly, on our hearts.

Martial Music.

Allow me to say, in concluding, that, a few weeks ago, an army officer, at home on a furlough, noticing that the minister was doing about all the singing on the Sabbath, kindly offered to lend me money enough to buy a Monitor organ, for use in the church, on the following terms: "As long as I wanted it, and without interest." Pretty good terms. I accepted his offer; and we expect, every day, the arrival of an organ worth $150.

A Concert.

Last week, we sent to Boston for fourteen copies of Dr. Kirk's "Songs for Public and Social Worship." On Friday evening of last week, after two months of drilling, the scholars of the Sabbath school gave a concert, for the benefit of their library. One hundred and ten tickets were sold, at twenty five cents each. All children were admitted free, and many tickets were given to poor people, who wished to attend, but could not pay. The concert was pronounced by all a "perfect success;" and the receipts, $27.50, will help our library very much. We are to give another concert; the proceeds to be used to furnish our soldiers and sailors, who are sick in hospitals, with reading matter.

From Rev. G. H. Woodward, Toledo, Tama Co.

He Taketh the Lambs in his Arms.

Sickness, especially among children, has been severe and quite fatal. This has called for special labor, as their minds have been very open to religious instruction. At their own request, I am frequently sent for to visit them; and when they are too feeble to see other friends, they request my presence. I have been instructed and reproved by their clear views of truth, and the evidence which some of them have manifested, of the teaching of the Spirit.

A lad of ten years died before the close of my last quarter. His mother is a member of our church, and his father quite a regular attendant in the sanctuary. He gave very striking evidence of spiritual light. He talked very freely and intelligently, of death and the future world; and so faithfully exhorted his father, to seek salvation, in earnest, that his father could not refrain from giving a promise which he seems disposed to redeem. The same parents have recently buried a little daughter. May their afflictions prove not in vain.

Somewhat earlier in the season, another little boy, fourteen years old, died. His mother is a member of our church. His father is not a member; nor has he heretofore cared much for these things. The little son lingered for some months, with a painful disease. All the while, God was opening his heart to divine impressions; and his clear mind so apprehended the truth, that his words became weighty even with his father. That father has been an attentive hearer of the Gospel every Sabbath since. The child seemed to meet death like a mature Christian.

About a month later, another lad of ten years, died. Like the others, already mentioned, he had been a regular attendant on our Sabbath school, and had usually been present at the Wednesday evening prayer meeting. His parents are both members of our church. The father is absent, a surgeon in the army. Domestic religion is very prominent in this family. The Bible is constantly studied; and, in the father's absence, the mother leads in family devotions, and each of the four children follows with a prayer. The fever preyed sadly upon little Freddie, day after day. He said, when taken ill, that he wished his pastor and all good people to pray for him; and often, in his lucid moments, asked his mother to read the Bible and pray with him. One day, the physician had thought him convalescent; but about midnight, he woke his mother, and putting his arms about her neck, kissed her, said he was going home, and asked her to read the Scriptures and pray with him, saying that Christ was his shepherd and his Savior.

Funeral sermons, specially prepared, were preached at the funerals of these dear children; and full and attentive auditories seemed to desire to know, what these things meant.

WISCONSIN.

From Rev. S. A. Dwinell, Reedsburg, Sauk Co.

Funerals.

This church has lost one member by death—the first in nearly five years—an exemption for which I am thankful to God. She died in great peace and triumph. During the quarter, I have attended one funeral, each month, in our meeting house, on the Sabbath. Many will attend on such occasions, who seldom or never are seen in the house of God on any other. I endeavor to make them especially profitable. This very dry season we have expected would bring unusual sickness; but upon my field we have not suffered more than usual.

The War.

During the quarter, the deaths in the army from my field have been larger than before. Many have fallen—most of them in battle. I united in marriage, last spring, three veterans, at home on their furlough. Two of them have fallen in battle. From Ironton, two brothers, leaving families, fell at Atlanta. Many are in deep sorrow among us; among them, several families of members of my churches. One has lost a husband; another, a son; another family has a son wounded and a prisoner, and another son very sick. More than usually, therefore, I have been called to be a minister of consolation.

Large numbers have left us, to labor in government service, aside from the army. Of twenty three families nearest me, in this part of our village, thirteen are in permanent or temporary widowhood and orphanage, made so mostly by the war.

Severe as are our trials we are not despondent. We expect that God will give us success in the army and at the polls. His hand has been most manifest, in lifting us up during the last few weeks, and in casting down the enemy, North and South.

Our sons have been with us, on veteran furlough of forty days, and have just left again for the front, in good health and spirits. They are in the Eighteenth corps. They enjoyed their much needed furlough very much, and I trust it was not without real spiritual benefit to them.

Our people are suffering severely from loss of crops and the drafts of the war. The taxes in our town, this year must be about $10 for each man, woman, and child, or $10,000 on a population of about 1,000. How it is to be met, many do not know. This does not include our road and school district taxes. To sustain the gospel ministry under such circumstances, will require much self denial and perhaps suffering, but I know of no minister of any denomination in these parts who is disposed to turn to other labor for a support. None will do so except as a last resort.

Our great need is, a baptism of the Holy Ghost. We hope and pray for it. Will you, brethren, unite your prayers with ours for this great blessing?

From Rev. W. W. Thorpe, Hudson, St. Croix Co.

Providentially Thwarted and Guided.

The long expected "commission" came safely to hand, about two weeks since; for which I am very thankful. It removes every apprehension with regard to continued support during the coming winter, and bids me go cheerfully forward with my work among this people.

In my present field of labor, I find great reason to "thank God and take courage." I am inspired with the conviction that God has sent me to deliver a message to this people. It was only after the most earnest solicitation, on the part of Rev. J. C. Sherwin, your Agent, that I consented to spend a few weeks in Hudson, and visit the surrounding country. I arrived here the third week in April. I was cordially received by one of our most prominent citizens and a leading man in this church. When he had read my letter of introduction he said, grasping my hand warmly: "We are very glad you have come among us. You are the man we have been praying for, these many months." I came with the fixed resolve that I would not, under any consideration, remain for any great length of time; but the people rallied around me, and urged the immediate demands of the church with so much seeming earnestness that I could not find it in my heart to refuse them the word of life. The failure of our own plans, and the disappointments with which we meet, serve, frequently, to bring us into spheres of labor, where we may accomplish far more for God and man than if our fondest hopes were realized.

"Our indiscretion sometimes serves us well

When our deep plots do pall; and that
should teach us,
There's a divinity that shapes our ends,
Rough-hew them how we will."

Providentially Rewarded.

I found the church in a lamentable condition of spiritual languor and decay. Numbers of her pious young men had gone into the army; many families which had added to her numbers and graces had removed; and many individuals who remained had become absorbed by other denominations. The Sabbath school, once prosperous, was reduced to ten pupils, under the care of a single female teacher, who labored on without "bating a jot of heart or hope." God bless that pious woman! The church edifice, though well designed, was out of repair, and, to some extent, in an unfinished condition. An old debt, of about two hundred dollars, lay like an incubus on the hearts of the few remaining members. And in addition to the calamities already enumerated, discord, arising from a claim of a former pastor, had driven his plowshare through a once happy and prosperous society. Indeed, the church was almost obliterated. On her closed portals seemed inscribed, "*ichabod;*" the glory has departed.

To resuscitate such a lifeless body, to breath into it the breath of life and impart to it a healthy and vigorous vitality, seemed, to all human view, a difficult undertaking. And yet nothing should be regarded as too hard for God. My labors here have, thus far, been successful, even beyond my most sanguine expectations. I have raised by subscription, $250 for painting, papering, and otherwise repairing our little church. The work is completed, and results in our having one of the finest edifices in the Northwest. The debt which has been standing more than five years, has been *liquidated.* Two hundred and fifty dollars have been paid on my salary. Forty dollars have been raised to defray the incidentals the coming winter. The little Sabbath school, numbering, six months ago, only ten, now has fifty pupils and a score of efficient teachers, and is rapidly increasing. The congregation, which during the first month of my administration numbered, all told, less than thirty, has increased to one hundred and fifty regular and attentive listeners to the word of God. Last Sabbath we commenced our evening service for the winter; and before the hour for worship arrived the house was filled. There is no other regular evening service held in the city, on the Sabbath; hence ours supplies a felt demand and promises well. The Wednesday evening prayer meetings and the monthly concert are largely attended by the old and the young; and on several of these occasions we have been led to exclaim, "The Lord is here." They are delightful gatherings, model meetings, in which nearly all who attend them take an active part. At our last communion I received two persons into the church on profession of their faith in Christ. Since that time, four others have come to my study, anxiously desiring to learn the way of life. Three are now hoping in the mercy of the Savior. May we not labor for and expect immediate results? "Say not ye, there are four months and then cometh harvest. Behold, I say unto you, lift up your eyes and look on the fields; for they are white already to harvest."

Need of a Bell.

But there is still one thing that we greatly need, and which would contribute much to our comfort and prosperity as a church: that is, a church *bell.* For years, there has been but one bell in the place, and that, a mere apology for one, made of *iron,* weighing only five hundred and nine pounds, the tones of which can not be heard over half a mile. Western men will not pull out their watches to see if it is time to go to church; for they, too often, care but little about the Sabbath; and we need a bell which will send its thrilling tones into their homes, into their saloons, into their *consciences,* awakening the associations of childhood, touching their hearts, reminding them of duty, and solemnly inviting them to attend the holy convocation. When I recall the remarkable fact, that every little native church on the Sandwich Islands is furnished with a first quality bell, transported, at great cost, from the United States, I sometimes wish we might be less heathenish than those heathen. It would be more than refreshing, to hear the tones of a bell ringing out on this clear, cold air, on a Sabbath morning; it would be heart thrilling, soul stirring music. We should forget that we dwell in a "city" in whose streets bears and wolves are killed almost every week, but should be transported, in imagination and heart, to our dear old homes in New York or New England, and live over again those Sabbath scenes of our childhood. But my people have done what they could. There is a last straw which breaks the camel's back. This current year, I can not conscientiously ask them to subscribe to this object, though they deeply feel and acknowledge its importance, and desire to secure such a boon. The country is comparatively new; the war has made fearful gaps and seams in their ranks; and they are poor. A good bell—and we want no other—weighing 800 lbs., with the transportation to Hudson, Wisconsin, will cost about $450. Is there not some benevolent individual in some of our Eastern churches who would delight to serve the common Savior by aiding us in the effort to secure one for our little missionary chapel? "Cast thy bread upon the waters."

MICHIGAN.

The Year's End.

Another year of Home Missionary labor has been expended—the last sand has fallen from its hour glass, and the record has gone on to the judgment. At the longest, I shall soon be there to meet it. The results of this year's labor I can not now gather up, nor is it for me to say what they will be. All I can say is, I have tried to be faithful to the trust committed to me; but in numerous instances, I can discern faults and failures, which sadden my mind and give me misgivings in sending in this closing report of the year's labor. I have not accomplished my heart's desire; this is an achievement that stretches itself far into the future, leaving room for weeks, and months, and years of toilsome labor. Nevertheless, I may say in truth—"perplexed, but not in despair, cast down, but not destroyed." Nor am I greatly discouraged. A lifetime of toil, perplexity, and self denial, would not make me any thing but an infinite debtor to the grace that comes to me through the Gospel.

Encouragements.

The following particulars may indicate the progress, if any, that has been made during the year. 1st. One year ago, the congregations averaged an attendance of less than fifty; but now over twice that number. 2d. The increase in our congregations has compelled us to enlarge our house. We were absolutely straitened for room; and so we cut the house in two, and put twenty two new seats into the center. This was quite a work and came heavily upon me; for in the scarcity of help I had the entire superintendence of the work, and many of the details to do myself. I was carpenter one day, and perhaps mason the next, and man of all work the next, and then paper hanger. I papered the entire audience room with my own hands. But we got through with the work, and reöpened the house with a dedication service; and although the enlargement and repairs cost over $700, it is all provided for; and the house looks enough better, to pay the cost; and the people are

All Satisfied

with it—so well satisfied, that the very next week after dedication they turned out, *en masse*, one evening, and came upon me, old men and women, young men and maidens, little girls and boys, taking me entirely by surprise—filled up the house and had every thing in general in their own way. The first thing in the demonstration was, to require myself, wife, and family, to take a position in the center of the crowd, and, with the people all surrounding us—the chairman of their committee, appointed for the purpose, read to us a very affectionate written address from the young people of the place, which closed with the presentation of their (the young people's) *gift of appreciation*—a very nice overcoat, the cost of which was $35. To my wife, they presented a purse containing $15, collected by a lady, entirely from "outsiders"—(I quote their own language)—"calling themselves sinners, or those who do not belong to any church." Next, they presented a dress to my daughter, and then changed the scene, by appointing a secretary and calling for voluntaries, which came in thick and fast, until the sum of $28.75 was made up and presented to me, to be used in whole or in part, according to discretion, for the other members of the family.

In the meantime, and while the excitement was going on, certain persons, who were that way inclined, availed themselves of the occasion and got into our wood house, by a back door, and committed such depredations as they were disposed unmolested; for when they were gone, and daylight came, we found that they had left behind them huge pumpkins, squashes, potatoes, turnips, apples, and even flour and butter, as the tokens of their *pleasure*.

Thus passed one of the pleasantest episodes in the experience of my lifetime—all the more valuable because unsolicited and wholly unexpected.

3d. Our Sabbath school has more than doubled its number during the year. Would that I could report a corresponding growth in grace and in holiness, during the year. My prayer is, that God will revive his work among us. Nor am I without some encouragement, that the day is not distant, when this may be the case.

Salary.

The church are making an effort to increase my salary, a little, if possible; which, for the year past—donations added—has not paid expenses, so that, for the first time, I close the year in debt. I have thought, once or twice before, that I should have to close in debt, but have escaped unexpectedly to myself, and may do so again; but the margin, this time, is almost too large, to justify the expectation. Expenses have been more than double what they formerly were. I have reported to the church the assurance "that the Home Missionary Society would meet the churches half way," in trying to raise their minister's salary; and under this encouragement they are trying to increase their subscriptions a hundred dollars.

ILLINOIS.

From Northern Illinois.

Germans.

In my last report, I mentioned that the constant influx of Germans into this portion of the State, is something of a hindrance, at present, to the multiplication and growth of our American Protestant churches. Since I came here, I have had more of an opportunity of acquainting myself with the German character than ever before; and, I am happy to say, I am rather favorably impressed.

They are industrious, and mind their own business. Were they acquainted with our language, when first coming among us, no doubt they would conform more readily to our usages. As it is, they are slow in uniting with us in society matters. Their churches (Lutheran) are multiplying about us. Their congregations are large—because all go to church; an example to us Americans. With one good, they have introduced among us one bad example—that of devoting the remainder of the Sabbath, after service, to visiting.

The Germans are inveterate smokers. The pious gait and becoming manners of a New England congregation on their way to the house of God, is in striking contrast with those of our Illinois Germans—going to their devotions, on Sabbath morning, with pipe in mouth, smoking as they go. That you may have an idea how large a portion of our population are from "Deutschland," I would say: We have three stores, one American, and two German; one hotel, German;—and a dreadful house it is, with billiards, gambling, drinking, and dancing, all under one roof.

OHIO.

Ministers Wanted.

We have many churches in this region destitute of ministers. The strength of many of these already feeble churches is still being drawn away, by the necessity of defeating the enemies of our government and overthrowing forever this great, slaveholders' rebellion.

If we, as soldiers of Jesus Christ can but faithfully hold the ground that we have already gained, and maintain deep-souled piety in the church, the Sabbath school, and the prayer meeting, which are the strong bulwarks of God on earth, for the resistance and overthrow of the powers of darkness, we can then have some reason to hope that at the close of this dreadful war, a brighter day will dawn upon us, when many, at least, of the great obstacles that are now in the way, of our spreading abroad the blessed Gospel, will be removed.

Twenty Years, Difficulty—Progress.

For twenty years I have labored under the kind patronage of the American Home Missionary Society; and were it not for the aid which I have yearly received, I could not have remained a single year; for I have never had any New England or New York families, to coöperate with me in building up the cause of freedom and the religion of Jesus according to that excellent pattern laid before us by our Puritan Fathers. The great majority of emigrants who have settled among these rough hills and valleys of Southern Ohio and almost in sight of old Virginia, are of Southern origin, and brought with them over the Ohio river many of the principles, habits and customs of the South. I have, for these twenty years, been obliged to contend against the poisonous influences of slavery, and have preached Jesus and him crucified amidst many discouragements and trials that to many, are quite unknown. I have been threatened, and many have, at times, withdrawn what little support they agreed to give, because I would not sympathize with slavery. In contending with such difficulties, and in overcoming such obstacles, with but few to sympathize with me, I have sometimes been ready to falter, and have longed for the free air of New England. But, by the help of a kind, Heavenly Father, I have continued in this field to the present time, with some happy results to comfort me. By the blessing of God, two Congregational churches have been organized among this people; two Congregational meeting houses have been erected, without much help from abroad; and about one hundred persons, the fruits of several revivals of religion, have made a public profession of faith in Christ. Our congregations are increasing; we have four Sunday schools in operation, larger the present season than ever before; and the spirit of freedom is in the ascendancy.

In looking back upon the past, I can behold the steady march of the principles of freedom and the Gospel in the Puritan style. I shall hope not to draw from your Society much longer; but for the present, shall still need aid; as we are about to make efforts to erect a larger and more comfortable meeting house, and it will tax every effort and all the means I can spare to accomplish our object.

NEW YORK.

Pray that Ye Fall Not.

The terrible scourge of intemperance has been exerting its baleful influence upon us. Some of our church members, who were formerly addicted to habits of drinking, have fallen repeatedly into this sin. We "have borne and had patience," I have sometimes thought, too long. But when there has been a willingness to confess, with other evident tokens of repentance, it has seemed to us a duty to forgive. But alas! after abstinence for a few weeks or a few months, another sad fall would occur.

Oh, how was I cut to the heart, when one or two of these falls took place during a series of religious meetings. There were evident tokens of a revival; God's people were greatly quickened; the impenitent were attentive at meetings; some of them were thoughtful and inquiring. It was indeed trying to us, at such a time, when we hoped to have our hands stayed up by the prayers and coöperation of every Christian, to be compelled to turn off from the great work of pointing sinners to the Lamb of God, for the purpose of looking after wandering brethren, who had brought a fearful scandal upon the church and upon the precious cause of Christ, by drinking even to intoxication. We endeavor to be faithful in efforts to restore the fallen. May God help them by his grace, to withstand the power of a morbid appetite, and the strong social and political influences which favor drinking customs. We have formed a Temperance organization among the children and youth, called the Band of Hope, which promises much good; we have engaged an able speaker to give us some lectures on Temperance; and we are hoping, laboring, praying for, and expecting a Temperance revival. And our waiting eyes and longing hearts are still towards the Lord for the descent of the Holy Spirit upon us.

MISCELLANEOUS.

The Connecticut Home Missionary Society.

This Auxiliary held its last Annual Meeting at the First Church, in Hartford, on Wednesday evening, June 22d, 1864. Prayer was offered by Rev. George J. Tillotson, of Putnam. The Annual Report of the Directors was read, and addresses were made by Rev. Isaac P. Langworthy, of Chelsea, Mass., Rev. Reuben Gaylord, of Omaha, Neb., and Rev. John P. Gulliver, of Norwich.

The following paragraphs are extracted from the Report of the Directors:

The Treasury.

The receipts of this Society for the year ending June 1, 1864, were $7,750.-01. During the same period, the receipts of the American Home Missionary Society from Connecticut were, $23,-594.95. Add the receipts of the Missionary Society of Connecticut, $2,299.-39, and it makes $33,643.35 — the amount contributed by our denomination in this State to Home Missions the present year.

The amount of disbursements for the year ending June 1, 1864, were $7,815.-84, in aid of 39 churches and congregations.

The State Missionary—His Work and Field.

Since the last meeting of the General Association the State Missionary has addressed 15 clerical and ecclesiastical bodies, 44 Sunday schools, and 126 churches, including all the churches now aided by the Connecticut Home Missionary Society. In the prosecution of this work, the missionary has been cordially received by the ministers and the churches; his measures, and the diligence and wisdom with which he has pursued them, have the entire and unanimous approval of this Board; and in the indications of his success we have evidence that his labors have been accompanied by the blessing of God. It does not seem necessary to exhibit publicly the details of his work; but the ample documents in possession of the Directors justify the commendations which we have thus expressed.

The duties assigned to him are threefold: (1.) The visitation of the aided churches—and of the self-supporting churches as he has opportunity—to encourage them to greater diligence in every department of church work. (2.) The calling of the attention of the churches to the necessity of effective labor in behalf of those in their own vicinity who do not attend public worship. (3.) The raising of funds for the promotion of the work of Home Missions as carried on by this Society in our own State, and by the American Home Missionary Society in the country at large.

The Work can be Done.

In our large cities there is an alarming increase of the non-church going population. In our rural districts there are large neighborhoods deplorably destitute of the influence of the Gospel. Is it credible that churches which have been able to devise means to reach the heathen of India, and to raise in a quarter of a century the Sandwich Islands from the depths of barbarism to the position of a civilized and christian land, are to be baffled by the problem of reaching the masses of our own citizens, educated in our schools, guided by our periodical press, intelligent in all the duties of freemen, and abiding under the very shadow of our churches? The supposition carries absurdity upon its face. This work can be done. The churches are even now prepared to enter upon it. They need only guidance and encouragement from their pastors and religious teachers. Let us not be faithless, but believing. Let us seek to fill our neglected sanctuaries by kindly visitation and personal solicitation. Let us send out bands of brethren and sisters to establish mission Sabbath schools. Let us build large churches with many and consequently cheap sittings. Let us appoint lay preachers, setting them apart to their special work by the vote and ordination of the churches to which they belong. Let this Society commission, as it did in its early operations, clerical missionaries who shall be local preachers or circuit preachers, wherever such labor is demanded. And let us not fail to inculcate upon the churches the great truth that we shall be held responsible by our Master for the salvation of the multitudes of the ignorant, irreligious, and neglected around us.

At the same time, in view of the large and increasing demands on the attention of the American Home Missionary Society, growing out of current political events, and in view of the consequent exigencies of its treasury, the necessity of increased attention to the matter of home missionary contributions becomes more grave than ever before.

Vermont Domestic Missionary Society.

This Auxiliary held its Forty Sixth Anniversary at Woodstock, June 22d, 1864. Rev. Charles C. Parker, Vice-President, presided, and prayer was offered by Rev. Henry M. Grout, of West Rutland. An abstract of the Annual Report of the Directors was read by the Secretary, Rev. Charles S. Smith, and addresses were made by Rev. ELDRIDGE MIX, Rev. C. E. FERRIN, Rev. W. J. HARRIS, and Rev. JOHN PIKE, of Rowley, Mass.

The following items are selected from the Report of the Directors:

Ordinary Department.

Thirty four missionaries have been employed, a part or the whole of the year, in thirty three churches, and have performed twenty eight years of labor. Twenty churches report hopeful conversions, amounting in the aggregate to ninety. In Barnet a gentle work of grace followed the week of prayer. In Underhill twenty eight, it is believed, have given their hearts to Christ. In Roxbury there has been a decided quickening of the people of God—a resurrection of the church, as it were, from the dead—and several cases of hopeful conversion. There have been added to the missionary churches 115 members—74 by profession, and 41 by letter; 23 have been dismissed, and 28 have died—leaving a gain of 64 members.

The contributions of the missionary churches show a large increase over previous years. It is believed that *relatively* they have given more for the great objects of christian benevolence than the self-sustaining churches. For the cause of Home Missions they have contributed $846.94; for other objects, $1,174.55—making a total, so far as reported, of $2,021.49.

The Itinerant Department

has been conducted much as in past years. As the Missionary Superintendent, appointed at the last Annual Meeting—Rev. W. W. Thayer—desired, in the present limited condition of the work, to be excused from acting, the labors in this department have devolved wholly upon the Secretary. There have been performed, by thirty five itinerant missionaries, 290 weeks of service, in twenty nine different fields. Twenty four of these laborers were students, under-graduates from five different theological seminaries, and have been, for the most part, faithful and efficient men. In eighteen of these fields there are feeble churches; in the other seven no church organizations exist.

In regard to the importance of the itinerant work, it can hardly be overestimated. There are nearly forty broken, discouraged, and destitute feeble churches in the State, that have not enough of energy and spiritual life left to make any persevering effort to arise and build. They need to be visited and encouraged, and to have a missionary sent to them, or they will soon cease to exist. It is doubtless too late to save some of them. Others may be resuscitated, and the communities around them preserved from Universalism, Spiritualism, and Infidelity—the forms of error that most quickly spring up from the ruins of decayed churches.

The Treasury

contained, at the close of last year, $2,463.92.

There have been received, for the Ordinary Department, from collections and donations, $5,079.99; from legacies and interest on notes, $1,201.57; for the Itinerant Department, in donations, $770; from the fields, $1,045.28—making the total resources for the year, $10,567.76.

There have been disbursed in the Ordinary Department, $4,093.72; in the Itinerant Department, $2,728.77—making the total disbursements, $7,632.49. There remains now in the treasury, $2,935.27.

Ladies' Home Miss. Soc. of the Center Church, New Haven, Ct.

This efficient Auxiliary has recently held its Annual Meeting, and reported its operations during the past year. It appears that it has expended in providing missionary families with clothing, etc., $2,008.75. If all the latent benevolence of the female members of the churches were as thoroughly organized and as effectively employed as in this church, every missionary family would soon be comfortably clad, and a flood of sunshine would light up the shady side of missionary life. We have room for but a single paragraph of the interesting Report of this Society:

Since its organization, this Society has forwarded to different and distant States more than eighty barrels of clothing, all of which have reached their destination safely and in good condition, with one exception. Our work has gone on as usual during the last year, and ten barrels have been sent away to eight different families. *Twelve* were sent last year, but the estimates of value can not well be compared in figures which represent the inflated prices of the times; but of the acceptableness of these supplies in the present emergency, it is unnecessary to speak; and of the continued need of such for the coming year, there can be no doubt. Indeed we feel sure that our work in this department will never cease being urgent; nor do we desire that it should do so, for besides its pleasant influence on ourselves and on our church, it consciously links our interests and our sympathies with the best prosperity of those wonderful emigrations which are peopling regions hitherto hidden from the tread of men and reserved—for what? That the answer to this inquiry is closely involved in the faithfulness of the present generation of Christians at the East, who can doubt? This is so often said that the repetition of the remark is exceedingly trite; but its truthfulness is becoming more evident in the assured fact that Home Missions have kept the northwestern section of the Union true to their place under the stars and stripes, and have inspired that lofty and heroic patriotism which commands our admiration.

Excursion to Middle Park.

The following graphic sketch of an excursion to the Middle Park of the Rocky Mountains is furnished by Rev. William Crawford, a missionary of this Society in Colorado. The journey it describes was an episode in missionary life, and the region to which it refers is not yet "missionary ground;" but we doubt not our readers will prize the information it contains respecting the Alps of this Western Hemisphere.

It was on Wednesday morning, Aug. 10th, about 9 o'clock, that we started out from Empire City—a little village by no means equal to its name, fifteen miles west of Central. Our party consisted of twenty one persons, among whom were the family of Gov. Evans, an Episcopalian minister, a Congregational minister, a banker, a Jewish merchant, a mining agent, seven ladies, three little boys, three servants, a guide, etc. We were mounted on ponies, our tents, provisions, and camp equipage being carried on three pack animals—a horse, a mule, and a Mexican donkey. Just as we were starting, three hunters joined us; and several friends from Empire rode out to escort us a few miles upon the way.

Clear Creek Valley.

A mile beyond Empire City we forded Clear Creek, there a rapid stream twenty feet wide, and came upon the Russell road, which extends some ten miles farther to the Berthond Pass. This road, bridging the creek three times, running along the precipitous mountain sides, and in some places penetrating through ledges of solid rock, is an achievement of considerable importance, and very creditable to the enterprise of Col. William H. Russell, under whose supervision it was constructed. It will be continued over the Range, through Middle Park, and onward toward Salt Lake City, and when completed, promises to be one of the great thoroughfares of California travel.

The scenery along Clear Creek is very striking. The valley is about an eighth of a mile wide, the mountains forming an abrupt boundary on either side. Below you, the water, clear and cold from the mountain snows, dashes and foams over its rocky bed. Pines and firs form a shade over your head, and flowers carpet the ground under your feet. Here and there the beavers have built their dams, which are still in good repair and filled with water; on your left, brooklets fringed with osiers thread their way down the steep mountain side; on your right, huge cliffs, blank and bare, rise perpendicularly more than a thousand feet. At noon we stop to rest and lunch by a crystal brook which laughs and sings among the evergreens and flowers. Here we find that the large Sibley tent, on which we were mainly depending for shelter, must be left behind. The pack animals are overloaded, and can not carry it. Indeed, they are not disposed to go any further at all, and only with considerable shouting and racing are they started again.

Vasquez Pass.

About four miles farther on we come to Vasquez Pass, by which we are to cross the Range, and the command comes from the guide, and is passed along the line, "Halt! tighten the girths!" All dismount, *cinche* the saddles as closely as possible, re-mount, and begin the ascent, turning off from Clear Creek to the right, and at a right angle with it. And now come two miles of such clambering as would appall a party fresh from the East. There is nothing but a narrow, zigzag trail, where, if your pony makes a mis-step, you are sure to roll to the bottom. To the left is a brawling streamlet, which tumbles down in a succession of cascades, giving moisture and support to many large, bright water flowers. One of the boys is frightened at the wildness of the place and begins to cry. Two or three ladies are dismounted and must be helped into the saddle again. The animals pant loudly, for we are now so high that the light atmosphere is very sensibly felt. The thunder begins to roll, and a hail storm beats upon us for half an hour, adding to the romance of our situation.

Vasquez Pass, at its highest elevation, is about twenty rods wide and a mile long, and bounded by peaks at least a mile high on either side. The trees here become stunted, bushy scrubs, which look as if they had grown against the sky and been beaten back. The grass is thin and crispy, hardly giving color to the ground. The flowers are brighter than in the valleys below—sunflowers, painted cups, ranunculus, and several species of cruciform flowers. On the western limit of the pass is an immense pile of snow, twenty rods long, of a reddish hue, and so hard that our animals walked over it with ease. This is the source of the little streamlet already mentioned. The flowers grow up to the very verge of the snow, and some of the hardier ones even shoot up through its margin.

View from the Summit.

Looking back across Clear Creek, a scene of indescribable wildness was presented. Just opposite to us, a winter torrent or an avalanche had rushed down the mountain, its course marked by a belt of shattered trees. A little higher up was a lode of iron or copper, with bright and varied hues, looking as if a stream of blood had flowed slowly down, spreading in ripples until it was spent. In another direction were some of the green plats of grass which are a conspicuous feature along the eastern line of the Range, their western arcs bounded by jagged walls of rock; and beyond them the peaks of the Snowy Range, still crowned with white.

The view in the other direction, consisting of the Middle Park, with its meadows, groves, and rivers, and the white mountains beyond, is no less imposing. We are now standing on the great water shed of the continent, which divides the waters from the waters.

"Camp Foul-weather."

The descent is even worse than the ascent; for the ground is now wet and clayey, and our ponies must pick their way with care. After riding about two miles — the last mile through yellow pines of ordinary size—we come to a little park, with rich, thick grass, where we camp for the night. The animals are turned loose, with a long lariat trailing after each one, so that they may easily be caught. The ladies' tent is pitched close by the woods, where we can easily gather fuel for the camp fires, and near a brook where we can draw water. A fire is lighted, the kettles suspended over it by a pole resting on two crotched sticks, and the party, stimulated by a sharp appetite, hasten to prepare the supper. The cloth is spread upon the ground, the food served on tin plates, and the coffee in tin cups; and we gather around on buffalo robes, in Oriental style. After tea comes the work of building booths, and collecting wood for the night. We are close by the highest points of the mountains, and the air will be sharp before morning. Just at dark the rain begins to fall, driving all into the ladies' tent. Here the evening is spent in telling stories, singing, and jollity, until the hour for retiring, when a hymn is sung, prayer offered, and we disperse for the night. The more cautious of us picket our ponies, allowing them to run to the length of the lariat, the prescribed measure for which is forty feet. Our men, we observe, have stretched themselves out in the open air, before a large fire, their beds made of rubber blankets, quilts, and robes, so that the rain might beat upon them all night without disturbing their slumbers. All you can see of them is several rolls of rubber cloth, as large as mummies and as still, pointing toward the fire. For us who were not so well provided for, suffice it to say, that we greeted the first gray dawn with delight, and with some doubts whether the Feast of Tabernacles (or booths) was really as joyous a festival as it is represented to have been. The morning is cold and misty—a "morning spread upon the mountains." (Joel 2: 2.) We name our camp "Camp Foul-weather."

To be continued.

Resignation of Rev. Mr. Noyes.

In reference to the resignation, by Rev. Mr. Noyes, of his office as a Secretary for

Correspondence of this Society, of which the public have already been apprised, the Executive Committee, at their meeting, January 3d, adopted the following minute:

Whereas, Rev. Daniel P. Noyes has tendered the resignation of his office as one of the Secretaries for Correspondence of the Society, in order to accept the Secretaryship of the Massachusetts General Conference of Congregational Churches, to which he has been appointed,

Resolved, That the Committee desire to record their testimony to the ability and acceptance with which Mr. Noyes has discharged the duties of a Secretary of this Society, for nearly eleven years since his first election to the office—that his intelligence, his fidelity, his kind and gentlemanly bearing, and his genial christian spirit have endeared him to our hearts; and that we deeply regret that he feels called, in Providence, to relinquish his connection with this Society, for another post of christian labor.

Resolved, That, as a Committee, and as individuals, we shall follow him, in his new sphere of responsibility, and in all his future pathway, with the deepest interest and sympathy, commending him to those who may be his fellow-laborers as one whom we have learned most highly to esteem, and to our Heavenly Father for his special guidance and blessing.

APPOINTMENTS IN DECEMBER, 1864.

Not in commission last year.

Rev. Peter Valentine, De Soto, Sterling, and Wheatland, Wis.
Rev. T. M. Ashley, Goodrich, Mich.
Rev. P. R. Van Frank, Otto, Mich.
Rev. Lemuel Leonard, McLean, Ill.
Rev. Walter P. Doe, Williamsbridge, N. Y.

Re-commissioned.

Rev. Charles Shedd, Mantorville and Wasioja, Minn.
Rev. G. S. Biscoe, Cottage Grove, Minn.
Rev. A. Blumer, (German,) Shakopee, Minn.
Rev. W. W. Allen, Council Bluffs, Iowa.
Rev. T. W. Judiesch, (German,) Grandview, Iowa.
Rev. Tudor Jones, (Welsh,) Georgetown, Iowa.
Rev. J. W. Pickett, Mount Pleasant, Iowa.
Rev. A. Wright, Durango and Concord, Iowa.
Rev. C. F. Veitz, (German,) Sherrill's Mount, Iowa.
Rev. A. Harper, Port Byron, Ill., and Le Claire, Iowa.
Rev. J. H. Langpaap, (German,) Lansing, Iowa.
Rev. Thomas A. Wadsworth, Sheboygan Falls, Wis.
Rev. R. Hassell, Leeds, Wis.
Rev. L. Bridgeman, Westfield, New Haven, and Packwaukee, Wis.
Rev. D. Jones, Arena and Mill Creek, Wis.
Rev. Fayette Hurd, Lansing, Mich.
Rev. James A. McKay, Lamont, Mich.
Rev. John R. Bonney, Mattison, Mich.
Rev. David Berney, Worth, Port Sanilac, and Bridgehampton, Mich.
Rev. R. Brown, Oswego, Ill.
Rev. N. C. Clark, Ringwood and Greenwood, Ill.
Rev. G. C. Judson, Westbrook, N. Y.

RECEIPTS IN DECEMBER, 1864.

MAINE—

West Bethel, Leonard Grover, $10 00

NEW HAMPSHIRE—

Received by Rev. B. P. Stone, D.D., Treas. N. H. M. S.—
Amherst, John Fletcher, to const. him a L. M., $30 00
Campton, legacy of Joseph Chandler, Jason Cook, Exr., 131 04
Derry, legacy of Alfred Reynolds, 314 92
Exeter, James D. Bell, 1 75
Fisherville, legacy of Rebecca Rolf, $200, less $12 U. S. tax, Asa H. Morrill, Exr., 188 00
Pelham, of which $10 is from Mrs. H. C. Wyman and Mrs. E. W. Taylor, $13 00 $678 71
Francestown, Joseph Kingsbury, to const. Albert J. Donnell a L. M., by Rev. Charles Cutler, 30 00

VERMONT—

Benson, "Two Individuals," 3 00
North Brookfield, A Friend, 3 00
Westminster West, Ladies' Benev. Soc., by Mrs. Ira Goodhue, 2 00

MASSACHUSETTS—

Massachusetts Home Missionary Society, by Benjamin Perkins, Treas., 3,000 00
Attleborough, Ladies' Miss. Sew. Circle, by Nancy M. Daggett, 4 00

Brimfield, balance of legacy of Lucy Bishop, by Solomon Homer, Exr., $19 00
Chicopee Falls, legacy of Elias Carter, by E. O. Carter, Exr., 100 00
Conway, Ladies' Benev. Soc., by Maria H. Avery, 4 00
East Hampton, Payson Soc., $310.75; Mon. Con., $140.43, by Seth Warner, Treas., 451 18
Fairhaven, First Cong. Soc., by Rev. John Willard, 3 00
Florence, Cong. Ch., to const. Rev. H. C. Hovey a L. D., Mrs. Helen L. Hovey, Dea. Leavitt Beals, and Dea. Anson B. Clark L. Ms, by A. L. Williston, 190 00
Hampshire Miss. Soc., by E. Williams, Treas.—
Hadley, legacy of Martha B. Kellogg, $400, less U. S. tax $20, by P. S. Williams, Exr., $380 00
Williamsburg, Cong. Ch., 70 06 450 06
Hatfield, Cong Ch. and Soc., by John A. Billings, Treas., 74 52
Kingston, Thomas Newcomb, 5 00
Lenox, Eldad Post, 5 00
Oxford, Mrs. Abigail Marsh, 50
Pelham, Rev. R. D. Miller, 1 00
South Amherst, Cong. Ch., by Rev. W. Barton, 21 50
South Hadley Falls, First Cong. Ch. and Soc., by Rev R. Knight, 89 00
Westfield, on account of legacy of Mrs. Hannah K. Mix, Dea. Henry Fowler Exr., by Gillett & Stevens, 400 00
West Newbury, L. P. J., 10 00

CONNECTICUT—

"A Connecticut Man," 50 00
Bethel, Cong. Ch. and Soc., 17 74
Bridgeport, First Cong. Ch. and Soc., Miss. and Benev. Soc., of which $30 is from Miss Ann B. Wordin to const. Edward Bradley a L. M., by E. E. Hubbell, Treas., 120 95
Center Brook, Cong. Ch. and Soc., by Rev. John G. Baird, 15 00
Central Village, Cong. Ch., by William A. Lester, 33 55
Cheshire, Cong. Ch., by J. A. Hitchcock, Treas., 33 00
Cornwall Bridge, Dorcas Soc., by Rev. S. Fenn, 6 50
Cromwell, A Friend, 5 00
Harwinton, 2 00
New Hartford, North Cong. Soc., "Anonymous," by H. W. Brown, Treas., 50 00
New Haven, Mrs. Ira Atwater, to const. herself a L. M., by Rev. William S. Porter, $30; Rev. Joel Mann, $5, 35 00
Southport, Ladies, by Miss V. M. Tompkins, 5 00
Stonington, Mrs. John D. Palmer, in full to const. Henry S. Stanton a L. M., by Annie Smith, 20 00
Terryville, Cong. Ch., Mon. Con., by Milo Blakesley, Treas., 5 00
Thompson, Cong. Ch., by Rev. A. Dunning, 21 00
Westbrook, Cong. Ch., by A. Bushnell, 19 03

NEW YORK—

Bellport, $10; Fire Place, $2, Cong. Chs., by Rev John Gibbs, 12 00
Brighton, Cong. Ch., to const. Joseph G. Wheeler a L M., by Rev. James Orton, 44 77
Brooklyn, Dea. E. Palmer and wife, by Rev. Edward Taylor, 13 00
Clinton Av. Ch., James W. Elwell, 500 00
Clarkson, Cong. Ch., by Joel Palmer, 15 90
Ellenburgh, Union Religious Soc., by Rev. George Hardy, 10 00
Geneva, on account of legacy of Henry Dwight, by Edmund Dwight, Exr., 2,100 00
Gouveneur, Miss Nancy W. Wright, 5 00
Hamilton, Mrs. Maria Manchester, in full to const. her a L. M., $10; Mrs. Gilbert Tompkins, $1, by Rev. W. R. Tompkins, 11 00
Harpersfield, Mrs. M. Boies and Sarah Hotchkiss, $5; Rev. Harper Boies, $2, $7 00
Knowlesville, R. S. Egleston, $5; Mrs. E. T Egleston, $3, 8 00
Lewiston, Presb. Ch., by O. P. Scovell, Clerk, 10 00
Livonia, legacy of Mrs. Susan Fowler, $100, less $5 U. S. tax, by James Richmond and Peres B. Pitts, Exrs., 95 00
Meredith, Cong. Ch., by Rev. G. R. Entler, 7 25
New Road, $28.35; Westbrook, $4.02; Sidney Center, $2.80, Cong. Chs., by Rev. G. C. Judson, 35 17
New York, Lloyd Aspinwall, by M. Howland, 100 00
Troy, Rev. Charles Redfield, 75 00
Warsaw, Cong. Ch., of which $30 is to const. A. Blake a L. M., by J. H. Darling, Treas., 55 00

NEW JERSEY—

Elizabeth, Wilmot Williams, 10 00

PENNSYLVANIA—

Centerville and Riceville, by Rev. U. T. Chamberlain, 30 00
Honesdale, legacy of Mrs. Elizabeth M. Speir, by C. P. Waller, Acting Exr., 25 00
Pittsburgh, Plymouth Cong. Ch., by Rev. J. H. Lyon, 30 00
Smithport, Mrs. B. P. Bond, 1 00
Sterrettania, Cong. Ch., by Rev. William Irons, 22 92

OHIO—

Cincinnati, Cong. Ch., by Rev. B. K. Maltby, 3 30
Elyria, Presb. Ch., by Rev. H. Lawrence, 25 00
Lebanon, Mrs. J. F. Gould, to const. J. Franklin Gould a L. M., 30 00
Ruggles, Bradford Sturtevant, 1 00
Siloam, Welsh Cong. Ch., by Rev. J. A. Davies, 15 00
West Mill Grove, Cong. Ch., by Rev. Samuel Kelso, 2 00

INDIANA—

St. Louis Crossing, Rev. Horace Bushnell, Jr., 1 00
Terre Haute, S. H. Potter, $1,000; "M.," $1, 1,001 00

ILLINOIS—

Received by Rev. E. Jenney—
Bunker Hill, Cong. Ch., $43 20
Galesburg, Cong. Ch., in part, 86 05
Waverly, Cong. Ch., to const. L. T. Hoyt a L. M., 52 30 181 55
Albion, Cong. Ch., Edwards Co., by Rev. T. H. Holmes, 25 00
Allen and Vienna, Cong. Chs., by Rev. S. R. Dole, 25 00
Atkinson and Shabbona Grove, Cong. Ch., $16; Cornwall, $7, by Rev. J. P. Richards, 23 00
Big Rock, Cong. Ch., by Rev. J. L. Richards, 14 00
Chandlerville, $10; Berlin, $2.50, Cong. Chs., by Rev. O. C. Dickerson, 12 50
Henry, Cong. Ch., by Rev. A. A. Whitmore, 8 00
Lawn Ridge, Cong. Ch., by Rev. L. Benedict, 16 00
Nora, Cong. Ch., by Rev. E. H. Avery, 12 20
Ontario, Rev. F. Wheeler, 5 00
Quincy and Fall Creek, Ger. Cong. Chs., by Rev. C. E. Conrad, 37 50
Rosemond, Cong. Ch., by Rev. E. B. Tuthill, 15 00
Roseville, Cong. Ch., by Rev. Alfred Morse, 2 35
Salem, Cong. Ch., by Rev. B. F. Worrell, 10 40
Udina, Cong. Ch., by Rev. R. R. Snow, 10 00

MISSOURI—

St. Louis, First Trin. Cong. Ch., by Samuel C. Cochran, Treas., $226 75

MICHIGAN—

Received by Rev. H. A. Read—
Alamo, $3 00
Allegan, Cong. Ch., 10 35
Cooper, Cong. Ch., 17 55
Galesburg, Cong. Ch., 19 35
Hudson, Cong. Ch., to const. Mrs. Sarah Smith a L. M., 30 00
Lodi, Cong. Ch., 10 00
Olivet, Cong. Ch., 24 35
Pontiac, Cong. Ch., 48 73
Port Huron, Cong. Ch., to const. John Johnston a L. M., 66 85
Rochester, Cong. Ch., 22 10
Leoni, Rev. A. St. Clair, in part to const. him a L. D., 35 00
Windsor, Cong. Ch., by H. H. Loomis, 2 00 289 28
Ada, $4.05, Dorr, $5.45, Cong. Chs., by Rev. N. K. Evarts, 9 50
Adrian, Plymouth Ch., by Samuel Lathrop, Treas., 26 00
Almont, Cong. Ch., by Rev. H. R. Williams, 27 55
Farmers' Creek, Cong. Ch., by Rev. G. Winter, 5 00
Grand Ledge, Jameson's School House, and De Witt, by Rev. W. P. Esler, 9 00
Kalamazoo, First Cong. Ch., of which $30 is from Dr. and Mrs. Hitchcock, to const. Charles W. Hitchcock a L. M., balance to const. Miss Frances Lewis a L. M., by Martin Willson, Treas., 76 79
Pinckney, Mrs. Jeane Affbak, 3 00
Pine Run, Rev. Jonas Denton, 2 00
Utica, Cong. Ch., by Rev. William Platt, 17 50

WISCONSIN—

Burlington, Plymouth Cong. Ch., by Rev. S. H. Barteau, 14 00
Geneva, Presb. Ch., by Rev. D. Clary, 15 36
Kenosha, First Cong. Ch., by L. G. Merrill, Treas., 20 00
Marquette, A Friend, 11 00
Oconomowoc, Cong. Ch. and Soc., by Rev. E. J. Montague, 9 00

IOWA—

Big Rock, $5.25; New Liberty, $3, by Rev. S. N. Grout, 8 25
Burr Oak, Cong. Ch., by Rev. George Bent, 7 00
Lansing, Cong. Ch., by Rev. J. B. Gilbert, 20 00
Quosqueton, Cong. Ch., by Rev. A. Manson, 11 00
Warren, Cong. Ch., by Rev. A. R. Mitchell, 10 00

MINNESOTA—

Faribault, Cong. Ch. and Soc., by H. Riedell, Treas., 13 00
Rushford, Cong. Ch., by Rev. W. W. Snell, 3 05
West Chain Lakes, by Rev. J. C. Strong, 1 00

CALIFORNIA—

Received by A. C. Nichols—
Downieville, Cong. Ch., $50 00
Rev. Mr. Rowell, 20 00 70 00
Received by Rev. J. H. Warren—
Clayton, $1 75
Downieville, 15 20
Dutch Flat, 23 05
San Francisco, Dr. J. W. Clark, 30 00 $70 00
HOME MISSIONARY, 32 00

$11,649 08

Donations of Clothing, etc.

Conway, Mass., Ladies' Benev. Soc., by Maria H. Avery, a barrel, $65 94
Fairhaven, Mass., First Cong. Soc., by Rev. John Willard, a barrel.
New York, by Mrs. Hannah Ireland, a bundle of clothing.
North Coventry, Ct., Cong. Ch., Ladies, by Rev. W. J. Jennings, a half barrel, and freight, 61 00
Southport, Ct., Ladies, by Miss V. M. Tompkins, a barrel.
Westminster West, Vt., Ladies' Benev. Soc., by Mrs. Ira Goodhue, a box, 30 00
Worcester—
Central Ch., Ladies' Miss. Sew. Circle, by Mrs. W. H. Sanford, a box, 119 00
Salem St. Ch., Ladies' Benev. and Social Soc., by Miss Emma Brown, a box.

Receipts of the Massachusetts Home Missionary Society, in November, 1864. BENJAMIN PERKINS, *Treas.*

Athol, Cong. Ch. and Soc., $10 50
Boston, A Friend, to const. Miss Lucy R. Kirby a L. M., $30; A Friend, $2, 32 00
Shawmut Ch. and Soc., 1,627 15
Dorchester, "A. S. F.," 10 00
Village Ch., balance, 1 00
Edgarton, Cong. Ch. and Soc., 25 00
Falmouth, Cong. Ch. and Soc., 172 55
Fitchburg, Calvinistic Cong. Ch. and Soc., to const. Philander G. Barrett, Jonathan Whitman, J. Calvin Spaulding, Mrs. Fanny Peirce, Mrs. E. L. Caswell, Mrs. Catharine Brown, Mrs. R. B. Miles, Miss M. L. Haskell, and Miss M. Goodwin, L. Ms., 305 60
Framingham, Hollis Evan. Ch. and Soc., 182 00
Grafton, Evan. Ch. and Soc., to const. Joseph Merriam, Jr., a L. M., 50 00
Haverhill, Center Ch. and Soc., to const. Frank S. McKenney and B. Milton Kimball, L. Ms., 74 60
Medway, legacy of Seneca White, 10 00
First Ch. and Soc., to const. Elbridge Clark, J. S. Walker, Mrs. Martha Richardson, L. Ms., 106 83
Middleton, Ladies' Sew. Circle, 10 50
Natick, John Eliot Ch. and Soc., 20 15
North Bridgewater, Porter Cong. Soc., to const. Mrs. E. Crocker, Miss M. E. Lewis, and Miss E. K. F. White, L. Ms., 90 00
North Weymouth, Rev. Mr. Emery's Soc., 101 13
Pittsfield, German Evan. Ch., 7 00
Rockport, Ladies' H. M. Soc., 22 15
Roxbury, Vine St. Ch., Mon. Con., 10 00
Salem, Tabernacle Ch. and Soc., 270 90
Walpole, Cong. Ch. and Soc., to const. Dea. Everett Stilson a L. M., 36 56
Watertown, Phillip's Ch., 31 25
West Amesbury, Cong. Ch. and Soc., $73.87; Mon. Con., $60, 133 87
West Gloucester, Cong. Ch. and Soc., 20 00
West Newton, H. B. Braman, 1 00
Weston, Mrs. M. A. H. Bigelow, to const. Rev. M. C. Stebbins a L. D., 100 00

$3,461 74

www.ingramcontent.com/pod-product-compliance
Lightning Source LLC
LaVergne TN
LVHW021103110826
845150LV00001B/151

* 9 7 8 1 4 2 5 5 6 6 6 5 4 *